S0-AER-585

REAL ESTATE

PRENTICE-HALL, INC., Englewood Cliffs, N.J. 07632

REAL ESTATE

PRINCIPLES AND PRACTICES

ALFRED A. RING
Professor Emeritus
University of Florida

JEROME DASSO
H.T. Miner Chairholder in Real Estate
University of Oregon

Library of Congress Cataloging in Publication Data

Ring, Alfred A.
Real estate principles and practices.

Includes index.
1. Real estate business. I. Dasso, Jerome J.
II. Title
HD1375.R5 1985 346.7304'37 84-18190
ISBN 0-13-765983-0 347.306437

Editorial/production supervision by Rick Laveglia
Interior design: Lee Cohen and Rick Laveglia
Cover design: Lee Cohen
Manufacturing buyer: Ed O'Dougherty
Cover Art:
Collection: State Museum
Kröller-Müller, Otterlo
The Netherlands

Real Estate, tenth edition
Alfred A. Ring/Jerome Dasso

Printed in the United States of America

10 9 8 7 6 5 4 3 2 1

ISBN 0-13-765983-0 01

PRENTICE-HALL INTERNATIONAL, INC., *London*
PRENTICE-HALL OF AUSTRALIA PTY. LIMITED, *Sydney*
EDITORA PRENTICE-HALL DO BRASIL, LTDA., *Rio de Janeiro*
PRENTICE-HALL CANADA INC., *Toronto*
PRENTICE-HALL HISPANOAMERICANA, S.A., *Mexico*
PRENTICE-HALL OF INDIA PRIVATE LIMITED, *New Delhi*
PRENTICE-HALL OF JAPAN, INC., *Tokyo*
PRENTICE-HALL OF SOUTHEAST ASIA PTE. LTD., *Singapore*
WHITEHALL BOOKS LIMITED, *Wellington, New Zealand*

Dedicated to the reader's understanding of real estate, a much more complex subject than most people realize, and to the wise use of our land resources.

CONTENTS

PREFACE

This book is written and designed for anyone seeking a clear understanding of the many decisions involved in acquiring, owning, and disposing of real estate. The real estate ownership cycle used herein provides an integrated, continuing frame of reference for this decision and action process. Some call this continuing cycle "the real estate process." The cycle is discussed in an urban land economic setting. Using and administering realty to maximize the self-interest of the investor, usually taken to mean maximizing wealth, is the assumed motivation or driving force in the cycle.

This material is for undergraduate students as well as for investors and practitioners seeking greater professional expertise. The content is intended to provide the student with a sound foundation for further study or research in real estate. The content also provides the investor or practitioner with a continuing awareness of the decisions to be made in any particular situation or transaction.

As with the ninth edition, the material is divided into six major parts, each of which takes up important components of the decision-making cycle. The parts are (1) defining property rights, (2) acquiring ownership, (3) markets and the investment climate, (4) financing, (5) value analysis and investment, and (6) ownership administration.

Each chapter, except the first and last, begins with a summary of the types of decisions to be discussed. This is a slight change in format from the ninth edition. Key terms and discussion questions continue to be provided. Case problems have been added for some chapters. Also, more illustrations have been added to make the material more easily understood. Note that while some topics may be mentioned in several places (such as taxation and deed restrictions), treatment in depth is provided only once, at the most appropriate place.

Great effort has been made, as usual, to provide accurate, up-to-date, authoritative information. However, the reader should recognize that this material is not meant to replace accounting, legal, real estate, or other professional advice. If expert assistance is needed, the services of a competent professional should be obtained.

ALFRED A. RING
Gainesville, Florida

JEROME DASSO
Eugene, Oregon

ACKNOWLEDGMENTS

Acknowledgment and grateful appreciation are extended to the following people who contributed directly or indirectly to the preparation of this work.

William Appleton
Richard F. Babcock
Raleigh Barlowe
Jay Berger
Charles O. Billings
Donald E. Bodley
Dave Boelio
Byrl Boyce
James H. Boykin
Jim Brown
Lawrence E. Brown
Robert Kevin Brown
William B. Brueggeman
Gary P. Cain
Neil G. Carn
Frederick E. Case
Walter H. Chudleigh, III
Richard Chumbley
John M. Clapp
Karel J. Clettenberg
Peter F. Colwell
Robert N. Corley
Gene Dilmore
Eugene F. Dunham, Jr.
James C. Downs, Jr.
Charles P. Edmonds
James R. Fallain
M. Chapman Findley, II
William B. French
Jack Friedman
James P. Gaines
Richard T. Garrigan
George Gau
Caroll L. Gentry
James Graaskamp
Charles D. Gray
Francis J. Grey
Terry V. Grissom
Jerome Y. Halperin
William G. Halm
Henry S. Harrison
Geoffrey D. Heath
John Heath, Jr.
Norbert Heath
Benjamin Henszey
Richard Hewitt, III
Dudley S. Hinds
Herbert A. Huen
Jane Jacobs
Austin J. Jaffe
Kate Jones
Sanders A. Kahn
Stephen D. Kapplin
William N. Kinnard, Jr.
Daniel B. Kohlhepp
Charles O. Kroneke
Gerald Kuhn
William F. Landsea
William H. Langdon
Rick Laveglia
P.F. Leighton
Donald R. Levy
Bruce Lindeman
Kenneth M. Lusht

Robert L. Lyon
Victor Lyon
Paul G. Martin
W.M. McClellan
Katty McIntosh
John McMahon
Herbert A. Meistrich
Ivan J. Miestchovich, Jr.
Stephen D. Messner
Mike Miles
Norman G. Miller
Stanley F. Miller, Jr.
Carl M. Moser
Edward A. Moses
Paul Nelson
Donald Nielsen
Hugh Nourse
Nicholas Ordway
Max F. Pachl, Jr.
Donald L. Pietz
Stephen A. Pyhrr
Joseph Rabianski
Ronald L. Racster
Wade R. Ragas
Richard U. Ratcliff
Arnold L. Redman
John T. Reed
Michael Rice
William J. Robert
Stephen E. Roulac
Elaine Schiff
Iving Schreiber
Arthur L. Schwartz, Jr.
Robert W. Semenow
Thomas W. Shafer
Harold Siegelaub
Herbert A. Simon
C.F. Sermans
Dave Sirota
Wallace F. Smith
Joseph L. Steinberg
George Sternlieb
Raymond J. Struyk
Dan L. Swango
Harold G. Trimble
Donald V. Valachi
James C. VanHorne
James Vernor
Robert L. Ward
Arthur E. Warner
James R. Webb
Paul F. Wendt
Robert J. Wiley
Wayne Winter
Larry E. Wofford
Lynn N. Woodward
Arthur L. Wright
Robert H. Zerbst

REAL ESTATE

CHAPTER ONE
INTRODUCTION AND OVERVIEW

The first man, who, having enclosed a piece of ground, bethought of himself saying, "This is mine," and found people willing to believe him, was the real founder of civil society.
ROUSSEAU

IMPORTANT TOPICS OR DECISION AREAS COVERED IN THIS CHAPTER

- The Real Estate Decision-Making Cycle
- Overview of Content and Organization
- Investor Goals and Constraints
- Decision-Making and Administrative Processes

Real estate has a myth and reality much like the myth and reality of the sirens of Greek mythology. The sirens, with their seductive singing, lured unwary sailors and adventurers to their deaths on rocky coasts. Real estate, with its promise of exciting careers and quick riches, entices many aspiring practitioners and unwary investors to their ruin on the reefs of ignorance and inexperience. Ulysses, with proper preparation, was able to hear the songs of the sirens while escaping the reality of their rocky coasts. In like manner, a newcomer to real estate, with proper preparation, may realize substantial financial rewards and/or career goals while avoiding its hidden reefs.

The world of real estate is very pragmatic and very dynamic. Providing proper preparation for maneuvering in this world is the overall purpose of this book. With mastery of its content, a reader will be able to make an informed decision as to whether to enter, and the best way to enter. To make mastery easier, an overview of perspective, content, and basic assumptions are all set forth in this chapter.

KEY CONCEPTS INTRODUCED IN THIS CHAPTER

Administrative process
Decision-making process
Economic person
Highest and best use
Investment value
Land use
Leverage
Market value
Rational investor
Self-interest
Title closing
Trade-off

THE REAL ESTATE DECISION-MAKING CYCLE

The viewpoint of a person making choices about owning, managing, and eventually disposing of real estate as a financial asset, termed the *decision-making cycle,* is used throughout this book. These ownership decisions may be divided into three phases: (1) *acquisition* or purchase, (2) *administration* and management during ownership, and (3) *alienation* or disposition as by sale. Every investor-owner goes through these phases. As one investor passes ownership on, another takes it up. The three phases may also be called the investment or ownership cycle. To satisfy the authors' sense of symmetry, these phases will be referred to as acquisition-administration-alienation. The cycle, with an indication of decisions to be made in each cycle, is shown in Figure 1–1.

Better investment decisions and results are realized if the cycle is looked at in its entirety prior to actual acquisition of ownership, because the phases are interrelated. For example, market analysis should precede investment analysis, both of which should precede negotiation for acquisition. And assuming a purchase contract, clear title has to be established at the same time that financing is being obtained. Failure of an investor

FIGURE 1–1
The real estate decision-making cycle

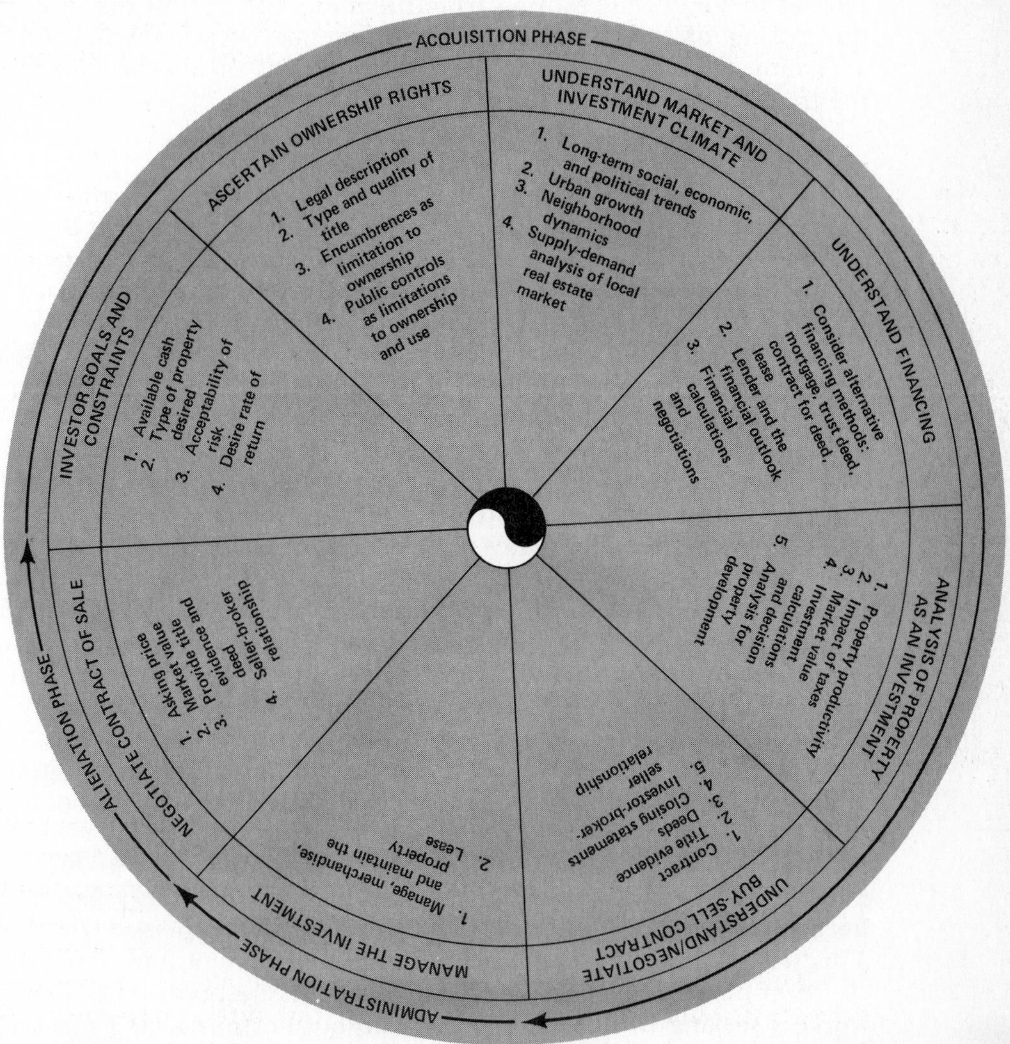

to give proper attention to any one of these areas may mean less than optimal results.

In looking at Figure 1–1, note that a major portion of the analysis and decision making connected with ownership takes place in the acquisition phase. Once a property is acquired (a contract signed, financing arranged, and title closed), an investor is locked in and may have a "proverbial tiger by the tail." Even so, acquisition takes only a relatively short time, typically from two to three months. On the other hand, ownership administration requires only occasional major decisions, even though it may last for five or ten years, or longer. Disposition may take several months or longer, measuring from the initial offering of the property to the closing of the sale. The main difference between acquisition and alienation decisions is that a specific investor is on the opposite side of the transaction.

Rational Investor versus Economic Being Assumption

The perspective or assumption of a rational investor, used in this text, is generally consistent with the "economic person" orientation commonly found in economic theory.[1] Both are presumed to act in self-interest. Both are strongly influenced by their institutional environment.

The *economic person*, by way of review, is often set up as a primary decision maker motivated to maximize his or her economic returns. But the economic person has an uncanny knowledge of the alternatives, and of what to expect under varying production, cost, and pricing situations. And the economic person looks at the use of land resources from the viewpoint of the typical investor.

A *rational investor* operates under different assumptions than does the economic person. Knowledge is less than total, which means that risk and uncertainty are present. Also, institutional considerations (laws and taxes, mainly) impact investors individually and specifically. These differences are the major reasons that the viewpoint of an individual, rational investor is preferred in making decisions about real estate as a financial asset.

Considering that our investor is a *rational being* who pursues, as logically as possible, the goal of maximizing self-interest (maximizing wealth) is an important assumption. The concept of a rational being was developed shortly after World War II by Herbert A. Simon, who won a Nobel Prize for his work in economic and decision theory in 1978.[2] Acting in self-interest, a rational being always selects the choice or alternative, within his or her range of knowledge, that gives the greatest personal advantage. This selection process is sometimes called "making a trade-off."

Self-interest is realistic as a supporting assumption, as evidenced by workers seeking to maximize wages and businesses seeking to maximize profits. Self-interest is neither good nor bad, desirable nor undesirable, per se. In a sense, self-interest is to people as gravity is to our world. We can curse gravity for keeping us from flying at will and requiring us to exert energy to conquer distance or elevation. But.gravity also works to our advantage. It causes rain to fall and rivers to flow downhill. It keeps

[1]See Raleigh Barlowe, *Land Resource Economics*, 3rd ed. (Englewood Cliffs, N.J.: Prentice-Hall, 1978), pp. 126–128.

[2]See Herbert A. Simon, *Administrative Behavior* (New York: Macmillan, 1947).

us on earth under predictable conditions and maintains our atmosphere. We even turn gravity to our advantage in our work and play when we irrigate gardens, ski, skydive, or play ball.

Self-interest is a force or motivation that causes us to try to maximize our satisfactions in life. We seek leisure, self-expression, travel, company of loved ones, thrills from skydiving, or social change out of self-interest. Most of us seek money (rents, profits, interest, wages) only as an intermediate goal. In our complex society, an investor seeking profits may be making a contribution to society as great as, or even greater than, a doctor seeking fees or a politician seeking power.

Self-interest acts to push real estate to its highest and best use. *Highest and best use* is that legal and possible employment of land that gives it its greatest present value while preserving its utility. A *land use* is that activity by which a parcel of real estate is made productive (generates services of value), as a residential, commercial, or industrial use.

Highest and best use of a parcel to the typical investor in the market may well differ from the highest and best use to a specific investor because of differences in what each is seeking to maximize. In turn, the market value of a parcel may not equal its value to the individual investor. A quick definition of *market value* is "most probable selling price" and represents the worth of the property to a *typical* investor. *Investment value,* on the other hand, is the worth of the property to a *specific* individual. This difference is the major reason a financial approach to real estate investment is needed rather than an economic approach. The effect is to provide the reader a highly useful model for numerous investment decisions about real estate as a financial asset.

Investor versus Practitioner Viewpoint

A practitioner benefits greatly from a knowledge of the investor viewpoint, be his or her specialty salesperson, broker, appraiser, building contractor, counselor, lender, planner, manager, housing analyst, escrow agent, or title analyst. Investor decisions and actions serve as the one commonality to all these specialties. For example, an architect must know a client's needs and life-style to design a suitable house. In a similar sense, each practitioner must know his or her client's needs and goals to render the best possible service. Further, a practitioner aware of an investor's perspective should more easily and quickly grasp an investor-client's needs. Mastery of the investor's perspective and of the decision-making cycle should also provide a better understanding of investment property, enabling a practitioner to convey a better image to clients, render a higher quality of services, and in turn earn higher fees.

Discussion centers on an investment property for two major reasons. The first is that the laws concerning ownership, conveyancing of ownership, and financing are essentially the same whether for a one-family residence or for an investment property. Therefore, the reader mastering this material has basic preparation for either residential or commercial-investment real estate. Second, readers are assumed to be interested in investing on their own or in rendering competent, professional investment services to others.

OVERVIEW OF CONTENT AND ORGANIZATION

The term "real estate" means different things to different people. It has three common meanings, which are interrelated. All three are covered here.

1. *A field of study.* Real estate as a field of study concerns the description and analysis of the occupational, physical, legal, and economic aspects of land and permanent improvements on or to land. The purpose is greater knowledge and understanding for decisions and actions. Books, magazines, courses, and other educational activities focusing on real estate as a business or commodity fit into this definition. Thus, this entire book concerns real estate as a field of study.
2. *A form of business activity.* People looking to real estate as their occupation, profession, or line of business activity are considered to be "in real estate." Appraisers, brokers, builders, lenders, planners, housing analysts, and investors are in real estate in this sense. In other words, real estate as a business activity focuses on human activities concerned with land and its use or improvement. Chapter 2 develops this meaning further.
3. *A financial asset.* Real estate as a form of property or financial asset begins with the land and includes all "permanent" improvements on or to the land. As a financial asset, real estate is a national resource, whether publicly or privately owned. It accounts for roughly two-thirds of the tangible wealth of the United States. This asset or property concept is the most common meaning of real estate and is also the object or focus of all other meanings. Except for Chapter 2, the remainder of this book is devoted to real estate as a financial asset. And, unless otherwise indicated, the terms real estate, realty, and real property are used interchangeably in referring to real estate as an asset or commodity.

Numerous ways of organizing an introductory book in real estate have been proposed. No one approach seems completely satisfactory. Perhaps the most accepted approach is to follow a sales transaction, in detail. Unfortunately, no two transactions are exactly alike. And such an approach does little to prepare the student for additional study.

The material here is organized by modules that represent advanced areas of study and that are also essentially consistent with the flow of the decision-making cycle in a sales transaction. Hence, the transaction is followed, but not in detail. The modules are (1) defining ownership rights, (2) markets and the investment climate, (3) financing, (4) value analysis, (5) conveying ownership rights, and (6) ownership administration. It is hoped that this compromise will facilitate reading, discussion, and understanding and at the same time better prepare the reader for advanced study.

INVESTOR GOALS AND CONSTRAINTS

Investors have varying goals depending on available resources (mainly money), age, and decision-making horizon. A recent college graduate with $5,000 to invest differs from an established family with investment experience and $50,000 to reinvest. And an elderly person with $500,000 looking for opportunity would be in a different class yet. Three case examples are presented here, for later referencing, to reflect the implications of these differences. Background is given first, followed by goals and motivations.

Case Examples

1. John Burgoyne graduated last June from East Coast University. He earns $21,000 a year in his new job. But after all deductions, his take-home pay is just over $1,000 per month. John likes the work and feels secure, and wants to do some investing in real estate. Combining graduation gifts and savings, John has $5,700 available. After living expenses, including payments on a recently purchased Toyota Celica, John usually is able to save about $250 per month. He is considering what issues or concerns should be important to him in starting his investment program.
2. Gerald and Nancy Investor, in their early thirties, have two children, Kelly in first grade and Ulysses in second grade. Gerald is a financial executive with the Diamond Distributing Company, the operations of which are limited to his state. Nancy works half-time for the county as a biologist. Together they earn after-tax income of $44,000 per year. After purchasing a home several years ago, they began investing small amounts in other real estate, most of which has done well. They spend considerable time managing the several properties involved and would like some relief from this chore. They have gained considerable knowledge and experience but now wish to adopt a less demanding approach.
3. Wendy Welloff, an elderly and wealthy widow, owns several quality pieces of real estate. She recognizes the need to begin changing her investment strategy because of her age. Also, she wants to arrange her affairs so as to pass on as much of her estate to her children and grandchildren as possible. Wendy is selling a property and will soon have nearly $500,000 to invest. She is considering what overall strategy would be best for her situation.

Motivations, Goals, Constraints

Self-interest is equated with wealth maximization in economic and financial theory. In life, however, self-interest takes other forms as well. Several of the more common human motivations and the implied goals for investment purposes are as follows.

MOTIVATION	GOAL OR OBJECTIVE
Gain/economy	Increasing rate of return, maximizing wealth
Protection/safety	Protecting purchasing power, hedging against inflation
Comfort/convenience	Avoiding undue risk, personal effort, or personal stress
Personal identity/prestige	Exhibiting power to control property and others; acquiring showpiece properties for ego satisfaction
Concern for welfare of others	Assisting or helping others, including relatives, by passing wealth on to them

Thus, one investor may want the comfort and convenience of owning a personal residence free and clear of any debt. A second investor may seek to own real estate as protection against inflation. A third enters real estate as a way of building prestige and maximizing wealth. In short, investors have different needs, wants, and resources as time, money, personal capability. Even so, real estate is such a large field that each may find a niche with search and analysis. On balance, a real estate investment strategy makes sense only if it is related to a individual's overall situation and desired life-style.

FACTOR	CONSTRAINT
Financial/economic	Wealth Income level Risk of alternative investments
Personal	Age (time horizon) Energy level and work preferences Time availability Investment analysis ability Executive ability Risk preference Location/mobility preferences

Age, analytical ability, executive ability, energy level, work preferences, and time availability all act as constraints on an investor. A young person can afford a longer time horizon than can an elderly person. A person with limited time or energy is probably best advised to invest in a medium requiring little effort. Likewise, a person with limited ability to analyze and administer investments is better off avoiding active investments, meaning most real estate investments. Locational preferences are self-explanatory as personal constraints.

Risk preferences are also very personal; some people seek risk and opportunity, others avoid risk with a vengeance. Certainly, anyone interested in real estate should weigh the risks against the expected rates of return. What type of risks? Risks in real estate are discussed at some length later on. But a brief overview is appropriate here.

Certainly, owning any type of real estate contains the possibility of value decreases because of lags in local economic activity or extremely high interest rates. Further, expected revenues may fluctuate due to variability in economic activity. These same conditions and the very nature of real estate itself tend to make it a relatively illiquid asset. Many people borrow to own real estate and to realize financial leverage; but this borrowing gives others prior claim should debt service on the loan not be met. Owners are also subject to having managers unable to operate the property efficiently or to adapting it to changing competition. Finally, owning real estate always involves the possibility of new legislation that affects the property adversely as rent controls, re-zoning, or increased taxes. Certainly anyone should take these types of risk into account in embarking on a real estate investment program.

Application

How are these motivations and constraints likely to affect our cast of characters?

John Burgoyne is primarily interested in gaining investment experience to increase his wealth and protect it against inflation. He is willing to take on extra risk, effort, and stress toward this end. His time horizon is quite long, whereas his cash resources are quite limited. The idea of being able to talk about "his" investment property turns him on. John does not feel tied to this community; in fact, he would like to relocate in a year or two with his next promotion or job change.

Gerald and Nancy Investor have adequate income for their present needs, by their own standards. They do not have great wealth and, therefore, are not able to get into very large properties. They have experience in real estate investing and are willing to undertake reasonable risks in investing. At the same time, they want to avoid extreme risks. They have adequate capital to acquire a moderate-sized property because of successful investments in the past. Both are satisfied with their work and the community; therefore, their preference is to limit their investing to the local area. Gerry has adequate ability to analyze and administer active investments for a financial management viewpoint. Neither has adequate time, energy, or desire personally to manage property on an everyday basis. Their goals are, as for many people, greater wealth, protection against inflation, and adequate time and money to travel. They do not feel the need for greater personal identity through development and management of property or control of people.

Wendy Welloff has considerable wealth, from which she obtains a comfortable income. She does not have or want a steady job. Wendy has adequate analytical and administrative ability to manage her own investments quite successfully. She takes great pride in owning good properties and exercising power. At the same time, she likes to travel and does not wish to be tied down with day-to-day details of property management. In short, she wants to continue enjoying the comforts and pleasures of life. She is well established in her community, having lived there most of her life. Wendy, in her late fifties, is beginning to shorten her time horizon; more and more she's thinking of ways to pass on as much of her wealth as possible to her children and grandchildren. Thus, she increasingly wants to preserve what she has rather than reach out and take high risks for greater gains.

DECISION-MAKING AND ADMINISTRATIVE PROCESSES

We make simple, everyday decisons about what to eat, wear, or do, about whom to see, or where to go, by feel, habit, hunch, or intuition. Actions generally flow out of the decisions in a very natural manner. As situations become more complex, it becomes worthwhile to devote more time to identifying alternatives and their implications prior to making a decision and taking action. It also becomes worthwhile to devote more time to administering or implementing the decision. The benefits of a good decision or the costs of a bad decision, at some point, become great enough to warrant spending extra time, money, and effort to reach the best choice. Choosing a career, a spouse, or a home are examples.

Higher costs of decision making are also justified in making real estate investments because of the high values involved. Investing in real estate is certainly an appropriate place in which to use these processes for a variety of reasons. Real estate is complex and relatively unique as a commodity. It has physical, legal, locational, and financial facets, which must all be analyzed prior to making decisions or taking actions about its use, purchase, sale, financing, and management. Before taking up the processes, a few comments seem in order about why real estate decisions are somewhat different from decisions about most other commodities.

1. *High value.* Real estate has relatively high value. This high value tends to be a market-limiting factor; that is, the ability of most people to own real estate is limited because of their relatively low wealth or earning capacity.
2. *Long life.* Real estate has a long life. Land goes on forever; buildings last for decades. It generates services and income over an extended time. And during this period, its services must be used as produced. They cannot be stored, to be used later, like toys, wheat, or cars. Each time period must stand on its own. If an apartment remains vacant during one month, the loss of rent cannot be made up in the next.
3. *Debt financing.* Debt financing is usually necessary as well as desirable. It is (1) necessary because most people cannot afford to purchase real estate outright and (2) desirable because the use of credit provides the opportunity for financial leverage and the possibility of a higher rate of return on the money invested.

Leverage, or "trading on the equity," results from borrowing money on a property at an interest rate lower than the property's rate of earning. Leverage is illustrated, by example, in the chapters on real estate finance and investment.

4. *High transaction costs.* In both time and money, costs of buying and selling real estate are high. At a minimum, several days are required to complete a simple closing and transfer of ownership. Several weeks is usual, and several months is not uncommon for large, expensive properties. A dollar transaction cost of 6 or 7 percent of the sale price of a property is also usual.

The Decision-Making Process

The decision-making process has five steps as identified by a number of scholars.[3]

1. *Recognize decision or problem situation.* Based on objectives or experience, the need for choice or some action becomes evident. For example, John Burgoyne, our novice investor, recognizes that real estate usually offers greater returns than do stocks and bonds. The objective, stated or unstated, is to maximize rate of return or wealth.
2. *Collect data.* In step 2, all pertinent data or facts within reasonable limits are collected, based on the importance of the problem and the time available to reach a decision. Our investor obtains data from securities dealers, real estate brokers, *The Wall Street Journal,* and other sources about various investment opportunities.
3. *Identify problems.* The collected information is studied, key issues or problems are identified, and, possibly, subproblems are recognized. Our investor determines, for example, that real estate really does offer better rates of return and is, therefore, worth pursuing. Important subproblems recognized are (1) getting more background in real estate ownership and investment, (2) learning about ownership and acquisition of titles, (3) finding out value trends in the community, (4) learning real estate finance because not enough money for 100 percent personal ownership is available, (5) learning tax implications of real estate ownership, (6) determining investment value of available properties, and (7) figuring out management needs, assuming acquisition.
4. *Pose alternatives.* Possible solutions or modes of action are listed, and the probable implications of each are considered. For example, our investor now has the alternative of not going into real estate at all, going in part way, or going in with all available assets. In short, it is a portfolio management and estate building situation.
5. *Make decision.* The entire situation is reviewed, and a choice is made of that action likely to give the best result. In our example, John decides to "try the water" by going after duplex ownership. It's time for action.

The decision-making process is not as clear or as clean cut in practice as presented here. Much going back and forth, or interweaving, between

[3]For a complete discussion of decision-making and administrative processes, see Herbert A. Simon, *The New Science of Management Decisions* (Englewood Cliffs, N.J.: Prentice-Hall, 1977). For early discussions, see Peter F. Drucker, *The Practice of Management* (New York: Harper & Row, 1954); Chester I. Barnard, *The Functions of the Executive* (Cambridge, Mass.: Harvard University Press, 1953); and Simon, *Administrative Behavior.*

the steps is likely. And, except for the last step, the sequence is likely to vary from situation to situation. The important consideration is the decision. The steps ultimately boil down to answering three questions: (1) What problem is to be solved? (2) What are the alternative solutions? and (3) Which of the alternative solutions is the best?

The Administrative Process

The administrative process is an extension of the decision-making process; it is action oriented rather than analysis oriented. It usually involves achieving objectives through people and also has five steps:

1. *Decide to achieve an objective.* In deciding to achieve an objective or desired result, much effort and study, termed the decision-making process, are often necessary. For our example, the objective decided upon is to invest in a duplex.
2. *Organize resources.* Money and people must be mobilized to accomplish an objective. In our example, our investor must now plan to learn about real estate ownership, investment analysis, and property management. Ability to work with brokers, lenders, counselors, and appraisers must also be developed.
3. *Exert leadership.* Action must be sparked to put a plan into action. A real estate broker must be informed of the need for a duplex, a counselor or appraiser may be engaged, and a loan arranged with a bank or savings and loan association.
4. *Control operation.* Efforts to achieve the desired objective must be coordinated and monitored on a continuing basis to assure conformance with the plan and achievement of the objective. Eventually, an appropriate property is located, financed, and purchased. Also, suitable arrangements must be made for the management of the property.
5. *Reevaluate periodically.* On a long-term basis, the investment must be reviewed periodically to determine if the past choices and actions are working out. In our example, this means comparing the risks and rates of return from stocks and bonds with the risks and rates of return from real estate and is a portfolio management strategy concern. More or larger real estate investments may eventually be desirable. And investment in different types of properties may become advantageous.

This is a very brief summary of the decision-making and administrative processes. For greater depth, the reader is referred to the sources cited in this Chapter. Successful investment does depend on selecting properties offering the greatest returns and on following through with a sound management system.

SUMMARY

The real estate decision-making cycle has three phases: (1) acquisition, (2) administration, and (3) alienation. A rational investor uses the cycle to gain perspective on maximizing returns and wealth. It is this self-interest that pushes real estate to its greatest value, which happens only when a property is in its "highest and best use."

Investors achieve better results by following the decision-making and administrative processes in setting up their programs. The administrative process has five steps: (1) deciding on an objective (make decision), (2) organizing resources, (3) exerting leadership, (4) controlling operations, and (5) reevaluating periodically. The decision-making process also has five steps: (1) recognizing problem situations, (2) collecting data, (3) identifying the "real" problem, (4) posing alternatives, and (5) making decisions.

QUESTIONS FOR REVIEW AND DISCUSSION

1. List and distinguish among the three most common meanings of real estate.
2. What are the stated goals and assumptions of the rational investor of this chapter? How can the approach of the rational investor be helpful to anyone interested in making real-world investments in real estate?
3. State and explain briefly at least three ways in which real estate decisions tend to be unique.
4. Indicate briefly some risks involved when investing in real estate. Might an investor avoid these risks?
5. List in order the steps in the decision-making process. Explain briefly how these apply in real estate decision making?
6. List in order the steps in the executive or administrative process. How do these apply to actions in real estate?
7. In 150 words or less, write down your main objectives in studying real estate. Discuss your objectives with others and revise as desired. Then save it until your immediate study or term is completed, as an administrative check on yourself.

APPENDIX
COMPUTER APPLICATIONS IN REAL ESTATE

"Home-Buying Process Is Changing Rapidly Because of Technology," according to a recent *Wall Street Journal* article.[1] The article goes on to describe a computerized loan search that enabled a buyer to obtain the best possible financing in a time of extremely tight money in just eight days.

In all areas of our lives, computers are revolutionizing the way in which we do things. Mainframe computers have been around since World War II. Microcomputers have only made substantial inroads in our way

[1] *The Wall Street Journal,* January 25, 1984, p. 1.

of doing business in the last decade. Both are having a significant impact on our personal activities as well as on real estate decision making. *With computers, analysis need no longer mean paralysis.*

In our concern with computer applications in real estate, the most attention is given microcomputers, because of their ever-wider use. In this discussion, hardware is taken up first, software second, and real estate applications third. Hardware, for the uninitiated, are the physical computers and their supporting equipment; software are the programs used to run computers.

HARDWARE

International Business Machines (IBM) has been a pioneer and leading force in mainframe computers from the beginning. Each year, its machines get more powerful. The IBM Personal Computer (PC) is undoubtedly the current standard for microcomputers. Apple, Radio Shack, and Pet led the way early with 8-bit processors. But when IBM entered the small-computer market, it quickly moved to the front for several reasons. IBM's 16-bit processor could access more memory than could the early leaders. Its machine could handle numbers, letters, graphics, and games with greater facility. Further, IBM used the soft sell of Charlie Chaplin's "tramp" to advertise its new product. Finally, manufacturers of peripherals were invited to plug into and add onto the IBM PC, which encouraged compatability with and standardization on the machine. Apple, Radio Shack, Hewlett-Packard, and the other manufacturers have been forced to adjust to the new reality.

Technical advances and competition have brought about another reality. Microcomputers of considerable capacity can now be owned and operated for less than five dollars a day. This makes their power and potential available for numerous applications that high-cost mainframe computers could not touch. In turn, much of the competition has shifted to software.

SOFTWARE

Software (programs) make it possible to use personal computers for everything from communications to word processing. The most popular software for the IBM PC, by category, according to a survey by *Softalk* follows.[2] The nature of each category is briefly explained following the listing of the software.

[2] "The Most Popular Software Poll RESULTS!" *Softalk for the IBM Personal Computer,* April 1984, p. 132.

Communications

1. PC Talk III
2. Smartcom II
3. Crosstalk

Communications software enables a single computer to access other computers or information files anywhere in the world that can be reached by telephone. The program simply organizes information into a orderly format that can be easily sent or received without loss of content or errors. ASCII (American Standard Code for Information Interchange) characters are used for the exchange of information between computers and files of all types.

A program that merely sends out information from a keyboard and displays incoming information on the screen is said to be operating in a dumb terminal mode and is said to be a "dumb" program. A "smart" program makes it possible to specify one disk file for transmitting information and another for receiving incoming information even while the computer operator is on line doing limited file editing. PC Talk III, the most popular communications program, is in the public domain and, therefore, may be used free of any charges, according to the *Softalk* article.

Games

1. MS Flight Simulator
2. Zork I
3. Olympic Decathlon

Video games were the first computer experience for many of us. Games may still be the leading use of personal computers. But games are not as widely associated with the IBM PC as with many other personal computers. For example, "Adventure," one of the first and most popular games is still not available on the PC. However, with ever-greater memory, speed, and graphics capability, entertainment programs of great diversity and sophistication should soon be available on all microcomputers.

General-Purpose Data Handlers (Data Management)

1. Lotus 1-2-3
2. dBase II
3. PC File

Management of data is essential in this day of information processing. Effective use of information requires that it be collected, organized, and stored in a format that can be applied, with relative ease, to a specific problem or task. Thus, programs for data management were developed. Data management programs are considered to still be in their infancy, and great improvements are expected in future programs.

Spread Sheets

1. Lotus 1-2-3
2. VisiCalc
3. Multiplan

Electronic spread sheet programs are widely credited as the primary reason for PCs having been accepted for business use so readily. Spread sheets, with rows and columns of figures, have been used by accountants for centuries. In a spread sheet format, numbers are much more meaningful for financial analysis. By hand, spread sheets take hours and days to prepare. Calculators greatly improved both accuracy and speed. In addition, on a PC, certain critical numbers can be changed and the spread sheet recalculated almost instantly in what is called "what-if" analysis. The result is that several varying assumptions may be tried for impact before a decision is made. Thus, a spread sheet is an essential analytical tool for accountants, financial planners, and anyone else concerned with comparing data, making alternative projections, and formulating strategy.

Lotus 1-2-3, with powerful data handling and spread sheet capability, was favored nearly three to one over any other program and is by far the most popular software package. Lotus has graphics capability in addition to its data management and spread sheet capability. An updated version of Lotus, called Symphony, that adds word processing and communications capability is expected to be released by mid-1985.

Word Processing

1. WordStar
2. MultiMate
3. Volkswriter
4. Word Perfect

Anyone who can type, even "hunt and peck," can be both more productive and more creative with word processing software. Text can be edited and rearranged until it is "just right." In addition, text can be saved on a disk for later recall and use in slightly different circumstances. Among other uses, word processing programs are used for writing correspondence; preparing reports, proposals, legal documents, school work, and technical manuals; keeping memoranda; and serving as family bulletin boards.

Wordstar is the most popular word processing program, largely because of its early start. Multimate, Volkswriter, and Word Perfect are gaining rapidly as they are considered easier to use or more powerful by many.

REAL ESTATE APPLICATIONS

The usefulness of word processing, in real estate and elsewhere, seems obvious. Games provide entertainment but are not really pertinent to computer applications in real estate. Communications, data storage and management, and spread sheet analysis are, therefore, the main areas of concern in our discussion. The potential applications in real estate of computers in each of these areas has long been recognized.[3] Programs with communications capability have no unique applications in real estate. *The Wall Street Journal* article cited earlier, which discusses computer networks to hasten a loan search, is an excellent example of a communications application in real estate, however.

Data Management

Information storage and retrieval is important in many areas of real estate. Several examples seem appropriate:

1. Listings for brokers and sales personnel
2. Sold properties for comparables by appraisers
3. Property characteristics for valuation, assessment, and taxation by assessors
4. Inventory of furniture and supplies, and occupancy status of units, by a property manager

Calculations and Analysis

Electronic spread sheets are able to do complex statistical and financial calculations quickly and accurately. This makes a spread sheet highly suitable for a wide variety of applications as investment, market, feasibility, and statistical analysis, all of which are important in making decisions. In turn, this flexibility gives a great economic advantage to a spread sheet as against special-purpose programs.

For years, special-purpose programs were written in computer languages such as FORTRAN or BASIC; they could handle only very specific types of calculations. In its software review, *PC World* lists some 1,200

[3] Jerome Dasso, *Computer Applications in Real Estate* (Storrs: Center for Real Estate and Urban Economic Studies, University of Connecticut, 1974), Exhibit 4, p. 20.

programs.[4] Increasingly, these programs are being made up and offered as "templates" for spread sheets for reasons of economy and flexibility in application. Programs written in FORTRAN or BASIC often list for from $500 to $2,000 and more; yet they can be used only for the specific type of problem for which they were developed. With a spread sheet program, as Lotus, the initial program costs $495. But once purchased, some 12 to 15 templates for a variety of problems can be obtained for from $35 to perhaps $75. The problems in this text were all developed and solved on Lotus.

So, what are some of the potential applications requiring many calculations?

1. Determine present worth of an income property based on expected cash flows, financing terms, and required rate of return on equity.
2. Determine various measures of yield under differing conditions or assumptions about an investment.
3. Produce closing statements based on sale price, old and new financing, adjustments between buyer and seller, date of sale, and other pertinent information.
4. Conduct sensitivity analysis under varying assumptions and conditions. Thus, in market, feasibility, or investment analysis, the question "what if" could be asked and a tentative answer generated.
5. Generate a linear or multiple regression equation from characteristics of sold properties to predict the most probable sales price of unsold properties.
6. Forecast market and economic trends based on linear and multiple regression analysis.

Some potential applications requiring both a data base and analytical calculations are as follows:

1. Maintain property management records, with periodic entries of rents due or received and of expenses incurred by tenant. As rent is received or expenses paid, accounts would be updated. Tenants might be sent notices of rent due toward the end of each month. Also, status of the loan on the property, as to payments for interest and principal repayment.
2. Maintain office and personnel records as accounts receivable, cash balances, accounts payable, payroll computation with update of taxes withheld by employee, and so on. Printouts of reports would be selective as to material desired.

The annual software review by *PC World* evidences software for many of these applications already exists. Examples follow. A listing here is not intended as an endorsement of a program.

1. *Real Realtor* performs "what-if" analysis on one piece of commercial real estate.
2. *Sell-a-House* helps to determine a buyer's borrowing power and price range.

[4] *PC World 1983/84 Annual Software Review,* San Francisco, 1984.

3. *Superval* analyzes cash flows for an investment for up to 50 years.
4. *Apartment House Manager* is a collection of five programs that assist owners and managers with their monthly and yearly bookkeeping chores.
5. *Real Estate Property Management* maintains income records for various types of rental properties.
6. *Real Estate Consultant* analyzes property investments from single-family homes to large, multitenant commercial buildings.
7. *SuperMarket Industry Performance Analysis* provides market analyses for the northeastern U.S. supermarket industry.
8. *Real Estate Tools I* analyzes mortgages and other cash flow situations.
9. *Residential Property Analysis* makes a ten-year forecast of the value, equity, tax payment, tax savings, and net cost of owning a single residential property.
10. *Construction Estimating* is an estimating program that records and stores information on up to 16,000 construction items.
11. *Construction Management Accounting System* is a job costing system designed for commercial construction contractors.

What Computers Cannot Do

A brief word about what computers cannot do seems appropriate here. Computers are smart, but they have their limitations. Sheila M. Eby listed eight problems a computer cannot solve.[5] These are

1. A computer will not solve broad, poorly defined problems.
2. A computer will not save money by eliminating workers. It will create new ways of doing things.
3. A computer will not clean up errors in your manual procedures. Thus, in accounting, "garbage in–garbage out."
4. A computer will not do forecasting or trend analysis until a few years down the road.
5. A computer will not solve problems that call for subjective evaluations.
6. A computer will not solve all your scheduling problems in production.
7. A computer's software will not accept changes made by amateurs.
8. A computer will not always be right.

---

[5] "Eight Problems a Computer Can't Solve," *Inc*, March 1982, p. 103.

CHAPTER TWO
THE REAL ESTATE BUSINESS

Our main ability is that we know how to win at this game of business. Society can make any rules it wants, as long as they are clear cut, the same for everyone. We can win at any game society can invent.
MICHAEL MACCOBY, *The Gamesman*

IMPORTANT TOPICS OR DECISION AREAS COVERED IN THIS CHAPTER

- Real property characteristics
- Market characteristics
- The players and their functions
- Rules of play
- History of the game

The activities and interaction of people involved in the buying, selling, exchanging, using, and improving of realty make up the real estate market. The commodity is rights in real property. Many of the people in the real estate business consider real estate to be a game in which everyone must play because we all need space in which to live. Some players have the same attitude as Michael Maccoby's gamesman. Even so, we all play at varying levels of intensity.

Extending the game analogy, each community constitutes a separate field of play, a distinct market. Each person keeps his or her own score. To win is to maximize self-interest, whatever that may be. The prize or payoff may be satisfactions from homeownership, profits or returns from investments, or fees from services rendered. The rules of play come from several sources, including contract and real estate law, licensure regulations, and professional and personal ethics.

KEY CONCEPTS INTRODUCED IN THIS CHAPTER

Accessibility
Agent
Appraiser
Architect
Blockbusting
Broker
Client
Contractor
Customer
Developer
Durability of investment
Eminent domain
Escrow
Fair housing laws
Heterogeneity
Immobility
Interdependence
Leasehold
Manager
Planner
Principal
Realtor©
Salesperson
Scarcity
Situs
Special-purpose property
Specific performance
Steering
Subdivider

REAL PROPERTY CHARACTERISTICS

Real property has distinct attributes or characteristics as a market product. For purposes of discussion, these characteristics are classified as physical, economic, and institutional. In practice, the distinction between the classes is sometimes uncertain. These attributes are as follows:

PHYSICAL	ECONOMIC	INSTITUTIONAL
Immobility	Scarcity	Real Property law
Indestructibility	Situs	Public regulation
Heterogeneity	Interdependence or modification	Local and regional custom
	Durability or fixity of investment	Associations and organizations

Physical Attributes

Immobility. Land is physically immobile—not movable in a geographic sense. Some of the substance of land—soil, minerals, oil—may be removed and transported, but the geographic location of a site remains fixed. An atomic bomb might destroy an entire city, but the geographic location of each parcel would be determinable by its latitude and longitude. It is *immobility* that causes land to be classed as real estate. Because of immobility, too, the market for land tends to be local in character; demand must come to the site. Immobility results in the value of each parcel changing in direct response to changes in its environment, for better or for worse. Immobility also means that taxes may be levied against a parcel and collected, in one way or another; the parcel cannot escape.

Buildings and other realty improvements are not necessarily immobile. But considerable expense must be incurred to move a house or other structure. This means that if the value of a site becomes great enough in a use inconsistent with the site's improvements, the improvements may be moved. In turn, the value of the improvements in a different location must exceed the cost of moving them.

Indestructibility. Land, as space, cannot be destroyed; it goes on forever; it is indestructible. The *indestructibility* of land tends to popularize it as an investment. A sophisticated investor, of course, distinguishes between physical indestructibility and economic (value) durability. Physically, land may go on forever, but its value may be destroyed by changing conditions. For example, the value of certain locations may disappear almost completely, as happened in "ghost towns." On the other hand, the permanence of land and space means that it may be used to support improvements and buildings with extremely long lives. The buildings themselves, however, tend not to be indestructible—in a physical or a value sense.

Heterogeneity. No two parcels of land are exactly alike. Differences in location, size and shape, topography, and so forth cause realty to have the attribute of *heterogeneity*, nonhomogeneity, or unlikeness. Parcels may be highly similar in location, soil type, and appearance. The parcels may be economically alike and substitutable for one another. But geographically all parcels differ.

Heterogeneity has caused land to be legally declared a "nonfungible" (not substitutable) commodity requiring specific performance in contracts involving use or sale. *Specific performance* means that the terms of a contract must be specifically complied with; for example, a particular property must be conveyed and not a similar or substitute property. Heterogeneity is the basis of problems in pricing or valuing realty because comparison of a site or property with similar but different properties is often a very complex undertaking.

Heterogeneity extends to buildings and other realty improvements. Structures usually differ in size, appearance, and complexity. Even if built to the same plan, workmanship and materials might differ slightly. At the very least, location and orientation are slightly different. In addition, differing owners and occupants lead to differing levels of use and maintenance.

Economic Attributes

Scarcity. Inadequacy in supply means scarcity. The physical supply of land is fixed for all practical purposes. But there is only relative scarcity of land or space as such. Thus, certain types of land of a given quality and in a desired location may be in comparatively short supply. But with money, time, and effort, the supply can be increased in response to demand. Even so, the fear of an ever-increasing population outrunning a limited physical supply of land has caused periodic land booms and busts.

Land in the United States today is relatively less scarce than it was a decade ago, despite continued growth in total population and ever-more extensive utilization of land and its mineral resources. The reason is greater and more intensive use of land (space) as a factor of production. Thus, today we use steel and elevators to build skyscraper office buildings and multistory apartment structures, each of which literally constitutes "a city in the sky." Whether land or buildings, increased demand means higher values. And higher space values mean new buildings or modification of existing structures to accommodate the demand.

Situs. The location of a parcel relative to other external land use activities is called *situs.* Both physical and economic location are involved, with the economic relationships being the more important by far. Situs is the result of choices and preferences of individuals and groups in selecting sites. Differences in situs cause otherwise similar parcels to have different uses and different values.

Factors influencing locational decisions of individuals and groups include direction of population growth, availability of services and utilities, shifts in centers of trade and manufacture, direction of prevailing winds, sun orientation, and changing standards in life-styles. Another factor affecting locational choice is *accessibility*—the relative costs (in time, money, and effort) of getting to and from a property. When the relative costs of movement to and from are low, a property is said to have high accessibility. In turn, the property's value is likely to be high. Alternatively, poor or difficult accessibility generally leads to low values. The use of, and the improvements or buildings added to, a parcel are largely the result of its situs or relative accessibility.

Interdependence or modification. The mutual interaction of uses, improvements, and values of parcels is called *interdependence.* Thus, the use and value of a given property is subject to modification by decisions and changes made about other properties. The development of a shopping center across the street strongly influences how I use my site. Or I may have a restaurant along a major highway that depends heavily on nearby motels for customers. Development of a bypass route may severely cut business of both the motels and my restaurant, with a consequent sharp drop in value of all properties. Under these conditions, the quality of the sites and their improvements would be secondary influences in determining their value.

Durability or fixity of investment. The long time required to recover costs of a site and its improvements is termed *durability.* Once a site is purchased and labor and capital committed to build a structure, the investment is "set" or "fixed" for many years from the viewpoint of the community or of society. Durability is directly related to the concept of duration as used in other areas of finance and investments.[1] Drainage, sewage, electric, water and gas facilities, or buildings cannot as a rule be dismantled and shifted economically to locations in which they would be in greater demand. The investment "sunk" in the realty is slow in returning during the economic life of the improvements. Furthermore, the immobility and fixity of land and land investment make real estate vulnerable to taxation and other social or political controls.

Durability does not preclude disposition of the property by one investor and acquisition by another. That is, the investment is not "set" for a specific owner.

Institutional Attributes

Real property law. Real property has its own laws for the most part. Real estate is owned as real property rather than as personal property. Several subsequent chapters are devoted to real property law.

Public regulation. In a fashion similar to real property law, public regulation also affects real estate as a commodity or a product. Community plans and zoning ordinances, rent controls, subdivision regulations, laws pertaining to mortgage finance, and building codes all go to shape the development and use of our realty. Chapter 5, Governmental Limitations to Ownership, looks at public regulation of real estate in some detail.

---

[1] M. H. Hopewell and G. C. Kaufman, "Bond Price Volatility and Term to Maturity: A Generalized Respecification," *American Economic Review,* September 1973, pp. 749–753. See also Jack Clark Frances, *Investments: Analysis and Management,* 3rd ed. (New York: McGraw-Hill, 1980), pp. 203–205.

Local and regional custom. Cape Cod houses are prevalent in one community, almost nonexistent in another. New York City is relatively compact, whereas Los Angeles has been described as "*suburbs* in search of a city." Bicycles are an accepted mode of transportation in some areas and firmly rejected in others. Subtle, local attitudes and customs do influence the nature, appearance, and use of real estate.

Associations and organizations. The National Association of Realtors (NAR), the National Association of Homebuilders (NAHB), and the Urban Land Institute all greatly influence the nature of the real estate business and the development of our communities. Homebuilders change their methods of construction in response to manuals published by the NAHB. The Urban Land Institute did much of the pioneer work to get planned unit developments, shopping centers, and curvilinear street systems accepted across the country. The National Association of Realtors emphasizes higher ethics and promotes multiple listings systems to improve the real estate business. The Federal National Mortgage association cooperates with other organizations to create and maintain a secondary mortgage market.

MARKET CHARACTERISTICS

The disorganized and inefficient appearance of the real estate market, by comparison with the stocks and bond markets, stems largely from real estate's unique nature as a commodity. What are the main attributes of the real estate market that give this appearance?

Market Attributes

Localized competition. Immobility, heterogeneity, and durability cause competition for real estate to be area specific. Inability to move real estate in response to changes in supply and demand conditions and lack of similarity and standardization means that a potential buyer must inspect each property of interest to understand fully its merits. Without easy means for buyers to compare one property with another, competition between properties is limited. Localized competition is more true of residential properties than of commercial investment and industrial properties. Investors and industrialists are usually more knowledgeable and have greater reason to look around carefully before buying a property.

Stratified demand. People generally seek and use real estate for a specific purpose. For example, a family looking for a detached home limits its search to one-family houses. A merchant seeking a property from which to sell furniture looks only at store buildings. An investor for dollar income looks only at income properties. The market responds accordingly. The market for apartments may be very active while the market for one-family residences may be very slow. Specializations develop and properties are classified according to this stratified demand; thus, brokers, appraisers, and managers may limit their activities to income or industrial real estate only.

Confidential transactions. Buyers and sellers usually meet in private, and their offering and agreed prices are not freely disseminated as a rule. Moreover, transactions are not made in a central marketplace but rather in homes, offices, restaurants, cars, planes, and dozens of other such locations. Decentralized and confidential transactions make market information difficult to collect and, therefore, costly.

Relatively uninformed participants. Most buyers and sellers lack adequate price and value information in making their decisions, because having information collected and analyzed is costly. Business firms increasingly use real estate specialists—negotiators—in buying and selling properties to overcome information limitations. But owners and potential purchasers often make less than optimal decisions in their real property dealings. Only people closely associated with the market have relatively easy access to price and value information. Nevertheless, sellers and buyers increasingly seek, and pay for, price information to maximize self-interest. Of course, this means higher transaction costs.

Supply fixed in short run. Supply, in the real estate market, is fixed for periods of a few years. If demand falls, it remains. If demand increases, from several weeks to several months or longer are required to build new structures. Conversion of existing properties is no less time consuming. In any given year, the total supply of space is increased by only 2 to 3 percent.

Demand in a specific area or community can be quite volatile in the short run. Thus, demand could advance sharply. The consequence is sharp price increases for space if demand runs too far ahead of supply. On the other hand, prices decrease only slowly if demand drops because owners resist taking losses on high-value, durable assets.

Concluding comment. *Localized competition, stratified demand, decentralized and confidential transactions, and relatively fixed supply all cause the real estate market to be less than ideal.* On the other hand, potential buyers and sellers usually do not have a tight time pressure regarding the completion of a transaction. A family just moving into a community may rent on a temporary basis while searching for a place to live, and an owner-occupant desiring a different home in the same community can generally take his or her time. Business firms may give themselves more lead time and hire more qualified personnel to realize better real estate decisions and locations. The point is that *most participants do have time to consider alternatives and otherwise prepare for an advantageous transaction.* Further, highly competent real estate service people are increasingly available to aid buyers and sellers, for a fee of course.

Classes of Property Traded

The classes or kinds of real properties bought and sold in the real estate market are several. Each class represents stratified demand and constitutes a submarket that is often the basis of specialization.

Residential. Residential real estate is generally considered to include one-family and multifamily residences up to six units and vacant land or lots that might be improved for anything up to six dwelling units, whether located in a city, a suburb, or a rural area. Technically, larger multifamily properties are also residential, but because of their higher value and greater complexity, they are more frequently classified as commercial investment properties.

Commercial investment. Large apartment buildings, stores, shopping centers, office buildings, theaters, hotels and motels, vacant commercial sites, and other business properties are termed commercial investment real estate. Most commercial investment properties are rental or income producing and are usually located in urban areas.

Industrial. Industrial real estate includes factories, warehouses, utilities, mines, and vacant industrial sites. Large industrial properties are usually located in or near urban areas because of their dependence on an adequate labor supply. Industrial plants may sometimes be located and developed in rural areas if the availability of raw materials and power so dictates. Labor will be drawn to the plant and eventually an urban area will grow up around or near the plant.

Rural (farm and land). Farms and ranches make up the bulk of the rural properties that are bought and sold. Recreational properties are often included, but they seem likely eventually to become a distinct class. Raw, vacant land near urban areas, though ripe for conversion to residential, commercial, or industrial use, is also typically included in this category.

Special purpose. Churches, colleges, and other educational institutions, hospitals, cemeteries, nursing homes, and golf courses are collectively termed special-purpose properties. These properties are bought and sold only infrequently, and no specialization has developed around them. They tend, for the most part, to be located in or near urban areas.

Public. Public agencies need real estate for highways, post offices, parks, administration buildings, schools, and numerous other public uses. Public properties are frequently acquired under the power of eminent domain, are held for a long time, and are sold only if considered excess property. *Eminent domain* is the right of a governmental agency to acquire property for public uses or purposes without consent of the owner, upon payment of just compensation. For the most part, public properties are not considered as being bought and sold in a free market. Even so, public agencies do acquire and dispose of realty through the free market.

THE PLAYERS AND THEIR FUNCTIONS

In the last half-century, player specialization has developed rapidly because no one person or organization can master all the knowledge available to us. Professionalization has developed hand in hand with specialization because "experts" want and need public recognition to set them apart. Professional recognition provides (1) prestige and distinction, (2) greater sales acceptance, and (3) social responsibility. In turn, new people entering any industry specialization, such as medicine, law, or real estate, must develop expertise and obtain professional recognition to compete.

Knowing specializations and professional organizations is, therefore, a great advantage to newcomers. In the real estate business, four player specializations (positions) must be recognized to know who does what and why:

1. Investors and lenders (primary decision makers and risk takers)
   - a. Equity investment
     - (1) Owner-user
     - (2) Owner-investor
   - b. Lender investment (primarily mortgage lending)
   - c. Leasehold investment
2. Property developers (specialized decision makers and risk takers)
   - a. Total development (from raw land to finished project)
   - b. Land subdivision
   - c. Speculative construction
   - d. Contract construction
3. Brokerage services (market catalysts or facilitators)
   - a. Residential
   - b. Commercial investment
   - c. Syndicators
   - d. Industrial
   - e. Farm and land
4. Specialized, nonbrokerage services (technical support)
   - a. Appraisal
   - b. Architecture
   - c. Counseling
   - d. Education
   - e. Escrows
   - f. Insurance
   - g. Management
   - h. Planning
   - i. Title analysis

Players often play two or more positions. For example, a broker may be a developer and an investor. Or an appraiser may be a counselor and a teacher.

Finance and Investment

Investors and lenders are the primary decison makers in the real estate business. They put up the money and take the risks. They account for all major financial interests in the use and operation of real estate. Generally speaking, the values of the interests of equity, lender, and leasehold (if any) total to market value.

Most owner-users and owner-investors hold property for long-term benefits. Some even develop or improve property to realize these benefits. On the other hand, some owner-investors, termed speculators, specialize in holding property for short periods in seeking quick gains. A license is not required to become an equity investor, although money and willingness to take risks are necessary. A leading trade organization of owners is the Building Owners and Managers Association (BOMA).

The investment of most lenders is in the loan to the owner, which is secured by the property. The lender's main concerns are that the property be kept operational and well maintained and that the loan be repaid on schedule. A substantial source of money for loans is obviously necessary to become a lender. Increasingly, financial institutions that were traditionally lenders are taking equity positions and, therefore, are becoming lender-owners.

Renters live in or use property in return for payments to the owner under a *leasehold agreement.* A leasehold position is gained simply by entering into the rental contract.

Property Development

Investor-developers, subdividers, and builders add to or modify the supply of real estate. They specialize in adjusting the quality and quantity of space, which is a major function of the real estate market. Contracting does not include any ownership risks. Leading trade organizations include the Urban Land Institute, the National Association of Home Builders, and the Associated General Contractors of America.

Brokerage Services

Brokers act as catalysts or stimulants to the real estate market. That is, they earn fees or commissions by bringing buyers and sellers together. Together with investors and lenders, brokers are instrumental in carrying out the exchange function of the real estate market.

All states and/or provinces require all brokerage personnel to be licensed. Anyone interested in becoming licensed may obtain specific information by calling the local realty board. Alternately, a letter requesting licensing information might be sent to the real estate commissioner at your state or provincial capital.

Briefly, obtaining a license requires that application be made and an examination passed. An examination fee must usually be sent in with the application, along with other information or documentation. In general, a person must be a high school graduate or its equivalent, be at least 18 years of age (in some states, 21), and be a citizen, to qualify to take the exam.

Upon applying, the stage is set for the following events. A notice will be sent to you stating when and where the exam may be taken, plus any additional response expected of you. Exam results will be sent to you within several weeks of taking the exam. If you pass, upon sending in the license fee, your license will be sent you. Anyone not passing, depending on state or provincial requirements, may usually take a second examination at a later time.

Several weeks are usually required for a license application to be processed. Hence, if you propose to take the exam upon finishing this book, you are advised to request application materials immediately.

Specialized Services.

Technical expertise or know-how is available to the finance and investment group on a fee or salary basis in many specializations. Appraisers and counselors collect and analyze market information for the decision makers. Appraisers specialize in making value estimates; counselors, who have wider background and experience, give advice for a variety of decisions or actions. Architects design and oversee construction of real estate improvements.

Real estate education is provided by people with many backgrounds at the licensure, professional, and college levels. Title analysts and insurance agents offer protection from loss to owners and lenders. Escrow agents hold money, legal instruments, and other valuables for contracting parties until all conditions have been satisfied. Title closing is the most usual situation where an escrow agent is used. Managers look after properties for owners. Planners coordinate development and change to protect the environment and to relate physical real estate to the social and economic needs of a community. Planners generally work for public agencies or very large private organizations.

Some states and/or provinces require appraisers, counselors, and others rendering real estate services to be licensed. Know-how, and frequently money, are necessary in these areas.

Professional Status

Specialization in real estate has developed rapidly in real estate because the field is too broad for any one person to master all its aspects. Professionalism has developed hand in hand with specialization, because the specialists want and need public recognition to maintain their status. The main specializations and trade or professional organizations are shown in Figure 2–1.

FIGURE 2–1
Real estate specialties and professional organizations

SPECIALIZATION	*ORGANIZATION*
1. Appraising	American Institute of Real Estate Appraisers*
	American Society of Appraisers
	International Association of Assessing Officers
	Society of Real Estate Appraisers
2. Architecture	American Institute of Architects
3. Brokerage	Farm and Land Institute*
	International Real Estate Federation*
	National Association of Real Estate Brokers
	National Association of Realtors*
	Real Estate Securities and Syndication Institute*
	Realtors National Marketing Institute*
	Society of Industrial Realtors*
4. Building/contracting	Associated General Contractors of America
	National Association of Home Builders
5. Counseling	American Society of Real Estate Counselors*
6. Developing	Urban Land Institute
7. Educating	American Real Estate and Urban Economics Association
8. Financing	American Bankers Association
	Mortgage Bankers of America
	National Association of Mutual Savings Banks
	U.S. League of Savings Associations
9. Insurance	American Institute for Property and Liability Underwriters
10. Managing	Institute of Real Estate Management*
11. Owning	National Apartment Owners Association
	National Association of Building Owners and Managers
12. Planning	American Planning Association

*Affiliates of the National Association of Realtors, 430 N. Michigan, Chicago, Ill. 60611.

RULES OF PLAY

Real estate is a high-value asset, the buying, selling, and financing of which involves large amounts of money. And people tend to act in strange ways and do bizarre things when large amounts of money are involved. Also, discrimination enters into the play at times.

To protect the public, to avoid legal problems, and to preserve professional reputations, government regulators and many established practitioners increasingly demand high ethical behavior in real estate transactions. Licensed practitioners, particularly brokerage personnel, are closely scrutinized in their daily business activities for violations of ethical behavior; a breach may result in loss of license.

Based on federal laws, rules of state and provincial regulatory agencies, and the Realtor Code of Ethics certain minimum standards of behavior are expected from most players, particularly licensed practitioners.

Fair Housing Laws

Real estate is a "public interest" commodity, and real estate brokerage is a "public service" industry. The average citizen uses the services of a real estate broker only every five or ten years and, consequently, is not usually knowledgeable about the services of brokers and the treatment to be expected from brokers. The U.S. government and some state governments, therefore, have laws, known as open or fair housing laws, to ensure equality of treatment of the public by brokers and, in some cases, by owners. Title VIII of the Civil Rights Act of 1968 is of greatest concern to brokerage personnel. Owners are subject to both the Civil Rights Act of 1968 and the Civil Rights Act of 1866, as upheld by the U.S. Supreme Court. Brokers and owners are expected to know and comply with these laws.

The Civil Rights Act of 1968. The Civil Rights Act of 1968 with its amendments requires that real estate agents (brokers) in their business dealings on behalf of principals (clients) must consider their product (real estate) as "open" and for sale, lease, mortgage, and so forth to all legally competent persons. The 1968 act, therefore, prohibits discrimination because of an individual's sex, race, color, religion, or national origin in real estate transactions. This act applies particularly to housing transactions. That is, one-family dwellings, apartment buildings, and even vacant residential parcels are covered.

The following acts are specifically prohibited or unlawful if they are based on an individual's sex, race, color, religion, or national origin:

1. Refusing to sell, rent, or negotiate or otherwise make a dwelling available to any person
2. Using terms, conditions, or privileges of sale or rental to deny or to discriminate against any person
3. Discriminating in the provision of services or facilities against any person
4. Using advertising or oral statements to limit the sale or rental of any dwelling
5. Falsely representing, as a means of discrimination, that a dwelling is not available for inspection, sale, or rental
6. Inducing for profit, or attempting to induce for profit, the sale or rental of housing because of entry, or prospective entry into a neighborhood of persons of a particular sex, race, color, religion, or national origin

In addition, denying access to, membership in, or participation in any multiple listing service, real estate brokers' organization, or other service or organization relating to the sale or rental of dwellings as a means of discrimination is unlawful.

Almost all the unlawful acts listed relate specifically to discrimination in sale or rental transactions. Steering and blockbusting are also prohibited. *Blockbusting* means using scare tactics (of neighborhood invasion by a minority group) to induce panic sales of houses by owners at prices below market value. The blockbuster buys the homes at reduced prices and later sells them at inflated prices to minority persons. *Steering* is channeling home seekers to specific areas to create a blockbusting situation or to maintain the homogeneous makeup (all white, for example) of a neighborhood.

Individual owners are exempt from the 1968 Civil Rights Act if

1. A sale or lease is arranged without the aid of real estate agents
2. A sale or lease is arranged without discriminating advertising
3. Fewer than three houses or fewer than four apartment units (one of which is owner occupied) are owned by the seller

For enforcement of the law, violations of, and complaints about, the 1968 Civil Rights Act must be reported to the Fair Housing section of any HUD office within 180 days of an infraction.

The Civil Rights Act of 1866. Fair housing had a banner year in 1968. A U.S. Supreme Court decision in June 1968 upheld the constitutionality of the Civil Rights Act of 1866. Under the 1866 act, owners of property are barred from discriminating in the sale or rental of real or personal property to anyone on racial grounds. This 1968 landmark decision derived from a lawsuit brought by a Mr. Jones against the Mayer Company, the builder of a community near St. Louis, Missouri. The Mayer Company had refused to sell Jones a home solely because Jones was black. Jones's attorney centered his case on the almost forgotten Civil Rights Act of 1866. The district court dismissed the complaint and the court of appeals affirmed. The Supreme Court, however, reversed, holding that the statute does cover discrimination on racial grounds and that the statute is constitutional under the Thirteenth Amendment to the Constitution.

In effect, this decision voids the exemptions given individual property owners, under the open housing law of 1968, who sell their homes without assistance from real estate brokers. A person seeking protection under the reaffirmed Civil Rights Act of 1866, however, must bring legal action personally. Support from government agencies is not provided for in the law. Aside from an injunction ordering sale, when a lawsuit is successful, the property owner faces no statutory penalty for damages and no fine under the Civil Rights Act of 1866.

State/Province Regulation of Licensees

Relations with customers. The public looks to practitioners, as specialists and experts in real estate, for reliable information upon which to make decisions on buying, selling, building, and leasing property, as follows:

1. There is to be no discrimination by reason of race, creed, sex, or place of national origin.
2. General knowledge possessed in such areas as planning, zoning, or economic trends is to be current and reliable.
3. All pertinent facts provided about a parcel of real estate shall be clearly and accurately stated; none shall be concealed, exaggerated, misrepresented, or otherwise caused to be misleading.
4. An appraiser may not have employment or size of fee contingent on the value to be estimated. Such a contingency leads to biased value estimates and destroys the professional image of appraisers.
5. Any written estimate of the value of a property shall include the following items (to avoid misuse of the estimate):
   a. Estimate of value
   b. Date of estimate
   c. Interest appraised
   d. Limiting conditions
   e. Description of entire property

Relations with clients. Some ethical guidelines to be expected by clients (principals) from practitioner-specialists (as agents) are as follows:

1. Market value shall not be misrepresented to an owner, as in trying to list a property.
2. Upon accepting an agency agreement, a practitioner owes complete fidelity to the principal. Full disclosure must be made of any personal interest in the client's property or of other conflicts of interest.
3. Compensation must not be accepted from more than one party in a transaction without full and prior disclosure to all parties in the transactions.
4. Owner-principals must be shown all offers as soon as they are received, whether from a prospective purchaser or another broker.
5. Any monies of principals or clients must be placed in special trust accounts until the transaction is completed or terminated.

Relations with fellow practitioners. Agents, to be effective, must build and maintain high levels of cooperation and communications with fellow personnel to further the principal's purposes. Sensitive areas of cooperation and communication among brokerage personnel are as follows:

1. Brokerage personnel must willingly and fully disclose, the nature of any listing to fellow sales personnel: open listing, exclusive right to sell, and so on.
2. All pertinent facts, negotiations, and communications must be promptly transmitted to an owner through the listing broker.

Realtors Code of Ethics

The Code of Ethics of the National Association of Realtors, first adopted in 1913, contains detailed standards of professional conduct for brokerage personnel and, therefore, embodies many of the already cited principles. Members of NAR agree to live up to the code. Licensing examinations for both broker and salesperson sometimes include questions on the code.

HISTORY OF THE GAME

Real estate transactions date back to the Old Testament. Jeremiah tells of buying a field from his cousin, Hanamel, for 17 shekels of silver.

Land subdivision and promotion is part of our heritage in the United States. For example, George Washington and Robert Morris actively engaged in land speculation in the newly laid-out Washington, D.C. Morris, a signer of the Declaration of Independence, died in poverty after serving over three years in prison as a result of his "speculation."

Until this century, most buy-sell transactions took place directly between owners and purchasers. After an agreement was made, lawyers were often called in to draw up the contract and to look after the detail of the transaction.

In the early 1900s, the real estate business was largely unorganized and fiercely competitive. An attitude of caveat emptor (let the buyer beware) generally prevailed. But the use of brokers and agents soon became established practice. The need for standardized brokerage practices soon led to trade organizations known as real estate boards. The boards proved so successful that the National Asssociation of Real Estate Boards (NAREB) was organized in 1908. In 1974, the association changed its name to the National Association or Realtors (NAR). Membership growth in the NAR is shown in Figure 2–2.

FIGURE 2–2
Real estate boards and membership in the National Association of Realtors, selected years, 1911–1980

YEAR	*NUMBER OF BOARDS*	*NAR MEMBERSHIP*
1911	43	3,000
1920	225	10,077
1930	608	18,916
1940	458	14,162
1950	1,100	43,990
1960	1,370	68,818
1970	1,590	98,400
1980	1,806	284,654

In 1917 both California and Oregon passed legislation requiring brokers and salespersons to be licensed. All states and provinces now require all brokeragepersons to be licensed. Contractors, appraisers, and managers and other real estate specialists must now be licensed in most states as well.

Employment in real estate and construction typically accounts for 5 to 7 percent of total employment in the United States. See Figure 2–3. The value of new construction approximates 10 percent of our gross national product. This output includes from 1.0 to 3.0 million new dwelling units each year.

FIGURE 2–3
Trends in employment in U.S. real estate and construction relative to total employment, selected years, 1940–1980 and 1983E.

YEAR	*EMPLOYMENT IN REAL ESTATE AND CONSTRUCTION*	*TOTAL EMPLOYMENT*	*PERCENTAGE OF TOTAL IN REAL ESTATE AND CONSTRUCTION*
1940	2,517,155	44,888,083	5.61%
1950	4,014,790	56,239,449	7.14
1960	4,415,057	64,639,256	6.83
1970	5,003,049	77,308,792	7.04
1980	4,346,000	100,907,000	4.31
1983E	4,943,000	102,454,000	4.83

E–Estimated.*Source*: U.S. Census of Population, 1940–1980, detailed characteristics. Calculations and some extrapolations by authors, based on data from *Survey of Current Business*..

SUMMARY

Real estate is a game in which everyone must play and in which the objective is to maximize personal benefits from realty. The players may be divided into four distinct groups: (1) finance and investment (the primary decision makers and risk takers), (2) brokerage services (catalysts and facilitators), (3) property development (specialized decision makers and risk takers), and (4) specialized services (supporters or helpers). Each community has its own real estate market or field of play. The commodity in this market is real property rights. The purpose of play, from an overall point of view, is to push real estate to its highest and best or most valuable use.

Physical and economic characteristics or real estate as a product are immobility, indestructibility, heterogeneity, scarcity, situs, interdependence, and durability. Characteristics of the real estate market are local competition, stratified demand, decentralized and confidential transactions, relatively uninformed participants, and a fixed supply, in the short run. The main classes of property and broker specializations are residential, commercial investment, industrial, and farm and land. Any competent adult may play the real estate game, although a license must be obtained to be eligible to render many of the services offered.

QUESTIONS FOR REVIEW AND DISCUSSION

1. List at least three physical attributes of realty and briefly give the implications of each.
2. What is situs and why is it important in real estate?
3. List at least two economic attributes of real estate, in addition to situs, and briefly give the implications of each.
4. Identify and explain briefly the implications of at least five characteristics of the real estate market.
5. Do the various classes of real estate (residential, commercial investment, etc.) have different-sized areas of market influence? If so, why? Discuss.
6. Name the four main classes or groups of participants in the real estate business and briefly explain the function of each.
7. What are the purposes of real estate licensing laws? Of real estate ethics? Are the purposes achieved? Discuss.
8. Explain the effect of the 1968 Civil Rights Act on real estate brokerage operations.
9. Give three reasons for belonging to a profession. Are these reasons valid in real estate? Discuss.
10. Do real estate investors have a responsibility to society? Discuss.
11. Are higher or special educational requirements desirable for entry into the real estate business? What are the requirements in your state or province, if any?
12. Most owners and potential owners are not well prepared to buy and sell property. Do you agree? Explain.
13. What are the main concerns and goals of a real estate specialist? Is the rational investor approach likely to be useful to someone interested in offering specialized real estate services? How?

CASE PROBLEM

Specify a real estate specialization that interests you most. Arrange an interview with a prominent local practitioner in this specialty. Ask about necessary preparation, everyday duties and activities, possible risks, and compensation levels. Discuss in class.

APPENDIX A
CAREER OPPORTUNITIES IN REAL ESTATE

Careerist *n.* a person interested chiefly in achieving his own professional ambitions, to the neglect of other things.
WEBSTER'S NEW WORLD DICTIONARY, 2nd college edition

Brokerage is most generally thought of first when discussing careers in real estate; actually, many other specializations are possible. The four categories of players, identified earlier, provide a ready framework for discussing career opportunities in the real estate game. However, we start with brokerage because of its dominant image.

BROKERAGE SERVICES

Brokerage is the largest single specialty in real estate, other than construction and development. The prominent image of brokerage comes about because brokers advertise widely and sales people move about freely in search of listings and sales. By way of extensive professional "know-how" and business contacts, brokerage personnel save clients time, trouble, and money. As indicated earlier, brokerage personnel act as the catalysts and facilitators of the real estate market.

Residential Brokerage

Most new licensees enter the real estate business through residential brokerage, and this is where most licensees earn their living. To begin with, a broad understanding of personal psychology and of real estate finance, law, and economics is needed. In addition, the work requires a good understanding of the community, that is, an awareness of income levels and life-styles by neighborhood, plus a working knowledge of local tax rates and zoning ordinances. Knowing the location and quality of schools, shopping facilities, and transportation routes is also important.

The work allows considerable independence in daily activity. Night and weekend work and an ability to maintain poise in a stress situation are sometimes needed. The product is mainly single-family houses, condominiums, and vacant residential lots.

Commercial Brokerage

Arranging the sale and exchange of properties, such as apartment buildings, office buildings, stores, and warehouses is the essence of commercial brokerage. The emphasis is on commercial or investment-type properties. Leasing and/or development of these properties may also be undertaken. And management of these property types for wealthy clients, engaged in other lines of work, may be necessary.

Current knowledge of population, income, and other economic trends, finance, and tax law are all necessary to structure transactions for greatest advantage to the parties involved. High income and great personal satisfaction may be derived from solving the high-value problems. Commercial practitioners have considerable prestige, independence, and numerous opportunities for personal investing, but long hours and considerable pressure is encountered when a transaction is "hot."

An outgrowth of commercial brokerage is securities and syndication brokerage. The work often requires changing the physical form (development) and the legal (creating a corporation or limited partnership) of real estate to make a more marketable package and, in turn, enhance value. Mainly large, high-value properties are involved because they must absorb the overhead of the syndication process.

Industrial Brokerage

Knowledge of a community's economic base and transportation is very important for industrial brokers as well as sources of raw materials and factors of production as water, power, and labor. An engineering or industrial management background is helpful because the work is frequently highly technical. Facts and figures must be collected, analyzed, and presented in a useful form to sophisticated industrial clients. The work is satisfying because complex problems are solved and prestige and high incomes may be gained. Entry and acceptance in the field may take considerable time.

Farm and Land Brokerage

Farm and land brokers specialize in the sale, leasing, and management of farms and ranches and in the sale and development of raw land. Properties handled may run from a 5-acre "ranchette" to a 160-acre farm to a 12,000-acre corporate spread. Obviously, a thorough knowledge of farming and ranching, and a rural background, are helpful. Specifically, knowledge of soils, crops, seeds, fertilizers, seasons, machinery, government subsidies, and livestock is needed, which in turn must be related to production costs and market prices of the products involved. Capable farm and land brokers have considerable independence, high earning capacity, and opportunities for personal investment.

SPECIALIZED, NONBROKERAGE SERVICES

Appraising

A professional appraiser must have an analytical mind, practical experience, technical knowledge, and good judgment. Capability in accounting, mathematics, computers, and writing is important for success in this line of activity. Poise is also necessary because appraisers are frequently called on as expert witnesses concerning value in court cases. Appraisers usually begin by valuing one-family residences. The more capable soon broaden their abilities so they can value a wide range of properties.

Appraising is one of the more respected specialties in real estate. Many appraisers are self-employed professionals, earning high incomes and much job satisfaction. Because of possible conflicts of interests, investment and speculative opportunities are not easy to come by. Some appraisers work for financial institutions or government agencies, which usually means fewer hours, less pressure, and lower pay.

Architecture

Architecture involves designing and overseeing the construction of improvements to land. The services of an architect are most used for complex and expensive buildings that must meet both aesthetic and economic standards. Considerable desire and talent is necessary to become an architect.

Most architects prefer private practice. Clients include school boards, corporations, governments, and individuals. Preparation in law, finance, computers, and real estate, in addition to architecture, is desirable. The work is highly creative, prestigious, and community-building. Much overtime and pressure are usually involved in designing and developing a project through to completion.

Community Planning

Planners usually work for local governments, civic groups, corporations, or developers or as consultants. Planners relate development and land use to a community's economic and social needs. Thus, planners coordinate the use of land and water resources in providing for new streets and highways, schools, parks, and libraries, as well as for residential, commercial, and industrial neighborhoods. Increasingly, urban renewal and renovation are an important part of planning. Planning is definitely a creative and community-building profession.

Counseling

A counselor gives expert advice on real estate problems, based on broad knowledge and considerable experience in the areas of brokerage, appraisal, development, financing, leasing, and investment. Needless to say, to maintain a reputation and a practice, the advice given must usually lead to success. Counseling is usually combined with some other specialty, such as appraising, research, education, or market analysis. Counseling, while a relatively young specialization, is growing rapidly.

Property Management

A property manager supervises real estate for an owner, usually to achieve the maximum financial return. Rents are collected, space is leased, and the property must be repaired and maintained. Management has grown rapidly as a specialization. In recent years, many corporations have created a new position, vice-president of real asset management, because of a new awareness that real estate constitutes nearly one-half, or more, of the firm's total assets. Experience in brokerage, construction, accounting, and appraisal is desirable for a career in property management.

Teaching

The demand for real estate education is considerable at the licensure, professional, and college and university levels. Even so, most real estate teachers do not work full time in education, except at colleges and universities. Many practitioners teach short two- or three-day courses in subject areas in which they are expert; many also teach at community colleges. Teaching helps to keep practitioners current in their specialty while at the same time exposing them to new clients.

Title Analysis, Title Insurance, and Escrows

Title search and examination and title insurance are involved in almost every real estate transaction, and escrow closing is increasingly being used. The purpose is to help people achieve secure ownership. Considerable knowledge of law and accounting is necessary for these specialties.

PROPERTY DEVELOPMENT AND CONSTRUCTION

Construction and development focus on the creation and modification of space. When demand exceeds supply, subdividers, builders, and developers construct new houses, stores, office buildings, warehouses, factories, and shopping centers. When demand for one use, say, office space, is strong while demand of another use is weak, contractors often remodel old buildings for office use rather than erect new buildings. Finally, when improvements are old and obsolete, they must be removed from the supply, often being replaced by a new and better improvement.

Subdividing

Subdivision is the splitting of a large parcel of land into lots or small parcels for sale to builders or the general public. Splitting and selling for single-family residences is the most common form of subdividing, although specialization for industrial, office, or retail uses is often followed.

Subdividing is an important and challenging specialty. Much management skill, negotiating ability, and marketing ability is required. Also, a sound knowledge of financing and local government regulations is needed. The work is creative and community-building, and the financial rewards can be substantial. The risks are also usually substantial.

Contracting

Contractors add or modify improvements to real estate, for profit, within the limits of local codes and ordinances. They convert an architect's plans and specifications into reality, be they for a one-family residence or a 40-story office building. Close accounting and control of material and labor costs are particularly important if a profit is to be realized. Engineering and business education is particularly helpful. The work is creative and satisfying, although at times much pressure is involved. Successful contractors enjoy great prestige. Investment and speculative opportunities are often encountered.

Property Development

A developer converts raw land into a complete operating property by adding roads, utilities, buildings, landscaping, financing, promotion, and other creative ingredients; thus, a developer combines the functions of a subdivider and building contractor. A developer is an executive who initiates and administers projects by coordinating the activities of architects, engineers, planners, attorneys, contractors, lenders, and others toward the completed project. A sound working knowledge of construction, building materials and methods, business matters, the law, and finance are necessary. Needless to say , the work is creative and satisfying, and considerable prestige and financial gain accrue to a successful developer. In many ways, a developer is the epitome of a decision maker and risk taker.

INVESTING AND FINANCING

Investors and lenders are the primary decision makers in real estate in that they own and finance real property. Most other specialties work or act for owners.

Lending

Most real estate investors borrow money to help finance the purchase and ownership of property. Lenders, for their part, advance monies in return for an agreement to repay and a pledge of the property as security for the loan. Banks, savings and loan associations, and insurance companies use salaried investment officers to initiate and administer the loans. The function of these officers is to locate financially sound properties on which loans may be made. Other officers of these financial institutions locate and attract money from savers. Some specialists work independently, earning substantial fees for bringing lenders and borrowers together in large deals.

Investing

Real estate investors lay out money today for uncertain payments to be received in the future; they usually borrow to help finance the purchase of the investment properties and to realize positive financial leverage in the process. The equity investor then owns the property but is responsible for keeping the property operational, for debt-service payments, and for any other risks and obligations that may develop.

Investors have many different modes of operation. Some investors regularly follow classified ads, visit brokerage offices, and maintain contacts with "cooperative" brokerage personnel in search of underpriced properties. Some investors develop properties for themselves. Others are particularly creative in adapting properties to changing local conditions to their own advantage. And still others specialize in leaseholds; they begin by renting an improved property, modernizing it, subdividing it, and subleasing portions at much higher rents; the eventual result is a sandwich lease position that involves no cash equity investment and that yields a high cash flow. This freedom and flexibility in operation is one of the main advantages of our free enterprise system. No license is needed by an investor handling his or her own properties.

APPENDIX B
BROKERAGE OPERATIONS AND PRACTICES

Nature magically suits a man to his fortunes, by making them the fruit of his character.
EMERSON, *Conduct of Life: Fate*

IMPORTANT TOPICS OR DECISION AREAS COVERED IN THIS APPENDIX

- The broker's function
- The listing process
- Selling the listed property
- Advertising real estate

Brokerage is an integral part of the real estate business. Hence, this appendix is included for those readers interested in entering brokerage. Brokerage personnel provide a critical service, namely, that of catalyst, in buy-sell transactions. Successful brokerage operations require a knowledge of everything covered here, that is, "putting it all together." In addition, brokerage personnel must master "on-the-job" listing, selling, and self-management.

KEY CONCEPTS INTRODUCED IN THIS APPENDIX

AIDA
Canvassing
Closing
Institutional advertising
Name advertising
Puffing
Specific advertising

THE BROKER'S FUNCTION

A broker must play many roles to market real estate successfully on a continuing basis. Among the more important of these roles are (1) negotiator and (2) manager.

The Broker as a Negotiator

A broker's primary function is negotiating sales. Listing a property at a reasonable asking price is a greater challenge, in some ways, than is selling the property. Both tasks involve sales or negotiating ability. The objective in either case is to persuade another person (or other persons) to make a major decision about property ownership.

Basic qualifications for negotiations include being clean and neat in appearance, being reasonably well dressed, and conducting oneself with self-confidence. Tact, good judgment, and reasonable knowledge of property and laws are equally important qualifications.

Important points that brokerage personnel should keep in mind as they seek to list or to sell property are as follows:

1. Never offer a property without having looked at it personally. An agent cannot sell what he or she does not know. And a person cannot know improved real estate without having inspected it thoroughly.
2. Analyze the property. Never offer anything without having thought it out clearly. Get your thoughts down on paper because almost everyone reads better than he or she listens.
3. Try to know enough about the property to answer almost any question about it.
4. Talk to the prospect in his or her own language. Never talk down to a prospect.
5. Always try to please the prospect. The prospect does not have to deal with a broker or salesperson and will not if irritated.

6. Remember that a prospect will not buy or sell unless he or she thinks it is advantageous. A prospect must be convinced that there is some good reason to act. Do not try to sell property unless in your judgment the prospect ought to buy it.
7. Never lie. Do not misstate. Almost all prospects are on the lookout for misstatements. And the salesperson is finished the instant he or she is detected making misstatements.
8. Never argue. A salesperson may be right and still lose the sale.
9. Get the prospect to the property as soon as possible. If there is more than one prospect, for instance, a husband and wife, get them all there. Do not handle them separately.
10. Concentrate on a few sales rather than putting in a little work on many and closing none.
11. Speak with discretion. Give your client ample opportunity to ask questions. Know when to stop; it is possible to talk oneself out of a sale.
12. Use the telephone to save time and steps. But bear in mind that if an issue is critical, a personal interview is better.
13. Never fail to submit an offer. It is not the agent's function to turn down an offer. Ridiculous offers are sometimes accepted. An agent cannot be absolutely sure of what a principal has in mind.
14. Look for business at all times. It is surprising how many listings may be picked up while working on something else.
15. Bear in mind that a prospect is a busy person. Do not waste his or her time.
16. Do not worry about competitors. Salespeople get their share of business if they work intelligently and diligently.
17. Never assume anything. Overconfidence has lost many a sale.

The Broker as a Manager

A broker must first organize his or her own time. In addition, a broker must set up and operate an organization for sales personnel and other employees. Attending to the details involved requires considerable managerial ability and attention to office, organization, and decision making.

The real estate office. Real estate offices are of many kinds and sizes. A few specialize in distinct kinds of work. Almost all transact all kinds of real estate business. Larger, well-rounded offices, with separate departments, each comprised of an executive and various subordinates, are found in larger cities. Some of the larger firms provide several, or all, of the following functions:

1. Appraising
2. Brokerage (property, mortgage, and exchange)
3. Counseling
4. Development and construction
5. Insurance
6. Management and leasing

The real estate organization. Each department has its own functions, but all are basically engaged in selling ownership, equity, or space. The small office consists of the "chief" and one or more sales personnel. The large office expands this organization. Naturally, the ambition of nearly every salesperson is to work up to an executive position and possibly to branch out into the operation of his or her own office. The broker-manager must obtain business, retain and train personnel, and maintain the organization.

Following through. The broker is the originator or source of drive in almost every organization. Sales and other office personnel attend to details, but the ultimate responsibility for the details falls back on the broker. The broker, through his or her organizational ability, must see that the details are taken care of for each transaction of the business. The broker's skill and persistence in following through on matters of listing, finance, insurance, accounting, property management, and closings provide the key to customer satisfaction and to success.

THE LISTING PROCESS

A successful and continuing brokerage program must (1) obtain, (2) service, and (3) sell listings. The first two are discussed in this section; the third is discussed in the next.

Listings may be secured by brokers and sales personnel from many sources. The most usual sources are (1) repeat business or referrals from satisfied customers; (2) friends and acquaintances, for example, who are members of the same clubs and organizations; (3) "for sale by owner" leads; (4) expiring listings of competing brokers, noted through a multiple listing pool; (5) leads based on births, deaths, marriages, promotions, or corporate transfers picked up from newspapers; (6) solicited office drop-ins of owners desiring to sell; and (7) canvassing, or contacting, property owners by telephone or in person without a prior appointment. Leads to a possible listing opportunity must be followed up promptly.

Obtaining the Listing

An owner must make at least the following four decisions in listing a property for sale:

1. Are the advantages of listing (hiring a broker) worth the brokerage fee or commission to be paid upon sale of the property?
2. Are the advantages of listing with one particular broker (your firm) greater than the advantages of listing with any other broker?
3. How will the listing price be set?
4. What length of time is to be allowed the broker to find a buyer?

Advantages of listing. To an owner the main advantages of listing a property for sale are obtaining (1) an objective negotiator, (2) professional assistance and service, (3) technical knowledge, and (4) broker cooperation.

A broker or sales agent can negotiate the sale without personal involvement. In any sale, and particularly in the sale of a home, the seller has strong feelings about the property and its worth. These feelings make direct negotiations with a buyer very difficult. In addition, very few people are skilled negotiators. Many owners try to sell their own homes and fail because they are unable to negotiate effectively with potential buyers. Personal selling efforts of owners often create a deep-rooted, negative feeling in the prospect. Eventually, these owners give up and list their properties with a real estate broker.

Owners also recognize that a broker can render professional assistance and service in the sale of properties. Professional assistance includes several items, one of which is advice on preparing the property to get a higher price and quicker sale. Another is advertising. Items of service include screening out unqualified prospects, showing the property to its best advantage, and always being present when a prospect visits the listed property. Brokerage service also includes looking after a property if the owner or owners move to another community.

Brokerage personnel generally have better technical knowledge than do owners. Brokers know the real estate market better. They also know financing better. A broker's knowledge of sources of mortgage money is particularly useful to sellers.

Owners also engage brokers to sell properties because there is greater market exposure through broker cooperation. Increasing the number of brokers, and people, who know about the property increases the likely sale price and shortens the time required for sale. Brokers who belong to multiple listing services offer an especially strong advantage to owners.

Specific broker advantages. Owners must decide whether or not the advantages of listing with one specific broker outweigh the advantages of listing with other brokers. The advantages of listing with a specific broker may be greater knowledge, better service, or more effective promotion and sales ability. A broker's reputation for professional, competent handling of listings helps greatly in obtaining listings. The broker's, or sales agent's, task in obtaining a listing is to convince the owner that the broker's firm can do a better job of selling the property than anyone else can.

The listing price. It is critical that a property be listed at a price not greatly in excess of its market value. Every owner wants to sell his or her property for as much as possible. At the same time, almost all owners recognize that they are limited by market competition as to how much they will actually realize from their property. Very few owners know the market value of their properties. And, usually, if they do have a value in mind, it is well above the property's actual value. Prudent brokers require that a property be listed at a price reasonably close to its market value and will not spend the time and effort promoting a property that is listed at too high a price.

A broker should have a fair idea of what a property will sell for when the listing is originally obtained. The most probable selling price of a property is the market value. The principles of market value appraising are explained in Chapter 19. Professional brokerage people use these principles to advise owners on a reasonable listing price for their properties. These brokers do not accept the owner's statement, "Let's list at my price; I can always come down." The broker should make a strong effort to persuade the owner to list at a price at which a sale can be made. "A property well listed is half sold." Calculations of commission amounts and net sales prices to owners are discussed in Chapter Six.

The listing term. A listing agreement may be written to run from one day to one year or more. Brokers prefer that a housing listing run for a minimum of three or four months to allow time for a reasonable promotion and sales effort. Usually, the larger and more valuable the property, the longer is the desired listing time. Some multiple listing boards have minimum listing periods.

Obtaining accurate listing information. All information likely to help sell a property should be obtained when the property is listed. Information taken at time of listing must be accurate and complete. The listing contract is often the first contact with an owner; therefore, making a good impression is important. Thorough inspection and accurate measurement of a property at time of listing are excellent ways in which to impress an owner of professional competence.

Specific information, as appropriate, should be recorded in listing a property. The listing form usually provides space for specific items, like the following:

1. Lot dimensions (frontage and depth) and area
2. Building dimensions and area or volume
3. Number and sizes of rooms
4. Kind of construction
5. Age and condition of structures
6. Equipment data (heat, water, electricity, etc.)
7. Financing offered by owner
8. Neighorhood data
9. Zoning (very important for vacant land)
10. Tax data

Additional items should be noted if they pertain directly to the sale of the property.

Servicing the Listing

Owners select brokers more on the basis of their sales results and of service offered than for any other reason. A reputation for sales and service performance must be earned.

Clear communication at the following times greatly helps to establish a reputation for service.

1. *Initial communication.* Upon taking a listing, a broker should advise the owner-seller specifically of what services are to be provided, who will provide each service, and why the services are necessary.
2. *Continuing communication.* Owner-sellers should be advised as to what services are being rendered and where results are to be expected. Personal contact (setting up showings of the listed property and explaining the results of a showing) are particularly important.
3. *Periodical review and recommendation.* A listed property that does not sell in a reasonable time requires a discussion between the owner and the broker. The history of the listing and selling prices of comparable properties or houses should be reviewed. The broker or sales agent should have recommendations in mind before the review. This review often takes place just before the expiration of the listing. If initial and continuing communications have been clear, and if all services have been performed, the owner should be receptive to extending the listing and following other suggestions. Both the owner and the broker are interested in getting the best price and terms as quickly as possible.

SELLING THE LISTED PROPERTY

Successful selling of listings involves three essential steps: (1) prospecting, (2) presenting and negotiating, and (3) closing. The broker or sales agent must sell himself or herself and the property throughout the process.

Prospecting

A broker's task is to sell properties once they have been listed. A sale cannot be made until someone is located who might be interested in the property. Locating potential buyers is called *prospecting*.

Several methods are used to locate prospects. The most widely used method is by advertising the property. Advertising is so important to locating prospects that the last major section of this chapter is devoted to the classes, methods, and principles of advertising. The main purpose of specific advertising of properties is to locate potential buyers for the properties. Other methods of locating prospects are used.

A well-run brokerage office maintains a file of properties wanted in addition to the listing of properties for sale. Every time an inquiry comes in for property that the office cannot supply, a memorandum of that fact and the details of the location, kind, and so on of the property desired should be noted. Whenever a listing of property for sale comes into the office, a check can at once be made in a short time.

A most likely source of prospects for any property is the tenants in a building. They usually do not want to move, and there is always the chance that the new owner may wish to occupy their unit. This is particularly true of business properties. The broker or salesperson should, therefore, interview the tenant or tenants at once. If the tenant does not want to buy, the other storekeepers on the street should be canvassed. One of them may be persuaded to stop paying rent and become an owner.

Personal contacts are always important and helpful. Friends who know that a broker is capable are likely to refer prospects to him or her. The same is true of old customers if they know that a broker is reliable and industrious. Thus, brokers and sales agents are wise to promote their listings verbally among friends and old customers.

Presenting and Negotiating

Prospecting leads to negotiations. Negotiations begin once the initial contact has been made. The contact may be the result of an advertisement and come in the way of a telephone call or an office drop-in.

A prospect must be carefully studied to determine whether he or she is serious or merely a "looker." An experienced salesperson can usually determine whether the prospect is serious or not early in the interview. Considerations such as urgency to move, newness to the community, or a recent birth in a family indicate serious intent. Time should not be wasted on a looker.

The broker must be a keen student of human nature. The first contact is usually brief; in many instances, the first impressions and analysis must be made in a few minutes. An older and more experienced broker sometimes seems to have a sixth sense. In reality, it is merely the ability to judge the prospect quickly and with a minimum of error.

Some prospects harbor an inner fear of real estate brokers and their sales associates. This fear is an internal defense against the power of persuasion or salesmanship that may lead the prospect to a premature decision or a disadvantageous position in the negotiations. This fear is generally no longer warranted, or justified, because of prevailing real estate practices. Almost all established brokers are conscious of the benefits that arise from "satisfied" customers and community goodwill. Thus, efforts are made not to sell the customer but to guide him or her in the purchase of what is needed and affordable. The broker is foolish to allow a customer to contract to purchase a home beyond the customer's means. It only results in the customer's failing to qualify for a mortgage loan. Or if the customer does get title, he or she later becomes unable to carry the property and loses it, creating ill will. A considerate philosophy of negotiating is beneficially reflected in the increasing number of services that the broker is called upon to render for the property owner. Negotiating, when carried forth in a spirit of service, not only wins friends but aids in building a professional reputation that is essential to sound business growth and continued success for the broker.

Having classified the prospect, the salesperson next shows the property or properties. The initial presentation is to a large extent oral, but it must always be borne in mind that most people learn more by seeing than by hearing. Ordinarily, the sales agent should tell his or her story simply and truthfully, never dressing up the truth and never exaggerating.

The sales representative should use the prospect's language. Few prospects are familiar with real estate terms, and some may be buying for the first time. The prospect should be taken out to the property as soon as possible. The salesperson should always make it a point to be familiar with a house before showing it to anyone. Thorough knowledge of the property inspires confidence in the prospect.

Sales personnel may legally engage in "puffing," or building up a property. *Puffing* is making positive statements and expressing overblown opinions about a property without misrepresenting facts and without an intent to deceive. The intent, or course, is to induce a purchase. Misstating facts is misrepresentation and the basis of fraud. Also, making superficial or inaccurate statements may cost the sale and injure the reputation of the real estate firm. A salesperson should go into detail, describing structural or property site weaknesses or faults in their true perspective. Good points, especially those that fit the prospect's needs or wants, should be stressed, with similar honesty.

It is usually helpful to have something in writing to show the prospective buyer. This often takes the form of a property brief. The property brief may be simple or complicated. If the subject of the transaction is an apartment house or office building, the brief will take the form of a pamphlet of several pages, including a description of the property, diagrams of the lot and the building, floor plans, elevation, information on nearness of mass transit, and a detailed financial setup of operating expense and income. If it is a home, the property brief should give a diagram of the lot and of the house, photographs of the building, and a financial statement showing the operating expense reduced to an average monthly carrying charge. Almost all realty boards have a special form for this purpose. Placing the brief in the hands of the prospect during the interview gives him or her something to look at that will probably be absorbed more readily than the sales associate's words. In addition, the prospect can take the property brief with him or her to study before making a decision.

The temperament of the prospect requires that the salesperson fit the general scope of the presentation to the prospect. In addition, the sales associate should find out various fact about the prospect's business as early as possible in the negotiations; for example, approximate family income, marital status, number and ages of children, if any, interests outside his or her business, where and how he or she has previously lived, and church and club connections, if any. Obviously, the sales associate who has these facts in mind can more readily appeal to the prospect's situation. For example, if there are any children, he or she could say, "This is a safe, healthy place in which to bring up children," adding, if the children are of school age and the prospect is in the average income group, "The public schools are convenient and very good, and the trip to and from schools is safe."

Closing

Closing is the stage in the negotiations at which the prospect is finally persuaded to purchase a property; that is, when negotiations are brought to a conclusion. Much has been written on this subject, but as far as the salesperson is concerned, there are no set rules. Experience will teach him or her when to bring the matter to a head.

Rarely does the psychological moment to close arrive at the first interview. The deal may be closed while the salesperson and the prospect are standing in the living room of the home that the prospect is about to buy. More often, however, there are several interviews, but there comes a time when the sales agent must frankly and tactfully bring the prospect to a decision. The trend of negotiations will usually indicate when the time is ripe.

The sales agent can learn to judge when to try to close by noting when the prospect has made the following key buying determinations: (1) recognition of the need for a new dwelling unit; (2) recognition of the house, condominium, or cooperative unit to fill the need; (3) acceptance, based on analysis, that the price is manageable; and (4) recognition that the time to decide is now. The sales agent, in continuing conversation with the prospect, must determine when the first three decisions have been made. When they have been made, the sales agent's task is to persuade the prospect to make an offer to purchase the property.

ADVERTISING REAL ESTATE

Real estate transactions are usually brought about by the combination of direct personal sales effort and advertising. Occasionally, a sales representative carries through an entire transaction without aid, but even here advertising almost always preceded the effort. Advertising is, therefore, an essential element to successful real estate brokerage operations.

Classes of Advertising

Real estate advertising falls into three general classes: (1) general or name, (2) institutional, and (3) specific.

Name advertising. General or name advertising places the broker's name and business before the public; the purpose is to establish identity and location in the minds of potential clients or customers. When these people need real estate services, they are likely to recall the broker who advertised. Name advertising is not intended to sell or lease a specific piece of property or to obtain a mortgage loan on a certain home.

Name advertising very often takes the form of "professional cards" in various places in newspapers. Occasionally, general advertising is used to indicate some specific field or kind of real estate in which the dealer is engaged. Examples would be a small box advertisement reading "JOHN JONES, real estate, factory sites," or "HELEN SMITH, real estate, mortgage financing." Advertisement like these often appear in real estate trade journals. Their function is largely to solicit cooperation with other brokers. Good examples are advertisements of lists of brokers and appraisers appearing in nationally known real estate magazines. It is through these ads that brokers in one area seek out alert brokers in another area when a prospect desires to reside there or to purchase property in that community for investment purposes.

Institutional advertising. Advertising to create goodwill and confidence in real estate organizations or groups is known as institutional advertising. This advertising is carried out by the National Association of Realtors, by local real estate boards, and by other groups that seek to inspire interest in district, city, or mode of real estate transaction, and to direct business to the group member firm. It seems reasonable to assume that the general public has greater confidence in an individual or firm governed by, or holding to, a code of ethics and business rules designed to protect its clients.

Specific advertising. Specific advertising pertains to the promotion of a particular property or article. It may take the form of a display or a classified ad. A publicity release is another means for a firm to get such information published. In any event, the purpose of such an ad or release, whether large or small, no matter where place or how arranged, is to sell a specific piece of real estate, to secure a mortgage loan on a definite property, or to lease a particular location. The greatest individual effort is expended in direct or specific advertising. It is in this form of advertising and in news releases that the enterprising brokerage firm can use its ingenuity and creative ability to draw attention to the offering of a specific good or service.

Advertising media

A survey to determine the effectiveness of the various methods of advertising and promotions that motivate homebuyers was conducted by the Association of Newspaper Classified Advertising Managers and covered ten cities in all parts of the country. This survey disclosed the following:

1. About 73 percent of homebuyers were motivated by newspaper advertisements.
2. Over 51 percent initially consulted real estate brokers.
3. Only 8 percent found the house through friends and neighbors.
4. About 9 percent were motivated by open house signs, billboards, and other advertising sources.

The various classes of advertising media obviously merit attention by anyone engaged in real estate brokerage and sales work. However, for our purposes, we will only recognize that advertising media may be divided into the following four general classes.

1. Newspapers
2. Billboards, signs, and posters, mainly outdoor
3. Direct mail, including pamphlets and circular letters
4. Miscellaneous

Advertising Principles

Advertising is absorbed primarily through the eye. Newspapers, billboards, signs, window displays, and direct-mail circulars must all produce a reaction when they are seen. Television and movie advertising are absorbed through the ear as well, and of course radio ads have to catch the listener's ears. In either case, the intended effects of advertising are (1) attention, (2) interest, (3) desire, and (4) action. The four effects are coded AIDA.

The first intended effect is to catch the eye or to get attention. No matter how good the property offered may be, no matter how much care may have been taken in preparing the copy, no matter how important the message, unless the eye of the prospect is caught, the advertising is ineffective.

Second, the advertisement must arouse interest. The readers' emotions or curiosity must be stimulated enough so that the entire message is read. The copy, letter, or other advertising vehicle must be interesting and human.

Third, the advertisement must arouse desire. The desire for the property or service must be strong enough to cause the reader to take the fourth step, action. Action, by the way of actual contact between a sales representative of the broker, is the goal of successful advertising. Once contact has been brought about, sales ability must take over where advertising left off.

Advertising Agencies

Many real estate firms engage advertising agencies to handle their accounts. The use of agencies is successful in connection with large campaigns, such as development or an auction of valuable properties. Ordinarily, however, the expense is far too great for the average parcel of real estate.

SUMMARY

Two important roles of a broker in real estate marketing are as a negotiator and a manager. A broker must organize and manage sales personnel as well as himself or herself. Negotiating a transaction usually means getting a buyer and a seller to agree to terms.

Brokerage involves both listing and selling properties. Listing involves getting an owner to grant authority to sell a property and later keeping the owner informed on selling efforts. The sales process involves prospecting or locating potential buyers, presenting and negotiating, and closing. Closing is persuading a prospect to make an offer to purchase the listed property.

Advertising is critical to successful brokerage operations. Three classes of advertising are (1) name, (2) institutional, and (3) specific. The main advertising media are (1) newspapers, (2) billboards and signs, and (3) direct mail.

QUESTIONS FOR REVIEW AND DISCUSSION

1. Explain the broker's function as a manager and as a negotiator.
2. Identify at least three key decisions an owner must make in listing a property.
3. Explain the real estate sales process from the viewpoint of the salesperson.
4. What are the three main advertising media used by brokers?
5. What steps or decisions must be made in purchasing realty?
6. What is AIDA?
7. Name and explain at least four motives for buying real estate.
8. An owner wants to list a service station with a broker for $330,000, which is about

$80,000 more than its market value. Should the broker accept the listing? If not, how might the broker proceed? What about an interested buyer?

9. What advantages does selling through a broker offer an owner? What disadvantages? Should an owner always sell through a broker? Discuss.

CHAPTER THREE
REAL PROPERTY RIGHTS AND INTERESTS

Property has its duties as well as its rights.
THOMAS DRUMMOND
(Letter to the *Tipperary magistrates,* 1838)

IMPORTANT TOPICS OR DECISION AREAS COVERED IN THIS CHAPTER

- Classes of Ownership Interests
- Business or Group Ownership
- Encumbrances to Ownership

Real property rights are the true commodity in the real estate market, even though attention is usually focused on the physical realty. The main ownership rights are control, possession and use (enjoyment), exclusion, and disposition. The quality and completeness of rights, and the absence of encumbrances, greatly affect the value of a specific property.

Ownership of real estate is traditionally considered as a bundle of rights. The bundle is wrapped in a government sheathing of law and order that serves to preserve, protect, and enforce the rights.

Knowledge of property rights is extremely important because decisions and actions an owner may take are implied in the rights owned. Also, the relative completeness and clarity of ownership translates directly into risk of loss of ownership because of poor title. *Title* means ownership of property. Having high-quality title of the right type reduces investor risks, enhances value, and increases investor flexibility in administering the property.

KEY CONCEPTS INTRODUCED IN THIS CHAPTER

Attachment lien
Community property
Condominium
Cooperative
Curtesy
Deed restriction
Dower
Easement
Encumbrance
Escheat
Estate
Fee, fee simple, fee simple absolute
Freehold estate
Homestead rights
Joint tenancy
Judgment
Lease
Leasehold estate
License
Lein
Life estate
Lis pendens
Mortgage
Partnership
Police power
Qualified fee
Restrictive covenant
Separate property
Statute of Frauds
Syndicate
Tenancy
Tenancy by the entirety
Tenancy in common
Tenancy in severalty
Title
Trust

CLASSES OF OWNERSHIP INTERESTS

Possessory interests in real estate property are termed *estates*, which divide into two major classes: (1) freehold and (2) leasehold. A *freehold estate* is considered real property, because, in legalese, it continues for an indeterminate period of time. That is, title to a freehold estate may be held for the lifetime of the owner or of some other designated person whose life expectancy is uncertain. Title to most freehold estates is held for the lifetime of the owner (unless sold or otherwise disposed of) and then passed on to an heir. The most common freehold estates are fee simple, qualified fees, and life estates and remainders.

A leasehold estate, on the other hand, endures for a determinate time only, that is, for a period measured in years, months, weeks, or days. Leasehold estates are personal rather than real property. A leasehold is also called a nonfreehold or less than freehold estate.

Freehold and leasehold estates are often called tenancies. That is, the terms tenancy and estate are often used interchangeably even though they technically do not mean the same thing. A *tenancy* is the manner of holding an estate. Again, an estate is a possessory right or interest. See Figure 3–1 for an overview of how estates and tenancies fit together.

Stating ownership by tenancy gives more specific information about the interest held. For example, identifying fee ownership as a tenancy in common gives more complete information about the interest. A leasehold estate, by itself, may mean anything from a tenancy for years to a tenancy at sufferance.

It should be noted that every state has a law applying to transactions involving interests of any consequence in real property, called a *Statute of Frauds.* A *Statute of Frauds* requires, among other things, that any contract creating or transferring an interest in land or realty must be in writing to be enforceable at law. Oral testimony to alter or vary the terms of such written agreements is not admissible as evidence in court.

Estates in real estate have three important dimensions: (1) quantity or completeness of the interest, (2) time when interest is active and benefits are realized, and (3) number and relationship of the concerned parties, which are summarized in Figure 3–1.

Completeness of Ownership

Fee simple. Fee, fee simple, and fee simple absolute all mean the same thing, namely, complete or absolute ownership of realty subject only to certain limitations imposed by the government. Fee simple is considered to be the most complete bundle of rights that anyone can acquire. The governmental limitations are police power, eminent domain, taxation, and escheat.

The owner of a fee simple may use it or dispose of it in any legal way, including passing it on to heirs or devisees by will. A fee owner may

FIGURE 3–1
Real property estates and tenancies

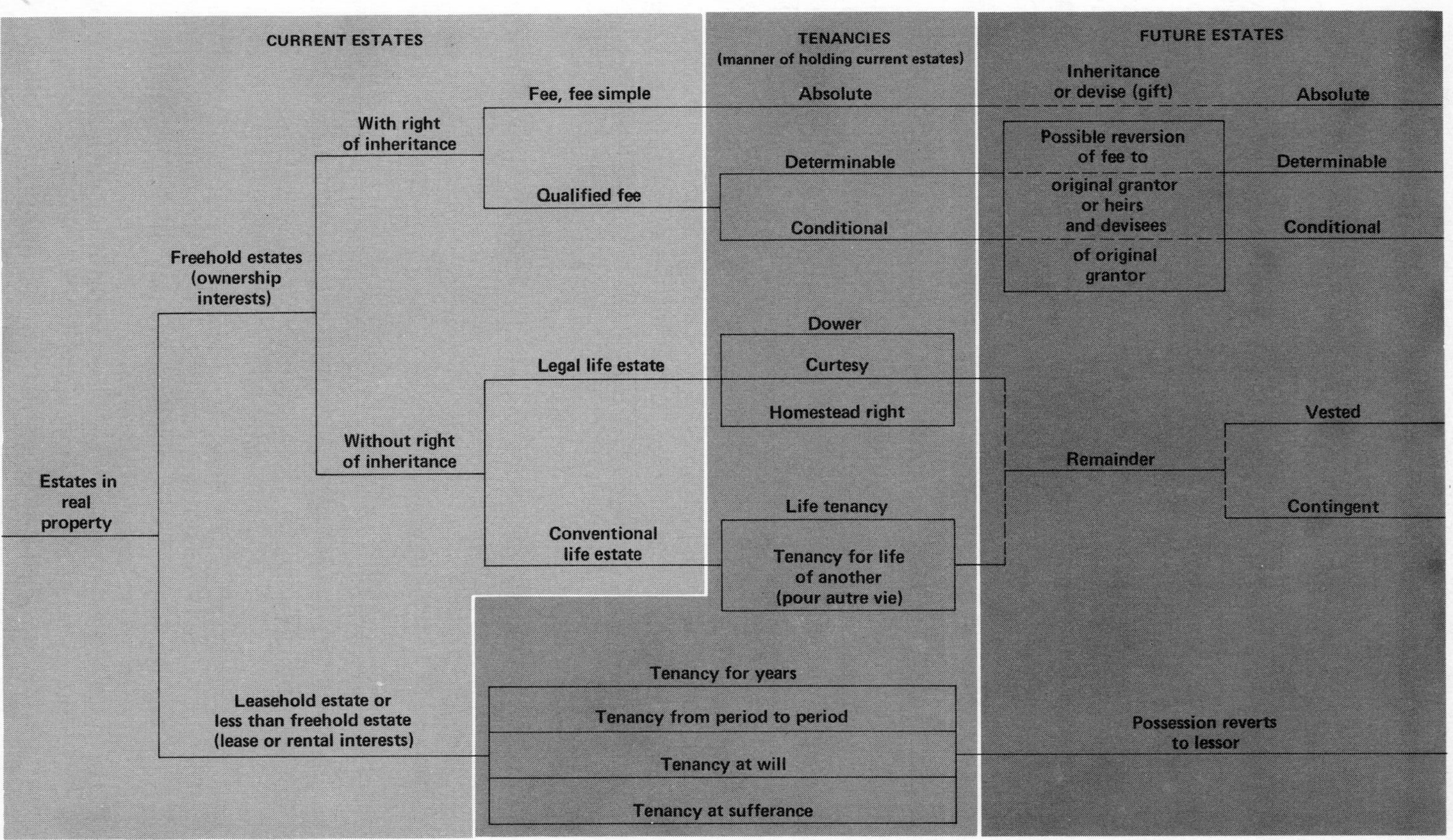

divide up the title, termed "fee splitting," as, for example, air rights, surface rights, and subsurface rights, or as between a present owner and a future owner. Splitting up the fee is usually in terms of completeness, time, or number of owners. An owner may also encumber or lessen the estate by allowing mortgages and other liens, easements, deed restrictions, and leases to be placed against it. In short, a fee simple owner may do anything with the property that does not interfere with the rights of others. Thus, a nuisance may not be maintained, as keeping pigs, goats, or chickens in an urban, residential neighborhood.

Most realty is held in fee simple and the term "ownership" ordinarily means such a position. All other estates are less than fee simple and, in fact, are some portion of it. All the lesser parts, when gathered together, make up a complete fee.

Qualified fee. A qualified fee is ownership in fee simple, with a limitation that may take title away and place it with another. Two types of qualified fees exist: fee determinable and fee conditional. The distinction between the two is that if the contingency occurs in a determinable fee, the ownership automatically reverts to the grantor. In the fee upon a condition, the shifting of ownership may only be brought about by reentry.

An illustration seems appropriate here. Assume that Brown deeds title to Green for as long as the latter refrains from smoking; the quality of the fee is determinable if only by Green's lifespan, which constitutes the maximum length of years over which this restriction is operative. On the other hand, assume that a property is deeded for as long as it is used for religious or education purposes by a church or university; now the fee is subject to a condition that might go on without end. These limitations are not used very often.

Conventional life estates. An ownership interest limited to the life of a certain person is a *life estate.* A *remainder* is the ownership interest that becomes effective at the end of a life estate; it is an interest of future ownership and possession. The person designated to receive the remainder interest is a remainderman (remainderperson??).

The creation of life estates is a common example of "fee splitting" by time. For example, a man wills land to his wife for as long as she lives and then, upon her death, to his daughter. Upon his death, his wife becomes a life tenant and owns a life estate, the right to full use of the property for life. His daughter obtains a remainder position, which is the right to receive and use the property after the wife's death. Upon the wife's death, the fee is reunited in the daughter, who then becomes the owner of a fee simple interest.

A life interest may be measured by the life tenant's own life or by that of another person, termed *pour autre vie.*

A life tenant has certain rights and duties. The owner of a fee simple estate may let the property fall into disrepair or disuse. The life tenant, however, must think of the remainderman. Hence, the tenant is entitled to the income and use of the land but is also obliged to keep the property in fair repair and to pay the usual, normal carrying charges, including taxes. The life tenant must also pay the interest on any mortgage. Any buildings erected on the land become the property of the remainderman. Because the rights cease at death, a life tenant is said to hold title without right of inheritance. Also, if the life tenant were to make a mortgage, the lien would automatically expire at the end of the life estate.

Legal life estates. Life estates may also be created by law, which are termed legal life estates. Dower, curtesy, and homestead rights are legal life estates. Dower and curtesy were developed under English common law and are almost extinct now. In states where they are recognized, the division of property in a divorce terminates them.

The estate for life given by law to a wife in all property owned by her husband at any time during marriage is termed *dower.* Where dower still exists, the requirements are (1) a valid marriage, (2) ownership of real property by husband, and (3) his death. The interest attaches as soon as the property is acquired or the marriage takes place and cannot be cut off without the wife's consent. For this reason, she usually signs the deed when she and her husband convey property by mutual consent. Upon his death she usually gets a one-third life estate in all the real property owned by her husband. Dower was intended to give her a means of support after his death. While the husband lives, the wife's rights are "inchoate" or inactive.

Curtesy is the interest given by law to a husband in real property owned by his wife. Requirements are (1) a valid marriage and birth of a child, (2) sole ownership of the property by the wife at her death, (3) her death, and (4) no disposition of the property by her will. This interest does not attach until the wife's death, and she may defeat it by deed in her lifetime or by her will, in either case without her husband's consent. If the curtesy right is created, it usually entitles the husband to all the net income as long as he lives.

A protection of residence that precludes its attachment or forced sale for nonpayment of debt, except for mortgage and tax liens, is a *homestead right,* also referred to as a homestead exemption. This exemption is statutory in origin; hence, its details vary from state to state. It usually has two purposes: (1) to exempt the home from debt and (2) to provide a widow (sometimes a widower) with a home for life. In most states, the value and area of the exempt homestead are limited. Usually, the dwelling must be occupied as the family home, and a written declaration of homestead must be filed. It is then free from general claims for debts except those that are a lien on the property, such as taxes and mortgages.

As a rule, a homestead right exists in favor of a head of a family residing thereon and may cover a maximum of 160 acres of land if outside, or half an acre if within, an incorporated city or town. A homestead right generally is not lost by a divorce if there are minor children whom the husband is bound to support and the spouse with custody does not abandon the homestead. Homesteads in a few states are exempt from taxes up to a stated assessed value.

Freehold Tenancies

Realty may be owned by one or more persons. One person holding ownership gives *sole* title and is termed a *tenancy in severalty.* Two or more people hold title together under tenancy by the entirety, community property, tenancy in common, or joint tenancy.

Tenancy by the entirety. A husband and wife, owning property as one person, is a *tenancy by the entirety.* The legal fiction of a husband and wife being one originated in English common law. As tenants by the entirety, neither can convey the property or force a partition during the marriage. If either dies, the entire property is owned by the survivor. A divorce converts the arrangement into a tenancy in common, unless the property is disposed of or awarded to one party. A tenancy by the entirety is very useful in the purchase of a home by a husband and wife, since it makes certain that the survivor will continue to own the residence even though a will is drawn. Tenancy by the entirety is not recognized in community property states.

Community property. Community property is a recognized form of ownership in eight states—Washington, Idaho, Nevada, California, Arizona, New Mexico, Texas, and Louisiana. The concept is of Spanish origin and applies only to property held by a married couple. Thus, community property is not designated as a tenancy, although it has the same effect.

The community property system recognizes two kinds of property, community and separate, rather than personal and real. *Community property* means that any property acquired by a husband and wife during their marriage, individually or jointly, is held equally by each of them. The death of either gives full title to the survivor.

Separate property is property owned by either the husband or wife before their marriage, or received by either after their marriage through gift or inheritance, which is specifically excluded from classification as community property. Separate property is free of any claim or interest by the other spouse. Each spouse, therefore, has full ownership and control of separate property and may sell, will, or give the property away, or place a mortgage against it. Income or profit from separate property is also separate property. All property not classed as separate property is community property. Dower and curtesy are not recognized in community-property states.

The rules are not uniform throughout the states that recognize community property. In most states, a wife or husband is automatically entitled to one-half of the real and personal property, or income, of the spouse. A divorce or mutual agreement dissolves the community ownership and divides the property between the two parties.

The law is continually challenged and modified. For example, "Do unmarried cohabitants, or *par vivants*, develop community property rights?" In one case, Lee Marvin, the actor, lived with Michelle Triola for several years, though he did not marry her. She did not work outside the domicile during this time, and she legally changed her last name to Marvin. Subsequently, they split up. She sued for one-half of his income during the period they lived together. The court ruled that Lee Marvin must only pay $104,000 "for rehabilitation purposes" in that no contract was reached. Subsequently, the award was overturned, on appeal. Other cases indicate that where couples live together, share assets, and jointly invest, a property settlement is appropriate.

Tenancy in common. Ownership of realty by two or more persons, each of whom has an undivided interest, is called *tenancy in common.* Upon a death, ownership passes to the heirs or the devisees of the deceased. The law expresses this principle by stating that there is no "right of survivorship" in a tenancy in common. That is, the surviving owner or owners do not become owners of the interest of one who dies. This seems to be fair and reasonable and is the relationship presumed to be intended, unless the instrument creating the ownership specifies to the contrary. Two or more heirs are presumed to receive and hold real property as tenants in common.

Tenants in common may have equal or unequal shares. They are entitled to share in the income and are obligated to contribute to expenses according to their shares. They may all join to sell the property, or one may sell his or her interest if he or she desires, in which case the purchaser becomes a tenant in common with the others. If one wishes the property to be sold and the others do not, an action may be brought for partition, in which event the property is sold at an auction and each owner is paid a proportional share of the proceeds.

Joint tenancy. Ownership of an undivided interest by two or more owners, with right of survivorship, is *joint tenancy.* That is, if one dies, his or her share or interest passes to the remaining owners. The death of one of the owners is often referred to as the "grand incident" of this form of ownership.

Joint tenancy is not favored by the courts. For a joint tenancy to stand up under court contest, it must be proved that the joint owners (1) have equal interests, (2) have acquired title by a single deed, (3) have acquired title at the same time, and (4) have the same undivided possession of the entire property. These are termed the *four unities* of joint tenancy. A breach of any one of them in a conveyance is interpreted as creating a tenancy in common rather than a joint tenancy. Many states have abolished joint tenancy, except that the right of survivorship may still be created if specified in the deed. The right of survivorship has caused joint tenancy to sometimes be referred to as a "poor man's will"; in fact, a will is not replaced because only one property is affected.

Leasehold (Less than Freehold) Tenancies

A lease is an agreement giving possession and use of realty in exchange for payment of rent. The owner who rents the property is a *lessor* or *landlord.* The person to whom the property is rented is a *lessee* or *tenant.* The rental property, if owned as a fee simple estate, is termed a *leased fee.* A *leasehold* or *leasehold estate* is the right of possession and use of a tenant in a leased property. A leasehold estate is not an estate of inheritance; possession is returned to the lessor at the end of a lease.

The lease or rental agreement need not be in writing to create a leasehold interest. And *a leasehold is considered personal property.* Even so, the Statute of Frauds requires that a lease for more than one year be in writing and signed by both the lessor and the lessee to be enforceable.

Four distinct tenancies are possible in a leasehold estate, based on the strength and duration of the leasehold interest. Again, tenancy means the manner or condition under which an estate or interest is held.

Tenancy for years. A leasing agreement for a specific or definite period of time is a *tenancy for years.* Such an agreement is usually for more than 1 year and is usually written. The time may actually be for 1 month, 6 months, 1 year, or more than 1 year. A written lease for 9 months creates an estate or tenancy for years just as a lease for 99 years does. In both cases, the time of occupancy and use is definite. The tenant is required to vacate the property and return possession to the landlord at the end of a tenancy for years without notice being required of the landlord.

Tenancy from period to period. A tenancy of uncertain duration, for example, month to month or year to year, is termed a *periodic tenancy* or *tenancy from period to period.* The tenancy is usually from month to month for apartments in urban areas, which continues until the landlord or tenant gives notice of termination. Usually, the rental period determines the length of notice required. That is, a week's notice is required to end a week-to-week tenancy. Only a month's notice is likely to be required to terminate a year-to-year tenancy, however. A lessee holding over from a tenancy for years, where rental payments are made monthly, is likely to create a month-to-month tenancy.

Tenancy at will. A lessee allowed to holdover with the consent of the landlord, subject to eviction at the will of the lessor, creates a *tenancy at will.* Note that the option to hold over is exclusive to the landlord. Almost all states now require that "reasonable" notice be given. This notice is important. For example, a farm tenant might hold over and plant crops; eviction before the crops could be harvested would be an injustice.

Tenancy at sufferance. A lessee holding over without any justification other than the implied consent of the lessor creates a *tenancy at sufferance,* which is the weakest possible estate in realty. The landlord suffers or tolerates the tenant to continue occupancy as implied by failure to interfere or prohibit. In the past, no notice to vacate was required of the landlord; however, even here, many states now require some minimum notice.

BUSINESS OR GROUP OWNERSHIP

More intense use of land and space during recent years for recreational, business, and residential purposes has caused rapid development of condominium and cooperative forms of ownership. In addition, business needs have long made it necessary for partnerships, corporations, syndicates, and trusts to own real estate. These needs are in addition to the individual and "personal" forms of concurrent ownership, discussed earlier as tenancy in common, tenancy by the entirety, joint tenancy, and community property. See Figure 3–2 for a comparison of these forms of real estate ownership for business purposes.

Condominium

Condominium ownership is holding a fractional interest in a larger property, part of which is separate and unique to each owner (the condominium unit) and part of which is held in general by all the owners (the common elements). Condominium ownership is similar to holding tenancy in common, except that a portion of the fractional share is held as a separate or divided interest. The larger property is, of course, the entire condominium development. An owner of a fractional share holds it in fee simple and may dispose of it without obligation to the other owner or owners.

Condominium co-ownership is most often used for multifamily residential properties. Each owner possesses an exclusive right to use, occupy, mortgage, and dispose of his or her particular dwelling, plus an undivided interest in the areas and fixtures that serve all owners in common. Each deed is subject to identical covenants and restrictions governing the repair and maintenance of the building. Owning an individual residential condo offers tax advantages identical to those enjoyed by owners of detached single-family properties.

Condominium ownership dates back to ancient Rome. Legislation introducing condominium ownership into the United States was initially passed in the early 1960s. As a rule, the legislation requires the separate assessment and taxation of each space unit and its common interests. The legislation, therefore, stops the assessor from treating any part of the common elements of the property as a separate parcel for taxation purposes. As a rule, too, statutes bar the placement of mechanic's or other

FIGURE 3–2
Comparison of ownership forms for real estate investment purposes

OWNERSHIP FORM	*LIABILITY EXPOSURE*	*TAX STATUS*	*LIFE DURATION*	*TRANSFERABILITY*	*MANAGEMENT FORM*
Individual (as condo or coop)	Unlimited	Full flowthrough, one level	Death terminates	Transferable	Personal
General partnership	Unlimited	Full flowthrough, one level	Terminated by death or withdrawal	Nontransferable	By mutual agreement, with equal say by each usually
Limited partnership	Limited for limited partners	Full flowthrough, one level	As agreed in organizational contract	Restricted transferability	Decisions by general partners, no say by limited partners
Corporation	Limited	No flowthrough, two levels	Perpetual	Easily transferable	Shareholder control, with board of directors
Subchapter S corporation	Limited	Full flowthrough, one level	Perpetual, if guidelines met	Easily transferable[1]	Shareholder control[1]
REIT	Limited	Substantial flowthrough, one level	Perpetual	Easily transferable[2]	Decisions by trustees

[1]Maximum number of stockholders is 35.

[2]Minimum number of shareholder-beneficiaries is 100.

liens on the common elements of a property held jointly by two or more owners.

The condominium arrangement does require formation of a central administrative body to act on behalf of all condominium owners for operation of the larger property as an integral whole. Thus, all co-owners must share the expenses of operation and maintenance, which are levied as monthly assessments to each according to his or her pro rata share. Owners, too, are bound to observe recorded rules and regulations governing use and occupancy of both individually owned premises and those held in common. An owner cannot ordinarily be ousted or dispossessed (as can a defaulting tenant) for infraction of bylaws or regulations but is subject to such court actions as necessary to compel compliance.

Condominium ownership is not limited to residential units. Business and industrial properties may also be subdivided into condominium units. Indeed parking ramps have been subdivided into condo parking spaces and yacht clubs have been broken into condo boat slips. Also, recreational housing is increasingly split into time-share condominiums; thus, a unit may have 50 different owners, each with the right of full use for one week per year.

Cooperative

Ownership of shares in a cooperative venture, entitling the owner to occupy and use a specific space or unit, usually an apartment, under a proprietary lease is *cooperative ownership.* The cooperative form of mutual ownership differs from a condominium entity in that the ownership of the entire property (land and improvements) is acquired by a corporation. The corporation as a rule finances the property by mortgaging the property for up to 70 or 80 percent of its value and by the sale of equity shares for the balance. Each buyer acquires a proprietary lease that is subordinate to obligations taken on by the corporation.

A *proprietary lease* is an agreement, with the attributes of ownership, under which a tenant-shareholder in a cooperative occupies space designated according to the shares owned. The lease terms stipulate the payment of rent to the corporation to cover pro rata shares of the amounts necessary to meet mortgage debt, maintenance expenditures, property taxes, and building-related expenditures, such as hazard insurance and sinking fund (replacement) reserves. By contrast, under condominium ownership, each family unit is separately mortgaged and insured; a default in payment by one owner does not affect the ownership rights of other owner-occupants. Under cooperative title ownership, the mortgage and the insurance are placed by the corporation on the entire property. And a default in payment by the corporation due to default in payment by some cooperative tenants affects occupancy and title of all cooperative participants.

Partnership

A partnership is an organizational arrangement whereby two or more people join their expertise and property to conduct business for profit. A partnership operates as a business entity, with its own name, even though it is only an association of individuals. In other words, it is not a corporation or trust. According to the Uniform Partnership Act, unless stipulated otherwise, profits and losses are shared by the partners according to contributions of capital and expertise. In addition, all partners have unlimited liability in the event of extreme losses. The arrangement may be oral or written, but articles of partnership are usually drawn up for partnerships of consequence.

Real property may be held in the name of the partners or of the partnership. Individual partners would hold as tenants in common or joint tenants. The partnership would hold the whole property under a *tenancy in partnership*, which would be an estate in severalty.

Two kinds of partnership interests are legally recognized: the general and the limited. The *general partner* (or partners) operates and manages the business and may be held liable for all losses and obligations of the entity not met by the other partners. A *limited partner* is exempt by law from liability in excess of his or her contribution. A limited partner, also termed a silent partner, may not participate in operations and management under penalty of losing the exempt or limited liability status. A partnership arrangement with silent partners is generally referred to as a limited partnership. A limited partnership must have at least one general partner who conducts business for the entity.

A real estate partnership is usually kept relatively small (under 25) in terms of number of partners. The general partner or partners act for the partnership in acquiring, managing, or developing and disposing of property. The limited partners then remain silent and often unknown outside the partnership. Unlimited liability of general partners means that, even though the partnership holds title to real estate, the effect is that the general partners hold title as tenants in common. When just a few real estate developers and investors buy and hold realty as a group, they do it as partners; this arrangement is sometimes called a syndicate.

Corporation

A *corporation* is a legal entity with rights of doing business that are essentially the same as those of an individual. The entity is owned by stockholders, who can be many in number, and has continuous existence regardless of any changes in ownership. A corporation limits the liability of owners to the amount invested in the organization. Substantial amounts of money may be raised from many investors by a corporation. A corporation ceases to exist only if dissolved according to proper legal process.

Corporations may own, buy, sell, and manage real estate. Many people may share ownership of realty under a corporate entity, that holds title as an estate in severalty.

The major disadvantages of the corporate form for real estate ownership and investment purposes are that (1) costs of organizing and maintaining the corporation are relatively high, (2) the profits are subject to double taxation—taxation of the corporation and taxation of the shareholder upon distribution, and (3) corporations are subject to more governmental regulation, at all levels, than are most other forms of business organization.

A Subchapter S corporation, a hybrid of the partnership and corporate forms of organization, is frequently used in holding real estate. The 1982 Tax Act greatly increased the desirability of this form of real estate investments. A Subchapter S corporation may now have up to 35 shareholders, all of one class, who enjoy limited liability. Unlike a limited partnership, these shareholders may participate in centralized management decisions without jeopardizing their limited liability status. Further, shares are more easily transfered than are limited partner interests. At the same time, profits are exempt from corporate income taxes if distributed to shareholders immediately at the end of each accounting period. Operating losses may also be passed through to shareholders, with certain restrictions, to be used as tax deductions. Finally, a Subchapter S corporation may have perpetual life, provided certain guidelines are not violated.[1]

Trust

A *trust* is a fiduciary arrangement whereby property is turned over to an individual or an institution, termed a trustee, to be held and administered for the profit and/or advantage of some person or organization, termed the beneficiary. The person setting up a trust is termed a trustor or creator. "Fiduciary" means based on faith and confidence as in money matters, primarily in the trustee. The trustee acts for the trust, which may hold property in its own name, just as an individual or a corporation does. The trustee is obligated to act solely for the benefit of the beneficiary. Two kinds of trust are mainly used in owning realty: a real estate investment trust and an express private trust.

A real estate investment trust (REIT) is much like a corporation. People buy shares (of beneficial interest) and, thereby, join together for the ownership or real estate with limited liability. At the same time, double taxation of profits may be avoided by meeting the requirements of the trust laws, that is, paying out earnings in the year earned.

---

[1]Unpublished paper by Professor Charles P. Edmonds of Auburn University and "The Appeal of Subchapter S," *Tierra Grande,* Issue 21, by Thomas L. Dickens.

An express private trust usually involves only a small number of beneficiaries, often a spouse and children. An express private trust may be created during one's lifetime (a living or inter vivos trust) or upon one's death (testamentory trust). The main advantages of a private trust are savings in estate taxes and extended protection for the beneficiary, who may not be familiar with business affairs.

Syndicates and Joint Ventures

Two other forms of organization often mentioned in regard to owning real estate are syndicate or joint venture; neither is a distinct legal entity, in and of itself. A *syndicate* is the coming together of individuals, and sometimes of individuals and organizations, to conduct business and to make investments. A syndicate may take the form of a partnership, corporation, or trust. Personal and financial abilities are pooled because the members believe that as a group they will be able to accomplish ends that each could not undertake and complete by acting separately. The term, "syndicate" is used because it connotes an organization that has limited goals, usually of an investment nature. A coming together of two or more persons or firms for a single project is commonly termed a *joint venture*; in fact there is little or no difference from a syndicate.

ENCUMBRANCES TO OWNERSHIP

An *encumbrance* is a claim against clear title of or a limitation on use of a property that comes about through either a defect in line of ownership or to some action, or nonaction, of the owner. An encumbrance is often referred to as a "cloud on title." Investor-owners need to know the causes and implications of encumbrances because the consequences of lack of knowledge can be substantial. For example, in 1973, a law student in Sacramento, California, went to small claims court to recover a $50 cleaning deposit plus $200 in damages from a building owner. The owner refused to pay. In 1976 the owner's property, a 95-unit apartment complex valued at $1.5 million was sold at auction to satisfy the claim. Only the student showed up at the auction, and in satisfaction of the default judgment, now put at $449, the student received a certificate of sale for the property. A one-year-and-one-day statutory period allowed for redemption of publicly auctioned property passed, without the certificate's being redeemed, so the student became legal owner of the property.

An encumbrance of a slightly less serious nature may result in title being unmarketable, meaning that a buyer need not accept a clouded title to a property. Most encumbrances are created voluntarily, but some are created involuntarily by action of law as when an owner ignores someone's rights.

Encumbrances take the form of liens, deed restrictions, leases, easements, and encroachments.

Liens

A *lien* is a claim to have a debt or other obligation satisfied out of property belonging to another. Common examples are mortgage liens, mechanic's liens, property tax liens, and judgment liens. A lien generally signifies a debtor-creditor relationship between the property owner and the lienholder. The creditor, if not otherwise satisfied, may initiate an action at law to have the debtor's property sold to satisfy the claim. In most cases, a lien results from a contract voluntarily entered into by an owner, but not always. Paying property taxes, for example, is certainly not done voluntarily, except by a great stretching of the imagination.

Note that a lien does not transfer title to the lienholder. And, where more than one lien is filed against a property, the one recorded first has highest priority of claim. The general rule is "First in time is first in line." However, property tax liens, imposed by law, take priority over all other liens.

A *mortgage lien* is created when property is pledged as security for a loan, as from a financial institution. A mortgage lien is specific to the property pledged.

Anyone performing work or furnishing materials toward the improvement of realty expects to be paid, of course. In the event of nonpayment, the worker or material supplier has a specific, statutory claim for payment against the property, termed a *mechanic's lien.* The rationale is that the labor and materials enhance the property's value, and it would be a great injustice to let an owner avoid payment of a claim so closely connected to the property's value.

A *tax lien* is a claim against property due to nonpayment of income, inheritance, or property taxes by an owner. A tax lien results from an implied contract in which the property owner owes tax payments to the government in return for protection, services, and other benefits received. The property tax lien is the most common and is property specific.

A *judgment lien* is a court declaration of individual's indebtedness to another, including the amount. A judgment lien means that a claim in the amount of the court declaration is placed against all property owned by the debtor. Thus, a judgment lien is a general, or nonspecific, lien.

Easements

An *easement* is a right or privilege to use the land of another for certain purposes, such as party driveways, ingress and egress, or drainage. An easement is a nonpossessory real property right, meaning that the holder of the easement does not have the right to occupy the property subject to the easement.

Easements are usually created by deed or by contract. For example, a rancher may sell off a section of land near a river but include in the sales contract and deed an easement to obtain and move water across the alienated land. Easements, except those for utilities and services, may be regarded as encumbrances to clear title in a sales transaction if detrimental to the use of the land. An investor should distinguish between the several types of easements and the implications of each.

Easement appurtenant. An access right-of-way across an adjacent property, a joint driveway, or the right to use a party wall are examples of an appurtenant easement. A *party wall* is an exterior building wall that straddles the property line and is used jointly by the adjacent property owners. Title is held to the part of the wall on one's own property, and an easement is held in the remainder. A written party-wall agreement is best used to create and control the use of this easement.

An easement appurtenant is considered part of the land and is said to "run with the land." Appurtenant means belonging to, or going with, another thing.

An easement appurtenant results in a slight gain or loss in real property rights (and values). The parcel benefited is known as the *dominant tenement.* The parcel subject to the easement is known as the *servient tenement.* The dominant parcel, of course, benefits and gains value, whereas the servient tenement becomes less desirable. Naturally enough, an easement resulting in a property's becoming a servient tenement is regarded as an encumbrance to clear or marketable title.

An easement appurtenant requires at least two parcels of realty owned by different parties. The parcels are usually but not necessarily adjacent. Although the parcels need not be adjacent, the dominant tenement must be at the beginning or end of the easement. For example, a road or right-of-way could cross several servient parcels (A, B, C, and D) to serve a dominant parcel (E).

Easement in gross. An easement in gross is a personal right to use the property of another. Neither adjacent nor nearby property need be owned to possess the right. Examples of easements in gross are rights-of-way for pipelines, power lines, sewer lines, or roads used by public service companies.

Easement by prescription. An easement by prescription is created by open, unauthorized, continuous use of a servient parcel for the prescriptive period. A prescriptive period is from 10 to 20 years in most states. The use must also have been under claim of right of use, without the approval of the owner of the encumbered parcel, and notorious to the point that the owner could learn of it.

Termination. Easements may be terminated by any one of several ways.

1. Consolidation or merger, as when the dominant and servient parcels are brought under one ownership
2. Agreement, as when the owner of the dominant tenement releases the right of easement to the servient owner, possibly for a price
3. Completion of purpose, as when the easement is no longer needed. A right-of-way easement of necessity ends if alternate access to the land-locked parcel is gained by its owner
4. Abandonment or lack of use

Deed Restrictions

A *deed restriction* is a covenant (promise) or condition entered into the public record to limit the nature or intensity of use of land. For example, a property may be limited by a deed restriction to one-family residential use or to having no residence smaller than 1,500 square feet. Or the requirement may be "not to keep goats, chickens, or pigs on the premises." Setback and sideyard standards may be imposed by deed restriction (see Figure 3–3) as well as by a zoning ordinance.

Restrictions were traditionally entered into the public record on a deed at the time of conveyance of title to another; hence, the term "deed restrictions." A more appropriate term for deed restrictions would be "title restrictions." Deed restrictions are now commonly entered into the public record by subdividers to enhance the quality of their developments. In effect, individual owners give up some rights to promote or enhance the value of the entire development. The purpose is to protect neighborhood quality and to preserve and enhance property values.

FIGURE 3–3
Typical encumbrances

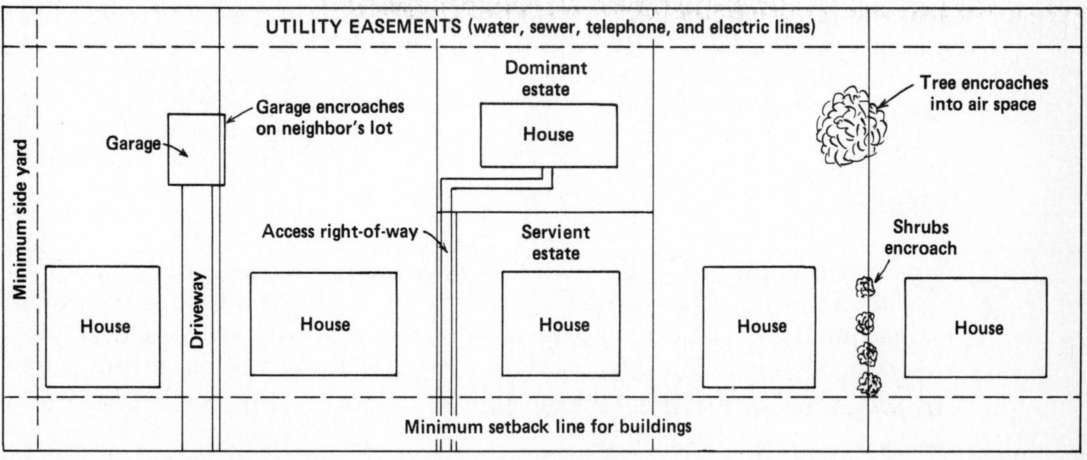

Enforcement is usually by proceedings at law or in equity against any person or persons violating or attempting to violate the covenants. In a subdivision or condominium development, the homeowner's association typically sees to enforcement.

Deed restrictions that do not contain their own time limit (effective for 30 years from this date, for example) are terminated by the law of the state in which the property is located. A deed restriction may be, but need not be, an encumbrance to marketable title; it depends on the effect of the restriction on the use and value of the parcel.

Encroachments

An *encroachment* occurs when a building or other improvement, such as a fence or driveway, illegally intrudes on or into the property of another owner. Intrusion of a garage overhang or tree limbs are examples. The owner of the property intruded upon can require removal, and failure to do so may weaken his or her title. On the other side, a new owner of the encroaching property may be stuck with the unexpected expense of moving a building or cutting back a stately tree. See Figure 3–3.

An abstract of title or title insurance policy is not likely to evidence an encroachment unless it existed and was picked up in a previous transaction. That is, a physical inspection of a property, and sometimes a survey as well, is needed to ascertain that an encroachment exists. An encroachment is a title encumbrance and must be cleared up for marketable title to be conveyed to a buyer.

Lease

A long-term lease extending beyond the closing date in a sales transaction is an encumbrance. A leasehold with periodic tenancy, tenancy at will, and tenancy at sufferance is not usually considered an encumbrance unless time of occupancy and use is of the essence to the buyer.

Licenses

A license is the privilege to use or enter on the premises, granted by someone in legal possession of realty. The right to attend a ball game after purchase of a ticket or to hunt or fish on a farmer's land are examples. As a general rule, a license may be canceled at the will of an owner and is not usually considered an encumbrance to clear title.

SUMMARY

Real estate ownership includes control, possession and use, exclusion, and disposition. Holding title in fee simple is the most complete form of ownership; in fact, all the lesser rights or interests, when taken together, make up the fee simple title. A fee simple title may be split up by time to create life estates and remainders or leasehold estates and reversions. It may also be split up by the number of owners as in tenancy by the entirety, community property, tenancy in common, or joint tenancy.

Business or group ownership may be held in several forms: condominium, cooperative, corporation, or trust. A syndicate actually has the legal form of a partnership, a corporation, or a trust.

Private limitations or encumbrances to clear title include liens, easements, deed restrictions, licenses, encroachments, and leases.

QUESTIONS FOR REVIEW AND DISCUSSION

1. Define and distinguish among the following:
   a. A freehold estate and a leasehold estate
   b. A conventional life estate and a legal life estate
   c. Estate and tenancy

2. Define and distinguish among the following:
   a. Tenancy in severalty
   b. Tenancy by the entirety
   c. Tenancy in common
   d. Joint tenancy
   e. Community property

3. List and explain briefly the four tenancies of leasehold estates.

4. List and explain at least four "voluntary" encumbrances of ownership to real estate.

5. Is government necessary for the existence of private property? Discuss.

6. Are there interests in real estate that do not involve ownership or possession? Discuss.

7. Compare condominium ownership with its Roman law origins, community property with its Spanish law origins, and tenancies with their English law origins. What are the similarities? What are the differences?

8. Does condominium ownership make sense in a rural setting? If so, are there some other forms of ownership that make more sense to accomplish the same purpose? Discuss.

9. Are the laws concerning ownership of real estate changing? In what ways? Give examples.

10. Distinguish between easement appurtenant and easement in gross. What is the usual purpose of each?

11. Identify and explain briefly two encumbrances, not due to defect in title, in addition to liens, easements, and deed restrictions.

12. Giving tax liens priority, by law, is unfair to other lienholders. Discuss.

13. It has been proposed that a statute of limitations is needed to remove encumbrances as clouds on title; thus, liens, easements, and deed restrictions would become ineffective after some stipulated period, say, 15 years. Discuss. What are the implications?

14. When is a deed restriction not an encumbrance? Discuss.

CASE PROBLEMS

1. Able, owner of 160 acres of land along a river, sold half to Baker. No frontage on the river was included, but an easement of access to use the river for recreation was written into the deed. Baker later sold off five 10-acre parcels to other persons. Are these subsequent purchasers entitled to use the access easement to the river? Discuss.
2. A, B, and C own land as joint tenants. C conveys his third to D and dies shortly after. A and B object, claiming that the conveyance is not valid without their approval. A and B further claim that the conveyance, if legal, makes D a joint tenant also. The case is taken to court. What is the result?
3. Francis Scott Key is looking to acquire a home. One property interests him but upon investigation he determines the following. What effect does each have on value?
   a. Garage encroaches on neighbor's lot
   b. Deed restriction prohibits occupancy by minority races
   c. Easement appurtenant to cross neighbor's lot to next street
   d. Utility easement for 9 feet along rear lot line
   e. Occupant's written lease for another six months
   f. Ownership by two brothers as tenants in common

CHAPTER FOUR

PROPERTY DESCRIPTIONS AND PUBLIC RECORDS

But that land—it is one thing that will still be there when I come back—land is always there.
PEARL S. BUCK, *A House Divided*

IMPORTANT TOPICS OR DECISION AREAS COVERED IN THIS CHAPTER

- From Mother Earth to Real Property
- Real versus Personal Property
- Legal Descriptions of Real Property
- Public Records

Having looked at ownership in the previous chapter, attention must now be given to ways of describing the real property that is owned. As a point of beginning, let us distinguish among land, realty, real estate, and real property. *Land,* of course, really means the solid part of the earth not covered by water, though traditionally land has been interpreted to mean real estate. *Realty* and *real estate,* are essentially identical concepts, which include land, land improvements, and the natural assets of land such as oil, water, and minerals. *Real property* is a legal, and somewhat more abstract, concept that means the ownership of rights in real estate. Included are the rights to possess, to use, to dispose of, and to otherwise capture the benefits of owning and controlling real estate. Except in this immediate discussion, we shall continue to consider the four terms as being identical in meaning.

An accurate, clear, and complete system of describing real property is important and necessary to an owner or investor for several reasons. A description provides for the physical identification of realty for the establishment of boundaries, for the calculation of area, for noting location relative to other properties, and for transfer of title from one owner to another. In a legal sense, it allows for the identification of rights owned, for example, air rights, water rights, or mineral rights. It provides a basis for law and order, and, in turn, for rational decision making about real property. In short, a system of property descriptions is the basis for packaging real estate as a commodity in our real estate markets.

KEY CONCEPTS INTRODUCED IN THIS CHAPTER

Acre
Actual notice
Base line
Benchmark
Constructive notice
Contract rent
Emblements
Fixture
Grantor-grantee index
Guide meridian
Land
Land use
Legal description
Metes and bounds
Monument
Personalty
Plat
Principal meridian
Range
Real estate
Real property
Realty
Rectangular survey system
Section
Tier
Township

Tract index
Uniform Commercial Code

FROM MOTHER EARTH TO REAL PROPERTY

In the beginning, the earth was only land and water. There were few people relative to the amount of land. As the population increased in number and crowded more closely on the land, a system of physical property descriptions gradually came into use.

Initially, only surface descriptions were of concern. However, with time, more complicated descriptions became necessary. Today, real estate consists of land and "permanent" improvements to the land. These improvements may be above or below the surface of the earth or may be something that affects the utility of a given parcel, as adding fertilizer to enrich the soil.

But real property is more than three-dimensional space, though we often begin with a physical description, as for a condominium unit. Property rights also are described as air rights, surface rights, and subsurface rights. And more difficult to describe are water rights and mineral rights. And a "right to light" (sunshine) appears to be evolving with our increasing dependence on solar power. Thus, real property, as the object of ownership, may be described in many ways.

Even so, the legal description of most real property begins with the physical boundaries of a parcel of realty. And most parcels have boundaries that extend in the shape of an inverted pyramid from the center of Mother Earth to the limits of the sky, as portrayed in Figure 4–1.

REAL VERSUS PERSONAL PROPERTY

Our concern is really only with real property. Therefore, before going further, we also need to distinguish between real and personal property. Invariably, in specific situations, a line must be drawn between the two.

We begin with a basic relationship: "personalty is to personal property as realty is to real property," based on our earlier discussion of realty. That is, if realty is the object of ownership for real property, then personalty is the object of ownership for personal property. *Personalty* means physical objects that are movable and not attached to the land. And *personal property* refers to ownership rights and privileges in these movable things, as cars, typewriters, and furniture. Also, whereas a deed is used to transfer title to real property, a *bill of sale* is used to transfer ownership to personal property.

FIGURE 4–1
Real estate extends from the center of the earth to the tops of the highest man-made improvements, above which common fly-over rights exist

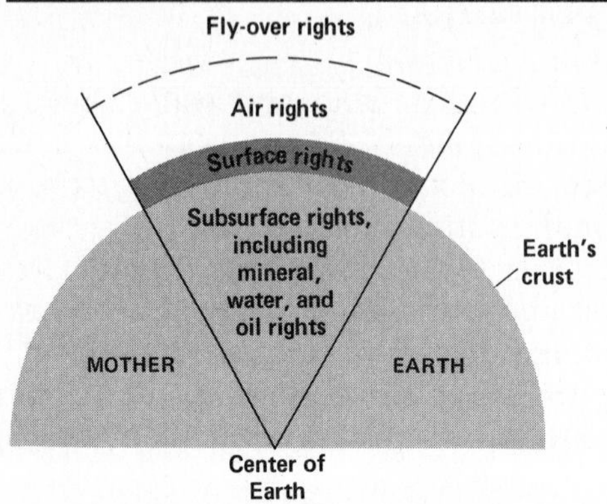

So, how do we know whether an object is personal or real property in specific situations? We begin by defining real estate more fully and then move on to a discussion of fixtures.

Land and Land "Improvements"

Real estate includes "permanent" improvements on a site as well as the land itself. Houses, stores, factories, office buildings, schools, outbuildings, fences, and landscaping, as "permanent" improvements, are clearly included. By law and tradition, conveying ownership of a parcel of land to another also conveys ownership of any improvements thereon. In a similar sense, trees, natural vegetation, and assorted perennial plants, which do not require annual cultivation, are considered real estate. The term for them is *fructus naturales* (fruit of nature). On the other hand, annual cultivated crops (e.g. corn, potatoes, and cotton) are considered personal property even though they are attached to the earth. They are called *fructus industriales* (fruit of industry) or *emblements.*

Fixtures

But, still, a "movable" item under one set of circumstances is considered to be personal property, or *chattel,* and under another set as real property. The bricks and windows in a building, for example, are usually taken to be part of the real estate and are termed fixtures. That is, an item of "movable" personal property annexed, affixed, or installed so as to be considered real estate is a *fixture.* At the same time, such items when not part of a building are considered personal property. A bathroom sink is personal property, a chattel, in a plumber's shop; it becomes a fixture and part of the real estate when installed in a house.

The determination is particularly important at the time of sale, of mortgaging, of lease termination, and of assessment for property tax purposes. A sales contract and deed convey ownership of land and fixtures but not of chattels. A fixture is part of the security for a loan while a chattel is not. A tenant installation, if a fixture, may not be removed at the end of a lease. And during the lease, an owner usually pays real property taxes on fixtures while the tenant pays personal property taxes on chattels.

Several tests are used to determine whether or not an article is a fixture. Meeting or passing the tests makes the item at issue a fixture and, therefore, real property.

1. *Manner of attachment.* Generally, if the article is specially adapted for use where placed, and if to remove it would leave the building or land incomplete, it is a fixture. Thus installed electrical wiring, water pipes, and furnaces are fixtures.
2. *Manner of adaption.* An article specially constructed or fitted to a particular structure, or designed and installed to carry out the purposes of the property, is usually considered a fixture. Thus drapes cut and sewn for particular windows, screens and storm windows fitted to a house, and a front door key are almost certainly fixtures.
3. *Intent of parties.* The reasonably presumable intent of the person placing the article is probably most important in making the determination of an item as a fixture. Kratovil and Werner say that tests 1 and 2 are important, but "once the intention is determined, it must govern."[1] The test is based on the nature of the article, the manner of adaption, the manner of annexation, and all pertinent circumstances. Thus an owner's statements to neighbors may show whether or not an article was intended to become a fixture. An agreement between parties before an item is annexed would make intent clear and avoid later differences and a possible legal suit.

The relation between parties is often such that a presumable intention is inferred by the courts. For example, an owner may be presumed to be permanently annexing the article. And a tenant is ordinarily bound to leave articles fastened to the building; nevertheless, if the property is leased for business, it is a general rule that trade fixtures, such as shelves, counters, and showcases, do not become real fixtures. But such equipment must be removed before the lease expires, and a renewal that fails to state that the equipment is to remain the tenant's property may deprive the tenant of ownership.

---

[1]Robert Kratovil and Raymond J. Werner, *Real Estate Law,* 8th ed. (Englewood Cliffs, N.J.: Prentice-Hall, 1983).

LEGAL DESCRIPTIONS OF REAL PROPERTY

In almost all states, real estate must be identifiable with reference only to documents. Courts consider a description legal if a competent surveyor can exactly locate the parcel of concern from the description. In other words, a *legal description* is a specific and unique identification of a parcel of real estate that is recognized and acceptable in a court of law.

A street address is the simplest form of property description, but a street address is not specific enough for most legal documents or for court purposes. Other methods of legally describing real estate are therefore needed.

The three accepted methods of legally describing real estate are (1) metes and bounds, (2) rectangular or government survey, and (3) recorded plat. A fourth method, the state plane coordinate system, is gradually being accepted as a supplement to the foregoing three methods.

Each of these methods provides for a description suitable for use in a sales contract, mortgage, deed, or court of law. Description by recorded plat is used mostly in urban areas. Metes and bounds descriptions are also frequently used in urban areas for describing residential, commercial, and industrial parcels that have been split off and developed as distinct parcels. That is, the parcels are not part of a larger recorded plat. The governmental survey system is used mainly in rural areas for large parcels; it is too crude for smaller, urban parcels. Except for condominium descriptions, these methods describe land only and do not describe the improvements on a parcel.

A brief discussion of the elements of surveying is appropriate before taking up the methods themselves.

Elements of Surveying

Several considerations are common to all systems of describing real estate. To begin, any land description should contain (1) a defininte point of beginning (P.O.B.), (2) definite corners or turning points, (3) specific directions and distances for borders or boundaries, (4) closure, or return to point of beginning, and (5) the area enclosed in accepted units of measurement.

A point of beginning is the point of take off in describing real estate. Ideally, a P.O.B. ties into a larger system of property descriptions so that the resulting legal description relates the subject parcel to other parcels and to the rest of the world. In addition, a basic knowledge of units of measurement for angles or bearings, distances, and areas is needed to understand fully legal descriptions.

Angle measurement. The full circle about a turning point contains 360 degrees. A *bearing* is a direction of measurement from an imaginary north-south line passing through a corner or turning point on a property. A bearing or angle of measurement is measured east or west of the imaginary line and cannot exceed 90 degrees. For example, assume a circular compass properly oriented and set exactly over the corner point of a property, as in Figure 4–2. A line running just slightly north of due east might have a bearing of "north, 89 degrees east." A 3-degree more southerly line would have a bearing "south 88 degrees east." A minute, in angle measurement, equals one-sixtieth of a degree.

Distance measurement. Distance measurements in surveying have traditionally been in miles, rods, feet, and inches. A mile equals 5,280 feet, or 320 rods. A rod, or stick 16½ feet in length, was a convenient unit of measurement in centuries past; it is not used much now because steel tapes and other new methods of measurement are faster and more accurate.

Area measurement. Areas are most commonly measured in square feet, acres, and square miles or sections. An *acre* is a measure of land that contains 43,560 square feet. A square mile covers 640 acres. More detail on area measurements is given in the appendix. The detail includes conversions to the metric system.

Elevation measurement. A final element of surveying is elevation. Elevations are usually measured from mean sea level in New York Harbor, which is the basic elevation datum or point of reference for the United States. Elevations are important in establishing limits on heights of buildings and other structures and in setting grades for streets and highways. Condominium developments also depend on accurate elevation data.

Permanent reference points, called *benchmarks*, have been created and are located throughout the country to aid surveyors in work involving

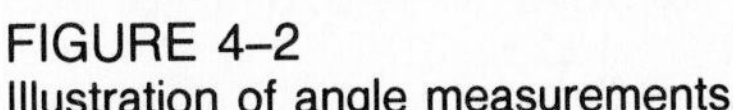
FIGURE 4–2
Illustration of angle measurements.

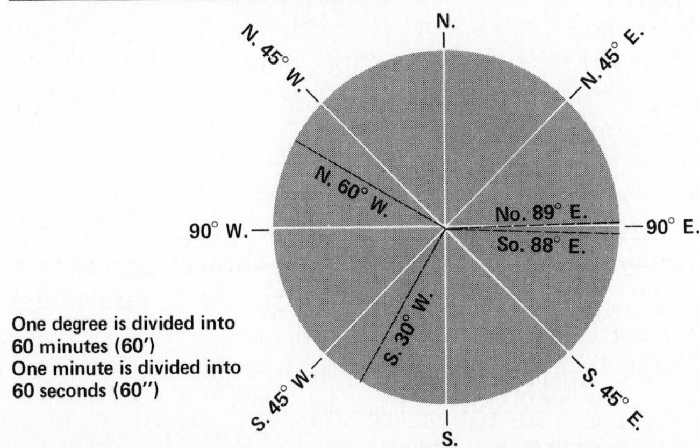

elevations. That is, a surveyor may take an elevation from a local benchmark and need not measure from a basic benchmark in the city of area that is miles from the parcel under survey. Benchmark locations may be obtained from the United States Geodetic Survey, if needed.

Metes and Bounds Descriptions

Metes and bounds descriptions are widely used in the eastern United States. They are also used throughout the country to describe irregular or nonplatted tracts in conjunction with the rectangular survey system. *Metes and bounds* means measures and boundaries; the edges of a property are, of course, its limits and boundaries. A metes and bounds description can be highly accurate when it is developed and written by a competent surveyor using precision equipment. A metes and bounds description for parcel Z, shown in Figure 4–3, might be as follows:

> All that tract or parcel of land situated in the Town of East Hampton, County of Suffolk and State of New York, bounded and described as follows: BEGINNING at the junction of the westerly line of land of James McKinney and the southerly side of Further Lane, and running thence along the land of said James McKinney,

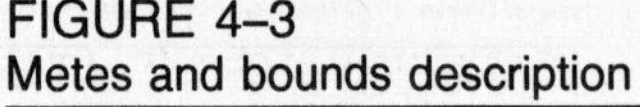
FIGURE 4–3
Metes and bounds description

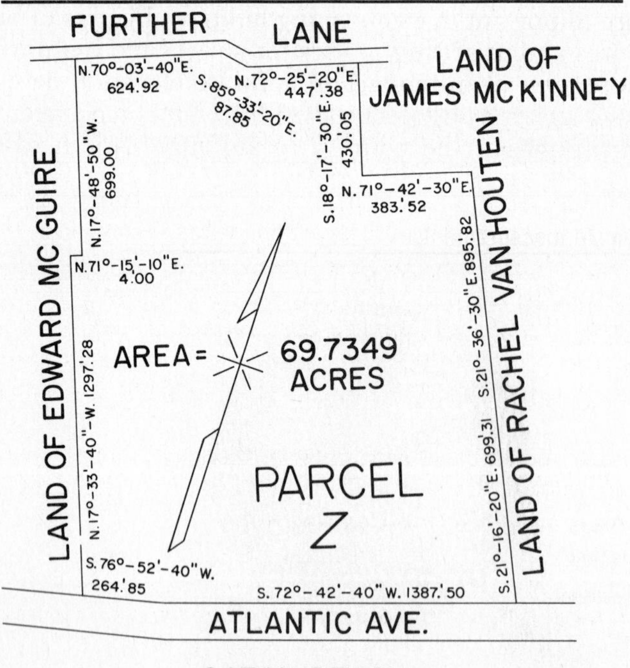

> south 18 degrees 17 minutes 30 seconds east 430 and 5/100 feet; thence along the land of said James McKinney north 71 degrees 42 minutes 30 seconds east, 383 and 52/100 feet to land of Rachel Van Houten; thence along the land of said Rachel Van Houten south 21 degrees 36 minutes 30 seconds east 895 and 82/100 feet to a point; thence still along the land of Rachel Van Houten south 21 degrees 16 minutes 20 seconds east 699 and 31/100 feet to the proposed Atlantic Avenue Highway, thence along said Atlantic Avenue south 72 degrees 42 minutes 40 seconds west 1387 and 50/100 feet; thence continuing along said Atlantic Avenue south 76 degrees 52 minutes 40 seconds west 264 and 85/100 feet to land of Edward J. McGuire; thence along the lands of said Edward J. McGuire north 17 degrees 33 minutes 40 seconds west 1297 and 28/100 feet, thence north 71 degrees 15 minutes 10 seconds east 4 feet; thence continuing along the land of said Edward J. McGuire north 17 degrees 48 minutes 50 seconds west 699 feet to Further Land Highway; thence along said Further Lane Highway north 70 degrees 3 minutes 40 seconds east 624 and 92/100 feet, thence continuing along said Further Lane Highway south 85 degrees 33 minutes 20 seconds east 87 and 85/100 feet; thence continuing along said Further Lane Highway north 72 degrees 25 minutes 20 seconds east 447 and 38/100 feet to the point or place of beginning.
>
> Containing by actual measurement as per survey dated April 10, 1971, of Nathan F. Tiffany 69,7349 acres. Atlantic Beach, New Jersey.

A simple variation of the metes and bounds system of identifying real estate is based on monuments. A *monument* is an identifiable landmark that serves as a corner of a property. A monument description, which does not require exact measurements or directions, is acceptable whenever land is not too valuable and the expense of a detailed, accurate survey would be out of proportion to the value. Monument descriptions are not widely used today, although at one time they were prevalent.

Monuments may be tangible or intangible. If tangible, they are either natural or artificial. Rivers, lakes, streams, trees, ricks, springs, and the like are natural monuments. Fences, walls, houses, canals, streets, stakes, and posts are artifical monuments. The center line of a street is an example of an intangible monument. Since all monuments are susceptible to destruction, removal, or shifting, they should be used only when necessary, and then every available identifying fact should be stated, for example, not merely "a tree" but "an old oak tree." Thus, even after the tree has become a stump, it may still be identified as oak and distinct from other trees.

A farm may be described without mention of metes or bounds per se. The farm of John Robinson at Pleasantville, Westchester County, New York, is bounded and described as follows:

> Beginning at the dock on Indian Creek at the foot of Dock Road; thence along Dock Road to the point where said road is met by the fence dividing the farms of [the seller] and Jones, thence along said fence to the side of Indian Creek, and thence along said Indian Creek to the Dock, the point of beginning.

FIGURE 4–4
Description by monuments

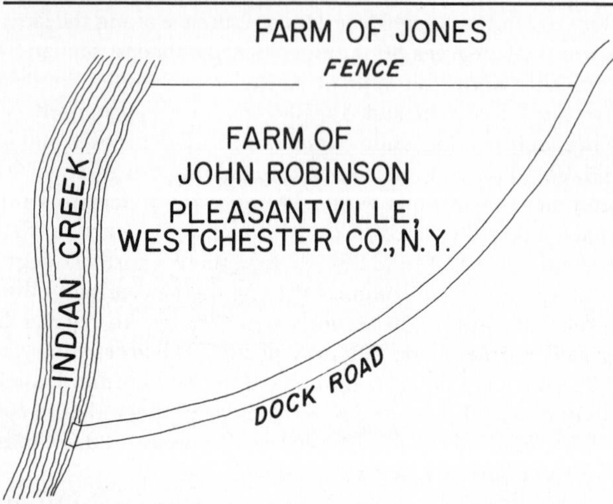

Rectangular or Government Survey Descriptions

The rectangular or government survey system was approved by the United States Congress in 1785 to establish a standardized system of property descriptions. It is relatively simple in operation, at least for rural lands, is easily the most general survey system, and is used in 30 states. The New England states, the Atlantic Coast states, southeastern Ohio, and Texas are not covered.

The general framework. This system is based on surveying lines that run north and south, called *principal meridians*, and east and west, called *base lines*. Principal meridians and base lines, created in pairs, were established and given a name and number by the land office in Washington, D.C. A map showing the location of the several principal meridians and their base lines in the United States is in Figure 4–5.

Guide meridians were established by the surveyors to minimize errors in measurement caused by the curvature of the earth. Guide meridians run parallel to the principal meridian at 24-mile intervals and converge as one goes north. In a comparable manner, *standard parallels* run east and west at 24-mile intervals north and south of the base lines. Thus, surveyors created areas called *checks* or *quadrangles*, 24 miles on each side.

These checks are further subdivided into 16 areas each measuring 6 miles by 6 miles (36 square miles) called *townships*. The townships are again subdivided into *sections*, each a mile square and containing 640 acres. In turn, the sections were further split up into halves, quarters, or smaller parcels as needed to describe individual land holdings.

To identify the exact location of a given 36-square-mile township, the east-west rows of townships, parallel to the base line, are numbered as tiers 1, 2, 3, and so forth, north or south, of a given base line. The

FIGURE 4–5
Principal meridians and their base lines within the United States

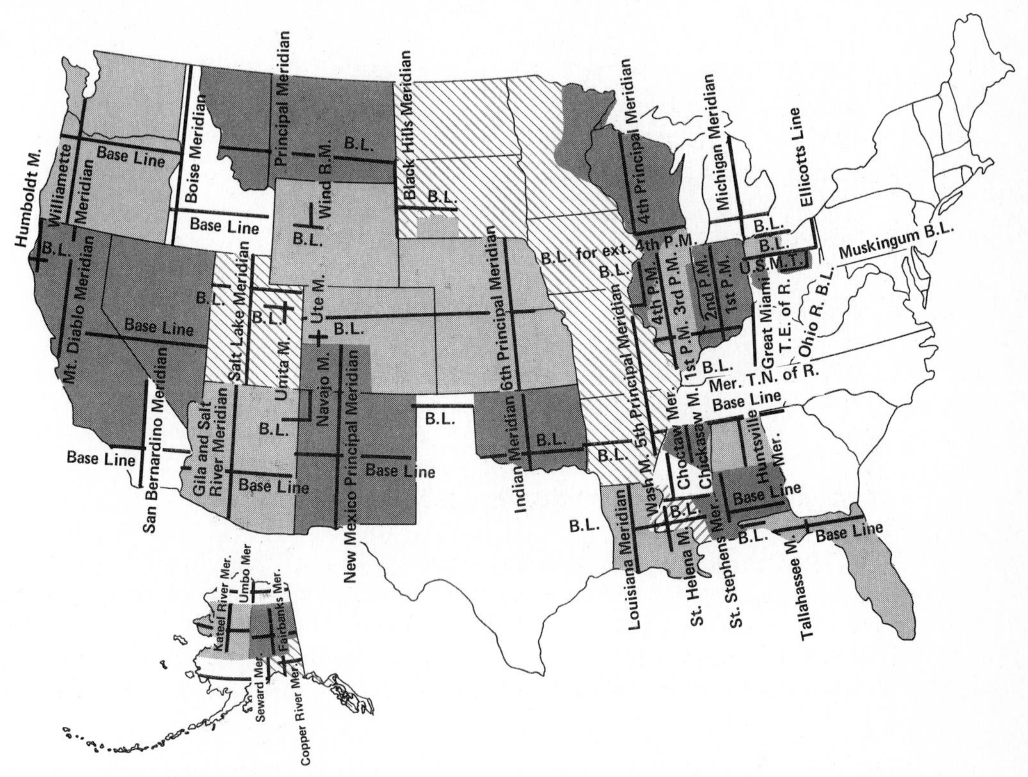

north-south columns of townships, parallel to the meridians, are called ranges and are numbered 1, 2, 3, and so forth, east or west of a principal meridian. The general system is illustrated in Figure 4–6.

Sections in a township are identified by number and are related to adjoining sections, as indicated in Figure 4–7.

In describing a section, as in Figure 4–7, it is customary to state first the number of the section, then tier and range: "Section 12, Tier 3 North, Range 2 East of the principal named meridian." It may be abbreviated: "Sect. 12, T.3N., R.2E., . . . County, State of . . .".

Specific description. The description of a specific parcel is relatively simple. For example, the parcel designated as "Parcel X" in Figure 4–8 is northeast one-fourth of the northwest one-fourth of Section 12, and so on. Parcel Y's description is "west one-half of the southwest one-fourth of Section 12," and so on.

The acreage of each parcel can be determined quickly by working backward in the legal description from the section area of 640 acres. For example, areas of parcels X and Y are calculated as follows:

FIGURE 4–6
Designation of townships by tiers and ranges

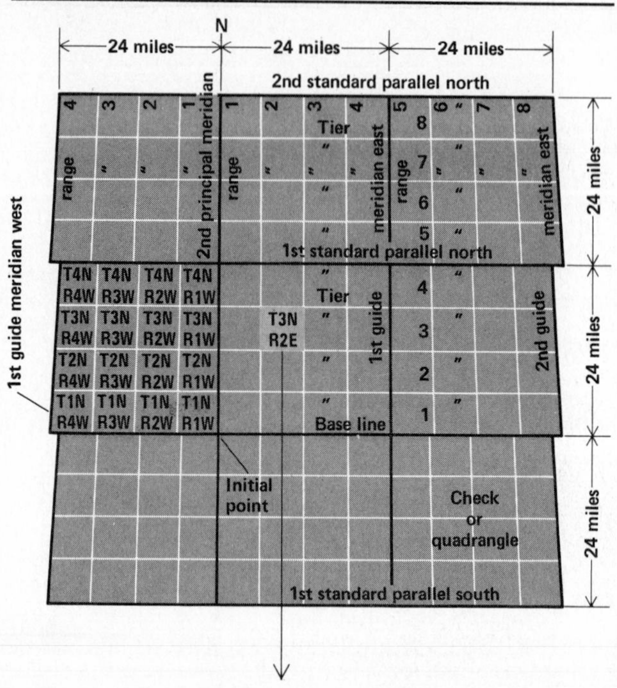

FIGURE 4–7
Designation of Section 12 by Tier 3 North, Range 2 East, and location relative to other sections

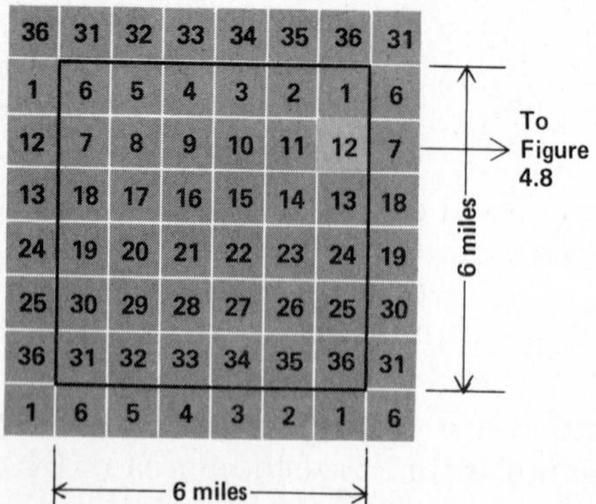

36	31	32	33	34	35	36	31
1	6	5	4	3	2	1	6
12	7	8	9	10	11	12	7
13	18	17	16	15	14	13	18
24	19	20	21	22	23	24	19
25	30	29	28	27	26	25	30
36	31	32	33	34	35	36	31
1	6	5	4	3	2	1	6

To Figure 4.8

6 miles

6 miles

FIGURE 4–8
Measurements and subdivisions of a section

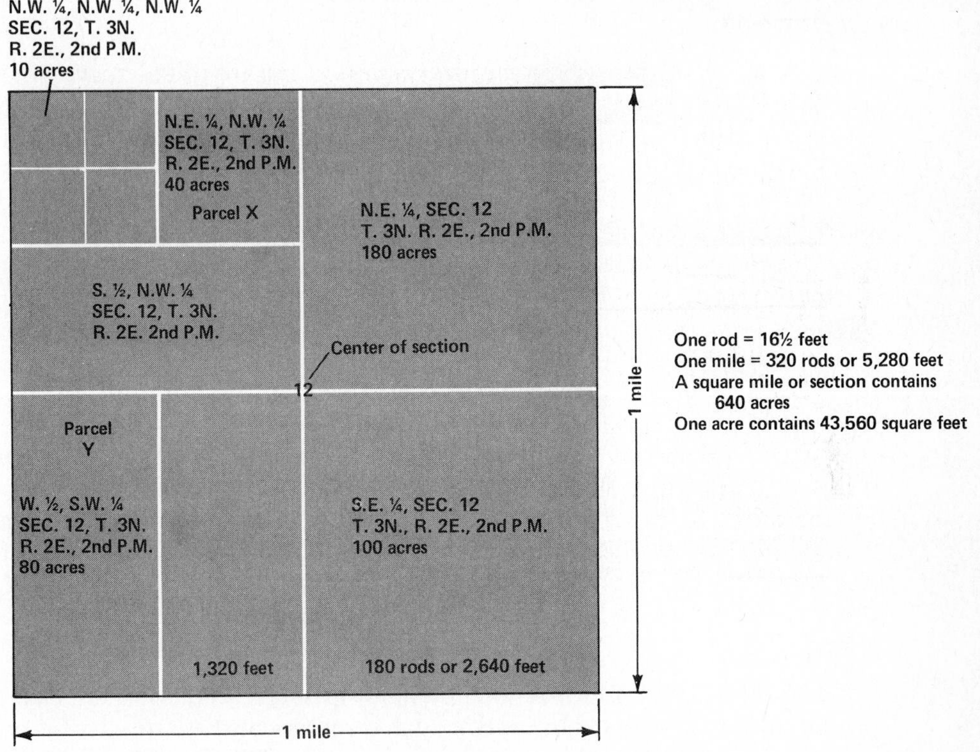

Parcel X:	NE ¼	of NW	¼	of	Section 12
	¼	×	¼	×	640 acres = 40 acres
Parcel Y:	W ½	of SW	¼	of	Section 12
	½	×	¼	×	640 acres = 80 acres

Occasionally, a section is incomplete because it extends into the ocean, a lake, or a river. Since some parcels in the section are irregular in shape, a standard legal description based on the government survey system is not suitable for them. These incomplete lots are called *government lots* or *irregular lots*. In these situations, a metes and bounds description is made up for the irregular parcel and tied back to a point of beginning based on the rectangular survey system.

Recorded Plat Descriptions

The government survey system is extremely cumbersome for describing the small parcels commonly found in urban areas. The descriptions become much too involved. A more efficient and widely accepted way of describing property is by recorded plat, as a subdivision or a condominium. A *plat* is a map or written plan showing actual or proposed property lines, buildings' setback lines, and so on, entered into the public record, as for a subdivision.

Subdivision plat. Subdividing requires a very accurate initial survey map of a tract of land. The land is then divided into streets and lots and blocks. Easements and deed restrictions are also often either included on the subdivision map or filed with it. The map, easements, and deed restrictions are all entered into the public record as a plat. The map assigns numbers to the various blocks and lots for convenience of identification, and the map usually bears a subdivision title, the owner's and surveyor's names, the date of survey, and the date of approval by community or county officials. Figure 4–9 is a simplified illustration of a small tract that the owner subdivided into lots.

The subdivision plat map describes exactly the size and location of each lot by the metes and bounds property description system. Once the subdivision plat map has been recorded, only the plat name need be referred to insofar as lots and blocks in the subdivision are concerned. Lot 8, Block 3, in Green Acres Subdivision, Rustic County, Wisconsin, would therefore constitute a complete and adequate legal description. Reference to the plat map would show the exact location, shape, size, and dimensions of the lot and would give considerable additional information about it.

Condominium plat. Condominium ownership is created by a special condominium law that permits individual interests and estates to be established within a total and larger property estate. The individual estates are technically established by use of vertical and horizontal planes (surfaces) that are usually identified vertically, such as the walls (not room partitions)

FIGURE 4–9
Green Acres subdivision, Rustic County, Wisconsin

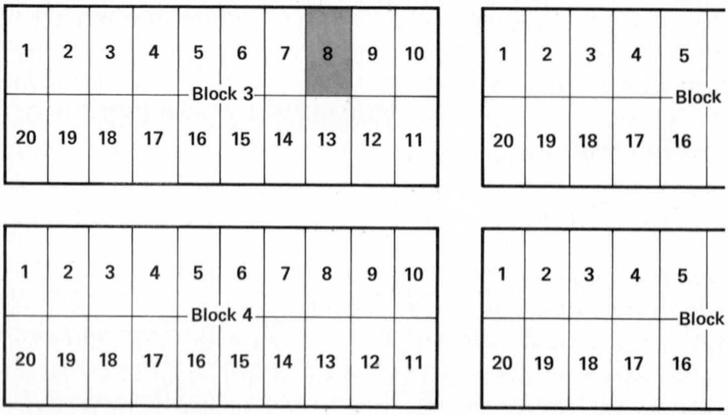

of the unit, and horizontally, such as the floors and ceilings of the unit. It is here that elevations above sea level become critical.

The exact location of the building or buildings on the site and the exact location of the unit within the buildings are described in the plat (location map) and in the architectural plans. Each is also described in legal language in a master deed. After all the individual unit estates have been described in the total property estate, all of what remains such as the land and the structural parts of the buildings becomes a common estate to be owned jointly by the owners of the individual unit estates. Thus, each condominium owner owns his or her individual unit estate and an undivided interest in the common estate.

Recording of the master deed extends the condominium laws of the state in which the condominium is located to the individual units of ownership. The master deed also establishes an association to look after the use and maintenance of the common estate. The association is governed by a board of directors, elected from among the owners of the individual units. Membership, with its attendant rights and responsibilities, applies to each unit in much the same sense that easements and deed restrictions apply to lots in a subdivision plat.

After recording, condominium units may be legally identified by reference to the plat or master deed. The complex three-dimensional descriptions need not be repeated in deeds, mortgages, or contracts.

The State Plane Coordinate System

The state plane coordinate system is intended to supplement other methods of describing real estate. The system provides a definite and very accurate means of identifying parcels, even if landmarks, monuments, and other points of origin are destroyed, moved, or otherwise obliterated.

The coordinate system is based on a system of coordinate grids for each state, with the state flattened mathematically into a level plane. Points in each grid are identified by longitude and latitude, much as a ship's navigator might do at sea; thus, the need for physical landmarks is avoided. Because of the complexity of the state plane coordinate system, property owners and lawyers are likely to continue to rely on traditional methods of describing realty. The system simply provides a certain means of locating critical points of beginning from which other methods of describing parcels may take off.

Description by Rights

Ownership may sometimes involve only air rights or riparian rights. Air rights are described in a similar manner to condominium rights. For example, rights of development over railroad tracks and cemeteries have been sold off in many larger cities. A legal description of air rights in a deed might convey all development rights 280 feet above mean sea level and up. To be useful, the description must also provide for the location and placement of footings and pillars among the railroad tracks, grave sites, and other surface uses, to support any structure built in the air space.

Riparian rights are usually not subject to physical survey per se. If they are, the survey is only incidental to more complex legal considerations involving interaction with other property owners, relocation of streams, and the rights to shut off or restrict the flow of water. These rights should be expressed as clearly as possible in any legal document.

A seller must use care to convey only what is owned. Generally, this can best be accomplished by using the identical description under which the property was acquired.

PUBLIC RECORDS

Anyone who has an interest in realty must give notice to the world to protect that interest. Notice may be actual or constructive. Possession of realty is legally considered *actual notice* to the world of an interest in the property. Entering a legal instrument that evidences an interest in real estate into the public records is considered *constructive notice.* In turn, the public record serves as a source of information to anyone about to enter into a transaction concerning real estate, such as lenders, potential tenants, or interested buyers.

Public records are maintained by local governments in all states in accordance with recording acts. Public records provide a central repository or storehouse for certain kinds of information. Recording acts provide for the registration of every legal instrument creating, transferring, mortgaging, assigning, or otherwise affecting title to realty. Public records thus are designed to protect against fraud and to reinforce the Statute of Frauds. The records are maintained by city, town, and county officials under titles like clerk, recorder, treasurer, or tax collector. Public records include many documents affecting title to real and personal property, taxes, special assessments, ordinances, and building and zoning codes.

Historically, possession of realty served as actual notice of an interest in realty and was adequate for almost all purposes. Modern society is complex, however, and a more efficient and effective system of notice became necessary. For example, A, an owner, might sell property to B, conveying title with a deed. But, if B does not take possession, A might also sell to C, who upon moving into occupancy acquires a claim of title superior to that of B. Or A might obtain cash under a mortgage from D, after the sale to B, and subsequently leave the area. Either situation involves fraud and many legal problems. Recording deeds and mortgages gives constructive notice of the interest to all parties and is recognized as notice equal to actual possession. As a general rule, recording acts give legal priority to interests according to the sequence in which they are recorded. "First in time is first in line."

Real Property Title Records

Recording of a deed is highly recommended to give constructive notice to all the grantee's interest in the property. The obligation and the benefit of recording both go to the grantee as the new owner. Recording is doubly important whenever vacant land is involved and whenever the grantee does not take immediate possession. Failure to record or to take occupancy leaves an opportunity for the grantor to sell and convey to a second grantee. If the second grantee records or moves into occupancy first, a claim of ownership superior to the first grantee's is realized. The first grantee's only recourse, for all practical purposes, is against the fraudulent grantor.

Two systems are used to maintain title records. The first is a grantor-grantee index; the second is a tract or lot and block index.

Grantor-grantee index. In a grantor-grantee system, deeds are indexed according to the last name of the previous owner (grantor) and of the new owner (grantee). Thus, a title search can be initiated and a chain of title can be run if the name of either is known. In running a chain of title, the grantor is regarded as a grantee in a previous transaction. When located in the grantee index, the previous grantor's name then becomes immediately available.

Tract index (lot and block). In a tract system, deeds are indexed according to the legal description or location of properties rather than by grantor-grantee. In urban areas, the name of the subdivision in which the property is located will often serve as the key to entering the index. Alternatively, maps of the area will include a distinct number for each block. Transactions involving individual lots on the block can then be ascertained by looking in the index itself.

Entry into a tract index is more difficult in rural areas because the classification system is more involved in that property has a distinct legal description. The general system of the tract index in rural areas is based on identifying properties by township and by section. A chain of title can be run more easily with a tract index because all transactions involving a specific property are recorded on the same page. A tract index, however, is considered more difficult and more expensive to maintain than is a grantor-grantee index.

Mortgagor-Mortgagee Records

In nearly every state, mortgages are accepted for recording in, and constructive notice is given by, a mortgagor-mortgagee index. The index functions are in a manner very similar to a grantor-grantee index. That is, the index may be entered with either the name of the borrower-mortgagor or the lender-mortgagee. When a mortgage lien has been satisfied, this also is entered in the index. In some states, mortgages are filed and recorded in the same grantor-grantee index that is used for deeds.

Plat and Plan Records

Maps, restrictions, architectural plans, and other pertinent information on subdivision and condominium plats are maintained as a part of the public record. The plats are a particularly excellent source of information on easements and restrictions on a specific plat. Parcel and building dimensions and building layout can also be readily determined from this source.

Secured Personal Property Records

Under the Uniform Commercial Code, items of personal property may be purchased on a conditional sales contract, which is also termed a security agreement. Legally, purchase by conditional sales contract means that title does not pass until full payment is made. In the meantime, a short version of the security agreement, termed a financing statement, is entered into the public record to give public notice of a collateral lien on the property. For owners of real estate, this notice is of considerable importance when items like water heaters, boilers, appliances, draperies, and other equipment frequently classed as fixtures are involved. The items do not become fixtures, or part of the real estate, until the security agreement is satisfied. That is, important components of a property may not actually be a part of the realty. Notice of the financing statement is usually entered in the mortgagor-mortgagee index.

SUMMARY

The need for legal descriptions came about from increasing numbers of people using the land. Real estate, as property, may be described physically or according to several types of rights, such as air, surface, subsurface, oil, mineral, and water rights. Realty refers to land and improvements as physical things. Realty is to real property as personalty is to personal property. A fixture is an item of personalty that meets the tests of intent, annexation, and adaptation and is, therefore, realty.

A legal description of real estate is a specific and unique identification of a parcel of realty that is acceptable in a court of law. The three accepted methods of describing real estate are (1) metes and bounds, (2) rectangular or government survey, and (3) recorded plat.

Any instrument showing an interest in real estate may be recorded to give constructive notice of the interest. Thus, new owners, lenders, lessees, and others frequently find it advantageous to record their interests.

QUESTIONS FOR REVIEW AND DISCUSSION

1. What is a fixture? When is the identification of a fixture important? Not important? When are the following fixtures important: key, storm windows, hot-water heater?

2. Explain the following methods of describing realty in detail.
a. Metes and bounds
b. The government survey system
c. The recorded plat

3. Are there occasions where the foregoing three methods or systems are not adequate to describe realty? Explain.

4. May the world's supply of "space" be increased? Explain.

5. What effects will adoption of the metric system have on legal descriptions of real estate, if any? Discuss.

6. The rectangular survey system is obsolete for describing real estate and should be replaced. Discuss.

7. Explain briefly the nature and use of the following public record indexes.
a. Grantor-grantee
b. Tract
c. Mortgagor-mortgagee
d. Secured personal property

8. Why should a deed be recorded from a grantee's viewpoint? A lender's? A lessee's?

CASE PROBLEMS

1. On a sheet of paper make a square approximately 2 inches or 5 centimeters on each side, to represent Sect. 31, T.2N, R.5W. Sketch the following parcels of land within the section: (a) N.E.¼, (b) S.E.¼ of the S.E.¼, (c) W.½ of the N.W.¼ of the S.W.¼, (d) S.W.¼ of the N.W.¼ of the N.W.¼, and (e) W.½ of the N.E.¼ of the N.E.¼ of the N.W.¼.
2. How many acres are in each parcel of 1(a)–(e)?
3. How many miles is it from the eastern edge of Sect. 31, T.2N, R.5W, to the western edge of Sect. 36, T.2N, R.3W?
4. How far from the northern edge of Sect. 31, T.2N, R.5W, to the northern border of Sect. 6, T.1N, R.5W?
5. Bridgett Bardow receives a deed to property she just bought from Blackstone. She moves into the property but does not record the deed. To what extent are her rights in the property protected?
6. Bridgett obtains a mortgage loan for $500,000 from Wayne Duke. Mr. Duke does not record the mortgage. To what extent is the mortgage valid?

CHAPTER FIVE

GOVERNMENTAL LIMITATIONS TO OWNERSHIP

Society in every state is a blessing, but government, even in its best state,
is but a necessary evil; in its worst state,
an intolerable one.
THOMAS PAINE, *Common Sense*, 1776.

IMPORTANT TOPICS OR DECISION AREAS COVERED IN THIS CHAPTER

- Police Power
- Eminent Domain
- Taxation and Special Assessments

The system of property ownership in the United States is a mix of the feudal and allodial systems of ownership brought over from England. Under the feudal system, a king or sovereign owned all the land, with subjects obtaining the use of the land in return for services and allegiance, whereas the allodial system recognizes individual ownership only; that is, in the allodial systems, no ownership rights are reserved by a sovereign authority. The mix of systems gives private ownership to the individual, with the state reserving the rights of police power, eminent domain, taxation, and escheat. The reservation of these four rights remains the same regardless of how the fee estate is split up.

Escheat is the reversion or automatic conveyance of realty to the state, upon an owner's death, when no will, heirs, or other legal claimants to title can be found. Escheat is seldom exercised in fact because someone almost always has a title claim. Also, for all practical purposes, escheat is not a restriction on ownership. Escheat serves simply to keep property owned and productive or "in the system." Real estate is too valuable to society to go unused.

Taxation, condemnation, and regulation are a substantial portion of the "rules of the game" for property owners; hence, an understanding of this chapter is crucial for intelligent investing in real estate. These powers are reserved by governments to maintain themselves; to look after the public health, welfare, and safety; and to facilitate growth and adjustment of their communities in response to changing social and economic needs. We look at how these three reservations of powers constrict our rational investor in the development and use of privately owned property. Even so, these restrictions are generally considered to yield positive results from the viewpoint of society.

KEY CONCEPTS INTRODUCED IN THIS CHAPTER

Ad valorem
Assessed value
Assessed value–sales price ratio study
Building code
Certificate of occupancy
Contract zoning
Density zoning
Development charge
Down zoning
Eminent domain
Enabling act
Environmental impact study
Exclusionary zoning
Floor-area-ratio (far) zoning
Just compensation
Land use control
Master plan
Multiple-use zoning
Nonconforming use
Performance zoning
Planned unit development
Police power
Rent control
Severance damages

Special assessment
Special use permit
Spot zoning
Subdivision regulations
Transferable development rights (TDRs)
Zoning
Zoning variance

POLICE POWER

Police power is a catchall term for those regulations of property, consistent with due process of law, considered necessary to protect public health, welfare, safety, and morals. *Police power regulations determine what an owner can and cannot do with a property.* Villages, cities, and counties all have rights of police power based on state enabling legislation or acts. An *enabling act* is the granting of express authority by a state legislative body to local governments to carry on certain activities. Police power enabling legislation provides the basis for planning, zoning ordinances, subdivision regulations, building and housing codes, and other land use controls. Even rent controls are imposed under the police power authority. No compensation need be paid for lowered property values resulting from the imposition of police power.

Planning

Community growth in population, commerce, manufacturing, and other activities results in demands that exceed the capabilities of physical facilities such as roads, sewers, water systems, schools, hospitals, and other public buildings. Depreciation and changes in technology also make changes necessary in these facilities. Designing and building such facilities requires large amounts of money. One major purpose of planning is to create and maintain a high-quality environment, one aspect of which is stabilized property values that result from orderly community growth and change. A second major purpose is to avoid wasteful mistakes that are the result of poor coordination, duplication, and overbuilding.

Planning is a systematic process involving data collection, classification, and analysis aimed at developing a master plan. A *master plan* is a comprehensive scheme setting forth ways and means by which a community can adjust its physical makeup to social and economic changes. The community may be a city, county, village, or metropolitan area. The plan or scheme concerns coordination of land uses with the provision of transportation, schools, parks, and other community services and facilities.

A master plan really consists of several lesser coordinated plans for land use, transportation, schools, and other public facilities. It must at the very least be based on studies of (1) population, (2) economic base, (3) land use, and (4) transportation of the area or community. In turn, the master plan provides the underlying rationale, "the big picture" for the community zoning ordinance, subdivision regulation, and building regulation, which are our most often employed land use controls. A *land use control* is a public or private means used to regulate and guide use of realty.

Experience shows that for a plan to effectively meet a community's needs, it must be

1. In scale with the population and economic outlook of the community
2. In scale with the current and future financial resources of the community
3. Balanced and attractive in design in relation to the environment to be created and maintained
4. In keeping with community sentiments on an attractive environment
5. Flexible and easily updated to accommodate changing conditions and projections

Zoning

Zoning is easily the most significant legal technique used by planners to regulate the use of land. *Zoning* is dividing a community (city, village, or county) into districts for the regulation of land use type (residential, commercial, and so forth) and intensity (one-family, multifamily, and so forth) and of height, bulk, and appearance of land use types specified. A zoning ordinance must undergo public review before being enacted into law by a city council, county commission, or other regulatory agency.

Increasingly, classes of uses, defined by performance standards, are permitted in the various districts. This is called *performance zoning*. Performance, as used here, means to meet the requirements of standards of the class. That is, performance zoning is establishing districts that allow or accept uses, regardless of type, if they meet certain standards relative to such things as density, appearance, traffic generation, and pollution origination. Thus, uses that do not adversely affect each other, and may, in fact, complement each other, are placed in the same class or district.

Let us look at several topics or issues to see the possible impact of zoning on investors.

Zoning ordinance content. A zoning ordinance usually includes a zoning map in addition to written regulations. Items generally regulated are land use, land coverage, height and bulk of buildings, and population density.

1. The community is divided into districts in which the land uses are controlled; for example, residential versus commercial versus industrial versus agricultural.
2. Standards limiting the height and bulk of buildings are set for each district.
3. Standards regulating the proportion of a lot that can be built on, including

detailed front-, side-, and backyard requirements, are set for each district.

4. Limits are set on population density in the various districts of the community by regulation of the foregoing factors; this procedure is called *density zoning.*

A zoning map is not the land use plan itself but, rather, just one way of implementing the land use plan.

A properly drawn zoning ordinance is not legally concerned with the following:

1. Specifying building materials and construction methods (governed by construction or building codes)
2. Setting minimum construction costs (not legal by public ordinance but may be set by private deed restrictions)
3. Regulation of street design and installation of utilities or reservation of land for park or school sites (governed primarily by subdivision regulations, along with street or public works department, the park department, and the school board)

Height, bulk, and area regulations. Building height and bulk restrictions prevent the usurpation of air, ventilation, and sunlight by one parcel at the unreasonable expense of another parcel. The restrictions also limit fire risks as well as population density and street congestion. Building heights are generally limited to a certain number of stories (i.e., one and a half, two, two and a half, ten).

Floor-area ratio (FAR) zoning is gaining acceptance as a means of allowing greater design flexibility in a district while limiting population and development density. FAR is the relationship of building coverage to lot area. For example, a FAR of 2.0 means that an owner is permitted to construct a two-story building over the entire lot, or a four-story building over one-half of the lot, or an eight-story building over one-fourth of the lot. (See Figure 5–1.) Any combination of proportion or fraction-of-lot coverage times the number of stories may not exceed the allowed floor-area ratio of 2.0.

Bonuses are sometimes added to the FAR of a parcel if the parcel is adjacent to open space or if the owner agrees to provide adequate off-street parking. FAR zoning is used primarily in multifamily residential and commercial districts. Other lot-coverage standards are not needed when FAR zoning is used. FAR zoning is an example of performance zoning.

Solar energy requires that adequate sunlight be available on a continuing basis. Thus, "right-to-light" zoning might modify FAR zoning, as shown in Figure 5–2.

Multiple-use zoning. Allowing several compatible, but different, uses in a district is called *multiple-use zoning.* Thus offices and small stores may be allowed in the same district as apartments or condominiums, an arrangement that may work to the benefit of all concerned. In fact, these uses may be combined into one project, termed a planned unit development,

FIGURE 5–1
Floor area ratio zoning, an example of performance zoning

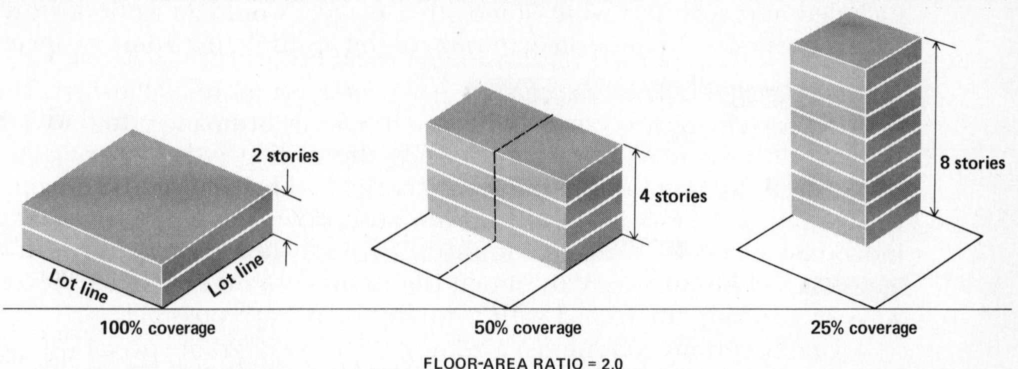

as a result of a transfer of development rights. In a *planned unit development (PUD),* improvements are added to realty at the same density as in conventional development, but the improvements may be clustered and surrounded by open, common areas. For example, assume a 10-acre parcel zoned for four dwelling units per acre. A developer is limited to 40 one-family houses by conventional zoning. With PUD, the developer could construct four closely clustered ten-unit buildings, leaving the balance of the acreage for open space. PUD may be used in residential, commercial, or industrial development. PUD zoning is also termed cluster zoning or density zoning.

A *transfer of development rights (TDR)* means that one parcel may be developed more intensely if another parcel is developed less intensely; the rights may be sold by one owner to another. Transfer of development rights adds flexibility and variety to an area without increasing its overall

FIGURE 5–2
"Right-to-light" performance zoning

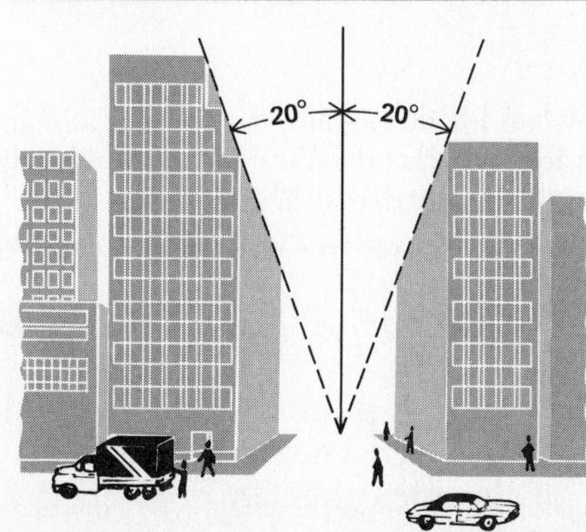

density. In the above PUD example, if commercial development rights were acquired by the investor in developing the PUD, stores could be included in the project while some other project would go without stores. This, of course, would be an extension of the multiple-use zoning concept.

Zoning challenge and/or negotiation. An owner, or potential owner, may petition for changes in, or relief from, a zoning ordinance. Initially, the key person to contact for information is the zoning enforcement officer of the area. In general, the officer is charged with literal enforcement of the zoning ordinance, with little or no authority to modify provisions in individual cases. A formal petition to a zoning board of adjustment or appeals may be necessary to obtain the desired change or relief. Several ways of reaching an accord with a zoning board are possible.

Under certain conditions, a zoning board may grant special use permits or variances. A *special use permit* gives the right to introduce a use into a zoning district where a definite need exists but where the use is normally not allowed. The introduction of a public utility substation into a one-family residential district, under controlled conditions, is an example. A *zoning variance* is a deviation from zoning ordinance granted because strict enforcement would result in undue hardship on a property owner. The usual rules are simply set aside as where a lot is so steep that front yard setback requirements cannot be met with reasonable expense. A variance must not violate the intent or spirit of the ordinance.

A technique known as contract zoning is sometimes used to fine tune a zoning ordinance. *Contract zoning* refers to an owner, who, by deed restriction or side agreement, limits a re-zoned property to a more restrictive use than that allowed by the new zoning classification. For example, a parcel is re-zoned as commercial, and at the same time the owner records a deed restriction limiting use to one-story professional offices. Contract zoning is not a recognized legal concept.

An owner may circumvent the zoning board of appeals by going through the courts and challenging the zoning ordinance itself on legal grounds. The legal requirements of a valid ordinance may be summarized as follows:

1. Use districts must be provided for by enabling legislation, and applicable regulations must be uniform for each classification and kind of building.
2. A reasonable basis for classifying districts differently must exist.
3. An entire jurisdiction (such as a city) and not just small, isolated areas must be zoned.
4. Parcels must not be zoned for uses that they cannot physically accommodate.

Effectively, a challenge on any of these points would mean that the ordinance is not based on a well-conceived land use or master plan. Also, a challenge might be based on the idea that an ordinance is arbitrary, unreasonable, destructive, or confiscatory in application.

Also, zoning may not be used to discriminate against minorities or low-income people as by exclusionary zoning. An ordinance that keeps low- and moderately low-income groups out of a high-income residential district, as by setting unreasonably large minimum lot sizes, floor-area requirements, or high construction quality standards, is *exclusionary zoning.*

Inconsistent uses. A parcel or small area may be zoned for a use or structure that is inconsistent with the rationale of the overall plan or ordinance; this is *spot zoning.* It is illegal for a zoning board to grant spot zoning. Therefore, an owner adversely affected by spot zoning of a neighboring parcel is likely to be able successfully to challenge such a re-zoning in court.

On the other hand, existing uses or structures may be inconsistent with the applicable zoning; these are termed *nonconforming uses.* If they were created before and existed at the original adoption of the ordinance, they are legal, nonconforming uses. Nonconforming uses are allowed to continue, subject to several provisions, because to require their removal would inflict severe financial hardship on owners. Generally, the provisions regulating a nonconforming use prohibit the following:

1. Enlargement
2. Rebuilding, or reconstruction, after a specified percentage of damage or destruction, usually 50 percent
3. Changing to another nonconforming use
4. Resumption after a stated period of discontinuance, usually a year

New uses and structures must conform to current zoning. To introduce a use or to build a structure inconsistent with the ordinance is to create an illegal nonconforming use, which would be subject to immediate removal without compensation.

Zoning and value. Zoning does not create value in land or realty, and zoning does not prevent value declines. Market demand for a use is the basis of value, whether it involves an office building, a shopping center, or an apartment building. At the same time, a well-conceived master plan along with appropriate zoning must be obtained for the full value potential, based on market demand, to be realized. If demand for a use is not present, commercial, industrial, or multifamily zoning does not enhance a property's value, except perhaps in the mind of the owner. Thus, inappropriate zoning may distort or alter the use to which a parcel is put, thereby limiting it to less than its highest and best use. Also, zoning cannot prevent the aging and depreciation of structures, factors that are likely to lower values.

Even so, an owner must be constantly aware of the possible down zoning of his or her property. Occasionally, communities, in updating a master plan and zoning ordinance will reclassify a property from a "high-value" use as commercial or industrial to a "low-value" use as single-family residential, which is *down zoning.* If demand for the high-value use exists, this would mean a substantial loss to the owner.

Subdivision Regulations

Subdivision regulations are locally adopted laws governing the conversion of raw land into building sites. The regulations work primarily through plat approval procedures, under which a subdivider or developer is not permitted to split up land until the planning commission has approved a plat of the proposed project. Approval is based on compliance with standards and requirements set forth in a subdivision regulation ordinance. For the most part, subdivision regulations apply at the fringe of communities where land is being converted from rural to urban uses.

In almost all states, a comprehensive plan, a major street plan, or an official map must have been adopted prior to subdivision regulations to provide a legal basis for implementation. Either plan serves as evidence that the regulations are not arbitrary or discriminatory. That is, either plan coordinates the layout of a particular subdivision with others in the area and also ensures provision for rights of way for major thoroughfares, easements for utility lines, and school and park locations.

Major elements controlled by most subdivision regulations are as follows:

1. Rights of way for streets, alleys, cul-de-sacs, highways, and walkways—location, alignment, width, grade, surfacing material, and possible dedication to community
2. Lots and blocks—minimum dimensions and building setback lines
3. Utilities—easements for sewer, water, and power; assurance of pure water and ability to dispose of wastes without health problems
4. Reserved areas for schools, parks, open space, and other public uses

The regulations in the jurisdiction where the land is located control its development. Development charges appear to be increasingly used by communities and incorporated into their subdivision ordinances and building regulations. A *development charge* is a fee imposed against a subdivider or developer by the community to pay the costs of new waste-disposal facilities, roads, water storage tanks, and the like, necessitated by the new subdivision or structure. The intent is that the tenants of the subdivision or structure will pay the marginal costs of these community facilities rather than the citizenry in general.

Environmental impact studies are required for large development projects. An *environmental impact study* (EIS) is an investigation and analysis to determine the long-run physical effects of a proposed land use on its surroundings and the long-run economic and social effects on other people. The purpose of an EIS is to bring together in one report the likely costs and benefits of a project before the project is approved for development. For example, the EIS for a proposed shopping center would document the expected effects on auto traffic, air quality, the waste-disposal system, energy demand, employment, and vegetation. If costs are too substantial, the proposal might not obtain approval, or modification might be required to avoid or ease expected problems.

Building Regulations

A *building code* is a local or state government ordinance, or series of ordinances, regulating the construction, alteration, and maintenance of structures. Almost all cities, towns, and counties have building or construction codes specifying structural requirements, material performance, and building arrangements that must be met when erecting or repairing structures. Protecting public health and safety is the obvious objective. Code requirements usually focus on fireproof construction, means of emergency exit, windows, load and stress, size and location of rooms, adequacy of ventilation, sanitation facilities, electrical wirings and equipment, mechanical equipment, and the lighting of exits. Several separate codes such as the electrical, plumbing, and fire code may make up the "building code."

The codes are particularly stringent for buildings likely to be occupied by large numbers of people, such as apartment buildings, schools, churches, hospitals, and office buildings. Special provisions also usually apply to unique or potentially hazardous structures such as amusement parks, canopies, roof signs, grandstands, grain elevators, or cleaning plants.

Building codes effectively take up where subdivision regulations leave off. That is, subdivision regulations apply mainly to land and building codes to improvements.

Enforcement begins with the requirement that a building permit be obtained for new construction or alterations. Both the zoning ordinance and the building codes must be complied with. Also, blueprints must pass examination before a building permit is issued. The permit is only evidence of compliance with public regulations and does not exempt or cure a violation of deed restrictions. Construction is inspected as it progresses. A certificate of occupancy must be obtained by an owner of a new or rehabilitated building before it can be put into use. A *certificate of occupancy* is an official notice that all code inspections were passed and that the structure is fit for use.

Rent Control

Rent control is a governmental limitation on the amount that may be charged for apartments or other dwelling units. Rent control is sought, often by tenant unions, on the argument that housing is a unique good that is required by everyone. Housing is unique in that everyone needs basic shelter, for which there is no real substitute. The same is not true of other goods. Many substitutes exist for foodstuffs, like pork, apples, and bread, or clothing, like pants, shirts, and shoes. Consumers can always shift to less expensive food or shop elsewhere for clothing. Further, housing tends to be unique in that supply cannot be expanded quickly in response to increased demand. Thus, tenants have little choice but to pay increased rents when demand outruns supply.

Rent controls may benefit those with a low income and the elderly at the expense of property owners. The effect is to transfer value or wealth from landlords to tenants. But providing relief or welfare for these people should fall on the whole of society rather than on property owners. In fact, the costs of controls to society as a whole appear to greatly outweigh the benefits. On this, both liberal and conservative economists agree.

Gunnar Myrdal, a labor-oriented economist, who won a Nobel Prize in 1974, has this view. "Rent control has in certain Western countries constituted, maybe, the worst example of poor planning by governments lacking courage and vision."[1] Frederick Hayek, a very conservative economist and also a Nobel Prize winner, has a similar view. "If this account seems to boil down to a catalogue of inequities to be laid at the door of rent control, that is no mere coincidence, but inevitable. . . . I doubt very much whether theoretical research into the same problem carried out by someone of a different political-economic persuasion than myself could lead to a different conclusion."[2]

What are the implications of rent control? Assuming inflation, the immediate effect is to squeeze profits from a landlord. This leads to neglect of property maintenance. Property values drop due to limited rents also. Property taxes to local government drop, resulting in a tighter budget and reduced services. Owners seek relief through efforts to convert to condominiums or to demolish and rebuild in a use that is not subject to control. If their efforts are unsuccessful and all profits are squeezed out of ownership, properties are abandoned. Thus, severe blight and slums result. The effect is one more step toward decline in the neighborhood life cycle. In the meantime, investors develop new housing projects only in locations or communities without controls. And lenders avoid making loans on properties in rent control areas. Again blight and urban deterioration result.

Miscellaneous Controls

Some communities maintain an official map that designates exact locations of existing and proposed street rights-of-way or proposed street-widening

[1]Sven Oydenfelt, "The Rise and Fall of Swedish Rent Control," in *Rent Control, A Popular Paradox, Evidence on the Economic Effect of Rent Control* (Vancouver, B.C.: The Fraser Institute, 1975), p. 169.

[2]A. F. Hayek, "The Repercussion of Rent Restrictions," in *Rent Control,* p. 80.

projects and of lands to be reserved for school sites, parks, and playgrounds. The official map is their equivalent of a master plan. Compensation will not be paid for any land improvements built in these proposed rights-of-way and reserved areas after they have been specifically designated or made a part of the map.

As a rule, fire and sanitation departments are empowered to make periodic inspections and to order compliance with directives to ensure safe and sanitary use and occupancy of buildings. Proper enforcement of fire control and sanitation ordinances may go a long way toward retarding housing blight and eventual elimination of unsightly and unsafe city slums. In almost all states, there are health regulations for wells, septic tanks, and other waste-disposal installations.

EMINENT DOMAIN

Eminent domain is the right of a governmental or quasi-governmental agency to take private property for public uses or purposes. The taking is without the consent of the owner and requires payment of reasonable or just compensation. This is sometimes called condemnation, or the right of expropriation. Semipublic organizations such as railroads and public utility companies may exercise eminent domain for limited purposes. And private, nonprofit institutions, such as universities, also have a limited right of eminent domain.

Eminent domain is based on the premise that an owner should sometimes be required to give up property, for fair or just compensation, so that the common good or welfare may be advanced. Land for streets, parks, schools, and other public buildings, and for other public or social purposes, is acquired through negotiation or eminent domain.

Most agencies and organizations seek to acquire desired properties by negotiation before exercising their right of eminent domain.

Need

The right of eminent domain is needed because our society and economy are growing and changing. For example, in the 1930s sociologists predicted that the U.S. population would mature and stabilize at 150 million by 1950. Nearly half the population lived in rural areas at the time. Automobiles were still a relatively new mode of transportation. Air travel was only for the wealthy. Most intercity passenger and freight transportation was provided by the railroads. Now, in the 1980s, the U.S. population exceeds 225 million people, about three-fourths of whom live in urban areas. Almost everyone drives an auto, and air travel is much more common than is travel by rail. Trucks haul a large share of intercity freight.

In a more specific sense, the power of eminent domain is exercised to acquire property for highway construction, public building sites, flood control projects, and airport expansion. The power has been legally exercised to acquire land for public parking lots to be operated by private concessionaires. The U.S. Supreme Court has even declared legal the acquisition of land in urban renewal areas for later resale and redevelopment by profit-seeking individuals and corporations. Thus, the emphasis is on public purposes and is not limited to public needs and uses per se.

Just Compensation

Just compensation is payment for property taken. If an entire property is taken, just compensation is almost universally defined as the fair market value of the property. Many states provide for payment of *severance damages* to the owner if only part of the property is taken but the value of the remainder is lowered as a result of the taking. That is, fair market value is paid for the portion of the property taken, and additional payment is made for any injury or reduction in value to the remainder.

Usually, compensation is not paid for certain damages suffered by an owner. Examples are

1. Loss of business profits or goodwill
2. Moving costs (although the federal government and some states do pay these in some situations, independent of the court's decision)
3. Additional costs of securing replacement housing or facilities
4. Adverse effects of having the proposed improvements as a new neighbor, such as an airport or a sewage treatment plant

TAXATION AND SPECIAL ASSESSMENTS

Property is taxed on an *ad valorem* basis, meaning that the tax is levied on property according to value, usually its market value. Each parcel is periodically appraised in ad valorem taxation and an assessed value placed on it. *Assessed value* means the worth or amount in dollars assigned to a parcel by the tax administrator. Assessed value may equal or be a proportion of market value, and it varies directly with market value.

Property taxes typically run about 2½ percent of market value, generally being lower in rural areas and higher in urban areas, a higher level of public services are provided. The percentage is generally lowest in the southern part of the United States and highest in the eastern parts and California. A *Wall Street Journal* article reported that the property tax rate in Newark, New Jersey, equaled $8.44 per $100 of market value, undoubtedly one of the highest in the country.

Taxes, if used wisely, may greatly benefit an owner. Taxes help to provide police and fire protection, schools, parks, and a road system, all of which, if of high quality, enhance the value of a property. Both the Constitution and statutory law contain safeguards against unfair or unreasonable taxation.

Uniformity in Assessment

A major concern of an investor-owner regarding a property tax should be the uniformity of assessment. The property tax burden in ad valorem taxation is fairly or equitably apportioned to real estate owners if all property is assessed at the same proportion of value. Thus, a store that sold for $100,000 and is assessed at $60,000 would be treated the same as a residence that sold for $40,000 and is assessed at $24,000. Each is assessed at 60 percent of its market price. The store stands to pay two and one-half times more in property taxes, regardless of the rate at which taxes are levied, because its value is two and one-half times greater. It would be unfair if the store and the house were both assessed at $24,000 because the store owner would not be paying a fair share of taxes.

When uniformity is lacking. Towns, cities, and counties tend to assess their properties at low levels to pay a lower share of taxes if the state levies taxes on local real estate. This assumes that the state would levy the tax as a fixed percentage of assessed value. To correct for differences in assessing levels, the state can make an *assessed value–sales price ratio study.* A ratio study is the analysis of a sample of recently sold properties to determine the relationship between assessed values and "market values" (approximated by actual market sales prices) in a taxing jurisdiction or district.

In using these studies, a ratio by property type for each taxing jurisdiction is determined. Thus, if a jurisdiction assesses properties at 80 percent of the sales price, an adjustment factor of 1.25 may be applied to its assessed values to bring them to market value. Prorating state taxes to be collected to cities and counties based on the market value of properties in them gives equity or fairness in ad valorem taxation.

Tax Exemptions

A second major item of concern to property owners is the amount of tax-exempt properties in their districts. Tax-exempt properties generally include all government property plus property owned by nonprofit institutions such as churches, hospitals, and private schools. The properties still require and get services like fire and police protection whether taxes are paid or not. Also, as in the case of military bases, the government property may house families who use local schools and public recreational facilities. In some cases, payments in lieu of taxes are made from one level of government to another in recognition of the extra burden placed on local facilities. In addition to the extra direct burden, however, large numbers of publicly owned properties mean that streets and sewer, water, and power lines must all extend greater distances to tie privately owned properties together. This constitutes an extra cost to private citizens of the community. Thus, where other considerations are equal, a private citizen might well prefer to locate where the amount of tax-exempt property is not unduly great.

On the other hand, exemption can benefit an owner. In many states, such as Florida, homeowners are given a homestead exemption on assessed value by statute. An exemption of $25,000 is typical, with it being doubled for owners who are 65 years of age and over. Each $10,000 of exemption means $300 less per year in taxes, assuming a 3 percent tax rate.

Special Assessments

Special assessments are charges upon real property to pay all or part of the cost of a local improvement by which the property will be benefited. They do not recur regularly, as taxes do, and are not always apportioned according to the value of the property affected. For example, all lots fronting on a certain street are benefited by the paving of the street and are equally assessed for it, even though the corner lots may have a greater value than inside lots. Buildings are not considered in apportioning a special assessment, it being assumed that the land receives all the benefit. Sometimes special assessments are spread over a large area, the property nearest to the improvement being charged with a greater proportion of it than the property more remote, the rate decreasing with the distance from the improvement.

Only where local improvements are beneficial—that is, where they increase the value of the affected properties—will courts sanction the levying of special assessments. In a court case, property owners in Miami Beach, Florida, challenged the right of the municipality to levy assessments for the widening of Indian Creek Drive in Miami Beach. The property owners contended that the widening of the drive from 25 to 40 feet was carried forth to relieve congested traffic on another street and that as a result of the widening, the affected street had turned into a noisy, heavily traversed thoroughfare and that the effect on property was to lessen the value and desirability of the sites for homes. The state supreme court in a 4-to-3 decision held for the property owners, reversing the Dade County circuit court, which had ruled in favor of the city. In the majority opinion, Justice Glen Terrell said: "Before the days of the automobile and creation of zoning ordinances, paving and widening of streets invariably conferred additional benefits to the abutting property. But this may be far from true at present. Commercial property is increased in value by widening and paving of streets . . . but who ever heard of making a traffic count to locate a home!"

Special assessments become liens when they are definitely known and fixed. In some states, a large assessment may be divided into installments payable over a period of five to ten years or more. Interest is charged on the deferred installments, however.

SUMMARY

Govermental limitations on real estate ownership are the powers to police, to condemn, and to tax. Police power is comprised of regulations to protect public health, welfare, safety, and morals. Eminent domain is exercised to enable community adjustment to changing social and economic needs. Taxation enables governments to provide needed public services and to maintain themselves.

Police power includes environmental planning, zoning, subdivision regulation, and building regulation. Zoning is the most significant of these controls, affecting land use, land coverage, height and bulk of buildings, and the population density. Zoning must be based on a rational master plan to be legally enforceable. Performance zoning, based on accepted standards or requirements concerning things as density, traffic generation, or appearance, is increasingly being used to give greater flexibility in land use control. Zoning does not regulate building materials or construction methods.

The exercise of eminent domain requires a public purpose. Just compensation must be paid for property taken and for damages caused a remaining parcel in a partial taking.

The power to tax makes the government a partner to the owner of real estate. Fairness requires that properties be assessed at uniform proportion of their market value. Overassessment or underassessment results in a loss or gain through tax capitalization.

QUESTIONS FOR REVIEW AND DISCUSSION

1. Briefly identify and explain the nature of the three main governmental limitations to private ownership of real estate.
2. Explain the need for land use controls. Name and briefly explain four controls. Does an owner have any rights relative to these controls? Explain.
3. Explain the need for eminent domain. What are an owner's rights relative to eminent domain?
4. Explain the need for taxation. Does an owner have any rights relative to taxation? Explain.
5. What is a special assessment?
6. Indicate and discuss the purpose or purposes of urban planning. Do you agree with them?
7. Does zoning create value? Might zoning destroy value? Discuss.

8. Is the real property tax system equitable and fair? Discuss.

9. A ceiling on property taxes, as a percentage of market value, is frequently proposed. What would be the effects of such a ceiling? Would a 3 percent ceiling affect your community? A 2 percent ceiling?

10. What are the trends in the use of police power? Eminent domain? Taxation? Discuss.

CASE PROBLEMS

1. Peter owns a 12,000-square foot lot zoned "residential 5,000," meaning that one dwelling unit may be built for each 5,000 square feet of area. Sales of similar lots show that lots sell for $8,000 per dwelling unit. Peter applies for a re-zoning to "residential 2,000."
   a. Assuming that Peter gets the re-zoning, how much increase in value does Peter stand to realize, assuming that the sale price per dwelling unit remains the same?
   b. What factors might make this value increment larger or smaller?
2. Paul owns the 12,000-square foot lot next to Peter's. His lot is also re-zoned to "residential 2,000." However, Paul's lot has a deed restriction limiting its development to a one-family residence. What impact on value is likely as a result of the zoning change?
3. Mary has owned a condominium unit on the twelfth floor of Lakeview Towers for 12 years. James is building a 20-story building across the street, which the zoning allows, thereby spoiling her view. Mary sues to have construction stopped, claiming that she has a scenic easement based on her continuous use of the view for more than the 10 years required to acquire an easement by prescription according to state law. What result? Discuss.

CHAPTER SIX
THE INVESTOR-BROKER RELATIONSHIP

Let us begin anew—
remembering on both sides that civility is not a sign of weakness,
and sincerity is always subject to proof. Let us never negotiate out of fear.
But let us never fear to negotiate.
JOHN F. KENNEDY, former U.S. President

IMPORTANT TOPICS OR DECISION AREAS COVERED IN THIS CHAPTER

- The Law of Agency
- Listing Agreements
- Critical Issues in the Listing Arrangement
- More on Commissions
- Selecting a Broker

A *real estate broker* is anyone engaged to negotiate the sale; purchase, lease, or exchange of realty; or arrange financing of realty—for a fee or commission. Brokerage specialization has now reached the stage where individuals—and entire organizations—limit operations to a single area, such as investments, commercial, industrial, land, or lease brokerage. Some organizations, however, do continue to provide a wide variety of functions and services, including appraising, brokerage, counseling, construction and development, financing, and insurance.

In looking at the investor-broker relationship, our concern is primarily with the buy-sell transaction. In this transaction, the broker is a negotiator and takes neither title nor possession of the realty. At the same time, the actions and success of the broker are of vital importance to the investor.

KEY CONCEPTS INTRODUCED IN THIS CHAPTER

Accountability
Agency
Agent
Disclosed principal
Dual/divided agency
Fiduciary relationship
Independent contractor
Listing agreement
Loyalty
Middleman
Principal
Procuring cause of sale
Ready, willing, and able buyer
Third party
Tort
Undisclosed principal

THE LAW OF AGENCY

Agency is the fiduciary relationship created when one person acts on behalf of, or under the control of, another. In a *fiduciary relationship* trust and faith are expected and necessary, for instance, in financial matters such as buying, selling, or leasing of property. The law of agency concerns the legal rights, duties, and liabilities of the principal, agent, and third parties based on contracts and/or relationships between them. The law of agency involves aspects of the law of contract and the law of torts. A *tort* is a wrongful or damaging act committed against another, for which a civil action may be brought. Causing personal injury to another, damaging another's property, fraud, and misrepresentation are examples of torts.

A person acting for or representing another, with the latter's authority, is an *agent.* Thus, a broker is an agent in selling property for an owner under a listing agreement. The person for whom an agent acts is a *principal.* An owner, therefore, becomes a principal when he or she signs a listing agreement with a broker.

Agency usually involves three parties: a principal (P), an agent (A), and a third party (T). A potential buyer, as an investor negotiating to purchase a property, is a *third party* in the typical real estate sales transaction.

A principal known or identified to a third party is a *disclosed principal*. A partially disclosed principal is one not known or identified to the third party, although the agent acknowledges that a principal is involved. Finally, an *undisclosed principal* is one who is secretly represented by an agent who appears to be acting in self-interest.

Duties, Liabilities, and Rights of a Principal

A principal's main duty is to compensate an agent in accordance with the contract of employment. Thus, with the typical listing agreement, the owner must pay a commission to the broker when a "ready, willing, and able" buyer has been found. An owner also has a duty to give the broker-agent complete and accurate information when listing a property to be sold, leased, or exchanged.

A principal is liable on all agreements or contracts made by an agent within the authority given the agent. Unauthorized agreements also become a principal's liability, if subsequently affirmed or ratified by a principal with full knowledge of the pertinent facts. Unauthorized agreements are agreements outside or beyond the authority given the agent. Most listing agreements clearly spell out the authority given a broker, and usually that authority does not include signing or accepting an offer to purchase the subject property.

A principal may become liable for torts committed by an agent. Thus, a tort committed by an agent within the scope of the employment agreement or under the direction of the principal becomes a liability of the principal. At the same time, a principal is not generally liable if the agent is an independent contractor. An *independent contractor* is a person retaining personal controls over work details while performing a service or task for an employer. A broker engaged to sell a property for an owner is almost certainly an independent contractor. A salesperson, engaged by a broker, may or may not be an independent contractor; the work relationship would be the primary determinant of whether the salesperson were an independent contractor. The greater the control exercised by the broker over the salesperson, the less the likelihood that the salesperson is an independent contractor.

A disclosed principal may enforce any contract made with a third party by an authorized agent for the principal's benefit. A real estate broker ordinarily does not enter contracts for a principal, but such is possible.

Duties, Liabilities, and Rights of an Agent

The duties of an agent to a principal are (1) to use reasonable care, (2) to obey reasonable instructions, (3) to exhibit accountability, (4) to be loyal, and (5) to give notice. Using reasonable cares means that the agent must be diligent and must act in good faith in representing the principal. And the agent is expected to follow or obey all reasonable instructions of a principal, assuming that the instructions pertain to the purpose of the principal-agent relationship. Following instructions includes keeping within the authority given by the principal. Instructions creating a tort or criminal situation would not be reasonable. An agent also has a legal duty of *accountability*—to account for all money or property to the principal, including keeping adequate records concerning such money or property. In addition, it is illegal for a broker to commingle or mix personal funds and funds of a principal.

Loyalty means that the agent must not benefit from the relationship except through compensation from the principal unless otherwise agreed. Faithful performance is another term for loyalty. A broker, therefore, may not represent both parties in a buy-sell transaction without the knowledge and consent of both. Representing two principals is called *dual* or *divided* agency. Contracts involving agent disloyalty are voidable at the option of the principal, in that the broker cannot get the highest possible price for the seller and at the same time get the lowest possible price for the buyer. It follows that the broker cannot collect a commission for arranging a voided contract. If the broker acts for both buyer and seller, with both having full knowledge of double agency, the double agency rule does not apply. In this situation the broker is often termed a *middleman*.

"Giving notice" to a principal means that any information given the agent must be communicated immediately to the principal. Any knowledge given the agent legally binds the principal. Therefore, it follows that the agent is bound to keep the principal informed of any important facts concerning the object of the agency arrangement.

An agent is generally not personally liable for contracts entered into for the benefit of the principal. However, an agent exceeding his or her authority does incur personal liability, unless such act is affirmed or ratified by the principal. A broker is usually engaged only to find a buyer and not to make a sales contract for the owner. Therefore, a broker's operations usually do not provide a situation where the authority of the agency agreement might be exceeded. However, if a principal lacks legal competence to make a valid agency contract (because of insanity or being underage), the agent incurs personal liability for any resulting contract.

In the matter of torts, agents and independent contractors are personally liable for their own acts. At the same time, agents and independent contractors are not liable for torts committed by their principals.

An agent has a right to enforce a contract of a principal against a third party in which an interest is held. Thus a broker may enforce a sales contract of an owner with a buyer because of an anticipated commission. Finally, a broker derives authority from an owner through the listing agreement. And to enforce the collection of a commission, a broker must have the agreement in writing. Ordinarily, the broker is authorized only to negotiate for the principal under a listing agreement. Most listing agreements provide that a broker may engage salespersons to help conduct the negotiations. The salespersons also operate under the law of agency, with the broker as the principal.

LISTING AGREEMENTS

After successfully completing a buy-sell or leasing transaction, the broker must show that a listing agreement was made with the owner, or the owner's agent, to enforce his or her right to the commission. A *listing agreement* is an oral or written contract of employment of a broker by a principal to buy, sell, or lease real estate. A listing agreement creates a principal-agent relationship, the broker being the agent. A *principal* is a person who employs another (an agent) as a representative. In turn, an agent is a person who represents or acts for another (a principal) by the latter's authority. A principal, in this situation, is usually an owner-seller, but not necessarily; a broker may act as an agent for a buyer.

The listing agreement is the foundation of the broker's business. Out of it arise the broker's relation or trust and confidence with his or her principal and the broker's rights for compensation. It is highly important, therefore, that any person engaging in the real estate business fully understand the rights and obligations underlying each of the listing contracts.

Strictly speaking, the typical "listing" is not a contract. At most, it may be classified as a unilateral contract that becomes an actual or bilateral contract upon performance by the broker. However, a listing agreement containing promises by a broker to make a diligent effort and by an owner to pay some minimum monetary consideration and a commission becomes a bilateral contract. Lacking consideration—until performance—a unilateral contract is revocable by either party at any time prior to performance, even though a definite time is stipulated in the listing agreement.

Five listing agreements are in general use: (1) open, (2) exclusive agency, (3) exclusive right to sell, (4) multiple, and (5) net. Open and net listing agreements may be reached orally in some states. However, to enforce a claim for the collection of a commission better, brokers prefer written listings. In fact, most brokers refuse to handle or promote properties not subject to written listings.

Open Listing

An open listing occurs when an owner-principal offers several brokers an equal chance to sell realty. The broker who actually arranges a sale receives compensation. The owner must remain neutral in the competition between the brokers to avoid obligation for a commission to more than one broker.

The owner may reserve the right personally to sell the realty without becoming liable for a commission, and usually does so.

The sale of the property terminates the open listing. Usually, the owner need not notify the agents, since under the law effective in almost all states, the sale cancels all outstanding listings. This safeguards the owner against paying more than one commission.

Exclusive Agency Listing

An exclusive agency listing is the engaging of only one broker to sell realty for a commission, with a right retained by the owner to sell or rent the property without obligation for a commission. An exclusive agency listing contains the words "exclusive agency." Under this form of list agreement, the commission is payable to the broker named in the contract. The purpose of the exclusive agency listing is to give the broker holding the listing an opportunity to apply "best efforts" without interference or competition from other brokers. In nearly every state, the exclusive agency listing binds the owner to pay a commission to the listing broker in the event of a sale by the listing broker or any other broker.

An exclusive agency listing does not entitle the broker to compensation when the property is sold by the owner to a prospect not procured by the broker. This listing is also revocable, unless a consideration was made. Further, the listing may be terminated if the broker has not performed, in which case the owner's liability is limited to the value of any services actually performed by the broker.

Exclusive Right-to-Sell Listing

An exclusive right-to-sell listing is the engagement of one broker to sell realty, with a commission to be paid the broker regardless of who sells the property, owner included. That is, the owner gives the rights personally to sell the realty and avoid paying a commission. An exclusive right-to-sell listing contains the words "exclusive right." This listing is similar in all respects to the exclusive agency listing except that under it, a commission is due the broker named whether the property is sold by the listing broker, any other broker, or even the owner, within the time limit specified in the listing contract. An owner may reserve the right to sell to certain parties, who are or have been negotiating with the owner for the property, by including their names as exceptions in the contract. Figure 6–1 is an exclusive right-to-sell listing contract that may also serve as a multiple listing agreement.

Multiple Listing

A multiple listing is actually a special version or a supplement to the exclusive right-to-sell listing whereby any member of a designated group

FIGURE 6–1
Real estate broker's employment contract

No. 678 © Rev. TT
Stevens-Ness L.P.Co.
Portland, Ore. 97204

REAL ESTATE BROKER'S EMPLOYMENT CONTRACT
(involving lease and lessee's interest only; Use Form 676)

APARTMENT, HOTEL, ROOMING HOUSE, MOTEL

Name of property Douglas Manor Tel.
Location 2001 Century Drive, Urbandale, Anystate, 00000 Legal Description Lots 16 & 17,
Edgewood South Subdivision
(If said property is incorrectly described, owner hereby expressly authorizes broker subsequently to write in hereon or attach hereto, the correct legal description thereof.)
City Urbandale, County Rustic, State and Zip Anystate 00000; for better description see owner's title deed on record, now made a part hereof.
No. of apts. 16; No. of rms. 72; No. of 4 rm. apts 8; No. of 5 rm. apts. 8; No. of rm. apts. Does structure need remodeling or renovating? Yes ☐; No ☒.
Selling price, free of encumbrances: $ 680,000; Terms: Cash
Is personal property included in this listing? Yes ☐; No ☐; if so, is signed inventory attached? Yes ☐; No ☐; to be attached? Yes ☐; No ☐.

September 1st 80

To Ivan M. Everready, Realtor Broker, City Urbandale State Anystate
FOR VALUE RECEIVED, you hereby are employed to sell or exchange the property described hereon at the selling price and on the terms noted. You hereby are authorized to accept a deposit on the purchase price. You may, if desired, secure the cooperation of any other broker, or group of brokers, in procuring a sale of said property. In the event that you, or any other brokers cooperating with you, shall find a buyer ready and willing to enter into a deal for said price and terms, or such other terms and price as I may accept, or that during your employment you supply me with the name of or place me in contact with a buyer to or through whom at any time within 90 days after the termination of said employment I may sell or convey said property, I hereby agree to pay you in cash for your services a commission equal in amount to 6% on 1st $100,000; 4% on excess of $100,000 (see below) % of the above stated selling price. I agree to convey said real estate to the purchaser by a good and sufficient deed, to assign the outstanding lease(s), if any, to transfer and deliver said personal property, if any, by good and sufficient bill of sale and to furnish title insurance in an amount equal to the selling price insuring marketable title to said real estate and good right to convey. I hereby warrant that the information shown hereon below is true; that I am the owner of said property, that my title thereto is a good and marketable title, that the same is free of encumbrances except as shown hereafter under "Financial Details" and except taxes levied on said property for the current tax year which are to be pro rated between the seller and buyer. In case of an exchange, I have no objection to your representing and accepting compensation from the other party to the exchange as well as myself. I hereby authorize you and your customers to enter any part of said property at any reasonable time to show same. Also, I authorize you, at any time, to fill in and complete all or any part of the "Information Data" below, except financial details. The following items are to be left upon the premises as part of the property purchased: All irrigation, plumbing, ventilation, cooling and heating fixtures and equipment (including stoker and oil tanks but excluding fire place fixtures and equipment), water heaters, attached electric light and bathroom fixtures, light bulbs and fluorescent lamps, venetian blinds, wall-to-wall carpeting, awnings, window and door screens, storm doors and windows, attached floor coverings, attached television antenna, all plants, shrubs and trees and all fixtures except: stove and refrigerators to be regarded as fixtures also.
The following personal property is also included as a part of the property to be offered for sale for said price none (or see signed inventory, if any attached). This agreement expires at midnight on December 31, 1980, but I further allow you a reasonable time thereafter to close any deal on which earnest money is then deposited. In case of suit or action on this contract, it is agreed between us that the court, whether trial or appellate, may allow the prevailing party therein that party's reasonable attorney's fees. It is further agreed that my signature affixed to the renewal clause below shall have the effect of renewing and extending your employment to a new date to be fixed by me on the same terms and all with the same effect as if the said new date had been fixed above as the expiration of your employment. Disposition of forfeited Earnest Money, if any, to be negotiated and set forth in the Earnest Money Receipt (Oregon only, delete if inapplicable).
*THIS LISTING IS AN EXCLUSIVE LISTING and you hereby are granted the absolute, sole and exclusive right to sell or exchange the said described property. In the event of any sale, by me or any other person, or of exchange or conveyance of said property, or any part thereof, during the term of your exclusive employment, or in case I withdraw the authority hereby given prior to said expiration date, I agree to pay you the said commission just the same as if a sale had actually been consummated by you.
I HEREBY CERTIFY THAT I HAVE READ AND RECEIVED A CARBON COPY OF THIS CONTRACT.

Accepted: September 1st, 1980 ____ Owner
Ivan M. Everready, Realtor Broker /s/ Wendy Welloff Owner
Owner's Address Unit 77, Condominium Towers, City Urbandale State Anystate Zip 00000 Phone 345-2020

FOR VALUE RECEIVED, the above broker's employment hereby is renewed and extended to and including ____, 19__
Accepted: ____, 19__ ____ Owner
____ Broker ____ Owner

FOLD ON DOTTED LINE FOR INSERTION IN RING BINDER

FINANCIAL DETAILS

Selling price (free of encumbrances)
$ 680,000 Terms: cash
Mortgage not assumable
Payments include: Prin. x Int. x Taxes x Ins. x
(Check items to be included in payments)
Interest on deferred payments none %
Fire ins. $ ____ Ann'l prem. $ ____
Taxes last fiscal year $ ____

	ENCUMBRANCES		PAYABLE
1st mtg. $	481,647	Int. 9 %	mo
2nd mtg. $	–	Int. – %	–
Contr. bal. $		Int. %	

Delinquent taxes $ none
Municipal liens $ none

OPERATION
Gross annual income $ 106,667
Gross annual outgo $ 34,000
Net annual income $ 72,667

CHATTELS
What included in this sale (check items involved)
Outstanding lease ____ Furniture ____
Fixtures x Equipment ____
Goodwill ____ Assumed Name ____
For details as to chattels included in sale:
See above ____ See signed inventory ____
Are chattels fully paid for ____ Are chattels mtg'd ____
Possession may be had at closing.

APARTMENT ☒ **HOTEL** ☐ **ROOMING HOUSE** ☐ **MOTEL** ☐ ☐
INFORMATIVE DATA Office Listing No. ____
(REAL ESTATE INVOLVED - WITH OR WITHOUT OUTSTANDING LEASE)
Name of property Douglas Manor
Location 2001 Century Drive, Urbandale, Anystate 00000
Name of owner Wendy Welloff Tel. 345-2020
Owner has: Abstract ____ Title Insurance ____ Cert. of Title ____ Contract ____ Deed ____
Type of construction: ____

LEASE
Is lease outstanding? Yes ____ No ____
Name of lessor ____
Name of lessee ____
Date of lease ____, 19__
Expiration date ____, 19__
Monthly rent $ ____
Are rents paid to date? Yes ____ No ____
Any option to renew? Yes ____ No ____
If so, for how long ____
If so, for what rent $ ____
Rent paid in advance? Yes ____ No ____
If so, how much $ ____
Is lease otherwise secured? ____
If so, how secured ____
Can lessee assign without lessor's consent? Yes ____ No ____

HOW MANY
Total No. of units 16
Furn. Un-F.
1 bedrm. apt. ____
2 bedrm. apt. 8
3 bedrm. apt 8
Rooms ____
Pvt. Pub.
Baths 16
Showers 24
Toilets 24
Elevator yes
Type Otis-auto
Garage Under-adequate for 28 cars

UTILITIES - METERS
Water 1 Gen. 16 Pvt.
Elect. Gen. 1 Pvt. 16
Gas Gen. 1 Pvt. 16
Phone Pub. 1 Pvt. Pay x
Sewer yes
Heating forced air
Type gas
Refrigerators yes
How Many 16
Type various
Ranges yes
How Many 16
Type various
Garb. Dis. 16
Laundry Fac. Coin op
4 washers
2 dryers

DISTANCES
City center 2-1/2 mis
Shopping center 1 mi
Bus stop in front
Grade school 6 blks
High School 8 blks
University-1 mi
waterfront-6 blk

EMPLOYEES
Operating help ____
Maids ____
Janitors ____
Other ____

Remarks commission 6% on 1st 100,000; 4% in excess of $100,000, payable only on closing
Listed by H. Ardent
Signs permitted yes
Will consider exchange for much larger property
Inspected by ____

BROKER'S COPY

7711

* TO MAKE NON EXCLUSIVE - Strike complete paragraph following asterisk * in Employment Contract and have owner initial deletion.

of brokers may sell the realty and share in the commission. Each broker in the group brings listings to the attention of the other members. If a sale results, the commission is shared between the listing and the selling broker, with a small percentage going to the multiple listing group or organization.

In a typical multiple listing organization, sales commissions may be divided as follows:

1. From 5 to 10 percent of the gross commission goes to the listing service to cover operating expenses and general overhead.
2. From 50 to 60 percent of the remainder goes to the selling broker.
3. From 40 to 50 percent (i.e., the balance) goes to the listing member.

Assume a $1,000 sales commission of 5 percent and a distribution of 50 percent and 50 percent of the remainder. The proceeds would be distributed as follows: $50 (5 percent of $1,000) to the listing bureau, $475 (50 percent of $950) to the broker effecting the sale, and $475 (50 percent of $950) to the broker who initiated the listing.

A multiple listing agreement is generally an exclusive right-to-sell listing, with the broker being granted authority to make the property known to other brokers. A multiple listing arrangement is advantageous to an owner-seller in that the property gets wider exposure, which tends to mean a higher price and a shorter selling time.

Net Listing

A net listing is an agreement whereby an owner engages a broker to sell realty at a fixed or minimum price, with any excess to be considered as the broker's commission. A net listing is, therefore, a contract to obtain a minimum price for the owner. The broker usually adds the commission to the quoted net price. In some states, the broker cannot lawfully obtain a compensation greater than the usual customary rate of compensation without the specific knowledge and consent of the owner. Because of the uncertainty of the agreed selling price, a net listing may give rise to a charge of fraud against the broker. This possibility is less with an experienced investor-owner than with a typical layperson homeowner.

Termination of Listing Agreements

A listing agreement is terminated by any of the following: (1) mutual consent of the parties, (2) performance by the broker in selling the property, (3) expiration of the agreed time, (4) revocation by the principal, (5) revocation or abandonment by the broker-agent, (6) destruction of the property, (7) death of the principal or agent, (8) insanity of the principal or agent, and (9) bankruptcy of the principal or agent. The first five represent termination by acts of the parties. The last four result from operation of the law.

CRITICAL ISSUES IN THE LISTING ARRANGEMENT

In most situations, the agreement in which a broker is engaged to sell a property for an owner, the listing contract, must be in writing for a broker to collect the commission. Several critical issues must be resolved for a satisfactory listing agreement.

Property Listing Price

In self-interest, an owner wants the highest possible price in selling a property. A broker ordinarily prefers to list a property at a price that is low enough to make it likely for the property to sell quickly. A broker, however, as an agent in a fiduciary relationship has a duty of keeping the principal informed of all material facts affecting the subject matter of the agency relationship, which includes providing knowledge of the market value of the property. Increasingly, the broker, as a real estate practitioner, has an obligation to document that any suggested listing price is not too low. Information from sales of comparable properties is one generally accepted way of documenting value. An owner is generally advised to list at a price above indicated market value, to take account of possible inflation in values and to retain room for bargaining. A property that sells too quickly may very well have been listed at too low a price.

Reservation of Right to Sell

A major distinction between listing contracts concerns who has a right to sell the property. The broker's control increases sharply in going from an open to an exclusive agency to an exclusive right-to-sell contract. And with greater control, the broker is likely to expend greater effort or go to more expense to bring about a sale.

In an open listing, any broker selling the property is entitled to a commission; of course, the owner may personally sell the property and pay no commission. In the exclusive agency, the listing broker is the only person legally entitled to a commission if someone other than the owner sells the property. That is, the owner may still sell the property and avoid paying a commission.

In an exclusive right-to-sell agreement, the listing broker is entitled to a commission if the property is sold by anyone. However, in entering an exclusive right-to-sell agreement, the owner may list exceptions (names of parties with whom negotiations have been or are being conducted), meaning that the owner may arrange a sale with one of them and avoid paying a commission.

Broker Compensation

The most usual arrangement is for a broker to get some percentage of the selling price for a commission. And commission rates are largely set by local area custom. However, brokers are prohibited from collusion in setting commission rates, according to the Sherman and Clayton Antitrust Acts, which prohibit monopoly and agreements in restraint of trade. The anticollusion law means that brokers may charge what the traffic will bear, and owners are free to negotiate the amount of commission to be paid with the broker. Brokers may not, in turn, cite local agreement or custom as reasons for not cutting a commission.

The amount of commission, or method of determining the amount of commission, is best included in the listing agreement. The situation is not too different from leasing. It follows that flat and percentage commissions are possible, individually or in combination. Also, a net listing may be used.

Flat commission. Certain basic costs are almost certain to be incurred in selling any property. These costs include advertising, office expenses, broker's time, and overhead in general. Thus some flat amount, say, $1,000, might be justified, whether a small lot or a large house is sold. An owner may quickly determine the net amount to be realized from a sale when a flat commission is to be paid. For example,

Sale price	$100,000
Less: Broker's "flat" commission	−1,000
Seller's net	$ 99,000

Percentage commission. Broker's typically get 5 to 7 percent of the sale price as commission. Thus, a sale for $100,000 with a 6 percent commission would net a seller $94,000.

Sale price	$100,000
Less: Brokerage commission	−6,000
Seller's net	$ 94,000

If a seller wanted to net $100,000 from a sale, the $100,000 would be 94 percent of the necessary gross sale price. To calculate the necessary sale price, the net amount would be divided by 0.94.

$$\frac{\$100,000}{0.94} = \$106,383$$

Six percent of $106,383 equals $6,383, when rounded to the nearest dollar.

Split commission. A brokerage fee might also be negotiated on larger properties that would give a higher rate of commission up to a certain base amount, with a lower rate for any amount of sale price above the base amount. A flat fee plus a percentage might also be negotiated. For example, a commission of 6 percent on the first $100,000 plus 4 percent of any price in excess of $100,000 might be agreed to in listing a property. A sale for $640,000 would result in a commission of $27,600 under this scheme:

Sale price			$640,000
Commission on first $100,000		$ 6,000	
Commission on price in excess of $100,000			
Sale price	$640,000		
Less: Base	100,000		
Excess	$540,000		
At 4% gives commission of	× 4%	$21,600	
Total commission		$ 27,600	$ 27,600
Seller's net			$612,400

The selling price, assuming that the owner wants to net $640,000 from a property, would be calculated as follows:

Net + commission on base $100,000 = $94,000 + $6,000 =	$100,000
Necessary sale price to net additional $546,000	
at 4% rate: $546,000/0.96 = $568,750	$568,750
Gross required sale price	$668,750

Proof:

$568,750 × 4%	$ 22,750
Commission on first $100,000 @ 6%	6,000
Total commission	$ 28,750
Gross sale price	$668,750
Net sale price desired ($668,750 − $28,750)	$640,000

Net listing/residual commission. A net listing means that the broker gets anything above the asking price stipulated by an owner. Net listings are illegal in some states because they invite fraud. Thus, a sale of a property for $750,000 for which the owner expected $640,000 would be almost prima facie evidence of disloyalty by the broker. The duties of loyalty and of keeping a principal informed would require the broker to make an owner aware that $640,000 was too low an asking price. An owner would have a strong case for avoiding the payment of $110,000 commission on a $750,000 sale, which calculates to 14.7 percent commission rate, far above the more usual 5 to 7 percent rates.

Duration/Termination of Agreement

A listing agreement may be terminated by action of the parties or operation of the law. Actions of the parties that end the agreement include (1) mutual consent of the parties, (2) completion of the agreement by sale of the property, (3) time expiration or running out, (4) revocation by the principal, and (5) revocation or abandonment by the agent. Operation of the law ends the agreement upon (1) destruction of the property, as by fire, (2) death of the principal or agent, (3) insanity of principal or agent, and (4) bankruptcy of the principal or agent.

A listing agreement is, of course, terminated by sale of the subject property and payment of the commission. And an agreement for a fixed period terminates at the end of the period unless an extension is arranged. Termination by completion of purpose or time expiration are the two most common ways in which listing agreements are ended. Some agreements contain a clause for automatic renewal or extension, meaning that the listing continues unless terminated by written notice. Automatic extensions are generally deemed to be unfair to an owner and are actually illegal in some states.

If no time limit is specified, a listing agreement expires after a "reasonable time." A reasonable time might be three months for a one-family residence and from six months to a year for a large office building. An owner may terminate any time up to the start of performance by the broker. Effectively, beginning performance converts the agreement from a unilateral contract to a bilateral contract. The broker is showing good faith toward consideration by making the effort to sell.

Broker Proof of Performance

An agent must complete the assigned task to earn compensation. A broker must also perform according to the listing agreement to earn a commission. Generally the broker's obligation is to produce a *"ready, willing, and able" buyer.* A purchaser acceptable to the seller or capable of meeting the seller's terms is such a buyer. The owner is not obligated to accept the offer of a third party even though the property is listed for sale. However,

failure to complete a sale through fault of the owner does not cancel a commission. Such failure might result because of title defects, refusal of a spouse to sign a deed, fraud, inability to deliver possession within a reasonable time, owner change of mind, buyer-seller agreement to cancel, or owner insisting on terms not included in listing agreement. In all these situations, a broker is entitled to a commission, whether or not the owner completes the sale to the aspiring purchaser.

An owner may include a "no-closing, no-commission" clause on a listing agreement. Such a clause means that, unless the transaction results in a conveyance of title, no commission need be paid. Also, courts are increasingly saying that a broker is better able to judge the ability of a buyer to obtain financing than is an owner. And, therefore, a buyer is not "ready, willing and able," until adequate financing has been obtained.

MORE ON COMMISSIONS

General Rules on Earning Commissions

To recover commissions, the broker must (1) show an agreement or contract of employment, (2) be the *procuring cause* in the sale, (3) bring about the deal on the terms of his or her employer, (4) act in good faith, (5) produce an available purchaser who under the general rule is ready and willing to purchase and also legally able to do so, and (6) bring about a completed transaction. We have already seen that double employment or secret sharing in profits violates the requirement that the broker acts in good faith. The purchaser obtained by the broker must meet all the terms as stated by the seller, unless the seller is willing to modify them. The broker must successfully complete the agreement. He or she cannot abandon the negotiations and expect that if the parties, later and in good faith, get together and make a deal, a commission can be claimed. The employer must give the broker a fair chance to complete the transaction once it is commenced. But having done so, the owner may refuse to negotiate further through the broker and may take up the matter directly or through another broker. Mere introduction of the parties by a broker or initiation of negotiations does not commit the owner to deal forever with the aspiring purchaser through the broker.

Who Pays the Commission?

The employer is liable for the commission in every case. The broker's employer is usually the owner or the owner's representative. In some cases a purchaser employs the broker to obtain the property for him or her. The rule on double employment has already been noted. It is no violation of this rule for the purchaser to employ a broker to procure the property with the understanding that whatever commission the broker is to receive shall be paid by the seller.

Persons not owning the property, or those acting in a representative capacity, are personally liable for a commission if they employ a broker toward buying a property. It sometimes happens that such a purchaser assumes, in the contract, the seller's obligation to pay the broker's commission. Also, subagents, as salepersons, look to their principal, as a broker, as their employer, for their commissions.

Commission on an Installment Sale

Installment sales are intended to minimize as well as to defer payments of capital gains taxes. Brokers, as a condition of employment, often agree to receive commission payments in proportion to the amounts of principal cash payments made by the purchaser to the seller or his or her agent. Thus, when the purchase agreement calls for 25 percent cash at closing and the balance in equal installments over a three-year period with interest on the purchase money mortgage debt at 10 percent on unpaid balances, the broker under the commission agreement may receive only 25 percent of the total commission at the time of closing and the balance in installments over the ensuing three years. The seller should expect that the deferred commission agreement will provide for interest payments on the commission balance at the same rate and in proportion to the amounts received under terms of the installment sales agreement. Deferred commission payments are still the exception rather than the rule and, when agreed upon, rarely extend beyond a contract period of five years.

Commissions on Exchanges, Loans, and Leases

The rules that apply to recovery of commission on sales apply also to exchanges. It is customary, however, for both parties to an exchange to pay a commission based on the value or price of their respective properties. A statement in the contract that each party shall pay the broker is sufficient notice to each that the broker receive a double commission.

The broker is usually entitled to a commission for procuring a mortgage loan only if the loan is actually made. The commission is also earned if the broker procured an acceptance of the loan and it failed to close through a defect in the title to the property or through a fault of the borrower. The reason for this is that there is rarely an enforceable agreement on the part of the lender to make a loan. The lender may agree to accept it, but this does not constitute a contract. In many jurisdictions, the rule is that a broker has earned a commission when a lender who is willing, ready, and able to make the loan on the terms offered has been procured.

The rule on making commissions on leases is similar to that for procuring loans. The broker is not entitled to compensation unless a lease or a complete agreement on its terms is obtained. The broker would, however, be entitled to a commission if the owner tried to impose new and unreasonable terms upon a prospective tenant and the lease was not made for that reason. When a lease has been made, the broker is entitled to a full commission, and this is so regardless of the tenant's subsequent default, unless, of course, the broker has made a binding agreement to the contrary.

Percentage leases are sometimes entered into with lessees of business property with a minimum rent required. In addition, an agreed percentage of the lessee's gross income from the business conducted on the leased premises must be paid for rent. In this lease, the broker is paid a commission at the time the lease is signed, based on the minimum rental. The broker receives a further commission on the accrual of the additional rental computed on the percentage basis set forth in the lease. Such further commission is usually payable at the end of each year.

SELECTING A BROKER

Experienced investors often buy properties through one broker and sell through another. In buying, these investors know that selecting the proper broker and/or agent may result in a price that is relatively low. They know that some brokers bargain/counsel their principals down rather than negotiate harder with buyers to make a high offer. Hence, a better buy may be made through them. Other brokers work very hard to get the highest possible price for their principals and, hence, provide a strong advantage to an owner in selling. The higher price may more than pay the broker's commission. Great care should be exercised in selecting a broker. The decision is too important for a sophisticated investor to leave it to chance, as by casually listing with a friend or relative.

Important considerations in selecting a broker are (1) office and agent specialization, (2) office location and procedures, (3) firm's attitude and reputation, and (4) a track record as evidenced by satisfied clients. Names of promising firms and agents may be obtained from fellow property owners. Also, names of firms specializing in the types of property of concern may be obtained from classified ads and multiple listing service books. Given several firm names, a survey to collect information necessary to making an informed selection is suggested. The first phase of the survey may be made by telephone. Later phases require personal contact.

Much background knowledge is obtained in making a survey. Such knowledge becomes useful in the immediate selection as well as for long-term purposes. Thus, while the investor may have one type of property in mind at the moment, another type may be of concern later on. Also, once a survey has been made, the broker selection process may be short-circuited in later selling situations.

The process of selecting a broker suggested here involved going from the general to the specific, from the firm to the individual. This process is intended to maximize chances of selecting the best broker-agent combination for an investor's needs.

An owner should not expect to get legal counsel from brokerage personnel. The law says that only licensed attorneys may give legal advice. At the same time, an owner is advised to get financial and real estate advice from brokers rather than from attorneys. Unfortunately, no law prohibits attorneys from giving financial and real estate advice, two areas in which many attorneys are not qualified. A broker may fill in the blanks on a listing agreement or sales contract, however.

Finally, an investor, when buying a listed property, should remember that sales representatives are agents of the owner. This means that the brokerage personnel owe care, obedience, accountability, and loyalty to the owner-seller, not to a buyer. The investor, in buying, is the "third party."

Firm Survey

The brokers or sales managers of firms likely to serve an owner's need are best interviewed first. This approach avoids the chance of an investor's getting locked in with a particular agent in a firm before it is clear that that agent will suit the investor's need best. The following questions are appropriate for asking:

1. Does your firm specialize in any particular property type? If so, what type?
2. Does your firm specialize in any particular areas or locations? If so, which locations?
3. What properties of ______________ type were sold by your firm in the last 12 months?
4. I'd like to contact some of the former owners of properties sold through your office. Would you give me the names of several?
5. How long has your office/firm been in operation?
6. During what hours does your office/firm operate?
7. Are your phones covered during off hours? If so, how?
8. What are your commission rates? Are they open to negotiation?
9. What listings do you currently have in ______________ types of properties? What are their ages? For how long are they?
10. Is your office affiliated with the multiple listing service?
11. Where does your office rank in its sales of ______________ types of properties relative to other firms/offices in this area/community? (Firm preferably is among the leaders.)
12. Do you personally own any properties of ______________ type? If so, which are they?
13. Does your firm have a continuing agreement with any financial institutions that might facilitate obtaining loans in times of tight money? If so, what institutions? With whom might I talk at these institutions about you?
14. Who are your leading salespersons for ______________ types properties? Does anyone clearly stand out above the others?
15. Is there anything else about your office/firm that you would like me to know?

This interview may be made by telephone and be terminated at any time if it is obvious that the firm is not suited to the owner's needs. After several such interviews, it will be likely that two or three firms will stand out. Follow-up interviews with former clients, lenders, and agents of these two or three firms then become a logical next step.

Agent Survey

At some point during an office survey, it usually becomes apparent that the choice is really among two, three, or four offices. It is at this point that the investor's emphasis shifts to selecting an agent or salesperson. The emphasis should continue to be on specialization and performance. Information from the salesperson may be obtained by asking the following questions, again by phone if desired:

1. Do you specialize in any particular type of property?
2. If so, in what type? In what locations?
3. How long have you specialized in these types of properties?
4. What properties of this type have you sold in the past 12 months?
5. What are the names of the former owners of these sold properties. I'd like to contact them for reference purposes.
6. Are you full time in real estate sales?
7. How long have you been licensed?
8. To what real estate organizations do you belong?
9. What real estate courses have you taken in the last four years?
10. Do you have any real estate designations? If so, what are they?
11. What real estate publications do you usually read?
12. Where do you rank in sales in your company? In sales of this type of property in the area?
13. What listings of property do you currently have?
14. Do you own any investment property? If so, of what type?
15. Do you have any other comments or information that I should be aware of about yourself or your firm?

Personal Interviews and Selection

Owner and lender references of firms and agents still under consideration may be checked out. And visits may be arranged to the firm offices to interview the agents, and possibly the sales managers, personally. Agents best measuring up to the "ideal agent" concept may be invited to the property. Each agent under consideration may then be asked to research the market as to the value of the property, how long a sale is likely to take, and so on. In responding to this situation, the agent is likely to reveal a great deal about his or her professional competence.

The responses may be compared as to probable sales value, consistency, and depth of analysis. Sales of comparable properties may be inspected as indicators of value. Conditions of sale may also be indicated by the agent, along with a marketing and advertising program. At some point, an owner-investor should be able to make an informed decision as to which agent-broker combination to select. At this point, the owner might negotiate for an exclusive agency listing agreement, considering that the agent is highly qualified and has undergone considerable review. If an exclusive right-to-sell agreement is entered into, specific reservations of possible buyers may be included.

SUMMARY

The investor-broker relationship becomes that of principal and agent when a property is listed for sale with the broker. The law of agency, therefore, applies. A principal's main duties in this relationship are to provide accurate information and to compensate the broker upon completion of a sale. A principal is liable on all agreements or contracts made by the agent within instructions or the authority given the agent. A principal is not liable for contracts made outside the agent's authority or instructions or for torts committed by the agent. An agent's main duties are care, obedience, accountability, loyalty, and giving notice. An agent is not responsible for torts committed by a principal.

Important considerations in the listing agreement from an owner's point of view are (1) the price, (2) reservation of the right to sell, (3) broker compensation, (4) length of listing period, and (5) point at which commissions are payable. Owners may make the commission payable at closing or on transfer of title rather than on the finding of a "ready, willing, and able" buyer. Commissions on installment sales, leases, and exchanges are often deferred in a manner consistent with the unfolding of the transaction.

Informed selection of a broker-agent may benefit an owner by more than the amount of a commission. Some investors buy through one broker and sell through another for greatest advantage. Important criteria in selecting a broker are (1) specialization, (2) office suitability as to location and appearance, (3) attitude and reputation, and (4) successful experience. In short, an owner seeks an experienced professional. A selection process of interviewing brokers, agents, and former clients is recommended.

QUESTIONS FOR REVIEW AND DISCUSSION

1. What is the law of agency?
2. What is a fiduciary relationship?
3. What duties does a principal owe an agent?
4. What duties does an agent owe a principal?
5. Identify and discuss at least four critical issues in listing a property from an owner's point of view.
6. List and discuss from an owner's point of view at least four important considerations in selecting a broker.

7. Identify and describe briefly at least four types of listing agreements; explain the use of each.

8. Outline and discuss the process suggested in this chapter for the selection of a broker.

9. Selecting and using the "right" broker in selling real estate may result in a benefit greater than the amount of a commission. Do you agree? Discuss.

10. How might a sophisticated investor best select a broker or agent through whom to buy?

11. Are there any advantages, from an investor's point of view, in using a broker as a buyer's agent in acquiring property, even though a commission would be required? Explain.

CASE PROBLEMS

1. A property sells for $320,000. Calculate the commission
   a. At 5 percent
   b. At a split rate of 6 percent on the first $100,000 and 4 percent of anything in excess of $100,000
2. An owner wants to net $85,000 from the sale of a residence. What selling price would apply, assuming that the brokerage personnel were to realize a 7 percent commission?
3. Baker, a broker, was hired by way of a listing agreement to sell Angus's house. Baker showed the property to Marlboro. However, before a sale could be arranged, the following occurred.
   a. Angus died. The executor later sold the house to Marlboro, directly, and refused to pay Baker a commission. Baker sued to collect a commission. What was the result?
   b. The house burned to the ground. Angus sold the lot and foundation to Marlboro shortly thereafter and refused to pay Baker a commission. Baker sued? What was the result?
   c. The listing expired. The next week, Angus sold the property to Marlboro, and refused to pay a commission. Baker sued. What was the result?
   d. Angus rented the house to Baker during the last month of the listing agreement. The listing expired. Baker sued Angus for a commission, claiming to be the "procuring cause" for the lease. What was the result?
4. Victor contacted a real estate broker, Alfredo, to sell his ranch. No written listing agreement was made. Shortly thereafter, Alfredo mentioned Victor's interest in selling to Ivan, another broker but not a business associate of Alfredo. Ivan arranged a sale of the ranch. Alfredo now claims that Victor owes him a commission, because he was the "procuring cause" of the sale. Is a commission owed? Why or why not?.

CHAPTER SEVEN

CONTRACTS FOR THE PURCHASE AND SALE OF REAL ESTATE

A verbal contract isn't worth the paper it's written on.
SAMUEL GOLDWYN, movie executive

IMPORTANT TOPICS OR DECISION AREAS COVERED IN THIS CHAPTER

- Essentials of a Valid Real Estate Contract
- Types of Sales Contracts
- Components of a Form Contract
- Remedies for Nonperformance
- Escrow Arrangements

A *contract* is a voluntary and legally binding agreement between competent parties calling for them to do or not to do some legal act, for consideration. A contract is also said to be a mutual set of promises to perform or not perform some legal act. In making a contract, the parties create for themselves a set of rights and duties that are interpreted and enforced according to a set of rules and customs concerned with the creation, transfer, and disposition of rights through mutual promises or agreements termed the *law of contracts.*

The emphasis in this chapter is on contracts of sale between a seller and a buyer, with secondary emphasis on listing contracts and escrow agreements. First, however, the essential elements of a legal contract are reviewed.

KEY CONCEPTS INTRODUCED IN THIS CHAPTER

Assignment
Binder
Breach of contract
Bulk transfer
Competent party
Consideration
Contract
Earnest money
Escrow
Financing statement
Fraud
Installment land contract
Land contract
Liquidated damages
Nonperformance
Option
Secured transaction
Security agreement
"Time is of the essence"
Uniform Commercial Code
Void contract
Voidable contract

ESSENTIALS OF A VALID REAL ESTATE CONTRACT

A contract for the sale or exchange of real estate must contain the five elements of any legal contract under the Statute of Frauds, which are

1. Competent parties
2. Bona fide offer and acceptance
3. Consideration
4. Legal object (including accurate property description)
5. Written and signed (some listing agreements are exceptions)

Competent Parties

A *competent party* is a person legally qualified to enter into a binding contract. To be competent, a party must be of legal age, 18 years in most states. The parties must meet on the same legal level or plane and must reach a meeting of the minds as to the subject matter of the contract. A party must not be under some mental handicap that makes for incompetency, such as being mentally retarded or insane.

Competence is also important when executors, administrators, trustees, people acting under a power of attorney, agents, and corporate officers are transacting real estate business. The persons must have legal authority to perform their duties. These persons have such rights and privileges only as contained in the legal instrument appointing them. For example, a corporation about to sell real estate must authorize its president or other officer, by resolution or bylaw, to execute the sales contract. Any real estate investor or practitioner dealing with such individuals is, therefore, strongly advised to demand evidence of their legal authority. Also, a contract with a minor is voidable; a *voidable* contract is one that may either be enforced or declared invalid, usually at the option of one of the parties, in this case, the minor.

Offer and Acceptance

The entire purpose of a real estate contract is to bind the buyer and seller to do something at a future time. Usually, we do not make written contracts to buy personal property that we pay for and then immediately take with us. But a real estate transaction is different. The seller claims ownership of the property, with good and marketable title, subject only to certain liens and encumbrances. None of these can be verified by a quick and simple examination of the property. The buyer must have the title searched and does not want to go to this expense unless the deal is relatively certain. The seller does not wish to remove the property from the market without a deposit and a commitment that binds the purchaser.

To safeguard the interests of both parties, a written contract is drawn. Each promises to do certain things in the future: the seller to give possession and title, the buyer to pay the price in accordance with specified terms. The offer and acceptance of contract terms must relate, of course, to a specific property. No contract is created unless there is a meeting of the minds. A mutual mistake voids the agreement. *Void* means that the agreement is not binding on either of the parties; thus no contract was ever created.

Consideration

Consideration is the promise made or price paid from each party to the other. Consideration is also what each party receives or gives up in the agreement. The amount paid for a property is consideration from a buyer. The conveying of title, evidenced by a deed, is consideration from a seller.

Consideration must be given by both parties for an agreement to be a legally binding contract. In other words, the promise of one party to the contract must be supported by an undertaking of the other. Each must undertake an obligation. A mere promise, even if made in writing, would not be binding upon its maker. A, seeing his good friend B, says to him, "B, I will give you my car tomorrow." B cannot enforce the delivery of the car. But if A offers to give B the car if B ceases to use tobacco for one week, and B accepts and agrees to cease use of tobacco for one week, then there is a mutual obligation or consideration. And if B performs, delivery of the car can be enforced.

Legal Object

An enforceable agreement must contemplate the attainment of an object not expressly forbidden by law or contrary to public policy. An agreement for the sale of realty to be used expressly for an illegal purpose is void and unenforceable, for its object is contrary to the law. Thus, an agreement by which A, a confirmed woman hater, promises B a house upon B's promise nevery to marry, is against public policy for it discourages marriage and is, therefore, unenforceable.

Written and Signed

The purpose of the Statute of Frauds is to avoid possible perjured testimony and fradulent proofs in the transactions of consequence. Thus, oral testimony is not admitted into court to alter the terms of a written agreement. *Fraud* itself means deceiving or using trickery to gain an advantage, as in business negotiations. Real estate contracts are governed by the Statute of Frauds of the state in which the subject property is located.

All real estate contracts coming under the Statute of Frauds must include the following:

1. Signature of buyer or buyers
2. Signature of any and all owners or sellers
3. Spouse's signature (necessary to release marital rights as dower, homestead, or community property)
4. Proper written authority, as power of attorney when an agent signs for a principal

The contract should also include all points of agreements between the parties, so that the provisions may be carried out without difficulty. A contract not carefully written may well give rise to disagreements, extended legal action, and much loss of time to all parties.

A real estate contract may be written up by all parties themselves or by their attorneys. Blank printed-form contracts are available and are widely used because almost all transactions are similar in nature and standard provisions therefore apply. There are, however, three problems in using blank printed forms: (1) What goes in the blanks? (2) Which clauses or provisions are not applicable and should be crossed out? (3) Which clauses or provisions (sometimes termed riders) need to be added? Remember that according to the Statute of Frauds, a real estate contract must be complete on its face.

The parties (usually buyer and seller) or their attorneys may prepare any contract or fill in the blanks on any printed forms. A property owner may prepare other legal documents connected with the handling of personal affairs. If form contracts are used, the parties usually initial near any additions or deletions.

A broker or salesperson may assist in completeing a form contract only to the extent allowed by state law. Brokers and salespersons are forbidden by law to give legal advice. And usually brokers and salespersons are not allowed to prepare other legal documents, as deeds and mortgages.

TYPES OF SALES CONTRACTS

A real estate sales contract holds an agreement together while the details are worked out. Neither the buyer nor the seller has assurance that the other can perform at the time the contract is drawn up. Time is needed to verify ownership, conditions of title, and the accuracy of representations concerning the property and to arrange financing. Also, time is needed for working out the mechanics of closing. The buyer and seller want to avoid the effort and expense of preparing for a title closing without assurance that the other party is bound to the agreement.

A property transfer may be arranged without a formal contract, of course. Title by deed could be directly exchanged for cash or other consideration. Direct property transfers are most uncommon in practice, however, and are subject to many pitfalls, particularly from the buyer's viewpoint. The quantity and quality of an owner's interest in a property cannot be ascertained without title search, which takes a certain minimum time. For example, Able conveys ownership of a house to Baker by warranty deed; in fact, Able is merely a tenant in the house. Baker, then, is also merely a tenant because Baker cannot get any rights that are greater than those possessed by Able, which in this case appears to be nothing. Baker could sue Able for damages and recovery of the money, of course—if Able can be found.

Real estate buy-sell contracts take the forms of (1) earnest money receipt, offer, and acceptance (for short-term transaction); (2) binder; (3) installment land contract (for long-term transaction); and (4) option. Of these, the first, calling for a relatively immediate transfer of title, is the most common and most important.

Earnest Money Form Contract

An earnest money receipt, offer and acceptance form is a special-purpose form contract. The form used here is typical of such contracts in use.

A cash deposit, termed earnest money, is expected of buyers at the time an offer is made. *Earnest money* is a down payment of money, or other consideration, made as evidence of good faith in entering an agreement. The deposit binds the prospective buyer to the offer by serving as evidence of an intent to live up to the proposed contract; failure to do so means forfeiture of the deposit. Typically, from 5 to 10 percent of the offered price is put up.

Earnest money paid a broker, in almost all states, must be held in a special trust, or escrow, account and not commingled with personal funds of the broker. A separate account is not needed for each earnest money deposit received, however; one account for all funds is sufficient. But complete and accurate records that fully account for each deposit must be kept.

A copy of the earnest money receipt, offer, and acceptance form is left with the prospective buyer to end the first step of negotiations. Both the prospective buyer and the broker, or the broker's agent, must have signed the form. Legally, the form is only an earnest money receipt and an offer at this point. A seller agreeing to and signing the offer constitutes the acceptance and second step.

Binder

Some sales transaction are very involved and not suited to a standard form contract. Also, one of the parties may insist that the contract be drawn up by an attorney so that particular provisions may be included. In either case, the deal is nearly ready for agreement, but time is needed to draw up a formal contract. The transaction must be "held together" until the detailed contract can be written up and agreed to by both buyer and seller. The solution is a binder.

A *binder* is a brief written agreement to enter into a longer written contract for the sale of real estate. The essential terms of the transaction and a brief description of the property are included along with a statement about the intention of the parties. A binder is, therefore, a valid contract, meeting the requirements of the Statute of Frauds. It is prepared in duplicate, with the buyer and seller each getting a copy. An attorney may then be contacted to prepare the more involved contract. If a broker is involved, a small earnest money deposit may be made by the buyer, for which a receipt is given. Also, a statement concerning the amount of a commission and who pays is usually included. A binder is shown in the documents appendix (Appendix A).

Installment Land Contract

An installment land contract is a written agreement for the purchase of real estate that calls for payments to be made over an extended period of time (two or more years) with title remaining with the seller until the terms of the arrangement are satisfied. An installment land contract is also know as a *land contract*, real estate contract, a contract for deed, or an agreement of sale.

A land contract is used when the purchaser does not have sufficient cash to make an acceptable down payment to the seller, as for the purchase of vacant lots. It is also used where a seller wishes to delay payment of taxes on capital gains realized in the sale. If title is transferred on a thin down payment, the cost to the seller of regaining clear title may exceed the initial down payment by the buyer. Yet the buyer would be willing to pay the price in installments. A contract is therefore drawn up specifying the amount and time of periodic payments. A completed installment land contract is shown in the documents appendix.

Option

An *option* is an agreement whereby an owner agrees to sell property at a stipulated price to a certain buyer within a specified time. The tentative buyer pays a fee or price or gives some other consideration to obtain this right of purchase. An option is sometimes included as part of a lease, which combination is called a lease option.

An option is used when a buyer is uncertain about whether or not to buy but is willing to pay something to the owner for the right to buy. For example, the buyer may be trying to purchase two or three adjacent properties to assemble a larger property. Each owner gets paid for holding his or her property off the market for the agreed time. If the last owner refuses to sell for a reasonable price, of course, the buyer may not want to purchase any of the optioned parcels. The buyer, in this instance, loses the cost of the options. Another common use of the option is to purchase a portion of a large tract for development, with the right to buy additional acreage if the development program on the first parcel goes well.

The option itself may contain all the terms of sale. Sometimes a proposed buy-sell contract, which includes important details relative to exercising the option, is attached to the option. A completed option is shown in the documents appendix.

COMPONENTS OF A FORM CONTRACT

In addition to the five essentials for legal validity, the type of deed to be used, the arrangement of financing, and the closing date and place are of crucial interest to buyer and seller. The purpose here is to identify and explain these elements as they appear in a typical form contract. Buyers and sellers may agree, as a part of the negotiation, to other conditions and provisions, of course.

A contract brought about by a broker or sales agent is also likely to include a receipt for earnest money put up by the buyer in making the offer. A broker's form contract also includes a seller's agreement to pay a commission.

Figure 7–1 shows the completed earnest money receipt, offer, and acceptance form contract explained throughout this section. It is designed to go with the flow of a transaction as it develops, being divided into six parts, A–F, as follows:

A. Earnest money receipt
B. Agreement to purchase
C. Buyer's and seller's agreement regarding deposit of earnest money
D. Agreement to sell
E. Acknowledgment by buyer of seller's acceptance
F. Seller's closing instruction and agreement with broker regarding earnest money if forfeited

Earnest Money Receipt

Before paying earnest money, a buyer wants the terms of the offer spelled out. Hence, the amount of consideration offered, the property description, the type of deed to be used, and the conditions related to financing are all stipulated in part A of our form contract.

The first five lines include the purchaser's name, the amount of the deposit, and the description of the property. In this case, the purchasers are Gerald and Nancy Investor. The amount of the earnest money is $32,000. By signing at the bottom of part A, Harvey Hustle, a sales representative of the Everready Realty Co., acknowledges getting $32,000 from the Investors, as evidenced by the opening words, "Received from."

Financing. The source of monies to finance the purchase price follows the legal description. The price offered is $640,000. The earnest money deposit is $32,000. The minimum conditional loan is $500,000. This means that the Investors may have to come up with an additional $108,000 in equity funds to see the transaction through. The offer is conditional on getting the $500,000 loan at 12 percent interest or less, with a life of 25 years or more and with monthly debt service. If any one of these conditions is not met, the buyer may withdraw from the transaction without penalty. On the other hand, if the seller can arrange financing with these conditions for the buyer, the buyer must continue with the transaction.

Title evidence and deed. The first three paragraphs of the form pertain to title assurance and deed requirements. Paragraph 1 calls for title assurance by a title insurance policy to be provided by the buyer at the seller's expense. Paragraph 2 says that the seller must provide for marketable title within 30 days of written notice or the earnest money is to be refunded to the buyer. Also, if the seller does not accept the offer, the earnest money reverts to the buyer. If, however, the seller accepts, and the buyer

FIGURE 7–1
Earnest money receipt and Real Estate Contract

FORM No. 671
Stevens-Ness Law Publishing Co.
Portland, Oregon TT

EARNEST MONEY RECEIPT

City Urbandale State Anystate, November 28, 19 80

A. RECEIVED FROM Gerald and Nancy Investor, husband and wife
(hereinafter called "purchaser") the sum of Thirty-two thousand Dollars ($ 32,000.00)
in the form of check (CASH, CHECK, DRAFT, NOTE) as earnest money and in part payment for the purchase of the following described real estate situated in the City of Urbandale, County of Rustic, State of Anystate, to-wit: Douglas Manor, 2001 Century Drive (Lots 16 and 17, Block 3, Edgewood South, Rustic County, Anystate)

which we have this day sold to said purchaser for the sum of Six hundred forty thousand Dollars ($640,000.00)
on the following terms, to-wit: The sum, hereinabove receipted for, of Thirty-two thousand Dollars ($ 32,000.00)
{ on owner's acceptance. **(Strike whichever not applicable)**
{ on ...., 19 ...., as additional earnest money, the sum of Dollars ($ ....)
Upon acceptance of title and delivery of { deed ~~contract~~ **(Strike whichever not applicable)** One hundred eight thousand Dollars ($108,000.00)
Balance of .... Dollars ($ - - - -)
payable as follows: conditional on obtaining mortgage loan for Five hundred thousand dollars ($500,000) or more, at ten (10) percent interest or less, with a life of twenty five (25) years or more, with monthly debt service; and no more than two points required to obtain financing. Also, conditional on closing in escrow, with escrow costs shared equally between seller and buyer.

1) A title insurance policy from a reliable company insuring marketable title in seller is to be furnished purchaser in due course at seller's expense; preliminary to closing, seller may furnish a title insurance company's title report showing its willingness to issue title insurance, which shall be conclusive evidence as to seller's record title.
2) It is agreed that if seller does not approve this sale within the period allowed broker below in which to secure seller's acceptance, or if the title to the said premises is not insurable or marketable, or cannot be made so within thirty days after notice containing a written statement of defects is delivered to seller, the said earnest money shall be refunded. But if said sale is approved by seller and title to the said premises is insurable or marketable and purchaser neglects or refuses to comply with any of said conditions within ten days after the said evidence of title is furnished and to make payments promptly, as hereinabove set forth, then the earnest money herein receipted for (including said additional earnest money) shall be forfeited and disposed of as stated in Section F below and this contract thereupon shall be of no further binding effect.
3) The property is to be conveyed by good and sufficient deed free and clear of all liens and encumbrances except zoning ordinances, building and use restrictions, reservations in Federal patents, easements of record and, none other, Title is to be conveyed by a general warranty deed.
4) All irrigation, plumbing and heating fixtures and equipment (including stoker and oil tanks but excluding fireplace fixtures and equipment), water heaters, electric light fixtures, light bulbs and fluorescent lamps, bathroom fixtures, venetian blinds, drapery and curtain rods, window and door screens, storm doors and windows, attached linoleum, attached television antenna, all shrubs and trees and all fixtures except No exceptions; stoves and refrigerators, one in each unit, to be considered as fixtures
are to be left upon the premises as part of the property purchased. The following personal property is also included as a part of the property for said purchase price:
(Any personal property to be conveyed by separate bill of sale.)
5) Seller and purchaser agree to pro rate the taxes which are due and payable for the current tax year. Rents, interest, premiums for existing insurance and other matters shall be pro rated on a calendar year basis. Adjustments are to be made as of the date of the consummation of said sale or delivery of possession, whichever first occurs. Encumbrances to be discharged by seller may be paid at his option out of purchase money at date of closing.
6) Possession of said premises is to be delivered to purchaser on or before Dec. 31, 19 80, or as soon thereafter as existing laws and regulations will permit removal of tenants, if any. Time is the essence of this contract. This contract is binding upon the heirs, executors, administrators, successors and assigns of buyer and seller. However, the purchaser's rights herein are not assignable without written consent of seller. In any suit or action brought on this contract, the losing party therein agrees to pay the prevailing party therein (1) the prevailing party's reasonable attorney's fees in such suit or action, to be fixed by the trial court, and (2) on appeal, if any, similar fees in the appellate court, to be fixed by the appellate court.

Address 41 East Third, Urbandale, Anystate   Everready Realty Co   ☐ Cooperating Broker ☐ Listing Broker
Phone 345-4321   By /s/Harvey Hustle, Sales Representative

B. AGREEMENT TO PURCHASE

We hereby agree to purchase and pay the price of $ 640,000 to purchase the property herein described in its present condition, as set forth above and grant to said agent a period of two days hereafter to secure seller's acceptance hereof, during which period my offer shall not be subject to revocation. Said deed or contract to be in the name of Gerald I and Nancy O. Investor, husband and wife   3:00 pm, November 28, 19 80
Address 3278 Exotic Drive, Urbandale   Purchaser /s/ Gerald I. Investor
Phone 686-3343   /s/ Nancy O. Investor

C. BUYER'S AND SELLER'S AGREEMENT RE DEPOSIT OF EARNEST MONEY   November 29, 19 80

The Earnest Money deposit in this transaction of $ 32,000.00 in the form stated above shall be deposited in the Client's Trust Account of the broker indicated above until this offer is accepted, whereupon the parties agree and direct that such funds be deposited (or retained) in the Client's Trust Account of Everready Realty Co., the listing broker to be held pending closing of this transaction.
/s/ Gerald I. Investor Buyer   /s/ Wendy Welloff Seller
/s/ Nancy O. Investor Buyer   Seller

D. AGREEMENT TO SELL   8:30 pm, November 29, 1980

I hereby approve and accept the above sale for said price and on said terms and conditions and agree to consummate the same as stated.
Seller's Address Condominium Towers, Unit 77   Seller /s/ Wendy Welloff (widow)
Urbandale, Anystate Phone 345-2020

E. Deliver promptly to buyer, either manually or by registered mail, a copy hereof showing seller's acceptance.
Buyer acknowledges receipt of the foregoing instrument bearing his signature and that of the seller showing acceptance 9:45 am Buyer /s/ Nancy O. Investor
Date November 30, 1980 /s/ Gerald I. Investor
Copy hereof showing seller's signed acceptance sent buyer by registered mail to buyer's above address (return receipt requested) on ...., 19....
Return receipt card received and attached to broker's copy ...., 19....

F. SELLER'S CLOSING INSTRUCTIONS AND AGREEMENT WITH BROKER RE FORFEITED EARNEST MONEY   November 29, 19 80

I, the seller whose signature appears below, agree to pay forthwith to said broker a commission amounting to $ 27,600.00 for services rendered in this transaction. In the event that the buyer's deposit is forfeited pursuant to sub-paragraph 2, above, said forfeited deposit shall be disposed of between broker and seller in the following manner:
One third (1/3) to broker ($10,667) and Two-thirds (2/3) to seller ($21,333)

Seller acknowledges receipt of a copy of this contract bearing signatures of seller and buyer named above.
Ivan Everready, Everready Realty Co. Broker   /s/ Wendy Welloff Seller
By /s/ Harvey Hustle, salesperson   Seller

NOTE: IF ANY BLANK SPACES ARE INSUFFICIENT, USE S-N No. 810 "HANDY PAD", TO BE SEPARATELY SIGNED BY BUYER AND SELLER.

7710   BROKER'S COPY - FILE IN DEAL ENVELOPE

defaults, paragraph 2 says that the earnest money is to be forfeited by the buyer. Paragraph 3 specifies type of deed and types of acceptable loans. Paragraph 4 defines items borderline to being fixtures.

Prorations, possession, and assignment. Prorations of taxes, rents, interest, and so forth are provided for in paragraph 5. Also, the condition in the offer (written in above) says that the transaction must be closed in escrow, with the costs shared equally between buyer and seller.

Paragraph 6 calls for possession by the buyer on or before December 31, 1980. Prompt performance in accordance with the contract is required of the seller because the paragraph also states, "Time is of the essence." Finally, assignment of buyer's rights is allowed only with written consent of the seller. *Assignment* means a transfer of one's rights in a contract to another.

Agreement to Purchase

Part B of the form contract contains an agreement to purchase the property "in its present condition" or "as is" for the price and under the conditions stated above. By signing the contract, the Investors make an offer to buy under the terms outlined in part A, which may contain stipulations and contingency clauses to protect the prospective buyer. The binding words are "We hereby agree to purchase and pay the price of $640,000." The offer is made at 3:00 P.M. on November 28, 1980. The two-day limitation means that an acceptance by the owner before 3:00 P.M. on November 30 would immediately create a binding contract. Of course, the offer may be withdrawn anytime before it is accepted. An acceptance after the expiration time would really be an offer by the owner to sell under the specified terms and conditions.

Interim Disposition of Earnest Money

The earnest money check must be cashed to protect the seller's and the broker's interests. If the check does not clear, the deal obviously does not hold together. But, once cashed, what happens to the money? In part C of the contract, both the buyer and seller agree that the $32,000 earnest money is to be held in the broker's client trust account until the contract is fulfilled or otherwise terminated. If a buyer and seller enter into a contract without a broker, the contract is likely to require that the money be held by an escrow officer.

Agreement to Sell

Part D of the form contract provides for acceptance of the offer to purchase at the price, terms, and conditions stipulated by the buyer. The seller may refuse to accept if the price and terms are not satisfactory. Or the seller may make a counteroffer. If no major change from the initial offer is involved in the counteroffer, it may be written on the same form. A major change from the price, terms, and conditions offered by the buyer is likely to necessitate the initiation of a completely new contract. In this example, Wendy Welloff, the owner, accepts the offer of the Investors at 8:30 P.M. on the day after the offer was initially made.

The contract is now complete and binding. The parties are competent; there is a bona fide offer and acceptance, with consideration by both; the object is legal, and both parties have signed. A copy is given to the seller as a record of the price and terms of the agreement. The buyer is entitled to a copy of the contract promptly after the seller signs it. Good brokerage practice requires that the buyer sign, acknowledging receipt of a copy of the contract, as shown in part E.

Forfeited Earnest Money

Part F shows the amount of the commission ($27,600) due the broker, Everready Realty, for negotiating the sale. However, if a forfeiture of earnest money occurs ($32,000), the split is to be one-third ($10,667) to the broker and two-thirds ($21,333) to the owner-seller. Forfeiture is prima facie evidence that the buyer is not ready, willing, and able to complete the transaction. The split gives the broker some relief for effort and expenses incurred in arranging the transaction. In turn, the owner-seller is entitled to compensation as the principal party in the transaction and also for holding the property off the market. By signing part F, the parties agree to the commission and also to the split. Needless to say, this signing takes place at the same time the agreement to sell, part D, is signed.

The contract is complete on its face as to the commission to be paid by the seller to the broker. This completeness eliminates the need to refer back to the listing agreement in closing the sale.

The Uniform Commercial Code

Investors acquiring properties must make decisions about the possible applicability of the Uniform Commercial Code to the transaction. The *Uniform Commercial Code* (UCC) is a set of laws governing the sale, financing, and security of personal property in secured transactions. A *secured transaction* is one in which a borrower or buyer pledges personal property to a lender or seller as collateral for a loan, with title remaining in a seller or lender until the loan is repaid. Thus, fixtures, growing crops, and standing timber have the possibility of being regarded as security for both personal and real property loans. A secured transaction is often evidenced by a financing statement that is filed in the public record as evidence of the lender's interest or claim. The financing statement, if properly recorded, would take precedence over the purchase contract and any deed conveying title.

REMEDIES FOR NONPERFORMANCE

Failure of a buyer or a seller to perform on a contract is variously called breach of contract, nonperformance, or default.

Buyer Remedies

A buyer has three alternative courses of action against a seller who is able but unwilling to fulfill a contract. First, the buyer may terminate the contract and recover the earnest money deposit plus any reasonable expense incurred in examination of the title. Second, the buyer may sue for specific performance, which means to bring legal action to force the seller to live up to the contract. Third, the buyer may sue the seller for damages; but this is not done very often. Damages would be the loss of the bargain or the difference between the market value of the property and the contract price. If the market value is less than the contract price, no damages have been suffered, of course. If a seller has acted in good faith, but is unable to perform, as by inability to convey clear title, the buyer's recovery in a suit for damages is likely to be minimal. Some contracts contain a liquidated damages clause to be invoked on nonperformance. *Liquidated damages* is the amount to be paid (usually a dollar amount) for nonperformance as agreed by the parties in making up the contract.

Seller Remedies

A seller has five alternative courses of action against a buyer who is able but unwilling to fulfill a contract. First, the seller may rescind or cancel the contract and return the earnest money deposit and all other payments received from the buyer. This, of course, is not very probable but would be highly acceptable to the buyer. Second, the seller may cancel the contract and keep the earnest money deposit and all payments received from the buyer. Third, the seller may tender a valid deed to the buyer, which, if refused, would provide the basis for a suit for the purchase price. The deed must be offered to the buyer first to force the buyer to live up to the contract or to default. Fourth and fifth, the seller may sue the buyer for specific performance or for damages. Again, liquidated damages may be stipulated in the contract.

ESCROW ARRANGEMENTS

Escrow is the depositing of money, legal documents (deeds, mortgages, options, and the like), other valuables, and instructions with a third party to be held until acts or conditions of a contractual agreement are performed or satisfied. Any real estate contract may be placed in escrow. The parties to the contract make up the escrow agreement (separate from the contract that contains instructions for the escrow agent). The escrow agreement also states the duties and obligations of the parties to the contract and the overall requirements for completing the transaction. The escrow agent must perform his or her duties in a "neutral" or "impartial" manner. That is, the escrow agent must not be a party to the contract and must not be in a position to benefit in any way from the main contract, except for the escrow fee. Escrows are commonly used in the closing or settlement of a sale, an exchange, an installment sale, or a lease.

In a sale, the escrow agreement states all the terms to be performed by the seller and the buyer. The escrow holder is usually an attorney, a bank, or a title institution. Sometimes, at the signing of the escrow agreement, the buyer's cash and the seller's deed and the various other papers that are to be delivered by each are all turned over to the escrow holder, who, when the title search has been completed, makes the adjustments, holds the title instruments, and remits the amount due to the seller. Other escrow agreements provide for initial payment of the deposit only and for the seller and buyer to deliver later the papers and monies needed to consummate the transaction. A completed "escrow instructions" form is shown as Figure 7–2.

Requirements of the buyer and seller in closing of a sale in escrow are the following:

The buyer provides

1. The balance of the cash needed to close the transaction
2. Mortgage papers if a new mortgage is taken out
3. Other papers or documents as needed to complete the transaction

The seller usually provides

1. Evidence of clear title (abstract, title insurance policy, or Torrens certificate)
2. Deed conveying title to the buyer
3. Hazard insurance policies, as appropriate
4. Statement from the holder of the existing mortgage specifying the amount of money needed to clear or satisfy the mortgage
5. Any other documents or instruments needed to clear title and to complete the transaction.

Instructions to the escrow agent contain authority to record the deed and the mortgage or deed of trust. When all conditions of the escrow agreement have been satisfied and clear title shows in the buyer's name, the escrow agent may disburse monies as provided in the instructions. The escrow agent has obligations to both the buyer and seller for performance according to the instructions.

Advantages of an escrow closing include the following:

1. Neither buyer nor seller need be present at the closing of title.

FIGURE 7–2
Escrow instructions

FORM No. 936
687 Stevens-Ness Law Publishing Co., Portland, Ore.

ESCROW INSTRUCTIONS

To: Hifidelity Escrow Services   Date December 1st, 1980

221 N. Main

Urbandale, Anystate 00000

Re: Wendy Welloff (Seller)   Gerald & Nancy Investor (Buyer)

Gentlemen:

The following checked items are enclosed for your use in closing the above transaction:

1. (x) Earnest money receipt
2. ( ) Exchange agreement
3. (x) Deed showing subject property description
4. (x) Previous title insurance covering subject property
5. (x) Fire insurance policy covering subject property
6. ( ) List of personal property included in sale
7. ( ) Rental list
8. ( ) Earnest money note executed by buyer
9. (x) Our check in the amount of $ 32,000 earnest money paid
10. ( )
11. ( )
12. ( )
13. ( )
14. ( )

You are directed to:

a. (x) Pay Multiple Listing Bureau 5 % of the commission
b. ( ) Pay ......% of the commission to
c. ( ) Pay ......% of the commission to
d. (x) Pay all commission (less MLB, if any), to I.M. Everready, Realtor
e. ( ) Have ...... prepare contract of sale
f. (x) Order title insurance from Hifidelity Title Co.
g. (x) Pro-rate taxes, fire insurance, if any, and make necessary adjustments as of closing date
   Start interest on contract/trust deed or mortgage as of
h. (x) split escrow fee evenly between buyer and seller.
i. (x) payoff existing 1st mortgage w/ 1st National Bank of Rustic Co. and record release.
j. (x) collect additional money from buyer as necessary to complete settlement.
k. (x) take account of and adjust other fees and charges as appropriate.

Please call undersigned and/or Harvey Hustle should you need further information.

Very truly yours,

/s/ Ivan Everready

Everready Realty Co.
41 East Third
Urbandale, Anystate 00000

Telephone 345-4321

Receipt of above mentioned items and instructions acknowledged.

By: /s/ Tom Barry

Form designed by
RUTH E. BEUTELL
MARION-POLK COUNTY ESCROW CO.
Salem, Oregon

2. The seller receives no money until the title is searched, found marketable, and is in the name of the buyer.
3. The seller has assurance that, if the title is found marketable, the contract will be carried out and monies will be forthcoming.

SUMMARY

A contract is a legally enforceable agreement to do (or not do) some legal act for consideration. The Statute of Frauds applies to real estate contracts. The five essentials of a valid real estate sales contract are (1) competent parties, (2) offer and acceptance, (3) legal object, including property description, (4) mutual consideration, and (5) a writing and signing. Additional items of import include (1) kind of title evidence and deed to be provided, (2) closing date and place, and (3) statement as to how the transaction is to be financed by the buyer. Real estate sales contracts are of four general types: (1) earnest money receipt, offer, and acceptance (form contract for an immediate closing); (2) binder (for an involved transaction); (3) installment land contract (for an extended transaction); and (4) option (for a flexible transaction).

Given nonperformance by a seller, a buyer may recover earnest money, sue for specific performance, or sue for damages. On the other hand, given buyer nonperformance, a seller may cancel the contract and keep the earnest money, sue for specific performance, sue for the purchase price, or sue for damages.

Listing agreements, creating a principal-agent relationship between an owner and a broker, are often used in selling property. The broker earns a commission upon selling the property. Five listing agreements are in use: (1) open, (2) exclusive agency, (3) exclusive right to sell, (4) multiple, and (5) net. Increasingly, real estate sales contracts are being closed in escrow. Title does not pass and funds are not disbursed in an escrow closing until all conditions are met.

QUESTIONS FOR REVIEW AND DISCUSSION

1. List and briefly explain the five essentials of a real estate sales contract. Are additional items important in making up the contract? If so, what are they?

2. List and explain briefly the four types of real estate sales contracts, including the functions of each. How does a binder differ from a form contract?

3. In what ways is the Uniform Commercial Code of importance in real estate sales contracts?

4. List and explain at least three alternative remedies for the buyer and the seller upon nonperformance by the other.

5. Explain the nature and advantages of closing in escrow.

6. Is there a legal requirement to have a written contract in the sale of realty? That is, is it possible to sell a property without a written contract?

7. May an owner and a buyer make up a valid real estate sales contract without a broker or an attorney?

8. Must fixtures be specifically mentioned in a sales contract? Is there any reason to do so?

9. Give at least four examples of persons not legally competent to make valid and binding contracts.

CASE PROBLEMS

1. Martin enters into a written agreement to sell a tract of land to Beverly. The boundaries are stated in the agreement. After the closing, with full payment to Martin, Martin discovers that the tract conveyed contained 10 acres rather than 5. Martin sues, contending that he had no intention of selling 10 acres to Beverly, that there was no meeting of the minds, and therefore that no contract existed. Can Martin get his land back? Why or why not?
2. Rita paid Steven $6,000 for a 90-day written option to buy Steven's farm. Thirty days later, a major highway improvement project is announced that will make the farm a prime location for a shopping center. As a consequence, the value increases tenfold. Steven refuses to convey title, claiming the consideration was insufficient. Rita sues. What result?
3. Joan agrees to sell her house to George for $110,000; a written contract is made up. Subsequently, Joan decides she wants to keep her house and offers to return George's earnest money. George asks you what remedies are open to him. Explain his alternatives.
4. If Joan were agreeable to performing, and George were not, what remedies are open to Joan in (3)?

CHAPTER EIGHT

TITLE ASSURANCE AND TITLE TRANSFER

Property is necessary
but it is not necessary that it should remain forever
in the same hands.
REMY DE GOURMONT, French critic and novelist

IMPORTANT TOPICS OR DECISION AREAS COVERED IN THIS CHAPTER

- Methods of Transferring Title
- Title Evidence
- Deeds
- Essentials of a Valid Deed

A person about to get ownership of real estate wants the best possible title, preferably marketable title. This is particularly true if substantial value, money, was parted with to acquire title; otherwise, the property may be very difficult to dispose of at a later time. This desire for high-quality title is true even if ownership were realized through inheritance or gift. Also, when dealing with an owner, lenders and lessees prefer that an owner has marketable title to assure their position.

Marketable title means an ownership interest that is readily salable to a reasonable, intelligent, prudent, and interested buyer at market value. Ultimately, it means title of adequate quality for courts to require its acceptance by a purchaser. The desire, of course, is for minimum risk of loss by an investor because of superior claims during ownership. And, as mentioned, the investor wants to avoid the possibility of loss upon disposition because the title has flaws or defects of some sort.

In addition, a prudent buyer wants the deed through which title is received to include the best possible assurance of good title from the *grantor*, the person conveying title. Finally, our buyer wants the public records to be as current and clear as possible so that mistakes in title search and analysis are avoided.

The purpose of this chapter is to explain the ways and means by which marketable title is assured and transferred, as by focusing on the following critical concerns.

1. The tentative grantor must actually have an ownership interest in the property that can be conveyed. This means that the chain or history of ownership must run to the grantor.
2. The legal description must be accurate and complete.
3. Encumbrances against the property must not preclude its use for the desired purposes and must not preclude reconveyance of clear title at a later time.
4. Documentary evidence from experienced, competent, professional people must be provided so that the preceding conditions are satisfied. Adequate public records are a substantial part of the means by which documentary evidence is provided.
5. The deed by which title is received gives the greatest possible assurances and protection to the recipient.

KEY CONCEPTS INTRODUCED IN THIS CHAPTER

Abstract of title
Acceptance
Acknowledgment
Administrator
Adverse possession, title by
Avulsion
Bargain and sale deed
Certification of title
Chain of title
Confiscation
Constructive notice
Decedent
Deed
Deed of release
Delivery
Dereliction
Devise

Donor/donee
Erosion
Executor
General warranty deed
Grantor/grantee
Intestate
Legacy
Marketable title
Mortgagor-mortgagee index
Patent
Quitclaim deed
Reliction
Special warranty deed
Testate
Title evidence
Title insurance
Torrens system
Warranty deed
Will

METHODS OF TRANSFERRING TITLE

Transfer of title to real estate takes place in one of three general ways. Transfer, as used here, means the manner in which a change of ownership is directed, controlled, or brought about. For example, a will is a transfer arrangement to become effective at an owner's death, while a gift by deed may be effective immediately. Acquisition by an investor, of course, is usually through purchase and a sales contract. Other means of transferring title are covered here to make the reader fully aware of the alternatives open to an owner in acquiring and disposing of real estate. The actual conveyance of ownership from one person to another is by a deed. The three general ways title is transferred are by (1) public grant, (2) private grant, as a voluntary act of an owner, and (3) action of law.

Public Grant

The original public domain was transferred to states, corporations (primarily railroads), and individuals by public grants to open up the land. Transfers to individuals were made under homestead laws to stimulate development and settlement of the West. Under homestead laws, several years of occupancy and the making of improvements were required to acquire title. The federal government used patents in making the original public grants of ownership. A *patent,* as used here, means a conveyance or grant of real estate from the U.S. government to a private citizen.

Subsequent transfers of ownership by grantees were expected to, and currently must, conform to the laws of the state in which the land is located. For all practical purposes, patents to the federal domain are no longer being issued.

Private Grant

An owner may voluntarily dispose of or transfer property by (1) sale or exchange for consideration, (2) gift, and (3) will. Technically, in some states, mortgaging also involves a voluntary title transfer. However, the owner retains possession and use of the property and the transfer is effectively only a lien on the title.

Transfer for consideration. An owner may sell or otherwise transfer an interest to another for consideration. A deed is used to convey the interest permanently. Any ownership right or interest in real estate may be transferred for consideration.

Transfer by gift. An owner may transfer title to an interest in real estate by a gift. The owner making the gift is termed a *donor*; the recipient is the *donee.* The transfer is not void because of lack of consideration. The donee, however, cannot enforce any covenants against the donor because of the lack of consideration.

Transfer by Will. A *will*, legally termed a last will and testament, is a written instrument directing the voluntary conveyance of property of property upon the death of its owner, and not before. An owner may write a will, or have one drawn up, at any time before death. And after making a will, an owner is free to sell or give the property away or to draw up a new will. The owner who makes a will is a *testator.* If an owner who has a will dies, he or she is termed a "decedent" and is said to have died *testate.*

The law requires certain formalities for the execution or carrying out of the will. The testator must be of legal age and mentally competent. The will must be written and signed, usually at the end. The will cannot cut off rights of a surviving spouse. In many states, two witnesses who have no interest in the will must acknowledge the signing. Upon the testator's death, the will must be submitted to probate court for judicial determination that it is the last will and testament of the decedent. Probate means to prove or establish the validity of the will left, or presumably left, by a decedent. A probate court is a court for probating wills and, when necessary, administering estates. If no valid objection is raised, the will is accepted for probate and entered into the public record.

The person empowered to carry out the terms and provisions of the will is an *executor*, also called a "personal representative" in some states. If a will does not name an executor, the probate court will appoint one. The executor settles the affairs of the decedent, which may involve selling off real property to raise cash for paying debts of the decedent or conveying property to designated persons, organizations, or causes. The giving of real property under a will is a *devise* and the recipient is a *devisee.* The giving of personal property under a will is a bequest or *legacy* and the recipient is a *legatee.* An executor's deed is used to convey title to real property in probating a will and settling an estate.

Actions of Law

Transfer by descent. Transfer of ownership by *descent* comes about when an owner dies without a will, or *intestate.* Owned property passes to certain relatives, termed heirs or distributees, of the decedent according to specific state statutes of descent and distribution. The rights of the surviving spouse are always protected by dower, community property, or "intestate share" laws, as they apply. A surviving spouse usually gets the entire estate in the absence of other surviving blood relatives of the decedent. Children, or lineal descendents of the deceased, share along with the spouse. If no children exist, parents of the decedent are next in line to inherit. Brothers and sisters, termed collateral heirs, are next in line to inherit. If no heirs exist, the property goes to the state, by escheat.

The affairs of a decedent who dies intestate are settled by an *administrator* (in some states, personal representative) who is appointed by a probate court. Generally, close relatives to the decedent are selected as administrators. The job of the administrator is essentially the same as that of an executor. Any real property sold is conveyed with an administrator's deed, which is exactly comparable to an executor's deed.

Transfer by lien enforcement. Failure of an owner to meet the obligations of a lien gives the creditor the right to enforce the lien. Thus, properties are sold as a result of mortgage default, unpaid taxes, or not meeting other lien obligations.

Transfer by adverse possession. Title may be seized or taken from an owner of record who fails to maintain possession and control of the premises; the process is known as *adverse possession.* Conditions for gaining title by adverse occupancy vary from state to state but are generally as follows:

1. Open
2. Notorious
3. Hostile to the interest of the true owner
4. Exclusive of the true owner
5. Uninterrupted
6. Underwritten claim of title
7. For a prescriptive period as required by law

The prescriptive period varies, but it generally runs from 10 to 20 years. It is long enough that a reasonably attentive owner has ample opportunity to defeat the developing claim. When the possessor pays taxes under "color of title," the prescriptive method may be as short as 5 years. Prescriptive, as used here, means according to legal precedent or established custom. To satisfy due process, at some point quiet title action is necessary to perfect the claim.

An occupant may acquire title by proving that all these circumstances exist. However, considerable proof of title is required of the claimant in selling the title; as mentioned, a buyer wants marketable title or a reduced price to compensate for the additional risk involved. The purpose of allowing title to be acquired by adverse possession is to keep realty productive for society.

Squatters occupy property without written color of title and without any legal right of possession. Squatters may develop a "prescriptive claim" but unless "cured," such title is not marketable in the legal sense of the word.

Transfer by condemnation. An exercise of right of eminent domain by a governmental or quasi-governmental agency may cause title to be transferred to the agency against the owner's will. Just compensation must be paid the owner. The use or purpose of taking title must be public.

Transfer by confiscation. The taking of property by a government in time of war, without compensation, is *confiscation.* Traditionally, only property of enemies of the government is confiscated.

Transfer by erosion. *Erosion* means the wearing away of land through natural processes, as by wind and water. An owner gains title by erosion or accretion when additional soil is brought to his or her property by natural causes. Title is gained by *reliction,* also called *dereliction,* when waters gradually recede, leaving dry land; this, however, is not necessarily transfer of title. Also, *avulsion,* the sudden breaking away of land from one owner and attachment to the land of another owner, as when a stream changes course, does not transfer ownership.

TITLE EVIDENCE

Documentary proof, termed *title evidence,* must be developed for prospective owners at some point before title is conveyed and accepted. Title evidence takes three basic forms: (1) an attorney's opinion or certification, (2) a title insurance policy, and (3) a Torrens certificate. The first two are based on a proper legal description, a proper chain of title, and a search of the public records. A *chain of title* is the succession of all previous holders of title (owners) back to some accepted starting point. A deed by itself is not evidence of title; it contains no proof concerning the kind or the conditions of the grantor's title.

Some judgment or interpretation may be required even after evidence of title is provided by one of the three forms. For example, certain easements or deed restrictions may or may not be acceptable to a buyer. Or, if an encroachment is suspected, a survey may be required; that is, an encroachment would not necessarily be brought to light by any of the three forms.

Opinion or Certificate of Title

A certification of title or an opinion that title is good is rendered by an attorney or other qualified person after examination of public records, an abstract of title, or other sources of information. Historically, the search and opinion were made by an attorney, who made up an informal abstract of title for personal use. But in recent decades, other persons, working for or through abstract companies, have qualified as abstractors and title analysts. If flaws or encumbrances stand in the way of clear title, they are listed as exceptions. An attorney's opinion of title is primarily used in rural areas of the United States. The trend is away from using abstracts and attorneys' opinions as evidence of title.

An *abstract of title* is a condensed history of the ownership of property, based primarily on instruments of record affecting the property. It has largely replaced the attorney's search of public records; that is, an attorney's opinion is increasingly based on the abstract only. Abstracting companies, which often maintain their own records, generally produce abstracts of title. An abstract contains a listing of documents bearing on title transactions, including summaries of important segments of the documents; thus such items as mortgages, wills, liens, deeds, foreclosure proceedings, tax sales, and other matters of record are noted. The information is arranged in chronological order, without any judgments made concerning the rights of the parties involved. A properly prepared abstract indicates the records examined, the period covered, and a certification that all matters of record are indexed against the owners in the chain of title are included. An abstract does not guarantee title. An attorney's interpretation of the abstract is required for title to be certified as good or to point out significant flaws and/or encumbrances.

In practice, title and abstract companies, attorneys, and other title analysts assume that a title is good or marketable at some early date. An irritating and expensive duplication of work in successive title examinations is involved nevertheless. And some meticulous attorneys want an examination carried back to an unreasonable date, as shown by the following tale.

In a legal transaction involving transfer of property in New Orleans, a firm of New York lawyers retained a New Orleans attorney to search the title and to perform other related duties. The New Orleans attorney sent his findings, which traced title back to 1803. The New York lawyers examined his opinion and wrote again to the New Orleans lawyer, saying in effect that the opinion rendered by him was all very well, as far as it went, but that title prior to 1803 had not been satisfactorily documented.

The New Orleans attorney replied to the New York firms as follows:

> I acknowledge your letter inquiring as to the state of the title of the Canal Street property prior to 1803. Please be advised that in 1803 the United States of America acquired the territory of Louisiana from the Republic of France by purchase. The Republic of France acquired title from the Spanish Crown by conquest. The Spanish Crown had originally acquired title by virtue of the discoveries of one Christopher Columbus, sailor, who had been duly authorized to embark upon the voyage of discovery by Isabella, queen of Spain. Isabella, before granting such authority, had obtained the sanction of His Holiness, the Pope; the Pope is the Vicar on Earth of Jesus Christ; Jesus Christ is the Son and Heir Apparent of God. God made Louisiana.

Remote lenders, and new owners, increasingly prefer title insurance to a certification of title as evidence of marketable title for several reasons. To begin, an attorney depends on an abstract, which may not disclose all possible defects of title. Also, the attorney's ability is uncertain. If a claim against the property is missed and subsequently proven with an attorney's certification, the purchaser or lender suffers. For example, a forged deed does not wipe out a dower interest. Recovering damages from an attorney for an error or omission is extremely difficult and costly. And recovering losses from a previous owner is often impossible because of death or change in location. With title insurance, defects such as these are automatically insured against if not listed as exceptions in the title policy.

Title Insurance Policy

Title insurance is protection against financial loss due to flaws, encumbrances, and other defects in the title of realty that existed but were not known at the time of purchase of the insurance policy. Therefore, title insurance is protection against events in the past rather than the future. The purchase of a policy simply shifts the risk of loss from a property owner or lender to the title insurance company. The premium or purchase price is only paid once, and the term is forever into the future. Title insurance, introduced in the late 1800s, currently provides ownership protection on more than half of all realty in the United States.

The insurance contract. Title insurance policies are usually made between the company and an owner (usually a new or purchasing owner), a lender, or a lessee. In return for the premium, the company contracts to reimburse or compensate against all losses due to title defects other than those listed as exceptions in the policy. However, typical of all insurance contracts, to collect, first a loss must be shown. An insurance company also agrees to finance the legal defense to protect an owner against a title lawsuit.

The main items insured against are as follows:

1. Flaws in the chain of title due to forged documents, improper delivery of a deed, incompetence or lack of capacity of a grantor, or lack of signature of a spouse
2. Errors and omissions in the title search and examination due to negligence or fraud by a company employee or due to improper indexing of public records
3. Possible lack of acceptability of title to a subsequent intelligent, prudent buyer, who may be unwilling to accept some minor encumbrance not listed as an exception in the title insurance policy; for example, a shared driveway easement

Items that may not be covered, unless extended coverage is obtained at some additional cost, are as follows:

1. Defects disclosed by title examination and listed as exceptions to the policy.
2. Defects that a survey or physical inspection of the property would disclose. Examples are encroachments, rights of an adverse possessor, unrecorded easements or leases, uncertain or incorrect boundary lines, and lack of access.
3. Defects known to the insured though not listed as an exception. Examples are a recorded mortgage known to the insured but missed by the title analyst and a violation of a covenant or condition.
4. Police power restrictions, which legally are not considered to make title unmarketable in any event.
5. Mechanic's liens not on record at time of policy issue.
6. Rights of parties in possession at time of title transfer.

The coverage provided a mortgagee or lessee in a mortgagee's or lessee's policy is basically the same as the coverage provided an owner.

Obtaining insurance. In a sales transaction, the seller or the broker usually arranges for the insurance that is to serve as evidence of clear title, from a title company. The title company frequently issues a preliminary title or informational report. The report lists the owner of record, unreleased liens, easements, restrictions of record, and other apparent encumbrances. The report indicates clouds that are likely to require removal. It is the seller's obligation to remove any serious encumbrances or "clouds" on title that block marketable title. After completing a reexamination of title, the title company issues a commitment to issue a title policy.

The commitment (1) names all parties involved, (2) gives the legal description of the property, (3) defines the interest or estate covered, (4) list exceptions, and (5) list terms and stipulations, including exceptions, of the policy. The policy is actually issued shortly after closing in a sale or refinancing transaction when all pertinent documents to the transaction have been recorded.

Use of title insurance. Title insurance is ever more widely used for several reasons. Costs of defending title are absorbed by the title company. Claims of loss are usually settled promptly. Remote lenders prefer title insurance because of the reputation and corporate integrity of title insurance companies, which, to the lenders, means quick, easy settlements. The main limitation to title insurance, from an owner's point of view, is that the amount of coverage is fixed. Reimbursement is only to the face amount of the policy even though improvements were added or land values increased sharply after the policy was issued.

Torrens Certificate

The *Torrens system* is a method of title registration in which clear title is established with a governmental agency, which later issue title certificates to owners as evidence of their claim. The Torrens system of title registration operates in a fashion very similar to that used by states for automobiles. Title is initially cleared and registered into the system on a voluntary basis, at which point a certificate of ownership is issued that serves as proof of title. Sales, mortgages, and other claims against the property must be registered to be effective; thus, the status of title may be determined at any time by checking with the registrar.

In theory, the Torrens system is considered ideal, but the high initial cost of registering a property in the system has worked against its wide acceptance. Also, some uncertainty about its operation exists because laws establishing Torren's registration vary from state to state.

DEEDS

A *deed* is a legal instrument that, when properly executed and delivered, conveys title to, or ownership of an interest in, realty from a grantor to a grantee. By definition and in accordance with the Statute of Frauds, a deed must be written. Proper execution means being signed by the grantor (or grantors), attested to by a witness or by witnesses, in nearly every state, acknowledged by a notary public or other qualified officer, and, in some states, sealed. A seal is a particular sign or mark to indicate the formal execution and nature of the instrument.

The circumstances surrounding the conveyance of real property vary greatly from one transaction to another. Generally, a grantor prefers to minimize the quality of title conveyed, consistent with the transaction, to avoid future obligation or liability to the grantee. Consequently, deeds take many forms to reflect the kind and quality of conveyance intended.

Deeds are sometimes classed as statutory or nonstatutory. Statutory deeds are short forms of the deeds in which any covenants or warranties mentioned are implied by law, as though written out in full. Nonstatutory deeds are usually written for special purposes or situations; thus only covenants, warranties, and terms included in the deed apply. The main statutory deeds are the general warranty, the bargain and sale, and the quitclaim.

General Warranty Deed

A general warranty deed provides a grantee the most complete set of assurances of title possible from a grantor. The grantor covenants (or warrants) good title, free of encumbrances, except as noted, which the grantor should be able to enjoy quietly; and if necessary, the grantor will protect the grantee against other claimants. A grantee cannot expect to receive a general warranty deed unles it is provided for in the sales agreement with the grantor. A general warranty deed is also known as a warranty deed.

The grantor legally incurs a continuing future obligation by the covenants when certain words, stipulated by state law, appear in a statutory deed. The statutes of each state must be examined to determine the exact stipulated words. Typical stipulated words indicating a warranty of deed are "warrant generally" or "convey and warrant."

Five covenants of promises are actually made in a general warranty deed; these may be set forth in the deed itself. Even if the covenants are not stated in the deed, they are binding on the grantor because of the deed's statutory basis. In some states, if covenants are added to a statutory deed, the statutory nature of the deed may be destroyed and only the written-in covenants or warranties apply.

1. *Covenant of seizing.* The grantor claims and warrants that he or she holds, or is seized with, ownership of the property conveyed and the right to sell it. If this covenant is breached or broken, the grantee may recover from the grantor any losses or expense up to the consideration paid for the property.
2. *Covenant against encumbrances.* The grantor claims and warrants that the property title is free of encumbrances except as stated specifically in the deed. If an encumbrance does exist against the property, the grantee may recover any expenses incurred to remove it from the grantor. Recovery is limited to the consideration given. Mortgage liens, easements, and deed restrictions are most likely to be noted as encumbrances.
3. *Covenant of quiet enjoyment.* The grantor claims and warrants that the grantee will be able to enjoy quietly or not be disturbed in the use of the premises because the title conveyed is good and superior to that of any third person. If the grantee, or any subsequent grantee, is dispossessed by a superior title predating the conveyance, the grantor is legally liable for any damages or losses incurred. Threats and claims of superior title by outsiders do not constitute a breach of this covenant.
4. *Covenant of further assurance.* The grantor warrants that any other instrument needed to make the title good will be obtained and delivered to the grantee. Under this covenant, if a faulty legal description were given in the deed, the grantor would be obligated to prepare a new deed, containing the correct legal description, for the grantee. Enforcement of this covenant is under a suit for specific performance rather than for damages.
5. *Covenant of warranty of title.* The grantor warrants forever the title to the premises, with monetary compensation to the grantee for any fault in the title, in whole or in part. This covenant is an absolute guarantee to the grantee of title and possession of the premises.

The first two covenants relate to the past and apply only at the time of sale or conveyance. The last three relate to the future and run with the land.

A warranty deed (see Figure 8–1) with covenants does not guarantee clear title. A grantor may be a complete fraud and plan to leave town immediately after collecting money from the sale. Or valid claims against the title may be outstanding even though not pressed by legal action. Therefore, evidence of clear title, independent of a warranty deed, is desirable even with the use of a general warranty deed.

Special Warranty Deed

A *special warranty deed* contains a single covenant that title has not been impaired, except as noted, by any acts of the grantor, which is a covenant against grantor's acts. This means that the grantor has liability only if the

FIGURE 8–1
A general warranty deed (statutory form)

FORM No. 963—Stevens-Ness Law Publishing Co., Portland, Ore. 97204

TN

WARRANTY DEED—STATUTORY FORM
INDIVIDUAL GRANTOR

Wendy Welloff (widow) *Grantor,*

conveys and warrants to Gerald & Nancy Investor, husband and wife

Grantee, the following described real property free of encumbrances except as specifically set forth herein situated in Rustic *County, Oregon, to-wit:*

Lots 16 & 17, Edgewood South Subdivision

(IF SPACE INSUFFICIENT, CONTINUE DESCRIPTION ON REVERSE SIDE)

The said property is free from encumbrances except

easements of record in subdivision plot

The true consideration for this conveyance is $ 640,000 *(Here comply with the requirements of ORS 93.030)*

Dated this 15th *day of* December, *19* 80.

/s/Wendy Welloff

STATE OF OREGON, County of Rustic *) ss.* December 15, *19*80

Personally appeared the above named Wendy Welloff

and acknowledged the foregoing instrument to be ...... voluntary act and deed.

Before me: /s/Alfred B. Culbertson

(OFFICIAL SEAL) *Notary Public for Oregon—My commission expires:* December 31, 1981

grantee is disturbed by a claim arising from or due to some act of the grantor. A special warranty deed gives a grantee much less protection than does a general warranty deed.

Bargain and Sale Deed

A bargain and sale deed is very similar to a special warranty deed. The grantor, in a bargain and sale deed, asserts ownership, by implication, of an interest in the property and makes no other covenants or claims, unless stated. The granting words are usually "grant, bargain, and sell," "grant and release," or simply "conveys." Thus, the grantee must demand or obtain good title evidence to be sure of receiving marketable title. Covenants against liens and other encumbrances may be inserted if agreeable to the grantor; the instrument is then called a bargain and sale deed, with covenants.

Quitclaim Deed

A *quitclaim deed* conveys the rights of the grantor, if any, without any warranty, claim, or assertion of title by the grantor. A quitclaim deed is the simplest form of deed and gives the grantor the least possible title protection. It conveys only an interest that a grantor may have when the deed is delivered. The operative words in a quitclaim deed are that (the grantor) "releases and quitclaims" (to the grantee). Title may be conveyed just as effectively and completely with a quitclaim deed as with a warranty deed, but without any warranties. The grantee has no recourse against the grantor, however, if no color of title is received.

Quitclaim deeds are widely used to clear up clouds on title. For example, a quitclaim deed is used whenever an heir might have a very weak title claim, or whenever a long-ago common law wife might have a dower claim. For a small consideration, the heir or "wife" gives up any claim held. A quitclaim deed to make right a legal description, names of parties, or some other error in a previously recorded deed is termed a deed of confirmation or a deed of correction. The obvious purpose is to clear up or correct the defect so that it does not become, or continue to be, a cloud on title. A quitclaim deed is shown in Figure 8–2.

Deeds of Trust and of Release

A deed conveying title to a third party (trustee) to be held as security for a debt owned a lender-beneficiary is known as a trust deed in the nature of a mortgage. It is also known as a trust deed or a deed of trust. A deed of trust is a nonstatutory deed. When the terms of the deed of trust have been satisfied (the debt has been paid off), the trustee reconveys title to the former borrower on a deed of release or of reconveyance. A deed or

FIGURE 8–2
A quitclaim deed (statutory form)

FORM No. 969—Stevens-Ness Law Publishing Co., Portland, Ore. 97204

TN

QUITCLAIM DEED—STATUTORY FORM
INDIVIDUAL GRANTOR

Wendy Welloff (widow) ....Grantor,
releases and quitclaims to Gerald & Nancy Investor, husband & wife
....*Grantee, all right, title and interest in and to the following described real property situated in* Rustic *County, Oregon, to-wit:*

Lots 16 & 17, Edgewood South subdivision

(IF SPACE INSUFFICIENT, CONTINUE DESCRIPTION ON REVERSE SIDE)

The true consideration for this conveyance is $ 640,000 *(Here comply with the requirements of ORS 93.030)*

Dated this 15th *day of* December *, 19* 80.

/s/Wendy Welloff

STATE OF OREGON, County of Rustic *) ss.* December 15th *, 19* 80
Personally appeared the above named ....
....*and acknowledged the foregoing instrument to be* her *voluntary act and deed.*

Before me: /s/Alfred B. Culbertson
(OFFICIAL SEAL) *Notary Public for Oregon—My commission expires:* ....

release is also used to lift or remove a claim from a dower, remainder, reversionary interest, or mortgage lien.

Miscellaneous Deeds

Many other deeds are used from time to time for special purposes or situations, frequently by court order. For the most part, the name of the deed indicates the nature of the purpose or situation. As fiduciaries, administrators, trustees, executors, and corporate officers do not wish to assume any greater future obligation than necessary when using these special-purpose deeds. They, therefore, include a covenant against grantor's acts in deeds they execute by stating that they "have not done or suffered anything whereby the said premises have been encumbered in any way whatsoever." In most cases, fiduciaries affect title only briefly and have no personal interest in the realty.

Administrator's deed. An administrator's deed is a nonstatutory deed used to convey realty of a person who died intestate to an heir or to a purchaser. An administrator is a person appointed by the court to settle the decedent's estate. The administrator executes the deed, which should recite the proceeding under which the court authorizes the sale or conveyance.

Executor's deed. An executor's deed conveys title to realty left by the person who died leaving a will to a purchaser or to a devisee. If more than one executor is designated in the will, all must sign the deed.

Deed of cession. A deed of cession is a nonstatutory instrument to convey street rights of an abutting owner to a municipality. The purpose should be recited. A quitclaim deed may be used for this conveyance.

Committee's deed. A committee's deed is a nonstatutory instrument to convey property of infants, mentally retarded persons, and other incompetents whose affairs are managed by a court-appointed committee. Authority from the court must precede any such conveyance.

Gift deed. An instrument conveying title from a donor-grantor to a donee-grantee is a gift deed. The usual consideration is "love and affection." The grantee has no recourse against the grantor if title is defective because no monetary consideration was given by the grantee.

Guardian's deed. A guardian's deed is an instrument used by a legal guardian to convey the realty interest of an infant or ward, upon permission of the court. Full consideration should be recited because the guardian is a long-term fiduciary.

Referee's deed in foreclosure. An instrument used by an officer of the court to convey a mortgagor's title, following a foreclosure sale, is called a referee's deed in foreclosure or, loosely, a "sheriff's deed" in some areas. It contains no other supporting covenants. The conditions surrounding the conveyance and the price paid by the purchaser should be cited in the deed.

Referee's deed in partition. Concurrent owners sometimes sue for partition or splitting up of jointly owned property. The instrument used following a partition judgment and sale is a referee's deed in partition. An officer of the court (the referee) conveys the interests of the former concurrent owners to purchasers with no other supporting covenants.

Deed of surrender. A deed of surrender is a nonstatutory instrument to convey a life estate to a remainderman or a qualified fee estate to the holder of the reversionary interest. These conveyances can also be accomplished with a quitclaim deed.

ESSENTIALS OF A VALID DEED

The formal requirements for a valid deed vary from state to state, but the following requirements are essential or basic to all states:

1. Name of grantor with legal capacity to execute the deed
2. Name of grantee, adequate for identification with reasonable certainty
3. A statement of some consideration
4. Granting clause or words of conveyance
5. Statement of the interest being conveyed
6. Description of realty in which interest is held
7. Habendum clause
8. Proper execution—signature of the grantor, notarized, with witnesses and seal when required
9. Voluntary delivery and acceptance

Grantor and Grantee

The conveyance must be from a competent grantor to a grantee capable of holding title. The rules of contracts usually apply in determining whether or not the grantor is competent to convey title to real property. Basically, the grantor must have reached the age of majority and be of sound mind. A deed signed by a minor is considered voidable (not void) at the option of the minor, until the legal age of majority is reached.

The names of the grantor and the grantee should be followed by their addresses to aid in their identification. The status of the parties should also be clearly indicated, for example, "John Jones and Mary Jones, husband and wife," or "brother and sister."

A deed conveying corporation property should be supported by a resolution properly passed by the corporate board of directors. The deed can be signed only by a corporate officer deriving authority from the corporate board of directors by resolution. Finally, the corporate seal must be affixed to the deed.

Consideration

Consideration is anything of value given in a contractual agreement—money services, love, and affection. Some consideration must always be stated in a deed. That shifts the burden of proving lack of consideration to anyone attacking the conveyance. Under the Statute of Frauds, the consideration cited in a deed cannot be disputed for purposes of defeating the deed. Dollar consideration is usually required except in a gift deed in which love and affect is sufficient. Even in gift deeds, a nominal consideration, such as "$12.00 and other good and valuable consideration," is customarily cited. Full dollar consideration is frequently not cited in a deed except when the deed is executed by a fiduciary.

Words of Conveyance—Granting and Habendum Clauses

The granting clause includes words of conveyance such as "convey and warrant," "grant and release," "grant, bargain, and sell," or "releases and quitclaims." Each of these terms of conveyance carries a different connotation concerning the warranties and obligations of the grantor. The interest being conveyed, including appurtenances, should follow the granting clause. Only a present interest in realty can be conveyed; that is, a deed to convey at some future time, for example, at the grantor's death, is invalid.

The description of the estate in the habendum clause should agree with the description in the granting clause. Deed restriction and other encumbrances are usually stated after the habendum clause.

Unique Description

A description must be used that identifies the property clearly and uniquely. Street addresses are often inadequate because ambiguity and uncertainty might result. Any description that would enable a competent surveyor to locate the property is considered adequate.

Proper Execution

Proper execution includes signatures, a seal, witnesses (in some states), and an acknowledgment of the signing before a public notary. Customarily, only the grantor or grantors sign a deed. If a mortgage is being assumed, the grantee must also sign, unless a collateral agreement is made. A grantor who is unable to write may sign with a mark in almost all states. A cross is usually used as a mark, with the grantor's name typed near the cross:

his
John (X) Brown (seal)
mark

The "X" must be made by the grantor, with two persons witnessing.

The word "seal" printed or written behind a grantor's signature is required in some states to indicate the formal nature of the deed. The signature of an authorized officer, in conveyance of corporate realty, must be followed by the corporate seal. In some states the signatures of the witnesses to the signing are also required for proper execution.

An *acknowledgment* is a formal declaration, before a notary public or other authorized public official, by a person signing a legal document that the signing is a "free and voluntary act." A justice of the peace, a judge, or a commanding officer in one of the military services may also acknowledge a signature. An acknowledgment is required for recording in nearly every state. The public official is expected to require proper identification of parties involved in an acknowledgment. The purpose of the acknowledgment is to prevent the recording of forged instruments. A deed without an acknowledgment is not a satisfactory instrument for most conveyance purposes. Deeds should be recorded as soon as received to give notice to the world of grantee's rights in the property received.

Delivery and Acceptance

The final requirement for a valid deed is delivery and acceptance. *Delivery* means that the grantor, by some act or statement, signifies intent for the deed to be effective. The grantor handing the deed to the grantee is the most obvious form of delivery. Similarly, the grantor's directing an attorney or an escrow officer to give a signed deed to the grantee also constitutes delivery. Delivery must take place while the grantor is alive. If several people share ownership of a property, for delivery to occur, all must sign and in some way indicate that the deed is to be effective.

The grantee must accept the deed for title to pass. *Acceptance* is agreeing to the terms of a deed. Since most people desire to own property, acceptance is ordinarily assumed. Thus, if a grantor records a deed conveying title to a grantee, the grantee must object and dissent immediately to avoid an acceptance.

Fraudulent Conveyances

Courts will occasionally inquire into the consideration in a conveyance if there is a possibility of fraud. For example, if a grantor who is being crowded by creditors conveys for apparently insufficient consideration to a friend or relative, inquiry is justified. If the conveyance is proved fraudulent, the courts will require a reconveyance to the grantor, making the property available to satisfy creditor claims. If the indebtedness to credits occurred after the conveyance, fraudulent intent must be proved to require a reconveyance to the grantor.

SUMMARY

A person owning, or about to own, real estate wants the best possible title, termed "marketable title." *Marketable title* means that quality is high enough that courts would require a buyer to accept the property at market value. Marketable title may be evidenced or documented by (1) title certification, (2) title insurance, or (3) a Torrens certificate.

The most common methods of bringing about a transfer of title are private grant (sale for consideration, gift, or will) and action of law (descent, lien enforcement, adverse possession, or condemnation). Deeds most commonly used to actually convey title are the (1) general warranty, (2) special warranty, (3) bargain and sale, (4) quitclaim, and (5) trust.

The essential parts of a valid deed are (1) names of grantor and grantee, (2) statement of consideration, (3) words of conveyance, (4) unique property description, (5) proper execution, including grantor's signature, and (6) delivery and acceptance. A deed, or any instrument showing an interest of consequence in real estate, is usually recorded to give constructive notice of the interest, which protects the owner of the interest.

QUESTIONS FOR REVIEW AND DISCUSSION

1. Briefly explain and distinguish among the following methods of transferring title:
   a. Contract for consideration
   b. Gift
   c. Will
   d. Descent
   e. Adverse possession
   f. Lien enforcement
   g. Erosion

2. Explain the use of an attorney's opinion of title, including any advantages or disadvantages from a prospective owner's or lender's point of view.

3. Explain title insurance in detail, including any advantages or disadvantages for a potential owner's or lender's point of view.

4. Explain the nature of a general warranty deed, including five accompanying covenants or warranties.

5. Explain the nature and uses of the following deeds:
   a. Special warranty
   b. Bargain and sale
   c. Quitclaim
   d. Trust

6. List and explain at least five essentials of a valid deed.

7. Title may be gained by adverse possession in 10 to 20 years. Should this law not invalidate most claims of title more than 20 years old because most real estate is now held under color of title? Are laws needed to make this situation clear to everyone? Discuss.

8. The Torrens system should be adopted nationwide in the United States. Discuss. What major obstacles would have to be overcome? What would be the probable effect on costs of title transfer?

9. What kind of deed would you prefer to use as a grantor of title? As a grantee? Why? How is the difference in attitude reconciled in practice?

10. Are deeds necessary? If not, what might be used instead?

11. What is an abstract of title? What is its use or purpose?

12. A property survey may be required to validate title. What purpose does a survey serve?

CASE PROBLEMS

1. Title to a property you recently bought is assured by title insurance, with typical coverage. Give three example situations in which you may not be protected by the insurance.
2. Henry notices 40 acres of unused land adjacent to his farm. He fences and farms the land for more than 20 years. The county assessor, in turn, levies and collects taxes on the land from Henry. In actuality, the land is a portion of an 800-acre spread owned by Marilyn, an attorney, who lives in a neighboring state. Marilyn dies. Upon settling the estate, the executor discovers Henry's use of the 40 acres. The executor sues for back rent. What is the result?
3. Helen brings an abstract of title up to date for a house that is being sold to Vincent. Carol, an attorney, examines the abstract and certifies the title as marketable. Title is conveyed to Vincent and the transaction is closed.
   a. After the closing, a forgery of an earlier deed is discovered, meaning that Vincent does not have marketable title. Vincent sues Carol for negligence. What is the result?
   b. Vincent also sues Helen, the grantor. What is the likely result if a quitclaim deed were used to convey title? A special warranty deed? A general warranty deed?
   c. Does Vincent have a basis for a valid claim for damages against the abstract company?
4. William is negotiating with Nancy about the sale of a bookstore he owns. Nancy verbally offers him $225,000 and asks him to think it over.
   a. William, thinking to accept, prepares and signs a deed and puts it in a drawer in his office desk. That evening he has a heart attack and dies. Is there delivery?
   b. If William had given the signed deed to an escrow agent, would there have been delivery?

CHAPTER NINE
TITLE CLOSING

Buy land. They ain't making any more of the stuff
WILL ROGERS, American humorist

IMPORTANT TOPICS OR DECISION AREAS COVERED IN THIS CHAPTER

- Preliminary Requirements (for Closings)
- Elements of Closing Costs
- Closing Statement Entries and Prorations
- Escrow Closing
- Title Conveyance

Knowledge of closing procedures and adjustments is advantageous to a prospective real estate buyer for several reasons. With an understanding of closing, an investor will have a better idea of "what's going on" in negotiations. The need for certain documents or information becomes much more obvious. Further, knowledge of closing procedures is absolutely essential for an agent or broker in arranging financing or closing and even in holding a deal together.

Earlier, we covered contracts for the purchase and sale of real estate. This chapter concentrates on closing procedures and settlement statements necessary to complete such a transaction. Necessary documents, typical closing costs, including prorations for the settlement statement, and recordation are all discussed.

The most common closing, which is the focus of this chapter, involves the sale of property that is financed by a new mortgage loan. This is actually a double transaction: a sale and a financing. The costs and adjustments may be substantial for the buyer, totaling between 3 and 8 percent for the majority of properties. Other common title closings are (1) sale of property financed by an existing loan, (2) exchange of two or more properties, (3) refinancing of a property under a continuing owner, and (4) sale of a leasehold. These closings are similar in procedures and details to the new financing closing and are, therefore, not discussed separately.

KEY CONCEPTS INTRODUCED IN THIS CHAPTER

Accrued expense
Affidavit of title
Credit
Prepaid expense
Prorate

PRELIMINARY REQUIREMENTS (FOR CLOSINGS)

Many details must be attended to between the signing of a sales contract and an actual closing. If an escrow closing is required, these details must be cleared through the escrow agent. Some of the more common and important details are shown in Figure 9–1. Parties primarily concerned with each detail are indicated.

The entire escrow closing process, within which these items must be processed, is shown in Figure 9–2. Even if a closing is not in escrow, the same considerations or details must be handled by the broker, lender, or others to complete the transaction.

Survey and Inspection

A survey specifically identifies the property and brings to light any encroachments onto or from the property. Encroachments must almost always be corrected by the seller before the closing can be completed.

FIGURE 9–1
Reports/documents/actions in preparing for a title closing

	PARTY PRIMARILY CONCERNED		
	BUYER	*SELLER*	*LENDER*
1. Survey	x		x
2. Inspection	x		x
3. Title search and report	x		x
4. RESPA disclosure			x
5. Encumbrances to be accepted by buyer	x		x
6. Encumbrances to be removed by seller		x	
7. Instruments			
Abstract of title or preliminary title report		x	
Deed	x		x
Mortgage or trust deed	x		x
Promissory note	x		x
Title insurance policy or certificate of title	x		x

If the property is an income property, a detailed property inspection is usually necessary prior to a closing to ascertain that conditions are as represented in the contract. The inspection is to verify such matters as names of tenants, rents, space occupied, lengths of leases, and amounts of security deposits. The inspection is also to make sure that no one in possession of any part of the premises has or claims any rights or ownership or other interest in the property. The law is clear in almost all states that possession gives public notice of an interest just as strongly as does a recorded instrument. An inspection should be made shortly before the closing in conjunction with the title search and analyses.

Title Search and Report

Having the title searched and obtaining the title report are probably the most important requirements from the purchaser's viewpoint. The purpose of the search and report is for the purchaser to be sure that the seller's title is clear or at least meets contract requirements. The seller usually provides title evidence in the form of a current abstract of title or title commitment from a title insurance company. If an abstract of title is provided, the buyer must obtain an option of title from an attorney. The title commitment or the title opinion sets forth liens, assessments, deed restrictions, and other encumbrances of record. The seller's title is subject to these limitations. The seller must remove any of these limitations that make the title unmarketable or otherwise do not meet the requirements of the sales contract.

Encumbrances: Acceptance or Removal

A marketable title must be delivered by the seller except for encumbrances specifically excepted in the sales contract. Customarily, the purchaser notifies the seller, shortly after receipt of the title report or opinion, of

FIGURE 9–2
The escrow closing process

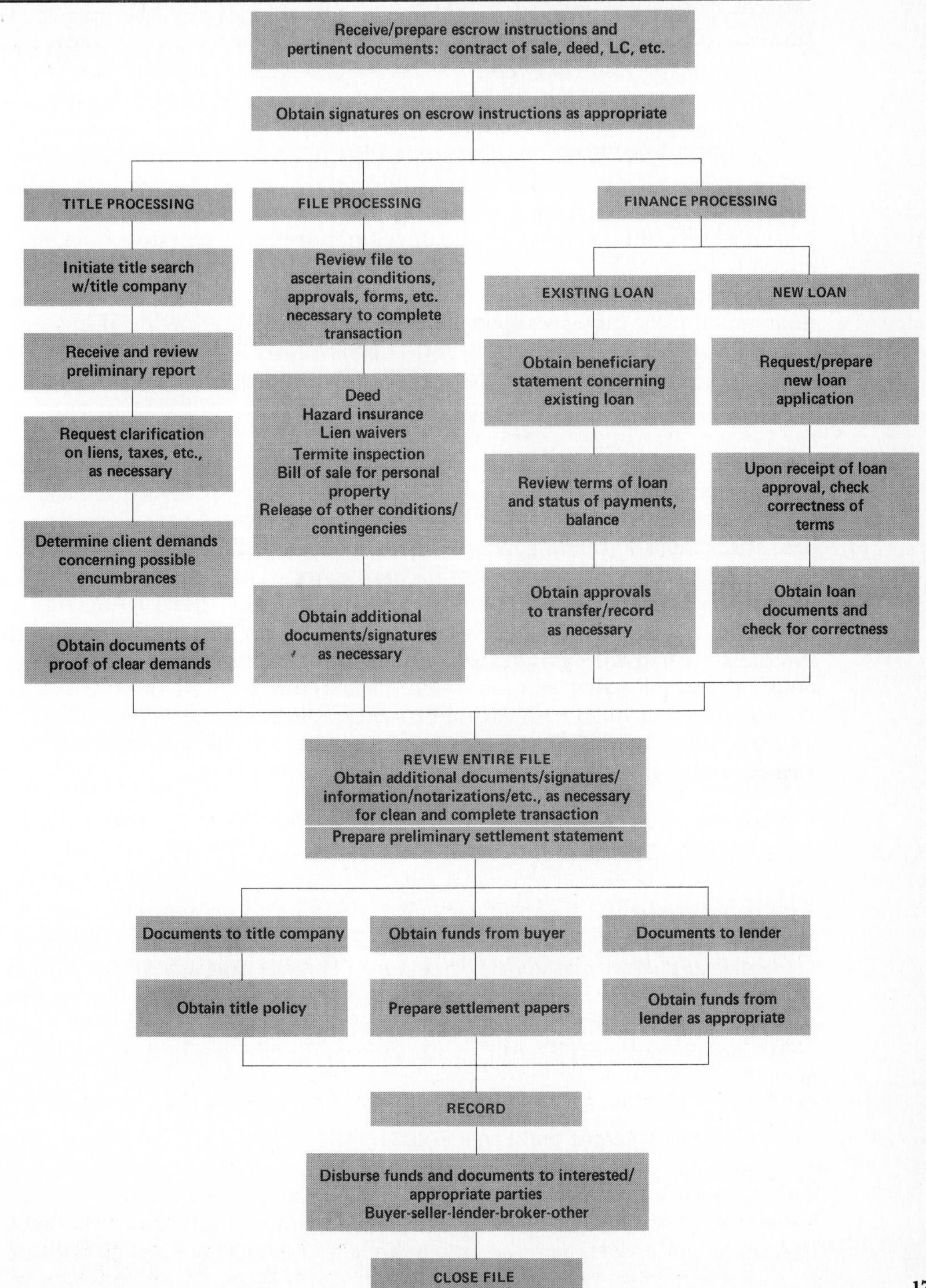

Receive/prepare escrow instructions and pertinent documents: contract of sale, deed, LC, etc.
Obtain signatures on escrow instructions as appropriate
TITLE PROCESSING
Initiate title search w/title company
Receive and review preliminary report
Request clarification on liens, taxes, etc., as necessary
Determine client demands concerning possible encumbrances
Obtain documents of proof of clear demands
FILE PROCESSING
Review file to ascertain conditions, approvals, forms, etc. necessary to complete transaction
Deed
Hazard insurance
Lien waivers
Termite inspection
Bill of sale for personal property
Release of other conditions/ contingencies
Obtain additional documents/signatures as necessary
FINANCE PROCESSING
EXISTING LOAN
Obtain beneficiary statement concerning existing loan
Review terms of loan and status of payments, balance
Obtain approvals to transfer/record as necessary
NEW LOAN
Request/prepare new loan application
Upon receipt of loan approval, check correctness of terms
Obtain loan documents and check for correctness
REVIEW ENTIRE FILE
Obtain additional documents/signatures/ information/notarizations/etc., as necessary for clean and complete transaction
Prepare preliminary settlement statement
Documents to title company
Obtain title policy
Obtain funds from buyer
Prepare settlement papers
Documents to lender
Obtain funds from lender as appropriate
RECORD
Disburse funds and documents to interested/ appropriate parties
Buyer-seller-lender-broker-other
CLOSE FILE

all encumbrances to be removed. The acceptability of encumbrances and other objections of title that show up on the title report or opinion must, therefore, be settled between the buyer and seller prior to closing. If acceptable or waived by the buyer and the new lender, these limitations need not be removed or "cured."

Typical liens or encumbrances to be removed are mortgage liens, tax liens, clouds on title because of improperly signed deeds, and unexpected easements or deed restrictions. Title restrictions and setback liens placed against the property by the developer are representative of exempt encumbrances.

A title report or opinion occasionally shows a title to be extremely unmarketable or clouded. After adequate opportunity has been given to the seller to remove the clouds and encumbrances, the buyer may reject such a title and rescind the sales contract. Upon rejection and rescission, the buyer is entitled to recover reasonable expenses incurred because of the seller's inability to perform according to the contract of sale.

Instruments to Be Delivered

The seller must sign and convey title either by a deed of the kind required by the sales contract or by one of higher quality. The new lender, in turn, provides a promissory note and a mortgage or trust deed to be signed by the buyer-borrower. If an existing loan is paid off as part of the closing, the old lender must sign and provide a mortgage satisfaction or deed of reconveyance. Finally, as mentioned earlier, the seller is often asked to sign an affidavit of title. If the sales contract calls for an escrow closing, all these instruments must be delivered to the escrow agent, along with escrow instructions.

ELEMENTS OF CLOSING COSTS

The main classes or types of closing costs and adjustments include (1) title assurance charges and legal fees, (2) loan-related charges and fees, (3) brokerage commissions and fees, and (4) taxes and other buyer-seller adjustments. Typical buyer closing costs range from 4 to 8 percent, not including adjustments for property taxes and special assessments. Tax adjustments and special assessments may double or triple these percentages.

Title Assurance Charges and Legal Fees

Title assurance means confidence or certainty in the quality of title. Title assurance is obtained through evidence or documentation. Title assurance charges include costs for the title search and examination and for title insurance. The cost of bringing an abstract of title up to date or the cost of title insurance is usually paid for by the seller. A buyer may incur fees for legal counsel to examine the title and otherwise look after the buyer's interests throughout the transaction.

Buyers and lenders both want assurances that the title to the property of concern has no hidden claims or liens filed against it. Therefore, a detailed search of various documents in the public record must be made to assure that hidden claims and liens do not exist. Title assurance evidence most generally consists of an attorney's certification of title or of a title insurance policy.

Loan-Related Charges and Fees

Major items of cost to a buyer in obtaining mortgage financing are for loan origination, discount points, property survey, appraisal, prepaid interest, hazard insurance, and the lender's attorney fee. A seller may be required to pay a penalty to a lender from prepayment of a mortgage loan. Prepayment penalties typically run from 1 to 2 percent of the loan balance paid off. For example, a seller prepaying a loan with a balance of $200,000 might be required to pay a 1 percent charge of $2,000.

Lender's service charge. Loan origination fees, payable by a borrower, typically amount to from 1 to 2 percent of the amount borrowed. The loan origination fee is also sometimes termed a lender's or a mortgage service charge. In addition, points must be paid by a seller of a FHA or VA loan because of below-market interest rates on these loans. Each discount point means 1 percent of the amount borrowed. In essence, the mortgage service charge is mortgage brokerage fee to cover the expenses incurred in initiating a mortgage loan with a lending firm.

Property survey. A property survey by a licensed land surveyor is sometimes required by lenders. Such a survey shows lot lines, dimensions, and the location of improvements with reference to lot lines. The costs for such surveys are customarily borne by the purchaser.

Appraisal fee. When the purchase funds are supplied by third parties or when the mortgage loan is guaranteed or insured by federal agencies, an appraisal report is generally required, with the cost charged to the purchaser.

Prepaid interest. Another charge that sometimes has to be accounted for at the title closing is prepaid interest. When a new mortgage is negotiated to cover part of the purchase price, prepaid interest is customarily charged from date of settlement to the end of the month. The first regular payment of debt service then begins at the end of the following month. This prepayment makes it unnecessary to compute interest for periods of less than one month's time. Whenever outstanding mortgages are assumed, an adjustment is made between the seller and the buyer, each bearing the respective interest costs—the seller to the date of the closing and the buyer from the next day hence. Whenever interest on an existing mortgage has accrued, an appropriate credit is given to the buyer for interest charges due up to and including the day of the settlement.

Hazard insurance. At closing a prudent lender requires the purchaser-mortgagor to provide hazard insurance on the property in an amount sufficient to protect the loan. This insurance is to protect the lender against loss by fire, windstorm, and other specified hazards. It is customary at the time of closing for the buyer to pay the premium for one year if new insurance is obtained. If the policy of the seller is being taken over, it is necessary to make an adjustment to pay the seller for any premiums in the reserve account. The buyer must also reimburse the seller for prepaid premiums, representing the remaining term of the insurance being taken over.

Commissions and Escrow Fees

When a broker is used to bring about a transaction, sales commissions typically run from 4 to 7 percent of the price. The seller usually pays this sales commission because the broker is usually the agent of the seller. Of course, if the buyer employs the broker, the buyer pays the commission. Commissions on sales of lots and land may run up to 10 percent. Unless otherwise agreed, escrow charges are usually split evenly between the buyer and the seller.

Taxes and Other Buyer-Seller Adjustments

Real property taxes may constitute a lien prior to the mortgage lien. Therefore, provision is usually made at the closing to provide for prepayment into a reserve account to allow the lender or mortgage service agent to meet the tax payments as they fall due. If a reserve account is required by the lender, the estimated real property tax for the year is prorated on a monthly basis and is added to the payments due each month for the mortgage interest, principal, and hazard insurance. In addition to having a reserve account set up, there must be payments made to cover tax adjustments pursuant to contract agreements reached between the buyer and the seller.

There are a number of "other costs" or miscellaneous charges that the buyer must be prepared to meet at the time of title closing:

1. Tax on mortgage and on bond or note. A mortgage is classified as personal property, and some states levy a documentary stamp tax on the promissory note, an intangible tax on the amount of the mortgage debt, and a fee for recording the mortgage document. These fees and charges must be paid to the

collector before the real estate mortgage may be recorded. Some states place the entire tax on the bond or note incorporated in the mortgage.

2. A credit report showing outstanding debt of the borrower, if any, and the borrower's credit relationship with various people and organizations with whom he or she has had financial dealings, is required by almost all lending agencies. The charge for this report is generally rather small.
3. Recording fees for deeds, mortgages, assignments, and mortgage satisfactions are customarily paid by the purchaser as part of the title closing costs. These recording fees vary with the length of the instrument and the recording fee customs.
4. Stamps on deeds required by state law are generally paid for by the seller and thus do not as a rule appear in the buyer's closing statement.

In addition to these costs and settlement charges, adjustments are made for accrued or prepaid rentals if tenants are occupying the premises.

CLOSING STATEMENT ENTRIES AND PRORATIONS

A written statement is needed at the closing to satisfy all parties involved, particularly the buyer and the seller. The statement shows the amount of money the buyer must pay to get title and possession. The statement also tells how much the seller will net after paying the broker's commission and other expenses. In this chapter, we show typical statements for the buyer and the seller.

Prorations and adjustments are necessary in preparing closing statements. To *prorate* means to divide proportionately, as between a buyer and a seller. The seller typically owes property taxes, has prepaid insurance, and owns reserve deposits, all of which require adjustments. The buyer wants these and similar items cleared at or before the closing. Also, if an existing mortgage is taken over by the buyer, adjustments for accrued interest to date of the closing are necessary. These adjustments are representative of the many that may be necessary at the closing.

General Rules of Prorating

The rules or customs applicable to the prorations vary widely from state to state. In some states closing rules and procedures have been established by the realty boards or bar associations. Rules most generally applicable are as follows:

1. The seller is generally responsible for the day of the closing. This means that prorations are usually made to and including the day of closing. (In a few states the buyer is responsible for the day of closing, and adjustments are made as of the day preceding the date of closing).
2. A year is presumed to have 360 days, with 12 30-day months, for prorations of mortgage interest, real estate taxes, and insurance premiums. The actual

number of days in a month may be used in prorations if specified in the sales contract. (Later in the chapter, Figure 9–4 provides an easy way to calculate prorations.)

3. Accrued real estate taxes that are not yet payable are prorated at the closing. The amount of the last tax bill is used in prorating if current taxes cannot be ascertained.
4. Special assessment taxes are increasingly paid by the seller and are not prorated at the closing, unless the buyer agrees to assume and prorate. Special assessments are technically not taxes but are charges for improvements that benefit the property, such as sewers, sidewalks, streets, and water mains. Special assessments are usually paid in annual installments over several years. If assumed by a buyer, the seller usually pays the current installment. Some purchasers demand that they get credit for the seller's share of the current year's interest on the remaining balance. Other arrangements may be stipulated in the sales contract.
5. The proration of rents is usally based on the actual number of days in the month of the closing. The buyer usually agrees in a separate statement to collect any unpaid rents for the current and previous periods, if any, and to forward the pro rata share to the seller. (The buyer is advised against taking uncollected rents as an adjustment in the closing statement because the buyer should not accept the responsibility for rents that the seller cannot collect.)
6. Tenants' security deposits for the last month's rent or to cover possible damages to the property must be transferred to the buyer without any offsetting adjustment. The deposits belong to the tenants and not to the seller. And, as the new owner, the buyer will be responsible for refunding these deposits at a later time. In some instances, tenant consent to such transfers may be necessary.
7. If closing is between wage payment dates, unpaid wages of employees working on the property are prorated, including amounts for social security and other fringe benefits.
8. Adjustments for chattels and fixtures must be made according to local custom. Unless otherwise stipulated in the sales contract, the following items are usually regarded as fixtures: plumbing, heating, built-in appliances, oil tanks, water heaters, light fixtures, bathroom fixtures, blinds, shades, draperies and curtain rods, window and door screens, storm doors and windows, wall-to-wall carpeting, shrubs, bulbs, plants, and trees. Hall carpets, refrigerators, stoves, and washers and dryers are also usually regarded as fixtures in apartment buildings.

Closing Statement Entries

Several items on a closing statement are direct entries and do not require adjustments between the buyer and the seller. These items are commonly called credits. A *credit* is an entry in a person's favor, as, for example, the balance in a bank account is in the depositor's favor. We also speak of "giving credit to someone" for doing us a favor or showing honesty or otherwise being financially trustworthy. A credit, as used here, is recognition to the buyer or seller for a contribution made to the transaction. See Figure 9–3 for a summary of closing statement entries.

The obvious first entry on a closing statement is the sale price, which is credited to the seller. Crediting the seller with the sale price is recognition of the seller's contribution of the property to the transaction.

If the seller has on hand coal, oil, cleaning suppplies, or other items

FIGURE 9–3
Settlement statement items

CREDITS TO BUYER	CREDITS TO SELLER
Direct Entry, No Proration Necessary	
1. Earnest money and down payments	1. Sale price
2. Remaining balance of outstanding mortgage loan, if taken over by buyer	2. Fuel on hand (coal or fuel oil) or supplies at current market price
3. Purchase money mortgage	3. Reserve deposits for taxes and hazard insurance (when existing mortgage is taken over by buyer)
4. Security deposits of tenants	
Proration Necessary	
1. Accrued general real estate taxes (seller's portion)	1. Prepaid hazard insurance premium (buyer's portion)
2. Accrued interest on loans (seller's portion)	2. Prepaid water and sewer charges (buyer's portion)
3. Accrued wages of employees, including vacation allowance (seller's portion)	3. Prepaid real estate taxes (buyer's portion)
4. Prepaid rents or rents collected in advance by the seller (buyer's portion)	

that are being taken over by the buyer, a direct entry for their current market price is also credited to the seller. The items are over and above the sale price of the real estate and represent additional seller contributions to the transaction, for which credit should be given. In a similar vein, the seller's reserve deposits that are being taken over by the buyer warrant a direct credit entry to the seller. Reserve deposits are commonly assumed by the buyer along with taking over an existing mortgage against the property.

The buyer is credited in the closing statement with any earnest money deposit or down payment made. In addition, if the buyer takes over an existing mortgage of the seller, a credit is due to the buyer. The buyer is taking over the responsibility of a seller's obligation relative to the property and deserves recognition by a credit on the closing statement. A buyer's giving a purchase money mortgage to the seller as part of the sale price has a similar effect. A purchase money mortgage is a mortgage given to a seller by a buyer to cover all or a portion of the purchase price of the property.

Tenants' security deposits, if carried as an obligation of the property owner, must also be treated as a credit to the buyer. The buyer is relieving the seller of the obligation to repay the security deposits, which constitutes a contribution to the transaction. Alternatively, if the security deposits are carried in escrow accounts, the accounts may be transferred to the buyer's name, with no adjusting entry on the closing statement.

Proration Calculations

Some items must be prorated between the buyer and seller rather than directly credited to one or to the other. A proration is necessary when a charge or a payment covers a time period for which both the buyer and the seller are responsible. Real estate taxes, accrued interest, prepaid hazard insurance, and rents collected in advance are representative of items that must be prorated. Refer to Figure 9–4.

Three considerations or steps are involved in proration:

1. Identify the item to be prorated (taxes, insurance premiums, etc.).
2. Determine whether a prepaid or accrued expense is involved.
3. Calculate the amount of the proration.

Figure 9–3 lists settlement statement items and indicates whether the buyer or seller gets a credit entry on the closing statement. Figure 9–3 also tells whether an item is an accrued expense or a prepaid expense. An *accrued expense* means accumulated charges, such as interest and taxes, owed but not yet paid. A *prepaid expense* is a charge, as rents or insurance paid in advance.

An accrued or prepaid expense, in turn, means a proration. For example, a hazard insurance premium prepaid by the seller means that the seller is due a credit for the portion of the premium that covers an ownership period of the buyer. Alternatively, accrued taxes of the seller, which the buyer eventually must pay, become a credit entry to the buyer on the closing statement.

Accrued expense proration. Real property taxes are a typical accrued expense. Assume that a tax is levied for a calendar year and is payable once a year, say, in late October. Then the accrued portion is for the portion of the year from January 1 to the date of closing, up to the time when the tax is paid. Once the tax is paid, it becomes a prepaid expense. Of course, the whole cycle is repeated beginning January 1 of next year.

An example is in order. Assume that a property is assessed at $640,000 with annual taxes of $12,000, or $1,000 per month. A closing on January 15 would mean accrued taxes for 15 days or ½ month. The amount of such taxes would be $500,

$$\$12{,}000 \times \frac{15}{360} = \$12{,}000 \times \frac{1}{24} = \$500$$

The $500 is credited to the buyer for assuming the seller's obligation to pay taxes.

A closing on September 18 (before the tax is paid for the year) would call for a buyer's credit of $8,600, covering 8 months and 18 days. The calculation is as follows. Monthly taxes equal $1,000 ($12,000/12 = $1,000). Eighteen days equals 0.6 month, for which taxes would be $600 ($1,000 × 0.6 = $600). Taxes for 8 months would amount to $8,000. Total taxes would then equal $8,600.

In similar fashion, interest on a 9 percent, monthly payment loan of

FIGURE 9–4
Buyer's closing statement or summary of buyer's transaction

ENTRY ITEM	*DEBITS/ CHARGES*	*CREDITS*
Contract sales price	$640,000	
Earnest money deposit		$ 32,000
New first mortgage		500,000
Buyer-seller adjustments		
Supplies on hand by seller	1,800	
Tenant security deposits (owed by seller)		7,040
Accrued property taxes (1/1–1/15/81)		500
Hazard insurance prepaid (1/16–11/30/81)	1,575	
Rents prepaid to seller (1/16–1/31/81)		4,200
Accrued water/sewer charges		48
Settlement charges to third parties		
Interest on new loan to 1/31/81	2,083.33	
Loan origination fee	10,000	
Lender's title policy (Hifidelity Title Co.)	420	
Appraisal fee (Allen Measure)	700	
Credit report (Rustic Co. Credit Bureau)	40	
Lender's attorney fee (Howard Light)	100	
Escrow fee (one-half)	210	
Buyer-borrower attorney fee (Sharpe and Brilliant)	180	
Recording fees (Rustic Co. recorder)	16	
Subtotals	$657,124.33	$543,788.
Cash/check required of buyer to balance		113,336.33
Totals (must balance)	$657,124.33	$657,124.33

$300,000 for the first 20 days of a month would be $1,500, calculated as follows:

$$\frac{9\%}{12} = \tfrac{3}{4}\% \text{ per month}$$

$$\$300{,}000 \times \tfrac{3}{4}\% = \$2{,}250$$

$$\$2{,}250 \times \frac{20 \text{ days}}{30 \text{ days}} = \$1{,}500$$

Assume a closing on the twentieth of a month (a seller's day) with the buyer assuming the seller's $300,000 mortgage as indicated. The buyer would be entitled to a $1,500 credit for assuming the seller's interest obligation. The buyer would also be entitled to a $300,000 credit for assuming the seller's mortgage loan obligation.

Prepaid expense prorations. A typical adjustment of a prepaid expense involves the premium for hazard insurance. Hazard insurance premiums are usually prepaid for 1, 3, or 5 years. A buyer frequently takes over the insurance coverage of a seller, as a matter of convenience. A careful check to determine correctly the period for which a premium has been paid is necessary prior to any prorating calculations. The number of future years, months, and days for which the premium has been prepaid must then be calculated. Two examples are given here to illustrate the usual methods of calculating the prepaid insurance expense. The first example concerns a 1-year prepayment, the second a 3-year prepayment.

Assume a seller's policy with an annual premium of $1,800 ($150 per month) that runs to November 30, 1981. A closing is on January 15, 1981. The buyer agrees to take over the seller's policy. What is the amount of the adjustment?

	YEARS	*MONTHS*	*DAYS*
Premium paid to 11/30/81	1981	11	30
Closing date 1/15/81	1981	1	15
Remaining coverage available	0	10	15

The end date of the prepaid periods is compared with the closing date. Then, beginning with the Days column, the closing date is subtracted from the end date. In this example, 10 months, 15 days of premium are prepaid as of the closing date. At $150 per month, this means a credit of $1,575 to the seller ($150/month × 10.5 months = $1,575).

In a second, more complex example, assume a 3-year premium of $5,400 for a policy that ends on November 12, 1983. Closing is assumed to take place on September 15, 1981.

	YEARS	*MONTHS*	*DAYS*
Premium paid to 11/12/83	1983	11	12
Closing date 9/15/81	1981	9	15
Future years, months, and days for which premium is prepaid	?	?	?

Again begin with the Days column. When the days of the end time (12) are fewer than the days in the line for the closing date (15), a month must be borrowed from the Months column. This increases the days column by 30, to 42. The 15 days on the lower line may now be subtracted from the upper line to give 27 future days for which a premium has been paid. Next move to the months column. The months in the lower line in (9) may be directly subtracted from the months in the upper line (now 10 after 1 has been borrowed) to give one prepaid month. If the months in the upper line were less that the months in the lower line, 12 months (1 year) would have to be borrowed from the years column.

	YEARS	MONTHS	DAYS
Premium paid to 11/12/83	1983	10	42
Closing date 9/15/81	1981	9	15
Future years, months, and days for which premium is prepaid	2	1	27

Finally in the Years column, 1981 is subtracted from 1983 to give 2 future years for which the premium is paid. In total, the premium has been prepaid for 2 years, 1 month, 27 days.

The $5,400 premium breaks down to $1,800 per year or $150 per month. Two years times $1,800 equals $3,600. One month at $150 per month equals $150. And 27 days or 0.9 month (27 days/30 days) at $150 per month gives $135. The total credit due the seller for a prepaid insurance premium is $3,885.

Prepayment credit for 2 years	$3,600
Prepayment for 1 month	150
Prepayment for 27 days	135
Total prepayment credit due seller	$3,885

ESCROW CLOSING

The closing involving the sale of Douglas Manor, a 16-unit apartment building, for $640,000 is used in an example. The seller is Wendy Welloff, a widow. Gerald and Nancy Investor are the buyers. Calculations for two adjustments in the example (property taxes and hazard insurance) are shown earlier in this chapter. The closing is handled by Hifidelity Escrow Services.

Data Inputs

The basic information for our example is presented as the Douglas Manor case. The data are intended to be representative. Some detail is omitted for greater clarity of illustration.

DOUGLAS MANOR—CLOSING CASE PROBLEM

On November 28, 1980, Gerald and Nancy Investor deposit $32,000 of earnest money toward the purchase of Douglas Manor for $640,000. On November 29 the owner, Wendy Welloff, agrees to sell. The sale was negotiated by Harvey Hustle of Everready Realty Company. The parties subsequently agree to a January 15, 1981 closing date. Escrow closing costs are to be shared equally, as per contract, and a 30-day month, 360-day banker's year is traditionally used for closing adjustments in the area. See Figure 7–1 for a copy of the Investor-Welloff contract.

The offer is conditional on the Investors' obtaining a 25-year monthly payment loan for $500,000 or more at 12 percent interest or less. The Urbandale Savings and Loan agrees to make a $500,000 loan, at 12 percent interest per year, with a 2 percent loan origination fee. Payments are to begin on March 1, so interest must be paid on the $500,000 to the end of January at the closing. The existing loan on Douglas Manor is $300,000 and is paid up to the end of December 1980.

Conditions in the transaction requiring noncash buyer-seller adjustments are as follows:

1. Cleaning supplies on hand worth $1,800 are taken over by the buyer.
2. Wendy Welloff holds $7,040 as security deposits of tenants. As the new owners, the Investors will be liable for repayment of these deposits as tenants leave.
3. Property taxes of $12,000 were paid for 1980. This amount is not expected to change for 1981.
4. A payment of $1,800 was paid as a 1-year hazard insurance premium for coverage to November 30, 1981. Buyer is agreeable to taking an assignment of the protection under the policy.
5. All rents for January 1981, totaling $8,400, are collected prior to closing.
6. Water and sewer charges run $288 per quarter for Douglas Manor, which amount is not payable until the end of the quarter.

Costs to the Investors in obtaining the loan include the following:

1. A lender's title policy from Hifidelity Title Co. costing $420 as a rider or addendum to the owners' title policy provided by the seller
2. A fee of $700 payable to Allen Measure for a market value appraisal of Douglas Manor
3. A credit report, required by Urbandale Savings and Loan, and costing $40, provided by the Rustic County Credit Bureau
4. A $100 fee payable to Howard Light, attorney, for looking over the title and loan documents and drawing up the mortgage and note for the lender

Other third-party costs payable by the buyer and/or seller in the closing costs are as follows:

1. Brokerage commission of $27,600 is payable by the seller to Everready Realty Co.
2. Escrow closing costs of $420 is to be shared equally.
3. Owner's title policy, provided by Hifidelity Title Co., for $1,680 is payable by the seller.

4. Buyer has Michael Sharpe, of Sharpe and Brilliant, attorneys, look over the title and loan papers, at a fee of $180.
5. Rustic County charges $4 to record seller's mortgage satisfaction for paying off exising loan. The county charges buyer $16 for recording the deed and mortgage lien papers.

Summary statements. Figures 9–4 and 9–5 summarize the necessary adjustments and prorations for the data presented.

TITLE CONVEYANCE

Assuming that all necessary payments are made, title is conveyed by delivery of a deed. In an escrow closing, title passes upon performance of all conditions in the escrow agreement, upon recording and delivery of the deed.

A grantor must be legally competent at the time of deed execution to legally convey title. Competency includes being of legal age and acting voluntarily and intentionally, with understanding.

All rights of the grantor cease upon delivery of the deed and conveyance of title. The closing or settlement statement becomes the buyer's and seller's permanent record of the transaction.

FIGURE 9–5.
Seller's closing statement or summary of seller's transaction

	DEBITS/ CREDITS	*CREDITS*
Contract sales price		$640,000
Buyer-seller adjustments		
Supplies on hand		1,800
Tenant security deposits	$7,040	
Property taxes (1/1–1/15/81)	500	
Prepaid insurance (1/16–11/30/81)		1,575
Prepaid rents	4,200	
Water/sewer charges	48	
Loan charges		
1st Nat'l., Rustic Co. payoff bal.	300,000	
Accrued int.	1,125	
Other settlement charges		
Everready Realty, commission	27,600	
Hifidelity Escrow Co., fee	210	
Hifidelity Title Insurance, fee	1,680	
Tangle and Webb, attorney, fee	250	
Rustic Co, recording fee	4	
Subtotals	$342,657	$643,375
Cash/check payout to seller	30,718	
Totals (must balance)	$643,375	$643,375

SUMMARY

Understanding closing procedures and settlement statements is advantageous for investors as well as for brokerage personnel. Preliminary requirements to an income property closing may very likely include a property survey and inspection, a title search and report, with subsequent removal of encumbrances, and an arrangement of financing. Instruments likely to be required at closing include an abstract of title, a deed, a mortgage or trust deed and a promissory note, and a title insurance policy or certificate of title.

Major types of closing costs include (1) title assurance charges and fees, (2) loan-related charges and fees, (3) other third-party charges and fees, such as brokerage and escrow fees, and (4) buyer-seller charges and adjustments, such as property taxes, hazard insurance, and fuel on hand. Closing costs typically range from 4 to 8 percent of the sale price.

A seller is generally responsible for the day of closing insofar as proration of charges for such things as taxes, hazard insurance premiums, or interest on loans is concerned. Direct-entry buyer-seller adjustments require no proration; examples are sale price, earnest money deposits, remaining balance of mortgage, and fuel on hand.

An escrow closing means that a neutral third party conducts the settlement to ensure that all acts or conditions of the contractual agreement are performed or satisfied. Costs of escrow are usually shared equally between a buyer and seller.

QUESTIONS FOR REVIEW AND DISCUSSION

1. Explain the nature and importance of (a) survey and inspections, (b) title search and report, and (c) the acceptance or removal of encumbrances to the title closing process.
2. List and briefly explain four classes of costs and adjustments in a title closing.
3. List and explain four rules of prorating.
4. Identify two buyer and two seller closing statement entries that do not involve proration.
5. Name two buyer and two seller closing statement entries that involve proration and discuss the nature of each briefly.
6. All closings should be in escrow, by law. Discuss.
7. An escrow agent is apparently an agent of both the buyer and the seller. What are the implications of such a role? Discuss.
8. Discuss the advantages of a closing's being handled by each of the following, from a buyer's point of view and from a seller's:
   a. Attorney
   b. Lender
   c. Broker
   d. Escrow agent

CASE PROBLEMS

1. Property taxes of $19,200 are payable for the current year. Closing is to be on November 10. Calculate the amount of the adjustment and indicate whether the buyer or seller gets the credit.
2. A 1-year hazard insurance premium of $660 provides coverage to April 15 of next year. Calculate the amount of the adjustment for a November 10 closing and indicate whether the buyer or the seller gets the credit.
3. Snuffy Smith, a building contractor, listed a four-unit apartment building that he was about to complete for sale on October 15, 1983 with the Red Hot Realty Company for $160,000. A commission rate of 5 percent on the first $100,000 and 3 percent on anything in excess of $100,000 was agreed upon in the listing contract. Dr. and Mrs. I. M. Rich agreed to purchase the property for $150,000, with a stipulation for an escrow closing as of April 30, 1984. Their offer was conditional upon their getting a new first mortgage for $120,000 at an interest rate of 12 percent, or less, compounded monthly, with amortization over 30 years. A loan at exactly these terms was obtained from the Ace S&L Association. A 10 percent earnest money deposit was submitted with their offer to purchase.

   Mr. U. R. Wise contracted to act as escrow agent for the closing. Adjustments required of Mr. Wise are as follows:

   (1) Premium for title insurance, $300.
   (2) Mr. Smith's construction loan was for $100,000, at 12 percent, with interest payments of $1,000 being required on the last day of each month. His last payment was made on March 31, 1984.
   (3) Taxes for 1984 are expected to be $3,000, a figure agreed to by both parties. Being new, the property was not taxed as a fully completed property in 1983.
   (4) All four units are rented as follows:
   (a) Lower 1: $400 per month, paid 4/7/84 for April
   (b) Lower 2: $400 per month, unpaid for April
   (c) Upper 1: $450 per month, unpaid for April
   (d) Upper 2: $450 per month, paid 4/2/84 for April
   (5) Escrow fee is one-half of 1 percent, all payable by the buyers because they insisted on an escrow closing.
   (6) Some yard improvements are to be made later in the spring. All parties agree that $2,200, left in escrow, would ensure completion.
   (7) Fuel oil of 840 gallons is on hand at 90 cents per gallon.
   (8) Hazard insurance was prepaid for 3 years, with $1,080 premium paid to run from September 21, 1983.
   (9) A part-time custodian cares for the property for $8.00 per day. He has not been paid for April.
   (10) A mortgage satisfaction recording fee of $8.00 must be paid.
   (11) Legal fee for drawing up deed to convey title is $50.00.
   (12) Cleaning supplies on hand, to be taken over by buyer, are valued at $210.

   a. Prepare a buyer's closing statement. (Additional amount to be paid by Dr. and Mrs. Rich, including escrow fee, is $17,186.)
   b. Prepare a seller's closing statement. (Amount to be paid to Snuffy Smith upon closing, after paying commission, is $42,618.)

CHAPTER TEN

LONG-RUN TRENDS AFFECTING THE CLIMATE FOR REAL ESTATE INVESTMENT

You won't have any trouble in your country as long as you have few people and much land,
but when you have many people and little land,
your trials will begin.
THOMAS CARLYLE, 1851

IMPORTANT TOPICS OR DECISION AREAS COVERED IN THIS CHAPTER

- Three Categories of Forces
- Physical and Biological Trends
- Economic Trends
- Institutional Trends

Fixity means that demand must come to each parcel of real estate. Fixity also means that the environment—the investment climate—around each parcel greatly influences its use and value. In this chapter, we take up the forces and trends that make up the real estate investment climate. The relative importance of each of the many forces is not easily determined; yet knowing about them should enable a person to make better investment decisions.

KEY CONCEPTS INTRODUCED IN THIS CHAPTER

Consumer choices
Consumer price index
Demography
Economic forces
Economics
Force
Gross national product
Institution
Institutional forces
Labor specialization
Opportunity cost
Personal income
Political force
POSSLQ
Social force

THREE CATEGORIES OF FORCES

For convenience in discussion and analysis, forces causing change in the use and value of real estate are traditionally classified as (1) physical and biological, (2) economic, and (3) institutional. These forces sometimes complement each other and sometimes offset each other. The net result of all these forces determines the direction and extent of change. Items making up these forces are summarized in Figure 10–1.

A *force* is an influence for change. In science, a force is considered to involve a certain magnitude of energy and direction. Gravity is a physical force pulling us toward the center of the earth, for example. When forces complement each other, they increase the influence or energy for change in a certain direction. When forces offset each other, a situation of stability, of little or no change, may result.

Physical and biological forces include the natural environment in which we live, the nature and characteristics of the various resources with which we work, and living organisms, including humankind. Land provides the physical support, the site for the activities of humans and animals. The earth, land, and water provide the raw materials (minerals, fuels, soil, climate, and so on) for our activities. The earth is, therefore, the physical setting or stage. Living organisms (humans, animals, plants, bacteria) are the players that interact on this stage.

Economic forces include the market and pricing system that allocates resources to various uses. Price usually means money, dollars, or some other monetary unit, paid or bid for something, such as the price of a house. But price also has a broader meaning, namely, opportunity cost.

FIGURE 10–1
Factors and forces influencing the development and use of realty

CATEGORY OF INFLUENCE	LEVEL OF INFLUENCE		
	NATIONAL AND INTERNATIONAL	REGIONAL	LOCAL
Physical and biological	Population	Population (natural increase and migration)	Population (natural increase and migration); age-sex distribution
	Natural resources (minerals, soils, climate, water, topography)	Resource distribution	Specific natural resources (soils, minerals, terrain)
	World locations for trade and commerce	Location relative to raw materials and markets	Location relative to raw materials and markets; fabricated structures/ constraints
Economic	Gross national product		
	Personal income		Personal income
	Employment and unemployment		Employment and unemployment
	Price levels (CPI)		Price levels (CPI)
	Money and credit (financial systems)		
Institutional Political	Federal powers and legislation	State powers and legislation	Local govermental powers and legislation
Religious Tradition, custom, and beliefs	Work ethic; attitude toward education		Attitude toward education; attitude toward architecture; chance

Opportunity cost is the value of what is given up in making a choice, as in trading a one-family house for a condominium.

Rational decision makers seek to maximize benefits and minimize costs in making choices. Consider, then, that raw materials, goods, and services can be used in only one way at any one time. For example, lumber to build a house cannot also serve as kindling wood. In a parallel, a person is not likely to maximize benefits by trying to be a medical doctor, an airline pilot, and a professional clown all at the same time. Likewise, raw materials of a country may be left in the ground, used to produce tractors and cars, or used to produce tanks for war. Thus even in a warlike nation, which decrees production of tanks, or in a primitive coutry, which leaves resources in the earth, costs or forgone opportunities are incurred. Thus, economics or a pricing system operates explicitly or implicitly.

Our third category, *institutional forces*, includes our culture, beliefs, religion, educational system, organizations, technology, and politics. Tradition, laws, governmental systems, and habitual ways of thinking are also included. In effect, institutional forces reflect the collective conditioning and ways of acting of people in a society. Thus our use of land in the United States, with our emphasis on manufacturing and trade, on wide use of the automobile, and on living in single-family dwelling units differs appreciably from the use of land in India, Hong Kong, or Ethiopia.

All factors or influences affecting real estate are included in these three categories. The forces continually interact. All must be understood and taken into account to achieve optimum decisions relative to the use of realty.

These many forces—physical, economic, and institutional—vary in the level at which their influence is exerted. Some are strongest at the national level, some at the local level. The approach taken here is to go from the general or national level to the specific or local level in discussing them.

Nationally, factors and forces of change affect real estate in only a general or nonspecific way. That is, we have national population, resources, production, income, and traditions. But these are seldom tied or linked directly to a specific parcel of land, except for federal government decisions pertaining to dams, military bases, national parks, and the like. In fact, national data are probably best viewed as the aggregate of many local events or activities. U.S. population, oil reserves, or gross national product are examples. Even so, national data are important in providing an overview for a real estate analyst or investor.

PHYSICAL AND BIOLOGICAL TRENDS

Population is the basic biological statistic at the national, regional, and local levels. The relative abundance and availability of natural resources constitute the major physical concern of most countries and communities. Location for production or trade is also a physical consideration. Population is more easily defined and interpreted than are resources or location and is, therefore, taken up first.

Population

U.S. demographic trends. The study of population characteristics and patterns is called *demography*. People—the population—serve as the interpreters and carriers of physical, economic, and institutional forces. In other words, the attitudes, motivations, and actions of people give life to the forces. What, then, are the U.S. population trends and characteristics?

The U.S. population was 76.0 million in 1900, 151.7 million in 1950, and 226.5 million in 1980. By the year 2000, we are projected to have a population of about 250 million, with a gradual leveling off thereafter at about 310 million by the year 2050. Figure 10–2 shows U.S. population projections to the year 2050.

The annual rate of increase to the end of the century, based on this projection, is about 0.6 percent. The annual rate of increase to the year 2030 is about 0.5 percent. From 1900 to 1970, our historical rate of increase was about 1.4 percent per year. A major reason for the declining rate is the increasing acceptance of the zero population growth (ZPG) concept. Reasons for the ZPG perspective include concern about running out of resources necessary to maintain our standard of living and the desire by individuals for personal freedom of choice in selecting a life-style.

Much of the current population increase comes from greater longevity. Average life expectancy at birth in the United States in 1976 was 72.8 years, that is, 69.0 years for males and 76.7 years for females. In 1900, average life expectancy at birth equaled 47.3 years. By 1920, average life expectancy at birth had increased to 54.1 years, with little difference between males and females. Average life expectancy increased rapidly to 68.2 years by 1950 but since has increased only by about 1 year per

FIGURE 10–2
U.S. population projections, 1975–2050

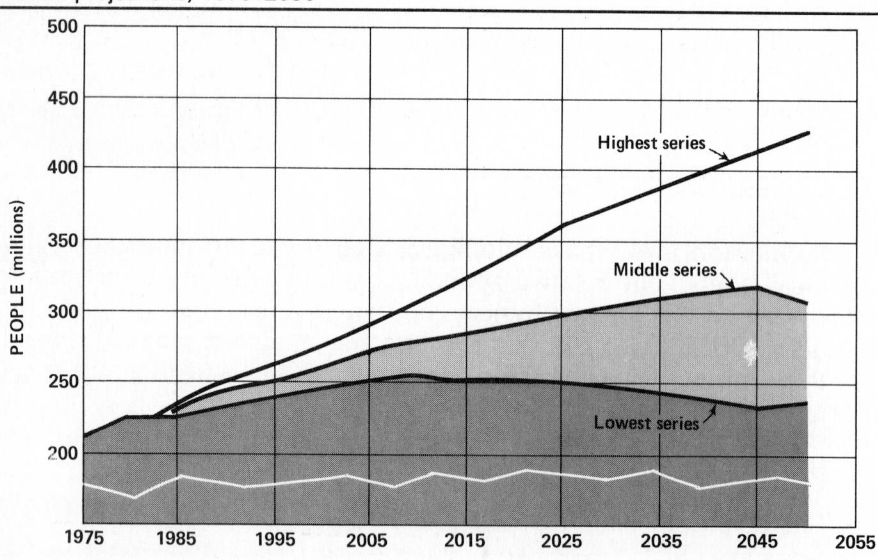

SOURCE: Bureau of the Census, *Population Estimates and Projections*, Series p. 25, no. 922, October 1982, Table 1.

decade. The result of greater life expectancy is an increase in the median age of our population. In 1900, the median age was 22.9 years and in 1950, it was 29.6 years. The baby boom following World War II caused this median age to dip to 28.0 years in 1970. But as these people mature, the median age is again expected to advance, reaching 30.1 in 1980 and 35.4 by 2000.

A direct relationship exists between population trends and real estate values. An increasing population means increased demand for real estate services and, in turn, higher values, other things being equal. A declining population has the opposite effect. Of course, other things usually are not equal. For example, on a national level, the thrust toward ZPG has several implications for real estate. First, even as the population stabilizes, per capita income is likely to continue increasing. Therefore, higher-quality space is likely to be demanded. With a stable population, pressures on resources and the environment will probably ease, meaning less air, water, and noise pollution. With an older and less venturesome population, lakes, waterways, hiking trails, ski slopes, and wilderness areas are likely to be less congested. At the same time, increased rehabilitation and redevelopment of existing urban areas will remain important because they exist at generally optimal locations and represent substantial investment in place.

Some new urban development will be necessary. As shown in Figure 10–3, dwelling units increased from 15.96 million in 1900 to 88.41 million in 1980. Our population in 1980 was 226.5 million, meaning that the number of persons per dwelling unit declined to 2.56. More people were living alone or in small households. In fact, from 1970 to 1980, the increase in dwelling units exceeded our population growth. Increasingly, dwelling units are occupied by two persons of the opposite sex sharing living quarters,' termed *POSSLQs* by the Census Bureau.

FIGURE 10–3
Total dwelling units in the United States, selected years, 1900–1980

YEAR	*POPULATION (MILLIONS)*	*DWELLING UNITS (MILLIONS)*	*POPULATION PER DWELLING UNIT*
1900	76.2	15,964	4.77
1910	92.2	20,256	4.55
1920	106.0	24.352	4.35
1930	123.2	29,905	4.12
1940	132.2	34,855	3.79
1950	151.3	42,826	3.53
1960	179.3	53,024	3.38
1970	203.2	63,450	3.20
1980	226.5	88,413	2.56

SOURCE: U.S. Department of Commerce Bureau of the Census, *Population Series Reports*, 1960, 1970, and 1980; and Census of Housing, 1980.

Population distribution. In 1980, 73.7 percent of the U.S. population lived in urban areas according to the *U. S. Statistical Abstract.* This is up sharply from 64.0 percent in 1950 and 39.7 percent in 1900.

By way of comparison, using comparative international statistics as reported in table 1505 of the *1984 Statistical Abstract of the United States,* 77.0 percent of the population of England (United Kingdom) and 76.0 percent of the population of West Germany are urbanized, whereas Russia is only 64.0 percent urbanized. Australia, a large country relative to its nearly 15.3 million, is the most highly urbanized country at 86.0 percent. China, on the other hand, with an estimated population of just over one billion people in 1982, is only 21.0 percent urbanized; and India, with an estimated 1980 population of 685 million people, is only 23.0 percent urbanized. While some differences in the definition of urban may be involved in these figures, it is clear that high population concentration count does not directly translate into high percentages of urbanization.

In regional terms, the distribution of our population shows a steady shift toward the West. See Figure 10–4. The Pacific states grew at a much more rapid rate than other areas, for a much larger share of total U.S. population. A less obvious tendency has been for the south Atlantic states to grow at a steady rate. These shifts are the result of people following the sun for economic opportunity and for life style.

Also, the increasing median age of our population has migrational implications. Elderly people increasingly demand retirement areas with mild climate, and thus, with housing, heating and clothing costs at a minimum. During the past decades, states such as California, Arizona, New Mexico, Texas, and Florida experienced extraordinary population gains, and consequently increased real estate market activity.

Natural Resources

Natural resources, or the lack of them, greatly influence the nature and extent of a country's development. Population, minerals, oil, water, location and complementary soils, terrain, and climate are all natural resources, and all are needed for balanced development of a country. Large countries, which are more likely to have all the basic ingredients, are, therefore, more likely to be world powers. The United States, Russia, and China are examples. Brazil, Canada, and Australia, while roughly equal in area, lack friendly climates and hence do not qualify as world powers. Japan and England are excellent examples of countries that have exploited advantageous locations for trade to have a considerable influence in world affairs. OPEC countries have exploited oil reserves to achieve power. And, of course, inadequacy of oil reserves has hurt the U.S. position of leadership in the world.

The lack of a balance of resources in some parts of the United States results in an uneven pattern of development. Thus the prairie states and

FIGURE 10–4
Population of United States by region, 1900, 1950, and 1980

	1900		*1950*		*1980*	
	POPULATION (THOUSANDS)	*% OF TOTAL*	*POPULATION (THOUSANDS)*	*% OF TOTAL*	*POPULATION (THOUSANDS)*	*% OF TOTAL*
United States	76,212	100.0%	151,326	100.0%	226,546	100.0%
Northeast	21,047	27.6	39,478	26.1	49,135	21.7
New England	5,592	7.3	9,314	6.2	12,348	5.5
Middle Atlantic	15,455	20.3	30,164	19.9	36,787	16.2
North Central	26,333	34.6	44,461	29.4	58,866	26.0
East North Central	15,986	21.0	30,399	20.1	41,682	18.4
West North Central	10,347	13.6	14,061	9.3	17,183	7.6
South	24,524	32.2	47,197	31.2	75,372	33.3
South Atlantic	10,443	13.7	21,182	14.0	36,959	16.3
East South Central	7,548	9.9	11,477	7.6	14,666	6.5
West South Central	6,533	8.6	14,538	9.6	23,747	10.5
West	4,309	5.7	20,190	13.3	43,172	19.1
Mountain	1,675	2.2	5,075	3.4	11,373	5.0
Pacific	2,634	3.5	15,115	10.0	31,800	14.0

*Numbers are sometimes slightly inconsistent because of rounding.

SOURCE: 1980 Census population, *Number of Inhabitants: United States Summary,* Table 8.

the mountain states of the West are less densely populated than are our eastern states. This means that resources become forces affecting the development and value of real estate only through the decisions and actions of people. On the other hand, little happens in an area unless resources are present.

ECONOMIC TRENDS

Economics is often defined as the allocation of limited resources to satisfy human needs and wants. Economic forces or adjustments are generated by humankind's efforts to maximize benefits in the uses of these limited resources. The resources may be water, oil, minerals, or land.

Real estate prices and values, real estate sales activity, and construction and developmental activity are directly influenced by the pace of economic activity and the sense of economic well-being at both the local and national levels. However, economic forces leading to this economic activity and sense of well-being cannot be observed or measured directly. Thus, an analyst or investor must look to economic statistics that measure the results of these economic forces. This section, therefore, has three divisions. The first identifies and discusses several of the more important and more enduring economic forces. The second concerns common and important measures of our national economic activity. The third takes up national economic indicators. Even so, not all measures of economic activity or all economic forces are covered in this discussion.

Economic Forces

The basic economic force, self-interest, motivates people to try to achieve the highest possible standard of living. Self-interest is also reflected in business decisions to maximize profits or wealth. It follows that both individuals and businesses tend to minimize transportation costs in the movement of people and goods.

In a more specific sense, what are economic forces? One study isolated four basic forces that lead to economic growth and regional change.[1] These are (1) technological change, (2) resources and their changing availability, (3) organizational change, and (4) shifting consumer choices.

Technological change. New technology has probably caused more change than has any other social, economic, or political force over the centuries. New technology accounts for "advances" in the art of war from sticks and stones to spears and arrows to rifles and cannons to tanks and planes to rockets and nuclear bombs. Likewise technology has advanced the peace-

---

[1] *Regions, Resources, and Economic Growth* by Harvey S. Perloff, Edgar S. Dunn, Jr., Eric E. Lampard, and Richard F. Muth (Baltimore, Md.: Resources for the Future, 1960).

time pursuits of human beings. Since 1900, the tractor has replaced the horse in agriculture. Commercial fertilizers are now widely used. The result is that whereas perhaps 5 or 10 percent of our population once lived in urban areas, now over 75 percent live in urban areas. In transportation, the progression has been from walking to horse-drawn carriages to autos, trains, and trucks to airplanes. In communications, the progression includes the telephone, radio, and television. Similarly, computers and calculators are strongly influencing information processing and analysis. And in construction, two major innovations have been structural steel and elevators to make skyscrapers possible.

Resources and their distribution. Resource availability goes hand in hand with technological change in determining where and how people live. With the Industrial Revolution, energy sources—water power, wood, coal, oil and gas, and eventually uranium for nuclear power—became critical to maintaining a desired standard of living. Likewise, minerals and other raw materials—iron, copper, gold, diamonds, salt, sulphur, phosphorus, and rare metals—were needed. The pattern became established. More resources and better technology meant more freedom and easier living. More freedom and easier living permitted more time to seek new resources and create new inventions. The result of this circular process is that people can locate almost anywhere in the world at a living standard well above any known in the past.

Organizational change. Organizational change, like technological change, helps to increase economic output per individual. The cost for any one person to manufacture a car or dishwasher or book would be extremely high, if indeed, one person could do the job. Yet, with labor specialization and mass production, these and many other products are available at a relatively low cost. Other examples of organizational change include supermarkets in place of corner groceries, corporations in place of sole proprietorships for businesses, and freeways in place of many local streets.

Shifting consumer choices. Change in what people eat and wear, where they live, and how they travel affect economic output and the regional distribution of economic opportunity. People can eat and wear only so much. Consequently, as a family's income increases, an increasing proportion of its income is spent on autos, recreation, and travel, whereas a smaller proportion is spent on food and clothing. Also, higher family income usually means more meat and fewer potatoes being eaten. That is, high-quality foods replace lower-quality foods; this type of shift directly affects what farmers produce and how they use their land. And, as an example of the interaction of the forces being discussed, an increasing proportion of our population prefers to work in Sun Belt states. Higher incomes also mean that people prefer to travel by auto and plane rather than by train or bus. Each shift in consumer choice, with higher incomes, means a higher level of social and economic well-being, that is, greater satisfaction of personal interest.

Measures of Economic Activity

Economic forces are difficult, if not impossible, to measure directly, even though they exert their influence anywhere people live. Thus, we resort to measures of economic activity. The most common and most important measures at the national level are (1) gross national products (GNP), (2) employment and unemployment, (3) consumer price index (CPI), and (4) personal income per capita. Statistics for these measures may be compared from one time period to another and, except for GNP, for one community or area to another at both regional and local levels. Figure 10–5 contains these statistics for the U.S. Each of these statistics may be integrated into the analysis for a specific community and/or property.

The Statistical Abstract of the United States, the *Survey of Current Business*, and the *Economic Report of the President* are reliable sources of national economic statistics. *The Statistical Abstract* contains an extensive appendix, "Guide to Sources of Statistics," which an analyst/investor might use to compile regional and local social and economic data. One section of this appendix, "Guide to State Statistical Abstracts," is a valuable source of state and local statistical data. Finally, most Standard Metropolitan Statistical Areas (SMSAs) have branch offices of the U.S. Department of Labor. These branch offices, listed in local telephone directories, readily provide data on employment and unemployment. Local economic conditions may easily be monitored based on varying levels of employment and per capita income.

Gross national product. *Gross national product* is the grand measure of economic activity. GNP aggregates, in dollars, the value of all goods and services produced in the United States for a year at current market prices. Thus, GNP measures the annual output attributable to the factors of production (land, labor, capital, and management) provided by residents of the United States. GNP includes the imputed rental value of owner-occupied dwellings plus allowances for depreciation. Using 1950 as a base, GNP increased fivefold during the 25 years to 1975. This steep surge includes rising prices caused by inflation as well as increased output.

Among other things, GNP tells us how well we are doing as a country, in economic terms, relative to our potential. Figure 10–6 shows this relationship in terms of 1972 constant dollars.

Employment and unemployment. A very sensitive measure of economic well-being is employment and unemployment. Unemployment is directly related to mortgage foreclosures and property tax delinquencies, as might be expected. People without jobs and earnings probably use any income they get (unemployment compensation, welfare) for food and clothing

FIGURE 10–5
Selected U.S. economic statistics, selected years 1950–1983

*YEAR**	*POPULATION (MILLIONS)*	*GROSS NATIONAL PRODUCT (BILLIONS)*	*PER CAPITA PERSONAL INCOME*	*PER CAPITA DISPOSABLE PERSONAL INCOME*	*CONSUMER PRICE INDEX (1967 = 100)*	*EMPLOYED (MILLIONS)*	*UN-EMPLOYED (MILLIONS)*	*PER-CENTAGE UN-EMPLOYED*
1950	151.7	$ 286.2	$ 1,491	$ 1,355	72.1	58.9	3.3	5.3%
1955		399.3	1,868	1,654	80.2	62.2	2.9	4.4
1960	179.3	506.0	2,212	1,934	88.7	65.8	3.9	5.5
1965		688.1	2,764	2,430	94.5	71.1	3.4	5.5
1970	203.2	982.4	3,911	3,348	116.3	78.6	4.1	4.9
1975	213.6	1,578.8	5,832	5,088	161.2	85.8	7.9	8.5
1980	226.5	2,631.7	9,503	8,032	246.8	99.3	7.6	7.1
1983[p]	234.2	3,309.5	11,707	9,968	298.4	100.8	10.7	9.6

*Unadjusted dollars.

[p]Data for 1983 estimated or based on latest figures available.

SOURCE: *Economic Report of the President, Statistical Abstract of the United States,* 1984, and latest Federal Reserve Bulletins

first, just to survive. Outlays for shelter have a lower priority, hence the higher foreclosures and delinquency rates.

Employed persons and unemployed persons, taken together, make up the labor force. *Employed* includes all persons working for pay or profit and all persons temporarily not working for pay or profit for noneconomic reasons (illness, bad weather, vacation, and labor-management disputes). *Unemployed* means all persons not working who made specific efforts to find a job in the previous month (such as applying for work with an employer or a public employment service) and who are currently available for work.

The number of employed gives hard evidence of growth trends and the economic health of an economy. For example, in 1983, 100.8 million people were employed in the United States and another 10.7 million were unemployed. The unemployment rate of 9.6 percent is high compared with a rate historically around 5 to 5.5 percent in the 1960s and early 1970s. The economic health of the United States was not very good in 1983. Thus it is no surprise that Figure 10–6 shows our actual GNP to be well below our potential or forecast GNP.

Local employment trends and projections closely affect population levels and potential demand for realty. For instance, in 1970, 38.7 percent of the total population in the United States was employed (78.6 ÷ 203.2 = 38.7%). Assuming a comparable ratio in 1980, the total popula-

FIGURE 10–6
U.S. Gross National Product, trend and forecasted, 1974–1988

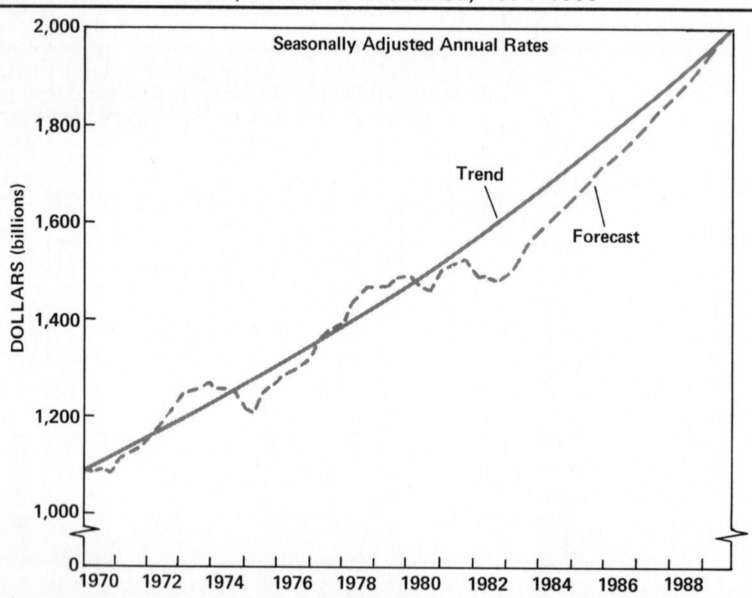

SOURCE: *Economic Report of the President, 1984*, p. 200.

tion in 1980 would approach 256.6 million; and 256.6 million people, at the 1970 figure of 3.2 persons per dwelling unit, means that 80.2 million dwelling units would be demanded to 1980, an increase of 16.7 million over 1970. And with greater demand, values go up and new construction is warranted. Actually, density per dwelling unit dropped, and 25 million units were added to our supply during the 1970's.

Per capita personal income. Personal income, as defined for national income accounting purposes, is the current income received by persons from all sources with contributions for social insurance (primarily social security) removed. Total personal income is an aggregate figure that is not directly useful for comparative purposes because communities vary in size. Thus, to say that community A, with 10,200 people, had total personal income of $61.2 million in 1975 has limited meaning when compared with community B, with a population of 78,600, and the total personal income of $393 million. But to say that in 1980 per capita income in community A was $10,000 and in community B was $8,000 is a useful comparison. Also, to say that per capita income in community A increased from $1,500 in 1950 to $10,000 in 1980 provides useful information.

Per capita personal income in the United States in 1983 was $11,707. Figure 10–7 shows regional per capita income for selected years from 1970. Disposable per capita income is an alternative measure of per capita income, adjusted for payments to governments, primarily taxes. Disposable personal income (DPI) is money that people may either spend or

FIGURE 10–7
Per capita income and ratio to U.S. per capita income, by region, for 1970, 1980, and 1982

	1970		*1980*		*1982*	
	AMOUNT (dollars)	*RATIO TO U.S. TOTAL*	*AMOUNT (dollars)*	*RATIO TO U.S. TOTAL*	*AMOUNT (dollars)*	*RATIO TO U.S. TOTAL*
United States	$3,893	100.0%	$9,503	100%	$11,107	100%
Northeast						
New England	4,245	109.0	9,989	105	11,916	107
Middle Atlantic	4,390	112.8	10,133	107	12,034	108
North Central						
East North Central	4,050	104.0	9,734	102	11,055	100
West North Central	3,657	93.9	9,234	97	10,789	97
South						
South Atlantic	3,562	91.5	8,786	92	10,376	93
East South Central	2,936	75.4	7,441	78	8,650	78
West South Central	3,323	85.4	9,086	96	10,938	98
West						
Mountain	3,557	91.4	9,010	95	10,528	95
Pacific	4,317	110.9	10,701	113	12,280	111

SOURCE: *Statistical Abstract of the United States, 1976*, Table 644; and *Survey of Current Business*, August 1983, Table 1.

save, at their discretion. Per capital disposable income increased almost five times between 1950 and 1978, going from $1,355 to $6,640.

Consumer price index. The *consumer price index (CPI)* measures changes in the cost of living, and therefore serves as a measure of inflation. The CPI does not measure changes in the total amount spent for living, however.

The consumer price index is based on the average change in prices or approximately 400 items of consumer goods and services purchased in urban areas. The index has several components: food, shelter, fuel oil and coal, apparel, transportation, and medical care. It is also broken down to all commodities and all services. The cost of shelter may thus be compared from one time period to another for a community under analysis to determine trends. The CPI given in Figure 10–5 is for all items.

The consumer price index may be used to determine changes from one time to another in real or constant terms. For example, U.S. per capita disposable personal income was $1,355 in 1950 and $8,032 in 1980. Dividing both figures by their respective consumer price indexes gives $1,879 in 1950 and $3,254 in 1980. Thus, per capita DPI increased by 73 percent during those 30 years in real terms. In other words, it might be said that the standard of living improved by 73 percent during this period.

Regional per capita income. The Census Bureau publishes annual data on regional shifts in population, as shown in Figure 10–4. In a similar manner, the Bureau of Economic Analysis estimates and publishes data on regional shifts in personal income per capita; see Figures 10–7 and 10–8. The

FIGURE 10–8
U.S. per capita income, by state and region, 1959, 1969, 1980, and 1982.

	AMOUNT (dollars)				*PERCENTAGE NATIONAL AVERAGE*	
STATE AND REGION	*1959*	*1969*	*1980*	*1982*	*1959*	*1982*
United States	**2,160**	**3,714**	**9,503**	**11,107**	**100%**	**100%**
New England	**2,364**	**4,048**	**9,989**	**11,916**	**109**	**107**
Connecticut	2,781	4,664	11,536	13,748	129	124
Maine	1,802	3,040	7,672	9,042	83	81
Massachusetts	2,378	4,073	10,089	12,088	110	109
New Hampshire	2,083	3,589	9,010	10,729	96	97
Rhode Island	2,139	3,690	9,174	10,723	99	97
Vermont	1,789	3,302	7,832	9,507	83	86
Mideast	**2,470**	**4,169**	**10,190**	**12,087**	**114**	**109**
Delaware	2,681	4,289	10,066	11,731	124	106
District of Columbia	2,741	4,434	12,296	14,550	127	131
Maryland	2,262	4,020	10,385	12,238	105	110
New Jersey	2,606	4,405	10,976	13,089	121	118
New York	2,630	4,408	10,283	12,314	122	111
Pennsylvania	2,190	3,684	9,389	10,955	101	99

FIGURE 10–8
U.S. per capita income, by state and region, 1959, 1969, 1980, and 1982.

STATE AND REGION	AMOUNT (dollars) 1959	1969	1980	1982	PERCENTAGE NATIONAL AVERAGE 1959	1982
Great Lakes	**2,320**	**3,930**	**9,734**	**11,055**	**107**	**100**
Illinois	2,584	4,287	10,471	12,100	120	109
Indiana	2,091	3,647	8,896	10,021	97	90
Michigan	2,269	3,970	9,872	10,956	105	99
Ohio	2,259	3,815	9,430	10,677	105	96
Wisconsin	2,162	3,564	9,347	10,774	100	97
Plains	**1,987**	**3,507**	**9,234**	**10,789**	**92**	**97**
Iowa	1,972	3,586	9,336	10,791	91	97
Kansas	2,062	3,523	9,942	11,765	95	106
Minnesota	2,005	3,636	9,688	11,175	93	101
Missouri	2,074	3,462	8,720	10,170	96	92
Nebraska	1,972	3,560	9,137	10,683	91	96
North Dakota	1,631	3,136	8,759	10,876	76	98
South Dakota	1,518	2,930	8,028	9,666	70	87
Southeast	**1,605**	**2,998**	**8,137**	**9,602**	**74**	**86**
Alabama	1,484	2,699	7,477	8,649	69	78
Arkansas	1,376	2,556	7,166	8,479	64	76
Florida	1,963	3,474	9,201	10,978	91	99
Georgia	1,620	3,107	8,061	9,583	75	86
Kentucky	1,563	2,878	7,648	8,934	72	80
Louisiana	1,647	2,854	8,525	10,231	76	92
Mississippi	1,215	2,339	6,680	7,778	56	70
North Carolina	1,543	2,999	7,753	9,044	71	81
South Carolina	1,358	2,756	7,298	8,502	63	77
Tennessee	1,556	2,896	7,662	8,906	72	80
Virginia	1,840	3,441	9,357	11,095	85	100
West Virginia	1,571	2,735	7,665	8,769	73	79
Southwest	**1,883**	**3,239**	**90,298**	**11,122**	**87**	**100**
Arizona	1,929	3,366	8,832	10,173	89	92
New Mexico	1,838	2,838	7,891	9,190	85	83
Oklahoma	1,804	3,085	9,187	11,370	84	102
Texas	1,901	3,292	9,538	11,419	88	103
Rocky Mountain	**2,048**	**3,303**	**9,092**	**10,754**	**95**	**97**
Colorado	2,201	3,569	10,042	12,302	102	111
Idaho	1,839	3,078	8,044	9,029	85	81
Montana	1,966	3,144	8,361	9,580	91	86
Utah	1,908	2,960	7,656	8,875	88	80
Wyoming	2,216	3,462	11,042	12,372	103	111
Far West	**2,570**	**4,181**	**10,689**	**12,238**	**119**	**110**
California	2,658	4,282	10,920	12,567	123	113
Nevada	2,653	4,335	10,761	11,981	123	108
Oregon	2,183	3,520	9,356	10,335	101	93
Washington	2,318	3,969	10,198	11,560	107	104
Alaska	2,422	4,253	12,916	16,257	112	146
Hawaii	2,103	4,191	10,222	11,652	97	105

SOURCE: *Survey of Current Business*, August 1983, Table 1.

combination of population and personal income trends tells much about what is likely to be happening to real estate in an area. That is, an area with sharp increases in population and personal income has greatly increased effective demand for real estate.

For example, Figures 10–4 and 10–7 show that the Pacific States (Washington, Oregon, California, Alaska, and Hawaii) have increased rapidly in both statistics since 1950. And these states have been growth areas for many years. Conversely, the West North Central States (Minnesota, Iowa, Missouri, North and South Dakota, Nebraska, and Kansas) increased only slightly in population and lag behind the U.S. total in per capita personal income growth. On a relative basis, these are slow-growth states. In turn, construction and real estate activity are probably not as strong as in many other states. Even so, urbanization trends may make real estate development and investment very attractive in some communities in the West North Central States.

National Economic Indicators

The data presented thus far are historical. The serious investor or analyst might find it advantageous to go an extra step—to consider national economic indicators and look into the future. It is the future that determines the success, or lack of success, of a real estate investment or development.

Figure 10–9 summarizes the national economic indicators by economic process and cyclical timing. Studies by the National Bureau of Economic Research (NBER) show that business and economic cycles vary in length and intensity. That is, they are not regular or rhythmic, so change cannot be anticipated with certainty. The cyclical indicators in Figure 10–9 have been singled out by the NBER as leaders, coinciders, or laggers, based on the general conformance to cyclical movements in general economic activity. The indicators are reported monthly in *Business Conditions Digest*, a publication of the U.S. Bureau of Economic Analysis.

INSTITUTIONAL TRENDS

An institution may be considered as an established arrangement or way of doing things. Being established, an institution may also be regarded as the influence of the past, and of other people, in defining "acceptable" action for individuals. Therefore, institutions provide structure for human activity. And institutions do change, though usually quite slowly.

An *institutional force* is the "influence" exerted through the acceptance by people of certain principles, laws, or beliefs. Real estate is owned and used in an environment containing numerous institutional forces, such as

FIGURE 10–9
U.S. economic indicators cross classified by economic process and cyclical timing.

ECONOMIC PROCESS	CYCLICAL TIMING		
	LEADING	ROUGHLY COINCIENT	LAGGING
Employment and unemployment	Average workweek, manufacturing New unemployment insurance claims, inverted	Nonfarm employment Unemployment, inverted	Long-duration unemployment, inverted
Production, income, consumption, and trade	New order, consumer goods, and materials*	Gross national product* Industrial production Personal income* Manufacturing and trade sales*	
Fixed capital investment	Formation of business enterprises Contracts and orders, plant and equipment* Building permits, housing		Investment expenditures, plant and equipment*
Inventories and inventory investment	Change in business inventories*		Business inventories*
Prices, costs, and profits	Industrial materials price index Stock price index Profits* Ratio, price-to-unit labor cost, nonfarm		Change in output per worker-hour, manufacturing inverted
Money and credit	Change, consumer installment debt*		Commercial and industrial loans outstanding Bank interest rates, business loans

*In constant prices.
SOURCE: National Bureau of Economic Research.

the law of property, land use controls, property taxation, accepted architectural styles, and the established use of the automobile for transportation. These forces may be generally subclassified as social and political/legal. Even so, they do not lend themselves to statistical measurement or presentation. Hence, our discussion must be of a slightly different nature than for economic forces.

Social Forces

A social force is the influence generated by the physical and psychological needs and desires of human beings. Beliefs, customs, and religion are social forces.

Many of our cities were initially laid out on a rectangular grid system; this customary way of laying out streets persisted for many decades even though other street systems would have been more suitable to accommodate to the hills, winding river valleys, and soil conditions encountered. Only since World War II have curvilinear streets, planned unit developments, and superblocks become acceptable.

Development and operation of real estate by religious bodies provided a focus for cities in Europe during the Middle Ages. Cathedrals and monasteries formed the nucleus of numerous communities. Prestige neighborhoods developed around the bishop's residence in the process, and the diocese was generally a stronger administrative unit at the time than were local and regional governments. Today, churches and most other religious facilities are exempt from property taxes. This tax-exempt status discourages the development and redevelopment of church-owned properties to what many people would consider their highest and best economic uses. The intrusion of church-owned properties into commercial areas often limits the development and growth of such areas also.

Religious beliefs affect the use of land indirectly also. One Hindu belief results in large local "sacred" populations of monkeys and cattle in India, which require space for living and feed. And consider the Christmas trees raised in the United States to help celebrate a religious season. Further, in some communities, taverns and nightclubs may not be located within certain distances, say, 300 feet, of a church, by local zoning ordinance.

Social forces tend to be more local and more informal in their operation than do political forces. Even so, social forces must sometimes be reckoned with by an investor. Neighborhood resistance to change has killed many an application for re-zoning that appeared economically justified.

Political Forces

Political forces, including laws, are the most obvious and probably the most significant of the institutional forces influencing our use of realty. A *political force* is an influence generated out of our efforts to organize and manage ourselves and others through government and laws. Political forces sometimes grow out of social and economic needs and wants (forces) and, therefore, represent the interaction of biological, economic, and institutional forces. For example, federal, state, and local elections reflect the competition for political power to write and/or enforce the rule or laws of our society. The winning party takes the lead in passing laws concerning energy, the environment, birth control, welfare programs, income taxes, and other current issues.

Political forces establish conditions, usually a stable environment, that social or economic forces cannot provide. For example, political forces bring about and maintain government and laws, thereby providing a setting of order and continuity for social and economic activities. Our system of private ownership of property, as opposed to state or federal ownership and control, is an another example of political/legal forces at work. Even so, these ownership rights are continually modified by legislative, executive, and judicial decisions and actions.

Governmental actions also constitute political forces. For example, the monetary policy and open market operations of the federal government directly affect real estate credit. Governmental tax policies—at the local, state, and federal levels—also impact real estate. On the other side, a governmental expenditure for a new highway, school, sanitary sewer line, urban renewal project, or dam definitely affect decisions by private investors.

Real estate regulation was almost entirely a matter of local concern until the 1930s. But lack of adequate housing and slums became recognized as a national problem. The Federal Housing Administration (FHA) and the Public Housing Administration (PHA) were created in a first effort to solve the situation.

World War II intervened, and finally, in 1949, a national housing act was passed that started an urban renewal program to assemble and clear slum lands for reuse. Also, city, urban, and regional planning programs were initiated about this time. All these programs helped, but urban and community and other real estate problems increased at a faster rate than they were solved by these acts and programs. During the 1950s, need for further federal legislation became apparent.

In the early 1960s, federal legislation providing for condominiums and real estate investment trusts, both new forms of ownership, was passed. By the late 1960s, environmental issues demanded attention; so the Environmental Protection Agency was created. In October 1973, the Organization of Petroleum Exporting Countries (OPEC) raised the price of oil from $2.25 to $11.00 per barrel to signal the world energy shortage. The federal Department of Energy (DOE) was created shortly thereafter.

What are some of the trends in legislation passed in the environment, energy, and housing areas in recent years?

Environment. The National Environmental Policy Act (NEPA) of 1969 (P.L. 91-190) easily dominates all environmental laws passed to date. Among other things, the act requires a detailed environmental impact statement on every major federal action that might significantly affect environmental quality. The statement must describe the environmental impact, and the unavoidable adverse effects, set forth and discuss alternatives and eventually resolve or reject the long-term, irreversible effects of the proposed action. Environmental impact studies are required of major private real estate developments as well. The act established the Environmental Protection Agency (EPA) as an enforcement authority.

Several acts complement the National Environmental Policy Act. These are the Clean Air Act of 1970 (P.L. 91-604), the Water Pollution Control Act of 1972 (P.L. 93-240), the Energy Supply and Environmental Coordination Act (P.L. 93-319), and the Coastal Zone Management Act (P.L. 92-583).

The purpose of the Clean Air Act is to establish acceptable national standards for air quality. The Energy Supply and Environmental Coordination Act provides for a review, before construction or development, of new sources of air pollution, including indirect sources. The two laws directly affect all real estate, particularly those uses or parcels emitting large amounts or high concentrations of pollutants. Indirect sources of pollution include shopping centers and airports, which while not emitting pollutants directly, attract producers of pollution, mainly cars. The Energy Supply and Environmental Coordination Act provides for transportation controls, such as bans on parking and limits or stoppage of auto use in urban area transportation patterns (central business districts) to reduce pollution.

The Water Pollution Control Act establishes water and sewage quality standards for citizen safety. The Coastal Zone Management Act calls for states to establish objectives, policies, and standards to guide public and private uses of land and waters in coastal areas. Salt-water and Great Lakes coasts are affected. The purpose is management, beneficial use, protection, and development of the land and waters of the nation's coastal zones.

Energy and Transportation

To date, not much energy legislation has been passed that directly affects realty. But some obvious conflicts with environmental goals and with owners' rights are apparent. For example, the federal strip-mining bill requires the owners of grazing rights on federal lands to give written consent before any underlying coal can be mined. This, of course, means that environmental quality has higher priority than does lower-cost energy. On the other hand, Congress set aside portions of the Environmental Protection Act to facilitate the construction of the Alaskan pipeline.

The energy shortage increases chances that private industry will get rights of eminent domain. By way of precedent, West Germany passed a Brown Coal Act in 1950 giving such right to mining firms. Under the act, a mining company must return land to its original condition, at its own expense, when the coal has been removed.

The Federal Energy Administration Act, as amended (P.L. 93-275) establishes and authorizes the Department of Energy to evaluate the nation's energy supplies and to take a wide range of actions to cope with energy shortages and pricing problems. The DOE's actions will have many significant implications for growth and location of economic activities in this country. Duties of the DOE include (1) administration of petroleum and gas distribution and consumption programs, (2) efforts to reduce demand for fuels and to increase fuel efficiency, (3) development of plans and programs to handle shortages in energy production, (4) promotion of stability in energy prices, and (5) development of strategy to reduce U.S. dependence on imported fuels (Project Independence). The impact of the act on real estate is likely to be mainly through locational economic effects.

Federal legislation concerning highways and mass transportation have great implications for real estate. Federal legislation provided for the planning, financing, and development of the Interstate Highway System. It also provided substantial financial support for the development and maintenance of a system of state roads and highways. Major items in the 1974 highway legislation (P.L. 93-643) include a uniform national speed limit of 55 miles per hour, bikeway demonstation programs, and stimulants for the organization of car pools.

A National Mass Transportation Act was also passed in 1974 (P.L. 93-503). The act increased financial assistance to urban mass transportation systems and provided for fare-free mass transportation demonstration projects. The act stipulates that "society depends on the provisions of efficient, economical, and convenient transportation within and between urban areas." With energy shortages imminent, revitalization of mass transporation systems seem critical to save fuel and to move people and goods rapidly and smoothly.

Most recently enacted transportation legislation concerns either energy conservation or preservation of environmental quality. Land use patterns of the future will reflect this shift in emphasis from "the auto is king" to "make way for mass transporation and car pools." Greater density of development should occur along main arteries where buses run or around stations on mass transit systems as a result of the shift. Also, the central business district should become more of a focal point for the community because most mass transportation lines run to, or through, the central area, making it the most accessible of all points in the community. The likely result, as usual, will be continued change in the patterns of land use.

Housing and Community Development

In 1949 Congress established as a national goal "a decent home and a suitable living environment for every American family." This goal has been the central theme of housing and community development legislation ever since. Housing and community development legislation calls for many changes and affects many areas at once. It is, therefore, the most important and the most wide-ranging of all federal laws affecting real estate and is often referred to as a form of omnibus legislation.

Seven specific objectives of housing and community development legislation are as follows:

1. Conserving and expanding the nation's housing stock
2. Using land and other national resources more rationally, including better arrangements of residential, commercial, industrial, recreational, and other land use activities.
3. Eliminating slums and blight and preventing the deterioration of property and facilities important to communities
4. Eliminating conditions detrimental to the public health, safety, and welfare through code enforcement, demolition, rehabilitation, and related activities
5. Expanding and improving the quantity and quality of community services that are designed principally for persons of low and moderate income
6. Reducing the isolation of various income groups within communities and geographical areas
7. Restoring and preserving properties of special value for historic, architectural, or aesthetic reasons

Typically, new or additional housing and community development legislation, in the form of a new federal act, is passed every two or three years. Specific information about these acts may be obtained from HUD field offices, which are located in most large metropolitan areas.

Political forces are usually not powerful at the regional level in that our political system is not organizaed on a regional basis. So, regional political forces exert energy at the national level or the state level. Political/legal forces may be extremely potent in their influence on real estate, however. We see this in property taxation, planning and zoning, rent controls, and eminent domain.

SUMMARY

Natural endowment and demand largely determine the use and value of real estate. A threefold framework—concerned with (1) physical and biological, (2) economic, and (3) institutional forces—is traditionally used in land economics to facilitate analysis of this demand and endowment. Physical and biological forces include land, land resources, and people. Economic forces are those created by our efforts to allocate limited resources for social and economic ends. An institutional force is created through people's acceptance of certain laws, principles, customs, or beliefs. Institutional forces may be subclassified as social or political/legal. A social force is generated by the physical and psychological needs of people. A political force is an influence generated out of people's efforts to organize and manage themselves, and others, through government and laws. These forces operate in the real estate market and are seldom found in the "pure" form.

QUESTIONS FOR REVIEW AND DISCUSSION

1. Identify and explain briefly the three components of the framework traditionally used for discussion and analysis in land economics.
2. What demographic characteristics are most important in relating population to real estate? Give examples.
3. Define economics. Give at least two examples of economic forces, and relate them to your definition of economics.
4. What is an institution? What are the two main categories of institutional forces? Give at least one example of each.
5. Define gross national product. What is the importance of GNP as a measure of economic activity?
6. Explain why personal income per capita is a better measure of local economic activity than is total personal income of the area.
7. Are levels of employment and unemployment related to GNP? Explain.
8. Basic economic forces are identified as (a) technological change, (b) changing availability of resources, (c) organizational change, and (d) shifting consumer choices. Are these forces likely to increase or decrease in strength in the years ahead? In what direction are they moving? Discuss.
9. The forces discussed in this chapter are said to make up the investment climate. Yet the forces cannot be directly related to any specific property. So are they useful and/ or important? Discuss.

CHAPTER ELEVEN
URBAN AREA STRUCTURE AND HIGHEST AND BEST USE

The test of a civilization is the power of drawing the most benefits out of its cities.
EMERSON, Journals, 1864.

IMPORTANT TOPICS OR DECISION AREAS COVERED IN THIS CHAPTER

- Urbanizing Forces
- Theories of Urban Growth
- Rent Theory and Urban Structure
- Determining Intensity of Improvement

Social, economic, and political forces interact with local physical characteristics to create functional areas, which are major components or building blocks of our urban areas. A *functional area* is a place where some specialized activity, for instance, manufacturing, is performed. Residential neighborhoods, commercial districts, and industrial districts are the most obvious examples of functional areas. Streets and other parts of our transportation system tie functional areas and specific land use activities together by facilitating movement of people and/or goods between them. Land use activities, functional areas, and the connecting transportation system, taken altogether, make up our urban areas.

Social, economic, and political forces influence where people live, play, work, and die because they push toward regional relocations and toward concentration or diffusion of human activity. An influence toward concentration of people, buildings, and machines is an *urbanizing force.* Manufacturing, trade, education, and government are prime examples of activities that are more advantageously carried on with people concentrated in one place. An influence toward scattering of people and activities is a *dispersing force.* Desire for isolation (e.g., a hermit) and the dispersion of Minuteman missiles for national defense are examples of these forces. Most economic, social, and political forces are urbanizing in their effect; hence, the long-term trend toward larger and larger cities.

Real estate, as a fixed physical asset, is highly dependent on its environment for value. The purpose of this chapter, therefore, is to look at the effect of these urbanizing forces on the nature and structure of our urban areas and on specific parcels of urban real estate. The physical, biological, economic, social, and political forces discussed in the previous chapter are, therefore, reconsidered here in regard to their influence on land use decisions at the local level.

KEY CONCEPTS INTRODUCED IN THIS CHAPTER

Comparative advantage
Concentric circle theory
Direction of least resistance
Dispersing force
Economic capacity of land
Economics of scale
Extensive margin
External economies of scale
Functional area
Intensity of use
Intensive margin
Internal economies of scale
Multiple nuclei theory
Proportionality, principle of
Rent
Rent triangle
Submarginal land
Urban infrastructure
Urbanizing force

URBANIZING FORCES

Most long-run trends in our society are urbanizing because they encourage concentration of activities. Because we are primarily interested in urban real estate, let us look at urbanizing forces in greater depth.

Components of Urbanizing Forces

History is filled with evidence of humankind's march toward urbanization. Manufacturing, trade, education, and government all benefit from a concentration of people and facilities.

Our early ancestors were hunters and nomads. They wandered about in response to the seasons, often with annual migrations. Gradually, they learned to harvest grains, berries, nuts, and other vegetation. With the shift to tilling the soil, they built permanent dwellings. Small villages developed as people banded together to share tools and benefit from mutual defense. Use of force to conquer and loot remained a way of life for many of the nomadic tribes.

Exchange, based on territorial specialization, soon became recognized as advantageous. Some areas had gold or silver to trade, other furs, other salt, others grain, and so forth. With trade, convenient transportation became advantageous. Settlements located near good harbors or on inland waterways tended to prosper most. Merchants found it more convenient to live near transport nodes, as did sailors. Inns or hotels and livery stables for traveling merchants prospered at these nodes. These strategic locations soon became important as military bases, particularly for the navy, and as political capitals. Specialization of labor, in manufacturing as well as in trade, soon developed, so productivity greatly increased. Individual skills increased as did the variety of manufactured products.

With modern modes of transportation (trains, automobiles, and airplanes) urban concentration soon became advantageous at other points. In addition, advances in technology increased the use of, and need for, raw materials like oil, copper, steel, coal, electricity, and rubber. Also, tractors replaced horses and oxen in agriculture, with a twofold benefit: tractors made greater production possible, and they did not require any part of the crop as feed. In turn, this change meant that a smaller proportion of the population had to remain on the land to grow food and fiber for those living in urban areas.

A number of urban analysts have studied these above forces and have broken them down into several elements. One of these analysts, Professor Wallace F. Smith of the University of California, lists six benefits or elements that make up the basis of urbanizing forces. In brief, these benefits are as follows:

1. Savings in costs of social interaction
2. Internal economies of scale to the firm

3. External economies of scale to the firm
4. Labor mobility or labor specialization
5. Greater consumer choice
6. Fostering of innovation[1]

Savings in costs of social interaction. Most of us like social interaction, preferably on a face-to-face basis. The closer we live together, and the better the transportation technology, the lower the cost of this interaction. Thus, cars, streetcars, buses, and bicycles, and the supporting road systems enable us to see friends and relatives with a minimum of effort. In addition, we are able to join in more exchanges and get greater personal satisfaction by living close together.

Internal economies of scale. Using specialized labor and machinery producing large numbers of units of output for one firm reduces the cost per unit and is termed *internal economies of scale.* Lower costs per unit mean lower costs to users and consumers, and a larger market. Henry Ford capitalized on the idea of mass production or economies of scale in producing automobilies. A firm, using this principle, must concentrate large numbers of people in one place and urbanization results.

External economies of scale. Firms realize lower costs by locating in a larger community where adequate support services and supplies are readily available from others at reasonable costs. The term for such action is *external economies of scale.* For example, large inventories are maintained by suppliers with several local customers, meaning that each firm can buy on a hand-to-mouth basis. Also, subcontractors are nearby to take over small jobs. In addition, law firms, accounting firms, machinery repair firms, and an adequate labor pool are readily available. Finally, users or consumers of the firm's product may be in the urban area, saving transportation costs to market for finished goods.

Jane Jacobs provides a vivid example of the importance of external economies of scale to a manufacturing effort:

> The Rockefellers, early in the 1960s, decided to build a factory in India to produce plastic intrauterine loops for birth control. At the same time they were undertaking to combat the Indian birth rate, they also wanted to curb the migration of rural Indians to cities. A way to do this, they thought, was to set an example of village industry, placing new industry in small settlements instead of cities. The location they chose for the factory, then, was a small town named Etawah in highly rural Uttar state. It seemed plausible that the factory could as well be located one place in India as another. The machinery had to be imported anyway and the loops were to be exported throughout India. The factory was to be small for with modern machinery even a small factory could begin by turning out 14,000 loops a day. The work had been rationalized into simple, easily taught tasks; no pre-existing, trained

[1] Wallace F. Smith, *Urban Development* (Berkeley: University of California Press, 1975), Chap. 2, pp. 21–47.

labor pool was required. The problem of hooking up to electric power had been explored and judged feasible. Capital was sufficient, and the scheme enjoyed the cooperation of the government of Uttar.

But as soon as the project was started everything went wrong, culminating in what *The New York Times* called "a fiasco." No single problem seems to have been horrendous. Instead, endless small difficulties arose: delays in getting the right tools, in repairing things that broke, in collecting work that had not been done to specifications, in sending off for a bit of missing material. Hooking up to the power did not go as smoothly as expected, and when it was accomplished the power was insufficient. Worse, the difficulties did not diminish as the work progressed. New ones cropped up. It became clear that—even in the increasingly doubtful event the plant could get into operation—keeping it in operating condition thereafter would probably be impractical. So after most of a year and considerable money had been wasted, Etawah was abandoned and a new site was chosen at Kanpur, a city of some 1,200,000 persons, the largest in Uttar, where industry and commerce had, by Indian standards, been growing rapidly. Space in two unused rooms in an electroplating plant was quickly found. The machinery was installed, the workers hired, and the plant was producing within six weeks. Kanpur possessed not only the space and the electric power, but also repairmen, tools, electricians, bits of needed material, and relatively swift and direct transportation to other major Indian cities if what was required was not to be found in Kanpur.[2]

Labor specialization. The larger an urban area, the greater is the feasibility of labor specialization. As individuals, we seek the work we do best or the work from which we derive the greatest satisfaction. At the same time, businesses want those workers who give greatest productivity or lowest costs per unit of output. An electrical engineer or a machinist has far fewer opportunities to specialize in a small town than in a large metropolitan area. And in the event of a layoff, the chances of a specialist's finding a satisfactory job locally are much higher in a metropolitan area.

Greater consumer choice. Economies of scale and labor specialization are limited by the size of the market. For example, unless the market can absorb 1 million cases of beer a day, it does little good to amass the facilities and people to produce 1 million cases of beer a day. But as a community grows larger, more and more firms find a market large enough for them to survive. Conversely, the greater the number of auto dealers, restaurants, law firms, schools, hardware stores, and shoe stores, the greater the choices available to citizens of a community.

Fostering innovation. An innovator or investor generally finds it easier to find needed equipment and services in a larger metropolitan area. This makes it easier to translate creative ideas into reality, though a determined innovator might succeed anywhere. The availability of supplies and services for an innovator is essentially an extension of the idea of external economies of scale, labor specialization, and wider consumer choice. Fos-

[2] Jane Jacobs, *The Economy of Cities* (New York: Random House, 1969), pp. 186–187.

tering innovation may be a small force relative to some of the earlier components of urbanizing forces, yet it does exert influence in the same direction.

Costs of urbanization. In fairness, some costs are also associated with urbanization. Urban life increases our exposure to contacts that are involuntary and often undesirable. Panhandlers, drug pushers, gamblers, and high-pressure sales people are all more likely to be encountered in metropolitan areas. We are also more tied to the "system" in urban areas. Thus, a strike of garbage handlers, of transportation workers, or of teachers is more likely in a city and tends to have a greater debilitating effect on us than it would in a rural area. In a similar vein, we are committed to a greater support of things we may not use or believe in. For example, we pay taxes to support municipal parks, schools, and hospitals even though we may not use them. Air and water pollution, congestion, and costs of commuting tend to be higher in urban areas. Hence, these items decrease the quality of life in cities and act toward decentralization or dispersal. Finally, anonymity is sometimes considered a cost of urbanization, although many people consider it a benefit.

Functional Basis of Urban Areas

All cities or urban areas exist for a reason. It follows that the investor or analyst who understands the forces that brought his or her community into existence is in a much stronger position to judge its future.

Cities, broadly speaking, may be classified as primary and secondary urban centers. A primary community is one that has its own economic base, that is, its existence is not dependent on the operations or well-being of other communities within the state or metropolitan area. A secondary community, on the other hand, is a satellite whose size and strength of orbit depends on the principal city to which it owes its existence. These satellite communities are better known as "bedroom" towns and cities, where commuters (people who work where they would rather not live) reside. The economic strength of a satellite community is entirely dependent on the strength of the primary community, of which it is a part.

Primary communities may be divided into classes, which in a general sense reflect their reason for existance, as follows:

Industrial cities	Detroit, Pittsburgh
Commercial cities	Chicago, San Francisco
Mining cities	Scranton, Pennsylvania; Wheeling, West Virginia; Butte, Montana
Resort cities	Miami; Atlantic City; Scottsdale, Arizona
Political cities	Tallahassee, Florida; Washington, D.C.; Springfield, Illinois; Salem, Oregon
Educational cities	Chapel Hill, North Carolina; Ann Arbor, Michigan; Champaign-Urbana, Illinois; Corvallis, Oregon

Many communities have a diverse economic base and may fall into two or more classifications. Thus New York City is industrial and commercial in character as well as a tourist Mecca. Miami, Florida, which started as a resort city, is presently one of the most important commercial centers in the South with one of the largest international airports in the country. And, Los Angeles, long known for movie making and citrus fruit is important today as an international shipping center second only to New York in shipping tonnage.

Urban location. Land is a resource necessary for almost all social and economic activities. But characteristics of land vary from place to place. Topography and soil characteristics are both important for urban development, although soil fertility is generally not important per se. Beyond these basic observations, what can we say about the location and growth patterns of cities?

Initially defense considerations were of primary importance in the location of cities because invasion and conflict were common realities. Hence, Rome was founded on seven hills, Paris on an island, and London and Moscow in swamps. Walled cities were common in the Middle Ages.

As trade developed, those settlements with the greatest comparative advantage for transportation and communication between producers and their markets prospered most. The *principle of comparative economic advantage* is that communities benefit most by specializing in producing goods or services providing the greatest advantage relative to other communities.

Locations of greatest advantage for trade were as follows:

1. At points on oceans or lakes with the greatest convenience between the hinterland and markets (e.g., San Francisco, Seattle, and Chicago)
2. At or near mouths of rivers (e.g., New York City, New Orleans, Philadelphia, and Portland, Oregon)
3. At branches of rivers or near other inland water transportation (e.g., Pittsburgh, St. Louis, Cincinnati, Omaha, and Syracuse)
4. At obstructions on the river requiring unloading and transshipment by another mode (e.g., St. Paul and Albany)
5. At river crossings (e.g., Rockford, Illinois, and Harrisburg, Pennsylvania)
6. At breaks in mountain chains or where mountain meets plain or intersections of land trade routes (e.g., Denver, Salt Lake City, and Albuquerque)
7. At points where modes of transportation require servicing, even temporary (e.g., Atlanta)

Note the importance of water transporation in the early development of the United States; large amounts of freight could be much more easily handled, at lower cost by water than by other means in our early history.

The emphasis on urban location and prosperity shifted to other factors with the coming of the Industrial Revolution. Comparative advantage continues to be important relative to these factors. The most significant factors are availability of raw materials, skilled labor, adequate power, and suitable climate. Nearness to market also tends to be important, particularly when product weight gain or loss are involved. Some examples seem appropriate.

1. *Raw materials.* (a) Relative availability of coal and iron ore were important in the development of Pittsburgh; Birmingham, Alabama; and Gary, Indiana. (b) Lumber mills were built near forests and at one time were prominent in the Midwest. Tacoma, Washington, and Eugene, Oregon, are leading mill towns now. But faster second growth of timber is causing the lumber industry to move to the Southeast.
2. *Power.* Fall River, Massachusetts; Minneapolis; and Spokane all owe much of their early growth to ready availability of low-cost water or hydroelectric power.
3. *Skilled labor.* The auto industry is concentrated largely in Ohio and Michigan because of the huge reservoir of skilled labor in these areas. Likewise, Seattle and Los Angeles have large reserves of skilled labor for airplane manufacture.
4. *Suitable climate.* Tuscon, Phoenix, San Diego, and Miami owe much of their growth to their pleasant climates. A general shift of economic activity to the Sun Belt is the current trend.
5. *Weight gain/loss.* A manufacturing process involving considerable weight gain is best located near the market for the product because the manufacturer avoids paying transportation costs on weight gain. Examples are soda pop, beer, and bread. Bulk, fragility, and perishability also increase market orientation. With considerable weight loss, the manufacturer avoids unnecessary transportation costs by processing near the raw materials. Examples are copper mining and processing and lumber manufacture. Some products, like grains, may be processed anywhere between producer and market, because little weight is gained or lost.

Manufacturing and trade, as leading economic activities in our society, locate for the reasons mentioned. Political capitals and educational centers, while having some economies of scale, are best located to serve with maximum convenience to the citizens or students. Madison, Wisconsin; Albany, New York; and Austin, Texas are clear examples of well-located governmental/educational centers. Ann Arbor, Michigan; Champaign-Urbana, Illinois; and Gainesville, Florida owe their existence largely to state universities located in each. Washington, D.C., is very definitely a governmental center and at one time was centrally located for all the states. Communities may also be founded as resort or health centers, as religious centers, or as military bases, with climate often a determining factor.

The Urbanizing Process

Most urban real estate is manufactured space. This space is created in response to physical, social and economic, and political forces. People locate to maximize satisfactions; businesses locate to maximize profits.

The space needs of people and businesses are negotiated in the real estate market, in what may best be described as the urbanizing process.

Initially, an urban area is raw land. Natural resources, such as oil, minerals, fertile soil, abundant snow (for skiing), or advantageous location may provide reason for a settlement. A community develops based on the beliefs, laws, political and financial systems, and other institutional considerations. Buildings and other improvements are added to the land, based on demand. These improvements constitute the supply of urban real estate. Opportunities for businesses, employment, or pleasure create the demand. Credit is usually needed to help create the supply as well as to help buyers in financing acquired realty. As time moves on, people buy and sell the existing supply of real estate, and new space may be built.

The combined activities of these buyers, sellers and builders and others make up the real estate market. Their investment and development activity results in the cities we see today. And with each passing year, the existing supply of space tends to become more dominant relative to new space added during the year. New construction typically adds only 2 or 3 percent to a community's supply of space in any one year. The market tends to be stable and predictable as a result. But what determines the structure and layout of the urban area?

THEORIES OF URBAN GROWTH

Cities or urban areas are built by people and are not gifts of nature. They are established and grow in response to need. The place of origin may be by design or by historical accident. But to fill a need, an area grows in spite of rugged topogrophy and unfriendly climate. Problems of water supply, waste disposal, transport, and schools are overcome as the occasion demands. Again, are there any theories to explain the growth and change of urban areas? Yes, many theories have been proposed, of which three have considerable applicability to our cities. These are (1) concentric circle, (2) direction of least resistance, and (3) multiple nuclei.

Concentric Circle

In 1826, Johann Heinrich von Thunen, an owner of a German estate, wrote *Der Isalierte Staat (The Isolated State)* to explain the allocation of land to various land use activities. Von Thunen began by assuming a walled city or village in the middle of a level, productive, and isolated field or plain. Climate, soils, topography, and transportation and other factors were all held constant so as not to influence or distort the analysis. Autos and railroads were not yet known, so goods to be moved had to be hauled by wagons, hand carried, or driven, in the case of livestock. Differences in land use could, therefore, be attributed entirely to differences in transportation costs or location. (See Figure 11–1.)

Von Thunen identified five zones or concentric circles outside the village or central city. Zone 1, immediately outside the walls of the city, would be used primarily for growing vegetables, milk cattle, and egg-laying hens. These activities are intensive, involving many trips from the village, with the products often hand carried into the city. Forest products production turned out to be the best use for zone 2. Forest products are both bulky and heavy and were used for fuel and construction in Von Thunen's day. Hence, production near the city saved considerable time and energy.

Production of heavy or bulky field crops—potatoes, grain, hay—would be the main use in zone 3. Grazing of cattle and sheep was the appropriate use for zone 4, in that the livestock could be driven to zone

FIGURE 11–1
Concentric circle allocation of space in an isolated state

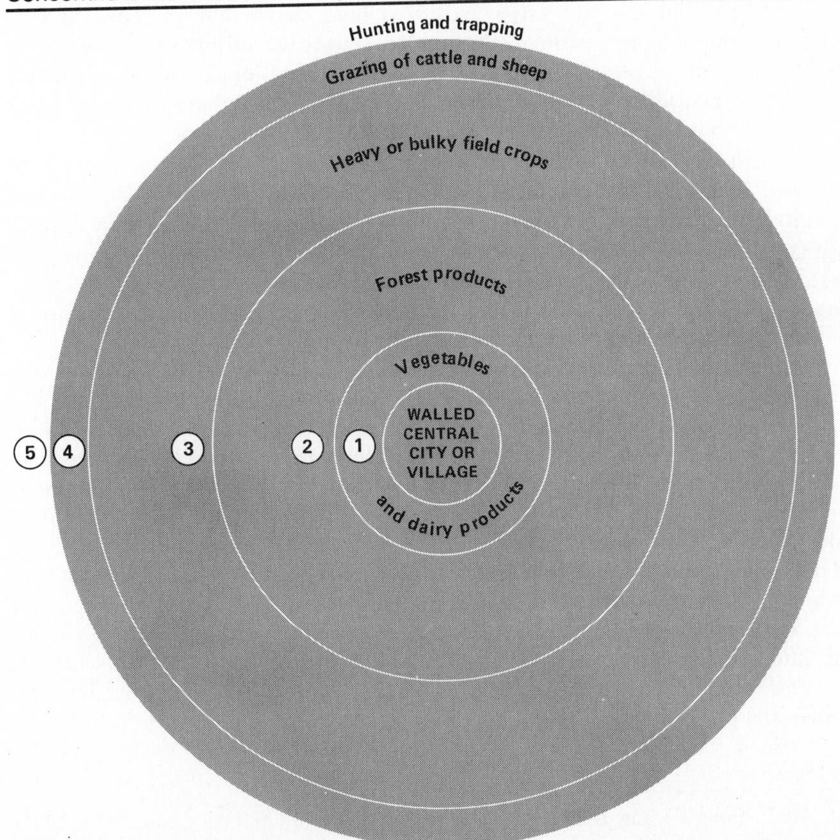

1 for slaughter or milking. The surrounding wilderness, Zone 5, was appropriate for hunting and trapping.

Direction of Least Resistance

Richard M. Hurd, a mortgage banker, compiled information on the expansion and growth of more than 50 American cities. In 1903, Hurd wrote that cities grow in the direction of least resistance or greatest attraction, or their resultants. He continues:

> The point of contact differs according to the methods of transportation, whether by water, by turnpike, or by railroad. The forces of attractions and resistance include topography, the underlying material on which city builders work; external influences, projected into the city by trade routes; internal influences derived from located utilities, and finally the reactions and readjustments due to the continual harmonizing of conflicting elements. The influence of modern topography, all-powerful when cities start, is constantly modified by human labor, hills being cut down, waterfronts extended, and swamps, creeks and lowlands filled in, this, however, not taking place until the new building sites are worth more than the cost of filling and cutting. The measure of resistance to the city's growth is here changed from terms of land elevation or depression, and hence income cost, to terms of investment or capital cost. The most direct results of topography come from its control of transportation, the waterfronts locating exchange points for water commerce, and the water grade normally determining the location of the railroads entering the city.
>
> Growth in cities consists of movement away from the point of origin in all directions. Except as topographically hindered, this movement being due both to aggregration at the edges and pressure from the centre. Central growth takes place both from the heart of the city and from each subcenter of attraction, and axial growth pushes into outlying territory by means of railroads, turnpikes and street railroads. All cities are built up from these two influences, which vary in quantity, intensity and quality, the resulting districts overlapping, interpenetrating, neutralizing and harmonizing as the pressure of the city's growth brings them into contact with each other. The fact of vital interest is that, despite confusion from intermingling of utilities, the order of dependence of each definite district on the other is always the same. Residences are early driven to the circumference, while business remains at the centre, and as residences divide into various social grades, retail shops of corresponding grades follow them, and wholesale shops in turn follow the retailers, while institutions and various mixed utilities irregularly fill in the intermediate zone, and the banking and office section remains at the main business centre. Complicating this broad outward movement of zones, axes of traffic project shops through residence areas, create business subcentres, where they intersect, and change circular cities into star-shaped cities. Central growth, due to proximity, and axial growth, due to accessibility, are summed up in the static power of established sections and the dynamic power of their chief lines of intercommunication.[3]

---

[3] Richard M. Hurd, *Principles of City Land Values* (New York: The Record and the Guide, 1903, 1924), pp. 13–15.

Considerable research and writing have been done since Hurd made his statement. Yet no simpler, clearer, or more comprehensive statement about urban growth dynamics has since been made. Direction of least resistance is really an extension or modification of Von Thunen's concentric circle theory. Concentric circle assumes no barriers to growth; direction of least resistance does.

Multiple Nuclei

In the 1930s, Homer Hoyt developed the sector theory, based on wedge-shaped neighborhoods surrounding the central business district. New, high-income residential areas were seen as developing along highways and next to other fast transportation facilities. In this sense, the theory is not too different from the route, or axial, theory suggested by a number of scholars. The axial theory says that an urban area tends to grow along its lines of transportation, owing to the economic advantage of convenience, made possible by the easy, low-cost movement. Both theories appear to be restatements of Hurd's line-of-least-resistance theory, and the power of these theories to explain urban growth and change, over and above Hurd's theory, seems limited.

Frederick Babcock, an appraiser, studying urban growth and change in the 1930s, characterized urban areas as sliding, jumping, and bursting in their growth.[4] One district expands by gradually encroaching or moving into neighboring districts in a sliding manner. Jumping means that a district will sometimes leap over a barrier, such as another well-established district, in its expansion. Thus, an expanding business district will jump a river, a civic center, or a university. Bursting means the scattering of a district to several new subdistricts. Thus, the pre–World War II central business district of large metropolitan areas burst and the suburban shopping center resulted. In like fashion, manufacturing areas scattered from the central city to the suburbs, taking the form of industrial parks and districts.

Ulman and Harris advanced the idea of multiple nuclei, or clusters of development, in 1945.[5] Essentially, their theory is an extension of Babcock's bursting explanation with physical, economic, and social considerations taken into account. It is also an extension of the ideas that cities are functional areas. Four reasons suggested by Harris and Ullman for the development of clusters or nuclei are

1. Some activities require specialized facilities.

[4] Frederick Babcock, *The Valuation of Real Estate* (New York: McGraw-Hill, 1932), p. 59.

[5] Chauncy D. Harris and Edward L. Ullman, "The Nature of Cities," in *Building the Future City, Annals of the American Academy of Political and Social Sciences*, November 1945, pp. 7–17.

2. Like activities tend to group together because they mutually benefit from cohesion.
3. Unlike activities are sometimes adverse or detrimental to each other.
4. Some activities can afford the high rents of the most desirable sites; others cannot and must take less desirable sites.

The multiple nuclei theory of land use arrangements is based strongly on the rent paying ability of the various uses. The use able to pay the highest rent gets the most desirable site for its purposes. The worth of a specific site or location depends on transportation and communication possibilities and the surrounding environment. Thus, business and industrial centers developed outside the central business district. Currently, these nuclei take the form of shopping centers, industrial parks, convention centers (often near major airports), and resort communities (functional areas). See Figure 11–2.

It should be noted that major changes occurred in transport as these theories developed. Until about 1900, trains, street cars, and buggies or wagons were the main modes of transport. The automobile gave everyone faster and greater flexibility of movement. It seems unlikely that central cities would have declined so sharply in the absence of widespread use of cars. But with increasing costs of energy, central cities seem to be getting new life, perhaps because they once again constitute the most accessible, least cost locations.

RENT THEORY AND URBAN STRUCTURE

Urban growth theory may be restated as rent theory to reflect the many decisions by individual owners about the use of their properties. In fact, it is the decisions by the individual owner-investors that make up urban growth theory. Also, rent theory, or value theory, is the means by which local economic activity is related to real estate. The key for rent theory is maximization of self-interest, expressed in monetary terms. Note that we are not talking of maximizing revenues or of minimizing costs but rather of maximizing net profits, rents, satisfactions, or benefits or, in some cases, minimizing net losses. In the immediate context, we are talking of maximizing net benefits from land and buildings.

Our discussion of rent theory begins by looking at the allocation of space in a large hotel, which concepts extend to allocation of land to alternative uses in rural and urban areas. We conclude our discussion with a general statement of rent theory.

Space Allocation in a Large Hotel

Which of all the uses in a large hotel gets its choice of location? Remember that owners and operators of hotels are rational and want to maximize

FIGURE 11–2
Allocation of space to functional areas (multiple nuclei) in an modern urban community

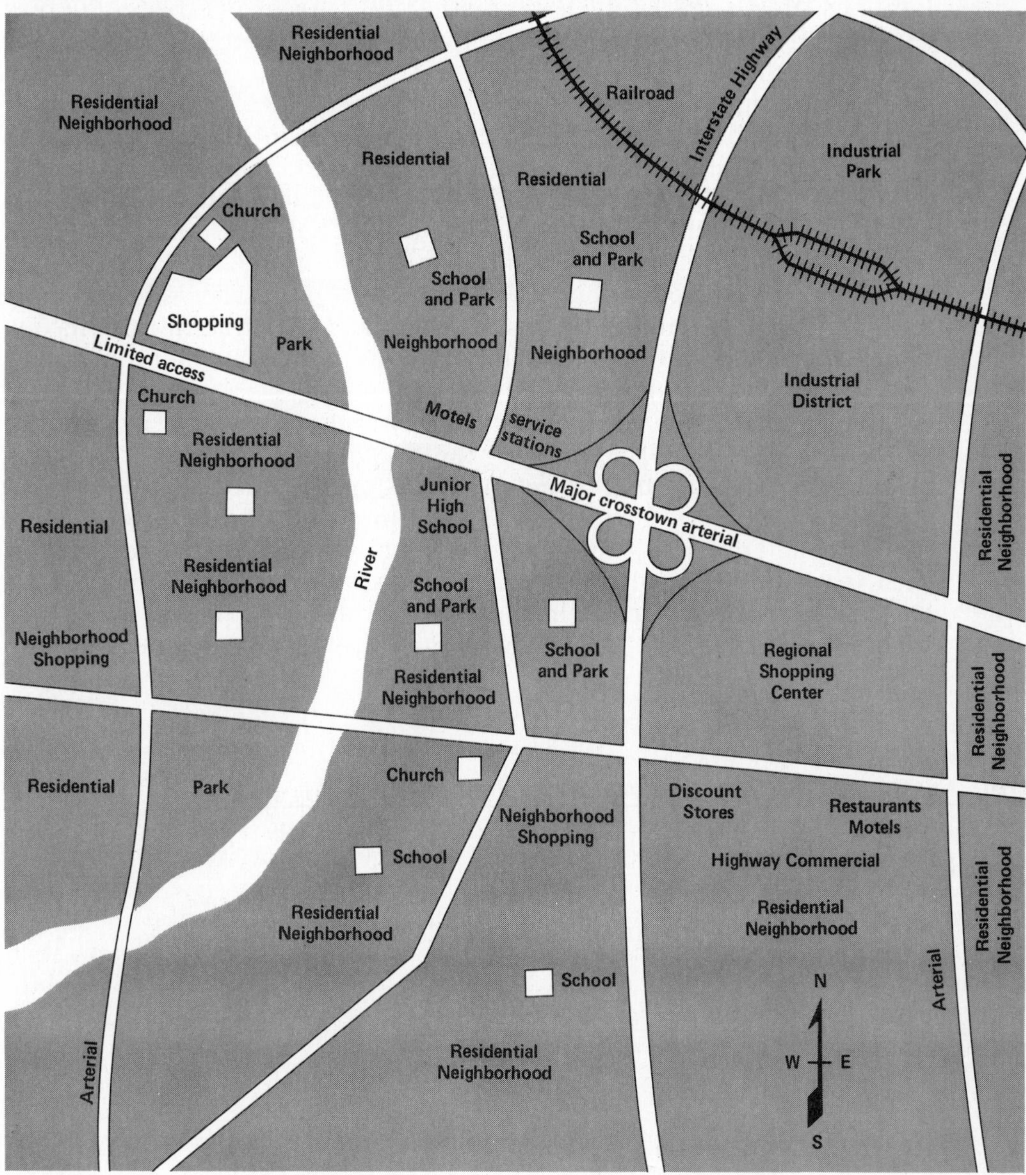

the profitability and value of the space under their control. In effect, once the hotel use has been decided on and approvals obtained, there are few limits on the use of space within the structure.

In most tall structures, the premium location is the top floor, followed by space at the street level. Brief reflection or observation shows that a bar or cocktail lounge is usually found in both these locations. Very large hotels often have four or five bars in the most accessible or desirable locations. Restaurants follow closely behind bars in this respect. From experience, owners know that these two uses are the most profitable and able to pay the highest rents.

Other common uses in slightly less advantageous locations are typically barber and beauty shops, drugstores, liquor stores, and newsstands. High-fashion clothing stores may also be included. The second to fourth floors are often devoted to ballrooms, meeting rooms, swimming pools, and health facilities. Auto parking is typically below ground or on the back of the building away from the main thoroughfare. Guest rooms occupy the space from about the fifth floor to just under the top floor. One must look carefully to find the lobby and registration desk in our newer hotels. The owners know that the guests will not be turned away by a slight delay in finding the registration desk.

This hierarchy of uses is illustrated by rent triangles in Figure 11–3. A *rent triangle* is a schedule showing the amount of rent a use or business activity can pay as an increasing amount of space is devoted to the use.

Thus, the cocktail bar in the Top of the Mark in the Mark Hopkins Hotel in San Francisco may be able to pay a rent of $300 per square foot each year. But as more space is allocated to serving liquor (more bars and restaurants are opened in the building), the rent-paying ability per square foot decreases. At some point, other uses—drugstores, news

FIGURE 11–3
Hierarchy of space uses in a large hotel based on profitability or rent-paying ability

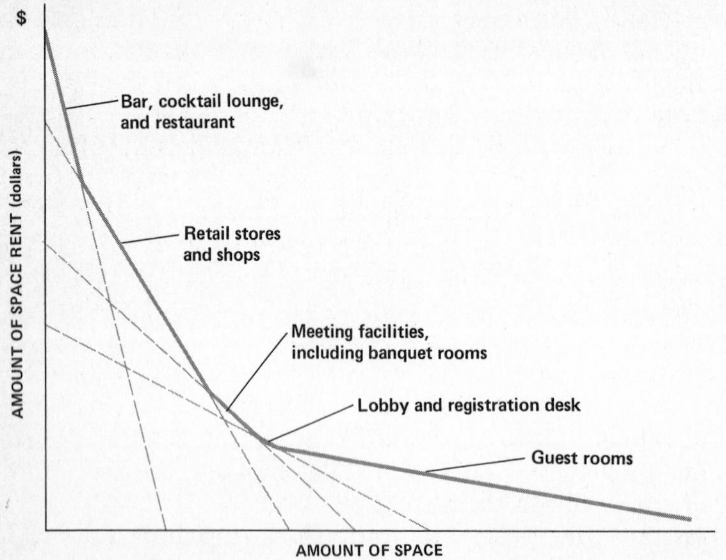

stands, guest rooms—offer a higher rate of return and, therefore, command the space. Each type of use has its own triangle or schedule of payments it can afford. The use paying the highest rent gets it choice of space.

An important exception to the hierarchy occurs in areas allowing gambling. The exception reinforces rent theory as a basis for space allocation. In Las Vegas, hotels devote much of their prime space at street level to slot machines and other gaming activities. This space is the most easily accessible to potential gamblers.

Rural Land Allocation

Fertile land in an area with a friendly climate is more productive than is land not so well endowed. That is, more bushels of corn, soybeans, wheat, and so on may be grown per acre on the productive land for a given amount of effort. In turn, each acre of the most productive land is more profitable and more valuable than is less productive lands, assuming that markets are available to use the crops grown.

An owner-operator of the more favorably endowed land would, therefore, use it to produce that crop giving the highest return per acre. A tenant-operator would also grow the crop or product giving the highest return. And an owner-landlord would charge a rent based on the profitability of the crop giving the highest returns per acre. Thus, self-interest pushes the use of land to that use giving the greatest return or value or to the highest and best use. In the Midwest, known for its productive lands, owners concentrate on growing corn and soybeans. The two crops reinforce each other in maintaining soil productivity and are about equally profitable. Moving west, the lands of Kansas and the Dakotas get less rain and are farther from the markets of the East. These areas concentrate on growing wheat rather than corn or soybeans. Grazing cattle and sheep is the most common use of lands in the drier areas of our western states.

Alternatively, rugged or inaccessible lands with abundant rainfall, as in the Southeast and the Northwest, are devoted to growing timber. Thus, we have lumber and wood products companies named Georgia Pacific and Boise Cascade. Finally, some lands (swamps, mountain tops, and deserts) yield no profit to human efforts and remain in their natural state and are termed *submarginal.* Figure 11–4 depicts broad uses of agricultural land in the United States.

Almost every state has some land better suited to growing vegetables than to field crops, because of the nearness of markets. Also, climate in California, Hawaii, and Florida favors the growing of oranges, grapefruit, pineapple, grapes, nuts, and produce over corn, wheat, or soybeans. But, as it turns out, these uses are able to pay higher rents and, therefore, give higher values to the land.

FIGURE 11–4
Allocation of land to alternative rural uses based on profitability or rent-paying ability

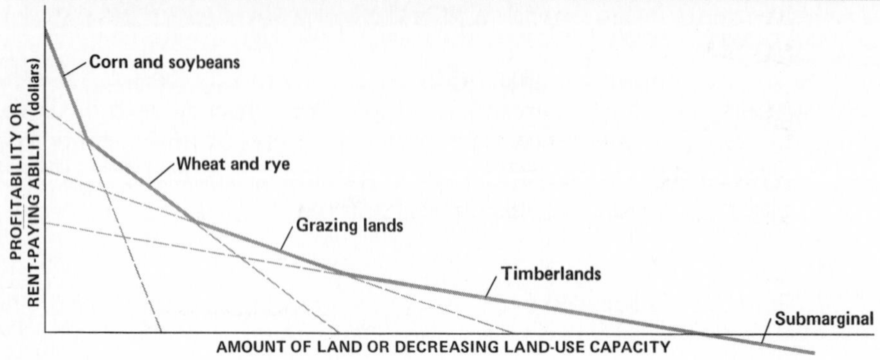

Space Allocation in Urban Areas

What land uses pay the highest rent or give the highest value to sites in urban areas? Location theory says that the most accessible site is likely to be the most productive or profitable. And unless rivers or hills intervene, the most central location is the most accessible in an urban area. And what uses dominate in our central business districts?

Early in this century, large department stores and other retail outlets occupied the prime sites in our major cities. Office buildings, hotels, apartment buildings, and manufacturing plants were usually located nearby. Moving out from the central city, one-family homes became a dominant land use. Individual commercial and industrial districts sometimes developed along major arteries as wedges or sectors. Lot sizes increased as the edge of the city blended into the countryside. The hierarchy of land uses is diagrammed in Figure 11–5.

With wide use of autos and trucks, industry moved to the suburbs after World War II. People and residential neighborhoods followed, pulling commercial districts with them. Satellite villages were often engulfed by the rapid urban expansion. Industrial parks, shopping centers, recreation centers, and residential neighborhoods combined to make up the community fabric. The land use structure became a pattern of more or less distinct functional neighborhoods or districts superimposed on a network of street and highways. The typical value pattern that developed is shown, in cross section, in Figure 11–6. Thus, land use patterns took on a structure that tended to minimize the costs of moving people and goods in the area and which is best described by the multiple nuclei concept, discussed earlier.

Rivers, lakes, marshes, and hills all act as barriers to the "normal" expansion of urban areas. In accordance with Hurd's direction-of-least-

FIGURE 11–5
Hierarchy of urban land uses based on profitability or rent-paying ability

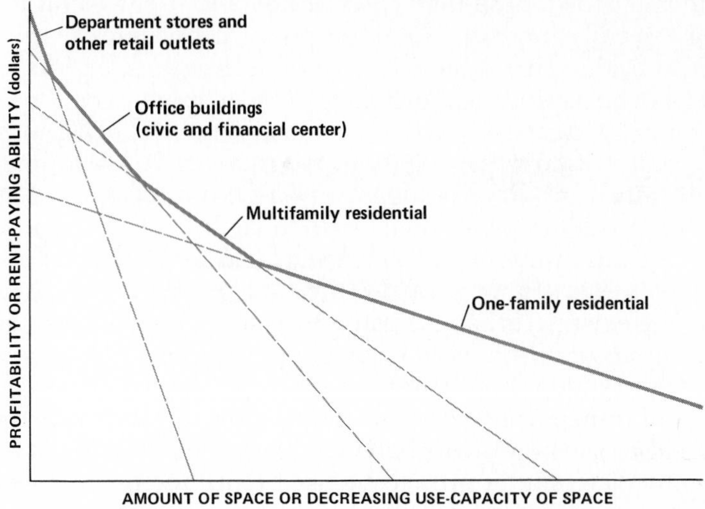

FIGURE 11–6
Schematic cross section of land uses and their rent-paying ability in a large metropolitan area

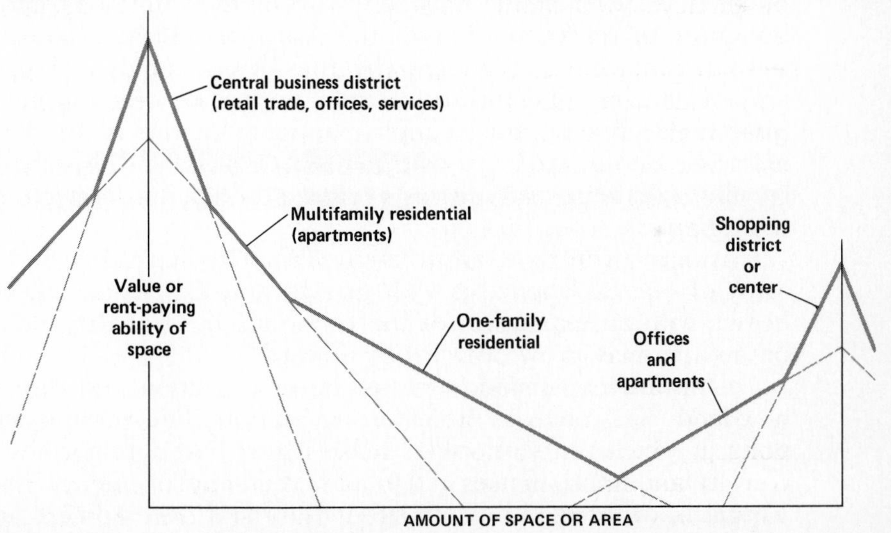

resistance principle, expansion takes place away from or around these barriers because the cost is less relative to the benefits realized. However, with time and growth, the time costs of travel to the urban fringe in other directions steadily increase. At some point, it becomes feasible to incur the costs to bridge rivers and lakes, to fill in marshes, and to expand into hilly areas. The Golden Gate Bridge of San Francisco, the Lake Pontchartrain Bridge near New Orleans, and the recent filling in of the tidal marshes near Newark, New Jersey, for industrial development are examples of "delayed" development outward from an urban center.

Existing realty improvements tend to lag behind social and economic needs of a community. That is, several one-family houses or a church must often be moved or torn down to make way for a discount store. Likewise, the existing urban infrastructure act to retard urban adjustment. *Urban infrastructure* is the basic installations and facilities of a community, such as schools, sewer and water systems, power and communications systems, and transportation systems, including streets, freeways, and subways. In either of these two situations, additional costs must be incurred for the immediate site or area to be used more intensely. At some point, the potential benefits may justify the additional costs.

Rent Theory Restated

Let us now summarize our discussion and restate rent theory as an explanation of urban growth and change. First, land use activities tend to locate at the point of greatest comparative advantage. If the site or location is not owned, it must be bought or rented. Land use competition is based on rent-paying ability. Over a period of time, those uses able to pay the highest rents or prices get the choicest locations. In addition, a hierarchy of land uses develops. Department stores, office buildings, and apartment buildings, therefore, tend to get the choice or central urban sites. Moving out from the center, the hierarchy goes to one-family residences to field crops to grazing and forestry to submarginal deserts and mountaintops. Subcenters of value, for example, shopping centers and industrial parks, intervene into urban areas as business operators and other citizens strive to minimize transportation costs relative to benefits received in accepting a location.

At any given time, an urban area may be expanding or contracting. Most of our experience is with growth and expansion. Growth usually begins with an expansion of the economic base of the community. An urban area may grow outward or upward.

Outward expansion, such as the urbanization and development of new lands, is growth at the extensive margin. The *extensive margin* is that point at which rents or values make it just barely financially feasible to convert land to urban uses and to add urban improvements. The extensive margin is symbolized by land subdivision and development at the urban fringe. The building of bridges and roads and the filling in of marshes are also activities associated with the extensive margin. See Figure 11–7.

Urban areas also expand upward or at the intensive margin. The *intensive margin* is that point at which rents or values make it just barely financially feasible to use urban land more intensely with the addition of more capital and labor. Replacing old houses with a discount store is an example. Alternatively, converting an old factory or cannery into a shopping center is another. Again, see Figure 11–7.

Note that intensity of use and rent are related but not identical concepts. *Rent* is the payment for the use of land, in an economic sense and in the sense used here. Rent is also the payment for the use of realty, in its more accepted meaning. *Intensity of use* refers to the relative amount of human and capital resources added in the use of land. Generally, the higher the value of the site, the higher its rent and the greater its intensity of use. That is, there must be a proportionality between the value of a site and the amount of improvements added to the land. Intensity of use, rent, and value are all closely related to highest and best uses of land.

Intensity of use is the key to understanding why urban areas grow upward as well as outward. Land, urban or rural, is not productive in and of itself. Corn, wheat, office space, or residential units all require labor, capital, and management in addition to land. These factors of production (land, labor, capital, and management) must be combined according to the principle of proportionality for each factor to get its greatest return. The *principle of proportionality* is that real estate reaches its maximum productivity, or highest and best use, when the factors of production are in

FIGURE 11–7
Intensive and extensive margins of urban land uses

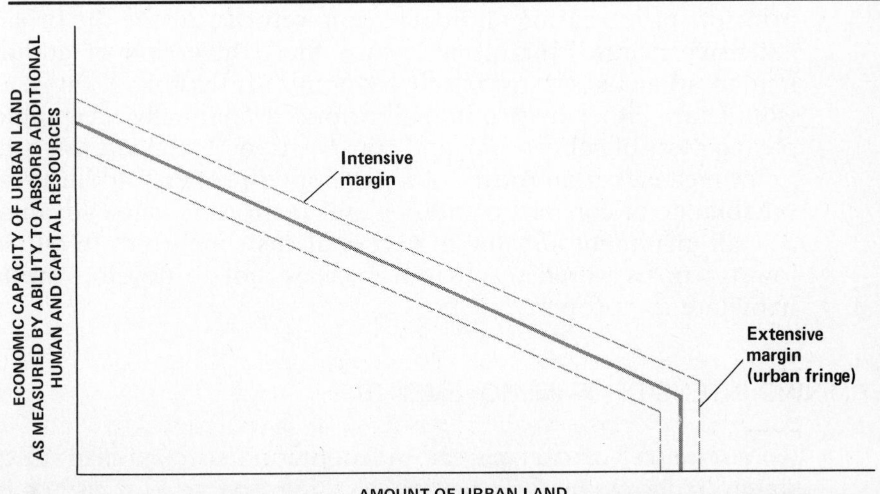

balance with one another. This is also known as the *principle of increasing and decreasing returns.* The ability of a site to absorb additional human and capital resources, under the principle of proportionality, is the *economic capacity of the land.*

Stated another way, the factors of production must be used in optimum balance to achieve the highest and best use of realty. How is the optimum determined? In the construction or modification of a property, expenditures should be made for those items adding the most to value, as judged by the market. Thus, $2,000 might be used for a fireplace, a third bathroom, or a patio.

	FIREPLACE	*THIRD BATHROOM*	*PATIO*
Marginal contribution to market value of property	$4,000	$2,500	$3,000

Adding the fireplace gives $2.00 of market value for every dollar expended, the patio gives $1.50 of market value, while the third bathroom gives only $1.25 of market value. Clearly, the addition of a fireplace is the best choice. And if another $2,000 is available, the addition of the patio would be second choice, with its $1.50 return for every dollar invested.

Obviously, the more money that is spent on improvements to the land, the more intensely the land is used. Intense development of land requires that high values (economic capacity) be justified. Urban uses are generally much more intense than are rural uses. And urban land values are generally higher than are rural. The highest and best use of a site is reached when no further value can be gained by the addition of resources. In fact, value may be decreased by more additions in accordance with the principle of increasing and decreasing returns. At the the urban fringe or extensive margin, this point means that conversion of additional rural land to urban uses is just barely economically feasible. That is, a developer would earn either no profit at all or only a minimally acceptable one after paying costs of subdividing and construction. At the intensive margin, this point means that an owner of a developed property adding resources (to rehabilitate or convert to another use) realizes no value advantage or only a small increment of value in excess of costs incurred. In either case, any lower returns would result in a decision not to develop the land or rehabilitate the property.

DETERMINING INTENSITY OF IMPROVEMENTS

An owner of a vacant parcel, in attempting to maximize its value, must weigh many alternatives before deciding how to best use it. In the end, that use that is physically possible, financially feasible, and legally acceptable and gives the greatest "net present value" to the site is selected. Part of this selection process is the evaluation to determine how many improvements should be added to the land.

Intensity of Land Improvements

Based on the principle of proportionality, improvements must be added to a vacant site to the point where a marginal dollar of input (cost) just produces a marginal dollars worth of output (value) for highest and best use to be achieved. To illustrate, let us consider a vacant site to be improved with an office building.

An investor acquired a 10,000-square-foot site for $600,000. Office space rents for $20 per square foot per year gross in the area, which gives a net operating income per square foot of $12. Net operating income equals gross income less operating expenses. Planning and zoning regulations allow 100 percent land coverage for commercial uses, as office space with no limit on height. The design of the building provides for 90 percent efficiency; that is, 90 percent of the building's area can be rented out. Finally, the ratio of annual net operating income (NOI) to sale price of comparable properties approximates 10 percent. Building costs vary from $105 per square foot for the first story down to $90 for the fourth and fifth stories, after which they increase by $5 per story. How many stories should the investor add to the land?

Figure 11–8 illustrates the calculations by which an investor-developer might make this determination. To begin, a one-story office building covering the entire site would provide 9,000 square feet of rentable area; see column 5 in Figure 11–8. At $12 per square foot, a net operating income of $108,000 would be realized in a year. Capitalized at 10 percent, the value realized would be $1,080,000 (column 10). However, the total cost for a one-story property would be $1,650,000 as shown in column 6; thus the investor would suffer a loss of $570,000, column 11. Adding a second story lowers the loss to $490,000 while yielding a positive marginal profit per square foot of rentable area added.

The marginal cost of a square foot drops as floors are added. Footings and other supports only have to be strengthed and one roof serves all floors. Offsetting these economies is the increasing costs to lift materials to ever-higher levels, to install elevators, and to solve similar types of problems.

The marginal profit per square foot, at $20, is maximized at four and five floors. Yet it is only at the fifth floor that value realized equals costs incurred. It is clear that the building must be built to at least five stories. Even so, it pays the developer to add more stories because marginal profit is positive and total profit is still increasing. See Figure 11–9 for a

FIGURE 11–8
Determining intensity of land improvements

ASSUMPTIONS:
$600,000 = site cost
10,000 = site area, square feet
90.00% = building efficiency
$12.00 = net operating income (NOI) per square foot
10.00% = overall capitalization rate (R)

BUILDING				COSTS OF DEVELOPMENT				PROFIT ANALYSIS				
1	2	3	4	5	6	7	8	9	10	11	12	13
No. of Stories	Marginal Cost per Square Foot	Marginal Cost per Story	Total Accumulated Cost	Net Rentable Area (square feet)	Total Cost (land and building)	Average Cost per Square Foot of Rentable Area	Marginal Cost per Square Foot of Rentable Area	Net Operating Income (annual)	Total Value (NOI/.10)	Profit (total value minus total cost)	Average Profit per Square Foot of Rentable Area	Marginal Profit per Square Foot of Rentable Area
1	$ 105.00	$1,050,000	1,050,000	9,000	$1,650,000	$183.33	$183.33	$ 108,000	$ 1,080,000	($570,000)	($63.33)	($63.33)
2	100.00	1,000,000	2,050,000	18,000	2,650,000	147.22	90.00	216,000	2,160,000	(490,000)	(27.22)	8.89
3	95.00	950,000	3,000,000	27,000	3,600,000	133.33	85.50	324,000	3,240,000	(360,000)	(13.33)	14.44
4	90.00	900,000	3,900,000	36,000	4,500,000	125.00	81.00	432,000	4,320,000	(180,000)	(5.00)	20.00
5	90.00	900,000	4,800,000	45,000	5,400,000	120.00	81.00	540,000	5,400,000	0	0.00	20.00
6	95.00	950,000	5,750,000	54,000	6,350,000	117.59	85.50	648,000	6,480,000	130,000	2.41	14.44
7	100.00	1,000,000	6,750,000	63,000	7,350,000	116.67	90.00	756,000	7,560,000	210,000	3.33	8.89
8	105.00	1,050,000	7,800,000	72,000	8,400,000	116.67	94.50	864,000	8,640,000	240,000	3.33	3.33
9	110.00	1,100,000	8,900,000	81,000	9,500,000	117.28	99.00	972,000	9,720,000	220,000	2.72	(2.22)
10	115.00	1,150,000	10,050,000	90,000	10,650,000	118.33	103.50	1,080,000	10,800,000	150,000	1.67	(7.78)
11	120.00	1,200,000	11,250,000	99,000	11,850,000	119.70	108.00	1,188,000	11,880,000	30,000	0.30	(13.33)
12	125.00	1,250,000	12,500,000	108,000	13,100,000	121.30	112.50	1,296,000	12,960,000	(140,000)	(1.30)	(18.89)

FIGURE 11–9
Total value and total cost curves for property improvement analysis

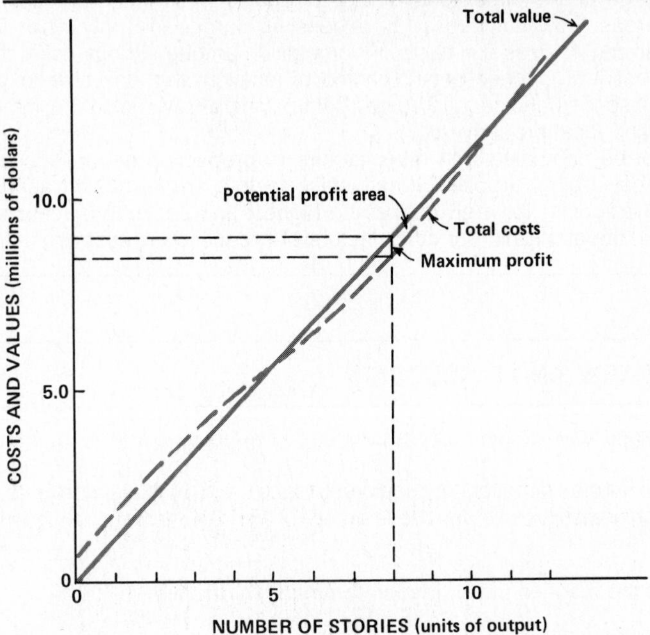

graphic summary, floor by floor, of the interaction of total costs and total value for this example.

The marginal cost of the eighth story, at $1,050,000, is just slightly exceeded by the marginal value realized of $1,080,000. The ninth floor would have a marginal cost of $1,100,000, $20,000 greater than the marginal value of the floor, meaning the point of diminishing returns had been reached and passed. Alternatively, it is in this area that marginal cost equals marginal revenue or profit, signaling that additional space produced will result in ever-greater losses. Thus, the office building should only be built to eight stories. At eight stories, profit is maximized at $240,000.

SUMMARY

Urban areas come about because of social, economic, and political forces requiring a concentration of people, buildings, and machines. Six major benefits of urbanization are (1) savings in the costs of social interaction, (2) internal economies of scale to a firm, (3) external economies of scale to a firm, (4) labor specialization, (5) greater consumer choice, and (6) fostering of innovation.

Three major theories of urban growth are (1) concentric circle, (2) direction of least resistance, and (3) multiple nuclei. Rent theory is an alternative explanation of alternative growth and change and is consistent with the foregoing three theories. According to rent theory, urban areas grow outward at the extensive margin and upward at the intensive margin. Ability to pay rents is the basis of competition among various uses; that use able to pay the highest rent or price gets it choice of location; that use able to pay the next highest rent gets second choice; and so on. Rent-paying ability is also the link between the local economy and local property values.

Land must be combined with other factors of production (labor, capital, and management) for most urban purposes. When these factors are combined according to the principal of proportionality for a given site, the highest and best use is realized. Land that does not warrant the application of other factors of production is submarginal.

QUESTIONS FOR REVIEW AND DISCUSSION

1. Explain briefly four benefits and three costs of urbanization.
2. Concentric circle, direction of least resistance, and multiple nuclei are prominent theories of urban growth and development. Are the theories related in any way? Explain.
3. Do any of the theories in (2) fit your community? Discuss.
4. Illustrate and explain briefly with rent triangles the allocation of space in a large hotel toward maximizing rent or value. In a department store.
5. Define the intensive and extensive rent margins relative to use of urban land. Give at least one example of each. What is submarginal land?
6. Explain the interrelationships, if any, among intensity of use, rent levels, value, and highest and best use for a specific site.
7. Is anonymity a cost or a benefit of urbanization? Explain.
8. Explain in general terms the interrelationships among site value, construction costs, and rent levels as they concern highest and best use of a specific site.
9. What is the principle of increasing and decreasing returns? How does it apply in the development of real estate?

CASE PROBLEMS

1. Survey your community. Note where development and redevelopment is taking place. Are there any bypassed hills or marshes that look ripe for development? Can you identify where development and redevelopment is most likely to take place in the next five years?
2. Refer to Figure 11–8. If the marginal cost per square foot of building started at $80 and increased $10 with each story added, what would be the optimal number of floors to be added to the site, all other assumptions remaining unchanged?

CHAPTER TWELVE

REAL ESTATE MARKETS

Fortune is like the market,
where many times, if you can stay a little,
the price will fall
FRANCIS BACON

IMPORTANT TOPICS OR DECISION AREAS COVERED IN THIS CHAPTER

- Market Types
- Market Characteristics
- Supply and Demand Forces
- Market Operation
- Local Market Indicators
- Market Functions

As commonly defined, market means (1) a meeting of people (buyers and sellers) who wish to exchange goods, services, and money; (2) a public place (as in a town) or a large building where a market is held; or (3) the course of commercial activity by which the exchange of commodities within a market area is effected. A real estate market is certainly not a meeting of buyers and sellers who truck and barter for commodities that are readily measurable as to quality and quantity. Nor would it be appropriate to describe it as a public trading place for commodities as produce, cattle, corn, or stocks and bonds.

The commodity of the real estate market is the elusive "property rights." And transactions are very diffused as to where they take place.

The real estate market is, therefore, more aptly described as a business activity in which an exchange of commodities is effected.

KEY CONCEPTS INTRODUCED IN THIS CHAPTER

Buyer's market
Cycle
Doubling up
Effective demand
Efficient market
Market
Perfect market
Potential demand
Prime rate
Seller's market

MARKET TYPES

In practice, real estate market operations are classified according to type of property traded. The kinds of real estate markets recognized as specialized fields of operation include (1) residential, (2) commercial, (3) industrial, (4) agricultural, and (5) special-purpose properties.

Each of these specialized fields may be subdivided further into smaller and more specialized market areas:

- Residential: (1) urban, (2) suburban, and (3) rural
- Commercial: (1) office buildings, (2) store properties, (3) lofts, (4) theaters, (5) garages, and (6) hotels and motels
- Industrial: (1) factories, (2) utilities, (3) mining, and (4) warehouses
- Agricultural: (1) timberland, (2) pasture land, (3) ranches, (4) orchards, and (5) open farmland (for produce, tobacco, cotton, and so on)
- Special-purpose properties: (1) cemeteries, (2) churches, (3) clubs, (4) golf courses, (5) parks, and (6) public properties (buildings, highways, streets, and the like)

Each of these specialized areas of the real estate market may be classified further as to rights of ownership or use. Thus, we may speak of (1) a rental market involving transfer of space and (2) an equity market involving transfer of ownership.

We might also recognize a buyer's market and seller's market. A *buyer's market* occurs when the supply of goods and services greatly exceeds demand, thereby enabling purchasers to bargain for lower prices and get them. Conversely, a *seller's market* occurs when demand greatly exceeds supply, thereby enabling sellers to bargain for higher prices and get them.

MARKET CHARACTERISTICS

Real estate has certain characteristics as fixed location, heterogeneity, indestructibility, durability, and situs that cause a real estate market to differ from other markets in several ways.

Local in Character

Fixity causes the market for real estate to be local in character. Since real estate cannot be moved from place to place, demand must come to the parcel. An oversupply of land or land improvements in a midwestern state is of no avail to fill a market demand for like land or improvements in another region or metropolitan center. Real estate is, therefore, extremely vulnerable to shifts in local demand.

Further, a real estate broker in Los Angeles, California, cannot well advise a homeowner or business executive seeking a site in Atlanta, Georgia. And absence, even for a few days, may leave a broker uninformed about significant changes in the local supply-demand relationships.

Transactions Private in Nature

Real estate transactions are very private. Buyers and sellers meet in confidence, often negotiating through brokers, and their bid and offering prices are rarely publicized. Also, deeds of record often do not specify the actual dollar amounts paid.

Commodity Not Standardized

No two parcels of real estate are exactly alike. Each parcel has its own unique location. Even with two physically adjacent properties, situs and legal characteristics may cause a difference in their relative values. To illustrate, two residential sites equal in width and depth may be improved with almost identical buildings, similar not only in floor plan and building material but also as to details of building construction and time of completion. Still, these two real estate properties, equal as far as inspection may disclose, may warrant different values or permit different uses because of intangible legal or economic considerations. One property may be zoned residential "A," the other "B," permitting different site utilization for one but not the other. One may be subject to deed restrictions limiting its use to high-income residential; the other may be free of any such limitations and thus open to any legal use.

Market Diffused

Fixity and heterogeneity account for the wide fluctuations in value and number of real estate transactions that characterize the real estate market. Such fluctuations occur from region to region as well as from state to state or community to community. The market for U.S. farmland, for instance, may be judged good (or "active")when based on number of sales and increases in overall values. But this "favorable" average may be a composite derived from the wheat, corn, tobacco, and cattle-raising regions, which more than offset unfavorable activity in the cotton-growing region. Likewise, real estate activity in Phoenix, Los Angeles, or Miami Beach may record sharp sales gains while sales activity in Tacoma, Washington, and Portland, Maine, drops through the floor.

Absence of Short Selling

Heterogeneity and the legal right to specific performance discourage speculation and prevent the market stabilizing operation known as short selling. *Short selling* is selling a security or commodity not owned, when prices are high, with delivery promised at some future date. Anticipating a drop in prices, the speculator hopes to cover these short sales by purchasing at lower prices prior to the delivery date the quantities previously sold. Short selling can, however, only be done with articles or goods that are legally fungible or substitutable, as grain, corn, or shares of stock. Real estate, as a commodity, is nonfungible and, therefore, is not subject to the market-stabilizing benefits of short selling. In the grain or security markets, short selling is both legally permissible and welcomed as a market-stabilizing influence; the speculator is "forced" to place a purchase order to fill short-selling positions when market activity might otherwise be low or even panicky.

Poor Adjustment of Supply and Demand

Fixity prevents equalization of real estate supply and demand on an area, regional, or national level. Durability causes maladjustments in supply and demand on a local market level as well. Land itself is indestructible. Improvements, if properly maintained, may last a hundred years or more. Thus, where demand suddenly falls, inability to adjust (withdraw) supply causes real estate to become a drug on the market. An oversupply of space results in a buyer's market, meaning lower purchase price offerings and keenly competitive trade practices. In a similar sense, a sudden increase in demand creates a seller's market because additional space cannot be quickly built.

SUPPLY AND DEMAND FORCES

A local real estate market is sensitive to changes in biological, economic, political, and social forces. Among the more important local forces are the following:

1. Population—number, age-sex mix, and family composition
2. Employment and wage levels and stability of incomes
3. Personal savings, availability of mortgage funds, and levels of interest rates
4. Sales prices, rent levels, and vacancy percentage
5. Taxation rates and land use controls, including rent controls
6. Availability and costs of land, labor, and building materials
7. Relative quality of existing structures and changes in construction technology

Population, employment, income, savings, and availability of credit combine to provide effective demand in contrast to *potential demand.* Population, by itself, represents raw or potential demand, in that the desire for land or space is without purchasing power. *Effective demand,* therefore, is desire armed with purchasing power.

Population

Population is a prerequisite of demand for most types of real estate. An increase in numbers of people means increased potential demand. And a decrease in population means declining demand. To become effective demand, the population must have wealth or income. For residential real estate, population is usually considered as number of households rather than as number of people.

Given population and purchasing power, demand then depends on characteristics of the population. For example, an elderly population means fewer children per household and, therefore, translates into demand for dwelling units with only one or two bedrooms. Alternatively, a community with many people under 18 years of age means strong demand for three- and four-bedroom, two-bath, dwelling units. More schools and playgrounds are also likely to be needed. A largely middle-aged population, most of whom work, is likely to translate into demand for two- and three-bedroom housing units of moderate to high value. With higher incomes, couples generally want larger and more attractive places in which to live.

Wage Levels and Income Stability

The real estate market is sensitive to changes in wage levels, employment opportunities, and stability of income. Rental payments and housing costs are closely geared to ability to pay. In fact, there are definite rules of

thumb accepted by mortgage lenders and federal housing agencies under which total housing costs should not exceed 25 to 35 percent of the wage earner's income. Homes, too, are purchased on time-payment plans, like other consumer goods, and payments are made out of income on a monthly basis. But food, clothing, and transportation generally take priority over housing. Hence, income and employment outlook must be positive for residential space demand to be strong.

Personal Savings, Credit Availability, and Levels of Interest Rates

Higher wage and salary payments are significantly reflected in the increase of total disposable personal income, which rose from $352.0 billion in 1960 to approximately $1,828.9 billion in 1980. During this same period, personal savings increased from $19.7 billion to $110.2 billion, more than five times. These personal savings and investments by financial institutions provide a great reservoir of mortgage funds, which in turn influence mortgage credit availability and interest rate levels.

Mortgage credit availability and interest rates act as a barometer of the residential real estate market activity. A tightening of money availability along with higher interest rates immediately and negatively influence home construction and existing home sales. Easier availability and lower interest rates have the opposite effect. Most homes are bought on credit. Terms, therefore, are an important part of a purchase transaction and often influence the transaction price. To many buyers with small equity down payments, price undoubtedly means size of monthly payments for principal, interest, insurance, and taxes, PIIT.

Rent and Vacancy Levels

The rental market is highly competitive. If rents are set too high in relation to servicing costs, tenants will economize on space, and vacancies will result. Housing supply cannot be withdrawn from the market, for all practical purposes. Competition to maintain full occupancy, therefore, forces prices into line. Vacancy rates exceeding 5 to 8 percent indicate either an oversupply or overpricing of rental space. In either case, construction cutbacks are likely until the market strengthens.

Taxation and Land Use Controls

Taxation is sometimes used as a governmental tool to compel or deter real estate development or to direct employment of land for particular uses. For example, vacant land is sometimes overassessed and taxed to stimulate its improvement. Likewise, homestead laws shift municipal costs to owners of business and tenant-occupied properties. Such tax policy is directly designed to encourage homeownership and the use of land.

Land use controls also affect real estate market operations. Tighter controls and permit requirements drive real estate prices upward and tend to discourage sales and construction.

Costs of Land, Labor, and Building Materials

Availability of land and the cost of land, labor, and building materials affect real estate supply. Although physically abundant, land that is economically usable may be in short supply. Improvements in the form of access roads, drainage facilities, water, and other community utilities must ordinarily be added to "raw" land before it can be subdivided and offered for sale. Such improvements are costly and often can be successfully made only with community sanction and on a relatively large scale. Scarcity of building sites, in turn, causes upward pricing of existing properties and adversely affects market sales activity. On the other hand, speculative optimism may lead to an oversupply of improved land or space, resulting in a depressed market for months and even years.

Construction Technology and Building Quality

More buildings are torn down than fall down. This destruction of often physically sound structures is caused by changes in the methods of building and by building obsolescence. Rapid advances in building design and methods of construction have sparked the demand for modern homes that offer greater conveniences and, hence, greater amenities of living. Improvements in home heating, lighting, insulation, soundproofing, air conditioning, and interior design have brought about an active demand for home modernization and replacement that is likely to last for many years. Similar comments apply to commercial and industrial buildings.

MARKET OPERATION

Supply and demand interact constantly in the real estate market causing both short-run and long-run adjusments.

Supply and Demand Dynamics

The real estate market acts much like the market of economic theory in response to changes in supply and demand. Imperfections, such as lack of product standardization, long lead times for production of new supply, use of leverage, and tax shelters cause some deviations from the theory. Suggested guidelines to understand real estate market dynamics are as follows.

1. Units or types of real estate comparable in size and quality tend to sell at similar prices.
2. Prices tend to be stable if supply and demand are in balance.
3. If demand outruns existing supply, a seller's market is created and prices advance. Higher prices cut back on the number of units demanded and, at the same time, stimulate construction of new units. Several weeks, and often several months, are required for new supply to be produced after the need is recognized. New construction will continue until supply and demand are again in balance and prices have stabilized.
4. If supply exceeds demand, as in a declining community or region, a buyer's market exists and prices decline. Falling prices stimulate demand while discouraging new construction. Prices will continue to fall until supply and demand are again in balance.
5. Changing cost of credit has significant impact with lower interest rates stimulating demand.

Short-Run Adjustments

Demand is much more dynamic than supply in the short run. If demand suddenly declines, the excess supply cannot be removed from the market area. And if demand suddenly surges, additional supply cannot be provided on short notice.

For illustrative purposes, consider the housing market in a medium-sized community that is not tied to a large metropolitan area by commuters and is, therefore, independent of outside influences. An assumption of standardized housing units is made to simplify our discussion. This assumption is not too unrealistic in that any one housing unit can be substituted for another of nearly equal quality. With many market adjustments possible, no great distortion in the operation of the market needs to result. The short-run interaction among supply, demand, and price is shown in Figure 12–1.

In Figure 12–1, curve D_0 represents the original demand schedule for housing. Curve S represents the supply schedule. The vertical axis can represent either the rental or sale price of one housing unit. The horizontal axis indicates the number of housing units demanded or supplied.

The demand curve means that fewer housing units will be demanded at a higher price than at a lower price. The supply curve, on the other hand, says that at a low price fewer housing units will be supplied than at a higher price.

Supply and demand forces are in balance at the point where curves D_0 and S intersect. The price at this point is P_0 at which level X units of housing are demanded. A sudden increase in population or income would shift the demand schedule to the right, curve D_i. Because new units cannot be readily produced, the price rises sharply to P_i. At this price, Y units are demanded and supplied. Alternatively, a decline in demand, curve D_d, would cause the price to drop to P_d, with fewer units, Z, being demanded.

FIGURE 12–1
Short-run supply, demand, and price relationships

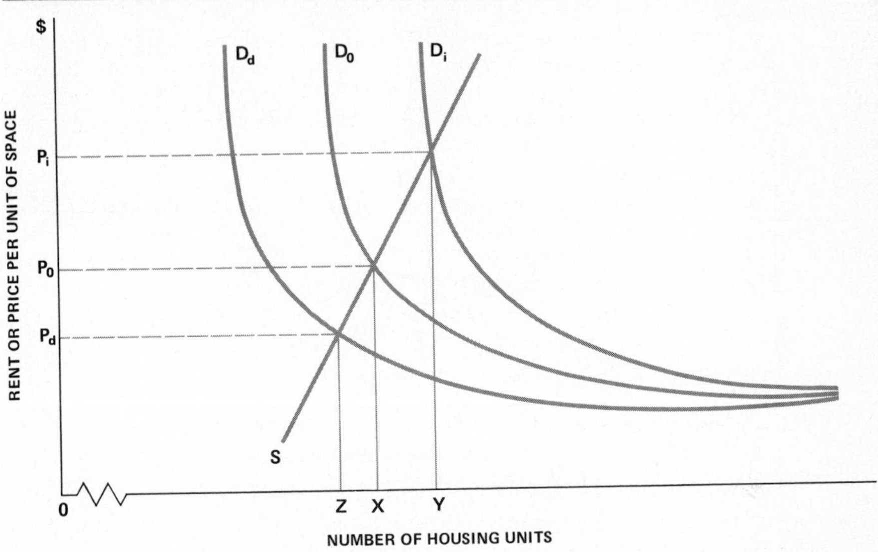

A sudden increase in demand cannot greatly increase the number of housing units supplied in the short run. Several weeks would be required as a minimum to increase supply, even though the price had increased to P_i. The additional amount of supply equals $Y - X$. This would come about first by vacancies being absorbed. Purchase and rental prices would then increase as demand pressed on supply. Some people would use their living space more intensely by *doubling up,* that is, by crowding more people into their dwellings. The motives might be to earn more rent or to help out friends and relatives forced out of other units by higher prices. Low-income people would be forced to double up because they could not afford the higher prices. Some families would find housing in the country or in the surrounding villages, thus commuting greater distances to work. Trailers, mobile homes, and seasonal housing would also be brought in and occupied to increase the community's housing supply.

Long-Run Adjustments

The cost of building new housing units enters into the long-run determination of a new equilibrium. Assume that several new industries move into our middle-sized community over a period of years. This is realistic, as many urban areas have steadily increased in population in recent decades. The successive increases in demand are represented by curves D_1 and D_2 in Figure 12–2. A long-run cost curve is also introduced in Figure

FIGURE 12–2
Long-run supply, demand, price, and cost relationships

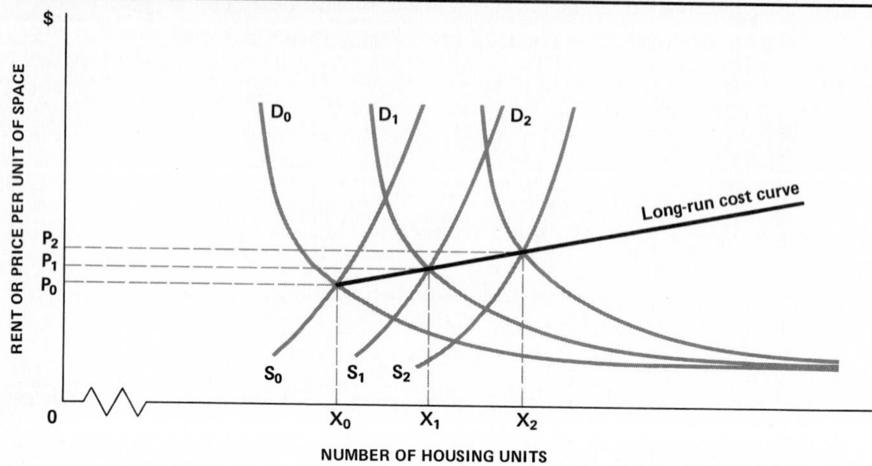

12–2 to introduce the cost of building an additional housing unit. The supply curves are short run because of the long lead time needed to build additional units.

In Figure 12–2, an increase in demand, from curve D_0 to curve D_1, increases the short-run price above the cost to produce a unit. This is represented by the intersection of curves S_0 and D_1. New housing units would be built (price exceeds cost) and eventually a new balance reached at the intersection of curves S_1 and D_1. Because the price at the intersection equals the cost of production, builders would not find it profitable to continue new construction beyond this point.

A second increase in demand, to curve D_2 (more new industry moving into town), would start the process again. With demand exceeding supply, prices again advance. Under conditions of steadily increasing demand, costs of land, labor, and building materials all tend to increase continually. That is, material suppliers and workers can bargain for higher prices and wages and almost always get the increase. Hence, the long-run cost curve slopes upward. Eventually, a new equilibrium is reached where the long-run cost curve and curves D_2 and S_2 all intersect. The new price level is P_2, whereas the number of housing units in the community has increased to X_2. The overall increase in housing units equals $X_2 - X_0$.

Little or no new construction would occur if demand decreased, that is, if the demand curve shifted to the left. The price would quickly drop below the cost curve, and no profit incentive would be present to justify starting construction of new housing units.

Real Estate Cycles

Some analysts and authors assert that population, income, and the economy interact to produce a regular rise and fall in real estate sales and construction *cycles.* Variations do occur in the level of these activities, as seasons and as economic conditions change. Seasonal changes or fluctuations are regular, with higher levels of activity usually occurring in the summer. But construction activity and real estate sales fluctuations have little regularity or rhythm in that they occur over periods of from three to seven or more years. Each period of expansion and interaction seems to be unique.

Real estate construction and sales activity seem more closely related to the cost and availability of financing than to any regular cycle. For example, shortages of credit in 1966, 1969–1970, 1973–1974, and 1979–1982 pushed interest rates up, resulting in sharp cutbacks in housing starts across the United States. Thus, an investor or developer might better look to current and likely monetary policy than to regular cycles in deciding whether to take on a new project. On an overall basis, real estate construction and sales activities have been more stable in recent decades because of better fiscal and monetary policies by our federal government.

Real Estate Market Efficiency

Markets range from perfect to imperfect in operation. A *perfect market* is one in which all information concerning future risks and benefits for each property is available to all participants. Full information is usually not readily available to all participants, particularly in real estate markets, which are generally considered to be imperfect. Real estate information costs considerable money, time, and effort to collect and analyze. Therefore, less wealthy investors find it relatively more expensive than wealthy investors to acquire information. Effectively, this means that not all investors operate from comparable levels of information. In turn, this means that market participants have differing expectations of returns and risks from real estate and differing values for a given parcel of realty.

Perfect or not, what is the efficiency of the real estate market? An *efficient market* is one in which changes in the information about the outlook for a given property are quickly reflected in the property's probable selling price or value. That is, favorable information about a parcel causes an immediate increase in its value, whereas negative or unfavorable information pushes its value down. In an inefficient market, participants with greater knowledge or skill can exploit other participants and thereby rapidly increase their wealth. Research has not provided a clear answer to the question. One thing is sure, information is generally captured and disseminated rather slowly in real estate markets. But once information is known, the value expectations of participants is influenced. This suggests that real estate markets are relatively inefficient in that those able to gain the greatest knowledge are also able to gain the greatest advantage in the market. This conclusion provides an extremely strong reason to study and follow cause and effect market indicators in investment real estate.

LOCAL MARKET INDICATORS

Market information is extremely important to an investor considering the development or purchase of a property. Levels of prices and values are uncertain and risky; they do not rise and fall in regular cycles. Uncertainty and risk may be reduced, however, by monitoring and interpreting local market indicators. Key market indicators for housing are discussed here. These same indicators may aid in interpreting change in other submarkets as well. The housing market is used as an example here because it is larger and more familiar and has more transactions.

Supply and demand and market theory, already discussed, must be understood to interpret these indicators. As buyers and sellers, most of us are opportunists, with a desire to buy low and sell high. Reading indicators enables us to follow this maximizing strategy better, insofar as it is possible. In short, market indicators help us identify "buyers' " and "sellers' " markets, possibly before they occur. But buyers must sometimes purchase in a sellers' market, and sellers must sometimes sell in a buyers' market. The result is that prices advance or decline according to the relative strengths of the supply and demand forces.

Four groups or categories of indicators are identified here. The basis of these groups are (1) demand, (2) supply-demand interaction, (3) financing, and (4) construction or new supply. (See Figure 12–3.) Supply indicators are conspicuous by their absence as a group, even though 95 to 97 percent of the space that influences market activity in any year already exists at the beginning of the year. Demand is the dynamic force in real estate markets. Trends, rates of change, and direction of change in these various indicators provide the most important information.

Demand Indicators

The four key demand indicators are (1) population, (2) employment, (3) unemployment, and (4) per capita personal income. Trends and fluctuations in these four variables tell a great deal about likely changes in effective demand.

Obviously, increases in population mean increased desire for housing. And an increase in employment, along with high levels of employment, indicates economic growth and is likely to result in immigration of ad-

FIGURE 12–3
Local real estate market indicators

CATEGORY AND ITEMS	SOURCES
1. Demand	
a. Population	Population center, Chamber of Commerce
b. Employment	Local U.S. Department of Labor office
c. Unemployment	Local U.S. Department of Labor office
d. Personal income per capita (wage levels)	Census data, local U.S. Department of Labor office
2. Supply-demand interaction	
a. Sales prices	Comparison of standard house with local sales prices
b. Rent levels	Comparison in market
c. Vacancy rate/utilization rate	Surveys, personal observation
d. Sales volume	Multiple listing service reports, want ads
3. Finance	
a. Relative availability of money	Survey of local lenders
b. Costs of money; interest rates	Survey of local lenders
c. Prime rate	News reports, local lenders
d. Foreclosure rates	Lenders, courthouse records
4. New supply	
a. Subdivision activity	Plat records, court house
b. Building permits	Local housing office/Dodge reports
c. Construction volume	Contractors, news reports
d. Construction costs	Contractors

ditional workers and population. Per capita personal income tells how much purchasing power is available for housing. Declines in population and income obviously mean decreased effective demand.

Many states have population centers, usually at a major university, from which population data may be obtained. The U.S. Department of Labor provides employment, unemployment, and wage (income) information for most communities. Planning commissions and chambers of commerce often publish reports containing population and labor force information. And most newspapers periodically publish reviews and comments on the economic outlook for an area or region.

Indicators of Supply and Demand Interaction

Price levels, vacancy rates, sales volumes, and rent levels tell what is happening in regard to supply-demand interaction in local real estate. For the most part, information on these variables must be captured on a personal basis. That is, data are not regularly published concerning the variables.

Price-level information may be obtained by comparing prices for certain "standard" houses through time. That is, typical two-, three-, and four-bedroom houses might be priced on a comparative basis every few months. In like manner, rent levels for one-, two, and three-bedroom apartments might be checked. The checking might involve asking prices in want ads or visits to dwelling units offered for sale or rent. Also a summary of completed transactions published monthly by a multiple listing service would serve as a source of price information. Sales volume may also be estimated from this summary. A further indication of sales activity is the volume of deeds recorded by a country recorder. Again, trends and rates of change are vital information.

Vacancy rates tell what portion of the existing supply of space is not being utilized. Thus, the rate of property utilization in a community is the complement or flip side of the vacancy rate. Post office surveys are sometimes made to determine vacancy rates. Checks with property managers and monitoring want ads may also indicate vacancy levels. New, unsold houses must also be counted as vacancies. An increasing vacancy rate foretells a weakening in prices or rents, while a declining rate suggests that rents and prices are likely to advance.

Financing Indicators

Key financing indicators are the relative availability of money, the interest rates being charged, the prime rate, and mortgage foreclosure rate.

The prime rate is the rate that major commercial banks typically charge large, well-established, financially sound companies on business loans. The rate tends to be uniform across the country and, in a sense, ties all financial markets together. An increase in the prime rate indicates a tightening in the money markets, while a decrease indicates easier money. Changes in the prime rate are widely quoted in the financial news. A change in the prime rate is usually followed by a comparable shift in mortgage interest rates.

Mortgage foreclosure rates tell of failures of borrowers to live up to their mortgage contracts. Deaths and divorces, two major causes, tend to be relatively stable through time in their incidence while unemployment fluctuates. Thus, a sudden increase in foreclosures is likely to be preceded by layoffs and declining economic conditions. Foreclosures translate into a decline in demand, at least in the short run.

New Supply Indicators

Development and construction mean increases in the supply of real estate. Developers and builders generally add to supply only if they expect sales prices or market values to exceed costs. Starting construction of a new building means that an aspiring homeowner or investor has decided that value exceeds cost. In the short run, construction may continue as a builder strives to keep a crew going, in spite of discouraging market outlook. Key statistics in this area are subdivision activity, building permits, construction volume, and construction costs.

Subdivision requires several months to a year from plat approvals to market availability of sites. Housing construction may take only from two to three months. And construction does not always follow immediately after the taking out of a building permit. Thus, lags must be taken into account in interpreting development and construction indicators.

Building permits and dollar construction value tell of short-term increases in supply. These increases must be related to indicated effective demand. Subdivision activity indicates that the long-run outlook is more promising, and increasing costs of construction result in higher costs of space. In turn, the cost of new space is at the margin; any increases tend to spread over the entire existing supply, given time. Ever-higher costs means that less space is likely to be demanded and used.

Interrelatedness of Indicators

Real estate supply and demand forces exert pressures in many directions. Increasing births or incomes translate into greater demand. At the same time, outmigration to better opportunities elsewhere decreases demand. Thus, supply and demand forces are interrelated in their effects. And market prices and sales volume are the result of these and many other conditions. Likewise, market indicators may not all point in the same direction. The investor-analyst must read and interpret the signs provided by indicators on a continuing basis.

MARKET FUNCTIONS

The primary functions performed by the real estate market are:

1. Exchange (redistribution of ownership) and the reallocation of land and existing space to alternative uses based on rent-paying ability
2. Providing price and value information to market participants for their use in making decisions.
3. Adjustment in the quality and quantity of space in response to changing social and economic needs.

The result of the market's operation is a physical pattern of land uses that reflects the social and economic tastes and needs of the community or area.

Exchange

Most sellers were buyers at one time, preferring property to the money. Through time, conditions changed to where the owner now prefers to give up ownership. New roads, new stores, and new factories may have been built. The tax shelter provided by the property may have been largely used up. A related business may have gone bankrupt. A spouse may have died or children married and left home. Any one of these would be reason for an owner to sell out and relocate.

A sale of property occurs in a free market only when it is mutually advantageous to both buyer and seller. The buyer would rather have the property than the money. The seller prefers the money. The real estate market, therefore, reallocates property ownership and redistributes space according to the preferences of property users with financial capability.

The value of each property, as well as how it might best be used, depends on its physical characteristics and its location. The owner wishes the property exposed to the greatest number of possible buyers to get the highest price possible. The expectation is that the buyer best able to use the property will pay the highest price. Each buyer, in turn, shops the many properties available, seeking the best possible property for his or her needs with price taken into account. The highest and best use for each site is expected to win out in the competition.

The exchange function includes rentals and tax-deferred exchanges in addition to outright sales. Attention here is focused on the sales transaction because it is most common. The concerns of a renter are essentially the same as those of a buyer, except that the control of the property is gained by leasing rather than by purchase.

Providing Information

Investors, lenders, managers, assessors, builders, developers, and brokers all want and use information about property sales for judgments and decisions that turn on value. An investor wishes to pay no more for a property than the amount for which a comparable property sold. On the other hand, an owner wishes to sell for no less. A lender does not want to make a loan on a property for more than it can be sold for. Managers need value information to set rent levels, assessors to establish assessed values. Builders and developers make value judgments on structures to be built or projects to be undertaken. And brokers need value information to show clients that transactions being proposed are sound. Price and value information are, therefore, important to the continuing operation and stability of the real estate market.

The price paid for property in one transaction can help other market participants develop ideas about value for subsequent transactions. Value is partially determined in the market, for a given type of property, by comparing actual prices paid for similar type properties. Value is also partially determined by a buyer's need and potential use of a property. An appraiser is often engaged to give an estimate of the market value (the most probable selling price) of a property.

Space Adjustment

Owners change the use of properties in response to market pressures and opportunities. Remodeling and renovation may be necessary to adjust to the changing need of the market. For example, assume that the value of a property in a possible use, such as for offices, exceeds the value of the property in its current use, residential, plus the cost of conversion. A rational owner is likely to convert the property to office space in this circumstance. If demand exceeds the current supply, raw land must be subdivided and vacant sites developed to increase the quanity of space. This is to say the value of new space exceeds the cost of providing it (site cost plus construction cost). If, however, demand for space decreases and property values decline, little or no space adjustment (remodeling or new construction) is likely.

SUMMARY

Property rights make up the commodity of the real estate market. Real estate markets are often classified as (1) residential, (2) commercial, (3) industrial, (4) agricultural, and (5) special purpose. A "buyer's market" or a "seller's market" may come about when supply and demand get out of balance.

Several relatively distinct characteristics of real estate markets are their (1) localness in character, (2) private transactions, (3) nonstandard commodity, (4) diffusion, and (5) poor adjustment of supply and demand. Some of the more important supply and demand forces are population, income levels, wealth, interest rates, rent and vacancy levels, government powers or controls, and construction technology. These forces interact to bring forth new space as long as the value of additional supply exceeds its cost. These forces also lead to fluctuations that vary in intensity and frequency in real estate sales and construction activity. Therefore, investors, lenders, builders, and brokers find market indicators extremely important.

Indicators may be grouped into four categories: (1) demand, (2) supply-demand interaction, (3) financing, and (4) construction or new supply. Three important functions of real estate markets are (1) exchange, (2) providing price and value information, and (3) supply adjustment in quantity and quality.

QUESTIONS FOR REVIEW AND DISCUSSION

1. Name at least two submarkets for each of the following market types of real estate: (a) residential, (b) commercial, (c) industrial, (d) agricultural, and (e) special purpose.

2. List and describe briefly at least four characteristics that make real estate markets relatively unique.

3. List and describe briefy four demand and four supply forces of local estate markets.

4. Describe briefly short-run and long-run adjustments in real estate markets. Illustrate with supply-demand diagrams.

5. Explain why market indicators are needed if real estate activity is cyclical.

6. Name and briefly discuss the nature of two market indicators in each of these four categories: (a) demand, (b) supply-demand interaction, (c) finance, and (d) new supply.

7. Identify and briefy describe three functions of real estate markets.

8. Would we need an urban real estate market if we did not have private ownership rights in real property? Discuss.

9. Property owners sometimes oppose community growth even though values generally go up as a result of growth. Is this rationale? Explain.

10. In earlier chapters we noted that real estate has characteristics of heterogeneity, durability, and interdependence. What implications do these characteristics have relative to stability in the real estate market? (Think hard, this is a tough one.)

CHAPTER THIRTEEN
REAL ESTATE MARKET AND FEASIBILITY ANALYSIS

He reads much; he is a great observer, and he looks quite through the deeds of men.
SHAKESPEARE, *Julius Caesar*

IMPORTANT TOPICS OR DECISION AREAS COVERED IN THIS CHAPTER

- Urban Change and Market Analysis
- Market-area Delineation
- Economic Base Analysis
- Supply-demand Analysis
- Current Market Conditions
- Market Study Conclusions
- Feasibility Analysis

Real estate market analysis is a study to predict changes in the amount and types of real estate facilities needed in an area. The emphasis is usually on urban space needs—that is, residential, retail trade, office, and industrial space needs. The time horizon used on a study varies from one or two years to ten years or more. The larger the probable size, the longer the study horizon is likely to be.

A real estate market study is a management tool for decision making as well as for planning and budgeting. An investor may wish to undertake a market study before purchasing a large apartment complex. The study could give assurance that the outlook for the property is sound. The study could also provide a basis for judging the amount to be bid for the property. Owners might want a market study to ascertain whether their property is being put to its highest and best use and is being merchandised to its greatest advantage.

A developer would use a study to judge whether a new shopping center is needed and where. Assuming that a new center is justified, the study helps a lender to decide how large a loan to make to finance its development. Tenants are induced to the center on the basis of the market analysis results. The study might also be useful in obtaining necessary approvals from planning officials.

Real estate market analysis is in the early stages of development; years will probably be required before the concepts, methodology, and applications are refined. In the meantime, much judgment will be required of the analyst and the decision maker. The discussion here assumes that the decision maker wants accurate, realistic information, not a report to justify an action or development that he or she has already decided to undertake or promote.

KEY CONCEPTS INTRODUCED IN THIS CHAPTER

Base activity
Comparative economic advantage
Economic base
Economic base analysis
Feasibility analysis
Locational quotient (LQ)
Market analysis
Service activity

URBAN CHANGE AND MARKET ANALYSIS

Urban areas constantly change, usually expanding, though in some cases, decline and contraction do set in. And all sectors of expanding areas do not share equally in the growth. The important considerations are when and where change will take place, and what types of change.

Economic Change and Land Use

An urban area grows and expands because its economic base grows and expands. An *economic base* is that activity that exports goods and services outside the community in return for money or income. The economic base provides employment and income on which the rest of the local economy depends. Employment and income in the rest of the local economy, often called service activities, expand and contract in direct relation to changes in base activities.

A local economy that is expanding attracts additional workers and population. With increased economic activity and population, the space needs of the area or community also increase. There are two major ways in which such change takes place. One is essentially growth outward; the other is growth upward.

Land development. Raw or vacant land is constantly converted from non-urban use to sites for productive urban space. Examples are the construction of shopping centers, industrial plants, or stadiums in previously open fields. A further example is the subdivision of open land with subsequent construction of houses. This type of growth and change usually occurs at the urban fringe and, thus, is growth outward.

Land use succession. Because urban areas are dynamic, the use of land and the improvements to the land tend to be in a constant state of flux. The changes came about in one or more of the following ways.

1. *Change in type of use.* A large old house being converted into an office building represents a change in the type of use. So also is the tearing down of a gasoline service station to make way for an apartment house. A change in the type of use involves the modification of an existing structure or its replacement by new improvements. The new use must be able to absorb the cost of conversion or replacement to be profitable and feasible.
2. *Change in intensity of use.* Adding another story to increase display and sales area is an intensity of use change. Converting a larger, old, single-family residence into several small apartment units is, also. Although the type of use is not changed, the amount of economic or social activity on the site is modified. If the intensity is increased, the additional benefits must be great enough to justify the costs of structural change usually involved in such a change.
3. *Change in quality of use.* The nature of the benefits of use of a property may be upgraded or downgraded. Creeping blight can lead to the gradual deterioration in the benefits generated by a residential neighborhood or a commercial area. The rehabilitation of the Georgetown area in Washington, D.C., on the other hand, is an excellent example of improving the quality of use. Upgrading the quality of use depends on an explicit act of a manager or owner plus a favorable set of environmental conditions for the property.

Urban areas tend to grow and expand along the lines of least economic resistance. That is, they grow in the direction in which values realized exceed costs incurred by the greatest amount for the additional space gained. For an economist, this is another way of saying that marginal growth occurs where the marginal profit is greatest.

The Study Framework

Several distinct phases are involved in making a market study. A decision regarding the type of real estate of concern—office space, warehousing, or apartments—is presumed to have been made before entry into these steps. An awareness of the relation of the national and regional economy to the local economy is also taken as a given.

1. *Market-area delineation.* The market area is largely determined by the range of influence or competitiveness of the type of real estate under consideration. A housing study might cover one community, for example. On the other hand, a study for a regional shopping center might extend for 50 to 75 miles from a study site.
2. *Analysis of the area's economy.* Analysis of an area's basic resources, employment, income, population, and economic trends provides a setting for later detailed consideration of real estate needs. This is commonly called an economic base analysis.
3. *Supply and demand analysis.* Real estate supply and demand factors are identified, followed by data collection and evaluation. Supply factors ordinarily include an inventory of space, plus current new construction, conversion, and demolition activity. Common demand factors are age-sex distribution of the population, per capita disposable income levels, and family size.
4. *Analysis of current market conditions.* Current market conditions reflect the interaction of the supply and demand factors. Thus, such items as prices and construction costs, rent levels and vacancies, and the availability and costs of financing must be considered as they relate to the specific type of real estate under study.
5. *Projections and conclusions.* Conclusions about the relative strength of market demand currently and into the future must be reached. The types of space needed at various prices or rent levels must be identified. Finally, a judgment on the share of the market that can be captured must be reached.
6. *Feasibility analysis.* The market study can be made more specific by a feasibility analysis. A feasibility analysis is a study of the profit potential in a proposed real estate project. The study must take into account market, physical, locational, legal, social, governmental, and financial factors.

A market study is usually conducted by an experienced analyst in that identifying and measuring significant variables is usually quite difficult. Even collecting existing data on important factors for a complete market and feasibility analysis is difficult, time consuming, and expensive. The decision maker's research budget is usually quite limited. Therefore, the intensity of emphasis given to each of the phases depends on the availability of data and on the size and type of decision to be made.

In interpreting a report, the decision maker needs to recognize data limitations as well as the sometimes loose interrelationships among the factors studied. In other words, judgment must be exercised.

MARKET-AREA DELINEATION

The range of competition of the type of real estate under study determines the market area. Criteria for defining a market area include physical, social, legal, and economic elements. These change from one type of use to another. And the importance given to each depends on the situation. Several brief examples illustrate the difficulty of the problem and how judgment must be used in delineating a study area.

Competition is communitywide for housing, except possibly in the largest metropolitan areas. People working in the central business district may live by themselves or with their families in a downtown apartment or a one-family suburban house. Workers in suburban factories, shopping centers, and offices are somewhat more likely to live near the urban fringe than in the central city. Therefore, the analysis of demand must be communitywide. The analyst can make some judgments about needs for apartments versus one-family homes and about needs for middle-income housing versus high-income housing to narrow the scope of the study. Even so, the market area continues to be communitywide.

By way of contrast, the market study area for a supermarket might be limited to a trade area or neighborhood. Groceries tend to be convenience goods; that is, people buy them on their way home from work. Or if they begin the shopping trip from their home, they usually go to one of the two or three nearest stores. Knowing this, the analyst can establish a trade area based on several considerations.

1. *Neighborhood boundaries.* Major streets and highways, freeways, railroad tracks, large parks, reservoirs, rivers, lakes, and steep hills all tend to serve as boundaries between neighborhoods.
2. *Social and economic groupings.* Neighborhoods tend to be made up of people of similar tastes and income levels. Observation of people's dress, cars, and housing gives a clue as to the extent of the similarity. Similar information can be obtained from census tract data.
3. *Travel patterns.* The mode of travel affects where people buy groceries. Thus, street and traffic patterns for motor vehicles and public transit become important in delineating the trade area.

Another example would be the market area for a regional shopping center. It is generally known that people will drive a hundred miles, and sometimes farther, to shop. Hence, this is the trade area and the area of competition.

Finally, competition for office and industrial space occurs on a regional and national basis. In locating a new plant or relocating its main office, a major corporation may weigh relative merits of several cities like New York, Chicago, Houston, Los Angeles, and Atlanta.

ECONOMIC BASE ANALYSIS

Communities, areas, or regions tend to grow or decline in direct proportion to some particular economic advantage they possess relative to the rest of the country and world. This is termed their *comparative economic advantage.* The activities providing this advantage, which results in exports of goods and services in return for money, are collectively called the economic base of a community or area. The economic base is sometimes considered the product for which a community is famous, such as cars in Detroit.

Specialization in the economic activity having the greatest comparative advantage takes place over time because the benefits or returns are maximized. For example, western Oregon and Washington excel in producing quality lumber, primarily Douglas fir, for export. Iowa farmers grow corn and soybeans rather than wheat or rice because the net returns per acre on the former are greatest. And Florida, Arizona, and southern California have built recreation and retirement into major industries because their climate is preferred to that in most other states.

Identifying the Economic Base

Economic activity is generally identified and measured in terms of employment, income, or business earnings. If Census data are used as a source, employment is most often used because it is more easily available and is more easily translated into population and demand for real estate. However, the Bureau of Economic Analysis of the U.S. Department of Commerce publishes reports that provide personal income, business earnings, and employment data, including projections. Data used in this chapter are taken from the U.S. Census Bureau.

In a base study, economic activity is divided into two categories: base and service or base and nonbase. *Base activity* produces goods or services that are exported to the outside world in return for money, which in turn is used to buy other goods and services from the outside world. The exchange enables the community or area to survive and to continue as an independent entity. Naturally enough, nonbasic or *service activity* produces goods or services for local consumption or use. That is, they are not exported. Base activity is also sometimes termed primary activity. In this event, service activity becomes secondary activity.

But how can base activity be identified? Frequently, people "know what the base is" and presumably can easily identify base activity. In fact, the problem is not so simple. For example, should a department store, a bakery, a service station, and a university be classified as base or service activities. The answer depends considerably on the size of the community or area being studied.

Almost all economic activity in the United States is service in that less than 5 percent of our production is exported. If the study unit is a relatively small city of 50,000 people, the answer is more difficult. To the extent that an activity satisfies the needs of a portion of the 50,000, it is a service. But to the extent that the department store draws farmers as customers or bakery goods are trucked to neighboring communities, the store and bakery are basic. Likewise, a service station, located on a highway and catering to through traffic, is basic. And if the university draws students and funds from outside the city, it contributes to the economic base of the city.

A *locational quotient (LQ)* is commonly used to distinguish between base and service portions of economic activity. An LQ is the percentage of total local activity in an industry relative to the percentage of total national activity in the same industry. For example, using 1980 industry employment as the measure, the locational quotient of the Oregon lumber and wood products industry is calculated as follows.

$$\text{Percentage of industry employment for Oregon for the lumber and wood products industry} = \frac{74{,}308}{1{,}138{,}425} \times 100 = 6.53\%$$

$$\text{Percentage of industry employment for the United States for the lumber and wood products industry} = \frac{1{,}229{,}394}{97{,}639{,}355} \times 100 = 1.26\%$$

$$LQ = \frac{\text{Percentage of Oregon business employment for the lumber and wood products industry}}{\text{Percentage of U.S. business employment for the lumber and wood products industry}} = \frac{6.53\%}{1.26\%} = 5.18$$

An LQ of 1 would mean that Oregon provided employment in the lumber and wood products industry at the same rate as the entire U.S. industry, on average. Hence, the industry, on balance, would be service only. A locational quotient of less than 1 would mean that Oregon did not meet its needs from this industry and, hence, had to import lumber and wood products. In actuality, the LQ is 5.18, meaning that Oregon produces over five times its needs in lumber and wood products. Obviously, the industry is very important to the economic base of Oregon.

Other LQs are shown in Figure 13–1. Note the LQ of 8.9 for the Eugene-Springfield SMSA. At the other extreme, the very low LQ in mining says that Oregon does not produce its proportional share of oil and minerals. Finally, not that non-base activities as trade, transportation, public administration, and services all have LQs very near one.

Base Projections

An analyst, working with employment data only, might project employment to 1990 based on trends and other information available.

Many local planning commissions make economic base analysis studies and projections. Thus, unless an investor has a specific need and is willing to pay for information, the data sources mentioned may be used.

SUPPLY-DEMAND ANALYSIS

Each land use has its own unique determinants of supply and demand to be considered in a market analysis. Supply determinants tend to be physical and economic, whereas demand determinants tend to be more social and economic.

Supply Factors

The existing inventory of space for the use under study marks the point of beginning in considering determinants of supply. At best, new construction increases the total supply from 2 to 3 percent in any one year. With strong demand, the amount of space for a specific use, other than housing, can be doubled or tripled in one year, however, by the conversion of space from alternative uses in less demand.

An example will make the point clearer. In 1970, the United States had about 75 million dwelling units. The construction industry, operating at peak capacity, could add about 2.5 million units in one year. During the same year, about 300,000 units would be removed because of fire, flood, urban renewal, street and highway projects, and miscellaneous factors. The net added to the supply is, therefore, about 2.2 million units, just slightly less than a 3 percent increase.

To extend the example, assume that housing represents 50 percent of the total supply of space. Assume further that commercial office space represents 10 percent of the total supply of space. This means that supply of office space could be increased approximately five times faster than supply of housing, with the same input of resources. All housing construction activities would have to be redirected toward creating new office space. If the demand were strong enough, apartment buildings, houses, warehouses, and garages might be modified to increase the supply of office space. Although the example is highly unlikely, the net result might be to double the amount of office space in one year. Our example can be extended further by narrowing the use; that is, the supply of office

FIGURE 13–1
1980 employment, employment distribution by industry, and location quotients for the United States, the State of Oregon, and the Eugene-Springfield SMSA

MAJOR INDUSTRY GROUP	UNITED STATES		STATE OF OREGON			EUGENE-SPRINGFIELD SMSA		
	NUMBER EMPLOYED (000)	PERCENT DISTRI-BUTION	NUMBER EMPLOYED	PERCENT DISTRI-BUTION	INDUSTRY LOCATIONAL QUOTIENT	NUMBER EMPLOYED	PERCENT DISTRI-BUTION	INDUSTRY LOCATIONAL QUOTIENT
Agri., forestry, & fisheries	2,914	2.98%	52,302	4.59%	1.54	3,752	3.20%	1.07
Mining	1,028	1.05%	2,699	0.24%	0.23	239	0.20%	0.19
Construction	5,740	5.88%	73,250	6.43%	1.09	6,668	5.68%	0.97
Manufacturing	21,915	22.44%	222,017	19.50%	0.87	21,804	18.57%	0.83
Durable goods: total	13,479	13.81%	168,424	14.79%	1.07	17,513	14.91%	1.08
Lbr. & W. Prod.	1,229	1.26%	74,308	6.53%	5.18	13,155	11.20%	8.90
Primary Metal Industries								
Fabricated Metal Industries								
Machinery, except Electrical								
Electrical Machinery								
Motor vehicles & other trans. eq.								
Other durable goods								
Non-durable goods: total	8,436	8.64%	53,593	4.71%	0.54	4,291	3.65%	0.42
Food & Kindred products								
Textile mill & fabricated products								
Printing, publishing, & Allied								
Chemical & allied products								
Other non-durable goods								
Transport, comm., & pub. utilities	7,087	7.26%	81,621	7.17%	0.99	7,850	6.69%	0.92
Wholesale trade	4,217	4.32%	53,277	4.68%	1.08	5,127	4.37%	1.01
			0					
Retail trade	15,717	16.10%	203,220	17.85%	1.11	23,211	19.77%	1.23
Finance, ins. & real estate	5,898	6.04%	71,228	6.26%	1.04	6,465	5.51%	0.91
Services	27,976	28.65%	321,809	28.27%	0.99	37,129	31.62%	1.10
Public administration	5,147	5.27%	57,002	5.01%	0.95	5,176	4.41%	0.84
TOTAL	97,639	100.00%	1,138,425	100.00%		117,421	100.00%	

SOURCE: Employment data from U.S. census; calculations by authors.

space for public accountants could be increased several times with little effect on the supply of space for other needs.

In a similar sense, the supply of space in Madison, Wisconsin, can be increased sharply by shifting contractors, workers, and materials from surrounding communities. Milwaukee, Chicago, and Rockford, Illinois, the nearby communities, might grow at a slightly lower rate as a result.

The principal considerations in increasing space supply are as follows:

1. The availability and costs of land and utilities
2. The availability and costs of materials and labor
3. The availability and costs of financing
4. The availability and willingness of a developer to organize these factors toward manufacturing new space.

Demand Factors

The economic base is the primary determinant of space needs in a community. The essential variables are employment, population, and income. The function of the real estate market analysis is to relate the type and amount of economic activity to the specific type of space or use under study. The spending pattern of the population provides a means of relating population, income, and land use.

The recent spending pattern of the U.S. population, by product or service, is shown in Figure 13–2. Each of the items purchased represents some type of real estate improvement. Food, beverages, clothing, and furniture are distributed through stores, for example. Housing is purchased directly or rented. Medical and other services are dispensed through doctors' offices, clinics, and hospitals. By applying these percentages to a community's income, as determined in the base analysis, the amount of money available to each land use may be estimated.

FIGURE 13–2
U.S. spending patterns, by product or service, 1982.

EXPENDITURE CATEGORY	*PERCENTAGE*
Food, beverages, & tobacco	21.2
Clothing, accessories, & jewelry	7.1
Housing	16.8
Household operation, incl. furniture	11.9
Transportation & related	13.5
Other durables	2.1
Other non-durables	5.4
Other services	22.1
TOTAL	100.1

SOURCE: Table 744, 1984 U.S. Statistical Abstract; calculations by authors.

Effective demand must be more specifically related to land use and location. For example, if the population is young and families are small, demand for living units in multifamily structures is likely to be relatively stronger. A few figures show the importance of age distribution in the population. In 1960, when family units usually included two or three children, only 22.8 percent of new housing starts were in multifamily structures. By 1970, the children were growing up and leaving the nest, and this proportion doubled to 45.2 percent. And by 1980, the percentage had declined to 31.3 percent as the "baby boom" generation paired up to have families and children of their own.

CURRENT MARKET CONDITIONS

Current market conditions are the result of the interaction of supply and demand in the past. The important indicators of current market conditions are unsold inventory and rental vacancies, prices and construction costs, and mortgage defaults and foreclosures. Many of these are the same as the market indicators identified and discussed in the previous chapter, but here we are concerned with their use in market analysis. With strong demand, unsold inventory, rental vacancies, and mortgage defaults should be down. Prices and construction costs are likely to be up or increasing. With weak demand, they are likely to point in the opposite direction.

Unsold Inventory, Prices, and Construction Costs

Prices must exceed total construction costs for new construction to be justified. If new houses sell for $25 a square foot and costs are $23, a contractor will continue to build these units. However, if not all units sell, an inventory of unsold units develops. The increasing inventory should eventually drive prices down and signal the contractor to slow the rate of construction. Of course, units selling quickly and a very low inventory signal strong demand and the need for more construction. The shorter the time horizon of the study, the more important these signals become.

Vacancies and Rent Levels

Vacancies are the equivalent of unsold inventory. If the amount of vacant space builds up, rent levels should fall, and construction of new space should be slowed, or stopped. Thus, for example, an office building developer might note an increase in the amount of unused office space and lower or not increase asking rental prices. On the other hand, an apartment house manager might note low vacancies and use the occasion to raise rents. Projected demand for an area must be reduced to the extent that vacancies exist because the vacant space is the equivalent of newly constructed space for market purposes.

Mortgage Defaults and Foreclosures

A small percentage of mortgages are constantly in default because of death, divorce, or other financial difficulty of mortgagors. But not all defaults end up in foreclosure. If conditions are not too severe, a borrower can usually find someone to take over the property, thus avoiding foreclosure. If current market conditions are extremely severe, lenders may have to take over a number of properties. The latter would be a strong signal that the market is down, and construction of new housing units should not be started until economic conditions improve.

MARKET STUDY CONCLUSIONS

A real estate market analysis should end with estimates of demand and competition for the use under study. The study may be extended to include a feasibility analysis. The report should be written in a clear and concise manner, with the data and the discussion logically leading the reader to the conclusions. Short- and long-run market outlooks should be blended into the discussion; extraneous or nonpertinent data should not be included.

As we shall see in Chapter 21 on real estate investment, the market study conclusions provide the basis for projecting cash flows and the resale value of a property under study. If the market outlook is for decline or no growth, the productivity and income of the subject property is likely to hold fast or even decline. Thus, market study conclusions are critical to the advisability and value levels of real estate investments.

FEASIBILITY ANALYSIS

A *feasibility analysis* is a study to determine the practicality of a specific investment or development proposal. It is an extension of the generality of the economic base and market analysis to a specific real estate development or investment problem. Included is a study of the profit potential in a proposed project, with market, physical, locational, legal, social, governmental, and financial factors taken into account. The project is considered feasible only if the value to be created exceeds the total costs to be incurred.

Everyone involved in an investment situation expects to benefit. The owner of the site or property wants to realize as much profit or value increase as possible. The user wants to get a property in a location that best serves his or her needs. The owner may become the user. The developer, brokers, architects, engineers, builders, lenders, and attorneys involved expect to receive reasonable fees or commissions. A feasibility analysis is made so that the initiator of action minimizes risk while getting the greatest benefits possible.

Feasibility analysis applies to three types of situations:

1. The owner of a site or property looking for a use
2. A user looking for a site or a property with improvements well suited to his or her needs
3. An investor or developer looking for the best profit opportunity available, with the pulling in of other equity investors or of getting support from a mortgage lender a possibility

Owner Looking for a Use

Costs must be incurred in developing a site or modifying an improved property to suit the needs of a proposed use. The problem is to find a use able to realize enough value or benefits from the completed project to justify the costs. An office building might be constructed on a site at a total cost of $8,400,000, for example. The present value of future rents or benefits must equal or exceed $8,400,000 for the project to be feasible. See the calculations in Chapter 11 on highest and best use.

Or, again, a developer has an option to buy an old abandoned cannery for $1 million. The property is located near the waterfront, which is a major tourist attraction. He is considering converting the cannery into a tourist shopping center at an additional cost of $2 million. The value in the new use must equal or exceed $3 million to justify the project. Thus, cost must be bumped against expected value.

The process of feasibility analysis in the case of a site looking for a use begins with selection of the three or four, or more most likely uses for the property. The total costs involved in preparing the site or property for each use is then determined. Categories of costs include

1. Cost of site, or market value if already owned
2. Site preparation costs—soil tests, grading, landscaping
3. Fees of architects, engineers, attorneys
4. Brokerage commissions
5. Construction costs of improvements
6. Financing charges
7. Developer's profit
8. All other costs incidental to the development of the project

The project is feasible if a reliable tenant can be found to pay a rent high enough to justify the costs. It is feasible also if the owner expects personally to use the property and considers the costs reasonable and within his or her financial capacity. If the project is to be rented to many tenants, the market analysis must show that sufficient effective demand exists. And if the project is conversion or rehabilitation, the higher rents or benefits must be sufficient to justify the costs of modification.

A feasibility analysis of an owner looking for a use ends with the selection of the use giving the greatest value to the site. That use is its highest and best use. The selection of that use is the principle of comparative economic advantage in action. For example, alternative uses might indicate site values as follows: office building, $200,000; department store, $180,000; and hotel, $140,000. The owner, acting in self-interest, would almost certainly choose to construct the office building.

A User Looking for a Site

A user values a property for the future returns it will yield. The costs of renting or owning must be less than the present value of the benefits to be realized for a property to be feasible. For example, after analysis of his situation, a merchant decides that the highest rent he can pay for a certain store is $54,000 a year. The owner wants $60,000. The property is not a feasible alternative for the merchant. Or a developer estimates that apartment rentals prices justify a value of $40,000 per dwelling unit on a certain site. The site would cost $8,000 per dwelling unit, and improvement costs are estimated at $30,000 per dwelling unit. The $40,000 value exceeds the costs of $38,000; the project is feasible.

A user begins with the results of a market analysis and estimates the amount of unsatisfied demand existing in a community. The demand might be for office space, retail luggage, or automobile parts and services. Several alternative sites are analyzed, based on their availability and suitability for the use under study. Street patterns and traffic flows, lot size, location, zoning, actual or potential building size and shape, and neighborhood quality would be important considerations in selecting each of the sites. Based on the specific characteristics of each site, the amount of business to be conducted or the gross rental to be realized is estimated. From this, the amount of annual rental that can be earned from the property, or the capitalized value of the rents, is calculated. The site or property best serving the user's needs is selected, assuming that the asking rent or price is less than that which the owner can afford to pay based on the analysis.

Little attention may be given to highest and best use unless the user is also the owner. In fact, a user-renter may well take a better property and location than his or her purposes justify if the asking rent is too low. Selection of the site that best meets the needs of the user ends the feasibility study.

Investor Looking for a Profit Opportunity

An investor may use market and feasibility analyses to locate, and to choose between, profit opportunities. In the simplest situation, the investor may

FAIRWAY MORTGAGE SERVICES

Fishkill, New York
~~896-4942~~

Poughkeepsie, N.Y.
~~473-1650~~

471-1070

Call Michael Domber for current rate quotes and free mortgage qualification.

Equal Monthly Payment to Amortize a loan of $1,000

TERM RATE	10	12	15	18	20	22	25	27	29	30
8%	12.14	10.83	9.56	8.75	8.37	8.07	7.72	7.55	7.40	7.34
8¼	12.27	10.97	9.71	8.91	8.53	8.23	7.89	7.72	7.58	7.52
8½	12.40	11.11	9.85	9.06	8.68	8.39	8.16	7.89	7.75	7.69
8¾	12.54	11.24	10.00	9.21	8.84	8.55	8.23	8.06	7.93	7.87
9	12.67	11.39	10.15	9.37	9.00	8.72	8.40	8.24	8.11	8.05
9¼	12.81	11.53	10.30	9.53	9.16	8.88	8.57	8.41	8.29	8.23
9½	12.94	11.67	10.45	9.68	9.33	9.05	8.74	8.59	8.47	8.41
9¾	13.08	11.81	10.60	9.84	9.49	9.22	8.92	8.77	8.65	8.60
10	13.22	11.96	10.75	10.00	9.66	9.39	9.09	8.95	8.83	8.78
10¼	13.36	12.10	10.90	10.16	9.82	9.56	9.27	9.13	9.01	8.97
10½	13.50	12.25	11.06	10.33	9.99	9.73	9.45	9.31	9.20	9.15
10¾	13.64	12.39	11.21	10.49	10.16	9.90	9.63	9.49	9.38	9.34
11	13.78	12.54	11.37	10.66	10.33	10.08	9.81	9.67	9.57	9.53
11¼	13.92	12.69	11.53	10.82	10.50	10.25	9.99	9.86	9.76	9.72

Equal Monthly Payment to Amortize a loan of $1,000

TERM RATE	10	12	15	18	20	22	25	27	29	30
11½	14.06	12.84	11.69	10.99	10.67	10.43	10.17	10.05	9.95	9.91
11¾	14.21	12.99	11.85	11.16	10.84	10.61	10.35	10.23	10.14	10.10
12	14.35	13.14	12.01	11.32	11.02	10.78	10.54	10.42	10.33	10.29
12¼	14.50	13.29	12.17	11.49	11.19	10.96	10.72	10.61	10.52	10.48
12½	14.64	13.44	12.33	11.67	11.37	11.14	10.91	10.80	10.71	10.68
12¾	14.79	13.60	12.49	11.84	11.54	11.33	11.10	10.99	10.91	10.87
13	14.94	13.75	12.66	12.01	11.72	11.51	11.28	11.18	11.10	11.07
13¼	15.08	13.91	12.82	12.18	11.90	11.69	11.47	11.37	11.29	11.26
13½	15.23	14.06	12.99	12.36	12.08	11.87	11.66	11.56	11.49	11.46
13¾	15.38	14.22	13.15	12.53	12.26	12.06	11.85	11.76	11.68	11.66
14	15.53	14.38	13.32	12.71	12.44	12.24	12.04	11.95	11.88	11.85
14¼	15.68	14.53	13.49	12.89	12.62	12.43	12.23	12.14	12.08	12.05
14½	15.83	14.69	13.66	13.06	12.80	12.62	12.43	12.34	12.28	12.25
14¾	15.99	14.85	13.83	13.24	12.99	12.81	12.62	12.54	12.47	12.45
15	16.14	15.01	14.00	13.42	13.17	12.99	12.81	12.73	12.67	12.65
15¼	16.29	15.18	14.17	13.60	13.36	13.18	13.01	12.93	12.87	12.85
15½	16.45	15.34	14.34	13.78	13.54	13.37	13.20	13.13	13.07	13.05
15¾	16.60	15.50	14.52	13.96	13.73	13.56	13.40	13.32	13.27	13.25
16	16.76	15.66	14.69	14.15	13.92	13.75	13.59	13.52	13.47	13.45

be trying to select the best of two or three investment properties available. The use and sites have already been joined into a going operation. The techniques for analysis and comparison in this situation are discussed in the chapter on investment analysis. The more investment value exceeds asking price, the greater is the profit opportunity.

In a more complex situation an investor-developer may strive to join uses and sites for profits. Thus, the investors may determine from market analysis that demand for a supermarket exists in a neighborhood. Search produces the two or three best sites, which are tied up on options. The investor then approaches supermarket chains to induce one of them to locate a store on one of the sites under option. The effort ends when the store is built and put into operation, yielding a large commission or a long-term sale and leaseback arrangement to the investor.

SUMMARY

A real estate market analysis is a study undertaken to predict changes in the amount and types of real estate improvements needed in a community or area. Much judgment must be exercised in making and using a market study because the concepts, techniques, and applications are not yet well developed. Market studies are useful in determining when land at the urban fringe should be improved as well as when the use of an improved site should be changed or increased in intensity.

The range of competition is a prime consideration in delineating the market area. An economic base analysis, which involves determining and projecting those activities that drive the local economy, serves as an umbrella for market and feasibility analyses. Real estate supply and demand factors must be studied to relate the economic base study to the use or site under study, taking both current and long-run market outlook into account. Study conclusions should take account of all the foregoing considerations as they relate to the site or use.

Feasibility analysis is a profitability study of a specific proposal, taking account of market, physical, locational, legal, financial, and governmental factors.

QUESTIONS FOR REVIEW AND DISCUSSION

1. Explain briefly the nature of a real estate market study and the uses of a study to a developer, an investor or owner, and a prospective tenant. In other words, why analyze the real estate market?

2. Explain why urban areas grow and change? Then distinguish among changes in intensity of use, quality of use, and type of use relative to land use succession.

3. List the six phases of a market study in sequence, and explain each phase briefly.

4. What considerations enter into delineating a market area?

5. In economic base analysis, what is a locational quotient? Explain the use of an LQ in identifying the economic base of a community.

6. Identify and explain briefly at least three supply and three demand factors of supply and demand analysis.

7. Identify and explain briefly the three types of situations for which feasibility analysis is suited.

8. Does a market study remove all the risk from a project for a developer of an investor? Discuss.

9. Is there a relationship among a market study, a feasibility study, and the highest and best use of a property? Explain.

10. What special factors would warrant consideration in making a market analysis for an office building? A shopping center? A supermarket? A warehouse?

CASE PROBLEM

(Environmental and market considerations are combined in this case. Thus, elements of this and the previous three chapters are involved. National economic and political conditions at the time of discussion provide the broader setting for this case and should be taken into account.)

Your aunt recently died and willed you 31 acres of land on State Highway 33 connecting Sun City and Parkridge, two rapidly growing communities in the Sun Belt. The property has been in your aunt's family for over 110 years.

The 31 acres is actually made up of two parcels on opposite sides of Highway 33. The southern parcel contains 7 acres, has a cotton mill and an old pole-type warehouse on it, and is bordered on the east by Avion Way that comes off the highway and provides direct access to the airport. Avion Way is scheduled to be widened to four lanes with a center boulevard during the next year. Also, a rail line runs along the property's southern edge. It is doubtful that the improvements are consistent with today's highest and best use of the parcel. The larger parcel is vacant, except for an old farmhouse where your aunt lived, fronts on Highway 33 for one quarter of a mile, and is bordered on both the eastern and western sides by public streets.

Highway 33 carries considerable traffic. The parcels along it generally range in size from ½ acre to 3 acres, with mostly mixed residential and highway commercial uses. Within 5 miles are many single-family residences, apartment buildings, commercial and office buildings, medical buildings, two colleges and a state university, several churches, and a large county park. The metropolitan airport, recently expanded, is about 3 miles to the south, just beyond the East-West Interstate Highway.

The Central Business District of Sun City, population 210,000 and 8 miles to the east, is undergoing a major face lift as part of an urban renewal project. The Jackson County court house is in Sun City. Downtown Parkridge, population 80,000, is 4 miles to the west. Parkridge is the more rapidly growing of the two cities. The cities are growing toward each other, for the most part. Most industrial expansion of consequence in the last two decades has been south of the interstate highway and the airport in unincorporated areas. Several high-technology firms have built plants there in recent years. Thus, the location of the parcels appears to preclude their being developed for industrial purposes.

Taxes on the two parcels amount to about $30,000 per year, or $2,500 per month. The net income from operation of the mill has been sporadic; in fact, it is likely that the mill has been operating in the red since your aunt's death, 18 months ago. Having just entered the work force, your income is only about $1,600 per month, gross. Clearly, you must make some decisions.

All estate and probate problems have been resolved. Now, as the new owner, you are free to take whatever legal actions you deem necessary to preserve your position and to operate the properties at a profit. Major problems you now face are as follows:

1. Not being familiar with this real estate, you clearly need information and advice about it and how to operate it. How would you go about getting such information? Alternatives range from looking in the Yellow Pages and arranging an appointment with the broker with the biggest ad to engaging a marketing and planning consultant, probably at a minimum cost of several thousand dollars.
2. The mill is only operating at partial capacity and probably at a loss. Might an adjustment in property taxes be sought? Assume that the assessed value and taxes are one-half on the land and one-half on the improvements. How might you find out about this?
3. Assume that property taxes are $16,000 on the smaller parcel and $14,000 on the larger. For the smaller parcel, the taxes on the land are $9,000 per year, which represents about 2 percent of its market value. What is a rough estimate of the market value of the land? Does this help in gaining a perspective of your problem? What limitations attach to estimating value by this method?
4. What steps might you take to develop some personal idea of the highest and best use of the properties?
5. Should the costs of demolition of the existing structures enter into your thinking and planning? What other alternatives are open to you regarding the improvements? Under what circumstances would you not demolish any structures?
6. Could and should the 7-acre parcel be developed independently of the larger parcel? What issues might be involved in making this decision?
7. In general, what effect are the following likely to have on the value of the land?
   a. Sun City downtown renovation?
   b. Industrial expansion to the south?
   c. The recently expanded airport?

   d. The mixed residential-commercial development along Highway 33?
   e. The rail line along the edge of the smaller parcel?
   f. The scheduled widening of Avion Way?
8. In your investigations, you uncover a rumor that Highway 33 is to be rerouted along the interstate highway. What probable influence on the value of your parcels, if true?
9. What, in your opinion, is the feasibility of preserving the buildings on the smaller parcel and converting it into a
   a. Neighborhood shopping center?
   b. Recreational center?
   c. Retirement home?
   d. Public market?
   e. Office complex?
   f. Research complex?

   What additional information might you want before making a decision on any of these?
10. What, in your opinion, is the feasibility of developing the larger parcel into
   a. A subdivision for one-family residences?
   b. A shopping center
   c. A medical office center
   d. An apartment complex
   e. A complex of four story office buildings?
   f. A race track?

   What additional information might you want before making a decision on any of these?
11. Would any combination of the foregoing uses make sense. Why?
12. Given that you now have a clearer idea of what your alternatives are, what are your next steps?

CHAPTER FOURTEEN
FINANCING ALTERNATIVES

If you want to know the value of money, go and try to borrow some.
BENJAMIN FRANKLIN

IMPORTANT TOPICS OR DECISION AREAS COVERED IN THIS CHAPTER

- Equity Financing
- Debt Financing
- Land Contract Financing
- Lease Financing

The total value of a parcel of real estate is financed by someone at all times. Financing an entire property from personal monies is known as 100 percent equity financing. *Equity* is, therefore, the owner's interest in the property. Alternatively, an owner may pledge the property as security for a loan, as with a mortgage. Taking out a loan to finance a property is termed *debt financing*. Making loans to help finance properties is termed credit financing, which means looking at the loan arrangement from the lender's point of view. Finally, for someone without any money or not wishing to make an equity investment, a property may be rented. Thus, to control a property, the choices range from 0 to 100 percent equity input.

"To borrow or not to borrow, that is the question" is a consideration facing most people when buying property. In practice, therefore, the main financing choices for anyone not able or willing to put up 100 percent equity financing to control real estate are (1) leasing, (2) contracting for title, and (3) debt financing with a mortgage or trust deed. An option to purchase may be viewed as a financing device as well, but only for short-term purposes. A thorough knowledge of these financing methods and their accompanying terminology is crucial to success in real estate.

A brief review of legal forms of ownership as they relate to equity financing opens this chapter. Reasons to borrow, loan terminology, and loan application requirements are taken up next. Last, lease and land contract financing are taken up as the main alternatives to borrowing from established financial institutions. In Chapter 15, we cover mortgages and trust deeds, which are so important and so widely used they deserve a chapter to themselves. Chapter 16 is devoted to loan calculations, which interrelate debt financing with investment decisions. In Chapter 17, we look at interest rates and sources of real estate credit.

KEY CONCEPTS INTRODUCED IN THIS CHAPTER

Credit financing
Debt financing
Debt service
Duration of loan
Equity
Financial leverage
Interest
Land contract
Loan-to-value ratio
Net lease
Principal of loan
Sale leaseback
Specific performance
Subordination
Trading on the equity

EQUITY FINANCING

An equity position may be owned by one individual or by two or more individuals and/or business organizations working together as a group. Thus, funds to acquire and control an equity position must be provided by an individual or a group. Also, the legal concepts of ownership, explained in an earlier chapter, are directly related to the equity positions described in this chapter, and some updating seems appropriate. The value of an equity position is generally increased as the debt is amortized or the property appreciates in value.

Equity funds, for acquisition or development of a property, come primarily from the personal resources of individuals or from monies accumulated by institutional investors. Some aspiring homeowners develop equity by providing work in kind—painting, labor, and so forth, in new construction, which is termed "sweat equity." Alternatively, a small fee may be paid by a speculator for a one-year option on a property expected to rise rapidly in value. If the value goes up, the property is sold and the option exercised, and a profit is realized. If the value does not increase, only the cost of the option is lost. In this situation, the cost of the option represents the equity funds—initially. Financial institutions as insurance companies, banks, pension funds, business corporations, trusts, and savings and loan associations may be equity investors or lenders. An institution, acquiring an equity position, is not lending money to the venture; it expects to share in the profits and the risks of property operations the same as other equity investors. Thus an institutional investor is in a significantly different position relative to the property than an institutional lender.

Individual Equity Financing

Typically, an individual uses personal savings as equity funds to gain undivided ownership of a property, which is termed "sole ownership" or "an estate in severality." Debt financing (e.g., a mortgage loan) may be used by the sole owner to help in acquiring and holding the property. A condominium interest in real property is also owned by an individual as an estate in severalty, even though debt financing is used to acquire the interest.

Group Equity Financing

An equity interest in real property may be owned and financed by a group, through a tenancy or a business organizational arrangement. Under either arrangement, individual members supply or provide the equity funds based on an agreement between the parties.

A major distinction between the arrangements is real property versus personal property. If property is held by a group as tenants, the laws of real property apply between and among the members of the group. If the property is held under a business organizational arrangement, the laws of personal property apply.

By tenancy arrangement. A husband and wife each own an undivided interest in the entire property under tenancy by the entirety and community property. The couple is considered as jointly putting up the equity funds to finance the property under either form of tenancy, except when the property is received as a gift or is inherited. At the same time, the couple usually borrows against the property as individuals.

Two or more persons may acquire and finance equal equity interests under a joint tenancy arrangement in some states. Partnerships sometimes use joint tenancy arrangements to hold and finance property to ensure continuity of the enterprise should one of the partners die. That is, the right of survivorship passes ownership to the surviving partners instantaneously. In return, life insurance is usually carried on each partner, and is paid for by the partnership, with the insurance benefits going to the deceased partner's spouse or estate. Again, debt financing may be used to help finance the purchase of the property.

The equity position may be split into equal or unequal shares under tenancy in common ownership. Each tenant owns an undivided interest in the property. Debt financing, if obtained, would require that all tenants in common sign the note and mortgage or other security agreement and be jointly and individually responsible for the debt.

Finally, a condominium arrangement may be used to own and finance a large, complex property. Each condominium unit must be financed by its individual owner, however. In turn, default by one condominium owner does not obligate other owners to pick up the payments to protect themselves. The unit in default simply goes through foreclosure proceedings the same as any other property owned in fee simple.

By business organizational arrangement. The main business organizational arrangements for owning and financing an equity position in property are the corporation, the trust, and the cooperative. Property owned by a partnership is usually held by the general partners as tenants in common or joint tenants. In a limited partnership, only the general partners hold as tenants. A syndicate may be a partnership, corporation, or trust, depending on which is most advantageous.

The financial structure of a corporation is usually made up of stocks and bonds. The stock represents equity ownership while the bonds represent debt financing. The stockholders enjoy limited liability but are subject to double taxation on income earned by the corporation—once at the corporate level and once at the personal level when dividends are received. The corporation may own an equity interest in real property against which a mortgage loan has been obtained.

A trust operates much in the manner of a corporation except that profits or proceeds go to specific beneficiaries rather than to stockholders. Cooperatives are either corporations or trust. The corporation or trust owns the real estate. Shareholders get a proprietary lease to a specified unit of space upon purchase of stock. The cooperative pays taxes and obtains needed debt financing on the property. If shareholder-proprietary tenants fail to pay their pro rata share of taxes and debt service, the burden of keeping the cooperative solvent falls on the remaining shareholder-tenants, who make up the group owning the equity interest in the property.

DEBT FINANCING

Any decision to own or control real estate must take account of its high value, which, in turn, makes an understanding of debt financing extremely important. With this brief introduction, let us look at reasons for borrowing and understanding loan terminology in some detail.

Necessity

Families borrow to buy homes because houses typically cost two to three times the homebuyer's annual income. That is, the average family only has savings equal to approximately 10 to 20 percent of its annual income or to about 5 to 10 percent of the purchase price of the desired house. Homebuyers usually prefer to buy and make payments on a loan rather than pay rent. In a similar manner, most investors find that they must borrow to buy real estate.

Financial Leverage

Financial leverage involves controlling a large investment with a relatively small equity investment. In science, leverage means the physical use of a lever or bar to gain a mechanical advantage in applying a force to an object. The longer the distance from the force being applied to a pivot point relative to the distance from the pivot point to the object, the greater the magnification of the force being applied. However, the force being applied must move a much greater distance as a compensation. The process works in reverse as well. Applying a force at the short end magnifies the distance moved by a point or an object at the long end. (See Figure 14–1.)

The concept of leverage carries over to economics and finance. An investor can magnify gains or losses by borrowing money to help finance an investment. *Positive financial leverage (PFL),* occurs when borrowing magnifies or increases the rate of return earned on the equity portion of the investment. For this to happen, the property or investment must earn at a higher rate than the interest rate charged for the borrowed money. If the property earns at exactly the same rate as the cost of the borrowed money, no leverage is realized. And if the property earns at a lower rate, *negative financial leverage (NFL),* results. Financial leverage is also termed "trading on the equity," meaning exploiting or taking the best possible advantage of an equity position in an investment. Two examples illustrate the use of financial leverage.

FIGURE 14–1
Physical leverage

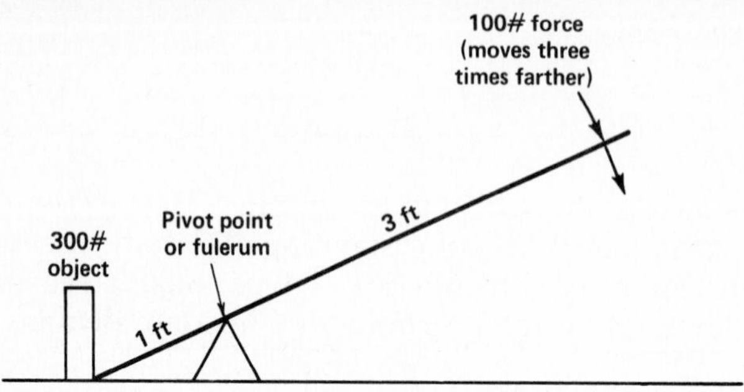

Assume that an investor owns a $1 million property with an $800,000 mortgage loan against it. The investor's equity in the property is $200,000. An increase of $200,000 in the market value of the property, to $1,200,000, accrues entirely to the owner-investor. Thus, positive financial leverage is realized as the value of the equity position doubles from $200,000 to $400,000. Thus, there is a 100 percent increase in equity resulting from a 20 percent increase in the property's value, which means positive leverage of 5:1. The debt, $800,000, remains unchanged.

INTEREST IN PROPERTY	*INITIAL FINANCING*	*FINANCING AFTER INCREASE IN PROPERTY VALUE*
Market value	$1,000,000	$1,200,000
Debt (fixed)	−800,000	−800,000
Owner's equity	$ 200,000	$ 400,000

A second example shows leverage on a rate-of-return basis. The facts are simplified to make the principle of leverage stand out. Assume that a commercial lot worth $1 million is under a long-term net lease for $100,000 per year. The tenant pays taxes, insurance, and all other costs of operation. Without debt financing, the rate of return to the owner is 10 percent. Suppose, however, that the owner obtains a long-term loan of $900,000 at 9 percent interest against the property, with no amortization required. That is, only interest payments of $81,000 need be paid each year ($900,000 × 9% = $81,000). The difference in income of $19,000 ($100,000 − $81,000 = $19,000) goes entirely to the equity position, which now is $100,000 ($1,000,000 − $900,000 = $100,000). The rate of return to equity has been leveraged up to 19 percent.

Total annual net income from lease	$100,000
Less: Interest on fixed debt ($900,000 × 9% = $81,000)	−81,000
Equals net cash flow to equity	$ 19,000
Divided by equity position's values ($1,000,000 − $900,000)	$100,000
Equals equity rate of return	19%

The advantages of leverage are not received without a cost. The borrower incurs increased risk of loss of income or of the property if reality does not live up to expectations. Thus, in the first example, if the property value declined by $100,000, negative financial leverage at a 5:1 ratio would result as the equity position would be cut 50 percent by a 10 percent decrease in the property's value. In the second example, a net income decrease by $10,000, or 10 percent, would reduce the rate of return on equity to 9 percent, a decline of slightly more than 50 percent. Under worse circumstances, the equity position might become a liability, as a result of the more severe negative financial leverage. Use of leverage always increases the risk of loss to the equity position. After-tax results must be used to determine the actual financial leverage expected or realized in any investments.

Loan Terminology

Clear, well-defined terms are necessary in negotiating and arranging a loan to avoid incorrect calculations and confused communications. For the most part, the terms or concepts are the same, whether a mortgage, trust deed, land contract, or some other instrument is involved. This is because the terms relate to the financing arrangement, not to the security instrument.

An $800,000 loan on a $1 million commercial property provides a convenient example to illustrate these loan terms and concepts.

Loan-to-value ratio. The proportion of a property's appraised market value borrowed is usually expressed as a percentage, called the loan-to-value ratio (LVR, sometimes LTV). Using the case example the loan-to-value ratio is 80 percent.

$$\frac{\text{Loan}}{\text{Market value}} = \frac{\$800{,}000}{\$1{,}000{,}000} = 80\% = \text{LVR}$$

The higher the loan-to-value ratio, the higher the risk to the borrower and to the lender. Therefore, maximum LVRs, for lending purposes, are set by law for most financial institutions. The LVR required of or used by a lender directly affects the amount of cash or equity down payment required of a borrower. If a lender is subject to a maximum LVR of 75 percent, a borrower with only $10,000 will not be able to bid for a property with a value in excess of $40,000. This is in contrast to a $100,000 property where a 90 percent LVR applies.

Loan principal. The principal of a loan is the number of dollars actually borrowed or the remaining balance of the loan. Almost all homeowners derive their income from wages or salaries; typically 25 to 30 percent of gross income goes for housing. The amount that homebuyers are able to borrow, therefore, depends directly on their income. In turn, the quality of housing they can command depends directly on how much they can borrow.

Interest rate. Interest is the rent or charge paid for the use of money. An *interest rate* is the amount paid to borrow money, calculated as a percentage of the amount borrowed. The higher the interest rate, the higher the interest charges. For example, at 6 percent, annual interest on $800,000 equals $48,000. At 9 percent, annual interest equals $72,000.

From a lender's point of view, the interest rate charged to borrowers reflects several factors: (1) the lender's cost of money, (2) the interest rates of other lenders, (3) the risks in the loan based on the characteristics of the property and the borrower, and (4) the yields available on competitive investments such as Treasury bonds and consumer loans.

Loan duration. The maturity date of the loan contract determines the duration or loan period. That is, the duration of a loan is the time given the borrower to repay the loan. The maximum acceptable duration is 40 years for loans to be bought and sold in the secondary mortgage market. However, most lenders have shorter loan periods based on management policy. A loan duration of from 20 to 30 years is typical for residential properties. The loan period for commercial loans tends to be between 10 and 20 years.

Loan amortization. *Amortization* means regular periodic repayment of the loan principal. The periodic repayment is usually made at the same time interest payments are made. The longer the amortization period, the smaller the required payments to repay the principal. If amortization is not required, interest must usually be paid periodically, with repayment of the entire loan principal on the last day of the contract. A loan may be partially amortizing, meaning that periodic payments are made to reduce the principal balance, but at some date the entire remaining balance must be repaid in a single, lump-sum payment.

Debt service. The periodic payment required on a loan for interest and, usually, principal reduction is termed *debt service.* If amortization is not called for (typical of construction loans), debt service is made up of interest only.

Debt service reflects the principal amount, the interest rate, the duration, and the amortization schedule of a loan, all discussed. Understanding the interrelationships among these loan elements is extremely important in arranging terms suited to a property's income or the income of a homebuyer.

The following are examples, with an $800,000 loan, as a standard, to show that debt service is a function of the principal, interest rate, duration, and amortization schedule:

---

1. The larger the principal amount, the greater the required debt service. Thus, monthly debt service on a $600,000, 12 percent, 25-year loan ($6,319.34) is less than that for an $800,000 loan on comparable terms ($8,425.793, carried to three decimal places for later reference).
2. The higher the interest rate, the greater is the debt service. Increasing the interest rate on the $800,000 loan in (1) from 12 to 15 percent increases the debt service from $8,425.79 to $10,246.64 per month.
3. Duration has an inverse impact on debt service. The longer the duration, the smaller the debt service, although the relationship is not proportional. Thus, increasing the term on the $800,000 loan from 25 to 30 years only lowers the monthly debt service from $8,425.79 to $8,228.90.
4. The more frequent the payments (monthly versus annual, for example), the smaller the debt service. Total annual debt service for our 12 percent, 25-year, $800,000 loan amounts to only $101,109.52, with monthly payments ($101,109.52 equals $8,425.793 times 12). With annual payments, total annual debt service comes to $101,999.98. The slightly lower amount comes about because principal repayment begins earlier with monthly payments. Thus, interest is paid on a slowly declining principal during the year.

LAND CONTRACT FINANCING

Buyers often lack adequate cash or equity to qualify for a loan from an established financial institution. Or it seems advantageous to preserve an existing mortgage loan on the property being bought. Or the property desired will not qualify for a mortgage loan, perhaps because of being vacant or being located in a blighted or run-down area. In all these situations, a land contract may well serve as a suitable financing alternative.

A *land contract* is a written agreement between a seller (vendor) and a buyer (vendee) for the sale of real property over an extended time, and with title remaining in the seller until the terms of the arrangement are met. The buyer normally takes possession when the contract is made. Payments are credited toward the purchase price in a manner parallel to that by which a mortgage loan is amortized. A land contract is also known as a "contract for deed," an "installment land contract," a "real estate contract," or a "contract of sale in escrow." See Figure 14–2 for a sample land contract.

FIGURE 14–2
Land contract

FORM No. 854—CONTRACT—REAL ESTATE—Partial Payments—Deed in Escrow. STEVENS-NESS LAW PUBLISHING CO., PORTLAND, OR. 97204

TT

38

CONTRACT—REAL ESTATE

THIS CONTRACT, Made this 31st day of February, 19 82, between Wendy Welloff, Unit 77, Condomium Towers, Urbandale, Anystate, hereinafter called the seller, and Gerald & Nancy Investor, 3278 Exotic Drive, Urbandale, Anystate 00000, hereinafter called the buyer,

WITNESSETH: That in consideration of the mutual covenants and agreements herein contained, the seller agrees to sell unto the buyer and the buyer agrees to purchase from the seller all of the following described lands and premises situated in Rustic County, State of Anystate, to-wit:

Douglas Manor, 2001 Century Drive, Urbandale
(Lots 16 & 17, Block 3, Edgewood South Subdivision)

for the sum of Six Hundred Forty Thousand and no/100 Dollars ($640,000) (hereinafter called the purchase price) on account of which thirty two thousand and no/100 Dollars ($ 32,000) is paid on the execution hereof (the receipt of which hereby is acknowledged by the seller), and the remainder to be paid at the times and in amounts as follows, to-wit:

Equal installments of $7,402.40 on the first day of each month for sixty (60) months, at the end of which the buyer is to arrange financing for the remaining balance of five hundred thousand dollars ($500,000) from another source, for which title will be conveyed.

All of said purchase price may be paid at any time; all deferred balances shall bear interest at the rate of one (1) per cent per ~~annum~~ month from March 1st, 1982 until paid, interest to be paid monthly and * in addition to / being included in the minimum regular payments above required. Taxes on said premises for the current tax year shall be prorated between the parties hereto as of this date.

The buyer warrants to and covenants with the seller that the real property described in this contract is (B)
*(A) primarily for buyer's personal, family, household or agricultural purposes,
(B) for an organization or (even if buyer is a natural person) is for business or commercial purposes other than agricultural purposes.

The buyer shall be entitled to possession of said lands on 1 March, 19 82, and may retain such possession so long as he is not in default under the terms of this contract. The buyer agrees that at all times he will keep the buildings on said premises, now or hereafter erected, in good condition and repair and will not suffer or permit any waste or strip thereof; that he will keep said premises free from mechanic's and all other liens and save the seller harmless therefrom and reimburse seller for all costs and attorney's fees incurred by him in defending against any such liens; that he will pay all taxes hereafter levied against said property, as well as all water rents, public charges and municipal liens which hereafter lawfully may be imposed upon said premises, all promptly before the same or any part thereof become past due; that at buyer's expense, he will insure and keep insured all buildings now or hereafter erected on said premises against loss or damage by fire (with extended coverage) in an amount not less than $ .... in a company or companies satisfactory to the seller, with loss payable first to the seller and then to the buyer as their respective interests may appear and all policies of insurance to be delivered as soon as insured to the escrow agent hereinafter named. Now if the buyer shall fail to pay any such liens, costs, water rents, taxes, or charges or to procure and pay for such insurance, the seller may do so and any payment so made shall be added to and become a part of the debt secured by this contract and shall bear interest at the rate aforesaid, without waiver, however, of any right arising to the seller for buyer's breach of contract.

The seller has exhibited unto the buyer a title insurance policy insuring marketable title in and to said premises in the seller; seller's title has been examined by the buyer and is accepted and approved by him.

Contemporaneously herewith, the seller has executed a good and sufficient deed (the form of which hereby is approved by the buyer) conveying the above described real estate in fee simple unto the buyer, his heirs and assigns, free and clear of incumbrances as of the date hereof, excepting the easements, building and other restrictions now of record, if any, and none other and has placed said deed, together with an executed copy of this contract and the title insurance policy mentioned above, in escrow with Hifidelity Escrow Services, Urbandale, escrow agent, with instructions to deliver said deed, together with the fire and title insurance policies, to the order of the buyer ,his heirs and assigns, upon the payment of the purchase price and full compliance by the buyer with the terms of this agreement. The buyer agrees to pay the balance of said purchase price and the respective installments thereof, promptly at the times provided therefor, to the said escrow agent for the use and benefit of the seller. The escrow fee of the escrow agent shall be paid by the seller and buyer in equal shares; the collection charges of said agent shall be paid by the buyer

(Continued on reverse)

*IMPORTANT NOTICE: Delete, by lining out, whichever phrase and whichever warranty (A) or (B) is not applicable. If warranty (A) is applicable and if the seller is a creditor, as such word is defined in the Truth-in-Lending Act and Regulation Z, the seller MUST comply with the Act and Regulation by making required disclosures; for this purpose, use Stevens-Ness Form No. 1308 or similar unless the contract will become a first lien to finance the purchase of a dwelling in which event use Stevens-Ness Form No. 1307 or similar.

Example

Assume that a 20-unit apartment building is being sold on a land contract for $1 million. The seller has an existing mortgage of $700,000 against the property at an interest rate of 8 percent. The owner's equity in the property is, therefore, $300,000.

Contract sale price	$1,000,000
Less: Seller's mortgage @8%	−700,000
Equals owner's equity	$ 300,000

The buyer makes a $50,000 down payment and agrees to make payments sufficient to cover interest and to reduce the balance due the seller from $950,000 to $800,000 by the end of five years. The buyer may refinance at any time and must refinance before the end of the sixth year. The interest rate on the unpaid land contract balance is a competitive 10 percent.

From a buyer's viewpoint, a land contract is similar to a partially amortizing loan in that payments go for interest and principal reduction. However, the buyer does not get legal title until all conditions of the land contract are satisfied and a deed is obtained. That is, the seller retains legal title and continues to pay debt service on the existing mortgage loan against the property. In so doing, both parties are likely to move into highly leveraged positions. The transaction now looks like this:

ITEM	*VALUE ALLOCATION*
Contract sale price	$1,000,000
Less: Buyer's down payment	−50,000
Equals amount of contract balance @10%	$ 950,000
Less: Seller's mortgage loan @8%	−700,000
Equals owner-seller's equity	$ 250,000

Amortization aside, the seller receives approximately $95,000 in interest in the first year (10% × $950,000), while paying approximately $56,000 interest on the mortgage loan (8% × $700,000). The difference is $39,000, while the owner-seller's equity equals only $250,000. This calculates to an approximate rate of return to the owner-seller of 15.6 percent ($39,000 ÷ $250,000).

Thus, the buyer gets a 95 percent loan-to-value ratio loan, and the seller both disposes of the property and stands to earn over 15 percent on the $250,000 loan to buyer.

Use

A land contract is extremely useful and extremely risky because it serves as a sales, financing, and tax-avoidance instrument. Generally, in a land contract, the buyer makes a nominal or "thin down" payment and agrees to make regular payments (usually monthly) over a number of years. The buyer also agrees to pay the seller a competitive rate of interest on the unpaid balance of the purchase price. Further, the buyer agrees to pay the annual taxes and insurance premiums on the property and to maintain the property in a reasonable condition.

A land contract may benefit a buyer, as in preserving a favorable mortgage loan, which would be lost if the property were completely refinanced in the transaction. At the same time, the thin down payment, or not getting a lot of money in the year of sale, enables the seller to defer taxes on capital gains until later years when the monies are actually received.

Because of the many risks involved, the rights and obligations of the buyer and seller over the years until the sale is consummated should be written out. Some of the more prominent concerns are as follows:

Seller considerations. Traditionally, land contracts have been written to protect the seller. The property involved may be difficult to finance from another source, possibly because of its run-down condition or its location in a blighted area. Some transactions need to be set up quickly, as in the sale of subdivision lots, where delay in arranging financing might allow a hot prospect to cool off. Or alternative financing may be difficult to arrange because of the buyer's thin down payment and relatively weak credit rating. In these situations, the seller wants to be able to recover the property, in case of buyer default, with a minimum of time and expense. Hence, the land contract makes possible the sale and financing of properties that would be very difficult to arrange in other ways while fully protecting the seller.

The seller (vendor) is advised to coordinate any required balloon payment or any prepayment privileges in the land contract with comparable privileges in any mortgage against the property. Failure to do so might mean that the buyer or vendee has the right to prepay the land contract, while the vendor is not able to prepay the mortgage. The vendor is then liable for a heavy prepayment penalty to the mortgagee or a breach of contract suit from the vendee for failure to deliver clear title.

Buyer considerations. A major buyer advantage in the use of a land contract is that only a small down payment is needed to control a property. A small down payment often means that the property and the financing are both being purchased. The arrangement gives a buyer time to build up equity in the property, at which time more traditional financing is possible upon the seller conveying title.

Several cautions should be exercised by a buyer in using a land contract. First, evidence of clear and marketable title should be required at the time the land contract is drawn up. Failure initially to assure clear title might mean that the buyer would make payments for several years only to find that the seller cannot deliver marketable title.

Second, the transaction should be handled in escrow. Failure to have a deed signed by the seller immediately and delivered into escrow might result in delay and added cost to the buyer if the seller dies or becomes incapacitated before signing a deed or conveying title. Also, it may be advisable to have periodic payments paid into escrow to insure that mortgage debt-service payments are made on schedule.

Third, the land contract or notice of the land contract should be recorded immediately, particularly if the vendee does not move into possession immediately, as with a vacant lot. Without recording or possession by the buyer, the seller could conceivably sell the lot several times and leave town. All the buyers would be left with a serious and expensive litigation problem.

Last, the seller should not be permitted to put the vendee's equity up as collateral for a loan. A simple clause in the contract to this effect, along with recording, would be one way to accomplish this restraint. To illustrate the problem, let us return to our earlier land contract example.

Assume that it is 5 years later and that the balance of the land contract has been paid down to \$800,000. Meanwhile, the value of the property increased to \$1,300,000. The buyer's equity should, therefore, be \$500,000. But suppose that the seller refinanced the property with a \$1,100,000 mortgage six months ago and left the area for whereabouts unknown. The vendee's equity has been reduced to \$200,000 (\$1,300,000 less \$1,100,000). Of course, the vendee also has a legal claim for \$300,000 against the seller, assuming that the seller can be found.

Default

Options open to the vendor if a buyer defaults include forfeiture, specific performance, foreclosure suit, or suit for damages.

The vendor may declare forfeiture of rights by the buyer and retain as damages any amounts paid or any improvements made by the vendee. Second, the vendor may require specific performance of the vendee. Specific performance is a court order compelling a defendant to carry out, or live up to, the terms of an agreement or contract. This option would probably be exercised if the unpaid balance of the land contract exceeds the value of the property and if the vendee is financially capable.

Third, the seller may file a foreclosure suit upon buyer default and seek to have the property sold. Finally, the seller may file suit for damages against the buyer if none of the foregoing options seems satisfactory.

Consumer Concern

Much criticism has been directed at the installment land contract because it so strongly favors the seller. Yet few laws have been enacted to modify or restrict its use, probably because of the great emphasis in our society on freedom to contract and because its wide use by individuals would make enforcement virtually impossible.

LEASE FINANCING

Controlling real estate by long-term lease rather than by purchase is often done to avoid ownership problems and to gain financial advantages. Insurance companies, pension funds, and universities are dominant among investors that own and finance properties for lease. Oil companies, motel chains, retail chains, supermarket chains, trucking companies, and public utilities all frequently lease rather than buy facilities to conserve working capital while expanding activities and services. Even the federal government frequently leases rather than buys post offices.

A sale-leaseback arrangement may be used to convert the equity in an older, existing property, on which the depreciation tax shelter has largely been used up, into working capital while retaining control of the premises. In the same transaction, a situation is set up whereby rental payments become fully tax deductible. Alternatively, a firm may buy vacant land, erect a new structure suited to its own specific purposes, and enter a sale-leaseback arrangement with an investor to release the monies for a subsequent and similar expansion effort at another location. Thus, a firm with limited working capital may expand very rapidly without tying up large amounts of money in real estate. See Figure 14–3 for an illustration of a long-term lease.

Common Considerations in Lease Financing

The rent, in a lease arrangement, is normally adequate to cover expected depreciation of the leased property and to give the owner a competitive rate of return on the investment. The tenant usually pays property taxes, insurance, and operating and maintenance expenses, an arrangement that is termed a *net lease* and sometimes a net, net, net lease. Presumably, the more "nets," the more the operating expenses paid by the tenant. Unfortunately, definitions are not standardized in this area. Thus, in negotiating a lease arrangement, clear communication between the parties is essential.

Unless otherwise agreed, the tenant-lessee receives the rights to occupy and use the premises and to sell the leasehold. At the same time, the owner-lessor may sell or assign the rights to the rental payments.

Long-term commercial leases run from 10 to 99 years and sometimes longer. The length of the lease, and any renewal option, are best specified, including a means of setting rents for any extensions. In addition to renewal options, many leases contain an option to purchase or, in a sale leaseback, to repurchase.

Mortgages enter into lease negotiations by way of subordination and the right of the lessee to make payments of debt service. A *subordination clause* pertains to the relative priority of claims on a property. Thus, for example, subordination of a lease to a mortgage means that in default, the lessee's right of occupancy might be completely wiped out by default and foreclosure. Lease subordination is frequently requested by an owner-lessor to obtain better financing terms on the property. In accepting subordination, the lessee should expect better rental terms and may even reserve the right to pay debt service directly to the mortgagee to prevent default.

Sale-Leaseback Arrangement

A sale-leaseback transaction is the transfer of title for consideration (sale) with the simultaneous renting back to the seller (leaseback) for a specified time at an agreed-upon rent. A sale leaseback might come about in the following manner. A supermarket chain has owned a store with high sales production for 14 years. The improvements have been largely written off or depreciated for tax purposes. Also, the property has tripled in value. The chain wishes to raise more working capital and, at the same time, to retain the store. A mortgage could be placed against the store for two-thirds of its value, but the loan would show up on the chain's balance sheet as a liability. A sale-leaseback arrangement is often a better alternative.

The store is, therefore, simultaneously sold to a private investor and rented back to the supermarket chain. The rent is set high enough to allow the investor a reasonable profit on the investment while writing off the improvements over the life of the lease. By treating the property as an income property and taking out a mortgage against it, the investment position is leveraged to gain a higher rate of profit. Therefore, both the supermarket chain and the investor gain from the transaction.

Some rapidly expanding business firms use buy-build-sell lease to get facilities designed and built specifically to the needs of the business but financed by someone else. The end structure is identical to that of the sale and leaseback arrangement. For example, a restaurant chain may buy land in a desired location, build a structure, sell the improved property to an interested investor, and simultaneously lease it back. After a working relationship has been established, the investor may even buy and improve

FIGURE 14–3
Long-term business lease—major provisions

*THIS INDENTURE OF LEASE, made and entered into this ....day of ...., 19........, by and between ....

hereinafter called the lessor, and ...., hereinafter called the lessee,*

WITNESSETH: In consideration of the covenants, agreements and stipulations herein contained on the part of the lessee to be paid, kept and faithfully performed, the lessor does hereby lease, demise and let unto the said lessee those certain premises, as is, situated in the City of.......................................; County of .... and State of ...., known and described as follows:

To Have and to Hold the said described premises unto the said lessee for a period of time commencing with the..............day of ...., 19........, and ending at midnight on the..............day of ...., 19........., at and for a rental of $............................for the whole of the said term payable in lawful money of the United States at ...., City of ...., State of ...., at the following times and in the following amounts, to-wit:

In consideration of the leasing of said premises and of the mutual agreements herein contained, each party hereto does hereby expressly covenant and agree to and with the other, as follows:

LESSEE'S ACCEPTANCE OF LEASE *(1) The lessee accepts said letting and agrees to pay to the order of the lessor the rentals above stated for the full term of this lease, in advance, at the times and in the manner aforesaid.*

USE OF PREMISES *(2a) The lessee shall use said demised premises during the term of this lease for the conduct of the following business: ....and for no other purpose whatsoever without lessor's written consent.*

(2b) The lessee will not make any unlawful, improper or offensive use of said premises; he will not suffer any strip or waste thereof; he will not permit any objectionable noise or oder to escape or to be emitted from said premises or do anything or permit anything to be done upon or about said premises in any way tending to create a nuisance; he will not sell or permit to be sold any spiritous, vinous or malt liquors on said premises, excepting such as lessee may be licensed by law to sell and as may be herein expressly permitted; nor will he sell or permit to be sold any controlled substance on or about said premises.

(2c) The lessee will not allow the leased premises at any time to fall into such a state of repair or disorder as to increase the fire hazard thereon; he shall not install any power machinery on said premises except under the supervision and with written consent of the lessor; he shall not store gasoline or other highly combustible materials on said premises at any time; he will not use said premises in such a way or for such a purpose that the fire insurance rate on the building in which said premises are located is thereby increased or that would prevent the lessor from taking advantage of any rulings of any agency of the state in which said leased premises are situated or its successors, which would allow the lessor to obtain reduced premium rates for long term fire insurance policies.

(2d) Lessee shall comply at lessee's own expense with all laws and regulations of any municipal, county, state, federal or other public authority respecting the use of said leased premises.

(2e) The lessee shall regularly occupy and use the demised premises for the conduct of lessee's business, and shall not abandon or vacate the premises for more than ten days without written approval of lessor.

UTILITIES *(3) The lessee shall pay for all heat, light, water, power, and other services or utilities used in the above demised premises during the term of this lease,*

REPAIRS AND IMPROVEMENTS *(4a) The lessor shall not be required to make any repairs, alterations, additions or improvements to or upon said premises during the term of this lease, except only those hereinafter specifically provided for; the lessee hereby agrees to maintain and keep said leased premises including all interior and exterior doors, heating, ventilating and cooling systems, interior wiring, plumbing and drain pipes to sewers or septic tank, in good order and repair during the entire term of this lease at lessee's own cost and expense, and to replace all glass which may be broken or damaged during the term hereof in the windows and doors of said premises with glass of as good or better quality as that now in use; lessee further agrees that he will make no alterations, additions or improvements to or upon said premises without the written consent of the lessor first being obtained.*

(4b) The lessor agrees to maintain in good order and repair during the term of this lease the exterior walls, roof, gutters, downspouts and foundations of the building in which the demised premises are situated and the sidewalks thereabouts. .... It is understood and agreed that the lessor reserves and at any and all times shall have the right to alter, repair or improve the building of which said demised premises are a part, or to add thereto and for that purpose at any time may erect scaffolding and all other necessary structures about and upon the demised premises and lessor and lessor's representatives, contractors and workmen for that purpose may enter in or about the said demised premises with such materials as lessor may deem necessary therefor, and lessee waives any claim to damages, including loss of business resulting therefrom.

LESSOR'S RIGHT OF ENTRY *(5) It shall be lawful for the lessor, his agents and representatives, at any reasonable time to enter into or upon said demised premises for the purpose of examining into the condition thereof, or any other lawful purpose.*

RIGHT OF ASSIGNMENT *(6) The lessee will not assign, transfer, pledge, hypothecate, surrender or dispose of this lease, or any interest herein, sub let, or permit any other person or persons whomsoever to occupy the demised premises without the written consent of the lessor being first obtained in writing; this lease is personal to said lessee; lessee's interests, in whole or in part, cannot be sold, assigned, transferred, seized or taken by operation at law, or under or by virtue of any execution or legal process, attachment or proceedings instituted against the lessee, or under or by virtue of any bankruptcy or insolvency proceedings had in regard to the lessee, or in any other manner, except as aboved mentioned.*

LIENS *(7) The lessee will not permit any lien of any kind, type or description to be placed or imposed upon the building in which said leased premises are situated, or any part thereof, or the real estate on which it stands.*

ICE, SNOW, DEBRIS *(8) If the premises herein leased are located at street level, then at all times lessee shall keep the sidewalks in front of the demised paemises free and clear of ice, snow, rubbish, debris and obstruction; and if the lessee occupies the entire building, he will not permit rubbish, debris, ice or snow to accumulate on the roof of said building so as to stop up or obstruct gutters or downspouts or cause damage to said roof, and will save harmless and protect the lessor against any injury whether to lessor or to lessor's property or to any other person or property caused by his failure in that regard.*

OVERLOADING OF FLOORS *(9) The lessee will not overload the floors of said premises in such a way as to cause any undue or serious stress or strain upon the building in which said demised premises are located, or any part thereof, and the lessor shall have the right, at any time, to call upon any competent engineer or architect whom the lessor may choose, to decide whether or not the floors of said premises, or any part thereof, are being overloaded so as to cause any undue or serious stress or strain on said building, or any part thereof, and the decision of said engineer or architect shall be final and binding upon the lessee; and in the event that the engineer or architect so called upon shall decide that in his opinion the stress or strain is such as to endanger or injure said building, or any part thereof, then and in that event the lessee agrees immediately to relieve said stress or strain either by reinforcing the building or by lightening the load which causes such stress or strain in a manner satisfactory to the lessor.*

ADVERTISING SIGNS *(10) The lessee will not use the outside walls of said premises, or allow signs or devices of any kind to be attached thereto or suspended therefrom, for advertising or displaying the name or business of the lessee or for any purpose whatsoever without the written consent of the lessor; however, the lessee may make use of the windows of said leased premises to display lessee's name and business when the workmanship of such signs shall be of good quality and permanent nature; provided further that the lessee may not suspend or place within said windows or paint thereon any banners, signs, sign-boards or other devices in violation of the intent and meaning of this section.*

LIABILITY INSURANCE *(11) The lessee further agrees at all times during the term hereof, at his own expense, to maintain, keep in effect, furnish and deliver to the lessor liability insurance policies in form and with an insurer satisfactory to the lessor, insuring both the lessor and the lessee against all liability for damages to person or property in or about said leased premises; the amount of said liability insurance shall not be less than $.................................... for injury to one person, $.................................... for injuries arising out of any one accident and not less than $.................................... for property damage. Lessee agrees to and shall indemnify and hold lessor harmless against any and all claims and demands arising from the negligence of the lessee, his officers, agents, invitees and/or employees, as well as those arising from lessee's failure to comply with any covenant of this lease on his part to be performed, and shall at his own expense defend the lessor against any and all suits or actions arising out of such negligence, actual or alleged, and all appeals therefrom and shall satisfy and discharge any judgment which may be awarded against lessor in any such suit or action.*

FIXTURES *(12) All partitions, plumbing, electrical wiring, additions to or improvements upon said leased premises, whether installed by the lessor or lessee, shall be and become a part of the building as soon as installed and the property of the lessor unless otherwise herein provided.*

LIGHT AND AIR *(13) This lease does not grant any rights of access to light and air over the property.*

DAMAGE BY CASUALTY, FIRE AND DUTY TO REPAIR *(14) In the event of the destruction of the building in which said leased premises are located by fire or other casualty, either party hereto may terminate this lease as of the date of said fire or casualty, provided, however, that in the event of damage to said building by fire or other casualty to the extent of .... per cent or more of the sound value of said building, the lessor may or may not elect to repair said building; written notice of lessor's said election shall be given lessee within fifteen days after the occurrence of said damage; if said notice is not so given, lessor conclusively shall be deemed to have elected not to repair; in the event lessor elects not to repair said building, then and in that event this lease shall terminate with the date of said damage; but if the building in which said leased premises are located be but partially destroyed and the damage so occasioned shall not amount to the extent indicated above, or if greater than said extent and lessor elects to repair, as aforesaid, then the lessor shall repair said building with all convenient speed and shall have the right to take possession of and occupy, to the exclusion of the lessee, all or any part of said building in order to make the necessary repairs, and the lessee hereby agrees to vacate upon request, all or any part of said building which the lessor may require for the purpose of making necessary repairs, and for the period of time between the day of such damage and until such repairs have been substantially completed there shall be such an abatement of rent as the nature of the injury or damage and its interference with the occupancy of said leased premises by said lessee shall warrant; however, if the premises be but slightly injured and the damage so occasioned shall not cause any material interference with the occupation of the premises by said lessee, then there shall be no abatement of rent and the lessor shall repair said damage with all convenient speed.*

WAIVER OF SUBROGATION RIGHTS *(15) Neither the lessor nor the lessee shall be liable to the other for loss arising out of damage to or destruction of the leased premises, or the building or improvement of which the leased premises are a part or with which they are connected, or the contents of any thereof, when such loss is caused by any of the perils which are or could be included within or insured against by a standard form of fire insurance with extended coverage, including sprinkler leakage insurance, if any. All such claims for any and all loss, however caused, hereby are waived. Such absence of liability shall exist whether or not the damage or destruction is caused by the negligence of either lessor or lessee or by any of their respective agents, servants or employees. It is the intention and agreement of the lessor and the lessee that the rentals reserved by this lease have been fixed in contemplation that each party shall fully provide his own insurance protection at his own expense, and that each party shall look to his respective insurance carriers for reimbursement of any such loss, and further, that the insurance carriers involved shall not be entitled to subrogation under any circumstances against any party to this lease. Neither the lessor nor the lessee shall have any interest or claim in the other's insurance policy or policies, or the proceeds thereof, unless specifically covered therein as a joint assured.*

EMINENT DOMAIN *(16) In case of the condemnation or appropriation of all or any substantial part of the said demised premises by any public or private corporation under the laws of eminent domain, this lease may be terminated at the option of either party hereto on twenty days written notice to the other and in that case the lessee shall not be liable for any rent after the date of lessee's removal from the premises.*

FOR SALE AND FOR RENT SIGNS *(17) During the period of .... days prior to the date above fixed for the termination of said lease, the lessor herein may post on said premises or in the windows thereof signs of moderate size notifying the public that the premises are "for sale" or "for lease."*

DELIVERING UP PREMISES ON TERMINATION *(18) At the expiration of said term or upon any sooner termination thereof, the lessee will quit and deliver up said leased premises and all future erections or additions to or upon the same, broom-clean, to the lessor or those having lessor's estate in the premises, peaceably, quietly, and in as good order and condition, reasonable use and wear thereof, damage by fire, unavoidable casualty and the elements alone excepted, as the same are now in or hereafter may be put in by the lessor.*

ADDITIONAL COVENANTS OR EXCEPTIONS *(19)*

HOLDING OVER *In the event the lessee for any reason shall hold over after the expiration of this lease, such holding over shall not be deemed to operate as a renewal or extension of this lease, but shall only create a tenancy from month to month which may be terminated at will at any time by the lessor.*

IN WITNESS WHEREOF, the respective parties have executed this instrument in duplicate on this, the day and year first hereinabove written, any corporation signature being by authority of its Board of Directors.

....

....

....

....

the land for subsequent lease to the business firm, without the firm's ever taking title.

Ground Lease with a Mortgaged Leasehold

Another major option of a business firm is to use leasing and mortgage financing in combination. A desired parcel of vacant land is rented on a long-term lease, which is termed a *ground lease.* Improvements are added and financed with a *leasehold mortgage,* which means that only the lessee's interest in the property is pledged to secure the loan. The lessee may depreciate the improvements completely for tax purposes over the life of the lease, with this arrangement. Thus, the firm keeps the depreciation as a tax shelter rather than pass it on to an investor. In addition, the rental payments for the land are tax deductible. Finally, over and above everything else, the firm is able to minimize its investment in real estate.

Default

A breach of rental terms, most likely nonpayment of rent, constitutes lease default. The owner-landlord then has a range of options that run from suing the tenant for specific performance to eviction and rerenting.

SUMMARY

Key terms relative to loan financing are (1) loan-to-value ratio, (2) principal, (3) interest rate, (4) duration, (5) amortization provisions, and (6) debt service. These terms apply whether real estate is being financed by a mortgage, trust deed, or land contract.

A land contract is sale of real estate with payments spread over an extended time, although the buyer usually goes into immediate possession. The buyer gets only equitable title until the contract is satisfied. The arrangement generally favors the seller. Important buyer considerations are to (1) obtain immediate evidence of clear title, (2) have deed placed in escrow immediately, (3) record if possession is not immediately taken, and (4) prohibit seller from pledging buyer's equity in any refinancing.

Lease financing covers 100 percent of a property's value and, therefore, conserves working capital for the lessee. Leasing to a strong tenant gives the owner-lessor a large, high-quality investment at a known rate of return. Chains of supermarkets, motels, and restaurants commonly use sale and leaseback financing to conserve working capital and make faster expansion possible.

QUESTIONS FOR REVIEW AND DISCUSSION

1. Explain fully the relationship between equity financing and debt financing as they pertain to a property's market value.

2. When is a tenancy arrangement most likely to be used in equity financing among a

group, where business or investment objectives are paramount? When might a business organizational arrangement (corporation, for example) be a better alternative?

3. Debt financing is used out of necessity or to gain financial leverage. Explain how financial leverage works. Is the use of leverage always advantageous?

4. Identify and explain or define briefly the six key financial terms to be negotiated in arranging debt financing.

5. How does a land contract work as a financing device? Give two key considerations in the use of a land contract by a buyer? A seller?

6. Is a land contract more a sales or a financing device? Discuss. What circumstances influence your answer?

7. Does the buyer or the seller have greater power in negotiating a land contract sale? Discuss. What considerations enter into your answer?

8. Is a land contract likely to have provisions pertaining to the applicability of payments for taxes, insurance, interest, and principal reduction? Why? If not, why not?

9. Discuss a long-term lease as a financing device, with emphasis on the sale-leaseback arrangement. When might such an arrangement be most advantageous?

10. Does the lessor or the lessee have the greater power in negotiating a long-term lease? Explain. Would it make any difference if a sale and leaseback were being negotiated?

CASE PROBLEMS

1. Joe Baloney buys a vacant lot on a land contract, agreeing to pay $24,000, with $4,000 initial down payment. Shortly after, re-zoning is requested and obtained, increasing the lot's value to $36,000.
   a. What percentage increase in property value and in equity has taken place?
   b. What leverage ratio does this represent?
2. Buck Montana buys a vacant lot on land contract, agreeing to pay $20,000 and paying $10,000 down. Black Bart, the seller, owns the lot free and clear. Buck and his wife move a mobile home onto the property and go into possession immediately. Due to the construction of a new bridge, the lot increases in value to $30,000. Black Bart subsequently mortgages the lot to a local bank to secure a $15,000 loan, based on the increased value, and leaves town. The bank files for foreclosure. What are the rights of the Montanas?
3. White leases a vacant lot from Green on a long-term net, net, net lease for $12,000 per year. Nothing is said about a subordination clause between White and Green. White adds improvements, financed by a mortgage loan of $150,000 from the Ace Savings and Loan Association. Subsequently, Green obtains $80,000 from the Third National Bank. White defaults. Ace S&L proposes to take the property over and re-rent it to Blue. The Third National objects. What result as between Ace and the Third National?

CHAPTER FIFTEEN
MORTGAGE AND TRUST DEED FINANCING

The house was more covered with mortgages than paint.
GEORGE ADE

IMPORTANT TOPICS OR DECISION AREAS COVERED IN THIS CHAPTER

- Applying for a Loan
- The Debt Financing Process
- Typical Provisions of Mortgages and Trust Deeds
- Types of Loans
- Loan Repayment Plans and Their Uses
- The Promissory Note
- Federal Laws Affecting Lending

Many of us in buying a car pledge the vehicle to a financial institution to get enough money to make the purchase. Likewise, most of us, in buying real estate, pledge the property to a bank or savings and loan association as security for a loan by way of a mortgage or trust deed.

As with obtaining an auto loan, a formal application is required. Beyond this, the process of obtaining a real estate loan in much more involved. And the legalities of mortgages and trust deeds during the life of a real estate loan are much more complex.

KEY CONCEPTS INTRODUCED IN THIS CHAPTER

Acceleration clause
Adjustable rate mortgage
Alienation clause
Balloon payment
Blended loan
Conventional mortgage loan
Deed in lieu of foreclosure
Default
Defeasance clause
Deficiency judgment
Equitable right of redemption
FHA loan
Fixed rate mortgage
Foreclosure
Graduated payment mortgage
Growing equity mortgage
Mortgage, subject to a
Mortgage assignment
Mortgage assumption
Mortgage satisfaction
Novation
Power of sale
Prepayment clause
Promissory note
Purchase money mortgage
Redemption, statutory right of
Renegotiable rate mortgage
Reverse annuity mortgage
Shared appreciation mortgage
Statutory right of redemption
Subordination
Trust deed
Usury
VA mortgage loan
Variable rate mortgage
Wrap around mortgage

APPLYING FOR A LOAN

A borrower usually seeks the lowest interest rate and the longest maturity available and, therefore, shops lenders and terms. A borrower may also negotiate to avoid interest rate adjustments and penalties for early repayment. A brief overview of the mechanics of the loan application process seems appropriate before getting into legalities and negotiations.

Exactly what is involved in obtaining a loan? Similar information and processing is usually required by lenders, regardless of the type of loan desired. Initial information requirements are well illustrated by the Federal Home Loan Mortgage Corporation/Federal National Mortgage Association (FHLMC/FNMA) loan application form. (See Figure 15–1.) The entire procedure involves several basic steps:

1. Borrower shops and obtains information on financial terms and repayment patterns of alternative lenders.
2. Prospective borrower completes and submits loan application form to lender of choice.
3. Lender provides a "good faith estimate of closing costs" to borrower.
4. Lender obtains credit report on applicant.
5. Lender obtains "verification of employment" form on applicant, if a residential loan is requested. If borrower is self-employed, or an investor, lender likely to ask to see borrower's income tax returns for at least the two immediately prior years.
6. Lender obtains a "verification of deposit" form to assure the existence and availability of equity funds.
7. Lender obtains a market value appraisal on subject property to assure that its value represents adequate security for the requested loan, that is, that an acceptable LVR is present.
8. Approval for loan insurance or guarantee obtained from FHA, private mortgage insurance company, or VA.
9. Loan committee of lender reviews all information and makes "go—no go" decision. If "go," loan is made. If "no go," applicant is notified, and file is closed.
10. Lender obtains evidence of marketable title (through title insurance or attorney's opinion), which also serves to detect presence of other claims that may exist against the subject property.

Borrower pays all costs, as for a credit report, an appraisal, a title report, attorneys, and recording. Some additional information and documentation would be required if FHA, VA, or private mortgage insurance is involved.

THE DEBT FINANCING PROCESS

Two separate and distinct legal instruments are executed in obtaining an enforceable loan on real estate. The first is either a mortgage or a trust deed.[1] The second is a promissory note or, in some states, a personal bond.

---

[1]A "security deed" or "deed to secure debt" is used in lieu of a mortgage in Georgia. Unlike the trust deed, this instrument involves only two parties, a borrower and a lender.

FIGURE 15–1
FHLMC/FNMA Loan Application

RESIDENTIAL LOAN APPLICATION

MORTGAGE APPLIED FOR	☐ Conventional ☐ FHA ☐ VA ☐	Amount $	Interest Rate %	No. of Months	Monthly Payment Principal & Interest $	Escrow/Impounds (to be collected monthly) ☐ Taxes ☐ Hazard Ins. ☐ Mtg. Ins. ☐

Prepayment Option

SUBJECT PROPERTY

Property Street Address	City	County	State	Zip	No. Units

Legal Description (Attach description if necessary)	Year Built

Purpose of Loan: ☐ Purchase ☐ Construction-Permanent ☐ Construction ☐ Refinance ☐ Other (Explain)

Complete this line if Construction-Permanent or Construction Loan	Lot Value Data Year Acquired	Original Cost $	Present Value (a) $	Cost of Imps. (b) $	Total (a + b) $	ENTER TOTAL AS PURCHASE PRICE IN DETAILS OF PURCHASE.

Complete this line if a Refinance Loan — Purpose of Refinance — Describe Improvements [ ] made [ ] to be made

Year Acquired	Original Cost $	Amt. Existing Liens $	Cost: $

Title Will Be Held In What Name(s)	Manner In Which Title Will Be Held

Source of Down Payment and Settlement Charges

This application is designed to be completed by the borrower(s) with the lender's assistance. The Co-Borrower Section and all other Co-Borrower questions must be completed and the appropriate box(es) checked if ☐ another person will be jointly obligated with the Borrower on the loan, or ☐ the Borrower is relying on income from alimony, child support or separate maintenance or on the income or assets of another person as a basis for repayment of the loan, or ☐ the Borrower is married and resides, or the property is located, in a community property state.

BORROWER	CO-BORROWER
Name — Age — School Yrs	Name — Age — School Yrs
Present Address No. Years ☐ Own ☐ Rent	Present Address No. Years ☐ Own ☐ Rent
Street	Street
City/State/Zip	City/State/Zip
Former address if less than 2 years at present address	Former address if less than 2 years at present address
Street	Street
City/State/Zip	City/State/Zip
Years at former address ☐ Own ☐ Rent	Years at former address ☐ Own ☐ Rent
Marital Status ☐ Married ☐ Separated ☐ Unmarried (incl. single, divorced, widowed) — DEPENDENTS OTHER THAN LISTED BY CO-BORROWER: NO. AGES	Marital Status ☐ Married ☐ Separated ☐ Unmarried (incl. single, divorced, widowed) — DEPENDENTS OTHER THAN LISTED BY BORROWER: NO. AGES
Name and Address of Employer — Years employed in this line of work or profession? ____ years — Years on this job ____ — ☐ Self Employed*	Name and Address of Employer — Years employed in this line of work or profession? ____ years — Years on this job ____ — ☐ Self Employed*
Position/Title — Type of Business	Position/Title — Type of Business
Social Security Number*** — Home Phone — Business Phone	Social Security Number*** — Home Phone — Business Phone

GROSS MONTHLY INCOME				MONTHLY HOUSING EXPENSE**			DETAILS OF PURCHASE Do Not Complete If Refinance	
Item	Borrower	Co-Borrower	Total		PRESENT	PROPOSED		
Base Empl. Income	$	$	$	Rent	$		a. Purchase Price	$
Overtime				First Mortgage (P&I)		$	b. Total Closing Costs (Est.)	
Bonuses				Other Financing (P&I)			c. Prepaid Escrows (Est.)	
Commissions				Hazard Insurance			d. Total (a + b + c)	$
Dividends/Interest				Real Estate Taxes			e. Amount This Mortgage	( )
Net Rental Income				Mortgage Insurance			f. Other Financing	( )
Other† (Before completing, see notice under Describe Other Income below.)				Homeowner Assn. Dues			g. Other Equity	( )
				Other:			h. Amount of Cash Deposit	( )
				Total Monthly Pmt.	$	$	i. Closing Costs Paid by Seller	( )
				Utilities				
Total	$	$	$	Total	$	$	j. Cash Reqd. For Closing (Est.)	$

DESCRIBE OTHER INCOME

B—Borrower C—Co-Borrower	NOTICE: † Alimony, child support, or separate maintenance income need not be revealed if the Borrower or Co-Borrower does not choose to have it considered as a basis for repaying this loan.	Monthly Amount
		$

IF EMPLOYED IN CURRENT POSITION FOR LESS THAN TWO YEARS COMPLETE THE FOLLOWING

B/C	Previous Employer/School	City/State	Type of Business	Position/Title	Dates From/To	Monthly Income
						$

THESE QUESTIONS APPLY TO BOTH BORROWER AND CO-BORROWER

If a "yes" answer is given to a question in this column, explain on an attached sheet.	Borrower Yes or No	Co-Borrower Yes or No	If applicable, explain Other Financing or Other Equity (provide addendum if more space is needed).
Have you any outstanding judgments? In the last 7 years, have you been declared bankrupt?			
Have you had property foreclosed upon or given title or deed in lieu thereof?			
Are you a co-maker or endorser on a note?			
Are you a party in a law suit?			
Are you obligated to pay alimony, child support, or separate maintenance?			
Is any part of the down payment borrowed?			

*FHLMC/FNMA require business credit report, signed Federal Income Tax returns for last two years, and, if available, audited Profit and Loss Statements plus balance sheet for same period.
**All Present Monthly Housing Expenses of Borrower and Co-Borrower should be listed on a combined basis.
***Neither FHLMC nor FNMA requires this information.

FHLMC 65 Rev. 8/78

FIGURE 15–1
(continued)

This Statement and any applicable supporting schedules may be completed jointly by both married and unmarried co-borrowers if their assets and liabilities are sufficiently joined so that the Statement can be meaningfully and fairly presented on a combined basis; otherwise separate Statements and Schedules are required (FHLMC 65A/FNMA 1003A). If the co-borrower section was completed about a spouse, this statement and supporting schedules must be completed about that spouse also. ☐ Completed Jointly ☐ Not Completed Jointly

STATEMENT OF ASSETS AND LIABILITIES

ASSETS		LIABILITIES AND PLEDGED ASSETS			
		Indicate by (*) those liabilities or pledged assets which will be satisfied upon sale of real estate owned or upon refinancing of subject property			
Description	Cash or Market Value	Creditors' Name, Address and Account Number	Acct. Name If Not Borrower's	Mo. Pmt. and Mos. left to pay	Unpaid Balance
Cash Deposit Toward Purchase Held By	$	Installment Debts (include "revolving" charge accts)		$ Pmt./Mos.	$
				/	
Checking and Savings Accounts (Show Names of Institutions/Acct. Nos.)				/	
				/	
				/	
Stocks and Bonds (No./Description)				/	
				/	
				/	
Life Insurance Net Cash Value Face Amount ($)		Other Debts Including Stock Pledges		/	
SUBTOTAL LIQUID ASSETS	$				
Real Estate Owned (Enter Market Value from Schedule of Real Estate Owned)		Real Estate Loans			
Vested Interest in Retirement Fund					
Net Worth of Business Owned (ATTACH FINANCIAL STATEMENT)					
Automobiles (Make and Year)		Automobile Loans		/	
Furniture and Personal Property		Alimony, Child Support and Separate Maintenance Payments Owed To		/	
Other Assets (Itemize)					
		TOTAL MONTHLY PAYMENTS		$	
TOTAL ASSETS	A $	NET WORTH (A minus B) $		TOTAL LIABILITIES	B $

SCHEDULE OF REAL ESTATE OWNED (If Additional Properties Owned Attach Separate Schedule)

Address of Property (Indicate S if Sold, PS if Pending Sale or R if Rental being held for income)	⇩	Type of Property	Present Market Value	Amount of Mortgages & Liens	Gross Rental Income	Mortgage Payments	Taxes, Ins. Maintenance and Misc.	Net Rental Income
			$	$	$	$	$	$
		TOTALS →	$	$	$	$	$	$

LIST PREVIOUS CREDIT REFERENCES

⇩ B–Borrower C–Co-Borrower	Creditor's Name and Address	Account Number	Purpose	Highest Balance	Date Paid
				$	

List any additional names under which credit has previously been received ________________

AGREEMENT: The undersigned applies for the loan indicated in this application to be secured by a first mortgage or deed of trust on the property described herein, and represents that the property will not be used for any illegal or restricted purpose, and that all statements made in this application are true and are made for the purpose of obtaining the loan. Verification may be obtained from any source named in this application. The original or a copy of this application will be retained by the lender, even if the loan is not granted. The undersigned ☐ intend or ☐ do not intend to occupy the property as their primary residence.

I/we fully understand that it is a federal crime punishable by fine or imprisonment, or both, to knowingly make any false statements concerning any of the above facts as applicable under the provisions of Title 18, United States Code, Section 1014.

________________ Date ________ ________________ Date ________
Borrower's Signature Co-Borrower's Signature

INFORMATION FOR GOVERNMENT MONITORING PURPOSES

Instructions: Lenders must insert in this space, or on an attached addendum, a provision for furnishing the monitoring information required or requested under present Federal and/or present state law or regulation. For most lenders, the inserts provided in FHLMC Form 65-B/FNMA Form 1003-B can be used.

FOR LENDER'S USE ONLY

(FNMA REQUIREMENT ONLY) This application was taken by ☐ face to face interview ☐ by mail ☐ by telephone

________________ ________________
(Interviewer) Name of Employer of Interviewer

FHLMC 65 Rev. 8/78 REVERSE FNMA 1003 Rev. 8/78

Mortgages and trust deeds serve the same basic functions and are handled alike for the most part. And the term "mortgage" is widely used in the trade to mean both mortgages and trust deeds, as in the secondary mortgage market. Even so, they are distinct instruments, with very different consequences in use, particularly in default. The generic term "mortgage" will be used here for both however, unless a specific distinction between the two instruments must be made.

Both pledge real property as security for a debt or other obligation. The borrower in the contract is generally called the *mortgagor*; the lender is the *mortgagee.* The *promissory note* is a written commitment to repay the debt, and it serves as evidence of the debt. A personal bond is an interest-bearing certificate containing a promise to pay a certain sum on a specified date, and thus is similar to a note. Usually only the mortgage or trust deed is recorded. Figure 15–2 summarizes loan documentation.

A mortgage or trust deed obligates the property pledged as security until cleared or satisfied. Although fee ownership of reality is usually pledged as security, any real property interest that is a legal object of a sale, grant, or assignment may be pledged. Thus a leasehold, a life estate, rights of a remainderman, or improvements apart from the land all provide a legal basis for a security pledge.

A trust deed increasingly is being used in place of a mortgage. The reasons are time and convenience to the lender. Upon default with a

FIGURE 15–2
Overview of loan documentation

DOCUMENT	*PURPOSE OR EFFECT*	*LEGAL REQUIREMENTS*
Mortgage or Trust deed	Creates and pledges a property interest for the protection of the mortgagee-lender Creates a property interest to be held by the trustee for the lender-beneficiary	1. In writing 2. Property adequately identified 3. Identify borrower, lender (and trustee) 4. Proper words to pledge a security interest 5. Signature of mortgagor-borower 6. Voluntary delivery and acceptance
Promissory note or bond	Creates a personal obligation of borrower to repay debt according to agreed terms or schedule	1. A written instrument 2. A borrower (obligor) with contractual capacity 3. A lender (obligee) with contractual capacity 4. A promise or covenant by borrower to pay a specific sum 5. Terms of payment 6. A default clause, including reference to the mortgage or trust deed 7. Proper execution 8. Voluntary delivery and acceptance

mortgage lien, foreclosure proceedings generally require from several months to two or three years to complete. *Default* is failure of the borrower to meet the terms of the contract.

A trust deed, instead of being a lien, conveys title to the pledged property to a third party (trustee) to be held as security for the debt owed the lender-beneficiary. A promissory note still evidences the debt. Upon default, the trustee usually has automatic power of sale. *Power of sale* means the right to sell without court proceedings, which considerably shortens the time required to get satisfaction by the lender. Thus, after three or four payments are missed, the lender may request sale, with satisfaction often realized in from 6 to 12 months. A trust deed is also referred to as a deed of trust or a trust deed in the nature of a mortgage.

Note that a trust deed arrangement is a three-party transaction even though it is used in place of a two-party mortgage loan arrangement. The owner-borrower-trustor receives money and, at the same time, conveys title to the trustee and gives a promissory note to the lender-beneficiary. The lender, therefore, becomes the legal owner and holder of the promissory note. The trustee holds title to the property as security for the lender in case of default by the borrower. Figure 15–3 shows the structure of the transaction.

A promissory note or bond, as mentioned, serves as evidence of the debt and makes the debt the personal obligation of the borrower. This expands the lender's rights in case of default. If only a mortgage or trust deed were used, the borrower might abandon the property, move elsewhere, and have no further personal obligation or liability regarding the loan. The note or bond, as a personal obligation, is enforceable wherever the borrower might take up residence.

The mortgage and promissory note used as illustrations in this chapter were developed jointly by the Federal National Mortgage Association (FNMA) and the Federal Home Loan Mortgage Corporation (FHLMC).

FIGURE 15–3
Trust deed financing

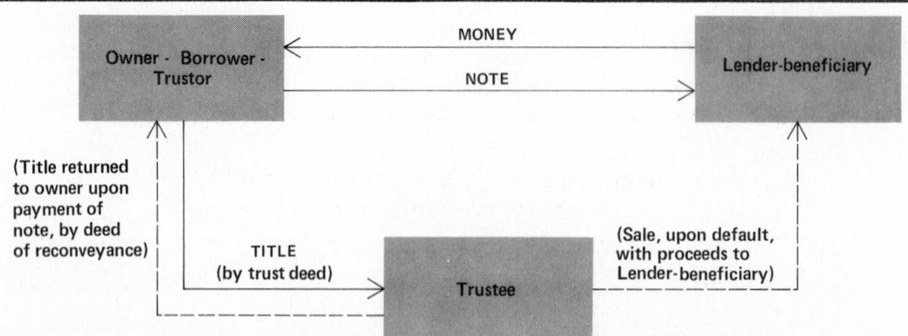

These instruments are as uniform as possible from state to state to facilitate their being bought and sold in the secondary mortgage market. In turn, the liquidity of the loan portfolios of lenders is greatly enhanced. With standardized wording, buyers of loans in the secondary mortgage market do not have to study each document in detail before acceptance of same. These instruments are representative of financing forms used throughout the country.

Incidentally, a mortgage or trust deed and the accompanying note are personal property, ownership of which may be sold or transferred by what is termed an *assignment.* Approval of the borrower is not required in an assignment, nor are the nature and enforceability of the note or pledging instrument affected. Assignment is a critical feature for mortgages to be bought and sold in the secondary mortgage market.

The debt financing process, for purposes of discussion, breaks down into three basic phases: (1) initiation, (2) interim or servicing, and (3) termination. These phases apply, regardless of the type of loan involved.

Loan Initiation

A lender must make several basic decisions in making the loan. The applicant must be judged to have an acceptable credit rating and adequate income as evidence of being financially responsible. Also, the relative size of the loan must be determined. A residential loan is not likely to be initiated in excess of 90 to 95 percent of the market value of the pledged property. For an income property, the loan may be limited to from 60 to 80 percent of market value. With an income property, the net operating income must be great enough to meet debt-service requirements, with some excess to serve as a buffer. For example, annual net operating income may have to be 1.25 times annual debt service. Thus, even though operating revenues dip slightly, the owner will still be able to make the necessary payments. Assuming that all the lender's criteria are met, the loan application is approved. The borrower signs the mortgage and note and meets other settlement requirements, and the loan contract is made.

Interim or Servicing Phase

As long as all terms of the contract are met, the agreement is continued without interruption. The borrower-owner most importantly must make scheduled payments of principal and interest to the lender and maintain the property in reasonable condition.

An owner-borrower may, unless prohibited by an *alienation* or *"due on sale" clause,* sell the pledged property without paying off the loan. The life of the loan is thereby continued even though ownership has changed. The buyer, in these circumstances, may take title "subject to" the mortgage or the buyer may take title and "assume and promise to pay" the mortgage.

The distinction between the two alternatives is substantial. Increasingly, lenders are including "due on sale" clauses in new loan agreements to prohibit the sale of the pledged property and continuation of the loan without prior consent from the lender.

Taking subject to a loan. A buyer, taking title subject to a loan, does not take over legal responsibility for the repayment of the debt. However, the buyer continues to make payments on the loan because it is in his or her self-interest. If unable to meet required debt-service payments, the buyer may simply walk away from the property without further obligation to the lender. That is, in case of default, the lender has no recourse or basis for action for debt satisfaction against the buyer-owner.

Even so, it is usually in the buyer-owner's interest to continue making payment of debt service as long as the buyer-owner has an equity interest in the property. However, if market value drops below the loan's balance, the new owner may be rational in walking away because a negative equity has developed. For example,

AT TIME OF PURCHASE		TWO YEARS LATER	
Purchase price	$100,000	Market value	$86,000
Initial loan	−90,000	Loan balance	−89,500
Cash equity	$ 10,000	Equity value	($ 3,500)

The original seller-borrower continues to be liable for the debt if the buyer defaults in making the payments.

Assuming and promising to pay a loan. Agreement by a grantee (usually a buyer) to accept responsibility for repayment of an existing loan against a property is termed *assumption.* The buyer agrees to pay debt service and and to pay any deficiency should a default occur. Unless released, the seller continues to be liable to the lender for payment of the loan as well. The release of a seller-borrower in an assumption is termed *novation,* which means that a *new* contractual obligation has been substituted for an old one by mutual agreement of all parties concerned.

Loan Termination

A borrower is, upon meeting all requirements of the mortgage loan contract, released from the obligation and is entitled to a *mortgage release, satisfaction,* or *discharge,* which is a receipt acknowledging payment. Recording a release ends the mortgage as a lien or claim against the pledged property. Under trust deed financing, the trustee is expected to provide a *deed of release* or *of reconveyance* to clear the record. Loan contracts are brought to an end in other ways as well.

Termination by mutual agreement. A borrower may refinance or recast a loan prior to complete repayment, provided that the lender or the contract so permits. *Refinancing* is generally taken to mean obtaining a new and larger loan, usually at new terms. *Recasting* means keeping the same-sized loan but changing the interest rate and/or the amortization period, usually to reduce required debt service. Finally, the loan may be prepaid, if the agreement contains a prepayment clause, as when a property is sold and the buyer obtains new financing.

Almost all mortgages and trust deeds contain a defeasance clause to protect the buyer if a lender refuses to give a release upon complete repayment of the loan. A *defeasance clause* states that if the loan and interest are paid in full, the rights and interests of the lender in the property cease. Thus, without a debt, a mortgage or trust deed has no life and is not enforceable.

A "deed in lieu of foreclosure" is sometimes "voluntarily" given by a borrower in default to a lender to avoid foreclosure problems and procedures. Such a deed is generally given when the owner's equity in the property is less than the expected costs of foreclosure. Such a compromise usually works to the advantage of both the borrower and lender.

It is when loan requirements are not met and a lender-borrower accommodation cannot be reached that serious complications develop. The complications are much different with mortgage default than with trust deed default. In fact, the critical distinctions between mortgage and trust deed financing surfaces in default and foreclosure. Also, it should be noted that in foreclosure, results differ from state to state, depending on whether title or lien theory applies.

Mortgage Loan Foreclosure

In early times, when real estate was used as security for a mortgage loan, the borrower deeded the property outright to the lender, who thereafter was its legal owner. The borrower usually retained possession, but upon default, the lender immediately took possession. The borrower only retained an equitable right for return of the property if the loan and back interest were fully paid. This right is now called the *equitable right of redemption.* Today, the transaction is still basically the same, although the property is now mortgaged, rather than deeded, to the lender. The distinction may be slight but the difference in outcome for commercial or income property may be substantial.

Theories of mortgage law. The two basic theories of mortgage law in the United States are title theory and lien theory. Some say that a third alternative is the "intermediate theory." For brevity and clarity, only the lien and title theories are emphasized here.

In title theory states, a limited form of legal title is conveyed to the lender when a property is mortgaged. On default, the lender receives the right of possession, which is not usually exercised for owner-occupied residences. For commercial and investment properties, the right is usually exercised through the collection of rents by the lender or the lender's representative. Even so, foreclosure proceedings must be initiated and completed by the mortgagee to clear the property's title.

In lien theory states, title remains with the borrower. The mortgagor may remain in possession even after default. The mortgagee must initiate and complete foreclosure proceedings to get satisfaction from the pledged property. In intermediate states, title remains with the borrower until default, at which point it passes to the lender.

Over the years the distinction between title theory and lien theory states has blurred. In both classes of states, an interest held through a mortgage is legally personal property. This interest must be accompanied by the note, as evidence of the debt, if sold or otherwise transferred. The main difference is, therefore, that rents from and possession of income properties are more readily realized by the lender in title theory states. Also, the foreclosure process is generally considered to be slightly faster in title theory states. In both classes of states, however, foreclosure means eventually offering the pledged property for sale and reducing or paying off the debt with the proceeds. Excess proceeds from the sale go to the borrower-mortgagor.

Termination by default and foreclosure. Lenders recognize that financial distress causes borrowers to miss debt-service payments occasionally and that most borrowers live up to their obligations if given an opportunity. In extended default, however, the lender eventually files a foreclosure suit. The suit demands immediate payment of the debt because the mortgage contract has been breached. The mortgagee-lender may, under certain conditions and in some states, take immediate possession of and title to the subject property as satisfaction of the debt, which is termed *strict foreclosure.* Alternatively, and much more commonly, the property is disposed of at a judicial or foreclosure sale to raise money to pay the debt. Figure 15–4 illustrates this most common mortgage foreclosure process.

Nearly every mortgage involves an acceleration clause to facilitate

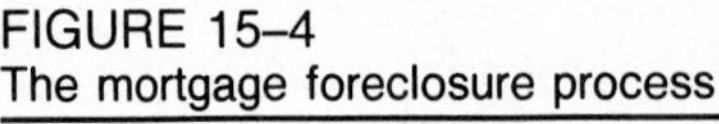
FIGURE 15–4
The mortgage foreclosure process

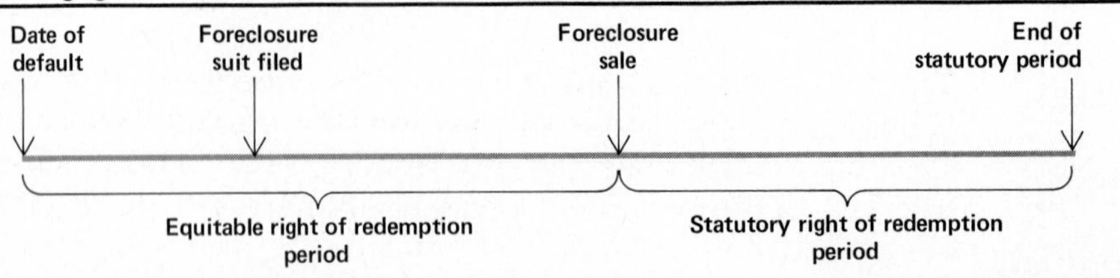

foreclosure. The clause is usually found in the note. An *acceleration clause*, upon default, gives the lender the right to declare all remaining debt-service payments of the loan due and payable immediately. Without an acceleration clause, a lender must sue for each payment as it becomes due.

A borrower may exercise an equitable right of redemption, up until the foreclosure sale, to recover or redeem the property. This right is also called the equity of redemption. In exercising the equitable right of redemption, the borrower must make up all back payments and pay any costs of foreclosure incurred by the lender. The equitable right of redemption cannot be waived or cut off except by a foreclosure sale.

Some states give the borrower a statutory right of redemption after the foreclosure sale. A *statutory right of redemption* allows a borrower to recover foreclosed property for a limited time after the judicial sale by payment of the sale price plus foreclosure costs plus any other costs or losses incurred by the lender. For example, a foreclosed borrower might well arrange another loan to redeem a property rapidly increasing in value. Or suddenly coming into a large inheritance might give a foreclosed borrower the means to recover a favorite property.

Any surplus in a judicial sale usually goes to the borrow-mortgagor. In some states, if the price is less than the debt plus interest plus foreclosure costs, a lender may obtain a deficiency judgment against the borrower. A *deficiency judgment* is a judicial decree in favor of a lender for that portion of the mortgage debt and foreclosure costs that remains unsatisfied from the proceeds of the judicial sale. The judgment attaches to real and personal property of the mortgagor.

Trust Deed Foreclosure

Upon default, the trustee has authority in almost every state to promptly carry out the terms of the trust deed arrangement, which usually means selling the property. Many of the time-consuming requirements of mortgage foreclosure are, therefore, avoided. And the borrower is usually not entitled to any redemption rights after the trustee's sale. On the other hand, a deficiency judgment is usually not recognized when a trustee exercises power of sale.

TYPICAL PROVISIONS OF MORTGAGES AND TRUST DEEDS

Lender experience governs the clauses and covenants in a pledging document, for the most part. The content of a mortgage or trust deed is, therefore, not usually negotiable between the parties. Even so, a prospective borrower needs to know and understand the specific clauses of the pledging document.

Mortgages and deeds of trust, as mentioned, are very similar except in foreclosure. Each clearly establishes that the realty is to secure the debt. Each refers to a promissory note as evidence of the debt. Each identifies the borrower and the lender. Each contains an accurate legal description of the pledged property. Each must be signed by all parties with an interest in the realty, although the lender usually signs neither.

The following are generally considered the more important borrower obligations and, hence, are consistently provided for in a mortgage or trust deed arrangement:

1. Make debt-service payments in accordance with the note.
2. Pay all real estate taxes as they are levied.
3. Provide adequate hazard insurance to protect the lender against loss if the property is damaged or destroyed by fire, wind, or other peril.
4. Maintain the property in good repair at all times.
5. Obtain authorization from the lender before substantially altering the property.

In addition, the following items are frequently but not always provided for in a mortgage or trust deed:

1. Reserve right of lender or noteholder to inspect and protect the property.
2. Stipulate that debt-service payments apply to taxes first, insurance second, interest third, and principal reduction fourth.
3. Stipulate that proceeds from insurance or condemnation go to the lender first, with any excess going to the borrower.
4. Reserve right of lender to approve transfer of ownership of secured property and assumption of the loan, including renegotiation of the interest rate (alienation or due on sale clause).

The FNMA/FHLMC uniform instrument for multifamily residential mortgages contains all these provisions, and more, with its 26 clauses or covenants. This instrument is, therefore, somewhat more extensive than the FNMA/FHLMC mortgage for one- to four-family residences. Whatever the property type, however, violation of any of the provisions by a borrower-mortgagor constitutes default and sets the stage for possible foreclosure.

The clauses are discussed here only briefly as to purpose or content. They are taken up in the same order as they appear in the document in Figure 15–5. The reader is encouraged to look over and study the specific wording of each covenant.

Uniform Covenants

1. *Payment of Principal and Interest.* Borrower agrees to make payments of debt service promptly and otherwise to live up to making payments as agreed, as for example, for a late charge.

FIGURE 15–5
FNMA/FHLMC uniform instrument

Uniform Covenants. Borrower and Lender covenant and agree as follows:

1. PAYMENT OF PRINCIPAL AND INTEREST. Borrower shall promptly pay when due the principal of and interest on the indebtedness evidenced by the Note, any prepayment and late charges provided in the Note and all other sums secured by this Instrument.

2. FUNDS FOR TAXES, INSURANCE AND OTHER CHARGES. Subject to applicable law or to a written waiver by Lender, Borrower shall pay to Lender on the day monthly installments of principal or interest are payable under the Note (or on another day designated in writing by Lender), until the Note is paid in full, a sum (herein "Funds") equal to one-twelfth of (a) the yearly water and sewer rates and taxes and assessments which may be levied on the Property, (b) the yearly ground rents, if any, (c) the yearly premium installments for fire and other hazard insurance, rent loss insurance and such other insurance covering the Property as Lender may require pursuant to paragraph 5 hereof, (d) the yearly premium installments for mortgage insurance, if any, and (e) if this Instrument is on a leasehold, the yearly fixed rents, if any, under the ground lease, all as reasonably estimated initially and from time to time by Lender on the basis of assessments and bills and reasonable estimates thereof. Any waiver by Lender of a requirement that Borrower pay such Funds may be revoked by Lender, in Lender's sole discretion, at any time upon notice in writing to Borrower. Lender may require Borrower to pay to Lender, in advance, such other Funds for other taxes, charges, premiums, assessments and impositions in connection with Borrower or the Property which Lender shall reasonably deem necessary to protect Lender's interests (herein "Other Impositions"). Unless otherwise provided by applicable law, Lender may require Funds for Other Impositions to be paid by Borrower in a lump sum or in periodic installments, at Lender's option.

The Funds shall be held in an institution(s) the deposits or accounts of which are insured or guaranteed by a Federal or state agency (including Lender if Lender is such an institution). Lender shall apply the Funds to pay said rates, rents, taxes, assessments, insurance premiums and Other Impositions so long as Borrower is not in breach of any covenant or agreement of Borrower in this Instrument. Lender shall make no charge for so holding and applying the Funds, analyzing said account or for verifying and compiling said assessments and bills, unless Lender pays Borrower interest, earnings or profits on the Funds and applicable law permits Lender to make such a charge. Borrower and Lender may agree in writing at the time of execution of this Instrument that interest on the Funds shall be paid to Borrower, and unless such agreement is made or applicable law requires interest, earnings or profits to be paid, Lender shall not be required to pay Borrower any interest, earnings or profits on the Funds. Lender shall give to Borrower, without charge, an annual accounting of the Funds in Lender's normal format showing credits and debits to the Funds and the purpose for which each debit to the Funds was made. The Funds are pledged as additional security for the sums secured by this Instrument.

If the amount of the Funds held by Lender at the time of the annual accounting thereof shall exceed the amount deemed necessary by Lender to provide for the payment of water and sewer rates, taxes, assessments, insurance premiums, rents and Other Impositions, as they fall due, such excess shall be credited to Borrower on the next monthly installment or installments of Funds due. If at any time the amount of the Funds held by Lender shall be less than the amount deemed necessary by Lender to pay water and sewer rates, taxes, assessments, insurance premiums, rents and Other Impositions, as they fall due, Borrower shall pay to Lender any amount necessary to make up the deficiency within thirty days after notice from Lender to Borrower requesting payment thereof.

Upon Borrower's breach of any covenant or agreement of Borrower in this Instrument, Lender may apply, in any amount and in any order as Lender shall determine in Lender's sole discretion, any Funds held by Lender at the time of application (i) to pay rates, rents, taxes, assessments, insurance premiums and Other Impositions which are now or will hereafter become due, or (ii) as a credit against sums secured by this Instrument. Upon payment in full of all sums secured by this Instrument, Lender shall promptly refund to Borrower any Funds held by Lender.

3. APPLICATION OF PAYMENTS. Unless applicable law provides otherwise, all payments received by Lender from Borrower under the Note or this Instrument shall be applied by Lender in the following order of priority: (i) amounts payable to Lender by Borrower under paragraph 2 hereof; (ii) interest payable on the Note; (iii) principal of the Note; (iv) interest payable on advances made pursuant to paragraph 8 hereof; (v) principal of advances made pursuant to paragraph 8 hereof; (vi) interest payable on any Future Advance, provided that if more than one Future Advance is outstanding, Lender may apply payments received among the amounts of interest payable on the Future Advances in such order as Lender, in Lender's sole discretion, may determine; (vii) principal of any Future Advance, provided that if more than one Future Advance is outstanding, Lender may apply payments received among the principal balances of the Future Advances in such order as Lender, in Lender's sole discretion, may determine; and (viii) any other sums secured by this Instrument in such order as Lender, at Lender's option, may determine; provided, however, that Lender may, at Lender's option, apply any sums payable pursuant to paragraph 8 hereof prior to interest on and principal of the Note, but such application shall not otherwise affect the order of priority of application specified in this paragraph 3.

4. CHARGES; LIENS. Borrower shall pay all water and sewer rates, rents, taxes, assessments, premiums, and Other Impositions attributable to the Property at Lender's option in the manner provided under paragraph 2 hereof or, if not paid in such manner, by Borrower making payment, when due, directly to the payee thereof, or in such other manner as Lender may designate in writing. Borrower shall promptly furnish to Lender all notices of amounts due under this paragraph 4, and in the event Borrower shall make payment directly, Borrower shall promptly furnish to Lender receipts evidencing such payments. Borrower shall promptly discharge any lien which has, or may have, priority over or equality with, the lien of this Instrument, and Borrower shall pay, when due, the claims of all persons supplying labor or materials to or in connection with the Property. Without Lender's prior written permission, Borrower shall not allow any lien inferior to this Instrument to be perfected against the Property.

5. HAZARD INSURANCE. Borrower shall keep the improvements now existing or hereafter erected on the Property insured by carriers at all times satisfactory to Lender against loss by fire, hazards included within the term "extended coverage", rent loss and such other hazards, casualties, liabilities and contingencies as Lender (and, if this Instrument is on a leasehold, the ground lease) shall require and in such amounts and for such periods as Lender shall require. All premiums on insurance policies shall be paid, at Lender's option, in the manner provided under paragraph 2 hereof, or by Borrower making payment, when due, directly to the carrier, or in such other manner as Lender may designate in writing.

All insurance policies and renewals thereof shall be in a form acceptable to Lender and shall include a standard mortgage clause in favor of and in form acceptable to Lender. Lender shall have the right to hold the policies, and Borrower shall promptly furnish to Lender all renewal notices and all receipts of paid premiums. At least thirty days prior to the expiration date of a policy, Borrower shall deliver to Lender a renewal policy in form satisfactory to Lender. If this Instrument is on a leasehold, Borrower shall furnish Lender a duplicate of all policies, renewal notices, renewal policies and receipts of paid premiums if, by virtue of the ground lease, the originals thereof may not be supplied by Borrower to Lender.

In the event of loss, Borrower shall give immediate written notice to the insurance carrier and to Lender. Borrower hereby authorizes and empowers Lender as attorney-in-fact for Borrower to make proof of loss, to adjust and compromise any claim under insurance policies, to appear in and prosecute any action arising from such insurance policies, to collect and receive insurance proceeds, and to deduct therefrom Lender's expenses incurred in the collection of such proceeds; provided however, that nothing contained in this paragraph 5 shall require Lender to incur any expense or take any action hereunder. Borrower further authorizes Lender, at Lender's option, (a) to hold the balance of such proceeds to be used to reimburse Borrower for the cost of reconstruction or repair of the Property or (b) to apply the balance of such proceeds to the payment of the sums secured by this Instrument, whether or not then due, in the order of application set forth in paragraph 3 hereof (subject, however, to the rights of the lessor under the ground lease if this Instrument is on a leasehold).

If the insurance proceeds are held by Lender to reimburse Borrower for the cost of restoration and repair of the Property, the Property shall be restored to the equivalent of its original condition or such other condition as Lender may approve in writing. Lender may, at Lender's option, condition disbursement of said proceeds on Lender's approval of such plans and specifications of an architect satisfactory to Lender, contractor's cost estimates, architect's certificates, waivers of liens, sworn statements of mechanics and materialmen and such other evidence of costs, percentage completion of construction, application of payments, and satisfaction of liens as Lender may reasonably require. If the insurance proceeds are applied to the payment of the sums secured by this Instrument, any such application of proceeds to principal shall not extend or postpone the due dates of the monthly installments referred to in paragraphs 1 and 2 hereof or change the amounts of such installments. If the Property is sold pursuant to paragraph 27 hereof or if Lender acquires title to the Property, Lender shall have all of the right, title and interest of Borrower in and to any insurance policies and unearned premiums thereon and in and to the proceeds resulting from any damage to the Property prior to such sale or acquisition.

6. PRESERVATION AND MAINTENANCE OF PROPERTY; LEASEHOLDS. Borrower (a) shall not commit waste or permit impairment or deterioration of the Property, (b) shall not abandon the Property, (c) shall restore or repair promptly and in a good and workmanlike manner all

Uniform Covenants—Multifamily—1/77—**FNMA/FHLMC Uniform Instrument** *(page 3 of 8 pages)*

FIGURE 15–5
(continued)

or any part of the Property to the equivalent of its original condition, or such other condition as Lender may approve in writing, in the event of any damage, injury or loss thereto, whether or not insurance proceeds are available to cover in whole or in part the costs of such restoration or repair, (d) shall keep the Property, including improvements, fixtures, equipment, machinery and appliances thereon in good repair and shall replace fixtures, equipment, machinery and appliances on the Property when necessary to keep such items in good repair, (e) shall comply with all laws, ordinances, regulations and requirements of any governmental body applicable to the Property, (f) shall provide for professional management of the Property by a residential rental property manager satisfactory to Lender pursuant to a contract approved by Lender in writing, unless such requirement shall be waived by Lender in writing, (g) shall generally operate and maintain the Property in a manner to ensure maximum rentals, and (h) shall give notice in writing to Lender of and, unless otherwise directed in writing by Lender, appear in and defend any action or proceeding purporting to affect the Property, the security of this Instrument or the rights or powers of Lender. Neither Borrower nor any tenant or other person shall remove, demolish or alter any improvement now existing or hereafter erected on the Property or any fixture, equipment, machinery or appliance in or on the Property except when incident to the replacement of fixtures, equipment, machinery and appliances with items of like kind.

If this Instrument is on a leasehold, Borrower (i) shall comply with the provisions of the ground lease, (ii) shall give immediate written notice to Lender of any default by lessor under the ground lease or of any notice received by Borrower from such lessor of any default under the ground lease by Borrower, (iii) shall exercise any option to renew or extend the ground lease and give written confirmation thereof to Lender within thirty days after such option becomes exercisable, (iv) shall give immediate written notice to Lender of the commencement of any remedial proceedings under the ground lease by any party thereto and, if required by Lender, shall permit Lender as Borrower's attorney-in-fact to control and act for Borrower in any such remedial proceedings and (v) shall within thirty days after request by Lender obtain from the lessor under the ground lease and deliver to Lender the lessor's estoppel certificate required thereunder, if any. Borrower hereby expressly transfers and assigns to Lender the benefit of all covenants contained in the ground lease, whether or not such covenants run with the land, but Lender shall have no liability with respect to such covenants nor any other covenants contained in the ground lease.

Borrower shall not surrender the leasehold estate and interests herein conveyed nor terminate or cancel the ground lease creating said estate and interests, and Borrower shall not, without the express written consent of Lender, alter or amend said ground lease. Borrower covenants and agrees that there shall not be a merger of the ground lease, or of the leasehold estate created thereby, with the fee estate covered by the ground lease by reason of said leasehold estate or said fee estate, or any part of either, coming into common ownership, unless Lender shall consent in writing to such merger; if Borrower shall acquire such fee estate, then this Instrument shall simultaneously and without further action be spread so as to become a lien on such fee estate.

7. USE OF PROPERTY. Unless required by applicable law or unless Lender has otherwise agreed in writing, Borrower shall not allow changes in the use for which all or any part of the Property was intended at the time this Instrument was executed. Borrower shall not initiate or acquiesce in a change in the zoning classification of the Property without Lender's prior written consent.

8. PROTECTION OF LENDER'S SECURITY. If Borrower fails to perform the covenants and agreements contained in this Instrument, or if any action or proceeding is commenced which affects the Property or title thereto or the interest of Lender therein, including, but not limited to, eminent domain, insolvency, code enforcement, or arrangements or proceedings involving a bankrupt or decedent, then Lender at Lender's option may make such appearances, disburse such sums and take such action as Lender deems necessary, in its sole discretion, to protect Lender's interest, including, but not limited to, (i) disbursement of attorney's fees, (ii) entry upon the Property to make repairs, (iii) procurement of satisfactory insurance as provided in paragraph 5 hereof, and (iv) if this Instrument is on a leasehold, exercise of any option to renew or extend the ground lease on behalf of Borrower and the curing of any default of Borrower in the terms and conditions of the ground lease.

Any amounts disbursed by Lender pursuant to this paragraph 8, with interest thereon, shall become additional indebtedness of Borrower secured by this Instrument. Unless Borrower and Lender agree to other terms of payment, such amounts shall be immediately due and payable and shall bear interest from the date of disbursement at the rate stated in the Note unless collection from Borrower of interest at such rate would be contrary to applicable law, in which event such amounts shall bear interest at the highest rate which may be collected from Borrower under applicable law. Borrower hereby covenants and agrees that Lender shall be subrogated to the lien of any mortgage or other lien discharged, in whole or in part, by the indebtedness secured hereby. Nothing contained in this paragraph 8 shall require Lender to incur any expense or take any action hereunder.

9. INSPECTION. Lender may make or cause to be made reasonable entries upon and inspections of the Property.

10. BOOKS AND RECORDS. Borrower shall keep and maintain at all times at Borrower's address stated below, or such other place as Lender may approve in writing, complete and accurate books of accounts and records adequate to reflect correctly the results of the operation of the Property and copies of all written contracts, leases and other instruments which affect the Property. Such books, records, contracts, leases and other instruments shall be subject to examination and inspection at any reasonable time by Lender. Upon Lender's request, Borrower shall furnish to Lender, within one hundred and twenty days after the end of each fiscal year of Borrower, a balance sheet, a statement of income and expenses of the Property and a statement of changes in financial position, each in reasonable detail and certified by Borrower and, if Lender shall require, by an independent certified public accountant. Borrower shall furnish, together with the foregoing financial statements and at any other time upon Lender's request, a rent schedule for the Property, certified by Borrower, showing the name of each tenant, and for each tenant, the space occupied, the lease expiration date, the rent payable and the rent paid.

11. CONDEMNATION. Borrower shall promptly notify Lender of any action or proceeding relating to any condemnation or other taking, whether direct or indirect, of the Property, or part thereof, and Borrower shall appear in and prosecute any such action or proceeding unless otherwise directed by Lender in writing. Borrower authorizes Lender, at Lender's option, as attorney-in-fact for Borrower, to commence, appear in and prosecute, in Lender's or Borrower's name, any action or proceeding relating to any condemnation or other taking of the Property, whether direct or indirect, and to settle or compromise any claim in connection with such condemnation or other taking. The proceeds of any award, payment or claim for damages, direct or consequential, in connection with any condemnation or other taking, whether direct or indirect, of the Property, or part thereof, or for conveyances in lieu of condemnation, are hereby assigned to and shall be paid to Lender subject, if this Instrument is on a leasehold, to the rights of lessor under the ground lease.

Borrower authorizes Lender to apply such awards, payments, proceeds or damages, after the deduction of Lender's expenses incurred in the collection of such amounts, at Lender's option, to restoration or repair of the Property or to payment of the sums secured by this Instrument, whether or not then due, in the order of application set forth in paragraph 3 hereof, with the balance, if any, to Borrower. Unless Borrower and Lender otherwise agree in writing, any application of proceeds to principal shall not extend or postpone the due date of the monthly installments referred to in paragraphs 1 and 2 hereof or change the amount of such installments. Borrower agrees to execute such further evidence of assignment of any awards, proceeds, damages or claims arising in connection with such condemnation or taking as Lender may require.

12. BORROWER AND LIEN NOT RELEASED. From time to time, Lender may, at Lender's option, without giving notice to or obtaining the consent of Borrower, Borrower's successors or assigns or of any junior lienholder or guarantors, without liability on Lender's part and notwithstanding Borrower's breach of any covenant or agreement of Borrower in this Instrument, extend the time for payment of said indebtedness or any part thereof, reduce the payments thereon, release anyone liable on any of said indebtedness, accept a renewal note or notes therefor, modify the terms and time of payment of said indebtedness, release from the lien of this Instrument any part of the Property, take or release other or additional security, reconvey any part of the Property, consent to any map or plan of the Property, consent to the granting of any easement, join in any extension or subordination agreement, and agree in writing with Borrower to modify the rate of interest or period of amortization of the Note or change the amount of the monthly installments payable thereunder. Any actions taken by Lender pursuant to the terms of this paragraph 12 shall not affect the obligation of Borrower or Borrower's successors or assigns to pay the sums secured by this Instrument and to observe the covenants of Borrower contained herein, shall not affect the guaranty of any person, corporation, partnership or other entity for payment of the indebtedness secured hereby, and shall not affect the lien or priority of lien hereof on the Property. Borrower shall pay Lender a reasonable service charge, together with such title insurance premiums and attorney's fees as may be incurred at Lender's option, for any such action if taken at Borrower's request.

13. FORBEARANCE BY LENDER NOT A WAIVER. Any forbearance by Lender in exercising any right or remedy hereunder, or otherwise afforded by applicable law, shall not be a waiver of or preclude the exercise of any right or remedy. The acceptance by Lender of payment of any sum secured by this Instrument after the due date of such payment shall not be a waiver of Lender's right to either require prompt payment when due of all other sums so secured or to declare a default for failure to make prompt payment. The procurement of insurance or the payment of taxes or other liens or charges by Lender shall not be a waiver of Lender's right to accelerate the maturity of the indebtedess secured by this Instrument, nor shall Lender's receipt of any awards, proceeds or damages under paragraphs 5 and 11 hereof operate to cure or waive Borrower's default in payment of sums secured by this Instrument.

(page 4 of 8 pages)

FIGURE 15–5
(continued)

14. ESTOPPEL CERTIFICATE. Borrower shall within ten days of a written request from Lender furnish Lender with a written statement, duly acknowledged, setting forth the sums secured by this Instrument and any right of set-off, counterclaim or other defense which exists against such sums and the obligations of this Instrument.

15. UNIFORM COMMERCIAL CODE SECURITY AGREEMENT. This Instrument is intended to be a security agreement pursuant to the Uniform Commercial Code for any of the items specified above as part of the Property which, under applicable law, may be subject to a security interest pursuant to the Uniform Commercial Code, and Borrower hereby grants Lender a security interest in said items. Borrower agrees that Lender may file this Instrument, or a reproduction thereof, in the real estate records or other appropriate index, as a financing statement for any of the items specified above as part of the Property. Any reproduction of this Instrument or of any other security agreement or financing statement shall be sufficient as a financing statement. In addition, Borrower agrees to execute and deliver to Lender, upon Lender's request, any financing statements, as well as extensions, renewals and amendments thereof, and reproductions of this Instrument in such form as Lender may require to perfect a security interest with respect to said items. Borrower shall pay all costs of filing such financing statements and any extensions, renewals, amendments and releases thereof, and shall pay all reasonable costs and expenses of any record searches for financing statements Lender may reasonably require. Without the prior written consent of Lender, Borrower shall not create or suffer to be created pursuant to the Uniform Commercial Code any other security interest in said items, including replacements and additions thereto. Upon Borrower's breach of any covenant or agreement of Borrower contained in this Instrument, including the covenants to pay when due all sums secured by this Instrument, Lender shall have the remedies of a secured party under the Uniform Commercial Code and, at Lender's option, may also invoke the remedies provided in paragraph 27 of this Instrument as to such items. In exercising any of said remedies, Lender may proceed against the items of real property and any items of personal property specified above as part of the Property separately or together and in any order whatsoever, without in any way affecting the availability of Lender's remedies under the Uniform Commercial Code or of the remedies provided in paragraph 27 of this Instrument.

16. LEASES OF THE PROPERTY. As used in this paragraph 16, the word "lease" shall mean "sublease" if this Instrument is on a leasehold. Borrower shall comply with and observe Borrower's obligations as landlord under all leases of the Property or any part thereof. Borrower will not lease any portion of the Property for non-residential use except with the prior written approval of Lender. Borrower, at Lender's request, shall furnish Lender with executed copies of all leases now existing or hereafter made of all or any part of the Property, and all leases now or hereafter entered into will be in form and substance subject to the approval of Lender. All leases of the Property shall specifically provide that such leases are subordinate to this Instrument; that the tenant attorns to Lender, such attornment to be effective upon Lender's acquisition of title to the Property; that the tenant agrees to execute such further evidences of attornment as Lender may from time to time request; that the attornment of the tenant shall not be terminated by foreclosure; and that Lender may, at Lender's option, accept or reject such attornments. Borrower shall not, without Lender's written consent, execute, modify, surrender or terminate, either orally or in writing, any lease now existing or hereafter made of all or any part of the Property providing for a term of three years or more, permit an assignment or sublease of such a lease without Lender's written consent, or request or consent to the subordination of any lease of all or any part of the Property to any lien subordinate to this Instrument. If Borrower becomes aware that any tenant proposes to do, or is doing, any act or thing which may give rise to any right of set-off against rent, Borrower shall (i) take such steps as shall be reasonably calculated to prevent the accrual of any right to a set-off against rent, (ii) notify Lender thereof and of the amount of said set-offs, and (iii) within ten days after such accrual, reimburse the tenant who shall have acquired such right to set-off or take such other steps as shall effectively discharge such set-off and as shall assure that rents thereafter due shall continue to be payable without set-off or deduction.

Upon Lender's request, Borrower shall assign to Lender, by written instrument satisfactory to Lender, all leases now existing or hereafter made of all or any part of the Property and all security deposits made by tenants in connection with such leases of the Property. Upon assignment by Borrower to Lender of any leases of the Property, Lender shall have all of the rights and powers possessed by Borrower prior to such assignment and Lender shall have the right to modify, extend or terminate such existing leases and to execute new leases, in Lender's sole discretion.

17. REMEDIES CUMULATIVE. Each remedy provided in this Instrument is distinct and cumulative to all other rights or remedies under this Instrument or afforded by law or equity, and may be exercised concurrently, independently, or successively, in any order whatsoever.

18. ACCELERATION IN CASE OF BORROWER'S INSOLVENCY. If Borrower shall voluntarily file a petition under the Federal Bankruptcy Act, as such Act may from time to time be amended, or under any similar or successor Federal statute relating to bankruptcy, insolvency, arrangements or reorganizations, or under any state bankruptcy or insolvency act, or file an answer in an involuntary proceeding admitting insolvency or inability to pay debts, or if Borrower shall fail to obtain a vacation or stay of involuntary proceedings brought for the reorganization, dissolution or liquidation of Borrower, or if Borrower shall be adjudged a bankrupt, or if a trustee or receiver shall be appointed for Borrower or Borrower's property, or if the Property shall become subject to the jurisdiction of a Federal bankruptcy court or similar state court, or if Borrower shall make an assignment for the benefit of Borrower's creditors, or if there is an attachment, execution or other judicial seizure of any portion of Borrower's assets and such seizure is not discharged within ten days, then Lender may, at Lender's option, declare all of the sums secured by this Instrument to be immediately due and payable without prior notice to Borrower, and Lender may invoke any remedies permitted by paragraph 27 of this Instrument. Any attorney's fees and other expenses incurred by Lender in connection with Borrower's bankruptcy or any of the other aforesaid events shall be additional indebtedness of Borrower secured by this Instrument pursuant to paragraph 8 hereof.

19. TRANSFERS OF THE PROPERTY OR BENEFICIAL INTERESTS IN BORROWER; ASSUMPTION. On sale or transfer of (i) all or any part of the Property, or any interest therein, or (ii) beneficial interests in Borrower (if Borrower is not a natural person or persons but is a corporation, partnership, trust or other legal entity), Lender may, at Lender's option, declare all of the sums secured by this Instrument to be immediately due and payable, and Lender may invoke any remedies permitted by paragraph 27 of this Instrument. This option shall not apply in case of

(a) transfers by devise or descent or by operation of law upon the death of a joint tenant or a partner;
(b) sales or transfers when the transferee's creditworthiness and management ability are satisfactory to Lender and the transferee has executed, prior to the sale or transfer, a written assumption agreement containing such terms as Lender may require, including, if required by Lender, an increase in the rate of interest payable under the Note;
(c) the grant of a leasehold interest in a part of the Property of three years or less (or such longer lease term as Lender may permit by prior written approval) not containing an option to purchase (except any interest in the ground lease, if this Instrument is on a leasehold);
(d) sales or transfers of beneficial interests in Borrower provided that such sales or transfers, together with any prior sales or transfers of beneficial interests in Borrower, but excluding sales or transfers under subparagraphs (a) and (b) above, do not result in more than 49% of the beneficial interests in Borrower having been sold or transferred since commencement of amortization of the Note; and
(e) sales or transfers of fixtures or any personal property pursuant to the first paragraph of paragraph 6 hereof.

20. NOTICE. Except for any notice required under applicable law to be given in another manner, (a) any notice to Borrower provided for in this Instrument or in the Note shall be given by mailing such notice by certified mail addressed to Borrower at Borrower's address stated below or at such other address as Borrower may designate by notice to Lender as provided herein, and (b) any notice to Lender shall be given by certified mail, return receipt requested, to Lender's address stated herein or to such other address as Lender may designate by notice to Borrower as provided herein. Any notice provided for in this Instrument or in the Note shall be deemed to have been given to Borrower or Lender when given in the manner designated herein.

21. SUCCESSORS AND ASSIGNS BOUND; JOINT AND SEVERAL LIABILITY; AGENTS; CAPTIONS. The covenants and agreements herein contained shall bind, and the rights hereunder shall inure to, the respective successors and assigns of Lender and Borrower, subject to the provisions of paragraph 19 hereof. All covenants and agreements of Borrower shall be joint and several. In exercising any rights hereunder or taking any actions provided for herein, Lender may act through its employees, agents or independent contractors as authorized by Lender. The captions and headings of the paragraphs of this Instrument are for convenience only and are not to be used to interpret or define the provisions hereof.

22. UNIFORM MULTIFAMILY INSTRUMENT; GOVERNING LAW; SEVERABILITY. This form of multifamily instrument combines uniform covenants for national use and non-uniform covenants with limited variations by jurisdiction to constitute a uniform security instrument covering real property and related fixtures and personal property. This Instrument shall be governed by the law of the jurisdiction in which the Property is located. In the event that any provision of this Instrument or the Note conflicts with applicable law, such conflict shall not affect other provisions of this Instrument or the Note which can be given effect without the conflicting provisions, and to this end the provisions of this

(page 5 of 8 pages)

Instrument and the Note are declared to be severable. In the event that any applicable law limiting the amount of interest or other charges permitted to be collected from Borrower is interpreted so that any charge provided for in this Instrument or in the Note, whether considered separately or together with other charges levied in connection with this Instrument and the Note, violates such law, and Borrower is entitled to the benefit of such law, such charge is hereby reduced to the extent necessary to eliminate such violation. The amounts, if any, previously paid to Lender in excess of the amounts payable to Lender pursuant to such charges as reduced shall be applied by Lender to reduce the principal of the indebtedness evidenced by the Note. For the purpose of determining whether any applicable law limiting the amount of interest or other charges permitted to be collected from Borrower has been violated, all indebtedness which is secured by this Instrument or evidenced by the Note and which constitutes interest, as well as all other charges levied in connection with such indebtedness which constitute interest, shall be deemed to be allocated and spread over the stated term of the Note. Unless otherwise required by applicable law, such allocation and spreading shall be effected in such a manner that the rate of interest computed thereby is uniform throughout the stated term of the Note.

23. WAIVER OF STATUTE OF LIMITATIONS. Borrower hereby waives the right to assert any statute of limitations as a bar to the enforcement of the lien of this Instrument or to any action brought to enforce the Note or any other obligation secured by this Instrument.

24. WAIVER OF MARSHALLING. Notwithstanding the existence of any other security interests in the Property held by Lender or by any other party, Lender shall have the right to determine the order in which any or all of the Property shall be subjected to the remedies provided herein. Lender shall have the right to determine the order in which any or all portions of the indebtedness secured hereby are satisfied from the proceeds realized upon the exercise of the remedies provided herein. Borrower, any party who consents to this Instrument and any party who now or hereafter acquires a security interest in the Property and who has actual or constructive notice hereof hereby waives any and all right to require the marshalling of assets in connection with the exercise of any of the remedies permitted by applicable law or provided herein.

25. CONSTRUCTION LOAN PROVISIONS. Borrower agrees to comply with the covenants and conditions of the Construction Loan Agreement, if any, which is hereby incorporated by reference in and made a part of this Instrument. All advances made by Lender pursuant to the Construction Loan Agreement shall be indebtedness of Borrower secured by this Instrument, and such advances may be obligatory as provided in the Construction Loan Agreement. All sums disbursed by Lender prior to completion of the improvements to protect the security of this Instrument up to the principal amount of the Note shall be treated as disbursements pursuant to the Construction Loan Agreement. All such sums shall bear interest from the date of disbursement at the rate stated in the Note, unless collection from Borrower of interest at such rate would be contrary to applicable law in which event such amounts shall bear interest at the highest rate which may be collected from Borrower under applicable law and shall be payable upon notice from Lender to Borrower requesting payment therefor.

From time to time as Lender deems necessary to protect Lender's interests, Borrower shall, upon request of Lender, execute and deliver to Lender, in such form as Lender shall direct, assignments of any and all rights or claims which relate to the construction of the Property and which Borrower may have against any party supplying or who has supplied labor, materials or services in connection with construction of the Property. In case of breach by Borrower of the covenants and conditions of the Construction Loan Agreement, Lender, at Lender's option, with or without entry upon the Property, (i) may invoke any of the rights or remedies provided in the Construction Loan Agreement, (ii) may accelerate the sums secured by this Instrument and invoke those remedies provided in paragraph 27 hereof, or (iii) may do both. If, after the commencement of amortization of the Note, the Note and this Instrument are sold by Lender, from and after such sale the Construction Loan Agreement shall cease to be a part of this Instrument and Borrower shall not assert any right of set-off, counterclaim or other claim or defense arising out of or in connection with the Construction Loan Agreement against the obligations of the Note and this Instrument.

26. ASSIGNMENT OF RENTS; APPOINTMENT OF RECEIVER; LENDER IN POSSESSION. As part of the consideration for the indebtedness evidenced by the Note, Borrower hereby absolutely and unconditionally assigns and transfers to Lender all the rents and revenues of the Property, including those now due, past due, or to become due by virtue of any lease or other agreement for the occupancy or use of all or any part of the Property, regardless of to whom the rents and revenues of the Property are payable. Borrower hereby authorizes Lender or Lender's agents to collect the aforesaid rents and revenues and hereby directs each tenant of the Property to pay such rents to Lender or Lender's agents; provided, however, that prior to written notice given by Lender to Borrower of the breach by Borrower of any covenant or agreement of Borrower in this Instrument, Borrower shall collect and receive all rents and revenues of the Property as trustee for the benefit of Lender and Borrower, to apply the rents and revenues so collected to the sums secured by this Instrument in the order provided in paragraph 3 hereof with the balance, so long as no such breach has occurred, to the account of Borrower, it being intended by Borrower and Lender that this assignment of rents constitutes an absolute assignment and not an assignment for additional security only. Upon delivery of written notice by Lender to Borrower of the breach by Borrower of any covenant or agreement of Borrower in this Instrument, and without the necessity of Lender entering upon and taking and maintaining full control of the Property in person, by agent or by a court-appointed receiver, Lender shall immediately be entitled to possession of all rents and revenues of the Property as specified in this paragraph 26 as the same become due and payable, including but not limited to rents then due and unpaid, and all such rents shall immediately upon delivery of such notice be held by Borrower as trustee for the benefit of Lender only; provided, however, that the written notice by Lender to Borrower of the breach by Borrower shall contain a statement that Lender exercises its rights to such rents. Borrower agrees that commencing upon delivery of such written notice of Borrower's breach by Lender to Borrower, each tenant of the Property shall make such rents payable to and pay such rents to Lender or Lender's agents on Lender's written demand to each tenant therefor, delivered to each tenant personally, by mail or by delivering such demand to each rental unit, without any liability on the part of said tenant to inquire further as to the existence of a default by Borrower.

Borrower hereby covenants that Borrower has not executed any prior assignment of said rents, that Borrower has not performed, and will not perform, any acts or has not executed, and will not execute, any instrument which would prevent Lender from exercising its rights under this paragraph 26, and that at the time of execution of this Instrument there has been no anticipation or prepayment of any of the rents of the Property for more than two months prior to the due dates of such rents. Borrower covenants that Borrower will not hereafter collect or accept payment of any rents of the Property more than two months prior to the due dates of such rents. Borrower further covenants that Borrower will execute and deliver to Lender such further assignments of rents and revenues of the Property as Lender may from time to time request.

Upon Borrower's breach of any covenant or agreement of Borrower in this Instrument, Lender may in person, by agent or by a court-appointed receiver, regardless of the adequacy of Lender's security, enter upon and take and maintain full control of the Property in order to perform all acts necessary and appropriate for the operation and maintenance thereof including, but not limited to, the execution, cancellation or modification of leases, the collection of all rents and revenues of the Property, the making of repairs to the Property and the execution or termination of contracts providing for the management or maintenance of the Property, all on such terms as are deemed best to protect the security of this Instrument. In the event Lender elects to seek the appointment of a receiver for the Property upon Borrower's breach of any covenant or agreement of Borrower in this Instrument, Borrower hereby expressly consents to the appointment of such receiver. Lender or the receiver shall be entitled to receive a reasonable fee for so managing the Property.

All rents and revenues collected subsequent to delivery of written notice by Lender to Borrower of the breach by Borrower of any covenant or agreement of Borrower in this Instrument shall be applied first to the costs, if any, of taking control of and managing the Property and collecting the rents, including, but not limited to, attorney's fees, receiver's fees, premiums on receiver's bonds, costs of repairs to the Property, premiums on insurance policies, taxes, assessments and other charges on the Property, and the costs of discharging any obligation or liability of Borrower as lessor or landlord of the Property and then to the sums secured by this Instrument. Lender or the receiver shall have access to the books and records used in the operation and maintenance of the Property and shall be liable to account only for those rents actually received. Lender shall not be liable to Borrower, anyone claiming under or through Borrower or anyone having an interest in the Property by reason of anything done or left undone by Lender under this paragraph 26.

If the rents of the Property are not sufficient to meet the costs, if any, of taking control of and managing the Property and collecting the rents, any funds expended by Lender for such purposes shall become indebtedness of Borrower to Lender secured by this Instrument pursuant to paragraph 8 hereof. Unless Lender and Borrower agree in writing to other terms of payment, such amounts shall be payable upon notice from Lender to Borrower requesting payment thereof and shall bear interest from the date of disbursement at the rate stated in the Note unless payment of interest at such rate would be contrary to applicable law, in which event such amounts shall bear interest at the highest rate which may be collected from Borrower under applicable law.

Any entering upon and taking and maintaining of control of the Property by Lender or the receiver and any application of rents as provided herein shall not cure or waive any default hereunder or invalidate any other right or remedy of Lender under applicable law or provided herein. This assignment of rents of the Property shall terminate at such time as this Instrument ceases to secure indebtedness held by Lender.

Uniform Covenants—Multifamily—1/77—**FNMA/FHLMC Uniform Instrument** *(page 6 of 8 pages)*

2. *Funds for Taxes and Insurance.* Borrower agrees to make monthly deposits with the lender for property taxes, hazard insurance, mortgage insurance, if any, water and sewer charges, if any, and rents or ground rents, if any. Lender is to make these annual payments when due.
3. *Application of Payments.* Noteholder is awarded some discretion in applying payments to taxes, insurance, interest, and rents. (For one- to four-family residence, payments apply first to insurance and taxes as necessary, second to interest on the principal, and third to reduction of the principal.)
4. *Charges, Liens.* Borrower agrees to pay any charges or liens against the property promptly. Also, the borrower agrees not to allow inferior or lower-priority liens to be perfected against the property.
5. *Hazard Insurance.* Borrower is required to keep the property insured against fire and other hazards up to the amount of the loan balance, and against rent losses, with the insurance proceeds payable to the noteholder and any excess paid the borrower.
6. *Property Preservation and Maintenance.* Borrower agrees to maintain the property in good repair and not permit its waste or deterioration. Borrower further agrees that fixtures, buildings, equipment, and other improvements shall not be removed or demolished without prior written consent from the noteholder.
7. *Use of Property.* Borrower agrees not to change the use of the property unless otherwise agreed to or required by law. Even a change in zoning is subject to review by the noteholder.
8. *Protection of Lender's Security.* Lender may protect the secured property by any actions necessary if the borrower fails to do so.
9. *Inspection.* Noteholder has reasonable entry to the property for inspections to assure its maintenance, safety, and proper operation.
10. *Books and Records.* Lender is permitted reasonable access to the borrower's books and other financial records concerning the property.
11. *Condemnation.* Proceeds from condemnation shall first go to pay lender expenses and the debt, with any excess going to the owner.
12. *Borrower Not Released.* Lender does not release the lien or forgive any of the borrower's repayment obligation by extending time for payment or by failure to press for payment. That is, the lender loses no rights by being courteous and considerate in dealing with the borrower or debtor.
13. *Forbearance by Lender Not a Waiver.* Noteholder forbearance—postponing action to a later time—does not waive or preclude exercise of a right or remedy. Thus, for example, in default, payment may be demanded immediately or at a later time, without damage to the note holder.
14. *Estoppel Certificate.* Borrower agrees to provide lender an estoppel certificate on demand. An estoppel certificate is a written statement that, when signed and given to another person, legally "stops" or prevents the signer from saying subsequently that the facts are different from those set forth. Such a certificate is usually used to verify the loan balance upon sale and assignment of the mortgage.
15. *UCC Security Agreement.* Borrower agrees to provide statements and to pay recording charges necessary to bring the mortgage into compliance with the Uniform Commercial Code.
16. *Leases of the Property.* Borrower promises to provide lender with copies of leases and side agreements with tenants, on request.
17. *Remedies Cumulative.* Lender remedies are distinct and cumulative and may be exercised concurrently, independently, or successively.

18. *Acceleration upon Borrower Insolvency.* Lender may require immediate repayment of the debt upon the borrower's insolvency, as evidenced by filing for bankruptcy.
19. *Transfer of Borrower's Interests: Assumption.* On sale or transfer of ownership, lender may require immediate repayment or renegotiate and extend the loan, as at a higher interest rate. This is often called the "due on sale" or alienation clause.
20. *Notice.* Certified mail must be used by the lender or borrower to give notice of changes of name or address, default and foreclosure, sale of the property, or damage or destruction to the property.
21. *Successors and Assigns Bound.* People taking over the legal positions of the lender and/or borrower at a later time are equally bound by the contracts provisions, jointly and severally.
22. *Governing Law and Severability.* Conflicts between the uniform instrument and local law are to be resolved according to the law of the jurisdiction in which the property is located. And any such conflict shall not invalidate the remaining provisions of the instrument. This division of the instrument into distinct, independent obligations or agreements, any one of which may be removed without affecting the others, is termed *severability.*
23. *Waiver of Statute of Limitations.* Borrower waives any statute of limitations rights to provisions in the mortgage.
24. *Waiver to Marshalling of Assets.* Right to the marshalling of assets (arranging in a certain order) in connection with default remedies in the contract is waived by the borrower, giving the lender greater freedom in pursuing remedies under the instrument.
25. *Construction Loan Provisions.* A construction loan may be made and tied into the instrument.
26. *Assignment of Rents.* Upon breach of a condition, and with proper notice, rents are to be paid to a receiver, to better protect the lender's interests. A *receiver* is an officer of the court appointed to take possession and control of the property of concern in a suit.

Nonuniform Covenants

State statutes are specific and often vary substantially. Thus, the FNMA/FHLMC instruments provide for state specific covenants to comply with such statutes. For the instrument in Figure 15–5, these nonuniform covenants are as follows.

27. *Acceleration: Remedies.* Lender may declare all sums secured by the mortgage to be due and payable immediately. Lender shall also be allowed to collect all costs of remedies as attorney's fees, abstracts, title reports, and other expenses.
28. *Release.* Lender will terminate this instrument upon payment of all sums due (defeasance clause).
29. *Attorneys Fees.* "Attorneys fees" shall include fees awarded by an appellate court.
30. *Future Advances.* Lender, at borrower's request, may advance additional monies, which also will be secured by this mortgage (open-end provision).

TYPES OF LOANS

Mortgage and trust deed loans are named in many ways. The terms are not completely unique or distinct in that some overlap often occurs from one name to the next. The more commonly used terms are taken up first, and their usage is briefly explained. Terms based on repayment plans are taken up in a subsequent section. The repayment plans are really provided for in the note, the financial portion of the transaction.

Construction Loan

A construction loan is made to finance the erection of a structure or the addition of other improvements. A construction loan to an investor generally runs until the completion of the proposed structure in accordance with plans and specifications included as part of the arrangement. Construction loans to builders usually extend to the sale of the property.

A construction loan is distinct in that the total of the loan is not initially fully paid out to the borrower. Instead, funds are paid out in installments at agreed stages as construction progresses. A lender representative usually inspects and certifies satisfactory progress prior to each payout. Some lenders allow land owners to convert their construction loans directly into permanent loans. Lenders also make conditional commitments to builders that if a financially responsible and capable buyer is found, the loan may be converted directly into long-term or permanent financing, as a conventional, FHA, or VA loan. Lien waivers are commonly used with construction loans to prevent the development and curing of mechanic's liens, which might take priority over the construction loan itself.

Conventional Loan

A conventional loan is one *not* backed by government, as insured by the Federal Housing Administration (FHA) or guaranteed by the Veterans Administration (VA). The term developed historically. When FHA loans were first introduced in the 1930s, borrowers were given the choice of an "FHA-insured" or a "conventional" loan. Conventional loans, being contracts between private parties, are much less subject to government regulation than are FHA or VA loans. Further, conventional loans are traditionally made at lower loan-to-value ratios than are FHA or VA loans because the lenders have less protection in default and foreclosure. Private mortgage insurance was added as an option with conventional loans in recent years to reduce the risk of lender loss on higher loan-to-value loans.

FHA-Insured Loan

The Federal Housing Administration insures lenders against loss in return for fees or premiums paid by borrowers by what are popularly referred to as "FHA loans." The FHA, as an agency of the U.S. government, only insures loans made by approved lenders under regulated conditions and terms and does not, itself, lend money.

FHA-insured loans may be made for up to 97 percent of value of newly built, low-cost homes. With this high loan-to-value ratio, the lender would be exposed to great risk if not protected by FHA insurance. In taking out an FHA loan, the borrower must agree to pay a premium for the insurance.

VA-Guaranteed Loan

A loan to an eligible veteran and certain others that is partially guaranteed against loss by the Veterans Administration of the United States is termed a VA or "GI" mortgage. The borrower pays no charge or premium for the guarantee. The VA sets no maximum amount for the loan, although there is a maximum to the guarantee, which is the lesser of $27,500 or 60 percent of the loan. Also, if no financial institution will make a loan to an eligible veteran, the VA will.

The guaranteed loan must initially be made to a qualified veteran or the dependent of a qualified veteran, usually a surviving spouse, and requires a "certificate of eligibility" from the VA. The lending institution then simply makes the loan from its own monies and gets the guarantee from the government. The loan may later be taken over by a nonveteran.

A number of states also sponsor loans to former service personnel, which are commonly referred to as "state VA" or "GI" loans.

Privately Insured Loan.

A conventional loan, on which the lender is partially protected against loss by a private mortgage insurance company in return for a fee or premium, is termed a privately insured loan. The insurance companies, therefore, compete directly with the Federal Housing and the Veterans administrations.

The industry began with the Mortgage Guarantee Insurance Company of Milwaukee, Wisconsin, in 1957. It experienced spectacular growth in the 1960s because of a much shorter turnaround time on loan insurance applications as compared with the "red tape"–bound competition, the FHA and VA. Also, interest rate ceilings on FHA loans hindered rather than helped borrowers in their efforts to obtain financing. Government acceptance of private mortgage insurance began with its approval for use by the Federal Home Loan Bank Board in 1971.

The effective cost of private mortgage insurance is roughly half that of FHA insurance. A one-quote comparison is not meaningful because of the differences in the way in which premiums are priced or calculated. For example, with a 10 percent down payment, a borrower would pay an insurance premium of one-half of 1 percent of the loan balance in the first year and one-fourth of 1 percent each year thereafter. The FHA, on the other hand, charges a continuing premium of ½ percent of the annual unamortized loan balance. However, private mortgage insurance covers only the top 20 to 25 percent of the initial amount of a loan, which is the portion most exposed to risk and loss. Further, the coverage runs out after several years because the principal balance is reduced to below the portion insured. FHA, on the other hand, insures the unamortized loan balance throughout its entire life.

Almost all states allow lenders to make loans up to 95 percent of value with private mortgage insurance. And like existing FHA and VA loans, loans insured by private companies are now regularly bought and sold among banks, saving and loan associations, insurance companies, and others.

Purchase Money Loan

A *purchase money mortgage* is one given by a buyer to a seller that secures all, or a portion, of the purchase price of a property. Thus, the seller is financing or partially financing the transaction. A purchase money mortgage or trust deed becomes active at the exact time that title is passed. The seller's claim is, therefore, considered to take priority to any lien that might develop against the property due to the purchaser's actions, provided that the deed and mortgage or trust deed are recorded together. The legal presumption is that since the property was pledged at the same time title passed, no other party could have developed a prior claim. The words "purchase money mortgage" are commonly included when the instrument is drawn up, to give notice of its special character.

In some states a deficiency judgment is not permitted on a purchase money mortgage. The law presumes that the seller-lender may recover the original property and thus is no worse off after foreclosure than if no sale had occurred and no mortgage was made.

Second or Junior Loan

A mortgage with priority as a lien over all other mortgages against a property is a first mortgage. A mortgage second in priority to another mortgage is a second mortgage. And a mortgage with two mortgages of higher priority is a third mortgage. Mortgages have been stacked six and seven deep as to priority. The collective name for mortgages lower in priority than the first mortgage is *junior mortgages.* It follows that the lower the priority of a mortgage, the greater the risk of loss to the lender-mortgagee.

The second or junior mortgage was commonly used in real estate financing prior to the depression of the early 1930s. In recent years, with tight money and wide use of creative financing, junior financing again became popular.

A key clause in junior mortgages anticipates possible default in a prior mortgage. A *default-in-the-prior-mortgage clause* provides that if the mortgagor defaults in the payment of interest, principal, or taxes on any prior mortgage, such interest, principal, or taxes may be paid by the junior mortgagee and added to the amount of the junior loan. Furthermore, the junior lender may forthwith declare a default and proceed to foreclose.

Another clause usually included is a *subordination clause,* which is usually included for the protection of the mortgagor. When the junior loan was originated, the subject property, already subject to a mortgage, was put up to secure the sum or sums advanced. Presumably, the second mortgage should continue in the same subordinated position. But without any provision to cover the sitution, the junior mortgage would automatically become a first lien upon full payment of all prior claims. Such a situation makes it difficult for the owner to refinance at a later time. In summary, a subordination clause "sets" the relative priority of a lien or claim. This priority of claim extends to other arrangements such as leases and land contracts.

Miscellaneous Mortgage Types

Loan arrangements may contain unique clauses for special situations or purposes, and consequently get special names such as (1) blanket, (2) package, or (3) open-end mortgages.

Blanket loan. One loan secured by two or more houses or other parcels of property is called a blanket mortgage. The most common use of a blanket loan is in subdividing, where an initial loan on raw acreage is continued after the land is split up into lots. Blanket mortgages usually include a *partial release clause* that provides for removal of parcels from the lender's claim in return for partial repayment of the loan.

Package loan. A loan contract that includes fixtures and other building equipment as collateral is termed a package mortgage. Equipment, widely accepted as security in a residential package mortgage, includes refrigerators, ranges, washing machines and dryers, and dishwashers. Package mortgages are often used in financing hotels, motels, and apartment projects.

Open-end loan. An open-end contract provides for later advances from a lender, up to but not exceeding the original amount of the loan. The interest rate on the loan may be renegotiated if the open-end provision is exercised.

LOAN REPAYMENT PLANS AND THEIR USES

In simpler times real estate was financed with *straight-term loans* that called for periodic payments of interest and a lump-sum repayment of the principal. Real estate loans are now made with a wide variety of repayment plans, each of which is designed to solve a particular problem. Needless to say, choosing between the alternative plans is a major decision for a borrower.

In the 1930s the FHA, and the Federal Home Loan Bank Board, introduced the amortizing loan, in which the periodic debt service pays interest on the loan and systematically repays the principal of the loan over the life of the agreement. Nearly all mortgages with an extended life include an amortization provision. Home loans are usually amortized by monthly payments. Commercial loans, on the other hand, may call for monthly, quarterly, semiannual, or annual debt service.

Beginning in the 1970s, numerous new repayment plans were introduced as a result of rapidly fluctuating interest rates and were facilitated by the increasing use of computers and calculators. A summary knowledge of the more widely used plans, and their advantages and limitations, is a must for any real estate decision maker.

Fixed Rate Mortgage

A fixed rate mortgage (FRM) loan means that the interest rate remains unchanged and debt-service payments remain equal or uniform in size over the life of the loan. Debt-service payments during the early part of the life go mostly to interest with a small portion to principal reduction. As the loan ages, the portion going to principal reduction increases while the portion to interest decreases.

Balloon Loan

A loan contract calling for repayment of a portion of the original principal over its life and the balance in a single lump-sum payment at the end of the agreement is a *partially amortizing mortgage.* The lump-sum payment at the end of the agreement in commonly called a *balloon payment.* An example is a loan setup with a 30-year amortization schedule while calling for a lump-sum principal repayment at the end of the twelfth year.

Wraparound Loan

A *wraparound mortgage* (WAM) is created when a second mortgage loan is made with the new lender taking over the debt service payments on the first loan. The face amount of the wraparound loan equals the total of the first loan plus the amount of money advanced by the second lender; hence, the "wrapping" or including of the amount of the first loan in a second. The amount of money actually advanced by the second lender equals the amount of the new loan less the amount of the existing first loan. The borrower pays debt service on the larger second loan only. This arrangement is termed an "all-inclusive trust deed" if a deed of trust is the security instrument.

ALTERNATIVE MORTGAGE INSTRUMENTS

The Federal Home Loan Bank Board, the Comptroller of the Currency, and the Federal National Mortgage Association caused the origination of more flexible mortgage instruments in the late 1970s to relieve the financial squeeze on lenders. These new instruments are known collectively as *alternative mortgage instruments* (*AMIs*). Several of the more popular of these AMIs that have gained considerable market acceptance are the following:

Adjustable Rate Mortgage

A loan agreement allowing the interest rate to increase or decrease directly with the fluctuations in an index beyond the control of the lender is called a variable rate mortgage (VRM) or an adjustable rate mortgage (ARM). The VRM loan was introduced by the FHA in the mid-1970s, but the specifications were too tight for the wild interest rate gyrations that followed. Consequently, it did not gain wide acceptance. Subsequently, the Federal Home Loan Bank Board and the Federal National Mortgage Association (FNMA) issued more flexible guidelines for ARM loans eligible for trading in the secondary mortgage market. In so doing, they made a due on sale clause mandatory in all ARM loans to enhance their negotiability in the secondary mortgage market.

ARM loans are amortizing, and debt-service payments usually remain level. If the interest rate increases, the life of the loan is simply extended, and vice versa. A maximum interest rate adjustment per year (interest rate cap) and a maximum payment adjustment per year (debt-service cap) may be included. The fluctuating index may be any of eight suggested by FNMA that is acceptable to both the lender and the borrower. Interest rate increases are at the lender's option, but decreases are mandatory.

Allowing the interest rate to fluctuate shifts the risk of increasing interest rates to the borrower; at the same time, any decrease in interest rates benefits the borrower. ARM loans are often made at slightly lower rates than are FRM loans because of this shift in risk. A flexible rate allows lenders to continue making loans in the face of increasing interest rates without fear of being locked into a below-market fixed rate loan. Hence, ARM lending tends to maintain a more even flow of funds into real estate. ARM loans apparently are becoming the dominant arrangement with many lenders.

FLIP Mortgage

A FLIP (*f*lexible *l*oan *i*nsurance *p*rogram) loan is very similar to a PAL (pledged savings account) loan. Both use a pledged savings account. Typically this type of loan is employed upon the purchase of a residence. All, or a portion, of the buyer-borrower's down payment is paid into the pledged savings account. A decreasing portion of the borrower's payments are met by withdrawals from the account. Thus the out of pocket payments required of the borrower gradually increase. The seller gives up all or a portion of the down payment but benefits by actual sale of the property that is otherwise very difficult to finance. The payment of the down payment into the pledged account is directly equivalent to the purchase of a buy-down loan by a seller. From a lender's viewpoint, a FLIP or PAL mortgage is a level payment loan.

Graduated Payment Mortgages

A graduated payment mortgage (GPM) provides for low initial debt-service payments with regular increases for several years until a level is reached where the payments will amortize the loan over its remaining term. Debt-service increases typically range from 2½ to 7½ percent per year. The interest rate may be fixed or variable. Sometimes payments in the early years will not cover all interest due on the loan, and the principal owed actually increases; this is termed "negative amortization." GPM loans are best suited to situations where the borrower expects steady increases in income at about the same rate as the scheduled increases in debt service. Thus, a GPM is sometimes called a young people's loan because it seems to suit best the needs of people who are just forming households and have increasing incomes. If the interest rate is adjustable, this becomes a GPAM (graduated payment adjustable mortgage) loan.

Growing Equity Mortgage

A growing equity mortgage (GEM) requires variable-sized payments that are tied to a borrower's ability to pay. However, the increase is not according to some fixed schedule, as is the GPM arrangement. A GEM loan is most likely to be made to a borrower with rising income expectations and, therefore, may be paid off well ahead of its maturity date. Increases in debt service above the original payment schedule go entirely to repay principal; hence, the borrower's equity builds up more quickly than with a more standard loan. The lender benefits from higher cash flow and greater liquidity. Payments are adjusted annually to reflect 75 percent of the rate of change in a national index of per capita disposable personal income.

Reverse Annuity Mortgage

The reverse annuity mortgage (RAM) loan was introduced by the FHLBB to enable elderly people to convert the equity in their homes into cash to meet living expenses. An elderly couple taking out an RAM loan would expect to live in their residence. Upon signing the loan agreement, the owner-borrower receives the money in one lump-sum payment or in periodic (monthly) payments. The loan is repayable, with interest, upon a specific event as sale of the property or death of the owner, or at a specific date. The cash flows with an RAM loan are, therefore, the opposite of those under a traditional mortgage arrangement; hence, the name. The interest rate on an RAM loan may be fixed or adjustable.

Renegotiable Rate Mortgage

Many lenders refused to renew the straight term loans in the early 1930s because of the uncertain times; this refusal resulted in many foreclosures and only served to worsen the depression. In response, the FHA introduced the long-term, fixed rate, fully amortizing loan. These long term FRMs acted like a straitjacket on lenders when interest rates sharply increased in the mid- and late 1970s. That is, the lenders could not increase the rates on the loans to bring them in line with the suddenly much higher rates required to retain deposits.

Straight term loans were reintroduced in Canada in the 1970s to give the lenders greater flexibility in adjusting their portfolios to changing economic conditions and were soon tabbed "Canadian rollovers." With wider acceptance by governmental agencies, rollover loans gradually became known as renegotiable rate mortgages (RRMs), perhaps to gain initials comparable to those of other repayment plans. Under the FHLBB plan, an RRM is a series of short-term (3, 4, or 5 years) loans secured by a long-term mortgage; that is, the lender is required to renew the loan, but at an interest rate adjusted to the market rate.

With an RRM, debt-service payments are smaller relative to amortizing plans, which enables borrowers to get higher cash flows in the early years of an investment and also to maintain a higher leverage ratio.

Shared Appreciation Mortgage

A loan in which any value increase in the subject property is split proportionately between the borrower and lender is termed a shared appreciation mortgage (SAM). In return for the right to share in appreciation, an SAM loan carries a below-market interest rate, which results in lower monthly debt service for the borrower. Further, debt service with an SAM loan is usually calculated on a long term, 25 to 40 years, even though the specified loan term is likely to be for a much shorter period, say, 10 years. The lender's share of the value increase is expected to bring the actual rate of return on the loan to an effective yield greater than the market rate of interest.

The borrower makes a lump-sum settlement if the property is sold or the loan is prepaid before the specified maturity date. If the loan runs its full term, the lender typically guarantees to refinance the entire property for the borrower, including the lender's share of the value appreciation.

An SAM loan involves risk for both the lender and borrower. For the lender, the higher rate of return may not be realized. For the borrower, a large value increase may require a much larger loan at a much higher and uncertain future market interest rate. Thus, the borrower may be unable to continue to afford the property.

Blended Mortgage

In refinancing a property or in a loan assumption in a sale, lenders and borrowers sometimes compromise on the interest rate. Thus, the new rate is somewhere between the low rate on the original, older loan and the current market rate. In effect, there is a blending of the two rates; hence, the new loan is often termed a *blended mortgage.* It should be recognized that such a compromise is not really an alternative mortgage instrument. The compromise is an extremely practical way of solving a knotty problem for all parties involved, however.

THE PROMISSORY NOTE

The debt, as evidenced by a promissory note or a personal bond, is a personal obligation of the borrower that gives life to a mortgage or trust deed. If the debt is unenforceable for any reason, the mortgage or trust deed is also unenforceable. A representative note, the content of which is discussed briefly, is shown in Figure 15–6.

FIGURE 15–6
Promissory note

NOTE

(Multifamily)

US $ 500,000 Urbandale, Texas
City
January 15, 19 81

1. For Value Received, the undersigned promise to pay Urbandale Savings and Loan Association, or order, the principal sum of Five Hundred Thousand and no/100 ($500,000.00) Dollars, with interest on the unpaid principal balance from the date of this Note, until paid, at the rate of 10 percent per annum. The principal and interest shall be payable at Urbandale Savings and Loan Association, 300 North Main, Urbandale in consecutive monthly installments of Four Thousand Five Hundred Forty Three and fifty/100 Dollars (US $ 4,543.50) on the 1st day of each month beginning March 1st, 1981, (herein "amortization commencement date"), until the entire indebtedness evidenced hereby is fully paid, except that any remaining indebtedness, if not sooner paid, shall be due and payable on the 1st day of February, 2006.

2. If the amortization commencement date is more than 30 calendar days from the date of this Note, the undersigned shall pay the holder hereof interest only on the outstanding principal balance of this Note at the rate of 10 percent per annum in one installments beginning 15 January, 19 81, and on no other thereafter until the amortization commencement date, at which time any remaining interest payable pursuant to this paragraph (and not paid as a part of the first monthly installment of principal and interest) shall be paid.

3. If any installment under this Note is not paid when due, the unpaid principal balance of this Note shall bear interest during the period of delinquency at a rate of 10 percent per annum, or, if such increased rate of interest may not be collected from the undersigned under applicable law, then at the maximum increased rate of interest, if any, which may be collected from the undersigned under applicable law; and, at the option of the holder hereof, the entire principal amount outstanding hereunder and accrued interest thereon shall at once become due and payable. Failure to exercise such option shall not constitute a waiver of the right to exercise such option if the undersigned is in default hereunder. In the event of any default in the payment of this Note, and if the same is referred to an attorney at law for collection or suit is brought hereon, the undersigned shall pay the holder hereof, in either case, all expenses and costs of collection, including, but not limited to, attorney's fees.

4. The undersigned shall pay to the holder hereof on demand a late charge of 2 percent of any installment not received by the holder hereof within 15 calendar days after the day the installment is due.

5. The undersigned shall have the right to prepay the principal amount outstanding hereunder in whole or in part at any time after the amortization commencement date, provided that the holder hereof may require that any partial prepayments shall be made on the date monthly installments are due and shall be in the amount of that part of one or more monthly installments which would be applicable to principal and further provided that the undersigned has given the holder hereof written notice of the amount intended to be prepaid at least five (5) days prior to such prepayment. The undersigned shall pay the holder hereof together with any prepayments (including prepayments occurring as a result of the acceleration by the holder hereof of the principal amount of this Note, but excluding prepayments occurring because of the application by the holder hereof of insurance or condemnation awards or proceeds pursuant to a Deed of Trust securing this Note) a percentage of the amount prepaid in excess of any amount upon which a charge is not permitted by applicable law as follows: 4 percent of the sums prepaid in the first year from the amortization commencement date, the percentage payable declining by the number one (1) each year thereafter until the percentage payable is 0 percent, which percentage shall be payable for the remaining term of the Note. Prepayments shall be applied against the outstanding principal balance of this Note and shall not extend or postpone the due date of any subsequent monthly installments or change the amount of such installments, unless the holder hereof shall otherwise agree in writing.

6. From time to time, without affecting the obligation of the undersigned or the successors or assigns of the undersigned to pay the outstanding principal balance of this Note and observe the covenants of the undersigned contained herein, without affecting the guaranty of any person, corporation, partnership or other entity for payment of the outstanding principal balance of this Note, without giving notice to or obtaining the consent of the undersigned, the successors or assigns of the undersigned or guarantors, and without liability on the part of the holder hereof, the holder hereof may, at the option of the holder hereof, extend the time for payment of said outstanding principal balance or any part thereof, reduce the payments thereon, release anyone liable on any of said outstanding principal balance, accept a renewal of this Note, modify the terms and time of payment of said outstanding principal balance or join in any extension or subordination agreement, and agree in writing with the undersigned to modify the rate of interest or period of amortization of this Note or change the amount of the monthly installments payable hereunder.

7. Presentment, notice of dishonor, and protest are hereby waived by all makers, sureties, guarantors and endorsers hereof. This Note shall be the joint and several obligation of all makers, sureties, guarantors and endorsers, and shall be binding upon them and their heirs, personal representatives, successors and assigns.

8. The indebtedness evidenced by this Note is secured by a Deed of Trust, dated of even date herewith, and reference is made thereto for rights as to acceleration of the indebtedness evidenced by this Note.

Douglas Manor
2001 Century Drive
Urbandale, Texas 00000
(property address)

/s/Gerald I. Investor

/s/Nancy O. Investor

TEXAS—FHLMC—2/72—Over Four Families

It is in the note that the financial terms of the loan are stated. The note shown here is for an FRM loan only. But if the arrangement is for an ARM, an RRM, or a GPM loan, the terms would show up here. Thus, the financial terms of a loan are much more negotiable than are the legal terms.

In the note shown, the amount and date appear in the heading, followed by numbered, specific clauses.

1. *Mortgagee and terms.* Mortgagee is identified, along with the interest rate, maturity date, monthly debt service, and place of payment. Payments are to be made on the first day of each month at the Urbandale Savings and Loan.
2. *Adjustment of payment date.* Interest only is to be paid for first partial month so payments may be scheduled on first of month.
3. *Default and acceleration.* Noteholder has right to accelerate or call for immediate payment of the entire outstanding principal plus accrued interest, if contract breached as by late payments. Acceleration is first step in foreclosure.
4. *Late charge.* If payment is over 15 days late, penalty is specified.
5. *Prepayment provisions.* Borrower may prepay, but only under stated conditions. Prepayment penalty as negotiated when the loan was taken out is included as part of the agreement.
6. *Negotiability.* The security and negotiability of the note is protected by stating that any modification to the terms shall not affect the obligation of the borrowers to abide by the terms and to repay the principal of the note.
7. *Joint and several.* Makers, endorsers, and others waive the right to protest or to deny the note as their obligation, individually or jointly.
8. *Reference to security instrument.* The security instrument of even date is identified and attached relative to acceleration rights in the note.

To be executed properly, the note must be voluntarily signed by all parties with an interest in the property. Finally, the note must be voluntarily delivered and accepted to complete the transaction.

FEDERAL LAWS AFFECTING LENDING

Federal laws increasingly extend into our lives so that what formerly was strictly private is now strictly regulated. Real estate financing is not exempt from this intrusion. Consumer protection is the most often cited motivation. The following brief summary is offered only to alert the reader to the many applicable regulations and their general content.

Equal Credit Opportunity Act

The Equal Credit Opportunity Act (ECOA), enacted in 1974, forbids discrimination by mortgage lenders because of race, color, religion, national origin, age, sex, or marital status or because all or part of an applicant's income is from a public assistance program. ECOA is implemented by the Federal Reserve System as Regulation B. Persons desiring credit must be informed of their rights under the act prior to completing an application. The reason for denial of credit must be given, upon request.

Real Estate Settlement Procedures Act

The Real Estate Settlement Procedures Act (RESPA) serves to (1) inform borrowers of costs of closing in purchasing a one- to four-unit residential property and (2) preserve to the borrower the right to select the parties providing services to the transaction, as attorneys, appraisers, and title companies. The act extends to lenders investing more than $1 million per year in one- to four-family residential loans and to all federally related first mortgage loans. Under RESPA, the lender must give a loan applicant (1) a copy of HUD's *Settlement Costs and You,* (2) a "good faith" estimate of settlement costs prior to the loan closing, and (3) a final statement of costs using a HUD uniform settlement form. RESPA is implemented by the Federal Reserve System as Regulation X. Note that RESPA does not regulate or limit fees and does not require disclosure of all the terms of any loan involved in the settlement.

Truth in Lending Act

The Truth in Lending (TIL) Act requires full disclosure of loan costs. TIL is, in truth, Title I of the Consumer Credit Protection Act and is implemented by the Federal Reserve System as Regulation Z. Under the act, a lender is required to provide advance disclosure of finance charges and loan terms, such as interest rate, origination fees, due date of payments, prepayment fees, and late payment fees so borrowers may shop for least cost or most advantageous credit terms. Note that the act does not regulate the cost of credit or set maximum allowable interest rates.

Coverage. To begin with, the TIL Act only applies to lenders who "regularly extend or arrange credit." Further, in real estate, Regulation Z applies to loans for personal, household, or family residences if four or more payments are involved. A lease in which the lessee's obligation is less than $25,000 is also covered if the duration is greater than four months. A private party taking back a purchase money mortgage on the sale of a residence is exempt. Also, credit transactions on investment property are exempt.

Finance charges and the APR. Finance charges are all the costs associated with a loan that are directly or indirectly payable by a borrower and required by a lender as a precondition to making a loan. Examples are interest, origination fees, finder's fees, and service or carrying charges. Real estate purchase costs that would be incurred whether the loan were taken out or not are not included in the finance charge. Examples are costs of title insurance, recording fees, appraisal fees, and legal fees. These costs must be itemized and disclosed, however.

Disclosure of finance charges must be made in terms of an annual percentage rate, APR. Regulation Z specifies how the APR is to be calculated. The disclosure must be to within one-fourth of 1 percent, based on monies actually disbursed. The APR states in one number the cost of the loan, which facilitates comparison shopping.

Rescission. Although Regulation Z provides for a borrower's right to rescind certain loans during a three-day waiting period, a borrower may not rescind or cancel a loan to purchase a personal residence and secured by a lien on the residence.

Usury Exemption Laws.

Usury is an unreasonably or unlawfully high interest rate. Prior to 1980, many states had usury laws setting a ceiling interest rate within their boundaries. FHA and VA loans were exempt from state usury laws by Congress in 1979. In 1980, Congress exempted conventional residential mortgage loans as well. However, each state could reenact a ceiling interest rate if it acted before April 1, 1983. The lifting of usury rates was intended to facilitate flows of funds.

SUMMARY

A mortgage is a pledge of real property as security for a debt or other obligation. The debt, evidenced by a promissory note, gives life to the mortgage. The mortgaging process involves the initiation, servicing, and termination stages. Terms are negotiated and agreed to in the initiation phase. A mortgage may be terminated by mutual agreement (paying off) or by default and foreclosure.

A promissory note summarizes the terms of the loan and is a contract. Typical provisions of a mortgage include agreements to (1) make debt-service payments, (2) make deposits for taxes and insurance, (3) maintain the property in good repair, and (4) obtain lender authorization before alteration or demolition of property improvements. In addition, control and assignment of rents are extremely important considerations in the financing of income properties.

Mortgages are commonly classified as conventional, FHA, VA, purchase money, or construction. Five payment plan classes of mortgages are (1) fixed rate, (2) rollover, (3) variable rate, (4) graduated payment, and (5) partially amortizing. A number of other mortgage instruments of importance are mortgage satisfaction, assignment, release, and subordination.

QUESTIONS FOR REVIEW AND DISCUSSION

1. Explain the mortgage financing process, including the main legal documents involved, the main parties involved, and the legal process of foreclosure upon default.

2. How does the debt financing process differ when a trust deed is used to secure the debt?

3. What purpose is served by the promissory note in debt financing?

4. State at least four major provisions of the security instrument that are common to both mortgages and trust deeds.

5. List and explain "mortgages" by classification as follows.
   a. Five by general type
   b. Four by payment plan
   c. Three by special provision

6. What are the purposes or functions of the following?
   a. Satisfaction of mortgage
   b. Assignment of mortgage
   c. Subordination of mortgage
   d. Power of sale
   e. Deed in lieu of foreclosure
   f. Deed of reconveyance

7. Compare "assuming a mortgage" with "taking subject to a mortgage."

8. Distinguish between an "equitable right of redemption" and a "statutory right of redemption."

9. Distinguish between a "deficiency judgment" and a "defeasance clause."

10. Does a prepayment privilege work to the advantage of the borrower or the lender?

11. First, second, and third mortgages are placed against a newly constructed apartment property. Which of these are senior mortgages? Which are junior claims? Explain.

12. Does the lender or the borrower have the greater power in debt financing negotiations. Discuss.

13. Explain the significance of the uniform documents promoted by FNMA/FHLMC relative to the secondary mortgage market.

CASE PROBLEMS

1. Evans mortgages his house to Thompson. Thompson does not record the instrument. To what extent is the mortgage valid relative to third parties?

2. Evans sells to Parker, who agrees to assume the mortgage. Parker defaults. Thompson forecloses, suing both Parker and Evans for damages suffered. Evans claims no liability. What is the result?
3. Butch Cassidy obtains a loan from the Apex National Bank that is secured by a FNMA/FHLMC mortgage. Later, Butch loses his job and cannot make payments. Finally, after more than a year, Apex files a foreclosure suit. Butch claims that Apex is estopped from foreclosing because it failed to act within a year. Is this true? Explain.

CHAPTER SIXTEEN
LOAN CALCULATIONS

Seven percent has no rest, nor no religion;
it works nights, and Sundays, and even wet days.
JOSH BILLINGS, American humorist and lecturer.

IMPORTANT TOPICS OR DECISION AREAS COVERED IN THIS CHAPTER

- Future Value or Compounding
- Present Value or Discounting
- TVM Factors
- Interest Calculations
- Mortgage Points—Discounts and Premiums
- Using Financial Calculators

One of the key concerns of an investor is interest, or the price paid for borrowed money. Thus, this chapter deals with time value of money (TVM) as applied in real estate financing. TVM as used in evaluating an equity investment position is taken up in Chapter 21.

Money has time value for at least three reasons. First, individuals prefer current consumption over future consumption and, therefore, must be compensated if they are to forgo current consumption. Second, individuals have alternative investment opportunities and, being rational, allocate money to the opportunities on the basis of comparative rates of return, the highest rates of return (risk adjusted) usually being preferred. Third, inflation causes people to demand a return on money held as cash to maintain purchasing power. In addition, the reality of interest rates in our economy provide a very pragmatic reason for their recognition; we cannot borrow money without paying interest.

This material is introductory in nature and covers only the basic ideas and applications of time value of money. A few essential formulas are taken up. Any reader interested in greater depth is referred to books on financial management and capital budgeting or the mathematics of finance. The problems discussed are difficult to work out by hand; therefore, the reader is encouraged to use a calculator to follow and verify the examples. TVM tables are provided in Appendix B. A much better alternative is a calculator with built-in TVM capability. Hewlett-Packard and Texas Instruments calculators are the largest sellers of these products.

KEY CONCEPTS INTRODUCED IN THIS CHAPTER

Compound interest
Contract interest rate
Discounting
Discount rate
Discounted cash flow
Dollar discount
Financial management of real estate
Interest in arrears
Internal rate of return
Loan discount
Loan premium
Market interest rate
Net present value
Percent discount
Present value analysis
PV1 factor (present value of 1)
PV1/P factor (present value of 1 per period)
Principal recovery factor
Time value of money

FUTURE VALUE OR COMPOUNDING

Understanding compound interest is essential to understanding the mathematics of finance. Compound means to mix or combine. It also means to increase or intensify by adding new elements, as to compound a problem. Both definitions apply when it comes to compound interest.

Compound interest means to compute additional interest on both principal and accumulated, unpaid interest. That is, interest on a loan or investment is added to or mixed with the principal, and consequently, interest is earned or paid on interest as well as on the original principal.

Let us look at a few problems or examples to illustrate the concept. First, consider an individual paying or depositing \$100 into a savings account to earn 5 percent interest, compounded annually. What amount or future value will the account contain at the end of one year? A simple equation showing the relationship solves the problem. Incidentally, EOY means end of year.

$$\begin{aligned} \text{Future value (EOY 1)} &= \text{Amount of deposit (1 plus the interest rate)} \\ \text{FV (EOY 1)} &= \text{Deposit } (1 + i) \\ \text{FV (EOY 1)} &= \$100\ (1 + 0.05) = \$105 \end{aligned}$$

At the end of two years, the future value equals \$110.25:

$$\begin{aligned} \text{Future value (EOY 2)} &= \text{Amount of deposit } (1 + i)(1 + i) \\ \text{FV (EOY 2)} &= \text{Deposit } (1 + i)^2 \\ \text{FV (EOY 2)} &= \$100\ (1 + 0.05)^2 = \$110.25 \end{aligned}$$

Thus, in the second year, interest at 5 percent is earned on the interest accumulated in the first year. That is, \$5 is earned on the initial \$100 deposit, and 25 cents is earned on the \$5 interest earned in the first year.

At the end of three years, the value of the account is \$115.76, calculated as follows:

$$\begin{aligned} \text{FV (EOY 3)} &= \text{Deposit } (1 + i)(1 + i)(1 + i) \\ \text{FV (EOY 3)} &= \text{Deposit } (1 + i)^3 \\ \text{FV (EOY 3)} &= \$100\ (1 + 0.05)^3 = \$115.76 \end{aligned}$$

Generalizing, the future value of a deposit at the end of n years may be calculated by the formula

$$\text{FV (EOY } n) = \text{Deposit } (1 + i)^n$$

where n is the number of years and i equals the interest rate.

The accumulation of interest for 10 years at 10 percent is shown in Figure 16–1. Interest being earned on interest shows up clearly in the interest-earned column. BOY means beginning of year.

FIGURE 16–1
Ten years of compound interest calculations at 10 percent on an initial investment or deposit of $1,000

YEAR	BOY VALUE	INTEREST EARNED DURING YEAR AT 10 PERCENT	FUTURE OR EOY VALUE
1	$1,000	$100	$1,100
2	1,100	110	1,210
3	1,210	121	1,331
4	1,331	133.10	1,464.10
5	1,464.10	146.41	1,610.51
6	1,610.51	161.05	1,771.56
7	1,771.56	177.16	1,948.72
8	1,948.72	194.87	2,143.59
9	2,143.59	214.36	2,357.95
10	2,357.95	235.79	2,593.74

The higher the interest rate, the faster the rate of increase in the deposit or investment. Also, the greater the number of periods, the greater the future value. Figure 16–2 shows the relative rates of compounding at interest rates of 5, 10, and 20 percent.

PRESENT VALUE OR DISCOUNTING

TVM calculations are necessary because a dollar in the hand is worth more than a dollar received next year or at the end of the decade. Calculating the present values of future cash flows enables us to analyze and compare *value differences* due to varying times of receipt or payment of these cash flows.

To illustrate present value calculations, assume that an investor wishes to sell the right to receive $1,000 at the end of each of the next two years. Other investors earn 10 percent per year on comparable investments. So, what is the value of our investor's position? What might other investors pay for the right to receive $1,000 at the end of each of the next two years? By comparing this with our earlier compounding example, we can ask, "What amounts invested today at 10 percent would grow to $1,000 at the end of each of the next two years?"

In calculating the future value of an immediate deposit (present value), we *multiplied* the initial deposit by $(1 + i)$, where i equaled the interest rate. Here, we have the future values and the interest rate. We can solve for the initial or present value by reversing the compounding process. Consequently, *dividing* the future value by $1 + i$, a process called *discounting*, gives us our desired result. For our example, the payment to be received at the end of year 1 has a present value of $909.09:

FIGURE 16–2
Future or compound value schedules of $1,000 at interest rates of 5, 10, and 20 percent

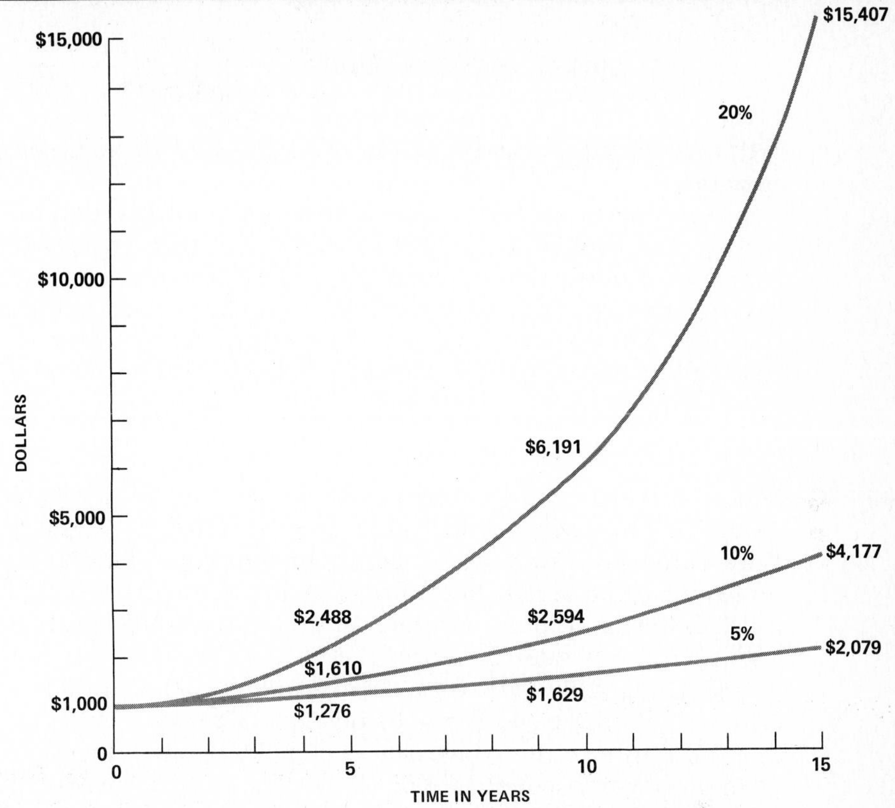

$$\text{Present value (BOY 1)} = \frac{\text{Future payment (EOY 1)}}{(1 + i)^1}$$

$$\text{PV (BOY 1)} = \frac{\$1,000}{1.10} = \$909.09$$

In like fashion, the present value of $1,000 to be received at the end of year 2 is $826.45.

$$\text{PV (BOY 1)} = \frac{\text{Future payment (EOY 2)}}{(1 + i)^2}$$

$$\text{PV (BOY 1)} = \frac{\$1,000}{(1.10)^2} = \frac{\$1,000}{(1.21)} = \$826.45$$

Thus the investor's position is worth $1,735.54 ($909.09 + 826.45).

The general formula for finding the present value of a future payment to be received at the end of year n, discounted at rate i, is

$$\text{Present value (BOY 1)} = \frac{\text{Future payment (EOY } n)}{(1 + i)^n}$$

The interest rate is usually called the *discount rate* in present value calculations.

Application of the equation results in the present value's getting smaller and smaller as the time of receipt extends farther into the future. Figure 16–3 illustrates the decreasing value of a future payment of $1,000 at discount rates of 5, 10, and 20 percent. According to Figure 16–3, for example, $1,000 discounted at 10 percent for 7 years is worth only $513.16, or about half the amount of the $1,000 payment.

TVM FACTORS

With tables of precalculated factors or multipliers, the appropriate $(1 + i)^n$ need not be recalculated for each problem. Even so, calculators are much faster, and more accurate, and able to handle problems involving atypical interest rates or terms.

In using tables, $(1 + i)$ is termed the *base*. Thus for a 5 percent table, (1 + 0.05) is the base. For a 10 percent table, (1 + 0.10) is the base.

To illustrate the construction of a TVM table, let us develop a few factors using a discount rate of 10 percent. Let us calculate present value

FIGURE 16–3
Present value schedules of $1,000 discounted at interest rates of 5, 10, and 20 percent

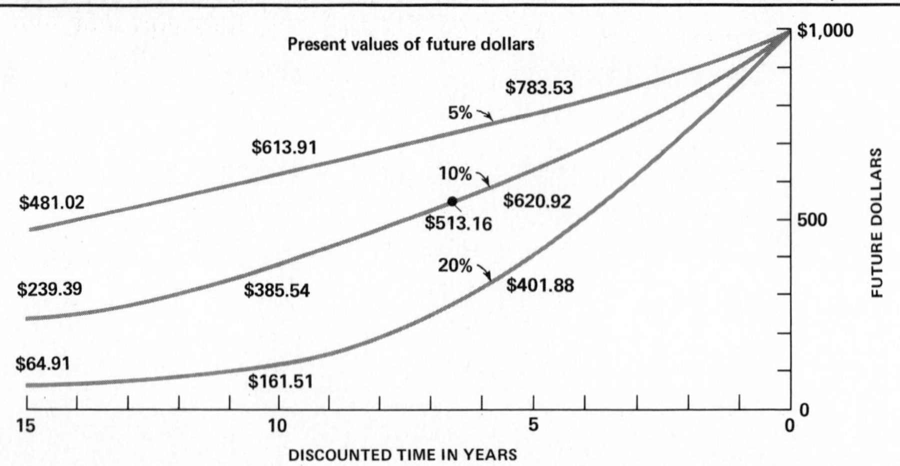

factors for payments to be received at the end of years 1, 2, and 3. The general equation is

$$PV = \frac{1}{(1 + i)^n}$$

The 1-year factor ($n = 1$),

$$PV = \frac{1}{(1.10)^1} = 0.090901$$

The two-year factor ($n = 2$),

$$PV = \frac{1}{(1 + 0.10)^2} = \frac{1}{1.21} = 0.826446$$

The 3-year factor ($n = 3$),

$$PV = \frac{1}{(1 + 0.10)^3} = \frac{1}{1.331} = 0.751315$$

In TVM terminology, the factors we have just calculated are present value of 1 (PV1) factors. The PV1 factor provides the means to calculate two other commonly used factors: the present value of 1-per-period factor (PV1/P) and the principal recovery factor (PR). Let us take up each of these.

PV1 Factor

The PV1 factors we have just calculated are shown in the PV1 column of the 10 percent annual TVM table in the appendix. The *PV1 factor* converts a *single payment* to be received in the future into a present, lump-sum value. (See Figure 16–4).

FIGURE 16–4

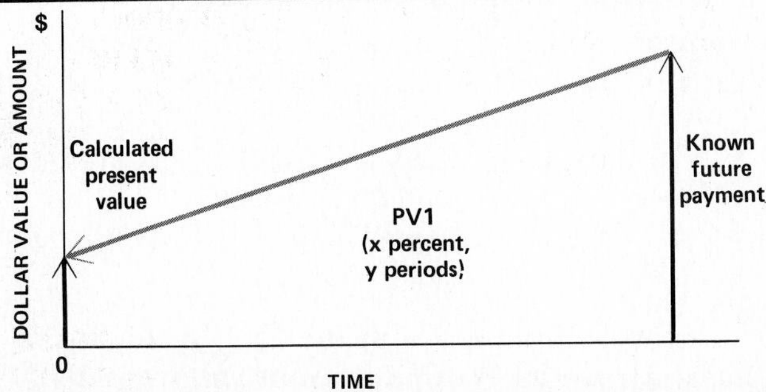

Several PV1 factors may be used in a single problem. Suppose that we expect to receive $20 at the end of each of the next 3 years. What is the present value of this series of payments using a discount rate of 10 percent? The answer is $49.74, rounded.

TIME	*PAYMENT EXPECTED*		*PV1 FACTOR*		*PRESENT VALUE*
EOY 1	$20	×	0.909091	=	$18.18182
EOY 2	20	×	0.826446	=	16.52892
EOY 3	20	×	0.751315	=	15.02630
			Total present value		$49.73704

PV1/P Factor

Given a PV1 table, we may calculate the present value of any series of future cash flows in a similar manner. However, when the future cash flows are all equal, the procedure may be simplified, as with the preceding series of $20 payments. For one thing, we can add up the factors and have them precalculated for any series.

TIME	*PV1 FACTOR*
EOY 1	0.090901
EOY 2	0.826446
EOY 3	0.751315
Total of factors	2.486852

The total of the PV1 factors equals 2.486852. Multiplying the equal payment, $20, times this 2.486852 also gives us $49.74. Thus, totaling PV1 factors gives us a new, shortcut factor, termed the present value of one-per-period factor (PV1/P). The PV1/P factor, used as a multiplier, converts a series of equal or level payments into a single, lump-sum present value. See Figure 16–5. A calculator with TVM capability can produce this same answer with only five or six keys being pushed.

A further example seems in order. Suppose that we wish to know the present value of a series of $20 payments to be received at the end of each of the next 4 years. The discount rate is 12 percent.

Payment	× PV1/P factor (12%, 4 years)	= Present value
$20	× 3.037349	= $60.74699

The factor is obtained from the PV1/P column of the 12 percent, annual table in Appendix B. The present value equals $60.75, rounded.

FIGURE 16–5

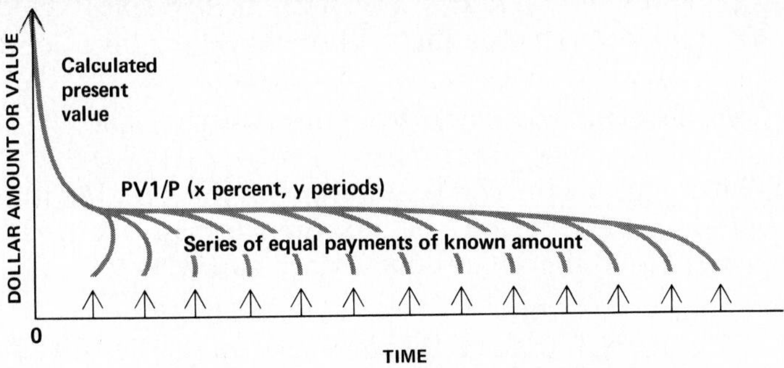

PR Factor

In making a mortgage loan, the lender exchanges cash for a series of debt-service payments from the borrower. Of course, interest is charged on the loan. Is there a definite relationship between the amount of the loan and the amount of the payments? Is there an easy way to calculate the necessary payments? The answer to both questions is "yes."

A principal recovery factor (PRF) is a reciprocal of and acts in exactly the inverse way from the PV1/P factor. The PV1/P converts a series of equal cash flows into a present lump-sum value. The PRF converts a present lump-sum amount (the loan) into a series of future cash flows (debt-service payments). In fact, the PRF is 1 divided by the PV1/P factor. See Figure 16–6.

As an example, suppose that a lender makes a $4,000 fixed rate mortgage loan at 10 percent to be repaid by equal end-of-year payments over 4 years. How much is each payment?

Present value or loan principal	×	PRF (10%, 4 years)	=	Required payment
$4,000	×	0.315471	=	$1,261.88

FIGURE 16–6

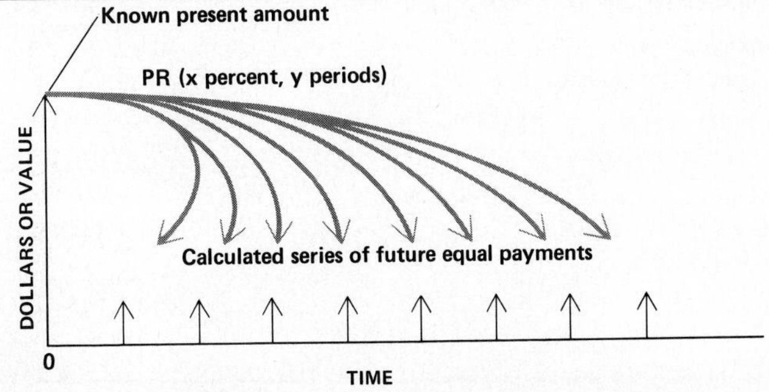

The PR factor allows us to calculate quickly the size of each payment. Let us follow up with a brief look at the amortization of the loan so we can feel assured that the arithmetic works out. See Figure 16–7.

Compounding/Discounting More than Once a Year

The equations for compounding and discounting must be modified when compounding periods of less than a year are used. The necessary adjustments in the United States are as follows:

1. The interest rate must be divided by the number of periods per year to get the effective rate for the shorter period.
2. The number of years must be multiplied by the number of periods per year to get the total number of compounding periods.

Thus, with monthly compounding, a 12 percent annual or nominal interest rate becomes a 1 percent per month effective interest rate.

$$\frac{12\%}{12 \text{ months}} = \frac{1\%}{\text{month}}$$

And a 25-year loan becomes a 300-month loan (25 × 12). Finally, annual payments become monthly payments, of approximately 1/12 the size. Thus the debt service on the $4,000, 10 percent, 4-year loan just discussed

FIGURE 16–7
Annual amortization of a $4,000, 4-year,10 percent loan on a level or fixed payment plan

Principal balance, BOY1		$4,000.00
Year 1 debt service	$1,261.88	
Interest (10% × $4,000)	400.00	
Principal reduction	861.88	−861.88
Principal balance, EOY1, BOY2		3,138.12
Year 2 debt service	1,261.88	
Interest (10% × $3,138.12)	313.81	
Principal reduction	948.07	−948.07
Principal balance, EOY2, BOY3		2,190.05
Year 3 debt service	1,261.88	
Interest (10% × $2,190.05)	219.00	
Principal reduction	1,042.88	−1,042.88
Principal balance, EOY3, BOY4		1,147.17
Year 4 debt service	1,261.89	
Interest (10% × $1,147.17)	114.72	
	1,147.17	−1,147.17
Principal balance, EOY4		$ 000.00

becomes $101.45 per month. In turn, annual payments total to $1,217.40 (12 × $101.45) versus $1,261.88.

Most mortgages call for monthly payments. Therefore, let us consider one more illustration. Suppose that a $500,000 loan for 25 years is obtained at 12 percent interest and that monthly payments are called for. How much is monthly debt service?

We must first refer to the 12 percent, monthly, TVM table in Appendix B. The monthly principal recovery factor (MPRF) for 25 years or 300 months is 0.010532. Monthly debt service equals $5,266.12 ($500,000 × 0.010532).

Elements of TVM Calculations

TVM factors merely express fixed mathematical relationships. It is up to a user to apply the factors properly. In any application, four elements are involved: (1) payment, (2) interest rate, (3) time, and (4) the lump-sum value. The equation simply expresses the mechanical relationship.

$$\text{Payment} \times \underset{(x\%,\ y\ \text{time})}{\text{Factor}} = \text{Value}$$

If any three of the elements are known, the fourth may be determined, although the process of deriviation may be involved. It is this ability to determine unknown information, along with making "what-if" calculations to aid judgment, that makes TVM analysis so useful in the financial managment of real estate.

INTEREST CALCULATIONS

Interest paid is a deductible expense for income tax purposes. Also, interest must be deducted from any loan payment to determine the amount of principal reduction included in the payment. Interest is usually payable at the end of each month or payment period, as a part of the loan debt service. In actuality, mortgage loan payments are customarily made at the beginning of each month. The payment, therefore, includes accumulated interest for the previous month plus the principal reduction amount for the current period. Interest payable at the end of each month is termed *interest in arrears.* Interest is sometimes payable at the beginning of a payment period, which is termed *interest due* or *interest due in advance.*

Several ways of making calculations for interest in arrears are used. For individual periods, when the loan balance is known, interest may be calculated by taking the rate per period times the remaining principal. For example, let us take our 12 percent, monthly payment, 25-year loan of $500,000. Monthly debt service is $5,266.12 as calculated earlier.

METHOD A		METHOD B	
	Period 1		
Loan balance, BOM 1	$500,000	Interest rate	12%
Times annual interest rate	× 12%	Divided by number of months	÷ 12
Equals interest/year	$60,000	Equals monthly interest rate	1%
Divided by number of months in a year	12	Times loan balance	$500,000
Equals interest for month 1	$5,000	Equals interest for month 1	$5,000

Monthly debt service of $5,266.12 less interest of $5,000 means a $266.12 principal reduction at the end of period 1. Thus, at the beginning of period 2, the principal balance is $499,733.88 ($500,000 less $266.12).

METHOD A		METHOD B	
	PERIOD 2		
Loan balance, EOM 1, BOM 2	$499,733.88	Loan balance	$499,733.88
Times annual interest rate	× 12%	Times monthly interest rate	× 1%
Equals interest on annual basis	$59,968.07	Equals interest for month 2	$4,997.34
Divided by number of months in a year	÷ 12		
Equals interest for month 2	$4,997.34		

Monthly calculation of interest has two major difficulties. It is tedious. And the exact beginning-of-month balance must be known. Also, monthly calculation is usually not necessary because interest expenses are generally needed on an annual basis for income tax purposes. Therefore, developing a loan progress schedule to summarize the end-of-year principal balances and the interest paid during each year is all that is generally necessary. The methodology is shown here using our $500,000, 12 percent, 25-year, monthly payment loan.

We know that debt service is $5,266.12 per month, or $63.193.45 per year (12 × $5,266.12). And, at the end of year 1, 24 years of debt service remain to be paid. The unamortized loan balance always equals the present value of these payments, discounted at the contract rate. In this case, 12 percent is the contract rate, and the EOY 1 balance is $496,625.

Monthly debt service	×	monthly PV1/P (MPV1/P) (12%, 24 years)	=	Principal balance (EOY 1, BOY 2)
$5,266.12	×	94.305647	=	$496,624.86

At the end of year 2, with 23 years of debt service remaining, the loan balance calculates to $490,033.

Monthly debt service	×	MPV1/P (12%, 23 years)	=	Principal balance (EOY 2, BOY 3)
$5,266.12	×	93.583461	=	$492,821.80

Taking the differences between the BOY and EOY loan balances for years 1 and 2 gives the amount of principal reduction or loan amortization in each year. Thus, for year 1,

$500,000 − $496,624.86 = $3,375.14 = Principal reduction, year 1

And deducting principal reduction from total debt service gives us the amount of interest paid during the year:

$63,193.45 − 3,375.14 = $59,818.31 = Interest paid

The process for the first two years is summarized in Figure 16–8.

Figure 16–9 summarizes the amortization process for the first 16 years of the loan. We refer to these balances later in case problems.

MORTGAGE POINTS—DISCOUNTS AND PREMIUMS

At times we are told to "discount" a statement or rumor made by a commonly known gossip or liar, that is, to take the statement at less than face value. Merchants run sales at discounted prices, meaning reductions from regular or list prices. Discounting, therefore, means to buy or sell, or offer to buy or sell, at a price less than face value. A premium is the opposite of a discount; a premium means to buy or sell, or to offer to buy or sell, at a price above face value.

A *loan discount* is an amount off or a reduction from the unamortized balance or face amount, as of a mortgage loan. A *loan premium* is an amount in addition to the unamortized balance. A discount or premium is calculated on the basis of the loan balance at the time the loan is originated, a sale is made, or an offer to buy or sell is made.

At one time, loans were discounted when originated to cover costs of obtaining credit reports, setting up amortization schedules, and pre-

FIGURE 16–8
Principal reduction and interest paid for first two years of a $500,000, 25-Year, 12 percent monthly pay loan

YEAR	*BEG-OF-YEAR BALANCE*	*END-OF-YEAR BALANCE*	*TOTAL YEARLY PAYMENT*	*PRINCIPAL REDUCTION*	*INTEREST PAID*
1	$500,000.00	$496,624.92	$63,193.45	$3,375.08	$59,818.37
2	$496,624.92	$492,821.80	$63,193.45	$3,803.12	$59,390.33

FIGURE 16–9
End-of-year amortization summary for a $500,000, 12 percent, 25-year, monthly pay loan (annual debt service equals $63,193.45) (rounded to nearest dollar amount)

YEAR	BEG-OF-YEAR BALANCE	END-OF-YEAR BALANCE	TOTAL YEARLY PAYMENT	PRINCIPAL REDUCTION	INTEREST PAID
1	$500,000	$496,625	$63,193.45	$3,375	$59,818
2	$496,625	$492,822	$63,193.45	$3,803	$59,390
3	$492,822	$488,536	$63,193.45	$4,285	$58,908
4	$488,536	$483,707	$63,193.45	$4,829	$58,364
5	$483,707	$478,266	$63,193.45	$5,441	$57,752
6	$478,266	$472,135	$63,193.45	$6,131	$57,062
7	$472,135	$465,225	$63,193.45	$6,909	$56,284
8	$465,225	$457,440	$63,193.45	$7,785	$55,408
9	$457,440	$448,667	$63,193.45	$8,773	$54,421
10	$448,667	$438,782	$63,193.45	$9,885	$53,308
11	$438,782	$427,643	$63,193.45	$11,139	$52,054
12	$427,643	$415,091	$63,193.45	$12,552	$50,642
13	$415,091	$400,947	$63,193.45	$14,144	$49,050
14	$400,947	$385,010	$63,193.45	$15,937	$47,256
15	$385,010	$367,051	$63,193.45	$17,959	$45,235
16	$367,051	$346,815	$63,193.45	$20,236	$42,957
17	$346,815	$324,012	$63,193.45	$22,803	$40,391
18	$324,012	$298,318	$63,193.45	$25,695	$37,499
19	$298,318	$269,364	$63,193.45	$28,953	$34,240
20	$269,364	$236,739	$63,193.45	$32,625	$30,568
21	$236,739	$199,975	$63,193.45	$36,763	$26,430
22	$199,975	$158,550	$63,193.45	$41,426	$21,768
23	$158,550	$111,870	$63,193.45	$46,680	$16,514
24	$111,870	$59,271	$63,193.45	$52,600	$10,594
25	$59,271	$0	$63,193.45	$59,271	$3,923

paring the documents and other costs of initiation. In more recent years, these costs have been shifted directly to the borrower while the origination fees have been kept to raise the rate of return on the loan or to provide negotiating flexibility in a market where interest rates tend to be "sticky." That is, with interest rates fluctuating around a certain percent, say, 12 percent, the origination fee, rather than the interest rate, can be raised or lowered to meet competition. In arranging an origination fee, debt service is based on the face amount of the loan rather than on the amount actually disbursed. Thus, debt service on a $50,000, 25-year loan at 12 percent, compounded monthly, would be computed on the basis of the $50,000 face amount; however, with a 2 percent discount, only $49,000 would be disbursed. A further reason for the use of origination fees is to adjust for risks in specific loans; thus, the higher the expected risk, the higher the origination fee.

Loan discounts and premiums are expressed in terms of dollars and of points or percentages. For example, a $10,000 loan that sells for $9,000 carries a dollar discount of $1,000 ($10,000 less $9,000). A sale price of $12,000 would mean a dollar premium of $2,000 ($12,000 less $10,000). A dollar discount of $1,000 on a $10,000 loan is a 10 percent discount, or a discount of 10 points.

$$\frac{\text{Dollar discount}}{\text{Face value}} = \frac{\$1,000}{\$10,000} = 10 \text{ points (or a 10\% discount)}$$

(unamortized balance)

A dollar premium of $2,000 on the same loan is also a 20-point premium.

Mortgage discounts and premiums come about on existing loans because the market interest rate of a loan differs from the contract or face rate. The *market interest rate* is the rate currently being charged by lenders. The *contract interest rate* is the rate in a specific note, which rate was agreed to when the loan was made. Through time, the market rate changes and a difference develops. In this situation, a lender-investor has the option of making new loans at market interest rates or buying existing loans at prices that give an interest yield equal to that offered by the market.

The following rules always apply when the market and contract rates differ.

1. When the market rate is higher, the market value of existing loans is always less than their face values or unamortized balances, and sales are at a discount.
2. When the market rate is lower, existing loans sell at premiums because the market value exceeds face value.

Long-term mortgages were historically prepaid in from 8 to 12 years; however, the initiation of adjustable rate loans in recent years may cause this time to lengthen. The futures market in GNMA loans assumes prepayment in year 12.[1] Prepayment comes about because a borrower (1) inherits money or otherwise suddenly becomes wealthy, (2) refinances, (3) sells to a buyer who obtains new financing, or (4) defaults, causing the loan to be foreclosed. Refinancing and sales occur much less frequently when interest rates are going up or are very high.

Case Problem

The Urbandale Savings and Loan Association makes a $500,000, 12 percent, monthly payment loan for 25 years. Now, 3 years later, the association needs money and decides to sell the loan. At what price will it sell under varying market conditions? What dollar and percent discounts or premiums?

---

[1] *A Guide to Financial Futures at the Chicago Board of Trade* (Chicago: Chicago Board of Trade, 1983), p. 30.

Discount, without prepayment. From previous work, Figure 16–9, we know that the monthly debt service is \$5,266.12 and the EOY 3 loan balance is \$488,536. A loan is discounted when the market rate exceeds the loan contract rate. Let us say that the market rate is 15 percent. Assuming no prepayment, a buyer of the loan stands to get \$5,266.12 per month for the next 22 years. See Figure 16–10.

The present value of \$5,266.12 discounted at 15 percent for 22 years (25 – 3) equals \$405,430.

Monthly debt service	×	MPV1/P (15%, 22 years)	= PV
\$5,266.12	×	76.988359	= \$405,429.94 (rounds to \$405,430)

The dollar discount is, therefore, \$83,106 (\$488,536 – \$405,430). And the discount off face value is 17.01 percent:

$$\text{Percentage discount} = \frac{\text{Dollar discount}}{\text{Loan balance (face value)}} = \frac{\$83{,}106}{\$488{,}536} = 17.01\%$$

Discount, with prepayment. Let us now change the case problem slightly and assume prepayment at the end of year 15 of the loan, or 12 years from the time of analysis. The prepayment equals the present value of the last 10 years of debt service at the 12 percent contract rate, or \$367,051.

$$\begin{aligned} PV &= \text{Monthly debt service} \times \text{MPV1/P factor (12\%, 10 years)} \\ &= \$5{,}266.12 \times 69.70052 \\ &= \$367{,}051 \end{aligned}$$

This amount may be verified in Figure 16–9.

FIGURE 16–10
Illustration of cash flows for loan discounting, no prepayment expected

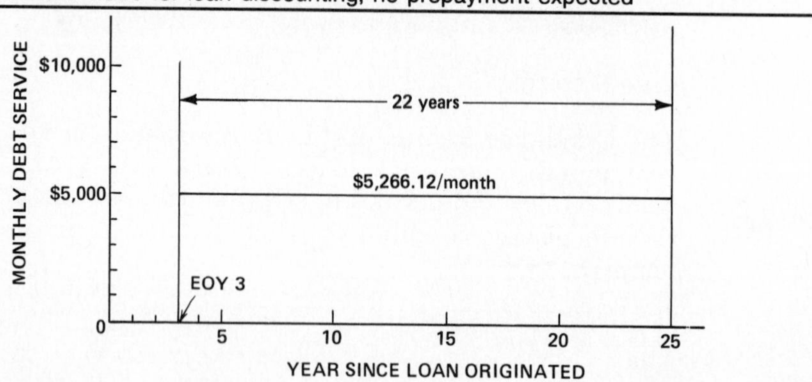

Therefore, at EOY 3 of the loan, a buyer would get the right to \$5,266.12 per month for 12 years plus the right to a one-time payment of \$367,051 at the end of year 12. See Figure 16–11.

The present value of \$5,266.12 per month for 12 years discounted at the market rate, 15 percent, is \$350,870. And the present value of the lump-sum prepayment (\$367,051), discounted 12 years at 15 percent, is \$61,354. Thus, the market value of the loan is \$412,224 (\$350,870 + \$61,354).

In turn, the dollar discount is \$76,313 (\$488,536 - \$412,224). This calculates to a discount off face value of 15.62 percent (\$76,313/\$488,536).

The prepayment reduces the discount off face value because the payments from time of prepayment to the end of the loan term are discounted at a lower rate, making their EOY 15 value larger. In turn, the market value of the loan is greater, meaning a smaller discount.

Premium, without prepayment. A market rate lower than the contract rate gives reason for a loan to have a market value in excess of face value. Remember, the lower the discount rate, the higher is the present value. Thus, with a 10 percent market rate, the last 22 years of debt service has a present value of \$561,273:

$$PV = \$5{,}266.12 \times 106.581844 = \$561{,}273$$

In turn, the premium is \$72,737, or 14.89 percent.

Premium, with prepayment. Figure 16–11 applies whether the market interest rate is 15 or 10 percent. In either case, at EOY 3 of the loan, a buyer would get the right to \$5,266.12 per month for 12 years plus the right to a one-time payment of \$367,051 at the end of year 12. However, a 10

FIGURE 16–11
Illustration of cash flows in loan discounting where prepayment is expected at EOY 15

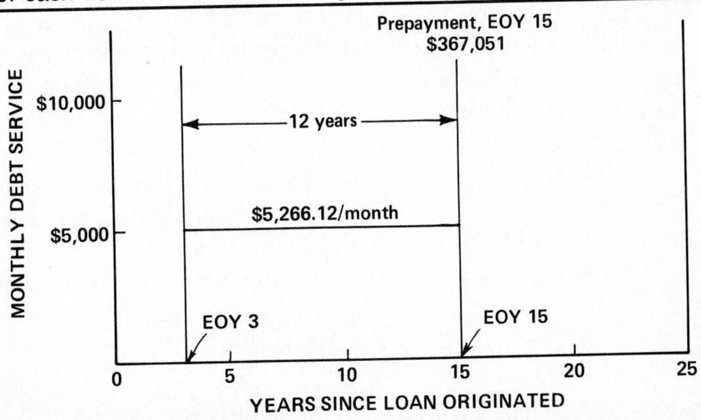

percent market interest rate means the cash flows would be discounted at 10 percent. The respective present values would total to $551,756 ($440,651 + $111,105), giving the market value of the loan in a 10 percent market.

PV of 12 years of monthly debt service = $5,266.12 × 83.676522 = $440,651
PV of EOY 12 prepayment = $367,051 × 0.302696 = $111,105

The dollar premium is $63,219 ($551,756 − $488,536), which gives a percentage premium of 12.94 percent ($63,219/$488,536).

With prepayment, the premium is reduced because a portion of the cash flows are discounted at the higher contract rate. Thus prepayment acts to lower a premium or discount from that expected without prepayment.

Balloon Loan

Balloon loans are sometimes made to keep debt service down and leverage up for the benefit of the borrower; at the same time a shortened maturity gives the lender greater liquidity in its portfolio. For example, the loan we have been working with could have been originated as a balloon loan. It would be described as a $500,000, 12 percent, compounded monthly loan, with debt service calculated on a 25-year amortization schedule, and a balloon payment called for at the end of year 15. Thus the monthly debt service would be $5,266.12 per month and the balloon payment at EOY 15 would be $367,051.

USING FINANCIAL CALCULATORS

All the calculations in this chapter can easily be performed on financial calculators, a number of which can be bought for less than $50. Only four or five key strokes are required to solve the simpler problems. Other problems can be broken down into two or three subproblems that can then be solved with four or five key strokes. Thus, using financial calculators is faster and more accurate than is using TVM tables.

The basic approach is the same, whatever the calculator. However, the keystrokes required vary from calculator to calculator; each takes an hour or two of practice to gain facility.

Most financial calculators have a row of five financial keys, as shown:

[N] [%i] [PMT] [PV] [FV]

The inputs for the keys are

N = number of periods
%i = periodic interest rate
PMT = periodic payment
PV = present value (of a stream of payments or of a single future payment)
FV = future value (of a stream of payments or of a single present value payment)

In most applications, known information for three variables must be fed in by pushing the appropriate keys. Pressing "2nd" or "CPT" (for compute) and the key representing the unknown information causes the desired answer to be displayed. Some examples based on calculations done earlier will illustrate the methodology. The answers given here were generated on a Texas Instruments MBA calculator.

1. Calculate the monthly debt service required on a $500,000 loan made at 12 percent for 25 years.

Keys	N	%i	PMT	PV	FV
Inputs	300 (25 × 12)	1 (12%/12)	—	500,000	—

Press	2nd	or	CPT	and	PMT
Answer					5,266.12071

Monthly debt service equals $5,266.12.

2. Calculate the balance of this loan at the end or its third year (after month 36). At the end of year 3, there are 264 payments remaining on the loan (22 years times 12 months or 300 − 36). Monthly debt service and the interest rate are unchanged:

Keys	N		%i		PMT	PV	FV
Inputs	264		1		5,266.12	—	—
Press	2nd	or	CPT	and	PV		
Answer						488,536.35	($488,536)

3. Calculate the amount of the EOY 15 prepayment. Then calculate the EOY 3 value of this prepayment in a 15 percent market. At EOY 15, 10 years or 120 payments remain to be made.

Keys	N		%i		PMT	PV	FV
Inputs	120		1		5,266.12	—	—
Press	2nd	or	CPT	and	PV		
Answer						367,051.36	($367,051)

The time difference from EOY 15 to EOY 3 is 12 years or 144 payments.

Keys	N	%i	PMT	PV	FV
Inputs	144 (12 × 12)	1.25 (15%/12)	—	—	367,051.36
Press	2nd or	CPT and	PV		
Answer				61,353.91	($61,354)

SUMMARY

Financial management of real estate is administering realty to maximize self-interest, which usually means maximizing wealth. TVM calculations provide a means of comparing cash flows through time to achieve this end. Time value of money involves both compounding and discounting. Compounding means computing interest on principal and on accumulated, unpaid interest to get a future value. Discounting is the opposite of compounding. Discounting is deducting interest in advance, as in converting a future value into a present value. Tables of precalculated factors are commonly available for making TVM calculations; also, electronic calculators increasingly have built in TVM capability.

TVM factors most frequently used in real estate are the present value of 1 (PV1), the present value of 1 per period (PV1/P), and the principal recovery factor (PR). TVM calculations are frequently used to determine the amount of interest paid in a year and to calculate the discount or premium on a mortgage note because the market interest rate differs from the face rate.

QUESTIONS FOR REVIEW AND DISCUSSION

1. What is the underlying concept of compound interest (and of time value of money calculations in general)? What is the importance of compound interest?
2. Explain the relation of compounding to discounting.
3. What is an annuity?
4. Explain the interrelation between the PR factor and the PV1/P factor.
5. How may the amount of interest paid on a monthly payment loan be determined for any one year?
6. Distinguish between buying a loan at a 5-point discount and discounting debt service for a loan at 5 percent.
7. The market rate is less than the contract rate of a loan. If the loan were sold by the lender, would it sell at a discount or a premium?

8. As an annuity lengthens, what happens to the present value of the most distant payment? What does this mean for the present value of all payments as the annuity goes to infinity?

9. Why is an error introduced in interpolating for present value with time value of money factors? Does the error increase or decrease as the distance between known factors increases?

10. The amount, term, and interest rate for two loans are identical; however, one calls for monthly compounding, the other for annual. Will the principal recovery factor (the amount to amortize one) for the annual compounding loan be more than, equal to, or less than 12 times the monthly factor? Why the difference?

CASE PROBLEMS

1. Ann Cook obtains a $100,000 loan from the University Savings & Loan Association at 15 percent to be repaid by monthly payments over 25 years.
   a. How much monthly debt service is required? ($1,280.83)
   b. How much interest would be paid in year 2 of the loan, assuming that all payments are made on schedule? ($14,910)
2. Joe Alum takes out a $100,000 loan at a 12 percent rate, with monthly payments to be made over 25 years.
   a. What is the monthly debt service?
   b. What is the amount of interest paid in year 2?
3. The market interest rate drops to 9 percent at EOY 2 from the time Joe Alum took out the loan. And the University S&L decides to sell the loan.
   a. What market value should a potential buyer place on the loan, assuming no prepayment is expected? ($122,572)
   b. What premium does this represent? (24.36%)
   c. Assuming prepayment at EOY 10 of the loan, what market value and what premium? ($114,722, 16.39%)
4. Suppose the market interest rate had gone up to 15 percent when the University S&L decided to sell the loan at EOY 2.
   a. Assuming no prepayment expected, what market value and what discount? (17.29%)
   b. With prepayment expected at EOY 10 of the loan, what market value and what discount? (13.44%)
5. A $200,000 loan is arranged at 10 percent interest, compounded monthly, to be amortized on a 30-year schedule, with a balloon payment due at EOY 12.
   a. How much is monthly debt service?
   b. What would be the amount of the EOY 12 balloon payment? ($175,542)
6. A 24-year loan is initiated for $50,000 at 9 percent with monthly payments called for.
   a. Assume that it is an RRM loan, with the interest rate subject to change at the end of every third year. At the EOY 3, the market interest rate is 12 percent. What are the loan balance and debt service at the BOY 4?
   b. Assume that it is an ARM loan, with a maximum change of 1 percent per year, all of which is to be reflected in higher or lower debt service. Shortly after initiation, the interest rate increased to 13 percent and remained there. What is the loan balance at end of years 1, 2, and 3? What is the monthly debt service in years 2, 3, and 4?

7. The Fifth National Bank of Clinton makes a $40,000 mortgage loan at 12 percent interest, compounded monthly, over 25 years to John L. Sullivan to finance a home he purchased. At EOY 6, the bank needs money and wishes to sell the loan in a 10 percent market.
   a. Assuming that monthly payments are made on schedule, what unamortized loan balance at EOY 6?
   b. Assuming no prepayment, at what price is the loan likely to sell? ($42,934)
   c. What dollar and percent discount for the loan in part (b)?
   d. Assuming prepayment at EOY 12 and sale at EOY 6, at what price is the loan likely to sell? ($41,011)
   e. Diamond Jim Brady buys the loan at EOY 6 for $40,000, assuming that it will not be prepaid. What yield should Diamond Jim realize? (11.1%)

CHAPTER SEVENTEEN

REAL ESTATE CREDIT AND OUR FINANCIAL SYSTEM

Bankers are just like anybody else, except richer.
OGDEN NASH

IMPORTANT TOPICS OR DECISION AREAS COVERED IN THIS CHAPTER

- Monetary Policy and Interest Rates
- Financial Markets and Money Flows
- Primary Lenders
- Secondary Lenders
- Lender Risks
- Lender Procedures and Commitments.

Money or credit is the lifeblood of real estate construction and sales activity. Money forms a very strong and a very direct link between national economic conditions and real estate market activity. With adequate money, termed *easy money*, interest rates fall or remain low, and, in turn, construction and sales activity tend to be brisk. With a scarcity of money in the economy, termed *tight money*, interest rates go up or remain up. Loans for building properties and refinancing old ones become difficult to obtain. In turn, investment opportunities are scarce, sales and construction activity lags, and incomes of builders, brokers, and sales people fall. Obviously, money is important to real estate.

Money generally comes to real estate through mortgage and rust deed arrangements, which are both commonly used to secure realty loans. To simplify discussion, the term "mortgages" is used in this chapter to mean both kinds of loans. In addition to knowing the importance of money to real estate, a borrower needs to know how to obtain a loan locally and to be aware of the federal laws that apply to obtaining a loan. A sound knowledge of financial institutions and governmental agencies that make up mortgage markets is also helpful. These topics are covered in this chapter.

KEY CONCEPTS INTRODUCED IN THIS CHAPTER

Borrower risk
Capital markets
Collateralized mortgage obligation (CMO)
Commitment
Disintermediation
Fannie Mae
Financial markets
Firm commitment
Freddie Mac
Ginnie Mae
Intermediation
Loan commitment
Money markets
Mortgage banker
Open market operations
Primary lender
Regulation Z
Reserve requirements
Right of rescission
Risk
Secondary lender
Secondary mortgage market

MONETARY POLICY AND INTEREST RATES

The president, the Treasury Department, and the Federal Reserve Banking System usually work together to achieve the economic goals of the country. The main goals are full employment, economic growth, and price stability. One of the major ways to achieve full employment and economic growth is to have an adequate supply of money in the economic system. Too much money puts more purchasing power (demand) in the system than can be satisfied by the available goods and services (supply) at existing price levels. The excess purchasing power competes for the available goods and services, driving prices upward. This increase in prices, of course, is not consistent with the third goal, price stability. Too little money in the economic system causes interest rates to go up, discourages economic activity, and may result in a recession. Adjustments in the money supply, termed *monetary policy,* are thus made to maintain a reasonable interest rate and to provide an acceptable balance in the economic goals.

Monetary policy is usually implemented through the Federal Reserve Banking System. The Federal Reserve Banking System, often called the Fed, is the most dominant financial institution in the United States. The Fed, in managing the nation's money supply, directly affects most private financial institutions as our commercial banks, savings and loan associations, and mutual savings banks.

These institutions are also called financial intermediaries. *To intermediate* means to act as a go-between. Thus, a financial intermediary is a go-between in money matters, taking deposits from savers and lending to borrowers for investment. The process is called *intermediation.* Intermediaries also serve to channel funds from capital-surplus areas, as the central city, to capital-deficit areas, as the suburbs. Sometimes savers withdraw monies from financial intermediaries and lend them directly to investors, which process is called *disintermediation.*

In addition to private financial institutions, a number of public and semipublic agencies exist to buy and sell mortgages and to promote housing policies of the federal government. Taken together, these institutions and agencies financially tie construction and real estate activity to the national economy. Therefore, it is very much in the interest of the investor, builder, developer, finance officer, and broker to watch these public institutions and agencies.

Costs and Availability of Mortgage Money

The availability of money and the level of interest rates greatly affect lending or borrowing terms. As money gets tighter, lenders raise interest rates; they may also shorten the term or life of loans made. The result can be a substantial increase in debt service for borrowers. For example, suppose that tighter money conditions cause a lender to raise the interest rate from 9 to 12 percent and to decrease the life from 30 to 25 years. On a $100,000 mortgage these changes would increase monthly debt service from $804.62 to $1,053.22 or by more than 30 percent. See Figure 17–1.

What does this 30 percent increase mean for an investor, a tenant, or a homebuyer? For income properties, debt service often runs to 80 percent of net operating income, or more. If cost of borrowed money

FIGURE 17–1
Monthly debt service on a $100,000 loan with varying duration and interest rates

LIFE (YEARS)	INTEREST RATE			
	6%	9%	12%	15%
15	$843.86	$1,014.27	$1,200.17	$1,399.59
20	716.43	899.72	1,101.09	1,316.79
25	644.30	839.20	1,053.22	1,280.83
30	599.55	804.62	1,028.61	1,264.44
35	570.19	783.99	1,015.55	1,256.81

goes up, an equity investor is also likely to want a proportionately higher rate of return because of greater risk. Thus, net operating income must go up by 30 percent, and rents to tenants must be raised accordingly. Or, alternatively, if demand for space is weak, property values fall with very negative impact on existing owners.

As for homeownership, assume that a typical family spends 25 percent of its income for PITI (principal, interest, taxes, and insurance) payments. Further, four-fifths of this 25 percent, or 20 percent, goes to loan debt service, principal and interest, and the remaining 5 percent to taxes and insurance. Thus, the income–to–debt service (PI) ratio is 5:1. The shift in borrowing terms means required monthly debt service on a $60,000 loan would go from $482.77 to $631.94. In turn, the annual income needed to borrow $60,000 for a typical home would also increase by more than 30 percent, from $28,966 to $37,916.

Obviously an increase of this amount would sharply reduce the number of buyers able to meet the demand of a $60,000 mortgage. This reduction in potential buyers would be true at all income levels and, if sustained, would reduce the number of units demanded and would eventually result in an across-the-board reduction in the quality of housing for the population.

The Lender's Viewpoint

The long-term upward trend in interest rates during the past two decades has severely squeezed profits of financial institutions with large mortgage portfolios. Normally, such institutions need a 1.5 to 2.0 percent spread or differential between the interest rate they pay on savings deposited with them and the interest rate they charge on mortgage loans. Mortgage loans have traditionally been long-term commitments with fixed terms. Interest rates are paid on all deposits, however, and tend to go up periodically with increasing interest rates in the economy. The result is a squeeze on profits.

As an illustration of the squeeze on profits, assume the following institutional assets in mortgage loans and cash: 30 percent of the loans—in dollar terms—were made over 10 years ago at an average of 8 percent,

30 percent were made from 5 to 10 years ago at an average of 10 percent, and 30 percent were made in the last 5 years at an average of 12 percent. The balance of the firm's assets are held as cash, buildings, or equipment and, hence, earn no income. The average interest rate paid by the institution on savings is expected to increase from 7.5 to 8.0 percent because of tightening money market conditions. What effect on profits?

30% × 8% =	2.4%
30% × 10% =	3.0%
30% × 12% =	3.6%
10% × 0% =	0.0%
Weighted rate of return	9.0%

The margin or differential equals 1.5 percent currently (9.0% − 7.5%). The expected increase in the rate paid on savings deposits will drop the differential to 1.0%., not enough to cover operating costs and leave a profit. It is this type of squeeze on profits that causes financial institutions to turn to more flexible financing arrangements, such as ARM, RRM, and GPM loans.

Under a typical ARM, an interest rate is agreed upon when the loan is made, to be increased or decreased in accordance with fluctuations in an index beyond the control of the lender, such as the interest rates paid on U.S. Treasury securities. Typically, the terms provide that rate changes can be made only twice a year, at a maximum of 0.5 percent per change. The change may fluctuate a maximum of 5 percent, in most cases, above or below the orginal loan rate. If the interest rate increases, the term increases while the debt service is held constant. If too large an increase occurs, an increase in debt service might become necessary.

The benefit of an adjustable rate mortgage to the lender is, of course, that an acceptable differential is maintained between the interest rate paid on savings deposits and the interest rate earned on mortgage loans. Also, with adjustable terms, lenders may make loans more readily in a time of rising interest rates because they avoid running the risk of being locked into a long-term fixed interest rate mortgage, at a rate below market. ARM lending is not widely accepted and, in fact, is strongly opposed by consumer interest groups.

Shifting Interest Rates

The two main methods used by the Fed in implementing monetary policy are (1) open market operations and (2) changing reserve requirements of member banks. Secondary methods are (1) changing the discount rate, (2) imposing selective controls when authorized by Congress, and (3) engaging in moral suasion. The process and effects to tightening or easing the money supply is summarized in Figure 17–2.

FIGURE 17–2
Effects of changes in the money supply

TO TIGHTEN MONEY SUPPLY	TO EASE MONEY SUPPLY
1. Federal Reserve System raises reserve requirements of member banks or sells bonds in open market to cause relative decrease in money supply.	1. Federal Reserve System lowers reserve requirements of member banks or buys bonds in open market to increase money supply.
2. Reserves of member banks are decreased. Money for new loans becomes limited.	2. Reserves of member banks are increased on relative basis. The reserves earn interest and produce profit only if put to work.
3. Member banks sell bonds and short-term notes to obtain money to meet demand of customers for new loans.	3. Member banks extend loans to customers more readily and buy bonds and notes with excess reserves.
4. As supply of bonds and notes offered for sale exceeds demand, prices drop; rate of return to buyers therefore increases.	4. As more bonds are purchased, demand exceeds supply offered for sale, and prices go up; rate of return to buyers decreases.
5. As rate of return increases, money is withdrawn from time and savings deposits to buy the bonds and notes. Also, bonds and notes are bought by savers in preference to putting new savings into time and savings accounts, which is *disintermediation*. Thus money is lost by banks and savings and loan associations.	5. As rate of return on bonds falls, more money is deposited in time and savings accounts in preference to more bond purchases. Therefore, *intermediation* increases as banks and savings and loan associations get more money to invest.
6. With less money to lend, banks and savings and loan associations raise lending standards and interest rates. Marginal borrowers are therefore unable to obtain credit.	6. With more money to lend, banks and savings and loan associations lower lending standards and interest rates. Marginal borrowers and therefore able to obtain credit.
7. Prepayment of mortgage loans and other low-interest debt drops off.	7. Prepayment of mortgage loans and other debt picks up as costs of refinancing drop.
8. Refinancing and new financing activity are slow because of higher interest rates and credit standards. Investment opportunities decline. Net result is reduced financial activity until money gets easier. Economy is slowed down, and inflation is hopefully brought under control.	8. Refinancing and new financing activity is brisk because of lower interest rates and credit standards. More investment opportunities become possible. Net result is increased financial activity as long as economy remains healthy and inflation remains under control.

Open market operations. Government bonds and notes may be bought and sold in the open market by the Fed through its *Open Market Committee.* Offering and selling large numbers of bonds drive bond prices down, as the supply exceeds demand. Individuals, banks, insurance companies, and other investors buy the bonds and pay by checks drawn on commercial banks, which reduces the number of dollars in the banks for loan purposes. This process makes money tight or scarce. Bankers ration out the scarce money by being more selective in making loans and by raising the interest rates charged on the loans. If the bankers cannot make sound loans at reasonable rates, they buy government bonds that are risk free and involve very low handling costs. Thus, the interest rate is pushed up and held up by the Fed's selling bonds on the open market. The Fed may buy bonds on the open market and lower the interest rate if easy monetary policy is the goal.

Changing reserve requirements. The Fed has the authority, within limits set by Congress, to raise or lower the *reserve requirements* of member banks. Reserve requirements are increased to make money tight or scarce. Since increasing requirements means that banks have less money to lend, the banks raise interest rates and credit requirements in making loans. For easy money, requirements are lowered so that banks have more money to lend. The banks, in turn, lower interest rates and act less selectively in making loans.

Monetary policy is usually not implemented by changing reserve requirements of banks because a small change in requirements results in a large change in the money supply. Changing reserve requirements is too crude a tool for day-to-day monetary policy purposes.

Secondary tools of the Fed. Members of banks may borrow from a federal reserve bank by pledging customers' promissory notes as collateral. The interest rate the banks pay when borrowing is termed the discount rate. By raising the rate of interest that member banks are charged for borrowing, the Fed can signal a desire for tighter money. Lowering the interest rate signals easy money. Banks usually do not borrow heavily from the Fed. Consequently, changing the discount rate does not greatly affect the interest rate that banks charge their customers.

Selective financial controls are sometimes authorized by Congress and administered by the Fed. Selective controls, in the past, have been used only in times of emergency, as when the Fed was authorized to raise down payment requirements on houses during the Korean emergency. *Moral suasion* is the effort by federal officials to convince banks to tighten or ease credit without any direct regulation.

Importance of Interest Rates to Real Estate Activity

In times of tight money, interest rates go up. Monetary policy is related directly to the availability and cost of mortgage money. If inflation is a national problem, monetary theory calls for a cutback in the money supply to decrease the purchasing power or effective demand for goods and services in the hands of the public. This, in turn, is meant to check further price increases. A limited or reduced money supply means that the available money will be directed to those users able to pay the highest interest rates. Thus, interest rates on mortgage loans must go up to attract money. If potential borrowers cannot or will not pay the higher rates, money is not channeled to them.

Alternatively, if unemployment and recession are national problems, one solution is to increase the money supply. With increased supply, funds begin to build up in financial institutions and must be lent out if interest is to be earned. The interest rate is lowered, and more business and individuals can afford the price. Hence, more mortgage money is available and interest rates drop.

An investor or builder might, therefore, key in on stated monetary policy in making decisions regarding the buying or selling of property or arranging to ensure future mortgage money availability. Of course, other considerations may complicate the decision. For example, in 1979 and 1980 the nation simultaneously experienced high unemployment, recession, and double-digit inflation. Economists and politicians were sharply divided on what goals to emphasize and what methods or policies to apply. No clear-cut indicator of policy was evident.

FINANCIAL MARKETS AND MONEY FLOWS

Mortgage lending represents only a portion of the total money flows in our economy. Before looking closely at mortgage markets, let us take a brief look at overall flows of money in our economy. Money flows are referred to as "flows of funds" by economists.

In the overall scheme of economics, payments must be made by our business sector to the factors of production in generating the gross national product, GNP. The factors of production are land, labor, capital, and management. We earlier defined gross national product as the total value of all goods and services produced by our economy, valued at market prices. GNP is made up of all goods and services produced plus gross domestic private investment. See Figure 17–3, which shows major money flows in our economy.

At the same time, the consuming sector of our economy, made up of the owner-managers of the factors of production, use the goods and services produced. These owner-managers get rents from land or realty, wages from labor, interest from money, and profits from ownership and management of business. The monies received go mostly to pay for the goods and services consumed. But some excess, or saving, is also realized by the consuming sector. This excess goes to the financial markets for investment. *Financial markets* are the places or the processes whereby those with funds lend to those wishing to borrow; money is exchanged for financial claims, such as bonds, bills, or mortgages.

In financial markets, a distinction is usually made between money markets and capital markets. *Money markets* involve the exchange of money for short-term money instruments and the subsequent buying and selling of these short-term instruments. Examples are notes and Treasury bills. Short term means that the instruments have 1 year or less to maturity. Financial institutions, and others, continually create and trade short-term instruments to adjust and maintain liquidity positions.

Capital markets refer to the creation and exchange of long-term debt

FIGURE 17–3
Simplified flow of funds with emphasis on money flows through financial markets

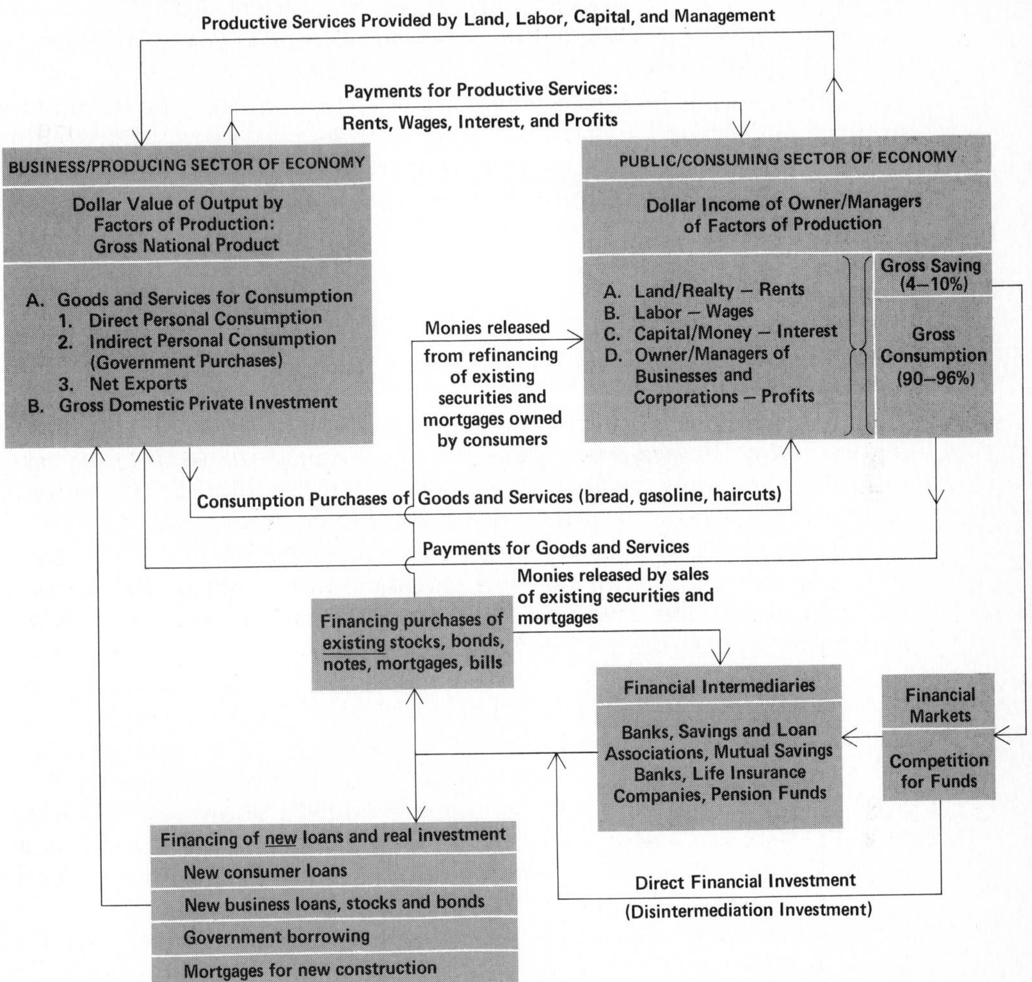

instruments (bonds, mortgages, commercial paper) and stocks for money. It follows that long term means that the instruments have maturity of longer than 1 year. Using 1 year as a dividing line is arbitrary but useful. And, of course, stocks generally have no maturity date at all. The mortgage market is basically a capital or long-term market.

Competition for funds is implicit in a financial market. The function of the market is to channel the nation's savings to its highest and best use, usually meaning that use most able and willing to pay the highest rate of return. As indicated by Figure 17–3, the competition for funds is between and among financial institutions as well as investment alternatives. The main institutions of concern are commercial banks (CBs), savings and loans (S&Ls), mutual savings banks (MSBs), and life insurance companies (LICs). The basic alternatives open to lenders are consumer loans, business loans, corporate stocks and bonds, government bonds, and mortgage loans.

Broadly speaking, mortgage market participants may be divided into primary and secondary lenders. These lenders frequently buy and sell existing mortgages and mortgage-backed securities among themselves, which activity is called the *secondary mortgage market.*

PRIMARY LENDERS

Primary lenders originate loans or supply funds directly to borrowers. Savings and loan associations, mutual savings banks, commercial banks, mortgage bankers, and life insurance companies make up the bulk of primary lenders. *Secondary lenders* buy loans from, or originate loans through, someone else. Federally supported agencies, pension funds, and some life insurance companies are the major secondary lenders. Some financial organizations act as both primary and secondary lenders.

Primary lending institutions originate nearly seven-eighths of all mortgage debt. The laws and regulations governing them are taken up here in the order of their relative importance.

Savings and Loan Associations

At the end of 1980, there were approximately 4,600 savings and loan associations in the United States and they held about $630 billion in savings deposits. These associations accounted for more than one-third of all mortgage loans outstanding, in dollar terms, and nearly one-half of all home mortgage loans.

Savings and loan associations have been active for over 100 years. Yet regulation of their lending activities on a regional and national scale did not begin until 1932 when Congress created the Federal Home Loan Bank (FHLB) System. Today, all federally chartered S&Ls are supervised by the FHLB System. In addition, almost all state-chartered S&Ls choose to be members of the system and subject to its regulations. A major reason for this is that members may borrow on short notice from a district home loan bank whenever funds are needed to pay off accounts of withdrawing depositors or to finance additional mortgage loans.

Almost all savings and loan associations, if qualified, also belong to the Federal Savings and Loan Insurance Corporation (FSLIC), which was created by Congress in 1934. FSLIC insures public deposits with member institutions for up to $100,000 per account. Depositor confidence in S&Ls is very high because of this FSLIC insurance and because of FSLIC's uniform lending policies and accounting supervision. As a result, S&Ls have grown rapidly in total assets and in mortgage loans outstanding.

S&Ls may make conventional installment loans for up to 95 percent of either the purchase price or appraised market value of any home offered as security, whichever is less. The loans must be amortized on a monthly basis and have a maximum life of 30 years. Almost all high loan-to-value ratio are made on an insured or guaranteed basis. According to FHLB System regulations, the loan must be secured by first mortgage liens on residences within the state of the home office of the association making the loan or within 100 miles of the office making the loan if outside the home office state. FHA and VA loans may be made up to any loan-to-value limits acceptable to the Federal Housing Administration or the Veterans Administration.

First mortgage loans may also be made on business and income properties, churches, and other improved properties up to the maximum loan-to-value ratio of 75 percent. Monthly loan amortization payments and a maximum of 25 years apply to these loans. Not more than 20 percent of an association's assets may be placed in "business property" loans. Savings and loan associations may also make loans for property improvement, alteration, repair, and equipment. Finally, mobile homes may be financed by S&Ls.

Commercial Banks

Commercial banks are required by law to maintain relatively greater liquidity in their assets than are other financial institutions because they are more subject to immediate withdrawal of deposits by the nature of their operation. Thus, although some 14,000 commercial banks control approximately one-half of Americans' savings, ($1,704 billion in assets at the end of 1980), their role in mortgage lending continues to be, for them, a secondary activity. Even so, CBs account for almost one-fifth of all mortgage loans outstanding. Making short-term commercial loans to local business firms is their primary lending activity. Short-term loans enable the banks to meet their liquidity requirements and at the same time to maximize their profits.

Commercial banks may make uninsured conventional loans on homes for up to 80 percent of the lesser of purchase price or appraised market value. The loans may be made, if fully amortized, for up to 30 years. Insured conventional loans may be made for up to 95 percent loan-to-value ratio. FHA-insured and VA-guaranteed loans may be made to any loan-to-value limits and terms allowed by the federal government. Commercial banks may also make construction loans for up to 24 months.

Commercial banks generally increase their mortgage lending activity when demand for local business loans is slow. They decrease mortgage lending activity when business loan demand is strong. That is, they tend to invest in real estate loans only when funds on hand exceed local business need. Recent improvements in secondary mortgage market operation has lessened the pressure on commercial banks to avoid mortgage lending activity. With an active secondary mortgage market, mortgages may be sold off at almost any time by a bank to increase cash on hand. Thus mortgage loans are now reasonably liquid assets.

Mutual Savings Banks

MSBs account for approximately one-eighth of all savings in the United States. About three-fourths of MSB-held savings are invested in mortgage loans. Thus, MSBs account for approximately 10 percent of all mortgage loans outstanding.

All of the approximately 450 mutual savings banks in the United States are state chartered. Nearly all are located in the Middle Atlantic States and in New England, with nearly seven-eighths in the states of New York, Massachusetts, Connecticut, Pennsylvania, and New Jersey. Mutual savings banks tend to be strong when savings and loan associations are weak, and vice versa. From the viewpoint of mortgage borrowers, the difference between S&Ls and MSBs is slight.

In almost all states, MSBs may make insured conventional loans up to 95 percent of value with a life of up to 30 years. Conventional, uninsured loans may generally be made up to 80 percent of value, also with an amortization period of up to 30 years. In a few states, uninsured conventional loans may be made up to 90 percent of value. FHA and VA loans may be made up to any loan-to-value ratios acceptable to the federal government.

Life Insurance Companies

Life insurance companies have shifted their mortgage lending emphasis since 1965 from one-family residences to multifamily and commercial properties. Larger loans and higher interest rates on loans for these properties make lending on them more profitable. Also, a share of the equity action, including participation in the income generated by these properties, is frequently arranged in multifamily and commercial lending. Investing in mortgage loans is particularly advantageous to LICs because of the long-term nature of their insurance policy obligations. Actuaries are able to forecast dollar requirements of their policy obligations and match them up with mortages of appropriate terms.

Larger insurance companies make mortgages on a national scale. Some loans are made through branch offices, but many are made through mortgage bankers and brokers. Extremely large loans are usually arranged from the home office. LICs have considerable flexibility in their mortgage lending, but they generally limit loans to two-thirds of appraised value with amortization periods up to 30 years. FHA-insured and VA-guaranteed loans are purchased in secondary mortgage markets from time to time when excess reserves pile up and investment opportunities are limited.

Mortgage Companies

Mortgage bankers and mortgage brokers hold little long-term mortgage debt. Instead, they service secondary lenders, as life insurance companies and government agencies, that wish to invest in mortgages. *Mortgage bankers* originate and service loans for these secondary lenders for a fee. *Mortgage brokers* originate loans for the fee but do not provide any servicing. The secondary lenders must then arrange for servicing elsewhere, often through mortgage bankers. Mortgage bankers sometimes originate loans first and look for a buyer later if the loan presents a profit opportunity.

Eastern and Midwestern banks and savings and loan associations sometimes become secondary lenders when they accumulate surplus funds that cannot otherwise be placed profitably; they use the surplus funds to buy loans, secured by properties in other regions, through mortgage bankers and brokers. The operations of mortgage firms become large in capital-scarce areas of the South and West where dependence on out-of-state funds is great.

Mortgage bankers generally charge three-eighths of 1 percent of outstanding loan balances per year as a servicing fee. Thus an outstanding loan balance of $10,000 yields $37.50 per year to a mortgage banker. This $37.50 must cover the cost of accounting, filing, making monthly statements, correspondence, and office overhead. This effectively means that the mortgage banker must service a high volume of loans to have a profitable operation.

SECONDARY LENDERS

If left to themselves, primary lenders would soon run out of money for loans in periods of tight money. The federal government has worked to develop secondary mortgage institutions such as the Home Loan Bank systems, FNMA, GNMA, and the Home Loan Mortgage Corporation to add liquidity to mortgage markets. These agencies either advance monies to primary lenders or buy mortgages from them. In both events, monies of primary lenders are released to make more mortgages.

The main secondary lenders include agencies of the federal government and life insurance companies. Banks and S&Ls also sometimes act as secondary lenders if profit opportunities elsewhere exceed local profit opportunities. Pension funds also increasingly invest in mortgages. The combined activities of all these lenders link the nation's capital and mortgage markets.

In addition, primary lenders frequently buy and sell mortgages among themselves. For example, New York MSBs with excess funds may buy mortgages from an S&L in Colorado where funds are scarce. Or life insurance companies may buy loans from mortgage bankers in several states. FHA-insured and VA-guaranteed loans facilitate this buying and selling of mortgages because of their standardized terms. Privately insured conventional loans on uniform FNMA/FHLMC instruments also give lenders protection and standardized terms. The result of this buying and selling activity among lenders is higher liquidity for mortgages and a broadening of the mortgage market. In addition, with commercial banks and life insurance companies being active in mortgage markets, mortgages must be directly competitive with other investments—stocks and bonds—in competing for excess funds. This competition means that mortgages and home construction are increasingly tied to the supply and demand for money in our entire economy.

A number of organizations promote loan safety, thus facilitating the purchase and sale of loans in the secondary mortgage market. These organizations offering protection to holders of mortgage loans include private insurance corporations, the Federal Housing Administration, the Veterans Administration, and the Farmers Home Administration.

Federal Home Loan Bank System

The Federal Home Loan Bank System was created by Congress during the financial crisis of the 1930s. The purpose was to establish a source of central credit for the nation's home financing institutions. This initial purpose has expanded into five functions as follows:

1. To link mortgage lending institutions to the nation's capital markets
2. To serve as a source of secondary credit for member institutions during periods of heavy withdrawal demand
3. To smooth out seasonal differences between savings flows and loan changes
4. To smooth flow of funds from capital surplus areas to capital deficit areas
5. To stabilize generally residential construction and financing

The FHLBS advances funds to members in need, consistent with the foregoing functions. The system does not operate as a secondary mortgage market facility per se.

The Federal Home Loan Bank System is made up of 12 regional banks and member institutions. Membership is open to savings and loan associations, mutual savings banks, and life insurance companies. By law, all federally chartered savings and loan associations must belong to the FHLBS. At the end of 1978, the system had 4,242 members: 4,158 S&Ls, 86 MSBs, and 2 life insurance companies. The system is governed by a three-member board appointed by the president of the United States.

Federal Home Loan Mortgage Corporation

The Federal Home Loan Mortgage Corporation was created by Congress in 1970. The nickname for FHLMC is Freddie Mac. Freddie Mac functions as a secondary mortgage market facility under the supervision of the FHLB Board. It buys and sells conventional, FHA-insured, and VA-guaranteed mortgages. In recent years, FHLMC has promoted the development of mortgage-backed securities such as the *collateralized mortgage obligation (CMO)*. Mortgage-backed securities generally pass through principal and interest, as received, to holders on a pro rata basis. The CMO provides a unique repayment structure to appeal to a wide variety of investors. CMOs are divided into three classes: short, intermediate, and long term. All holders receive semiannual payment of interest at the certificate rate. Holders of first-class, short-term certificates receive all payments of principal from the collateralized loans until they are fully repaid. Next, holders of intermediate certificates receive all payments of principal. And, of course, long-term holders are repaid their principal last. This unique repayment schedule reduces the uncertainty of holders as to the length of their investment. Pension funds have found the intermediate- and long-term certificates particularly attractive.

The declared goal of the FHLMC is to make mortgages as highly liquid, and equally as attractive, as other securities to investors. In the past, mortgages have been considered a relatively illiquid investment. *Liquidity* refers to the ease of quickness with which an investment can be converted into cash and to the cash-to-value ratio realized. The easier the conversion into cash and the higher the cash-to-value ratio, the more liquid the investment. An active secondary mortgage market gives mortgages liquidity equal to that of stocks and bonds.

The FHLMC seeks to accomplish its goal in several ways:

1. Development, in conjunction with the Federal National Mortgage Association (FNMA), of uniform conventional mortgage instruments so that a lack of standardized terms would no longer be a major deterrent to the ready buying and selling of conventional mortgages.
2. Purchase and sale of conventional mortgage loans on a whole and a participation basis. Participation means that two or more investors or lenders share or participate in the ownership of the loan.
3. Purchase and sale of FHA-insured and VA-guaranteed loans on a continuing basis.

Federal National Mortgage Association

The Federal National Mortgage Association (FNMA) was created by Congress in 1938. FNMA carries the nickname of Fannie Mae. Fannie Mae is a government-sponsored corporation, but its stock is privately owned. This unique combination of interests makes FNMA a private corporation with a public purpose.

The basic purpose of FNMA is to provide a secondary market for residential loans. FNMA buys, services, and sells loans to fulfill this purpose. It deals in conventional, FHA-insured, and VA-guaranteed loans. Operationally, FNMA buys mortgages when loanable funds are in short supply and sells them when funds are plentiful. FNMA and FHLMC jointly developed uniform instruments for conventional mortgage loans to facilitate their use in the secondary mortgage market.

Government National Mortgage Association

The Government National Mortgage Association (GNMA) was created by Congress in 1968. GNMA is referred to in the trade as Ginnie Mae. Ginnie Mae is entirely owned by the federal government, and its financial activities are supported by borrowings from the federal government. In fact, Ginnie Mae is an agency of the Department of Housing and Urban Development and has its operating policies set by the HUD secretary. The Government National Mortgage Association has three main functions: (1) special assistance for disadvantaged residential borrowers, (2) raising additional funds for residential lending, and (3) mortgage portfolio management and liquidation.

The special assistance function involves providing funds for low-cost housing and for residential mortgages in underdeveloped, capital-scarce areas. The fund-raising function is to stabilize mortgage lending and home construction activities. The primary technique used to accomplish these two functions is government-guaranteed securities.

GNMA guarantees mortgage-backed securities secured by government-insured or -guaranteed loans, namely, FHA and VA loans. The loans underlying the guarantee are pooled, a covering security is issued, and repayments from the pool are used to pay off the security. Two basic types of securities are issued: the passthrough and the bond. The passthrough provides for monthly payments to the security holder. The bond provides for semiannual payments of principal and interest. Debt service from the pool of mortgages is used to make payments on the securities. The funds raised from sale of the security are used to purchase additional mortgages.

These above programs, of course, result in GNMA's carrying a very large portfolio of mortgages, which requires continuing management. GNMA may buy, service, and sell mortgages in an orderly manner that will have a minimum adverse effect on the residential mortgage market and result in minimum loss to the federal government.

Private Mortgage Corporations

Some private mortgage insurance corporations organize subsidiary mortgage corporations to invest reserves in mortgages. Prepayments and monthly debt service on the mortgages are used to pay claims on insured mortgages on which lenders lost money. These companies constitute a private, secondary mortgage lender or investor. The largest of these firms is the MGIC Mortgage Corporation. The nickname for the MGIC Mortgage Corporation is Maggy Mae.

LENDER RISKS

An investor or homebuyer can almost always obtain real estate credit if he or she is willing to pay the price by way of interest rate and other terms of borrowing. A knowledgeable investor or homeowner makes it a point to know the procedures of borrowing and, in addition, to borrow in the most opportune way and at the most advantageous terms.

Advantageous borrowing begins by understanding money market conditions. For example, the inverse relationship between money market supply and interest rates is an economic fact of life. The time required for a change in monetary conditions to be reflected in a changed level of residential construction is uncertain and depends on several complex factors. Nevertheless, the basic relationship continues; when plenty of money is available, interest rates drop, and vice versa.

A further consideraton for the potential borrower is approaching the right institutions for the kind of loan desired. Savings and loan associations and mutual savings banks lend much more readily on one-family houses than do life insurance companies or commercial banks. Commercial banks and life insurance companies, however, are more likely to make loans on farms and commercial properties. And, of course, individual lenders must be approached for purchases money mortgages and land contracts, as on undeveloped land.

A third major consideration in arranging a loan is lender's risks, of which a potential borrower must be aware. Lenders continually balance opportunities for profits against chances of loss of profit and principal. Lenders operate on the principle that as risk increases, profits should also increase. Mortgage lenders have three major types of risk: (1) borrower, (2) property, and (3) portfolio.

Borrower Risk

A lender's analysis of borrower risk in making a loan begins with the borrower. The borrower's situation must not possess undue risks that cause it to be screened out by lenders if a loan is to be obtained. The categories of concern in the analysis generally are (1) credit rating, (2) assets, (3) earning capacity or income, and (4) motivation. A lender is likely to have accept-reject guidelines for each category.

A credit rating may be obtained simply by ordering a credit report on the prospective borrower. The borrower's credit experience and reputation must show an acceptably stable performance, including job and income patterns and family life. The credit report and the borrower's application provide information on assets owned or net worth, including savings and checking account balances.

Third, the borrower's monthly or annual income must show a capability of meeting the principal, interest, taxes, and insurance (PITI) requirements of the proposed loan. For a homeowner's loan, the usual rule is that the PITI must not exceed one-fourth of 25 percent of the borrower's gross monthly income. In addition, PITI and other debt obligations must not exceed one-third of the borrower's gross monthly income. The lender looks more to the property for security in making a loan on investment property, and these rules do not necessarily apply.

The borrower's motivation is the final and perhaps the most important of the four categories. Motivation means that the borrower has sufficient incentive and desire to meet the requirements of the loan. A young family wishing to own their own home is usually considered highly motivated. Motivation may be judged in several ways. A strong credit report, a steady accumulation of assets, and rising income all indicate strong motivation.

Property Risks

In analyzing property risks, three categories of concern must be addressed: (1) on-site characteristics, (2) location, and (3) marketability. Borrower risks are generally more important than are property risks for owner-occupied dwellings. But for investment properties, where the value may be many, many times the borrower's income, the property must be looked to more strongly for security. Property risks are largely evaluated in a market value appraisal.

The size, shape, and topography of a site are the first considerations in judging on-site characteristics. These characteristics must be complementary to the improvements and the use. Next, the size, condition, functional capability, mechanical equipment, and appearance of any improvements are taken into account.

Location means relative ease of accessibility to begin with. The exposure or environment of a property is also an important locational consideration. By way of example, a house with a pleasing view in a well-kept neighborhood is preferable to a house opposite a junkyard in a blighted neighborhood.

Marketability risks pertain largely to market value and the economic makeup of the community. A growing community with diversified industries provides greater marketability, for example, than does a community with one industry that is declining. Also, stable employment and economic patterns are preferable to cyclical patterns. Property valuation is taken up in more detail in Chapter 19.

Portfolio Risks

A portfolio, in finance, is all the securities, or investments, owned or managed. Undertaking the owning and managing a large number of investments includes many risks, termed *portfolio risks.* For a mortgage lender, these risks may be categorized as (1) administrative, (2) investment, and (3) mix and turnover, or diversification, perils.

Administrative risks are perils inherent in making and servicing loans that might lead to losses. The chance of error in the property file and in keeping records of payments is ever present. Other administrative risks include overlooking some item in required periodic inspections to ensure upkeep and maintenance.

Investment risks are chances that an adequate rate of return will not be realized on loans. A loan may go sour for two reasons. First, the borrower might not be able to keep up with increasing costs of operation, in which event, abandonment or foreclosure would result. Second, the property's value may decline faster than the loan is amortized. Thus, in a foreclosure, the unamortized principal plus foreclosure expenses might exceed the disposition value of the property.

Risk Ratios

Lenders use risk ratios to ascertain how large a loan might safely be made on a given property. The loan-to-value ratio, previously discussed, is most commonly used. Commercial lenders use several financial ratios, in addition, to ascertain the relative risk of a loan. For income property, lenders want to ascertain (1) that the property's expenses are a reasonable proportion of its gross income and (2) that the property can carry the proposed loan by itself without dependence on the investor-borrower because of the exculpatory clause. The specific ratios are taken up in Chapter 21 on investment analysis because we have not taken up all the required inputs yet. Also, an investor may want to calculate and study the ratios personally *before* applying for a loan from an institutional lender.

LENDER PROCEDURES AND COMMITMENTS

Making an application is the first step in obtaining a loan. Information required by lenders includes (1) the amount of the loan desired, (2) identification of the property to be pledged as security, and (3) annual income, kind of employment, and other financial information on the applicant. If the property and the applicant look acceptable to the lender, a loan commitment is given the borrower.

A *loan commitment* is a written pledge, promise, or letter of agreement to lend or advance money under specified terms and conditions. The amount, the interest rate, and the life of the loan are stated along with any other terms demanded by the lender. In most cases, the applicant has the right to shop with other lenders if the amount and terms of the commitment are unacceptable. At the same time, the lender is usually likely to include a termination date on the commitment, after which the offer to make the loan is withdrawn.

The four commonly used loan commitments are (1) firm, (2) conditional, (3) takeout, and (4) standby. The first two commitments, firm and conditional, are most applicable to consumer loans on residential properties. Takeout and standby commitments are important to builder-lender transactions as well as to transactions between lending agencies themselves.

VA, FHA, and private mortgage insurers make commitments to guarantee or insure loans. The terminology of these commitments is comparable to that of commitments by lenders.

Firm Commitment

A *firm commitment* is a definite offer to make a loan at stated terms and conditions. For all practical purposes, the borrower-applicant need only accept the offer and prepare for the loan closing. Nearly all commitments to homebuyers and small investors are firm commitments.

Conditional Commitment

An agreement to make a loan, subject to certain limitations or provisions, is a *conditional commitment*. The provision may be completion of construction or development of a property. The Federal Housing Administration commonly issues conditional commitments for loan insurance to builders that depend on the builder's finding an acceptable buyer-borrower for the speculative house. The builder, therefore, accepts the risk of finding an acceptable buyer. Because the property is already approved, the conditional commitment facilitates the sale of the house.

Takeout Commitment

A *takeout commitment* is an agreement by one lender to make a permanent loan to "take" another lender out of a temporary or construction loan. A takeout commitment is also a firm agreement to buy a loan for an originating lender at a definite price.

A takeout commitment is commonly used between financial institutions and government agencies. For example, a takeout commitment may be given by a governmental agency, such as the Government National Mortgage Association, to a local lender, such as a bank. The government agency agrees to buy and take over a mortgage loan from a local lender as soon as the loan is closed and all contingencies surrounding the loan are satisfied. The local lender is usually considered contractually bound to sell the loan at the stipulated price. The price to be paid for the loan is included in the written commitment. Takeout commitments usually involve properties under construction or development.

Standby Commitment

A *standby commitment* is the promise to buy a loan from a second lender, without the initial lender being obligated to sell the loan. That is, standby commitment gives the owner of a loan the option to sell or not to sell the loan at the stipulated price. The option to sell is obtained for a fee payable in advance, and the price may be lower than the market value of the loan.

A standby commitment is usually issued by a large institutional lender, as a life insurance company, to a local bank or mortgage banker. An owner or developer may pay the fee for the local lender to obtain construction financing. With a standby commitment, the local lender is able to make the construction loan with assurance of being able to sell it promptly at a definite price instead of keeping it as a large loan on the books. If a higher price can be obtained elsewhere, the local lender has the right to take advantage of it and to realize a higher profit.

SUMMARY

Monetary policy to achieve national economic goals directly affects and ties real estate construction and sales activity to the general economy. Monetary policy is intended to achieve national economic goals. Easy money and low interest rates help to realize the goals of economic growth and full employment. The combination of tight money and high interest rates slows inflation, to achieve the goal of price stability. In periods of tight monetary policy and high interest rate, real estate activity tends to decline, whereas easy money tends to stimulate real estate activity. The main financial institution for implementing monetary policy is "the Fed."

Real estate competes for money or credit in our capital markets. Financial intermediaries or go-betweens, mainly S&Ls and banks, channel money or savings from the public to real estate. Real estate credit accounts for about one-fourth of all public and private debt in the United States. In times of tightening money conditions, disintermediation, or direct investment by the public, sometimes occurs and traditional financial intermediaries are bypassed.

Our mortgage markets are made up of primary and secondary lenders. Primary lenders originate loans with homebuyers, builders and developers, investors, and businesses. Secondary lenders buy loans. S&Ls, CBs, MSBs, and LICs make up the bulk of our primary lenders. LICs, pension funds, private mortgage companies, and governmental agencies make up our secondary lenders. The buying and selling of existing mortgages and of mortgage related securities is termed the seconday mortgage market. "Fannie Mae," "Ginnie Mae," and "Freddie Mac" are the main governmental agencies involved in secondary lending. Mortgage lender risks are (1) borrower risks, (2) property risks, and (3) portfolio risks. The main concerns in analyzing borrower risks are credit rating, assets, income, and motivation. Market value relative to loan amount and marketability are the main property risks of a lender. Portfolio risks include administration, investment, and diversification considerations. Four types of commitments used in mortgage markets are (1) firm, (2) conditional, (3) takeout, and (4) standby.

QUESTIONS FOR REVIEW AND DISCUSSION

1. Identify our national economic goals. Explain how monetary policy helps to achieve these goals. How is monetary policy carried out?
2. Define or explain intermediation and disintermediation. When are these two concepts important?
3. What is the relationship of monetary policy and conditions to real estate construction and sales activity? What does this mean to a sophisticated investor?
4. Is the mortgage market a money or capital market? Why? What happens in capital markets?
5. What is the secondary mortgage market?
6. Identify and explain the three major classes of lender risk.
7. What is a primary lender? What financial institutions are most likely to be primary lenders?
8. What is a secondary lender? What institutions make up the bulk of secondary lenders?
9. Distinguish among conditional, takeout, and standby loan commitments.
10. Does real estate get its fair share of public savings? Explain how our various financial institutions affect the allocation of monies to real estate. What other considerations influence the portion of public savings channeled into real estate?
11. Real estate construction and sales activity are causes rather than effects of changing monetary conditions. Discuss.

CASE PROBLEMS

1. The Ace Saving and Loan Association's assets earn at the following rates of return, based upon when the loans were made or what function the assets serve:

- 20% earns at 8% rate
- 40% earns at 11% rate

- 30% earns at 13% rate
- 10% earns at 0% rate (operating cash, buildings, etc.)

What is Ace's weighted rate of return on its assets?

2. Ace pays the following rates for its monies:

Passbook	40% at 5%
Money certificates	50% at 11%
Owner's equity opportunity costs	10% at 15%

What is Ace's weighted cost of capital?

3. What spread does Ace realize between its earnings rate and its cost of capital? Is this rate acceptable?
4. What actions can Ace take to improve its chances of maintaining an acceptable spread?
5. What type of risks does Ace S&L incur when doing the following:
   a. Makes loans that require borrower to devote 30 percent of ASI to housing expenses?
   b. Restricts its loans to employees of the Uplift Fork Truck Manufacturing Corporation?
   c. Consistently lends at 90 percent LVR without requiring mortgage insurance?
   d. Concentrates its loans on residences in the west side of the city?

CHAPTER EIGHTEEN
PROPERTY PRODUCTIVITY ANALYSIS

We shape our dwellings, and afterwards our dwellings shape us.
WINSTON CHURCHILL

IMPORTANT TOPICS OR DECISION AREAS COVERED IN THIS CHAPTER

- Property productivity
- Site analysis
- Improvements analysis
- Locational analysis
- Measuring Productivity

Productivity means the ability of the property to provide a flow of services and benefits. Productivity is the net result of a property's site, improvement, legal and locational characteristics. Measuring productivity is the first step toward determining a property's market and investment value. The same information is used in either case, but the interpretation differs.

KEY CONCEPTS INTRODUCED IN THIS CHAPTER

Accessibility
Convenience of location
Costs of friction
Effective gross income
Exposure
Functional efficiency
Functional obsolescence
Functional utility
Income ratio
Linkage
Locational obsolescence
Net operating income
Operating ratio
Physical deterioration
Productivity
Reserves for replacements
Utility

PROPERTY PRODUCTIVITY

Real estate provides services or is productive in many ways. It provides services in the form of shelter for a homeowner and renter; of fertile land that enables a farmer to grow corn, wheat, and cattle; or of a well-located place of business, as for a jewelry store, a service station, or a warehouse. In all these cases, the real estate satisfies a need and, therefore, has utility and value.

Utility—The Basis of Value

The ability of a property to render services that are in demand means that the property has utility. *Utility* is the usefulness of a thing based on its ability to satisfy a need. Utility can also be considered the benefit that comes with owning or using a thing. Utility, whether it is obtained from diamonds, wine, gasoline, medical service, or shelter, commands dollars in the marketplace. Thus, to say that real estate has utility is to say that it has value.

To know how much value a property has requires a judgment of the quality, quantity, and duration of services that it can render. More detailed knowledge of the contributions of site, improvements, legal status, and location to productivity is required to make such a judgment. Even further, it is necessary to measure productivity and property value in dollar terms for most real estate decisions and transactions.

How Productivity Is Realized

Productivity of real estate is realized in three different ways:

1. *Ownership for self-use.* Property is acquired for self-use as a house is bought by a family for shelter. A store is built and occupied by a jeweler as a place of business. An insurance company acquires an office building to serve as a branch office. Ownership is desired to obtain greater security, to give greater flexibility, to avoid paying rent to someone else, or to obtain and control an advantageous location.
2. *Ownership for cash flow.* People frequently invest savings with an eye for a regular return on their money. Thus they acquire apartment houses, warehouses, office buildings, or shopping centers to rent out space. The return is generally stable and predictable and can be used to supplement occupational income and to reinvest for building an estate. Included here is owning to gain tax shelters for other income.
3. *Ownership for appreciation.* Raw land, vacant lots, and timberlands are often purchased because appreciation in value is anticipated. It is hoped that during the waiting period, the property will earn enough to cover carrying costs, although such will not necessarily happen. Thus, in some cases, additional monies might have to be advanced. The plan might call for the raw land to be subdivided at some future time.

Owners may hope to realize the benefits of property productivity in all three ways, and often do.

Sources of Productivity

Productivity results from a property's physical capability and its location. *Physical capability* refers to the type of services that the property can render and for how long the services can be rendered. Location refers to where the services are rendered relative to where they are in demand as well as the quality of services rendered.

The physical capability of a property depends entirely on its on-site characteristics. This means the site and the improvements on the site. Generally, the improvements determine how a property will be used, and therefore, they greatly influence its productivity. For example, an office building is constructed on a site. For all practical purposes, this precludes the property's use as a motel, a warehouse, or an apartment building. A new use is feasible only if it is so profitable that it can absorb the cost of conversion of the existing improvements to its needs.

How long improvements can render services—their durability—affects the quantity of services to be derived from a property. The size or extent of the improvements also directly affects the quantity of services to be rendered. That is, a 2,000-square-foot building does not compare with a 200,000-square-foot building in satisfying the needs of an insurance company as a home office.

How well a property renders services is termed its functional efficiency. *Functional efficiency* is the quality of service in a given use rendered by a property relative to the quality of services that could be provided by a new property designed for that use. Thus, an old gasoline service station converted into a drive-in restaurant is not likely to be as efficient as a new facility designed and built as a drive-in restaurant.

Location concerns the relation of the property to its surroundings; location is a combination of the two real estate characteristics, fixity and situs. Location has two dimensions. One is the relation in terms of movement of people or goods to and from other properties (e.g., students going to and from school, customers going to and from a supermarket). The second involves the environment around the property, in an aesthetic sense. A residence located near a school, a park, and a pleasant lake is preferred by most people over a residence located in a slum area that is subject to considerable air pollution from nearby factories. This second dimension of location is realized without moving from the site.

Location determines whether demand exists for the services that a property, at a fixed site, is capable of rendering. This is the principal reason that market and feasibility analysis studies are made before developing a property. Location also affects the costs of rendering services. A hotel in the desert may be physically capable of rendering services, but if no demand exists, productivity cannot exist. And if the demand is present, the costs of getting workers, foods, water and the like may be much higher than if the hotel were located near an urban community.

SITE ANALYSIS

Property analysis refers to the study of on-site characteristics of real estate as they relate to productivity. Road improvements and public utilities are necessary for the parcel to be productive and to have value and are, therefore, included as part of property analysis. Property analysis begins with the site. Legal issues, zoning, title restrictions, easements, and so on are a vital part of site analysis.

A complete listing of all factors affecting site productivity is probably impossible. Some factors are physical, some are legal, some are economic. The following categories of factors account for those considered most important. Physical factors in site analysis tend to be less important to property productivity if the property has been developed and is in use; they no longer determine the size and type of improvements to be added to the site. However, if the site is unimproved, physical factors are a primary determinant of the highest and best use to which a property might be developed.

Size and Shape

Size and shape are of prime importance to productivity, particularly in urban areas. Lots that are small or of odd or irregular shape are difficult to develop and can accommodate only a limited number of uses. As a consequence, their worth per unit of area is generally lower than is that for parcels of standard size and shape.

For example, a lot that is triangular in shape does not lend itself to the siting of a rectangular building. As a result, either land is wasted or a triangular building is erected with higher construction costs and inefficient interior space arrangements. Long narrow lots are not desirable either; a lot 10 feet by 600 feet would not be practical as a site for a single-family residence even though it contained 6,000 square feet, a typical size lot in many communities.

Generally, land value per unit of area declines as the size of parcels increases and the method of measuring area changes. In rural areas, land values are lower and size is stated in terms of acres or sections rather than square feet.

Sometimes a value increment, called plottage, or plottage value, can be realized by bringing two or more smaller parcels of land under one ownership. *Plottage value* means that the value of the several parcels, when combined, is greater than the sums of values of the parcels taken individually under separate owners. Plottage comes about because the larger unit of land can be used more intensively or with lower costs than would be possible with the smaller parcels treated independently. Thus, combining two triangular business lots could provide a site able to accommodate a rectangular building. The benefit, as against two triangular-shaped buildings, would be lower construction costs and more efficient space arrangements. Another example of plottage would be the combining of two single-family lots to make a larger site on which a four-unit apartment building might be built, when allowed by the zoning ordinance.

Topography and Geology

A site must be able physically to accommodate, at a reasonable cost, the use to which it is put. The topography and geology of the earth's crust determine the suitability of a site for support of buildings, or for cultivation, and may limit the uses to which a site can be put.

Topography, the contours and slopes of the surface, must generally not be unduly rough for business, industrial, or agricultural uses. Rough terrain increases the costs of putting in roads and streets, installing utilities, and landscaping, in addition to increasing building costs. Improved amenities—view and relative privacy—frequently result in builders of upper-income housing seeking hilly terrain even though the costs are greater.

Topography also has an important bearing on the drainage and susceptability to erosion of a parcel of land. This applies to adjoining land as well as to the subject site. The possibility of flooding is always an important item. Stagnant or polluted waters can be a ready source of mosquitos or disease and, therefore, a hazard to health.

Soil and subsoil conditions bear directly on the income-producing ability of farms. Fertile soils produce more and better crops and are more valuable. In urban areas, marshy conditions or subsurface rock usually mean much greater difficulty, and expense, in development. Soil fertility tends to be of less importance. In urban fringe areas not served by city sewer lines, the soils must be relatively permeable to adequately absorb septic tank effluent if healthy, relatively dense development is to occur.

Topography and geology must work together to produce desirable sites. The contours of the land affect water flow and drainage. Subsoil conditions also affect drainage. Fertile soil eases landscaping problems. In developing a site, test boring helps to foretell excavation and foundation needs. Rocks, gullies, quicksand, cliffs, or bog underlayment present special problems in this sense.

Street Improvements and Public Utilities

Access to the street and road system is essential for each privately owned parcel of land in a community. The system facilitates movement between and among all sites and thus serves them all. Without ready accessibility, transportation costs might become so great that most uses could not absorb them. Thus a farm on a good road, or an industrial plant on a railroad and an interstate highway tend to be prime property. The value of a farm or plant that is inaccessible except by foot is almost certain to be extremely low in comparison. And a completely inaccessible site, as in the snowbound Antartic or the jungles of Brazil, has no value for all practical purposes.

In a similar sense, other public utilities are important to most sites. Telephone, gas, and electrical services are needed for rapid communication and for power. Sewer and water mains are necessary if septic tanks and wells cannot be accommodated. In many areas storm water sewers must be installed to prevent periodic flooding.

The value of a site is likely to be reduced where these various services are not immediately available. That is, a site without water is worth less than is a site with water. That means that the value or price of a site is generally on an "as is" basis. The penalty should reflect the loss in benefits suffered because of the absence of the service. If improvements and services are in but not paid for, the value of the site is reduced by the amount of the unpaid costs or assessments.

Zoning and Other Legal Limitations on Use

The highest and best use of a site can be limited by zoning, deed restrictions, easements, leases, or liens. In the absence of limits or constraints on use, highest and best use is determined by supply and demand considerations only. Thus, if the zoning is consistent with the use in demand, the site is likely to be developed to its highest and best use. If zoning is for a less intense use than the use in demand, the zoning controls. Of course, if the zoning is for a more intense use than the use in demand, then demand should control. To develop to the intensity allowed by the zoning ordinances would be to go beyond the point of diminishing returns. In a similar sense, title restrictions or lease arrangements that are at odds with the use in demand may serve as limitations on the potential use and value of a site.

If several legal constraints apply, the most limiting takes precedence. Thus, a site may be suitable by demand for a high-rise apartment building, zoned for a two-story apartment building, and limited by deed restriction to development for a single-family residential site. The single-family use governs. If the deed restriction were removed, the zoning would control.

Thus, restrictive zoning, an easement, or an awkward lease can reduce the productivity and, therefore, the value of a site just as surely as can poor drainage, lack of access, or inconvenient size or shape. The cause is less tangible, but the effect is just as real.

Title Encumbrances

Lack of clear title or other title problems can also limit use and productivity. For example, three brothers may inherit a property as tenants in common. Unless all the brothers agree (preferably in writing) to the terms necessary for development, efforts by an investor to develop it would be fruitless. Another example of an encumbrance limiting use and productivity is a power-line easement across a site. Assume that the easement limits construction to 32 feet in height. Even though demand justifies a seven-story building, which would be allowed by zoning, the use would be limited to a three-story building.

IMPROVEMENTS ANALYSIS

Improvements involve the main structure plus miscellaneous items such as garages, utility buildings, and landscaping. Improvements must be compatible with the site and with one another for highest and best use to be realized.

Structural Analysis

Structures are the main on-site improvements for most real estate, generally making up more than half the cost or value of the total property. A primary purpose of structures is to provide shelter from the elements—wind, rain, sun, cold. Many modern buildings even provide year-round climate control for their inhabitants. Buildings also provide privacy. And they provide space for storage and for carrying on economic activities under controlled conditions.

Structures are increasingly designed to accommodate specific activities. Thus, a plant for the production of baby foods will differ greatly from a foundry. And an insurance office building will differ from a warehouse. An additional purpose of some structures is to project an image of prestige, as with a bank or luxury hotel.

The concern in structural analysis is to weigh the value generating characteristics of a building as they relate to its use and ability to provide services and benefits. In a more specific sense, the concern is with the amount of services provided, with how well the services will be rendered, and with how long the services will continue. Thus, the size of the structure must be considered along with its functional utility, its appearance, and its durability. Building equipment must also be given attention.

Loss of utility, *depreciation,* must be taken into account in structural analysis. Loss of utility comes about because of physical deterioration, functional obsolescence, or location obsolescence. Depreciation may be curable or incurable. *Curable depreciation* means that the cost to correct is less than the value added because of the correction. Incurable depreciation exists when the cost to correct exceeds the value added by correction.

Physical Capability and Durability

The size, efficiency, and physical soundness of a structure determines the quantity and duration of the services it renders. Other things being equal, a large structure will give more services than a small one.

The physical soundness of a building depends on the quality of materials and workmanship used in its construction. A properly constructed building can render services for decades without maintenance costs becoming excessive. Loss in ability to render services—diminished productivity—results from physical deterioration. A building suffers physical deterioration in three ways:

1. Wear and tear through use—a ball going through a window, trim getting nicked from being bumped, or a stair railing torn loose.
2. Faults due to poor initial construction as a cracked foundation or sagging superstructure or damage as a result of actions of war, fire, explosion, or neglect.

3. Deterioration due to aging and actions of the elements. Examples are the need for replacement of a roof or for repainting. Damage due to storms or extreme temperatures might also be included here.

Although the cause is physical, the effect of deterioration is economic. Physical deterioration is generally not considered to be a major cause of ending the useful life of a building. Buildings are more frequently demolished because they become functionally or locationally obsolete. They are usually removed to clear the site for a higher and better use (structure); hence, the saying, "More buildings are torn down than fall down."

Functional Utility

To function means to work or operate. To have utility means to have the ability to satisfy a need. Thus, to evaluate a structure's ability to provide a useful service is to analyze the amount of functional utility that it contains. This judgment must be made in relationship to the nature of intended employment of the structure. A dwelling unit is therefore tested against the needs and demand of family living and possibly for prestigious location. A warehouse is measured by the amount of storage it provides and the ease with which items can be put into or taken out of storage. A supermarket is tested against needs for storage, displays, checkout stations, and customer parking. The standard is a new property specifically designed for the intended use.

Functional efficiency, as mentioned, is a measure of how well a building (or property) is suited to its actual or intended use relative to a new building (or property) specifically designed for the use. A property that performs well relative to a new property designed for the use is said to have a high functional efficiency.

Any deficiency relative to the new property is functional obsolescence. *Functional obsolescence* is, therefore, the decreased ability of a property to provide the benefit or service relative to the new property designed for the use. Functional obsolescence results in diminished productivity because of higher costs of operation and maintenance, reduced ability to generate revenues, or lowered amenities. Functional obsolescence might also be regarded as the relative inability of improvements to perform the functions for which they are intended or used. Current market standards of acceptability provide the basis of this judgment. Functional obsolescence is inherent in a structure and, in turn, a major source of property depreciation.

Some examples seem appropriate here. A five-bedroom house with only one bath is an underimprovement and has diminished productivity. Outdated equipment such as electrical wiring or plumbing means diminished functioning relative to a new structure. An inadequate floor plan, as all traffic between bedrooms going through a living room, lessens the desirability of a residence.

New technology and methods of organization result in the continuing functional obsolescence of buildings. Elevators caused walk-up apartments and office buildings to be outdated. New and better household appliances sharply reduced the need for servant's quarters. The automobile, with its high demand for convenient parking spaces, gave rise to the shopping center and caused the decline of many downtown business districts. Motels replaced hotels for the same reason. Self-service supermarkets made old corner grocery stores obsolete. Modern, clear-span office buildings and factories continually replace older structures with their many load-bearing walls and inefficient layouts.

The relation of the structure to the site needs to be taken into account also. Many older shopping centers provide too little parking space relative to sales space and are, therefore, relatively obsolete when compared with newer centers. An industrial plant with too little parking space for employees is in the same category. A four-bedroom house on a small lot cannot have a yard large enough for the outdoor living demands of today; the house is too large for its site and is an overimprovement. Too small a structure is an underimprovement. In either case, some loss in value from the optimum occurs.

Functional utility is optimal when the site, structure, and equipment are combined in proper proportion with no distracting features. The building design should be suited to meet the requirements of typical users or purchasers in the price range and location.

Even building appearance is a consideration in functional utility. An older apartment house of forbidding appearance that deters tenants is functionally obsolete. Tastes change and architectural styles come and go. A property should meet reasonable standards of simplicity, harmony, and balance to minimize functional obsolescence due to appearance.

Miscellaneous Improvements

Other site improvements, besides the main structure, contribute to or detract from the productivity of a property. Examples include (1) walks and driveways; (2) accessory buildings such as garages; (3) landscaping, including lawn, trees, shrubbery, and gardens; (4) fences and terraces; and (5) retaining walls.

LOCATIONAL ANALYSIS

Location concerns relationships external to a property only and has two distinct dimensions. One, termed "convenience" or "accessibility," concerns the relative costs of getting to and from a parcel. The second, called "exposure," concerns the environment around the parcel. If these external factors are negative, thereby diminishing utility, the property is said to have *locational obsolescence.* Locational obsolescence is usually outside the control or remedy of an owner and is, therefore, almost always incurable.

Convenience

A social or economic activity takes place on a site as only one of many possible uses to which the parcel could be put. For example, a given site might be used for a residence, a professional office building, a gasoline service station, a dry-cleaning pickup station, or a tavern. What determines which use will win out in the competition among them?

If all possibilities are open, convenience or location is usually the dominant consideration in the competition among the alternative uses. *Convenience* or *accessibility* means that a property is easy to get to or that the relative costs in time and money of getting to it tend to be minimal.

Linkages. Social and economic activities are interdependent. Families in residence tend to be tied to schools, stores, churches, work centers, and friends in other dwelling units. Lawyers are typically in frequent contact with court proceedings and records, clients, abstracting and title companies, and financial insitutions. A drive-in restaurant attracts customers, takes orders for deliveries of food and drink, and is the daily workplace of its employees. Each of these relationships is termed a *linkage* or a relationship between two land use activities that generates movement of people or goods between them.

A child going to school is a linkage. So is a parent going to the office or a parent going to the store for ice cream. A car getting gas at a service station constitutes a linkage, as is wheat going from the farm to the flour mill. The movement of cars from a factory in Detroit to a distributor in Denver is a linkage. All involve movement of people or goods.

FIGURE 18–1
Linkages of a residential unit (outward orientation)

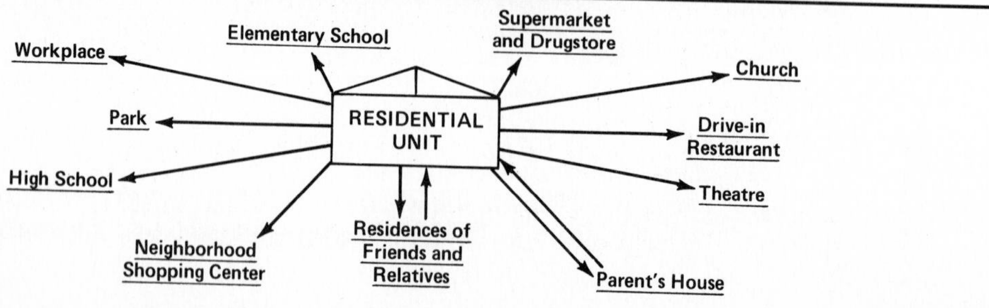

A residence is considered to have an "outward orientation"; the trip originates at the dwelling unit. See Figure 18–1. On the other hand, a shopping center, a factory, or an office complex has an "inward orientation"; most trips are initiated elsewhere and come to the activity. See Figure 18–2.

Costs of friction. Moving people or goods between linked activities involves four types of costs, termed *costs of friction.* Costs of friction are measured in time and energy as well as in dollars. Some costs of friction cannot be easily estimated in dollar terms.

1. *Transportation costs.* The out-of-pocket costs of movement are measured as fares on public transit or operating expenses for privately owned vehicles.
2. *Time costs of travel.* Time is required for a person or good to move from one site to another, from one economic activity to another. The speed of alternative transportation modes, traffic controls, congestion, and the efficiency of the street and road system all affect time costs of travel. The dollar cost of a trip can be calculated based on the time required for the trip and the value of the traveler's time. For goods, estimating the dollar cost is much more difficult. It is a function of lost business because of the goods not being on hand, of spoilage due to delays in transit, or of lost personnel or work time because of interrupted schedules.
3. *Terminal costs.* Many types of linkage involve expenses at one or both ends. Terminal costs include dollars spent for loading docks as well as for moving goods onto and from a truck or train. Storing an automobile during a downtown interview involves paying a parking fee, which is a terminal cost. Shopping centers absorb or internalize terminal costs to improve accessibility and reduce aggravation costs.
4. *Aggravation costs.* Traveler irritation and annoyances caused by delay, congestion, bumping and shoving, and heat or cold are costs of travel that, on a personal level, enter into the costs of friction. Aggravation costs are very difficult to measure in dollar terms.

In measuring the costs of friction connected with an economic activity, the most important (number of trips times cost per trip) are considered first. The costs are measured as disutilities (dollars, time, aggravations).

FIGURE 18–2
Shopping center linkages (inward orientation)

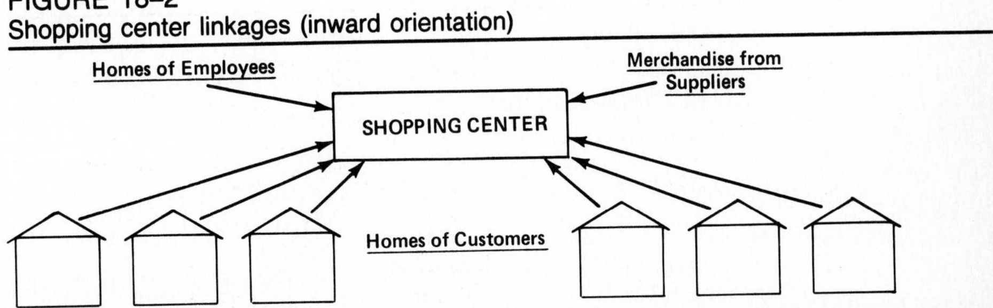

For each linkage the costs of friction equal the product of the costs of each trip times the frequency of the trips. Subjective judgment is sometimes required for this calculation. The site with the lowest total costs of friction provides, by definition, the greatest convenience or accessibility for a use.

Examples of convenience. The importance of convenience can best be shown with an example. Retail trade activity sharply shifted from central business districts (CBDs) to shopping centers following World War II. The prices charged in the shopping centers were not any lower and were possibly a little higher. The centers provided free parking and could be reached easily by auto. Congestion and delays were minimal compared with reaching the CBD. The out-of-pocket costs to reach the centers were in some cases greater than were those required to reach the downtown area, and it was not unusual for shoppers to circumvent CBD to reach a center on the other side of town. But overall, the centers were much more convenient for the population. And, in turn, the centers captured most of the dollar growth in retail sales in recent years while CBDs have held steady.

A more recent example of the interrelationship between location and productivity is the revival of Atlantic City. In 1976, Atlantic City's economy was faltering and its famed hotels were in severe disrepair. In late 1976, casino gambling was legalized for Atlantic City. Subsequently, the local economy surged and building remodeling and construction boomed. The nearness of the population centers of the East enables Atlantic City to tap the demand for gambling that formerly had been satisfied through illegal local bookies or by the casinos of Nevada.[1]

Exposure

A good view, pleasant breezes, or nearness to centers of prestige and fashion are said to give "favorable exposure" to a property and thereby make its ownership and use more desirable. On the other hand, the productivity of a property subject to loud or untimely noises, to foul-smelling odors and smoke, to unduly high property taxes, or to a distressing view is said to have "unfavorable exposure." Exposure affects the senses of people and is realized or experienced without moving from the site. Some considerations such as the social mix of a neighborhood may be considered favorable or unfavorable, depending on the user's perspective. *Exposure* is the environment around a property as experienced by a user of the property.

Favorable exposure. The primary benefits of exposure are aesthetic satisfactions and prestige, as tree-lined residential streets or a Wall Street

---

[1]See "Gaming Fever: Atlantic City Bets Casinos Will Revive Its Faltering Economy," *The Wall Street Journal,* June 22, 1977.

address for a financial house. High ground tends to possess these attributes to a greater extent than do low-lying areas. These factors coupled with the ability to outbid low-income families are the reasons upper-income areas tend to dominate the hills in most urban areas.

Social and business prestige are important determinants of location also. In Washington, D.C., Georgetown or Chevy Chase addresses carry high social acceptance. The same is true of the Gold Coast north of the Chicago Loop. Likewise, a Madison Avenue addresss in New York City is important for acceptance in the world of advertising. Every large metropolitan area has several premium areas. As might be expected, these are usually associated with desirable aesthetic qualities.

Unfavorable exposure. A social or economic activity prefers to avoid conditions that are distasteful, inharmonious, or objectionable. More than one slaughterhouse has been banned from a business district because it produced noxious odors. Slum areas are not inviting for high-income housing developments. Factories emitting excessive smoke cause residential areas downwind to become blighted. Polluted lakes and streams, trash dumps, open sewers, and sewerage-disposal plants are all undesirable neighbors for most land use activities. The result of unfavorable exposure is usually lower property values.

Locational Dynamics

The elements of location are constantly changing. Four types of change should be taken into account in any analysis to select a site for locating or relocating a specific social or economic activity. Failure to take account of them is likely to result in locational obsolescence.

Changes in linked activities. Tendencies and trends of linked activities to relocate must be noted and taken into account. For example, Sears, Roebuck developed a policy of relocating at the edge of downtown areas in the new shopping centers, following World War II. Montgomery Ward chose to be conservative and stay downtown. For over three decades, Sears far outstripped Ward in growth, although the two firms started out approximately even.

Changes in channels of movement. New modes of movement or new channels of movement mean new travel patterns. Thousands of motels, truck stops, and gasoline service stations were "done in" by the construction of the interstate highway system. If higher energy costs cause a shift toward greater use of mass transit, central or downtown locations for restaurants and motels would increase in demand. On the other hand, drive-in restaurants would probably be seriously hurt by the shift.

Changes in nonlinked establishments. The development, removal, or relocation of unrelated activities may have widespread effects on nonlinked land uses. The development of a civic center may break up a retail shopping pattern. A large new office building may touch off a whole series of moves by attorneys, engineers, realtors, and business services, leaving numerous vacancies in the process. Lower rents in the older buildings tend to allow a shift in the makeup of local office users to such types of business as bill collectors, insurance adjustors, printing agencies, and cheap photography studios. An "innocent" newsstand owner may find that the clientele has largely left, forcing either a move or a change in operational methods.

Changes in nature of an activity. The influence of changes in technology and in ways of conducting business on the functional utility of a property was discussed earlier. The replacement of the corner grocery by a supermarket because of a change in distribution methods was cited as an example of functional obsolescence because supermarkets can serve larger areas and must be located on or near major traffic arteries.

Protection from Adverse Land Uses

A social or economic activity may gain protection from encroachment of undesirable land uses in several ways:

1. A physical buffer against impending blight, as provided by freeways, a line of hills, or a river, may be taken into account in selecting a site or a location.
2. Legal action may be initiated to curtail or close down nuisance activities that create smog, dust, or unpleasant odors.
3. Requests may be made for enforcment of public and private land use controls. Or a site may be selected because of the protective planning, zoning, or deed restrictions that go with it.

MEASURING PROPERTY PRODUCTIVITY

The gross annual income for which a property can be rented serves as an initial index or measure of its productivity as judged by the market. This information is the point of beginning in valuing an income property. The income, and expenses, must be projected into the future to ascertain the total flow of benefits to be expected by an owner-investor. The forecast may be only a best estimate; yet it does provide a basis for judgment and decision making. With computers and techniques such as discounted cash flow analysis, the forecast can easily be made on an annual basis and could be made on a monthly basis if necessary.

The productivity of a nonincome-producing property, as a one-family house or vacant lot, is measured by the price for which it sells or would probably sell. The theory is simple; the greater the sale price or value, the greater is the productivity of the residence. In evaluating a residence that has not yet sold, an analyst or homebuyer may have to make individual and subjective judgments of the utility possessed by the residence relative to other residences that have sold or that are offered for sale.

Income Property Productivity

Property managers, investors, and others who work with income properties use a pro forma annual operating statement to measure property productivity. The statement shows both gross and net operating income, plus operating expenses. *Net operating income* (NOI) equals the amount left over after operating costs, necessary to maintain the property's earning capability, have been deducted from the gross income.

Realistic estimates of income and expense must be used in preparing an operating statement. That is, the statement should reflect actual market behavior because it is the source of useful and important accounting information for analyzing the property as an investment. The annual operating statement of Douglas Manor Apartments is representative, shown in Figure 18–3. Figure 18–1 provides the starting point for a series of income and expenses projections, termed cash flow analyses, taken up in detail in Chapter 21.

Gross income. The total rents a property should earn in a year constitute its gross scheduled income. The use of "should" here is important. If the

FIGURE 18–3
Pro-forma annual operating statement, Douglas Manor Apartments

GROSS SCHEDULED INCOME, GI			$108,000
Less vacancy & credit losses @ 4%			$4,320
EFFECTIVE GROSS INCOME, EGI			$103,680
Less total operating expenses:			
Fixed			
Property taxes	$20,908		
Hazard insurance	$1,460		
Licenses & permits	$250		
		$22,618	
Variable			
Gas, water, & electricity	$2,035		
Supplies	$1,350		
Advertising	$385		
Payroll, including payroll taxes	$2,555		
Management, as percent of EGI @ 5%	$5,184		
Miscellaneous services	$1,160		
Property maintenance	$4,393		
		$17,062	
TOTAL OPERATING EXPENSES			$39,680
NET OPERATING INCOME, NOI			$64,000

owner or manager leases the premises for less than their market rental, that gross income is not an accurate reflection of the property's productivity or earning capability. Too low an income might be reported because of a long-term lease or because of ignorance or incompetence on the part of the owner or manager. Market rent, also termed economic rent, rather than contract rent, should therefore be used in estimating gross income. *Market rent,* or the number of dollars for which a property could be rented if made available to the market at the present time, is determined by current supply and demand conditions.

Contract rent is the number of dollars to be paid in rent for a property based on a lease or rental agreement. Contract rent is likely to equal market rent at the time a lease is negotiated. Later, contract rent may exceed or fall below market rent owing to changing economic conditions that are not accommodated in the lease. Contract rent should be used in estimating gross income for a determination of investment value, at least for the duration of any long-term lease.

Properties frequently rent subunits of space on a month-to-month basis, as with an apartment house. However, office buildings, shopping centers, and even warehouses also are operated on this basis. By way of example, our sample property, Douglas Manor Apartments, contains 16 apartments—8 one-bedroom units and 8 two-bedroom units. The rents are $525 and $600 per month, respectively. Gross scheduled income would be calculated as follows:

		ONE-BEDROOM UNITS		TWO-BEDROOM UNITS
Monthly market rental per unit		$ 525		$ 600
Times number of months	×	12	×	12
Annual market rental per unit		$ 6,300		$ 7,200
Times number of units	×	8	×	8
Gross scheduled income from units		$50,400		$57,600

The total gross scheduled income equals $108,000 ($50,400 plus $57,600).

No income is earned if a subunit of space, such as an apartment, is not rented for a month or if it is rented but the tenant fails to pay. Therefore, gross scheduled income must be reduced by the amount of income not realized. The term for this deduction is *vacancy and collection losses.* In the sample operating statement, Douglas Manor Apartments is expected not to collect 4 percent of gross scheduled income because of vacancy and collection losses, based on experience in the area. A deduction of $4,320 is therefore made. The resulting figure, *effective gross income* (EGI), is the amount of money the manager or owner actually collects.

Operating expenses. *Operating expenses* are out-of-pocket costs necessary to provide services to tenants and to maintain the income stream. The costs fall into three general categories: fixed expenses, variable expenses, and reserves for replacements.

Property taxes and hazard insurance are the two main fixed costs. *Fixed costs* are outlays that remain at the same level, regardless of the intensity of use of the property. Property taxes, for example, are levied on an annual basis and do not increase if occupancy climbs to 100 percent, nor do they decrease if occupancy drops to 65 percent.

Variable expenses, on the other hand, tend to fluctuate with the level of occupancy. More gas, water, electricity, and supplies are used with full occupancy than with 75 percent occupancy. Management is usually calculated as a percentage of EGI rather than of gross income to give the manager a stronger incentive to keep the property as fully rented as possible. Calculation in this way also causes the management fee to fluctuate with the level of occupancy. Repairs and miscellaneous services also tend to rise and fall with the number of tenants.

Building parts and many items of equipment have lives longer than one year but much shorter than the expected life of the building. Stoves, refrigerators, elevators, roofs, boilers, washers, dryers, carpeting, and air conditioning are examples. Yet these items must be replaced, as periodic out-of-pocket expenses. Accountants used to believe that the annual deduction for replacement of equipment and building parts should be placed in a special account called *reserves for replacements.* But, until the expense is incurred, it is not recognized by the IRS. Deductions may still made on the operating statement under this heading however. If deducted, the amounts must be added back in for calculating taxes. Also, the monies are not necessarily placed in a special account. Straight-line depreciation, dividing the cost of an item by its expected useful life, is the usual method used in calculating this deduction. Thus a roof with an expected life of 15 years and a cost of $9,600 is expensed at $640 per year, $9,600/15 years. Reserves for replacements are taken account of as out-of-pocket property maintenance expenses in Figure 18–3.

Net operating income. The amount left over after total operating expenses have been deducted is called net operating income. NOI is the bottom-line amount a property can earn in a year in competition with other properties that offer similar services. Average or typical management is assumed to avoid rewarding or penalizing the property for superior or inferior management. NOI directly reflects property productivity and, as such, is a basic input into income capitalization techniques to find value.

NOI is preferred to gross income as a measure of productivity because it is a standardized concept. Differences in costs of operation or leasing terms are taken into account in reaching NOI. Thus, NOI allows comparison of the subject property's productivity with that of other properties.

A prestige office building that generates high rents but that also has extremely high operating costs can be compared with a more modest office building on a long-term net lease.

Some items, often considered by an owner-investor in analyzing an income property, must not be included in the operating statement because NOI is supposed to indicate what a property can do on its own. Thus, financing costs, owner's income taxes, depreciation, and corporation taxes are excluded. These items, though important to an investor, have no effect on a property's ability to generate net revenue.

Mortgaging does not affect a property's income-producing capability, one way or the other. Likewise, the owner's income taxes on money earned from the property reflect the owner's tax situation and not the productivity of the property. The same is true if the property is held under corporate ownership; so corporate taxes should not be deducted as an operating expense. Other items to be excluded are outlays for capital improvements, business expenses of the owner in owner-occupied, income-producing properties, and personal property taxes of the owner.

Neither is building depreciation deducted as an operating expense because it is really a recovery of capital. Depreciation does not affect productivity and is not necessary to produce gross income. Thus, its function as an expense differs from that of other operating expenses. Operating expenses are required to maintain the property's flow of services. Depreciation is simply a loss in value that may be taken as an income tax deduction. This loss in value is taken into account in the capitalization process.

Forecasting future productivity. Future expected benefits are the basis of investing. An investor's central task then is to forecast and evaluate expected future benefits before investing. The forecast is a prime input into determining the value of the property for investment purposes. The forecast depends on the property's physical and functional capability and its location. The forecast also depends on local market conditions. These topics have already been discussed.

The forecast cannot be precise because the world is an uncertain place. But the current revenues, expenses, and NOI provide a takeoff point of some certainty. Unless secured by a lease with a strong tenant, a forecast is only a secular trend or tendency. Short-term influences will cause fluctuations above and below a projected trend. One can assume, however, that over time, the up and down movements will offset each other, and the average will reflect the underlying long-term forces. Certain ratios concerning current income and expenses are helpful as background in making the necessary forecast.

Productivity ratios. Standardized accounting terms and formats are used in classifying and reporting property income and expense information, making possible the calculation of useful operating ratios. Considerable experience and caution are needed in interpreting the ratios. Even so, the potential usefulness of ratios is so great that it appears almost certain that this area of real estate analysis will be expanded.

Thus far, the best operating data have been reported for apartment buildings, shopping centers, and hotels and motels. The Institute of Real Estate Management annually publishes *Apartment House Income—Expense Experience.* The Urban Land Institute publishes *Dollars and Cents of Shopping Centers* every third year. And the Building Owner's and Manager's Association and specialized accounting firms periodically publish operating information on hotels and motels, office buildings, and other specialized property types.

Two of the more useful ratios for evaluating property productivity are the income ratio and the operating ratio. The *income ratio* is the proportion of gross scheduled income represented by net operating income.

$$\text{Income ratio} = \frac{\text{Net operating income}}{\text{Gross scheduled income}}$$

For Douglas Manor Aparments, the income ratio equals 59.3 percent.

$$\text{Income ratio} = \frac{\$64{,}000}{\$108{,}000} = 0.593 = 59.3\%$$

The higher the income ratio, the greater the productivity of the property. This might be the result of good management—keeping the property fully rented while keeping control of operating expense. It might also be the result of high-quality construction that minimizes costs of repairs and maintenance. An alternative ratio emphasizing controls of expenses thus becomes necessary for cost-control purposes.

An operating ratio reflects operating expenses as a percentage of gross scheduled income:

$$\text{Operating ratio} = \frac{\text{Total operating expenses}}{\text{Gross scheduled income}}$$

$$= \frac{\$39{,}680}{\$108{,}000} = 0.367 = 36.7\%$$

The use of the operating ratio might be as follows. New apartment buildings typically have an operating ratio between 35 and 40 percent. As the building ages, costs of repairs and maintenance go up. And the ratio gradually increases toward 50 percent and eventually 60 percent. The ratio tells the experienced investor or lender if an operating statement is realistic. A ratio of 32 percent for a new apartment building would indicate that perhaps not all expenses were reported. Or that expenses might have been understated. Operating ratios vary from property type to property type, that is, from apartment house to office building to hotel, and so on.

Nonincome-Producing Property

The productivity of properties like single-family homes and churches cannot easily be measured in dollars of annual income. Productivity is realized through self-use. Very few of these property types are rented out. Vacant lots, timberlands, and owner-occupied stores and factories are other property types for which productivity measurement is difficult.

Productivity may be estimated by comparison, even though they are owner-occupied. That is, the rent-producing capability of owner-occupied stores, warehouses, offices, and factories can be estimated by comparison with similar-type properties that are rented out for income. For example, if a similar office building rents out for $16 per square foot per year, it is likely that the subject office building would rent out for $16 per square foot per year. Based on this information and typical productivity ratios for the property type, the net operating income potential of the subject property can be estimated.

Productivity for property types that are not usually rented out but sell frequently can be based on comparative sale prices. Single-family residences are the classic example of this situation.

A sale price is the capitalized expression of property productivity; the price indicates the value for family living purposes placed on the services to be rendered by a one-family house by the buyer. In turn, the productivity of a 6-year-old, four-bedroom, three-bath house can be estimated by comparison with prices recently paid in the market for similar houses. The value estimate represents the utility of the property to the typical person in the market for that type of property. Vacant lots may also be judged for productivity in this way.

SUMMARY

Productivity is the ability of a property to render a flow of services and benefits. Productivity analysis is the first step toward ascertaining a property's value.

The benefits of productivity are realized through ownership for self-use, for cash flow, or for value appreciation. Productivity results from a property's physical capability to render service and from a property's location.

Property analysis means study of on-site characteristics of real estate, with primary attention given the site and the structure. Major categories of study in site analyses are (1) size and shape, (2) topography and geology, (3) street improvements and public services, (4) zoning and other legal limitations on use, and (5) title encumbrances. Major categories of study in structural analysis are (1) physical capability and durability and (2) functional utility. The functional efficiency of a property is the quality of services rendered in a given use relative to the quality of services rendered by a new property designed for that use.

Locational analysis concerns convenience and exposure of a property or off-site characteristics. Convenience is measured in terms of the costs of movement involved in carrying on a social or economic activity on a site; the lower the costs, the greater the convenience. Costs of movement are (1) transportation costs, (2) time costs of travel, (3) terminal costs, and (4) aggravation costs. Exposure is the relation of the property to its environment. Favorable exposure means that the environment is pleasing or prestigious.

The amount of net operating income earned or the amount for which the property could be sold provides an index of a property's productivity. Net operating income equals gross scheduled income less vacancy and credit losses and less operating expenses. The income ratio (net operating income divided by gross scheduled income) and the operating ratio (operating expenses divided by gross scheduled income) are highly useful in analyzing and comparing the relative productivities of income properties.

QUESTIONS FOR DISCUSSION AND REVIEW

1. What is property productivity? What is it based on? How is it realized? Explain.

2. Explain briefly how each of the following site characteristics relates to property productivity.
   a. Size and shape
   b. Topography and geology
   c. Street improvements and public utilities
   d. Zoning
   e. Title encumbrances

3. Define the following concepts briefly, and then explain how each relates to the productivity of structures. Give examples where possible.
   a. Physical capability, physical deterioration
   b. Functional efficiency, functional obsolescence
   c. Locational convenience, locational obsolescence

4. Four "costs of friction" are incurred in moving people or goods between linked activities. Identify and briefly explain the nature of each.

5. What does "exposure" mean to a property in a locational sense? Give at least one example of positive and negative exposure.

6. How is productivity measured for an income property? For a detached one-family residence?

7. Write up an outline showing the major sections of an annual operating statement for an income property. State briefly the nature of the inputs or items in each section.

8. Is all property productive? Does all property have value? Discuss.

9. Is a property's productivity related to economic and social activity on a regional basis? On a local basis? Discuss.

10. Is there a relationship between the energy crunch and the location of real estate? Explain or discuss.

CASE PROBLEMS

1. Classify the following items of depreciation as physical, functional, or locational. Also indicate whether the deficiency is likely to be curable or incurable.
   a. Small rooms
   b. Paint blistered and cracked
   c. Rotting wall studs
   d. Cracked foundation
   e. Rough flooring
   f. One-car garage in two-car garage neighborhood
   g. Ultrahigh ceilings
   h. Commercial development intruding into a residential neighborhood
   i. Leaky roof
   j. Industrial odors in residential neighborhood
2. Organize the following items into a pro forma annual operating statement. All quantities are on an annual basis (NOI = $15,060).

Gross income	$24,000	Mortgage debt service	$6,400
Miscellaneous	200	Property maintenance expense	1,000
Property taxes	2,000	Owner's income taxes	4,600
Supplies	800	Salaries, maintenance and operations	2,000
Management 5% of effective gross income		Hazard insurance	600
Vacancy and credit losses, 5% of gross income			

3. After considerable research, you obtain the following information about a property you are analyzing. All quantities are on an annual basis. Develop a pro forma annual operating statement based on this information.

Mortgage debt service	$72,000	Vacancy and credit losses as % of gross income	5%
Owner's income taxes	12,800	Management, as % of effective gross income	5%
Maintenance and operating salaries	4,800	Property taxes	$10,200
Property maintenance expense	4,000	Supplies	1,800
Hazard insurance	1,200	Utilities	3,000
Security deposits	8,000	Miscellaneous	600
Gross scheduled income	96,000		

4. A pro forma annual operating statement for Hawaii Towers appears as follows.

Gross scheduled income	\$380,000
− Vacancy and credit losses @ 5%	19,000
= Effective gross income	\$361,000
− Total operating expenses	131,000
= Net operating income	\$230,000

a. Calculate the income ratio for Hawaii Towers.
b. Calculate the operating ratio.

CHAPTER NINETEEN
APPRAISING FOR MARKET VALUE

Nothing can have value without being an objective of utility.
If it is useless, the labor contained in it is useless, cannot be reckoned as labor, and cannot therefore create value.
KARL MARX, *Capital*

IMPORTANT TOPICS OR DECISION AREAS COVERED IN THIS CHAPTER

- The Need for Appraisals
- Value
- Principles of Appraising
- The Appraisal Process
- Market or Direct Sales Comparison Approach
- Income Capitalization Approach
- Cost Approach
- Reconciliation

An *appraisal* is an estimate or opinion of value of a property, or some interest therein, rendered by an impartial person skilled in the analysis and valuation of real estate. The *appraisal process*, an orderly, well-conceived set of procedures, is used in making the value estimate. An appraisal is usually followed by an appraisal report setting forth the value estimate along with any reservations or limiting conditions attached to it. Of course, a specific description of the property being evaluated and the date of the value estimate must also be included. Supporting data and analysis are also usually included as documentation of the value estimate.

Market value is the focal point of rational real estate decision making. Whether a person is buying, selling, investing, developing, lending, exchanging, renting, assessing, or acquiring property for public use, market value must be known for the decision and action to be sound. As a consequence, anyone engaging in these activities needs a working knowledge of appraising principles and procedures.

Obviously, all theoretical and practical knowledge necessary to become a professional appraiser cannot be condensed into one chapter in an introductory real estate text. The objective of this chapter, therefore, is limited to defining terms and to providing a basic explanation of appraising for market value.

KEY CONCEPTS INTRODUCED IN THIS CHAPTER

Appraisal
Appraisal process
Capitalization
Cost approach to value
Cost of replacement
Cost of reproduction
Depreciation
Direct income capitalization
Direct sales comparison approach to value
Gross income multiplier
Income approach to value
Market price
Market rent
Market value
Objective value
Overall capitalization rate
Principles of:
  Change
  Contribution
  Highest and best use
  Substitution
Reconciliation
Subject property
Subjective value
Value in exchange
Value in use.

THE NEED FOR APPRAISALS

Everyone uses real estate and must pay for its use in one way or another, usually by purchase or rental. Transactions or situations in which a decision must be made, an action taken, or a policy established usually turn on a value estimate of the property of concern, the *subject property;* hence the need for appraisals and appraisers.

Almost all decisions or actions fit into one of the following classifications:

1. Transferring property ownership or possession
2. Financing a property interest
3. Taxing a property interest
4. Compensating for loss of a property interest
5. Making up a property utilization program

The value most usually sought in an appraisal is market value. Simply stated, *market value* is the most probable selling price of a real estate interest.

Transferring Ownership or Possession

Market value serves as a benchmark to both the owner and the prospective buyer in negotiating the sale or purchase of real estate. For example, assume that the market value or most likely selling price of an apartment building is $600,000. A prudent buyer would be very likely to open negotiations at a lower level, say, $550,000, and would not want to pay very much in excess of $600,000, as negotiations progressed. The owner, as a prospective seller, certainly would not want to begin by offering to sell or list the property at less than $600,000. Most likely, the initial asking price would tend toward $650,000 or $700,000. Further, the owner would not be likely to accept less than $600,000 unless the pressure to sell were very great. Without market value, both would find the negotiations much more uncertain.

Market value is also important in negotiating the rent to be paid for a property; rent is usually a percentage of market value. In fact, some leases call for property reappraisal every 5 or 10 years as the basis for periodic adjustments in the rent. Market value estimates are also needed to establish a fair basis for tax-deferred exchanges of real property or a minimum bid in an auction sale.

Market value estimates are helpful in group negotiations as well as in settling an estate in which a number of parcels are involved and in which several people are designated as heirs on a pro rata basis. In this situation, it is often preferable to assign properties to individual heirs rather than to sell the properties and distribute the proceeds to the heirs.

If there were no objective value estimates, some of the heirs might believe that they received less than their fair share of the estate and considerable bitterness and litigation could result. In a similar vein, an objective value estimate is needed as a basis for the reorgnization or the merging of interest in which multiple properties or owners are involved. This need even extends to transactions such as corporate mergers, the issuance of new or additional stock by a corporation or trust, or corporate bankruptcy.

Financing a Property Interest

Large amounts of money are involved in almost all real estate loans. And the lender's first line of defense, or security, is the property. Therefore, the lender wants assurance that the most probable selling price of the property pledged as security is greater than the amount of the loan.

To illustrate the problem, suppose that a 90 percent loan were requested to finance the purchase of the apartment building mentioned earlier, which sold at the owner's initial asking price of $700,000. A $630,000 loan is implied, which is $30,000 more than the $600,000 market value and $90,000 more than the $540,000, or 90 percent of market value. If the $630,000 loan were made, the lender would have little or no cushion if the foreclosure became necessary within a few years. The risk to the lender would be much greater than implied by the 90 percent loan-to-purchase price ratio.

Extending this line of reasoning, the prospective purchaser of mortgage bonds also wants assurance that adequate security or protection is provided by the property. Of course, insurers of mortgage loans, for example, the Federal Housing Administration, also want assurance that the security exceeds the insured principal by an established percentage.

Taxing Property Interests

In most taxing jurisdictions, assessed value is some portion of market value. Assume that assessed value is supposed to equal 60 percent of market value. And assume that the apartment building with an actual market value of $600,000 is overappraised at $700,000. The $100,000 difference converts into a $60,000 overassessment. With a 3 percent tax levy, the extra annual taxes on the building would amount to $1,800. An error in estimating market value thus can directly affect the amount of property taxes levied against a property.

The amount of annual depreciation allowance that may be taken in an income tax return depends on an appraisal to allocate the costs of assets, or basis, between land and depreciable improvements. The allocation is frequently made in direct relation to the distribution of assessed value between the land and depreciable improvements. An investor may disagree with the assessor's distribution, in which case, an appraiser may

be hired to make the determination. The market value of gifts and inheritance (of which a part may be real property) must also be determined to ascertain the amount of any taxes payable to federal and state governments.

Compensation for Property Loss or Damage

Owners take out insurance to protect against risk of property loss or damage due to natural disasters as fire, wind, flood, lightning, and earthquake. In some cases, this insurance is for the cost of replacement or reproduction of the property rather than for market value. But if the loss is realized, the insurance adjustment or settlement depends on an appraisal.

Likewise, eminent domain properties constitute a continuing and major need for appraisals. If an entire property is condemned, the owner is entitled to just compensation equal to at least the market value of the property. If only part of the property is taken, the owner is usually entitled to compensation equal to the value of the part taken plus the amount of any damages to the remainder. Frequently, the taking authority and owner will each have two or three appraisals made as a basis for determining just compensation. If a settlement cannot be negotiated, the appraisers may have to testify at a court hearing.

Property Utilization Program

Determining highest and best use involves investigating all alternative ways of using land or realty to find the one or several ways that give the greatest present value to the property. For all practical purposes, each investigation constitutes a market value appraisal. This analysis is closely akin to market and feasibility analysis and should precede any decision or action concerning development or redevelopment of realty.

VALUE

Five attributes must be present for real estate to realize its full value potential. The first is utility, or the ability to satisfy human needs and desires, as by providing shelter, privacy, or income. Effective demand must be present for the services or amenities that the property produces; effective demand is need or desire for the service or amenity backed up by purchasing power or financial capability. The third is relative scarcity; the supply must be limited relative to demand. The fourth is transferability, meaning that the rights of ownership can be conveyed from one person to another with relative ease. Finally, the realty must be located in an environment of law and order so that, when people invest in real property, they will not sense a risk of loss because of legal or political uncertainty.

Market Value

The two most widely accepted meanings of value in real estate are (1) the amount in dollars, goods, or services for which a property may be exchanged and (2) the present worth of future rights to the income or amenities generated by a property. The value under these definitions varies, depending upon the person involved. In this sense, value is subjective or dependent on the nature or mental attitude of the person making the exchange or judgment.

If the viewpoint of the *typical person* exchanging or evaluating a property is taken, the resulting value estimate is the most probable selling price of the property, as given earlier. Market value can usually be estimated in an *objective manner* by methods shown later in this chapter. In applying the methods the following assumptions must be made about the market and the property.[1]

1. Real estate buyers and sellers act with reasonable, but not perfect, knowledge. This is realistic because almost all market participants gather information about conditions before they act.
2. Buyers and sellers act competitively and rationally in their own best interests to maximize their income or satisfactions.
3. Buyers and sellers act independently of each other, that is, without collusion, fraud, or misrepresentation. If this were not the case, some transaction prices might be severely distorted.
4. Buyers and sellers are typically motivated; that is, they act without undue pressure. This means that properties placed on the market turn over or sell within a reasonable period. Thus a forced sale or a sale occurring after the property has been exposed to the market for an extremely long time would not be considered typical.
5. Payment is made in cash in a manner consistent with the standards of the market; that is, the buyer uses financing terms generally available in the local market.

Market Value versus Market Price

Market value does not necessarily equal market price. In fact, market value for a property may be greater than, equal to, or less than its sale price in an actual market transaction. *Market price* is the amount negotiated between a buyer and a seller, who were not necessarily well informed, free from pressure, or acting independently. Market price is an accomplished fact. Market value, on the other hand, is an estimated price made by an objective, experience, knowledgeable appraiser. The estimate is made after looking at and studying a number of actual transactions and other market data. Market value is more akin to the most likely sale price for the property as of a given date.

---

[1]See market value in *Real Estate Appraisal Terminology*, rev. ed., compiled and edited by Dr. Byrl N. Boyce under the joint sponsorship of the American Institute of Real Estate Appraisers and the Society of Real Estate Appraisers (Cambridge, Mass.: Ballinger, 1981).

Market Value versus Cost of Production

Market value may also be greater than, equal to, or less than the cost of a property. As used here, cost means the capital outlay (including overhead and financing expenses) for land, labor, materials, supervision, and profit necessary to bring a useful property into existence. In appraisal analysis, cost means the cost of production. It does not mean the cost of acquisition, that is, price.

A rational owner, subdivider, or builder creates lots or constructs new buildings only if the expected sale price (market value) equals or exceeds the cost of production. To subdivide or develop property or to remodel property otherwise would mean proceeding even though a loss were expected. Developing a major property without adequate market analysis also ignores the simple truth that cost does not necessarily mean value.

Value in Use versus Value in Exchange

Each property has a subjective value to anyone considering its ownership and use. *Value in use* is the worth of a property to a specific user, based on the utility of the property to the user. The utility may be based on expected amenities, income, or value enhancement. Value in use depends on the specific judgments, standards, or demands of the user. Thus, value in use is synonymous with *subjective value.* Value in use does not depend on identifiable market information.

Value in exchange, on the other hand, is based on the explicit actions of buyers and sellers. *Value in exchange* is the amount of money or purchasing power (in goods and services) for which the property most probably might be traded. Value in exchange is, therefore, synonymous with objective value or market value in that it is based on observed or explicit actions of market participants.

A rational owner retains a property as long as value in use exceeds value in exchange. With time, however, depreciation is used up as a tax shelter, community change makes a location obsolete, or an owner decides to retire to the Sun Belt. Thus, for a variety or reasons, value in use drops down to and eventually below value in exchange or market value. At this point, disposition becomes advantageous and market activity results. Note that, in a special sense, value in exchange becomes value in use when disposition becomes desirable.

PRINCIPLES OF APPRAISING

Over the years professional real estate appraisers have developed several principles of real estate valuation. Although only implied, the principles treat real property interests as a commodity and are, therefore, applied economic theory. The principles are the following:

1. *Supply and demand.* The market value of real estate is determined by the interaction of supply and demand as of the date of the appraisal.
2. *Change.* The forces of supply and demand are dynamic and are constantly creating a new real estate environment, thereby leading to price and value fluctuations.
3. *Competition.* Prices are kept in line, and market values are established through continuous rivalry and interaction of buyers, sellers, developers, and other market participants.
4. *Substitution.* A rational buyer will pay no more for a property than the cost of acquiring an equally desirable alternative property.
5. *Variable proportions.* Real estate reaches its point of maximum productivity, or highest and best use, when the factors of production (usually considered to be land, labor, capital, and management) are in balance with one another. (This is also termed the principle of balance or the principle of increasing and decreasing returns.)
6. *Contribution or marginal productivity.* The value of any factor of production, or component of a property, depends on how much its presence adds to the overall value of the property.
7. *Highest and best use.* For market valuation purposes, real estate should be appraised at its highest and best use so that maximum value is recognized.
8. *Conformity.* A property reaches its maximum value when it is located in an environment of physical, economic, and social homogeneity or of compatible and harmonious land uses.
9. *Anticipation.* Market value equals the present worth of future income or amenities generated by a property, as viewed by typical buyers and sellers.

The first four principles involve the real estate market. The next three apply primarily to the subject property itself. The eighth principle concerns the neighborhood or area around the property. The ninth principle looks at the property's productivity from the viewpoint of a typical buyer or seller.

The principles of substitution, change, contribution, and highest and best use are generally considered most important and, therefore, merit further explanation.

Substitution

According to the *principle of substitution,* "A rational buyer will pay no more for a property than the cost of acquiring an equally desirable alternative property." An equally desirable alternative means one of equal utility or productivity, with time costs or delays taken into account. In appraising, a buyer is presumed to have the following three alternatives:

1. Buying an existing property with utility equal to the subject property. This is the basis of the market or direct sales comparison approach to estimating market value.
2. Buying a site and adding improvements to produce a property with utility equal to the subject property. This is the basis of the cost approach to estimating market value.
3. Buying a property that produces an income stream of the same size and with the same risk as that produced by the subject property. This is the basis of the income approach to estimating market value.

Change

The *principle of change* states that "the forces of supply and demand are dynamic, thereby leading to price and value fluctuation." It is this principle that necessitates that a specific date be attached to each value estimate. That is, physical, social, political, and economic conditions are in a continuing state of transition: buildings suffer wear and tear, people move, laws change, and industries expand and contract. The appraiser's task is to recognize cause and effect in these forces and to make a "snapshot" estimate of their effect on the subject property.

Contribution or Marginal Productivity

The *principle of contribution* says that "the value of any factor of production, or component of a property, depends on how much its presence adds to the overall value of the property." Alternatively, the value of the factor or component can be measured by how much its absence detracts from the overall value. For example, the absence of a garage or a second bath reduces the value of a residence by some incremental amount. This principle serves as the basis for making adjustments between properties in the direct sales comparison approach in value. It also provides the basis for estimating depreciation due to property deficiencies in the cost approach.

Highest and Best Use

Finally, the *principle of highest and best use* says that "real estate should be appraised at its highest and best use for market valuation purposes." There is a simple logic behind this principle, namely, that a prudent owner will, in self-interest, put a property to that use that yields the greatest value or return. To do otherwise would not be rational. And it is this value that is critical to any decision to be made about the property.

In applying this principle, it must be recognized that the value of an improved property in its highest and best use may not be as great as that of the site, if valued as vacant and available for an alternative highest and best use. This would be the case, for example, if a house were on a commercial site and not suited to its highest and best use. The value of the site exceeding the value of the total improved property would mean that the improvements made no contribution to value and should be removed. On the other hand, as long as the property value was greater, it would pay the owner to continue the use dictated by the improvements.

THE APPRAISAL PROCESS

In a specific assignment, several elements or steps that make up what professional appraisers call the "appraisal process" or "framework" must be developed. These elements, when taken up in the order presented, provide for systematic analysis of the facts that bear upon and determine the market value of a specific parcel. See Figure 19–1.

Defining the Problem

The appraisal assignment must be agreed upon jointly by the appraiser and by the owner or the owner's agent to ensure that the analysis and conclusions serve the decision or action to be made. In defining the problem, agreement must be reached on the following:

1. Identify, in a very specific manner, the subject property, preferably by address and by legal description.
2. Identify the specific legal rights to be valued: fee simple, leased fee, leasehold, or other.
3. Specify the purpose of the appraisal: sale, financing, insurance, condemnation, or other.
4. Specify the date for which the value estimate is desired.
5. Specify or define the value to be estimated: market value, assessed value, condemnation damages, or other. Market value is the objective in most fee appraisal assignments.

Making a Survey and Plan

Next, the scope, character, and amount of work involved must be determined. In valuing a one-family residence, this is quite simple and routine. But a check with data sources, such as brokers, lenders, title companies, and other appraisers, is often necessary when a major property or complex legal rights are involved. The highest and best use alternatives of the property must also be considered. Based on obtainable information, the appraiser must also decide which alternative approaches to value can be utilized, the effort likely to be involved, and the fee. This determination constitutes the appraisal plan. If not already agreed upon, the fee is usually cleared with the employer at this time.

FIGURE 19–1
Elements or steps in market value estimating (also termed the appraisal process or the appraisal framework)

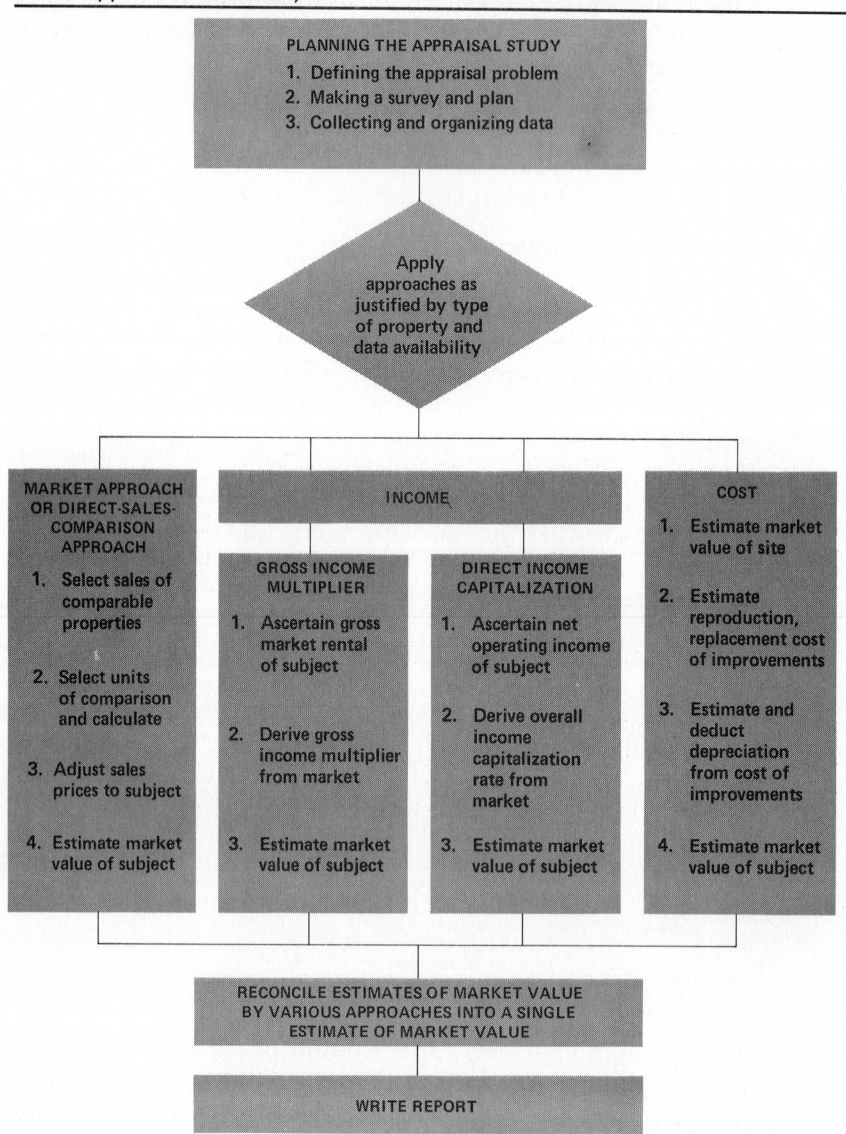
PLANNING THE APPRAISAL STUDY
1. Defining the appraisal problem
2. Making a survey and plan
3. Collecting and organizing data
Apply approaches as justified by type of property and data availability
MARKET APPROACH OR DIRECT-SALES-COMPARISON APPROACH
1. Select sales of comparable properties
2. Select units of comparison and calculate
3. Adjust sales prices to subject
4. Estimate market value of subject
INCOME
GROSS INCOME MULTIPLIER
1. Ascertain gross market rental of subject
2. Derive gross income multiplier from market
3. Estimate market value of subject
DIRECT INCOME CAPITALIZATION
1. Ascertain net operating income of subject
2. Derive overall income capitalization rate from market
3. Estimate market value of subject
COST
1. Estimate market value of site
2. Estimate reproduction, replacement cost of improvements
3. Estimate and deduct depreciation from cost of improvements
4. Estimate market value of subject
RECONCILE ESTIMATES OF MARKET VALUE BY VARIOUS APPROACHES INTO A SINGLE ESTIMATE OF MARKET VALUE
WRITE REPORT

Collecting and Organizing Data

The appraisal generally begins with an on-site inspection of the subject property, followed by a written description of it. Included here would be a pro forma annual operating statement, if an income property is under study. With these data on the subject property in hand, the appraiser is in a much better position to collect data on comparable sales, cost, and capitalization rates. Once data are collected, they are sorted according to the sale comparison, cost, and income approaches, thus enabling the appraiser to concentrate analysis on one approach at a time.

National, regional, community, and neighborhood data must also be collected and analyzed to provide the setting for the more specific approaches to value. The focus and nature of much of this background analysis are discussed in earlier chapters. By way of example, the following considerations would be important in a residential appraisal:

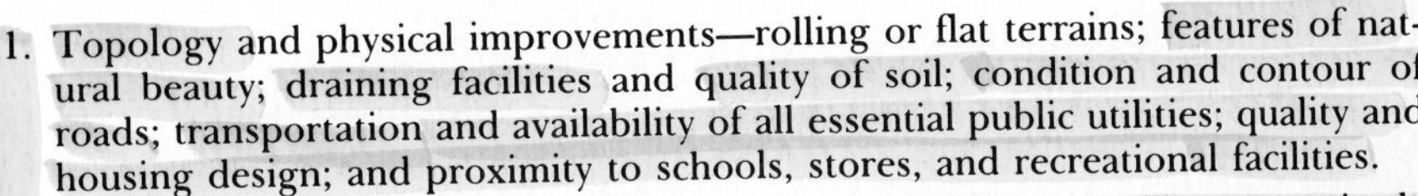

1. Topology and physical improvements—rolling or flat terrains; features of natural beauty; draining facilities and quality of soil; condition and contour of roads; transportation and availability of all essential public utilities; quality and housing design; and proximity to schools, stores, and recreational facilities.

2. Nature and characteristics of population—living habits; care of homes; attitude toward government; homogeneity of cultural interests; and percentage of homeowners.
3. Economic data—homogeneity of professional or business interests; index of earnings and income stability; frequency of turnover and market price trends; tax and assessment levels; building mortality; vacancies; and percentage of area development.

MARKET OR DIRECT SALES COMPARISON APPROACH

The market approach, also termed the direct sales comparison approach, provides for the estimation of market value by referring to recent sales, listings, and offerings of comparable properties. The underlying assumption is that an investor or potential owner will pay no more for the subject property than would probably have to be paid for another property of equal desirability or utility.

The direct sales comparison approach to value involves four basic steps, as shown in Figure 19–1.

Adjustments

The process is to discover recent sales of properties similar to, and competitive with, the subject property and then to adjust the prices to the subject property based on differences between the properties. Generally speaking, the greater the likeness between a comparable and the subject property, the fewer the necessary adjustments and the more reliable the resulting value estimate. If sufficient sales of comparable properties cannot be found, listing and offering prices of comparables may be used.

Square footage is almost always used as a unit of comparison in making adjustments. In addition, number of rooms and number of units are usually used in comparing motels, hotels, and apartment buildings.

Cubic footage is an important unit of comparison for warehouses and storage facilities. The number of frontage feet is also often important in valuing vacant sites and commercial facilities.

Differences that require adjustment between comparables and a subject property fall into four general categories: (1) location, (2) property characteristics, (3) date of sale or value estimate, and (4) terms and conditions of sale. Locational adjustments mainly involve differences in neighborhoods or areas. Items of locational adjustment for one-family houses include age, kind, size, condition of houses, zoning, prevalence of deed restrictions, and the general price ranges of houses in neighborhoods of comparables relative to the neighborhood of the subject. Items of adjustment for property characteristics include size, age, condition, number of rooms, number of baths, the presence or absence and size of a garage or carport, and special features like fireplaces, air conditioning, or a swimming pool.

An adjustment must be made for the time of sale if market activity, money availability, or sale prices in general changed between the date of the sale of the comparable property and the date of the value estimate for the subject property. Finally, if a buyer or seller were under pressure, if an unusually high down payment were required, or if one party knew more about market conditions that the other, a terms and conditions adjustment would be necessary.

FIGURE 19–2
Direct sales comparison adjustment analysis of apartment properties

		COMPARABLE SALE		
ITEM OF COMPARISON	*SUBJECT PROPERTY*	*730 OAKWAY*	*3320 HILYARD*	*1720 PARK*
Sale price	—	$610,000	$745,760	$680,000
Number of units	16	14	16	16
Sale price/unit	—	$43,571	$46,610	$42,500
Number of rooms/unit	4½	4½	4½	4½
ADJUSTMENTS				
1. Location	fair	fair	excellent	fair
2. Physical characteristics			−10%	
a. Condition	rundown	excellent	fair	excellent
		−10%	−5%	−10%
b. Garage spaces/unit	1½	1	2	1½
		+2%	−2%	—
3. Date of sale		current	2 months	4 months
			+2%	+4%
Net adjustment		−8%	−15%	−6
Adj. S.P./unit of subject		$40,085	$39,618	$39,995

An Example

Figure 19–2 gives an example of adjustments that might be made in the direct sales comparison approach to value as applied to an apartment house.

Note that all adjustments are made from comparables to the subject property. The adjusted sale prices per unit represent the probable sale price of the subject property by comparison with each respective comparable property. The range is from $39,618 to $40,085. Using this information, an indicated market value of $40,000 per unit for the subject property could easily be justified. Thus, on an overall basis, the subject property, with 16 units, has indicated market value of $640,000.

16 units × $40,000/unit $640,000.

Note also that analysis on a per unit basis allows comparisons between different-sized properties. That is, a 14-unit property may be compared with a 16-unit property or a 20-unit property if other things are generally the same.

Finally, recognize that comparisons and adjustments are actually much more complex than indicated here. Considerable judgment and experience are required. But our purpose here is to illustrate the concept and the process.

Uses and Limitations

The direct sales comparison method is well suited to making an objective estimate of a property's market value. It depends entirely on market information. Including several comparable sales almost ensures that the thinking and behavior of typical buyers and sellers are taken account of in the resulting value estimate. Also, the approach takes account of varying financing terms, inflation, and other market elements that influence the typical purchaser. Consequently, courts place greater emphasis and reliance on this method than on any other.

The method is most applicable when the market is active and actual sales data are plentiful and readily available. This means the direct sales comparison method is most appropriate for a property type that is widely bought and sold, such as vacant lots, one-family houses, and condominium units. In fact, lack of adequate market data is the method's major limitation. By default, then, the method is not applicable to the kind of property that is infrequently bought and sold or is of a unique character. Two other limitations are that sales of truly comparable properties must be selected and that the value estimate is based on historical data. An underlying assumption is that market trends of the past continue on to the date of the value estimate.

INCOME CAPITALIZATION APPROACH

The income approach uses a ratio, derived from the market, to convert income generated by a property into market value. By the principle of substitution, the underlying assumption is that a potential owner should pay no more for an income property than the cost of acquiring an alternative property capable of producing an income stream of the same size and with the same risk. One of the two most basic versions of the income approach, termed the *gross income multiplier (GIM)*, relates the total income generated by a property to its market value. The second, termed *direct income capitalization*, relates net operating income to market value.

Gross Income Multiplier

The basic steps in using the GIM technique to find market value are set forth in Figure 19–1.

Ascertaining current market rental. Current market rental of the subject property is obtained by comparing the subject property with similar properties that are rented. *Market rent* means the amount that a property would command if exposed to the market for a reasonable time and rented by a reasonably knowledgeable tenant. Market rental is analogous to market value except that rental instead of a sale price is involved. Annual rental is commonly used for income properties. And adjustments are made in rental price from the comparable property to the subject property in much the same way that a sales price is adjusted from the comparable to the subject in the market approach to value. Thus, if rental prices for three comparable one-bedroom apartments, after adjustment to the subject, equal \$510, \$525, and \$535 per month, the subject may be considered to have a gross monthly market rental of \$525 per month. This \$525 would be multiplied by 12 to get the annual rental of \$6,300 for the unit (\$525 × 12). And, if eight one-bedroom units were in the building, the gross annual income for the units would amount of \$50,400 (\$6,300 × 8). In a similar manner, eight two-bedroom units with a market rental of \$600 per month would give an annual rental of \$57,600 (\$600 × 8 × 12). Gross annual rental for the property would equal \$108,000 (\$50,400 + \$57,600).

Deriving the GIM. Dividing sales price by the monthly gross income of comparable properties that recently sold gives the gross income multiplier. The calculations are made as follows:

$$\frac{\text{Sale price}}{\text{Gross income}} = \text{Gross income multiplier (GIM)}$$

$$\text{Comparable A:} \quad \frac{\$610,000}{\$101,400} = 6.02$$

$$\text{Comparable B:} \quad \frac{\$745,760}{\$124,500} = 5.99$$

$$\text{Comparable C:} \quad \frac{\$680,000}{\$113,200} = 6.01$$

A market GIM of 6.00, therefore, seems reasonable for apartment houses in this particular neighborhood at this time. A GIM changes through time. Thus, a GIM once derived is not a "once and for all" rule of thumb that applies to all similar properties.

Applying the GIM. The indicated market value of the subject property is $648,000, as calculated by multiplying its gross income by the market GIM. For example,

Gross income × market GIM = Indicated market value
$108,000 × 6.00 = $648,000

Monthly rental income is usually used in making these calculations for one-family residences. The ratio is then called a *gross rent multiplier (GRM).*

Uses and limitations. The multiplier technique is a quick, simple, and direct technique for estimating value whenever properties are rented at the same time they are sold. Many appraisers use the technique early in their appraisal analysis to develop a "quick and dirty" idea of market value to aid their judgment in applying other techniques.

One limitation is that sales of rental properties are not always available for deriving the multiplier. Another is that gross rents are used instead of net operating incomes. In addition, the ratio is subject to some distortion because adverse zoning, lack of maintenance, or heavy property taxes will negatively influence sale price with little effect on rental levels. Thus, unless the comparables are similar in all respects to the subject, a distorted GIM may be derived from the market. Finally, in deriving a GIM, the presence or absence of extras, for example, range, refrigerator, and furniture, must be the same for the comparables as for the subject to avoid distortions.

Direct Income Capitalization

The direct income capitalization approach is based on the premise that market value equals the present worth of future rights to income after operating expenses as judged by the typical investor. This means that the market value of a subject property depends directly on its annual net operating income. The conversion of expected future income payments into a lump-sum present value is termed *capitalization.* Direct income capitalization is most meaningfully applied to investment properties (apartment buildings, office buildings, warehouses, stores).

The basic steps of the direct income capitalization process are shown in Figure 19–1.

Deriving the capitalization rate. Direct income capitalization begins with ascertaining gross market rental. Deductions must be made for vacancy and credit losses and total operating expenses, giving NOI. (See Figure 18–3.) The concern here centers on deriving a capitalization rate from the market and subsequently applying it. Assuming comparable properties, the only information required about each property is its net operating income and its sale price. Dividing the sale price into the net operating income gives a ratio or capitalization rate. This ratio is termed an overall capitalization rate, designated as "R," by convention:

$$\frac{\text{Net operating income}}{\text{Sale price}} = \text{Capitalization rate} = \text{“R”}$$

Using three comparable properties, the calculations are as follows:

$$\text{Comparable D:} \quad \frac{\$59{,}400}{\$600{,}000} = 0.0990 \text{ or } 9.9\%$$

$$\text{Comparable E:} \quad \frac{\$74{,}800}{\$740{,}000} = 0.1011 \text{ or } 10.11\%$$

$$\text{Comparable E:} \quad \frac{\$46{,}500}{\$468{,}000} = 0.09935 \text{ or } 9.94\%$$

An overall capitalization rate of 10 percent seems reasonable based on these ratios.

Applying the capitalization rate. Finding an indicated market value of the subject property merely involves dividing its NOI by the overall capitalization rate. The formula is

$$\frac{\text{Net operating income}}{\text{Overall capitalization rate}} = \frac{\text{NOI}}{\text{R}} = \text{Market value}$$

Using the $64,000 NOI from the operating statement for our subject property, we obtain a value of $640,000:

$$\frac{\$64{,}000}{0.10} = \$640{,}000$$

Uses and limitations. The income approach obviously is applicable only to income properties, such as apartment buildings, office buildings, and rented warehouses and store buildings. In fact, it is best suited to larger-income properties that have stable net operating incomes and are sold fairly frequently. Because of the manner in which the capitalization rate is derived, the approach yields value indications very similar to those generated by the market approach.

One major limitation of the direct capitalization technique is that sales of some income properties occur only infrequently; thus the derivation of a capitalization rate must be based on limited information. In addition, obtaining or verifying the NOI of an income property that has been sold is often very difficult. Chance for error is introduced in calculating net operating income for the subject property because estimates of expense items are often based on judgment; and any error in estimating NOI is magnified severalfold in the capitalization process. Further, the limitations that apply to deriving the GIM also largely apply to deriving "R"; for example, units, equipment, and so on, must be comparable. Finally, the technique is not useful for properties that are unique or that generate income in the form of amenities.

COST APPROACH

The *cost approach to value* provides for the estimation of market value based on the cost of acquiring a vacant site and constructing a building and other improvements to develop a property of equal utility. The underlying assumption is that a rational potential owner will not pay more for a subject property than the cost of producing a substitute property with equal utility and without any undue delay. Note that the cost involved is to the typical, rational, informed purchaser and not to a contractor or builder. The cost approach is also sometimes called the summation approach.

The Basic Steps

The basic approach to value involves the steps shown in Figure 19–1. Land value is first established by the direct sale comparison with similar sites. The most usual method of determining the cost of buildings is to multiply their area or cubic content by the current cost of construction per square foot or cubic foot. Two techniques of estimating cost new are used. The first, cost of replacement new, involves determining the cost of producing a building or other improvement with utility equal to that of the subject property's improvement. Modern materials, design, and layout may be used, but the utility must be the same. Cost of reproduction new, the second technique, involves determining the cost of producing an exact replica of the subject property's improvements, including materials, design, layout—everything.

Depreciation is loss in value of a property due to diminished utility. Depreciation is deducted from replacement cost new or reproduction cost new to arrive at an indicated market value. Three types of depreciation are recognized in appraising. The first, physical depreciation, is loss in value brought about by the wear and tear of use, acts of God, or actions of the elements. The second, functional obsolescence, is loss in value because of a subject property's relative inability to provide a service as compared with a new property properly designed for the same use. The cause may be poor layout and design or inefficent building equipment. In short, the improvements are old and out of date. The third class of depreciation, termed economic, locational, or environmental obsolescence, is loss in value of a site or property because of external or environmental factors that unfavorably affect the flow of income or benefits from the property, including blight and declining demand. Note that we are talking of market depreciation here and not tax depreciation.

An Example

An example of the cost of reproduction less depreciation approach to market value is appropriate here. Assume that the cost of producing the subject property in its present condition is estimated at $639,400. Thus the indicated market value by the cost approach is $639,400. But cost is not value. And only if market value exceeds cost would a buyer or investor choose this alternative.

Land value (by direct sales comparison)		$ 88,000	
Plus: Landscaping, walks, drive, etc.		12,000	
Total site value		$100,000	$100,000
Reprodduction cost of new improvements:			
Main structure: 24,800 sq. ft. @ $30/sq. ft.		$744,000	
Garage area: 6,000 sq. ft. @ $8.00/sq. ft.		48,000	
Miscellaneous (blinds, storage areas, etc.)		41,600	
Total cost new		$833,600	
Less: depreciation			
physical deterioration	$106,000		
functional obsolescence	86,000		
locational obsolescence	101,600		
Total depreciation	$294,200	−294,200	
Depreciated value of improvements		$539,400	539,400
Indicated market value by cost approach			$639,400

Uses and Limitations

The cost approach to value has greatest application in estimating the value of unique or special-purpose properties that have little or no market, for example, churches, tank farms, or chemical plants. It is also well suited to new or nearly new properties where estimating depreciation is not too involved or difficult. The cost approach has long been used in assessing for property tax purposes, which involves mass appraising and, in the past, has demanded standardized methodology. Property insurance adjustors rely on the cost approach because improvements often are only partially damaged or destroyed and must be restored to their original design and layout or else completely torn down. Finally, the approach is very suitable in analysis to determine the highest and best use of a vacant site.

One major limitation of the cost approach is that depreciation is very difficult, if not impossible, to measure for older properties. Another is the great difficulty in allowing for differences in quality of improvements that result from design and style, kind and quality of materials, and quality of workmanship. This limitation applies to both estimating cost new and estimating depreciation. Further, even getting an accurate estimate of costs-new is difficult because costs often vary substantially from one builder to another. For these reasons, the cost approach is not as applicable as other approaches for older properties or properties that are frequently sold. Also, it is nearly impossible to find vacant lot sales to serve as comparables in determining site value in older, established neighborhoods.

RECONCILIATION

Each approach yields a distinct indication of market value. For the apartment property discussed in this chapter, the approaches produced indications as follows:

Direct sales comparison approach	$640,000
Income approach	
Gross income multiplier technique	648,000
Direct income capitalization technique	640,000
Cost less depreciation approach	639,400

These estimates must be reconciled into a single estimate of market value. *Reconciliation* is the process of resolving differences in indications of value and of reaching a most probable sales price estimate. Increasingly, appraisers are attaching a range to the market value estimate, based on the standard deviation from statistical analysis.

Reconciliation involves weighting and comparing the indications according to the quality of the available data and the appropriateness of the approach for the kind of property and the value being sought. That is, reconciliation is a thought and judgment process; it is not the simple averaging of the value indications.

The direct sales comparison approach is generally regarded as giving the most reliable indication of market value when adequate data are available. The GIM, on the other hand, is often regarded as a rule-of-thumb technique. The direct income capitalization technique and cost less depreciation approach strongly support the direct sales comparison indication in our example. Therefore, a market value judgement of $640,000 for the subject property would seem reasonable and defensible.

SUMMARY

Appraisals are needed for decisions in such situations as: (1) transferring of property ownership or possession, (2) financing a property interest, (3) assessing a property for taxes, (4) determining compensation for property loss or damage, and (5) developing a property utilization program.

The most common objective of an appraisal is to estimate the market value, a property's most probable sale price. Market value may be greater than, equal to, or less than either the sale price or the cost of the reproduction of a property. The most important principles of market value appraising are (1) substitution, (2) change, (3) contribution, and (4) highest and best use.

The three approaches to value are (1) market or direct sales comparison, (2) cost less depreciation, and (3) income capitalization. The income approach is divided into the gross income multiplier and the direct income capitalization techniques. All three approaches are based on the principle of substitution. Reconciliation is the resolution of the three indications of market value generated by the techniques into one estimate of market value.

QUESTIONS FOR REVIEW AND DISCUSSION

1. List and explain briefly three major reasons or needs for appraisals.
2. Define and/or distinguish among the following:

market value	value in use
market price	value in exchange
cost of reproduction	subjective value

3. List and explain at least three principles of market value appraising, including the principle of substitution.

4. Briefly explain the following in relation to the direct sales comparison approach to value:
   a. The four basic steps
   b. Two appropriate applications
   c. Two major limitations

5. Relate the following to the income approach to value.
   a. Three basic steps of GIM technique
   b. The basic steps of the direct income capitalization technique
   c. Two appropriate applications of each
   d. Two limitations of each

6. Explain the purpose and process of reconciliation.

7. Depreciation need not be considered in market value appraising because it is more than offset by inflation. Discuss.

8. In what directions would the adjustments be for a comparable sale involving extremely low down payment and a first and second mortgage? Explain your reasoning.

9. Is depreciation taken account of in the direct sales comparison and income capitalization approaches to value? If so, how? Explain.

10. How do market values adjust or change in response to changes in demand? How is the changing value incorporated into estimates of value by appraisers? Discuss.

CASE PROBLEMS

1. You are appraising a vacant downtown site, 1½ blocks from the main business area of Park City. The owner is contemplating a long-term lease to a local parking lot operator. Vacant parcels are being leased to local operators with good credit experience at 12 percent of market value. The parcel is 80 feet × 120 feet; is located in the middle of the block, level, on grade with the street; and has a public rear alley. The offer is for $12,000 per year, net, to the owner. Three sales and a leased parcel are available for comparables:

   - *Comparable 1* is a parcel 90 feet × 115 feet directly across the street that sold for $82,000 two years ago. It is on grade and has a rear alley.

   - *Comparable 2* is a corner parcel, 60 feet × 120 feet, one block south of the subject, that sold two months ago for $100,000. It also is on grade and has a rear alley.

   - *Comparable 3* is 80 feet × 120 feet, located in the middle of the next block to the south from the subject, that sold six months ago for $105,000. It is very similar to the subject in all physical respects.

   - *Comparable 4*, an 80-foot × 120-foot site in the next block north was leased a year ago for 30 years at a net rental of $9,600 per year. It is at grade with the street and has a rear alley.

Appropriate adjustments are as follows:

- *For Time:* Up 10 percent per year.

- *For Location:* Subject area is considered to be 10 percent better than that one block to the north and 10 percent less desirable than that one block to the south. Site across street is comparable to subject. A corner site is 20 percent superior to a midblock lot.
  a. Diagram the locations of the vacant sites. Include some indication of relative desirability and values.
  b. Set up a grid to adjust sale prices on a per square foot basis.
  c. Estimate the market value of the subject site, and give recommendations for or against the proposed lease.

2. A new zoning ordinance, allowing for less intense development of parcels, has just been initiated and makes the usual rules of thumb for valuing parcels obsolete. The following three sales of parcels, all zoned for multiresidential use, were made in the year just previous to the change:

- Price = $180,000, area = 12,000 square feet
  Number of one and two bedroom apartments allowed = 30.
- Price = $221,400, area = 14.250 square feet
  Number of dwelling units allowed = 36.
- Price = $166,000, area = 11,000 square feet
  Number of dwelling units allowed = 28.

The subject site contains 18,000 square feet, but under the new zoning, it can only be developed with 36 apartment units. Considering all factors, what is the probable value of the subject site?

3. An owner of a commercially zoned parcel, with an established market value of $50,000, approaches your lending institution for a $100,000 mortgage loan. The improvements are to cost $110,000. No depreciation or diminished utility is expected because this would be a well-designed structure. Your institution has an established policy of a 65 percent maximum loan-to-value ratio on commercial loans. The building is expected to have a 50-year economic life. The current interest rate is 12 percent. Expected gross annual income is $30,000, with vacancy and credit losses and operating expenses coming to 40 percent of gross. Local gross income multipliers for this type property typically run about 5.2. Overall capitalization rates range from 11.1 to 11.3 percent in the area. No sales of comparable properties are available.
   a. What is the indicated market value by the cost approach?
   b. What is the indicated market value using the GIM technique?
   c. What is the indicated market value using the overall cap rate?
   d. What is your estimate of market value upon reconciling the several approaches?
   e. Is the loan request within the LVR guidelines of your company?
   f. Would the property be able to carry the debt service comfortably assuming a 25-year term? A 15-year term?

CHAPTER TWENTY

FEDERAL TAXES AFFECTING REAL ESTATE

The art of taxation consists in so plucking the goose
as to obtain the largest amount of feathers
with the least amount of hissing.
JEAN BAPTISTE COLBERT

IMPORTANT TOPICS OR DECISION AREAS COVERED IN THIS CHAPTER

- Basic Tax Concepts
- Four Classes of Real Estate (for tax purposes)
- Tax Basis
- Tax Depreciation or Cost Recovery
- Tax Credits
- Disposition of Income Property

"Taxes are what we pay for civilized society," according to a 1904 U.S. Supreme Court ruling.[1] But in 1947 Judge Learned Hand said,

> Over and over again courts have said that there is nothing sinister in so arranging one's affairs as to keep taxes as low as possible. Everybody does so, rich or poor; and all do right, for nobody owes any public duty to pay more than the law demands: taxes are enforced extractions, not voluntary contributions. To demand more in the name of morals is mere cant.[2]

[1] *Compania de Tobocas* v. *Collector*, 275 US 87, 100, 1904.

[2] *Commissioner* v. *Newman*, 159 F.2nd 848 (2d. Cir., 1947).

Thus, no person is obligated to place himself or herself in the highest possible tax-paying position. Rather, the prudent person is expected to practice *tax avoidance,* which means to plan and conduct affairs and transactions to minimize the amount of taxes paid. Such planning requires that the citizen be well informed on tax law. Tax evasion, on the other hand, is illegal and punishable by fine, imprisonment, or both. Padding expense accounts, making false and fradulent claims, and failing to submit a return are forms of *tax evasion.*

The federal tax regulations that most directly affect real estate are set forth in this chapter, in generalized form; major provisions of the Tax Reform Act of 1984 are included. Basic concepts pertinent to a personal income tax return are taken up first, to provide a framework. Then examples and explanations of how the concepts apply to real estate are given.

Tax law is very complex and sticky. Because of this, it is sometimes called a bramblebush; everyone working in the field gets stuck at one time or another. Many books and manuals have been written to explain the subject. Millions of dollars are spent in tax litigation each year. No last word is possible because the law coming out of the tax courts is changing on a daily basis. Decisions, therefore, should not be based solely on the material presented here. Further checks should be made with competent accountants and attorneys and other reliable sources.

Our federal income tax laws are administered and enforced by the Internal Revenue Service, alternately referred to as the IRS or the "infernal revenue service." The IRS is a division of the U.S. Treasury Department. Everyone earning annual income above a certain minimum, currently $3,300, must file an Individual Income Tax Return, Form 1040. Under special circumstances, the minimum drops to $1,000.

KEY CONCEPTS INTRODUCED IN THIS CHAPTER

Accelerated cost recovery system
Adjusted cost basis
Adjusted sale price
Alternative minimum tax
Book value
Boot
Capital gains income
Date of sale
Dealer
Depreciation recapture
Excess depreciation
Installment sale

"Like kind" of property
Nonresidential property
Ordinary income
Realized gain
Recognized gain
Residential rental property
Tax avoidance
Tax basis
Tax credit
Tax-deferred exchange
Tax depreciation
Tax evasion
Tax shelter

BASIC TAX CONCEPTS

Federal tax laws affect most real estate decisions regardless of the type of property involved. The effect becomes very apparent in the income reported and the tax paid. Discussion begins with income as tax basis, tax shelters, depreciation methods, capital gains, and disposition methods are all interrelated through it.

Classes of Taxable Income

Taxable income is divided into two classes: ordinary and capital gains. Each class has its own tax treatment.

Ordinary income. Wages, salaries, commissions, professional fees, and business income make up ordinary income. Dividends, interest, rental, and royalty income also fit into this class. Expenses incurred to generate this income and exemptions may be deducted to determine the ordinary income that is taxable. Annual net taxable income is taxed at rates from 0 percent at very low levels to 50 percent for higher levels ($162,400 plus for a joint return). See the schedule in Figure 20–1. Corporations pay taxes at the rate of 15 percent of the first $25,000 of earnings, 18 percent on the second $25,000, 30 percent on the third $25,000, 40 percent on the fourth $25,000 and 46 percent on earnings in excess of $100,000.

Capital gains income. A capital gain is realized when a capital asset, such as real estate, is sold for more than its book value or traded in a taxable exchange. Any value realized in excess of book value is capital gains income and is subject to capital gains tax treatment. *Book value,* for capital gains purposes, is value based on accounting calculations and events. For example, an investor pays $300,000 for an apartment property, on which $90,000 in tax depreciation is taken during a 6-year ownership period.

FIGURE 20–1
Marginal tax computation for personal taxable income, 1984 and after

Unmarried individuals		*Married, Joint Returns*	
If taxable income is:	*The tax is:*	*If taxable income is:*	*The tax is:*
Not over $2,300.	No Tax.	Not over $3,400	No tax.
Over $2,300 but not over $3,400	11% of the excess over $2,300	Over $3,400 but not over $5,500	11% of the excess over $3,400.
Over $3,400 but not over $4,400	$121, plus 12% of the excess over $3,400.	Over $5,500 but not over $7,600	$231, plus 12% of the excess over 5,500.
Over $4,400 but not over $6,500	$241, plus 14% of the excess over $4,400.	Over $7,600 but not over $11,900	$483, plus 14% of the excess over $7,600.
Over $6,500 but not over $8,500	$535, plus 15% of the excess over $6,500.	Over $11,900 but not over $16,000	$1,085, plus 16% of the excess over $11,900.
Over $8,500 but not over $10,800	$835, plus 16% of the excess over $8,500.	Over $16,000 but not over $20,200	$1,741, plus 18% of the excess over $16,000.
Over $10,800 but not over $12,900	$1,203, plus 18% of the excess over $10,800.	Over $20,200 but not over $24,600	$2,497, plus 22% of the excess over $20,200.
Over $12,900 but not over $15,000	$1,581, plus 20% of the excess over $12,900.	Over $24,600 but not over $29,900	$3,465, plus 25% of the excess over $24,600.
Over $15,000 but not over $18,200	$2,001, plus 23% of the excess over $15,000.	Over $29,900 but not over $35,200	$4,790, plus 28% of the excess over $29,900.
Over $18,200 but not over $23,500	$2,737, plus 26% of the excess over $18,200.	Over $35,200 but not over $45,800	$6,274, plus 33% of the excess over $35,200.
Over $23,500 but not over $28,800	$4,115, plus 30% of the excess over $23,500.	Over $45,800 but not over $60,000	$9,772, plus 38% of the excess over $45,800.
Over $28,800 but not over $34,100	$5,705, plus 34% of the excess over $28,800.	Over $60,000 but not over $85,600	$15,168, plus 42% of the excess over $60,000.
Over $34,100 but not over $41,500	$7,507, plus 38% of the excess over $34,100.	Over $85,600 but not over $109,400	$25,920, plus 45% of the excess over $85,600.
Over $41,500 but not over $55,300	$10,319, plus 42% of the excess over $41,500.	Over $109,400 but not over $162,400	$36,630, plus 49% of the excess over $109,400.
Over $55,300 but not over $81,800	$16,115, plus 48% of the excess over $55,300.	Over $162,400 but not over $215,400	$62,600, plus 50% of the excess over $162,400.
Over $81,800 but not over $108,300	$28,835, plus 50% of the excess over $81,800.	Over $215,400	$62,600, plus 50% of the excess over $162,400.
Over $108,300	$28,835, plus 50% of the excess over $81,800.		

The investor then sells the property for $345,000. The realized capital gain or profit is $135,000, calculated as follows:

Sale price, EOY 6		$345,000
Purchase price	$300,000	
Less: Tax depreciation	− 90,000	
Book value of property*	$210,000	− 210,000
Capital gain or profit		$135,000

*technically called the tax basis or adjusted cost basis. The tax or bookkeeping depreciation accounts for $90,000 of the gain; market-value appreciation accounts for the other $45,000.

The rationale for distinct tax treatment of capital gains and losses is that the gain or loss takes place over an extended period. With our progressive income tax, the impact would be magnified if all the gain or loss were attributed to the year of sale or exchange. And it is not practical to revalue each and every capital asset each year to determine possible gain or loss. So the government simply applies special rules to gains and losses realized from capital assets held for longer than 6 months, termed long-term capital gains (LTCG) or losses. The 6 month holding period was initiated by the Tax Reform Act of 1984 and is due to expire in 1987, unless extended. Capital gains or losses on assets held 6 months or less, termed short-term, are treated the same as ordinary income.

A capital gain must be realized to be taxable. A *realized gain* means that cash or "boot" was obtained in the sale or exchange of the capital asset. *Boot* is cash or the value of personal property given or received to balance equities in the transaction. A known increase in the value of a capital asset that is not realized as boot or cash is termed *recognized gain.* Recognized gain is not taxable until it is realized. That is, a recognized gain may be transferred from one capital asset or property to another without being subjected to taxation, as in a tax-deferred exchange.

Since November 1, 1978, only one method of taxing long-term capital gains of individuals has applied. Very simply, 60 percent of the gain is exempt from taxation. Or 40 percent of the long-term capital gain is added to other, ordinary income, all of which is taxed according to ordinary income tax rates. Therefore, for the capital gain of $135,000 cited, $54,000 ($135,000 × 40% = $54,000) is taxable at ordinary income tax rates. Assuming an investor in the 50 percent marginal tax bracket, the tax on the $135,000 gain would be $27,000 ($135,000 × 40% × 50% = $27,000).

Note that with only 40 percent of a long-term capital gain being subject to tax and a maximum tax rate of 50 percent, the maximum tax rate on long-term capital gains works out to be 20 percent (40% × 50%). Taxpayers in lower brackets pay lower maximum rates; thus, someone in the 40 percent bracket would have a maximum rate of 16 percent (40% × 40%).

The corporate tax rate on long-term capital gains is a flat 28 percent. The 60 percent deduction does not apply. However, where corporate income is less than $100,000, a rate of 16 percent applies on the first $25,000 of income and of 19 percent on the next $25,000.

Tax Shelters

A *tax shelter* is a means of reducing taxes on income, either by deferring realization of the income or by changing the class of the income from ordinary to capital gains. Income realization may be deferred by using a bookkeeping loss, an expense not involving an expenditure of cash, to avoid paying taxes on income as it is received. Such expenses are termed "artificial losses."

Tax depreciation on buildings is an example. The IRS recognizes buildings as wasting assets; therefore an owner may take an annual depreciation allowance to recover an investment in a wasting asset even though the building does not decline in value as judged by the market. The allowance is deducted as an expense from the income generated by the property. Thus, the NOI of $64,000 for Douglas Manor may be reduced by $30,000 as a cost recovery or depreciation allowance (see Figure 21–4). In addition, interest on borrowed funds is deductible, as $59,818 in year 1 on Douglas Manor. This means that taxable income is a minus $25,818 in year 1, for a tax saving of $10,327 in year one (again see Figure 21–4).

Land is not considered a wasting asset and therefore no depreciation expense may be taken against it. The market value of the property must not, in fact, decline. If it does, the depreciation allowance is really a recovery of the investment and no advantage has been gained. And, in turn, no off setting capital gain or profit will be realized upon sale of the property.

Deferring or changing the class of income is particularly important when disposing of real property if capital gains are present. In real estate, the amount of money involved is often very large. Thus, in addition to getting capital gains treatment on realized profits, installment sales and tax-deferred exchanges come into play. A *tax-deferred exchange* is the trading of property held for productive use in a trade or business or for investment for "like kind" property held for productive use in a trade or business, or for investment. No gain is realized for tax purposes in a well-structured exchange, and hence no tax must be paid. In an installment sale, taxes must be paid on gains as they are received.

Alternative Minimum Tax

The alternative minimum tax was enacted in 1978 to ensure that taxpayers taking certain types of large tax deductions, termed tax preference items, pay some tax. A *tax preference item* is a special deduction or exemption, as accelerated depreciation or a mineral depletion allowance, allowed in regular tax computations. Taxpayers pay the alternative minimum tax to the extent that it is more than the regular tax owed.

FOUR CLASSES OF REAL ESTATE

For tax purposes, four classes of real estate are recognized: (1) property held for sale, (2) property held for use in trade or business, (3) property held for investment, and (4) property held for personal use, as a residence. Tax treatment differs from class to class.

Property Held for Sale

Property held for sale is considered inventory for tax purposes and not a capital asset. Lots being held by a subdivider or condominiums being held by a builder are examples. The purpose of the owner is sales for profits as opposed to generation of income from rents or investment appreciation for capital gains. The owner is termed a *dealer*.

Income or losses from dealer property receive the same tax treatment as income and losses on merchant inventory. All gains are treated as ordinary income and all losses as ordinary losses. Thus, houses held by a developer would be the equivalent of cars held by an automobile dealer. No depreciation allowance may be taken. And neither capital gains and losses nor a tax-deferred exchange is recognized.

Property Held for Use in Trade or Business

A service station owned by an oil company, an industrial plant owned by a manufacturer, or a store owned by a merchant are examples of property held for use in a trade or business. The real estate is considered a factor of production in much the same sense as equipment in a factory rather than as merchandise held for sale. Tax treatment is according to Section 1231 of the Internal Revenue Code; hence, trade or business property is often termed "1231 property."

1. Depreciation may be taken on the wasting asset portion of the property, along with other expense of operating and maintaining the property. There is no recapture of "excess depreciation" on sale if the straight-line depreciation method is used.
2. If owned longer than six months, gains and losses may be taken as long-term gains and losses or as ordinary income and expenses, depending on which gives greater advantage to the taxpayer. In all likelihood, gains would be taken as capital gains and losses would be taken as ordinary losses because they could be used to offset other income on a dollar-for-dollar basis. Also, as ordinary losses, they can be used to offset income in previous years to get a tax refund.
3. The property may be traded for like kind of real estate in a tax-deferred exchange. Thus, deferring capital gains taxes in relocating or in trading up in property size is possible.

Rental property qualifies as 1231 property, with the owner considered to be in the "rental business," that is, in the business of owning and renting apartments or offices. Owners of apartment houses, stores, warehouses, shopping centers, and the like are, therefore, better off to take the 1231 classification.

Property Held for Investment

Investment property is held primarily for capital appreciation rather than the production of income; that is, an investment motive must exist. Lots, unimproved land, and a condominium in a resort area fit into this class. Nominal income, as that from rental for grazing or signboards, is not sufficient to move property from this class to that of trade or business property.

Owners of investment property face the following tax implications:

1. Long-term capital gain and loss treatment is available if the property is held for longer than six months.
2. Interest payments may be "expensed" only up to the amount of "nominal" investment income earned by the owner or owners from this and other property. Interest payments beyond nominal income must be capitalized, that is, added to the tax basis. All interest expense may be capitalized if the investor wishes.
3. A depreciation allowance cannot be taken because the property is regarded as not producing income.
4. The property must be traded in a tax-deferred exchange for like kind of real estate.

Property Held for Personal Residential Use

A single-family house and a condominium used as a personal dwelling are examples of property held for personal use. Tax treatment of personal residential property is looked at in detail in the chapter on Home Ownership. For now, its tax treatment, in summary, is as follows.

1. Depreciation may not be taken as an income tax deduction.
2. Real property taxes and interest on a loan against the property may be taken as income tax deductions.
3. Sale or exchange results in a capital gain or a nondeductible loss. The taxation of gain, if held longer than six months, is the same as for other long-term capital gains. But, if sold for less than the purchase price, the loss may not be used as an offset against other income.
4. A personal residence does not qualify as "like kind" of property in a tax-deferred exchange for other classes of real property.

TAX BASIS

Basis is an expression of property value or cost for tax purposes that is determined at the time of acquisition. In an accounting sense, basis is book value. Basis is necessary to determine the amount of depreciation expense (tax shelter) that may be charged off for income tax purposes. Basis is also needed to determine the amount of gain or loss on disposition. With time and change (the taking of depreciation, the making of improvements, and exchanging), tax basis must be adjusted to ascertain the gain or loss upon disposition. After basis has been modified, it is called the *adjusted tax basis* or *adjusted cost basis* (*ACB*).

Acquisition of Tax Basis

The initial purchase price or cost of real estate becomes its basis. The use of credit to help finance the purchase has no influence on the amount of basis acquired by the new owner. Thus, a property purchased for $200,000 has an initial basis of $200,000, even if a $150,000 mortgage loan were used to help finance the purchase. Special rules, not taken up here, determine the basis to a new owner when property is acquired by other means as gift, inheritance, or exchange.

Allocation of Tax Basis

Only the wasting-asset portion of a real estate investment may be depreciated for income tax purposes. Thus a new owner must allocate the purchase price or basis to the land and improvements. The ratio of this allocation must be based on the fair market value of the land and the improvements at time of acquisition, according to the IRS. Two methods of making this allocation are used most often:

1. The ratio of land value and improvement value to total property value as determined by the local tax assessor.
2. An allocation of property value to land and improvements provided by a qualified fee appraiser.

The allocation process is quite straightforward. For example, assume a property is purchased for $200,000. Its assessed value is $100,000, or 50 percent of market value. The assessor's records show an allocation of $15,000, or 15 percent, to the land and $85,000, or 85 percent, to the improvements. In turn, $170,000, or 85 percent, of the purchase price can be depreciated by the new owner.

Changes in Tax Basis

The tax basis of a property changes through time. A common way of increasing basis is to make capital improvements, such as building an addition or installing an elevator. The purchase of adjacent property will increase the basis. And carrying expenses, property taxes, and loan interest may be capitalized to increase further the basis for investment property. Taking depreciation, selling off a portion of a property, or an uninsured casualty loss (such as fire) decreases the basis.

An example may be helpful here. An investor buys two vacant lots for $40,000. He adds $120,000 worth of improvements to one lot. He sells the other for $60,000. And he takes $16,000 of depreciation. What is the current adjusted cost basis of the property?

ACTION	AMOUNT	CHANGE IN BASIS	ACB
Purchase lots	$ 40,000	$ +40,000	$ 40,000
Add improvements	120,000	+120,000	160,000
Sell lot 2	60,000	−20,000	140,000
Take depreciation	16,000	−16,000	124,000

The adjusted cost basis is $124,000. Note that in selling lot 2, only the basis attributed to lot 2 is deducted in making the adjustment to basis. The $40,000 profit on lot 2 (sale price less cost or $60,000 less $20,000) is reported as a long-term capital gain, provided that lot 2 was held longer than 6 months.

TAX DEPRECIATION OR COST RECOVERY

The Economic Recovery Tax Act (ERTA) of 1981 greatly simplified tax depreciation rules. A major change was going from allowing tax depreciation deductions over the useful or economic life of a wasting asset to cost recovery deductions over periods specified by the act. Another change initiated by ERTA was the discontinuance of component depreciation.

ACRS

The 1981 Tax Act initiated a 15-year write-off period for most real property (buildings), which could be taken by straight-line (S/L) or the accelerated cost recovery system (ACRS). ACRS applies to wasting or depreciable property placed in service after 1980. The Tax Reform Act of 1984 extended the write-off period to 18 years except for low income housing, which retains the 15-year period. An extended life of 35 or 45 years may be used in lieu of the 18 years with straight-line (S/L) recovery to gain a slower depreciation schedule.

As mentioned, a taxpayer has the choice between taking straight-line cost recovery or accelerated cost recovery, both based on a prescribed life for the type of asset. Under the 1984 act, straight-line cost recovery calculates to 5.6 percent per year; (100%/18 years = 5.6%).[3]

Example. In July, Glen Livet purchased an office building for $250,000, of which $200,000 is allocated to the building. Glen, a calendar year taxpayer, decides to use an 18-year, straight-line cost recovery schedule. As ownership was for 6 months in year one, Glen can take 6/12 of 5.6

[3] As of this writing, the ACRS schedule is not known. The reader should be able to obtain copies from the IRS and accounting firms. If the 175 percent declining balance method is retained, the crossover from accelerated to straight line should be at about 8.7 years.

percent for cost recovery. No proration would be necessary in year 2 and after.

Unadjusted basis × percentage = Depreciation expense.
Year one \$200,000 × (5.6% × 6/12) = \$5,600
Year two \$200,000 × 5.6% = \$11,200

Excess Depreciation Recapture

In 1964, recapture of excess depreciation was begun. Excess depreciation occurs when accelerated depreciation methods are used. *Excess depreciation* equals the cumulative surplus of accelerated over straight-line depreciation. When recaptured, excess depreciation is taxed as ordinary rather than as capital gains income. Straight-line depreciation is used in our examples to focus attention on the workings of the discounted cash flow model, and not on the intricacies of tax law.

The 1981 act made a major distinction between residential and nonresidential real estate, insofar as depreciation recapture is concerned. *Residential property* is realty deriving at least 80% of its income from rentals to long-term tenants; thus, motels and hotels are not classified as residential property. It follows that nonresidential properties are basically commercial and industrial, as warehouses, stores, factories, office buildings, and motels and hotels. Recapture rules, in summary, are as follows:

1. If straight-line cost recovery is used, upon sale of either residential or nonresidential property, No recapture is ever required.
2. If accelerated cost recovery is used, Recapture is always involved.
   a. Upon sale of residential property, *only excess depreciation* is recaptured.
   b. Upon sale of nonresidential property, *all depreciation* taken is recaptured.

TAX CREDITS

The Internal Revenue Code provides for investment tax credits to encourage rehabilitation of older buildings, energy conservation, and the installation of pollution controls. A *tax credit* is a dollar-for-dollar offset against taxes due and payable.

Industrial, commercial, and other income-producing buildings (factories, office buildings, retail stores, hotels and motels) qualify for rehabilitation tax credits. However, residential rental structures do not qualify, except when certified historical structures. Costs of acquisition or enlargement of the property are not recognized expenses. In addition, 75 percent of the existing exterior walls must be retained. The tax basis of the rehabilitated property is reduced by the amount of the credit. And straight-line cost recovery must be used following rehabilitation. The amount of the allowable tax credit varies with the age and use of the building, according to the following table.

REHABILITATION EXPENDITURES FOR	*INVESTMENT CREDIT PERCENTAGE*
30–39-year-old nonresidential structure	15%
40-year-old plus nonresidential structure	20
Certified historical structure—residential or non-residential	25

Example. Alfa Romero buys a 39-year-old office building for $100,000, and then waits one year before spending $120,000 renovating it. The property qualifies for a 20% investment tax credit, which amounts to $24,000 ($120,000 × 20%). What is the effect on Alfa's taxes? What is Alfa's tax basis in the property following renovation?

Effect on Alfa's taxes.	
Tax liability prior to investment credit	$60,000
Less investment credit	−24,000
Equals net taxes payable	$36,000

Tax Basis of property following rehabilitation:

Acquisition price	$100,000
Plus renovation costs	120,000
Total invested	$220,000
Less investment tax credit	24,000
Equals tax basis	$196,000

An investment tax credit is subject to recapture upon early disposition of the rehabilitated property, as follows.

Disposition in 1st year	100 % recapture
2nd year	80 %
3rd year	60 %
4th year	40 %
5th year	20 %

Thus, if Alfa sells the building in year three, a $14,400 increase in tax liability is incurred ($24,000 × 60 %) for the year.

DISPOSITION OF INCOME PROPERTY

After several years of ownership, it is often advantageous for an investor to dispose of or "get out of" a specific property, mainly because the depreciation tax shelter has largely been used up. This change in position can be accomplished by cash sale, installment sale, or a tax-deferred exchange. Tax implications vary with each of these techniques.

Cash Sale

Cash sale means that the seller gets all his or her equity in the year of sale. Cash sale is desirable when a taxpayer wishes to change the makeup of his or her investment portfolio. Also, cash sale may be desirable if the taxpayer needs to release equity for personal reasons, such as to establish a retirement annuity.

Example. Ben Franklin sells a fourplex that he owned for four years, for $150,000 in December. He used straight-line depreciation since buying the property, and his present tax basis is $90,000. Assuming Ben is in the 40% tax bracket, what is the tax?

Sale price	$150,000
Less: Present tax basis	– 90,000
Equals long-term capital gain	$ 60,000
Minus 60% L.T.C.G. exemption	– 36,000
Equals taxable gain	$ 24,000
Times average rate of taxation	40%
Equals tax on gain	$ 9,600

The tax bite is quite stiff with a cash sale. All capital gains and excess depreciation recapture must be reported and taxes paid accordingly. Investors, therefore, prefer to dispose of their properties by alternative methods to defer taxes.

Installment Sale

An installment sale takes place when the buyer makes payments over a number of years. An installment land contract and a first or second purchase money mortgage are typical vehicles for deferring payments. The Internal Revenue Code allows a taypayer to make pro rata payments of taxes as each installment is received. What effect would a restructuring to an installment sale have on Ben's taxes?

Example. Assume that Ben negotiates to get a 20 percent down payment, with equal payments spread over the next four years. What is the impact? First, a brief restatement of the situation.

Sale price	$150,000	(Contract price)
Less: Present tax basis	– 90,000	(three-fifths of contract price)
Equals long-term capital gain	$ 60,000	(two-fifths of contract price)

Ben will receive the full $150,000 over 5 years, of which $90,000 is a return of capital. The remaining $60,000 is the gain. Of every dollar received, three-fifths ($90,000/$150,000) is return of capital and two-fifths ($60,000/$150,000) is long-term capital gains.

Thus, in the year of sale, Ben's situation would look like this.

Down payment received	$30,000	(one-fifth of contract price)
Less: Basis	– 18,000	(three-fifths of installment)
Gain reported for year	$12,000	(2/5 of installment)
Less 60% exemption	– 7,200	
Taxable gain	$ 4,800	
Times Ben's tax rate	40%	
Equals tax payable	$ 1,920	

Ben's tax payable in year of sale is $1,920, or one-fifth of his payment in a cash sale. The calculation of tax is identical with the cash sale, except for the proration by installment. Comparable calculations would be made as payments are received in subsequent years. Thus, taxes are deferred. And, given that Ben would probably be in a lower marginal tax bracket, the total tax bill could be greatly reduced.

Tax-Deferred Exchange

The exchange of property for like kind of property without taxation of economic gains is allowed under federal tax law. The gain, though realized in an economic sense, is not recognized for tax purposes. A transaction of this type is frequently referred to as a "tax-free" exchange; a more accurate statement is that it is a *tax-deferred exchange*. Under current tax law the advantages of a well-structured exchange are substantial. As a result, an ever-increasing proportion of income and investment property transactions are exchanges rather than sales.

Tax basis, market value, mortgages, and equities must all be taken into account in arranging an exchange; They tend to be very complex. For this reason, other than to stipulate elements of an exchange, the subject will not be pursued further here. The elements that must be present in an exchange to qualify it for nonrecognition of gain or loss:

1. The transaction must be an exchange as distinguished from a sale and separate purchase.
2. The exchange must involve "like kinds" of or similar properties. Business and investment properties may be exchanged for each other. But a personal residence may not be exchanged for a business property, with taxes deferred. City real estate may be exchanged for country property. A warehouse may be traded for a supermarket. But a tax-deferred exchange of real property for personal property is not recognized. Nor may "dealer" real estate be exchanged on a tax-deferred basis for investment real estate. Like kind therefore refers to business or investment property that is exchanged for business or investment property.

Considerable planning is required to structure a tax-deferred exchange properly. Usually some unlike kinds of property (remember "boot") must be added to balance the equities in the transaction. To the extent that boot is used and gain is recognized, taxes must be paid as a result of the transaction.

SUMMARY

A prudent real estate investor uses tax shelters in owning and disposing of properties, legally practicing tax avoidance, so as to minimize the amount of income taxes payable. A tax shelter is reducing taxes on income, either by deferring realization of the income of by changing the nature of the income from ordinary to capital gains. Ordinary income tax returns range from 0 to 50 percent, depending on an investor's tax bracket. And only 40 percent of long-term capital gains is subject to ordinary income tax rates; that is, the maximum tax rate on long-term capital gains is 20 percent (40% × 50%).

A long-term capital gain results when the sale price less disposition costs exceeds the adjusted tax basis of a property that has been held longer than 6 months. Taking tax depreciation is a major way that tax basis is reduced. Tax depreciation is a bookkeeping expense allowed by the IRS even though the property may not decline in value. Tax depreciation is calculated by straight-line or ACRS over an 18-year life for most real property. Tax depreciation may not be taken on property held for sale by a dealer.

QUESTIONS FOR REVIEW AND DISCUSSION

1. Distinguish between ordinary and capital gains incomes, and describe the methods of calculating tax payable on each.
2. What is a tax shelter? Give at least three examples or illustrations.
3. List four classes of real estate for tax purposes, and briefly explain the tax treatment applicable to each.
4. What is tax basis? How is it initially established? How is it changed?
5. Investors are generally advised to take accelerated depreciation or cost-recovery. Why?
6. Why might a business not take accelerated cost recovery? Explain.
7. Explain briefly the calculation of depreciation by the straight-line and ACRS methods. Then briefly explain when each method is best used.
8. Are investment and market values of real estate influenced by tax factors? If so, how?
9. Is depreciation different for tax purposes than for appraisal purposes? If so, must there always be a difference? Discuss.

CASE PROBLEMS (For some of these problems, an 18-year ACRS schedule is needed; obtain from the IRS or other reliable sources.)

1. What is the marginal tax rate for an unmarried individual with a taxable income of $51,500? For a married couple with the same taxable income and filing a joint return?
2. For the taxpayers in (1), determine the value of an additional $2,000 cost recovery deduction. Is the value higher for the unmarried individual or the married couple? Why?
3. Jennie purchased a vacant lot for $100,000 and added $600,000 in improvements create a residential income property. Rentals started as of January 1. Determine the cost recovery allowance (per year and total) by both the 18-year straight-line and accelerated systems for the first four years of ownership.
4. Jennie sells the property of (3) above at EOY 4. Assuming that she used the 18-year ACRS, how much of the cost recovery allowance would be subject to recapture?
5. The sale price for Jennie is $900,000. What is the tax liability from the sale, assuming a 50 percent marginal tax bracket and use of 18-year straight-line depreciation?
6. What is Jennie's tax liability assuming an 18-year ACRS was used? How much is the difference?
7. If the property is an office building and an 18-year ACRS is used, what is Jennie's tax liability? How much is the difference from a residential income property?
8. Jim sells a property for $250,000 on an installment sale with $50,000 down and the balance scheduled for equal payments over the next five years. His present basis is $200,000. What is the tax in year of sale? What is the tax in subsequent years?

CHAPTER TWENTY-ONE

REAL ESTATE INVESTMENT ANALYSIS

Never follow the crowd.
BERNARD BARUCH, *American financier and governmental advisor*

IMPORTANT TOPICS OR DECISION AREAS TAKEN UP IN THIS CHAPTER

- Nature of Real Estate as an Investment
- Characteristics of Property Types as Investments
- Investment Strategy
- Determining Investment Value
- Risk Ratios
- Negotiation and Rate of Return

We have already looked at various components of the real estate decision-making cycle: (1) investor goals and constraints, (2) ownership rights, (3) markets and the investment climate, and (4) financing. In this section, we have looked at topics closer to the investment decision: property productivity, market value, and tax considerations. These are all inputs into the investment decision, the point where our investor moves from passive theorizing to active commitment. Prior to the decision, costs are relatively low, and control is almost entirely with the investor. But, upon making a decision to invest, other people get involved, and a large monetary commitment may be required. In short, the game gets serious. It also gets exciting. And the time span is quite short relative to the probable holding period of any property acquired.

The viewpoint is that of a real estate investor, not that of a speculator or developer. The lines of demarcation between these three roles are not always obvious or clear-cut. For our purposes, an *investor* puts money into real estate based on careful analysis of expected benefits and risks, with the expectation of realizing profit over an extended period. In effect, an investor looks for both annual income and long-term capital gains. A *speculator* buys and sells realty with the expectation of realizing quick profits due to sharp price changes. A speculator is roughly synonymous with a dealer, operating with a short time horizon. A *developer* prepares and improves land for use, usually by the construction of buildings. A developer's time horizon is usually several years.

All three take risks, although speculator risks are generally considered the greatest. In fact, a speculator may be regarded as a risk seeker, hoping to beat the market and thereby realize higher profits. Speculators are sometimes considered to operate on the "bigger fool" theory. The theory is that buyers pay current prices based on trends in market prices rather than on analysis of underlying value, with the expectation of reselling to a "bigger fool." The owner holding title when the bubble bursts is the ultimate fool.

Investment in only one property is considered, for several reasons. To begin with, real estate is a "lumpy" investment; that is, a large amount of equity investment is necessary to buy even one property. At the same time, usually only a small portion of all investment properties is offered in a market at any one time. Further, considerable analysis is required to evaluate even one property. In fact, a calculator with TVM capability is almost a must for the type of analysis presented here. Finally, only one property is needed to make a decision when an investor operates on a required rate of return basis. That is, if the investment value of the subject property exceeds market value at the required rate of return, an offer to purchase becomes a logical next step.

This chapter concludes with a discussion of negotiating strategy because even though the investment value exceeds market value, an investor wishes to pay no more for a property than necessary. That is, the lower the purchase price, the higher the realized rate of return to the investor, *ceteris paribus.*

KEY CONCEPTS INTRODUCED IN THIS CHAPTER

After-tax cash flow to equity
After-tax equity reversion
Business risk
Financial risk
Internal rate of return

Investment value
Leverage
Liquidity
Market risk
Political risk
Purchasing power risk
Pyramiding
Required rate of return
Sensitivity analysis

NATURE OF REAL ESTATE AS AN INVESTMENT

Advantages

An investment is the act of putting money into property or a business to obtain income or profits. Real estate is like many other investments in its ability to provide periodic income and/or value appreciation. During the 1970s, however, real estate provided a much higher rate of return than did stocks, bonds, and many other investment media. Of course, periodic losses and value depreciation are possible for real estate as well as for these other investments. Many of the advantages of real estate as an investment are in its surrounding traditions and institutions.

Leverage. As explained in an earlier chapter, positive leverage is the use of borrowed monies to increase the rate of return earned from an equity investment. This presumes that the investment earns at a higher rate than is paid on the borrowed monies. It does not matter whether the rate of return is from periodic income or from value enhancement. Traditionally, real estate investors borrow from 60 to 90 percent of the value of any properties owned or acquired, which is a much higher ratio of leverage than is available on most other investments.

The higher the leverage ratio, the higher is the rate of return on equity. For income property, this often means a higher dollar cash flow per dollar of equity investment. Also, a high leverage ratio increases the likelihood that tax depreciation will shelter most of the cash flow. Of course, a high loan-to-value ratio carries lots of risk to the investor-borrower if the property becomes distressed. For this reason, many investors negotiate for and get exculpation clauses in any loan terms when borrowing money. An *exculpation clause* is a provision in a mortgage or trust deed holding the borrower blameless in default and, therefore, limiting the borrower's personal liability. Without limited liability, the borrower might lose all personal assets if the investment fails. And, of course, from the borrower's point of view, that is not good.

Leverage also enables an investor to control more property with a given amount of money. And by maintaining high leverage through slow repayment or frequent refinancing, an investor may pyramid investments more quickly. *Pyramiding* is controlling ever more property through reinvestment, refinancing, and exchanging, while keeping leverage at a maximum. The objective is to control the maximum value in property with given resources. Needless to say, pyramiding carries high risk of a total wipe-out during a recession.

Tax shelter. Tax depreciation, long-term capital gains, tax credits, installment sales, and tax-deferred exchanges all enable a real estate investor to minimize or defer income taxes. These tax shelters concern federal taxation, as discussed earlier, but often apply to taxation at local and state levels as well.

Purchasing power protection. Real estate is unusual in the inflationary protection it offers. This protection has been specially evident during the steep inflationary period that began in 1964.

Whereas most capital assets have lost in terms of purchasing power of their dollar value, adequately improved realty, especially apartments, shopping centers, and selected commercial properties, have increased in terms of constant dollars. The rise is a result of rapidly increasing costs of construction and the rising cost of money as reflected in interest rates that reached statutory usury levels in states with usury laws. In the absence of rent and price controls, real property, like a ship upon ocean waters, floats above its purchasing power–constant dollar line irrespective of depth or rise in the level of prices. It is this purchasing power integrity that has, in recent years, popularized the demand for shares of real estate trusts and syndicates. For this real value holding power to be true of a specific parcel of income real estate, the property must be well located, have rentals that can be adjusted periodically, and not be subject to sudden sharp increases in operating costs.

Pride of ownership. Many investors gain identity by being "in the game" of real estate or "shrewd operators." Some investors also realize great satisfaction from owning something tangible that can be touched, felt, and shown to friends and relatives.

Control. The immediate and direct control of an owner over realty enables the owner or an agent to make continuing decisions about the property as a financial asset and as a productive property. This control enables the investor to manage property to meet personal goals, be they to maintain the property as a showpiece for pride of ownership or to operate the property for maximum rate of return. Many owners experience a sense of power and independence in this control.

Entrepreneurial profit. A last important advantage is that profit may be realized by building or rehabilitating a property, and the profit is immediately invested in the property without being taxed. Thus, many investors also develop property. Other investors combine real estate investing with brokerage or property management.

Disadvantages

Lack of liquidity. Investment *liquidity* is judged by the ease with which an asset can be converted to cash and the ratio of the conversion. Any asset, of course, can be converted into cash if the price is low enough. An asset is considered to have high liquidity when it can readily be sold for cash at or near its market value. High-value real estate is generally considered to have low liquidity.

Lack of liquidity continues to be the economic Achilles' heel of real estate despite the ready availability of syndicate and real estate investment trust shares on national stock exchanges. A well-informed capable investor, therefore, balances his or her investment portfolio so as to weather impending and generally short-range economic fluctuations. Thus, with a balanced portfolio approach, the relative nonliquidity of real estate need not be a serious handicap to garnering its long-term benefits of net return and capital safety. Also, in an urgent situation, as an opportunity for an alternative investment, an investor has the option to raise cash by refinancing, giving a second mortgage, or making a partial sale of the equity position, thereby entering into joint ownership.

Risk. Risk is the chance of damage or loss. Most risks associated with real estate investment may be classified as either business or financial.

Business risk is the probability that projected or predicted levels of income will not be realized, or will not be adequate to meet operating expenses. Real estate productivity is a function of physical capability, function capability, and location in an environment where the services of a property are in demand. Each of these factors is subject to fluctuation and change and to misinterpretation. Therefore, predicting productivity and income involves some uncertainty or risk. For example, a new freeway or bridge can destroy the locational advantage of a service station; likewise, a new shopping center can undercut a downtown department store. Or an unexpected decline in the economic base of a community can result in higher than expected vacancy rates for apartment houses. To the extent that events like these adversely influence the productivity of a property, business risk is involved.

Fluctuation in projected income must not be confused with business risk, however. If fluctuations in productivity are certain and predictable, an investor need only take the fluctuations into account. For example, in many university communities, occupancy levels in student housing drop below 50 percent in the summer months. An investor, by observation and analysis, can determine the nature and extent of fluctuations and thus remove uncertainty. In the analysis of business risk, the emphasis should be on the *relative certainty* of the prediction, *not on the level or pattern* of the prediction.

Financial risk is the extra uncertainty created when money is borrowed to help finance a property. An investor who does not borrow has no financial risk. At the same time, no leverage is realized, and the rate of return on equity may be quite low. In borrowing to increase the rate of return, both the investor and lender relate the loan contract to the productivity characteristics of the property. Thus, a farm loan may call for only one payment per year, in the fall when the harvest is assumed to be sold. On the other hand, a loan on an apartment house, that earns monthly rental payments, is likely to call for monthly debt-service payments.

Financial risk might be rather slight for a wealthy owner with strong financial carrying capacity. And, of course, the higher the loan-to-value ratio, the higher the risk. This risk would also show up when annual debt-service requirements are related to net operating income (NOI). The higher the debt service as a proportion of net operating income, the greater the risk. Note that a change in the financing for a property does not influence its NOI, or productivity. Productivity and income are determined by the market; the financing pattern is the result of a decision by a specific owner.

Several additional risks are involved in owning real estate. One, *market risk*, is the chance of a drop in market value. We have already pointed out that real estate tends to ride with inflation; therefore, market risk and purchasing power risk are usually rather small for real estate. But values do sometimes drop sharply as when a major business closes a plant or when the local economy takes a nose dive because of changing economic conditions. Market risk is much more applicable to securities, however, because their values can drop 20 or even 30 percent in a matter of a few months. *Legislative or political risks*, which tend to be area specific, must also be recognized. That is, all properties in a jurisdiction are likely to be affected by governmental actions, as when a city changes its zoning ordinance, initiates rent controls, or increases property taxes.

Risk and Return

The equity rate of return expected by a specific investor should be, in part, a function of the risk involved in owning the property. A safe and sure return to the investor justifies a relatively low equity rate of return. As risk and uncertainty increase, the expected rate of return should also increase. Thus, an investor who borrows money to gain leverage assumes greater risk in return for the potential of a higher equity rate of return.

But, even when leverage is not used, some risk is involved. And increasing attention is now paid risk assessment. However, lest we expect too much, we might note some pitfalls facing decision makers as described by William Clark in recasting and updating the fable, "The Lady or the

Tiger." The story applies equally to homebuyers or investors in high-value, commercial properties.

> The young man could open either door as he pleased. If he opened the one, there came out of it a hungry tiger, the fiercest and most cruel that could be procured, which would immediately tear him to pieces. But, if he opened the other door, there came forth from it a lady, the most suitable to his years and station that His Majesty could select among his fair subjects. So, I leave it to you, which door to open?
>
> The first man (investor) refused to take the chance. He lived safe and died chaste.
>
> The second man hired risk assessment consultants. He collected all the available data on lady and tiger populations. He brought in sophisticated technology to listen for growling and detect the faintest whiff of perfume. He completed checklists. He developed a utility function and assessed his risk averseness. Finally, sensing that in a few more years he would be in no condition to enjoy the lady anyway, he opened the optimal door. And was eaten by a low-probability tiger.
>
> The third man took a course in tiger taming. He opened a door at random and was eaten by the lady.[1]

Comparing Investment Media

Real estate requires good financial management if the investor is to realize as many benefits and to avoid as many costs or disadvantages as possible. In fact, a prudent investor would compare the costs and benefits of all alternative investment media to determine that one or that combination that best serves his or her personal needs. Many subjective judgments would be involved in such a comparison. Therefore, we will limit our attention to real estate.

The real estate investment cycle has three phases: (1) acquisition/development, (2) administration/use, and (3) alienation. Considerable attention is paid to acquisition/development because most of the major decisions determining the success of an investment are made in this phase. It is much easier to finish right if you start right. Legal, financial, market, and tax factors must all be taken into account early for the optimal investment decision.

More than dollar costs are involved in real estate investing. Even so, some dollar costs have been overlooked and deserve brief attention here.

Costs incurred in finding and adminstering real estate are often overlooked by investors because they are not picked up as part of the transaction. Examples include investor payments for transportation, meals, lodging, telephone calls, and counselors while looking for, buying, and selling properties. These costs may be substantial and obviously deserve

---

[1]William Clark, "Witches, Floods, and Wonder Drugs: Historical Perspectives on Risk Management," in Richard C. Schwing and Walter A. Albers, Jr., eds. *Societal Risk Assessment—How Safe is Safe Enough?* (New York: Plenum Press, 1980), p. 302.

FIGURE 21–1
Generalized characteristics of real property investment types

PROPERTY TYPE	MAIN VALUE DETERMINANTS	INVESTMENT CHARACTERISTICS	PRINCIPAL RISKS	MOST LIKELY INVESTOR TYPE
VACANT OR RAW LAND	Expansion of demand Convenient location Travel patterns Planning/zoning/ highest and best use	Passive Illiquid Limited leverage Rate of return by value appreciation No tax depreciation Capital gains taxation Expenses capitalized	Carrying costs: Must be fed, "alligator," distress sale possible Value appreciation uncertain ("Tax payer" may be used to help carry)	Speculator Developer Estate as store of value
RESIDENTIAL RENTALS (APARTMENTS)	Expanding population Rising incomes Location —convenience —favorable exposure Prestige, sometimes	Moderately active Moderately liquid High leverage, LVR R. of R. by periodic income and value appreciation Tax dep'n., accelerated possible Ordinary and capital gains taxation	Start-up when new Management (Probably necessary to hire professional for larger projects) Tenant harassment	High income benefiting from tax shelter Suitable for anyone but must be able to put up initial equity investment
OFFICE BUILDINGS	Expanding local economy Location linkages Prestige/status sometimes important Tenant-mix compatibility	Active, unless leased to one firm Moderately liquid R. of R. by periodic income and value appreciation Tax depreciation Ordinary and capital gains taxation	Start-up when new Management—high level of service required Competitive facilities Obsolescence Shift in location of business activity	High income needing tax shelter Suitable for anyone if professional management hired and if able to put up initial equity investment
WAREHOUSES	Commercial/ industrial activity Location for ease of movement Structural design to endure change	Mostly passive—often on long-term lease Moderate liquidity Moderate leverage R. of R. mainly by periodic income Tax depreciation Ordinary and capital gain taxation	Obsolescence due to changes in materials-handling, equipment techniques, and equipment	Retired—desiring high cash flow and limited management Anyone desiring tax shelter with adequate initial equity capital
NEIGHBORHOOD SHOPPING CENTERS	Community growth Effective demand —population —income Convenient location relative to competition Adequate parking Tenant mix relative to spending patterns and effective lease negotiation	Moderately active Liquidity limited Moderate leverage R. and R. by periodic income and value appreciation Tax depreciation Ordinary and capital gains taxation	Start-up—getting proper tenant mix Management—provide adequate level of service Vacancies Competitive facilities Obsolescence	High value, large equity investment likely, therefore reasonably wealthy Anyone able to use tax shelter plus other benefits

FIGURE 21–1
Generalized characteristics of real property investment types

HOTELS/MOTELS	Location—linkages and convenience Demand—conference, tourist, resort, business Mix of facilities and services	Active Liquidity Moderate to poor leverage R. of R. by periodic income and value appreciation Tax depreciation Ordinary and capital gains taxation	Management—high tenant turnover (professional management almost a necessity) Competing facilities Larger than certain minimum size—economies of scale apply	Anyone able to use tax shelter and with adequate initial equity capital Smaller properties siutable for investors also willing to manage and maintain

recognition when comparing investment media. Some of these expenses are tax deductible as well; records of these out-of-pocket expenses, therefore, should be kept by an investor.

And more than money is involved in real estate investing. Considerable time for data collection and analysis, for negotiation, and for management is invested also. Aggravation costs are also sometimes incurred, as when an owner is harassed by tenants and others. An owner is wise to log these costs also and fix a dollar value to them. Only then can a truly valid comparison of investment media be made.

CHARACTERISTICS OF PROPERTY TYPES AS INVESTMENTS

Differing property types offer distinct advantages to specific investors. Figure 21–1 summarizes these comments.

Vacant or Raw Land

The supply of land is limited. Demand is growing. Therefore, investing in land is a sure thing. This analysis is generally valid, but it is also limited. Land is only one of several real estate alternatives open to an investor.

Rate of return from land must be realized through value appreciation, which involves supply and demand. The supply of land is limited. But the supply of urban land may be increased simply by extending roads, water and sewer lines, and electrical services. Demand for land depends on expansion of demand in the specific community. Location relative to local road and travel patterns goes far to determine the demand for a specific parcel of realty. Finally, planning, zoning, and probable highest and best use greatly determine chances for value enhancement.

Land is passive and illiquid as an investment medium. Low loan-to-value ratios make it difficult to leverage land very highly. Owning land gives no tax depreciation; carrying costs must be capitalized. And rate of return on the investment must be realized through value appreciation subject to capital gains tax treatment.

In that land earns little or no income, an investor must pay carrying costs from other income. Such an investment is sometimes called an "alligator" because it has to be fed. If the owner suffers reduced income, a distress sale may be necessary. The rate and amount of value appreciation likely to occur over a period adds additional risk to investment in land.

The most likely investors in land are speculators for short-term gains and developers for long-term operating needs. Estates and others seeking a store of value and an easily managed hedge against inflation are also likely investor types for vacant or raw land.

Apartments

Number of households and income levels are the primary determinants of value for residential real estate. Some apartment buildings also realize value based on prestige considerations. Location, in terms of convenience and of environment, also greatly influences value.

Apartments require moderately active attention as an investment. And apartments are more liquid than are most realty investments because investors are more knowledgeable in residential properties than in other types of investment properties; the market is broader. Also, up to 90 percent, and sometimes higher, loan-to-value ratios may be obtained, giving high leverage. Accelerated tax depreciation may be taken. Rate of return may be by both periodic income and value enhancement, which, respectively, are subject to ordinary and capital gains taxation.

The major risks in apartment investment are during the start-up period of new properties and in obtaining or providing quality management on a continuing basis. For large complexes, professional management is almost a must because of the considerable "know-how" required to manage these complexes and because of the need to avoid harassment from tenants and others. Smaller properties, roughly 12 units or less, may be managed and maintained by an owner with adequate time. Personal management gives the owner closer control in addition to "payment" for the services rendered.

Office Buildings

The value of office buildings depends heavily on the business health of the area. Location for convenient linkages, a compatible tenant mix, and a prestigious image also add to value.

Office buildings generally require active participation of an investor unless leased to a single firm. Tenant demands must be dealt with. Liquidity and leverage are generally moderate. Accelerated tax depreciation may be taken on improvements but all is subject to recapture upon sale. Rate of return is by both periodic income and value appreciation.

The main risks with an office property are during start-up, maintaining high-quality management, and obsolescence, all of which are within the control of the owner. Shifts in location of business activity and development of competitive facilities are risks outside the direct influence of the owner.

Likely owners of large office buildings are wealthy or high-income investors, who are likely to have the high initial equity investment required as implied by "moderate leverage." Also, high-income owners gain more benefit from the tax depreciation. Syndicates are sometimes organized to own office buildings, thereby opening the investment opportunity to persons of more moderate means.

Warehouses

Warehouses obviously depend heavily on the level of commercial and industrial activity for value. To maintain value, warehouses must be designed and built to accommodate changes in methods of handling materials. Ceilings too low and aisles too narrow to accommodate forklift trucks caused many warehouses to become obsolete in the 1950s and 1960s, for example. Warehouse value also depends on a location that allows easy movement throughout a community.

Many warehouses are on long-term leases to one firm and, as a consequence, are a passive type of investment. Leverage and liquidity are moderate. Cash flow tends to be somewhat higher as a proportion of value than with some other improved properties because less value appreciation is expected. In turn, people desiring high cash flow and limited management requirements find warehouses an excellent investment. In most other respects, warehouses are similar to apartment and office buildings.

Small Shopping Centers

The value of shopping centers depends heavily on adequate purchasing power in their tributary area, meaning people and incomes. The location must be convenient for the population, and parking must be plentiful. Finally, the tenant mix must be suited to the demands of the population in the tributary area. Supermarkets, small variety and discount stores, restaurants, and gasoline stations are typical tenants.

Active management is required to establish and maintain a center as an investment. Effective lease negotiation is important. Liquidity is limited because few investors have the broad knowledge needed to manage a center; also, leverage is moderate. The tax treatment of shopping center investment is similar to that of other commercial properties. Vacancies and lease negotiation, obsolescence, and development of competitive facilities are the main risks of center ownership. Also, as with office buildings, a reasonably large equity investment is required. In other respects, any investor for periodic income and capital gain would find shopping center investment inviting.

Hotels/Motels

Hotels and motels depend primarily on tourist and business people for their demand. Tourists look to hotels and motels for rest, relaxation, and recreation. Traveling sales people and executives make up a large portion of the continuing clientele. And in recent years, it has been in vogue to hold business conferences in hotels and motels. Having a location and the facilities to satisfy this demand with ease is a large determinant of value.

Hotels and motels are active investments with limited liquidity and offer moderate-to-poor leverage. They receive tax treatment as business property.

Major risks in hotel/motel investment are maintaining adequate sized and competent management. Economies of scale apply. And high tenant turnover means that management must be effective. Obsolescence and the development of more adequate competing facilities are also major risks.

Large hotels and motels require considerable equity investment and are, therefore, limited to syndicates or wealthy investors. Smaller properties are suitable for less affluent investors who are also willing to personally manage and maintain the property.

INVESTMENT STRATEGY

In Chapter 1 we looked briefly at the decision-making process relative to managing real estate as a financial asset. We use our knowledge now by looking briefly at goals and constraints to be taken into account in developing an investment strategy.

Key Variables

Austin Jaffe and David Walters independently conducted sensitivity analysis of real estate investment to determine the most significant *variables involved.*[2] *Sensitivity analysis* is the study of the impact of various factors of an investment decision on the rate of return earned from a property or

[2]Austin Jaffe, *Property Management in Real Estate Investment Decision Making.* (Lexington, Mass.: D.C. Heath, 1979), Chaps 5–7. David W. Walters, "Just How Important Is Property Management?" *Journal of Property Management*, July–August, 1973.

on the investment value of a property. The factors are varied under controlled conditions to determine which exerts the most influence, which the second most influence, and so forth. The results help an investor to know which are the most critical variables in an investment decision. The research results of Jaffe and Walters are very similar.

The six most important variables were found to be (1) operating expense, (2) loan-to-value ratio or leverage, (3) effective gross income (EGI), (4) property value growth rate, (5) mortgage loan interest rate, and (6) purchase price. The significance of these variables to an investor are as follows. Property management is quite important to successful investment because operating costs (1) must be kept under control, whereas effective gross income (3) must be kept high. To keep EGI up, a manager must keep rents at market while keeping vacancy and collection losses low. Financing also showed up as important in that high leverage (2) gives substantial advantage and also keeps the interest rate low (5). The last two variables, property-value growth rate (4) and cost or purchase price (6), effectively mean buy low and sell high. Buying low is the result of good analysis and shrewd negotiation. Selling high is the result of managing the property well during ownership and careful negotiations on disposition.

The importance of variables drops off sharply after these first six. Other variables considered include loan term, tax depreciation, investor's tax rate, expected holding period, and rate of return required by investor. Alternative tax depreciation rates (straight-line versus accelerated) do not show up as significant; however, it does not follow that tax depreciation is not significant to a successful investment.

Strategy

In Chapter 1 we concluded that Nancy and Gerald Investor have the knowledge and the capability to conduct a very successful investment program. They have a reasonable amount of money. Their main constraints are wanting to invest locally and not wanting to manage property personally any longer. By selling off their smaller properties and refinancing one other property, they generate enough cash equity for a larger property, Douglas Manor, at $640,000. They thereby meet both constraints. Several of the smaller properties required considerable attention from them; large properties may be managed by professionals at an acceptable percentage fee.

With a larger property, the Investors expect to better realize cash flow and equity appreciation. They also realize high leverage by investing in residential rental property. They pay extra capital gains taxes to make the transition but consider the cost acceptable because they also benefit from a shorter, 18-year, write-off period for depreciable assets. The purchase of Douglas Manor would complete their transition. Further, the

Investors now have more time for family life, and Gerald is better able to attend more closely to financial management of investments rather than to the everyday details of property management.

The extra ACRS tax shelter is expected to be especially beneficial as the investor's income goes up. The size, 16 units, and high value, $640,000 or more, stretch the Investors slightly insofar as coming up with the initial cash equity is concerned. Fortunately, the age and condition of the property appear such that no unduly large expenditures or capital improvements are likely to be needed for several years.

Wendy Welloff plans to sell off Douglas Manor because much of her depreciation shelter had been used up. Also, she wants to release money to reinvest in vacant land for appreciation so more of her income comes in the form of capital gains. She now earns considerable periodic income from investments. Also, she wants several smaller parcels of property that can more easily be passed on to heirs in an estate. Finally, she plans to do some property development before retiring. She can do the analysis and arrange financing. She hopes to improve individual parcels in joint venture arrangements with local developers.

DETERMINING INVESTMENT VALUE

Investment value is the worth of a property to a specific individual or group. Personal assumptions or judgments about the property are considered to be included in this value. By way of contrast, market value is based on the assumptions and judgments of the *typical investor* for the particular type property under consideration. A case property, Douglas Manor Apartments, is used here to illustrate the elements and techniques needed to determine investment value on an after-tax basis. The viewpoint of Gerald I. and Nancy O. Investor is used.

The analysis is conducted in dollar terms only. An investor may have preferences over and above the economic analysis, but these should be exercised after the investment value of the property is known. In this way, the investor is able to ascertain the cost of the preferences in making a decision. The analysis includes an after-tax cash flow projection, discounted at a 15 percent required rate of return (RRR) to determine the net present value of the equity position. Subsequently, the internal rate of return is calculated, assuming purchase at a price less than investment value.

Data on Douglas Manor Apartments

Much of the data needed to determine the investment value is discussed earlier in this book. These data, plus additional assumptions or inputs for Douglas Manor Apartments, are provided here for easy reference.

1. Net operating income is $64,000, as presented in the pro forma operating statement in chapter 18, on Property Productivity Analysis.
2. Market value for Douglas Manor Apartments is taken at $640,000, as determined in chapter 19, Appraising For Market Value. This $640,000 is also the assumed purchase price for purposes of the depreciation schedule which was developed in chapter 20 on federal income taxes.
3. The property is to be financed with a 25-year, 12 percent mortgage requiring monthly payments and made at a 78 percent loan-to-value ratio. The loan is therefore $500,000 with debt service of $5,266.12 monthly or $63,193 yearly. An end-of-year loan amortization schedule is shown in chapter 16, Financing Calculations, Figure 16–9.
4. Improvements are assumed to make up 84.4 percent of the purchase price, or $540,000. Using the 18-year ACRS life, as allowed by the Tax Act of 1984, with straight-line write-off, gives $30,000 as annual tax depreciation. See Figure 20-2 developed in chapter 20, Federal Taxes Affecting Real Estate. Use of a straight-line depreciation schedule avoids problems of depreciation recapture upon disposition in our example. Actually, most investors would probably use accelerated depreciation.

5. The Investors are assumed to be in the 40 percent tax bracket insofar as annual income from this property is concerned. In the year of disposition, the long-term capital gains are expected to push them into the 50 percent tax bracket.
6. The Investors have a minimum of 15 percent per year after-tax required rate of return on any equity investment.
7. The property is assumed to be held for 4 years, during which time its market value increases at 5 percent per year to $777,924. A 4-year cash flow projection is used to make the analysis of Douglas Manor Apartments easier to follow. According to a study by Dr. Daniel E. Page, the most popular projection (holding) period is actually 10 years.[3] The cash flow projection gives ownership a time dimension in which NOI is assumed to increase by 5 percent per year. Disposition costs upon resale are taken at 7 percent of sale price.
8. Time value of money factors from the Appendix are used to calculate the present worth of future payments. By convention, monthly payments are assumed on mortgages unless otherwise stated and annual payments of cash to equity.

Figure 21–2 provides a visual summary or overview of the process by which investment value is determined. Investment value equals available credit financing plus the present value, at the RRR, of after-tax cash flows to equity from annual income and equity reversion. See Figure 21–3.

The Investment Value of After-Tax Cash Flow

The taxable income from real estate equals operating income less the depreciation allowance and less interest paid on money borrowed to finance the property. See Figure 21–4. Multiplying the taxable income times the tax rate gives the tax payable on income from the property.

[3] Daniel E. Page, "Criteria for Investment Decision Making: An Empirical Study," *The Appraisal Journal*, October 1983, p. 505.

FIGURE 21–2
Projected cash flows and market value levels, Douglas Manor Apartments

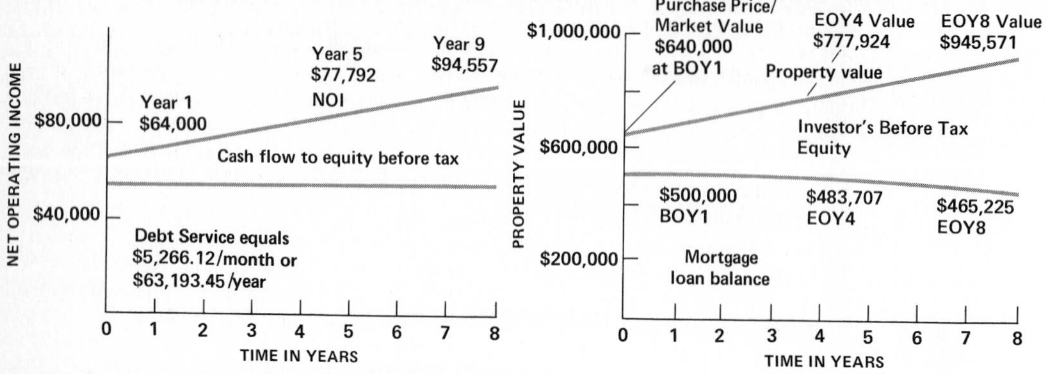

For year 1 in Figure 21–4, taxable income is actually a minus $25,818 because depreciation and interest exceed net operating income:

Net operating income	$64,000
Less: Depreciation	−30,000
Less Interest paid	−59,818
Taxable income	$25,818
Income tax rate	40%
Income tax payable (tax savings)	$10,327

The minus income offsets $25,818 of other income, meaning a tax savings of $10,327 on income from other sources, which is its value to

FIGURE 21–3
Investment value equals the present value of annual after-tax cash flows and after-tax equity reversion plus available credit financing

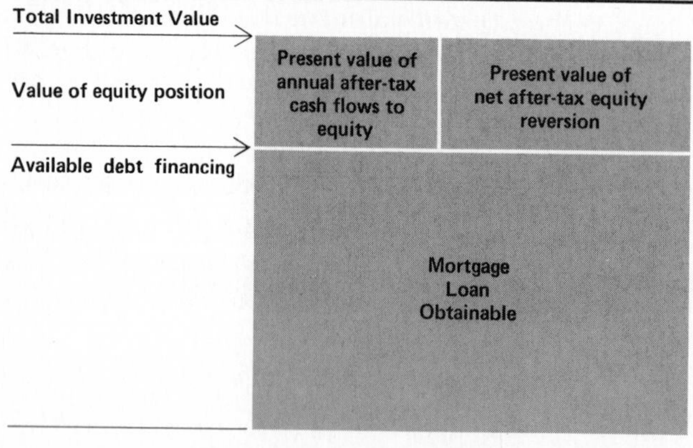

FIGURE 21–4
Douglas Manor cash flow projection and calculation of annual tax on income to equity owner in 40 percent tax bracket

ACCOUNTING ITEM	YEAR 1	2	3	4
NOI, Rate of Change = 5.00%	$64,000	$67,200	$70,560	$74,088
– S/L Tax Depreciation	30,000	30,000	30,000	30,000
– Interest Paid	59,818	59,390	58,908	58,364
= Taxable Income	($25,818)	($22,190)	($18,348)	($14,276)
× Investor's Tax Rate	40.00%	40.00%	40.00%	40.00%
= Income Tax Payable	($10,327)	($8,876)	($7,339)	($5,711)

the investor. The effects of depreciation to shelter income and interest paid to leverage the property lead to this result. By year 4, NOI has increased, and interest payments have declined so that the tax savings on income from the Douglas Manor Apartments is reduced to $5,711.

The next step in valuing the annual cash flow from a property is to determine the actual after-tax income realized. Before-tax cash flows equal NOI less annual debt service. Subtracting the tax payable on the income from the property yields the after-tax cash flow that can be pocketed. Finally, because the cash is realized in the future, it must be discounted back to the present at the investor's desired rate of return.

For year 1 in Figure 21–5, the before-tax cash flow to equity equals the NOI of $64,000 less annual mortgage debt service of $63,193, or $807. The minus income tax (tax saving) is deducted from this to give an after-tax cash income of $11,134.

By convention, the income is assumed to be received at the end of the year and is discounted with annual TVM factors. The 15 percent, present value of one factor for 1 year is 0.8696; therefore, the present value of the after-tax cash flow for year 1 is $9,682. For year 4, the present

FIGURE 21–5
DOUGLAS MANOR: Calculation of the present value of annual cash flow after tax

ACCOUNTING ITEM	YEAR 1	2	3	4
Net Operating Income	$64,000	$67,200	$70,560	$74,088
– Annual Debt Service	63,193	63,193	63,193	63,193
= Cash Flow Before Tax	$807	$4,007	$7,367	$10,895
– Income Tax Payable	(10,327)	(8,876)	(7,339)	(5,711)
= Cash Flow After Tax	$11,134	$12,883	$14,706	$16,605
× PV1 Factor @ 15.00%	0.8696	0.7561	0.6575	0.5718
= P.V. of Annual CFAT	$9,682	$9,741	$9,669	$9,494

value of the after-tax cash flow is $9,494; the projected annual increase in NOI is more than offset by decreasing tax savings and a decreasing PV1 factor.

Net operating income	$64,000
Less: annual debt service	−63,193
Before-tax cash flow to equity	$ 807
Less income tax payable	−10,327
After-tax cash flow to equity	$11,134
Times annual PV1 factor (15%, 1 year) (col. 1)	×0.8696
Present value of cash flow after taxes to equity	$ 9,682

The BOY 1 value of the after-tax cash flows to equity for all 4 years is $38,586 ($9,682 + $9,741 + $9,669 + $9,494).

The Investment Value of the After-Tax Equity Reversion

The present value of the after-tax equity reversion expected upon disposition is also needed. Some of this reversion will, of course, be a return of the initial cash investment. And to the extent that tax depreciation is taken in excess of the market depreciation, capital gains are recognizable upon disposition. Also, to the extent that value appreciation occurred during the ownership period, capital gains are generated and taxed. Costs must also be incurred in disposing of the property. The net after-tax equity reversion equals the sale price less disposition costs, less the amortized mortgage balance, and less capital gains taxes.

Let us look again at Douglas Manor Apartments. They are projected to have increased in value by more than 20 percent, so that a disposition sale price of $777,924 is realized. This figure is arrived at by taking the expected NOI for year 5, $77,792.40, and dividing by the 10 percent overall capitalization rate we developed earlier. At the end of 4 years, the mortgage balance has been reduced to $483,707. Disposition costs at 7 percent are estimated at $54,455.

The long-term capital gain equals $203,469, of which 60 percent is excluded from taxable income.

Disposition Price, EOY 4		$777,924
Less T/C @7.00%		54,455
Equals Net Disposition Price		$723,469
Less Adjusted Tax Basis		
Purchase Price	$640,000	
− Accum. S/L Tax Dep'n at $30,000 per year	120,000	520,000
Equals Long-Term Capital Gain		$203,469

Minus Exclusion of 60.00%	122,082
Equals Taxable Portion of LTCG	$81,388
× Investor's LTCG Tax Rate:	50.00%
Equals Tax Payable on LTCG	$40,694

The estimated overall tax rate applying to the capital gain is 50 percent. Thus, total taxes on this long-term capital gain are taken at $40,694. Because tax depreciation was taken on a straight-line schedule, no excess depreciation needs to be recaptured.

The following summary of the calculation shows that the BOY1 present value of the net after-tax equity reversion amounts to $113,818.

Disposition price		$777,924
Less:		
Transaction costs @ 7%	$ 54,455	
Loan balance, EOY 4	483,707	
LTCG taxes	40,694	
	$578,856	578,856
Net after-tax equity reversion, EOY 4	–	$199,068
Times annual PV1 factor (15%, 4 years)	×	0.571753
Equals BOY 1 Value of the after-tax equity reversion		$113,818.

Total Investment Value

The investment value of the equity position under the stated condition equals the present value of the annual after-tax cash flows and of the net after-tax equity reversion. Total investment value equals equity value plus the obtainable mortgage. The total value of Douglas Manor Apartments to Gerald and Nancy Investor, based on a 15 percent required rate of return on equity, equals $652,400, calculated as follows.

	CALCULATED	*ROUNDED*
Investment value of annual cash flow after taxes to equity	$ 38,586	
Investment value of net after-tax equity reversion	$113,818	
Investment value of equity position	$152,404	$152,400
Plus available mortgage loan		500,000
Equals total investment value of Douglas Manor		$652,400

Therefore, the maximum that the Investors can pay for the property and still realize their objective of earning a RRR of 15 percent on equity invested is $652,400. Naturally, the investors would prefer to purchase the property for less. Figure 21–6 shows how these values combine to equal investment value.

RISK RATIOS

An investor-borrower may wish to calculate financial risk ratios prior to bidding for a property or applying for a loan, thereby knowing in advance that any proposal submitted is within reasonable limits from a lender's point of view. The numbers used in calculating these ratios are explained in this or earlier chapters.

Operating Ratio

An income property must incur operating expenses to earn rents and to maintain its earning capability. An operating ratio is used to determine if the net operating income reported for a property is realistic. An *operating ratio* equals total annual operating expenses divided by gross annual scheduled income.

$$\text{Operating ratio} = \frac{\text{Total annual operating expenses}}{\text{Gross annual scheduled Income}}$$

A ratio of between 38 and 40 percent is typical for newer multifamily residential properties. For older properties, costs increase and the ratio may approach 50 percent. Other ratios apply for other properties (office buildings, warehouses, stores). Too low a ratio indicates that some expenses may be unaccounted for; too high a ratio indicates slipshod management.

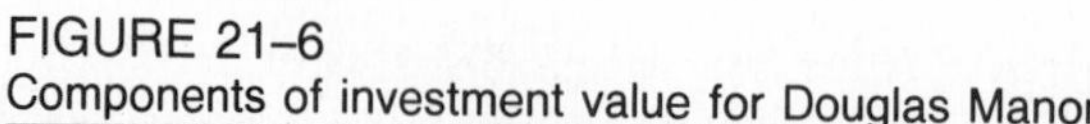

FIGURE 21–6
Components of investment value for Douglas Manor

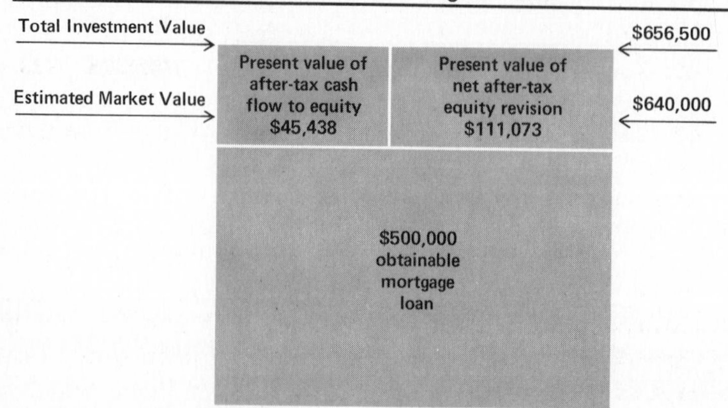

Debt-service coverage ratio. Net operating income is the amount left over after all operating expenses are accounted for; NOI indicates the amount available for debt service. Thus, NOI can be compared with the debt service required of a loan to determine whether adequate income is available to service the loan. The debt-service coverage ratio equals NOI divided by annual debt service for principal and interest.

$$\text{Debt service coverage ratio} = \frac{\text{Annual net operating income}}{\text{Annual debt service}}$$

A DSC ratio is normally expected to exceed 1.20 on a residential income property for a loan to be considered safe by a lender. Anything less is almost certain to result in a refusal of a loan application.

Break-even occupancy ratio. A third ratio, which is another way of measuring the security offered by a property, is the break-even occupancy (BO) ratio. The BO ratio identifies the point at which a property's earnings exactly equals all operating expenses plus required debt service:

$$\text{Break-even occupancy ratio} = \frac{\text{Total annual operating expenses plus annual debt service}}{\text{Annual gross scheduled income}}$$

Obviously, a lender wants some buffer for vacancy. The industry standard for residential income properties is that a 10 to 15 percent vacancy must be allowed for. Thus, an acceptable BO ratio would be from 85 to 90 percent.

NEGOTIATION AND RATE OF RETURN

An owner wants to sell for as much as possible and is not likely to accept less than market value. An interested investor wants to buy for as little as possible and is unlikely to agree to pay much more than market value, even though investment value is higher. Even so, undue pressure on a buyer or seller, differences in negotiating ability, lack of adequate information, and changing market conditions might result in an agreed price being above or below market value.

The market value of Douglas Manor Apartments was estimated as $640,000. The investment value is $652,400. An investor needs both these figures going into negotiations. If the property can be purchased for $640,000 rather than 652,400, the investor accomplishes several things. The cash equity invested is reduced to $140,000, and, in turn, the equity rate of return will be greater than 15 percent, if all other assumptions hold. Further, the investor has over $12,000 left over, which might be invested in another property, possibly at 15 percent or more. Investing in more than one property also spreads out the investor's risk.

Realized Equity Rate of Return

Assuming purchase of the property for $640,000, the equity rate of return can easily be calculated—if no other factors vary. To begin, an equity rate of return high enough to give a total investment value less than $640,000 must be used to discount the cash flows to equity, including the net after-tax equity reversion. A 20 percent rate is used here. After-tax cash flows calculated earlier and presented in Figure 21–5 are used in that they are not influenced by an increase in the RRR to 20 percent.

EOY	Amount of cash flow after taxes	×	PV1 FACTOR (20%)	=	BOY 1 Value of Payment
1	$ 11,134		0.83333		$ 9,278
2	12,883		0.69444		8,947
3	14,706		0.57870		8,510
4	16,605		0.48225		8,008
4*	199,068		0.48225		96,001

*(revision)

Total equity investment value	$130,744
Available mortgage loan	500,000
Total property investment value	$630,744†

†Rounded to $630,700.

Now the equity rate of return may be calculated. The total investment value of Douglas Manor Apartments at alternative equity rates of return is as follows:

15%	$652,400		
		$12,400	
Unknown, target rate = x%	$640,000		$21,700
20%	$630,700		

The investment values at 15 and 20 percent bracket the expected purchase price and market value of $640,000. Therefore, with purchase at $640,000, the expected equity rate of return, or internal rate of return, is between 15 and 20 percent. The *internal rate of return* (IRR) is that rate of discount that makes future cash receipts equal to the initial cash investment. In fact, the IRR would be approximately $12,400/$21,700 of the way from 15 percent to 20 percent, which calculates to 17.86 percent, by interpolation.

$$x = 15\% + 5\% \left(\frac{\$12{,}400}{\$21{,}700}\right)$$
$$= 15\% + 5\%\ .5714$$
$$= 15\% + 2.86\%$$
$$= 17.86\% = \text{Internal rate of return to equity}$$

Negotiating Strategy

According to the Jaffe and Walter studies mentioned earlier, purchase price and value appreciation are two of the most important items in a successful investment. Negotiation directly affects both figures, one when buying and the other when selling. What can an investor do to improve negotiating performance? Entire books have been written on negotiation, but for our purposes, four items stand out.

1. An investor must understand his or her personal goals and negotiating style. What are the relative priorities of the goals? What negotiating style best suits achieving the goals?
2. The property must be understood. What is its highest investment value to me as a buyer-investor? What is the lowest price at which I will sell, as an owner (market value, unless in distress)? What influence will terms have on these prices?
3. Know the opponent and his or her goals. In buying, look in the public records to find out how much the seller paid for the property and how long it has been owned. Is the owner's tax depreciation about used up? Also, estimate owner's mortgage balance and terms, if not included in the listing. Are there other liens against the property? Under how much pressure to sell is the owner?
4. In negotiating, remain objective. Losing one's temper or getting highly emotionally involved leads to mistakes and to failure to achieve goals. Have high expectations in the negotiations; be determined while pursuing them, but also be courteous. Recognize that no transaction occurs unless both parties expect to benefit. In buying, the property must have as high, or higher, a value in use to you that it does to the seller. The owner is selling because the value in exchange exceeds value in use. And once a bargain is struck, look for ways in which to improve it by modifying terms. Cooperative negotiations are better for both parties in the long run.

SUMMARY

Real estate, as do many investments, promises periodic income and value appreciation. The main advantages of real estate as an investment are (1) leverage, (2) tax shelter, (3) purchasing power protection, (4) pride of ownership, and (5) control. For builders and developers, real estate investing also offers an opportunity for entrepreneurial profit. Disadvantages are lack of liquidity and risks—business, financial, market, and political. Business risk is the chance that predicted incomes will not be realized. Financial risk is the added uncertainty caused by use of debt financing.

The most common property types of real estate for investment are vacant lands, residential, office buildings, warehouses, hotels and motels, and small shopping centers. Each has its own characteristics and risks.

Sensitivity analysis shows that the key variables in income property investing are (1) operating expenses, (2) leverage or loan-to-value ratio, (3) effective gross income, (4) property value growth rate, (5) interest rate on loans, and (6) purchase price or cost. Wealth maximization is the primary investor goal according to financial theory. Other possible investor goals include purchasing power protection, avoidance or risk and personal stress, power to control property and others, and pride of ownership. Common investor constraints are wealth or income level, risk avoidance, time availability, investor analytical and administrative ability, and locational preferences.

Investment value equals equity value plus obtainable debt financing. Equity value equals the present worth of periodic after-tax income to equity and of the net after-tax equity reversion. The investor's required rate of return is used in finding the present worth of the cash flows to equity.

QUESTIONS FOR REVIEW AND DISCUSSION

1. Distinguish among an investor, a speculator and a developer.

2. List and explain briefly at least four advantages of real estate as compared with most other investment media. What are the major risks or disadvantages of investing in real estate?

3. Compare vacant or raw land with an office building as an investment. On what bases or criteria should the comparison be made?

4. What are the six key variables in income property investing, according to sensitivity analysis research?

5. List and explain briefly at least five common constraints to real estate investors.

6. Explain in general terms the process of determining the investment value of an income property.

7. Outline the accounting steps to calculate each of the following:
   a.) Tax payable on annual income from a property
   b.) Long-term capital gain or loss from sale of property
   c.) Net after-tax equity reversion

8. How might an investor best estimate the amount of a loan obtainable on a property of interest for the purpose of analysis? Discuss.

9. Is there a difference between investment analysis and market value analysis? Discuss.

10. It has been said that a skilled negotiator can buy for 20 percent less than can a typical citizen. Does this apply to real estate as well? Discuss.

CASE PROBLEMS

1. Popeye is considering the purchase of University Towers, a student apartment building, for $640,000, of which $118,000 is attributable to the land. He thinks he will use an 18-year straight-line cost recovery schedule. What is the cost recovery allowance each year?
2. Academic Savings and Loan agrees to lend Popeye $540,000 to help finance University Towers, on an RRM loan with a 30-year amortization period and with the interest rate at 12 percent, compounded monthly.
   a.) What is the monthly debt service? The annual debt service?
   b.) What are the loan balances at the end of years 1, 2, and 3, assuming that all debt-service payments are made on schedule? ($538,040, $535,832, $533,344).
3. NOI is $64,000 in year 1 and $68,000 in year 2. At the end of year 2, Popeye assumes that he will sell for $720,000. Popeye has a 14 percent after-tax required rate of return on any real estate investments he makes. And he is in the 42 percent tax bracket.
   a.) What are the present values of the annual after-tax cash flows from operations?
   b.) What is the present value of the after-tax equity reversion from disposition at end of year 2?
   c.) What is the investment value of the equity position? [Combine answers to (a) and (b).]
   d.) What is the total amount that Popeye can pay for the property and still realize his objective of a 14 percent after-tax rate of return? (Combine investment value of equity position and available loan.)
   e.) Should Popeye buy University Towers?
4. If Popeye buys the Towers for $640,000 with the aid of the $540,000 loan, what is the internal rate of return to equity?

CASE PROBLEM FOR QUESTIONS 5–9

As a developer, you just completed Case Center, an apartment complex. The land cost $2,000,000 and the improvements, $8,000,000; therefore, total development costs are $10,000,000. You obtained 70 percent financing, $7 millions, on a 30-year RRM loan with interest at 12 percent, compounded monthly. You are in the 50 percent tax bracket. Also, you opt to take 18-year straight-line cost recovery. In year 1 of operations, NOI is $900,000, and in year 2, it is $1,200,000. At the end of year 2, you receive an offer you cannot refuse and sell Case Center for $12 millions, net after transaction costs.

5. Determine the cash flow after taxes for both years of the investment.
6. Determine depreciation recapture and tax payable upon disposition at EOY 2.
7. Determine after-tax equity reversion from sale at EOY 2.
8. Assuming that you have a 15 percent after-tax required rate of return, what would the investment value of the equity position have been at BOY 1?
9. Given a $10,000,000 total development cost, what after-tax internal rate of return (ATIRR), was earned on equity?

CHAPTER TWENTY-TWO
PROPERTY DEVELOPMENT AND REDEVELOPMENT

City building is just a privilege of citizenship.
ROBERT THORNTON, Sr., former mayor of Dallas

IMPORTANT TOPICS OR DECISION AREAS COVERED IN THIS CHAPTER

- History and Economics of Property Development
- Site Selection and Analysis
- Analysis for Property Development
- The Property Development Process
- Analysis for Redevelopment/Modernization

An understanding of property development and redevelopment is important to a real estate investor for several reasons. Vacant land may be bought and improved to create an investment as an alternative to buying a property already improved. Or an older property might be bought and redeveloped by an investor. Or, after owning an improved property for several years, an investor might consider when it is best modernized or redeveloped.

Whatever the situation, an investor must recognize that realty, whether vacant or improved, must produce a surplus, or profit, to warrant its improvement and use. That is, in development, a specific parcel of land is combined with other factors of production (labor, capital, and management) only if each factor stands to obtain a return sufficient to attract it to the project. Combining these factors in optimum proportions gives the highest value to the property, meaning that the property is in its highest and best use.

A parcel of land that does not promise a margin of profit is termed *submarginal.* Deserts, jungles, arctic areas, marshes, and mountain tops are examples of submarginal lands. A parcel may be submarginal in one use and yet promise a surplus in another. Thus, a parcel may have value as a residential lot but not as a site for a service station.

Competition to control and develop desirable properties is often very keen, sometimes making acquisition necessary well before a property is ripe for actual development. A *ripe property* is one that yields a maximum profit to a developer after all other factors of production have been satisfied. With advance acquisition, *carrying costs* (expenses and outlays of holding) must be met until a property is ripe. Thus, downtown sites are often devoted to interim uses, known as *taxpayers* (parking lots and one-story fast-food outlets are common), to meet carrying costs.

An economic anomaly that applies more to real estate development than almost any other activity is worth noting at this time. Real estate developments, as apartment houses, shopping centers, office buildings, and hotels are often designed and built as "one-of-a-kind" projects. In turn, total cost also becomes average cost and marginal cost. The developer is working in a batch rather than a flow process. Thus, the developer must be extremely alert in each project as it builds from scratch because the costs of mistakes apply only to the project at hand; there are no second, third, or fourth projects over which the costs of mistakes can be spread.

KEY CONCEPTS INTRODUCED IN THIS CHAPTER

Carrying costs
Land development.
Land use succession
"Ripe property"
Land subdivision
Submarginal land
"Taxpayer"

HISTORY AND ECONOMICS OF PROPERTY DEVELOPMENT

Property development and redevelopment are simply responses to the changing social and economic space needs of a community. Initially, the need is for urban space, meaning the extension of roads and utilities and the adding of structures to individual parcels. Subsequently, the issue becomes adjusting obsolete and inefficient rigid physical structures, with their long lives, to the changing need for real estate services of a dynamic society.

Subdividing versus Developing

Subdividing and developing, while sometimes used interchangeably, have distinct meanings in practice. *Subdividing* means the breaking up of a large parcel of vacant land into smaller sites. The sites may be for one-family houses, office buildings, or warehouses. In most communities, the subdividing must be done in accordance with the regulations of the city, village, or county in which the land is located. Also, to provide identification and an adequate legal description, the plat must be entered into the public records.

Developing is a broader concept, generally taken to mean combining land and improvements to produce a completed, operational property. Adding improvements to subdivided land is also considered development. Much more coordination of activities is involved in developing.

Changing Development Practices

During the "boom" period following World War I, land speculators often took advantage of the naïveté of people desiring homes and of the unconcern of community and governmental leaders. Planning, zoning, and subdivision regulations had not yet been initiated. Subdivisions sprang up at random, principally in remote suburban places and often miles away from connecting utility services as electricity, water, and waste disposal. Often too, imposing pillars were erected at the entrance to the proposed subdivision. Promotional schemes were then set in motion and supported by extravagant advertising campaigns. Municipal authorities, in turn, frequently "jumped" on the bandwagon and agreed to extend utilities, install paved roads, build schools, provide police and fire protection, and otherwise encourage the new development. Except in isolated cases, the mad rush to the suburbs failed to occur, and the cities found themselves heavily burdened with the long-term bonded debt floated to finance the ill-fated improvements.

The Great Depression of the 1930s brought home to citizens everywhere the serious consequences of the hasty faith that municipal leaders had placed in the overtures of fast-working real estate speculators. Subsequently, states and federal agencies acted to prevent a recurrence of runaway subdivisions and their attendant civic burdens.

Today most cities have strict subdivision controls. Whenever subdivisions are proposed, assurance must be given that all costs, including the grading and paving of streets and the installation of conduits for municipal services, can and will be borne by the subdivider. Generally, necessary land for schools and other civic facilities must be dedicated to public use. Proof of subdivision demand, too, must be provided in many jurisdictions before authority to proceed with site improvements is granted.

However, abuses continue to occur, primarily in interstate land sales. Typical examples, cited by the Comptroller General in the "Need for Improved Consumer Protection in Interstate Land Sales," make the point.[1]

> A purchaser of a lakefront lot in Texas reported that there had never been any water in the man-made lake areas.
>
> A purchaser of a lot in Arizona attempted to resell his property but was told by the developer that he could not sell the lot until the subdivision was completely developed. He was not informed of this restriction when he purchased the lot.
>
> A purchaser of a lot in Florida reported that he was advised that monthly charges would be on the unpaid balance of the contract. He later learned that monthly interest was computed on the original balance due, without considering payments made.
>
> A purchaser of a lot in California reported that a drainage easement on his property had rendered the land useless.

Notwithstanding the foregoing excesses, developers are much more responsible now than in the past. The public expects greater livability in its communities and buys from the developers offering the best values. Also, more land use controls (community plans, zoning ordinances, subdivision regulations, building inspections) are in effect now than in the past. Consequently the quality of development has steadily improved since World War II.

Land Use Succession—The Reason for Development

As discussed in the chapter on highest and best use (Chapter 11), land, or real estate, tends to go to that use paying the owner the highest return (rent) or giving the owner the greatest value. There are examples all around us. Forest lands are cleared or marshes are drained to make way for farms. Farmland is developed into residential neighborhoods, shopping centers, and industrial parks. Older houses are remodeled and converted to office use. Old factories, mills, breweries, and canneries are

---

[1] *Report to the Congress by the Comtroller General of the United States* (Washington, D.C., U.S. General Accounting Office, 1973), pp. 31–33.

rehabilitated for shopping centers and other commercial uses. Houses and stores are removed to make way for bridges and freeways.

Each successful change increases the intensity of use, productivity, and value of the land involved and adds to the general welfare at the time it is made. In effect, each parcel is continually seeking its highest and best use, whether urban or rural. The highest and best use will be realized unless prevented by institutional limitations (such as community plans and zoning ordinances) or lack of owner insight and initiative. Thus, each parcel is subject to development and redevelopment, a process termed *land use successsion.*

The reason for land use succession may better be visualized with the aid of a graph. Effectively, each new or succeeding use must be so productive or profitable that it can absorb the old use. Figure 22–1 illustrates the process. In the figure, use B might be a high-rise office building replacing an old, obsolete apartment building. The value of the site in office use is, therefore, great enough to absorb the value of the site in residential use plus the value of the depreciated building. Where remodeling is involved, the new use must absorb the value of the property in its old use plus the construction costs involved.

Our cities historically developed outward, or at the extensive margin, until recent years. The energy crunch of the early 1970s, and other factors, apparently brought about a turning point toward more growth upward, or at the intensive margin. Energy conservation means more compact urban areas, or less travel, of course. Construction costs have inflated so rapidly that it is now often more economical to rehabilitate older buildings than it is to build new ones. Rehabilitation is also advantageous because our cities are optimally located for the most part and involve a substantial infrastructure of streets, utilities, and civic buildings. And a centrally located older building is generally preferable to a new building at the urban fringe. Further, with zero population growth (ZPG) becoming a reality, it seems likely that high-quality space is going to be in greater demand than is simply more space. Finally, tax incentives favor rehabilitation of existing buildings as against construction of new buildings for business uses. Thus, our present communities, with their houses, apartments, schools, recreational, and cultural facilities, shopping centers, industrial districts, and churches all tied together by the transportation system, seem likely to endure for many years. In turn, it seems likely that rehabilitation of existing structures will become increasingly more important relative to construction of new buildings.

SITE SELECTION AND ANALYSIS

Judging a site suitable for development is probably the most basic decision of an investor-developer. Most other decisions in the development process

FIGURE 22–1
Land use succession results when a new use is so profitable that it can absorb the value of the property in its older use

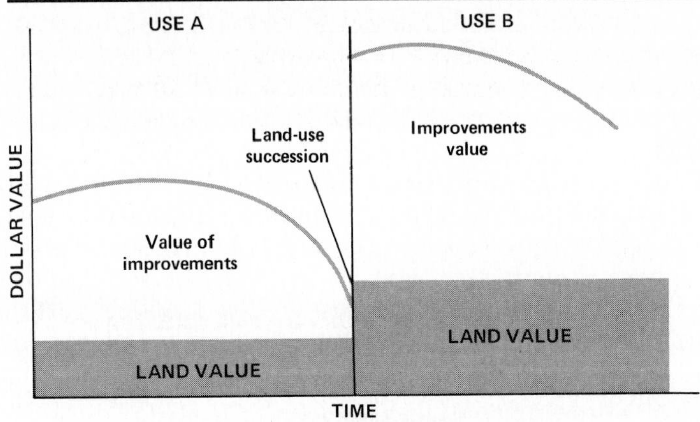

flow from the site selection decision. In many cases, the site selection decision is made twice. Acquisition of the site or even committing resources to study a site and its potential for development is the first decision. Committing resources to subdivide and/or develop a site is the second one. The second decision is of greater importance than the first. An acquired site may be sold or held vacant as well as developed.

Major elements of consideration in site selection and analysis are

1. Location or sites
2. Accessibility
3. Size and shape
4. Physical characteristics
5. Utilities and services
6. Applicable public regulations
7. Cost or value

We consider these elements briefly as they apply to the major alternative uses of any site, namely, residential, commercial, and industrial.

Residential

Location is the relation of a site to its environment, namely, to other land uses. Showing a site on a vicinity map enables a developer to visualize its location relative to existing or future schools, churches, shopping centers, major roadways, and other urban facilities. Desirable residential location includes living amenities. Thus, adverse or conflicting land uses, such as air-polluting industrial plants, are best avoided. Location and accessibility are closely related. Accessibility, you will remember, is the relative ease of getting to and from a particular parcel. Most trips from homes are to schools, shopping facilities, places of work, and homes of friends or relatives. Thus, close proximity to schools and shopping is important. Most wage earners are willing to commute up to an hour if the neighborhood and living environment are otherwise acceptable. Beyond close proximity, immediate access to freeways and mass transit is important to having good accessibility.

Each site is unique in its size, shape, and physical characteristics. The size and shape of a parcel must accommodate reasonable layout for residential use. Similarly, the topography, soils, hydrology, trees and bushes, and other physical characteristics of a site must be suitable to residential development. The most desirable topography is gently rolling hills that allow adequate drainage and facilitate the creation of an interesting living environment. Fertile soils that support vegetation are also advantageous.

The relative availability of utilties, such as water, sanitary sewers, and storm sewers, is critical to most residential development. These utilities may be provided through private or public systems, with public being much preferred to assure continuity of services at a reasonable cost. The installation of these utilities and of streets is a major cost in residential development. On the other hand, electrical and telephone services are extended to most urban sites at time of development, without costs to the project. In many areas, gas is available on a no-cost basis also.

Public regulation of development increased dramatically in the 1960s and 1970s, to become one of the major costs of development. The situation became so serious that in 1976 the Urban Land Institute published *The Permit Explosion* to state the seriousness and to encourage greater coordination in permitting procedures by public agencies. Permits add to development costs, both directly and indirectly. The direct cost is the charge made to obtain them, and the indirect cost is the long delay in getting the many required approvals and inspections. Also, increasing permit requirements tend to bar entry into development, making it easier for existing owners and developers to ask for and get higher prices.

Cost or value is a final major consideration in selecting a site for development. If the cost or asking price is so high that little developer profit is likely, all things considered, the site is unacceptable. On the other hand, if the value of an owned site on the market is higher than a developer considers justified, the site may be sold rather than developed.

Commercial

A distinct trade area is the prime consideration in locating a convenient commercial district. The size of the population and income levels must be examined in the market analysis and must justify the development. Then the most accessible site to the residences, one that cannot be readily cut off by competition, becomes important. Easy accessibility from several directions, without undue congestion and with easy entry onto the parcel itself, makes up a substantial part of this locational and accessibility need. High visibility to passing traffic is a location plus.

The size and shape must be suited to the type of development proposed. For example, a 5- to 10-acre site is needed for a neighborhood shopping center, while 80 to 100 acres or more are needed for a regional center. A large discount store might need 5 to 10 acres. Fast-food outlets and service stations increasingly need from 1 to 3 acres. Commercial sites must accommodate not only a necessary structure but also easy and adequate parking for customers.

A level site, at or slightly above street level, is desirable for commercial development. That is, uneven terrain, or sites substantially above or below street level, discourage entry by potential customers and are avoided by developers. All urban utilities and services are necessary for most commercial development. Proper zoning and other public approvals must be obtained in developing a commercial center or district, as for other types of development. In addition, an environmental impact statement is required. And, finally, the cost or value of the site must be consistent with the proposed use to allow the developer an acceptable profit.

Industrial

Primary concerns in location and accessibility for industrial purposes are raw materials, labor, supplies and component parts, and the market for the finished product. Larger firms, such as metal and mineral processors, are tied to raw materials. Weight-gaining industries must locate near their markets. Most other manufacturers need only be sure of readily obtaining component parts, supplies, and services from suppliers. That makes proximity and access to a freeway or interstate highway highly important to them. Large plants may need railroad or water access in addition. Immediate airport access is becoming increasingly important. An adequate labor pool with appropriate skills is necessary for any plant. But except for the most specialized processes, labor may be readily obtained almost anywhere in the United States because of the high technical capability of our population.

An industrial park may occupy several hundred acres in a large metropolitan area. Of course, many parks and districts are much smaller. The size and shape of the parcel must accommodate a reasonable layout. That is, the parcel must not necessitate sites of odd and inefficient shape. The topography must be level for the most part, and the soil must have high load-bearing capability. That is, sites with soft ground, such as marshes, are best avoided as they may not be able to support large buildings and heavy machines.

All utilities are required in an industrial area. In many cases, the utilities may have to be oversized to handle the many wastes resulting from the processes. Likewise, gas and electrical services may have to be oversized.

Highly restrictive local air- and water-pollution regulations discourage industrial location in many areas. Some communities, in addition, have a "no-growth" posture, which results in reluctance to accommodate the needs of prospective industries. An environmental-impact statement is required in creating any industrial park or district.

As with residential and commercial parcels, the cost or value of a site intended for industrial purposes must be in line with its profit potential.

ANALYSIS FOR PROPERTY DEVELOPMENT

The analysis preparatory to developing a real estate investment is quite similar to that required when buying an investment. The main difference is that the cost of land plus improvements is incurred instead of a purchase price. Also, in development, the details of construction management must be handled, and the delay for construction must be taken into account. A specific example seems appropriate at this point.

Black Oaks Case Data

Let us consider that Wendy Welloff expects to net, after taxes, $300,000 from the sale of Douglas Manor and that she is considering reinvesting this money in developing a new apartment building, Black Oaks. She has obtained cost estimates for land and improvements to develop Black Oaks that round off to $1,006,000. See Figure 22–2. Wendy has also had the market analyzed and has come up with a proforma annual operating schedule that indicates a NOI of $97,134 for Black Oaks. See Figure 22–3.

FIGURE 22–2
Black Oaks Apartments: project cost summary

LAND (including road improvements and installation of utilities)	$196,000
IMPROVEMENTS	
Building costs, including architectural fees	571,395
Financing and legal costs	96,080
Contingencies	40,000
Developer fees and profit	102,500
TOTAL	$1,005,975
Round to:	$1,006,000

FIGURE 22–3
Black Oaks Apartments: proforma annual operating statement

GROSS SCHEDULED INCOME:				
1 BR unit w/1½ baths 20 @$450 per month			$9,000	
2 BR units w/2½ baths 4		600	2,400	
3 BR units w/2½ baths 4		695	2,780	
Gross Monthly Income			$14,180	
Gross monthly income times 12				$170,160
Less: Vacancy & credit losses @5.0%				$8,508
Equals: Effective gross income (EGI)				$161,652
Less: Total operating expenses (TOE)				
Fixed:				
Real Estate Taxes	$24,503			
Hazard Insurance	1,702			
Licenses	200			
Variable:				
Management @ 5.0%	8,083			
Resident Manager	6,000			
Custodian and Yardman	8,000			
Workman's Comp. & Soc. Sec.	1,555			
Advertising	1,021			
Utilities	1,455			
Elevator Service	1,800			
Supplies	1,200			
Other—Pool, etc.	2,400			
Repair and maintenance	6,600			
Total	$64,518			64,518
Equals: Net operating income (NOI)				$97,134

In shopping financing, Wendy obtained a commitment for a $700,000 loan through ABC Mortgage Bankers. Debt service would be based on a 30-year amortization schedule, a 12 percent interest rate initially, compounded monthly, with renegotiation every 5 years, and a balloon payment at the end of year 15. Monthly and annual debt service would therefore be $7,200.29 and $86,403, respectively.

If developed, Wendy expects the NOI and value to increase 6 percent per year. Wendy decides that 15-year, straight-line depreciation would be best for her purposes. Further, Wendy has an after-tax required rate of return of 16 percent on any ventures she undertakes. Also, to determine feasibility, she considers a 4-year projection and analysis adequate. If feasible in four years, she considers that she then has flexibility to sell or exchange as opportunities occur. Annual interest payments on the loan in the first four years would therefore be $83,863, $83,541, $83,178, and $82,769. Straight-line cost recovery on the $810,000 in land improvements would be $45,000 per year.

FIGURE 22–4
Black Oaks Apartments: Cash flow projection and calculation of annual income tax to equity owner in 42% tax bracket

	YEAR			
ACCOUNTING ITEM	*1*	*2*	*3*	*4*
NOI, Chng/yr = 6.00%	$97,134	$102,962	$109,140	$115,688
−S/L Tax Depreciation	45,000	45,000	45,000	45,000
−Interest Paid	83,863	83,541	83,178	82,769
= Taxable Income	($31,729)	($25,579)	($19,038)	($12,081)
× Investors' Tax Rate	42.00%	42.00%	42.00%	42.00%
= Income Tax Payable	($13,326)	($10,743)	$7,996)	($5,074)

Wendy is usually in the 42 percent tax bracket, which would go up to 50 percent if Black Oaks were sold at the end of year 4 and a long-term capital gain realized. Given this information, the question comes up: "Is developing Black Oaks a worthwhile venture for Wendy?"

Equity Analysis

In a manner comparable to that used in Chapter 21 on investment analysis, Figures 22–4 and 22–5 show the BOY 1 value of annual cash flows after taxes are $20,739, $20,290, $19,689, and $18,976 when discounted at 16 percent; the total is $79,693. Figure 22–6 shows the calculations leading to the BOY 1 value of the after-tax equity reversion, $233,277.

Figure 22–7 summarizes the analysis. Note that the investment value of the equity position equals $312,970. In that Wendy Welloff's initial cash investment would be $306,000, this appears to be a viable investment for her. She would have to add $6,000 to the $300,000 realized from the sale of Douglas Manor. Note also that the total investment value is $1,012,970 (round to $1,013,000), which is some $7,000 greater than the

FIGURE 22–5
Black Oaks Apartments: Calculation of the present value of annual cash flow after tax

	YEAR			
ACCOUNTING ITEM	*1*	*2*	*3*	*4*
Net Operating Income	$97,134	$102,962	$109,140	$115,688
−Annual Debt Service	86,403	86,403	86,403	86,403
= Cash Flow Before Taxes	$10,731	$16,559	$22,736	$29,285
−Income Tax Payable	(13,326)	(10,743)	(7,996)	(5,074)
=Cash Flow After Taxes	$24,057	$27,302	$30,732	$34,359
× PVI Factor @ 16.00%	0.8621	0.7432	0.6407	0.5523
=P.V. of Annual CFAT	$20,739	$20,290	$19,689	$18,976
Accum' PV of CFAT	$20,739	$41,028	$60,717	$79,693

FIGURE 22–6
Black Oaks Apartments: Beginning of year one value of after-tax equity reversion from EOY 4

Disposition Price, EOY 4		$1,270,052
Less T/C @ 7.00%		88,904
Equals Net Disposition Price		$1,181,148
Less Adjusted Tax Basis		
Development cost	$1,006,000	
−S/L Cost Recovery	180,000	826,000
Equals Long-Term Capital Gain		$ 355,148
Minus Exclusion of 60.00%		213,089
Equals Taxable Portion of LTCG		$ 142,059
Times Investor's LTCG Tax Rate		50.00%
Equals Tax Payable on LTCG		$ 71,030
Disposition Price EOY 4		$1,270,052
Less:		
Transaction Costs	$ 88,904	
Loan Balance	687,738	
LTCG Taxes	71,030	
	$847,671	847,671
Net After-Tax Equity Reversion		$ 422,381
Times Annual PVI Factor @ 16.00%		0.552291
BOY 1 Value of After-Tax Equity Reversion		$ 233,277

total development cost. Thus, the investment is feasible in that value, based on Wendy's resources and criteria, exceeds cost.

Risk Analysis

Analysis of the financial risk would be important to the undertaking. Unless the risk ratios, as discussed in Chapters 17 and 21, on real estate credit and investment, meet the criteria of lenders, debt financing for the venture would not be obtainable. The ratios for Black Oaks are shown in Figure 22–8.

FIGURE 22–7
Black Oaks Apartments: BOY 1 investment value equity position and total property, if developed

BOY 1 Value of Annual CFAT to Equity	$79,693
Plus BOY 1 Value of After-Tax Equity Reversion	233,277
Equals Investment Value of Equity Position	$312,970
Plus Available Mortgage Loan	700,000
Equals Total Investment Value of Black Oaks	$1,012,970

FIGURE 22–8
Black Oaks: financing risk ratios

1. Operating Ratio	=	TOE / GI	=	$64,518 / $170,160	=	37.92%
2. BO Ratio	=	(TOE + ANN.D.S.) / GI	=	$150,921 / $170,160	=	88.69%
3. DSC Ratio	=	NOI / Ann. D.S.	=	$97,134 / $86,403	=	112.42%
4. LV Ratio	=	Loan, BOY 1 / M.V.	=	$700,000 / $1,006,000	=	69.58%

Briefly, the operating ratio at 37.92 percent is acceptable. A range of 38 to 40 percent is generally considered reasonable for new residential properties. The break-even occupancy ratio, at 88.69 percent, is at the high end, but acceptable also. A BO ratio over 90 percent is generally considered a "no go." Effectively, Black Oaks could have a vacancy rate of slightly over 11 percent and still meet debt service. The DSC (debt-service coverage) ratio of 112.42 is on the low side; a ratio of over 1.20 is preferred by lenders. Finally, the LVR, loan to value ratio, at 69.58 percent is well within acceptable limits for almost any lender. With a growth expectation of 6 percent per year and Wendy's extensive experience, ABC should find these ratios within acceptable bounds and be willing to make the loan, subject to negotiating the details.

THE PROPERTY DEVELOPMENT PROCESS

Successful property development requires a series of positive decisions by the many interests concerned with a particular project. First, the developer must judge that the project is feasible and coordinate the development process, much like a maestro. The landowner, if not the developer, must be satisfied as to the price and terms for the land. Consumers or other uses must be satisfied that the space provided suits their needs at an acceptable price. Planners and other public officials must accept the project as meeting applicable zoning and subdivision regulations and as being in the public interest generally. Realtors, financiers, engineers, architects, and attorneys must also solve problem situations to make the project "go." The development process only moves forward with positive decisions and actions by the players noted. One negative or "no-go" decision may shut down an entire project. Hence, the developer's skill in coordinating the many participants in a project is critical to success. All elements in a project are interrelated, and a weakness or inadequacy in any one element may endanger the entire project.

FIGURE 22–9
The property development process

STAGE OF DEVELOPMENT	TYPE OF CONSIDERATION				
	PHYSICAL	INSTITUTIONAL		ECONOMIC	
	PHYSICAL DESIGN AND DEVELOPMENT	GOVERNMENTAL	LEGAL	FINANCIAL	MARKETING AND PROMOTION
PRELIMINARY PLANS	Locate property if not already owned Complete preliminary design	Discuss possibilities with planning agency and others Tentative approvals	Arrange for option to purchase land if not owned	Make estimate of cost and value of land Locate financial backing Feasibility analysis	Market analysis Highest and best-use analysis
FINAL PLANS	Details of final plat	Work with planning and other agencies to get final approvals of proposed development Approvals obtained	Develop land-use controls Purchase land, if not owned	Make up initial capital and operating budgets and solvency statement Verify backing Make up final budgets	Marketability study Develop marketing and promotional program based on market analysis
DISPOSITION OR START-UP	Install utilities and streets Build houses, etc., if part of operation	Record plat and controls	Transfer parcels as sold	Recheck profit picture Pay bills, watch money come in	Initiate marketing program Rent space if ownship to be retained

These many decision may be classified into a physical, institutional, and economic framework, as shown in Figure 22–9. Study of Figure 22–9 makes apparent the need for careful coordination in the development process. Institutional considerations break down into legal and governmental limitations and constraints. Zoning ordinances, subdivision regulations, and approvals by the planning commission are examples of governmental constraints. Legal constraints include options to purchase, obtaining clear title, and preparing private plans and actions. The process involves three stages: preliminary plans, final plans, and disposition or start-up. The process, as presented here, is schematic only. In fact, it varies from one project to another.

Preliminary Planning Stage

In the preliminary planning stage, a developer must search for a property suitable for improvement if one is not already owned. Once a property is located, its development possibilities must be checked out with the planning commission and other governmental agencies. A market analysis is necessary to ascertain the probable demand, if the property were to be approved by local governmental agencies and the value, and probable cost, if the land were to be purchased. If the situation looks right, an option to purchase is arranged with the owner. Assuming that these constraints or limitations are satisified, the highest and best use of the property must be determined and financial backing located. A preliminary plan is drawn up and submitted to the planning commission and other agencies for tenative approval. Upon receipt of tenative approval, the financial planning stage is entered. No definite time limit applies in the preliminary planning stage, but several months to a couple of years is typical.

Final Planning Stage

In the final planning stage, details of the plat map to be recorded are worked out. This means removing or satisfying any reservations or conditions attached to the approval of the preliminary plan by governmental agencies. Private land use controls must be written. Capital and operating budgets must be worked out to determine if the project is feasible and likely to leave the developer solvent. Based on these accounting statements, financial backing must be arranged if not already in hand. Also, concurrently, a marketing and promotional program must be drawn up. Toward the end of the final planning stage, governmental approvals must be in hand and final budgets firmed up. If everything continues to appear feasible, the land is purchased if not already owned. One year is usually the maximum time from preliminary plan approval to final plat approval. The maximum time will be stipulated in local regulations. If this time is exceeded, the developer is likely to have to begin all over again, which frequently involves having additional conditions attached to the project.

Construction/Disposition/Start-up Stage

Upon getting all permit approvals and recording the appropriate documents, the developer suddenly becomes largely independent of outside influences except for the market. Utilities and streets must be installed or a performance bond put up, and deed restrictions must also be recorded if appropriate. Also, a marketing program must be initiated. Finally, if improvements are to be added, arrangements must be made for architects, landscape architects, contractors, and others. The adding of improvements and the rent up or disposition of the properties may take several years.

If the project is an urban subdivision, model dwellings must be built as demonstration homes. On sale, clear title must be conveyed. If the project is an income property being developed for use as an investment, space must be leased and a management plan initiated. The disposition stage continues until all parcels are sold or all space is rented out.

ANALYSIS FOR REDEVELOPMENT/MODERNIZATION

Modernization/redevelopment is necessary from time to time to keep a property productive and in its highest and best use. The question becomes: "At what time is modernization/redevelopment suitable?"

In simple terms, modernization is appropriate when the marginal value created exceeds the marginal costs. Or, in financial management terms, when the present value of the marginal revenues, discounted at the required rate of return, exceeds the costs of modernization. A case example based on Douglas Manor and Gerald and Nancy Investor illustrates the approach to be taken. The DCF model will continue to serve as the analytical framework.

Case Data

Gerald Investor, having completed his analysis of Douglas Manor, recognizes that some modification and modernization is needed. The additional cost would be $30,000. The lender agrees that the modernization is desirable and is willing to lend an additional $20,000 toward it at the original terms: 25 years, 12 percent, with monthly compounding, based on Gerald's analysis.

Modernization will increase the annual NOI by $4,800 in year 1 to $68,800. Jerry Investor considers that his tax bracket will be raised to 42 percent as a result of the modernization and some other changes in his and Nancy's investment situation. The $30,000 modernization would be

FIGURE 22–10
Douglas manor modernized: cash flow projection and calculation of annual income tax to owner in 42.00% Tax Bracket

ACCOUNTING ITEM	YEAR 1	2	3	4
NOI, Rate of change = 5%	$68,800	$72,240	$75,852	$79,645
−S/L Tax Depreciation	31,667	31,667	31,667	31,667
−Interest Paid	62,211	61,766	61,264	60,699
=Taxable Income	($25,078)	($21,193)	($17,079)	($12,721)
× Investor's Tax Rate	42.00%	42.00%	42.00%	42.00%
=Income Tax Payable	($10,533)	($8,901)	($7,173)	($5,343)

FIGURE 22–11
Douglas manor modernized: Calculation of the BOY 1 values of annual cash flows after taxes discounted at 15%

ACCOUNTING ITEM	YEAR 1	2	3	4
Net Operating Income	$68,800	$72,240	$75,852	$79,645
−Annual Debt Service	65,721	65,721	65,721	65,721
=Cash Flow Before Tax	$3,079	$6,519	$10,131	$13,923
−Income Tax Payable	(10,533)	(8,901)	(7,173)	(5,343)
=Cash Flow After Tax	$13,611	$15,420	$17,304	$19,266
× PV1 Factor @ 0.15	0.8696	0.7561	0.6575	0.5718
=P.V. of Annual CFAT	$11,836	$11,660	$11,378	$11,016

amortized over 15 years, meaning an additional $1,667 per year for straight-line cost recovery; thus, total cost recovery would be $31,667 per year. All other investment assumptions regarding Douglas Manor, from chapter 21, would hold as before.

DCF Analysis

Figures 22–10 and 22–11 show the revised annual cash flow projections for Douglas Manor, including income taxes payable and the cash flows after taxes. The format is almost identical to that in Figures 21–4 and 21–5. Cash flows after taxes for years 1 to 4 respectively are $13,611, $15,420, $17,304, and $19,266.

Figures 22–12 A & B show the calculation of the net after-tax equity reversion from EOY 4, assuming modernization. The amount is $227,795. Again, the calculations are directly parallel to the calculations of Chapter 21.

Marginal NPV and IRR

Annual cash flows after tax before and after modernization are shown in Figure 22–13. The marginal revenues resulting from the modernization are also shown. Note that after-tax equity reversion from EOY 4 is combined with CFAT from operations in the figure. The marginal equity investment for modernization is $10,000. In accordance with the RRR of the Investor's the marginal cash flows are discounted at 15 percent.

Figure 22–13 shows that the present value of all marginal cash flows after taxes is $15,319. In turn, the net present value, (NPV), of the modernization investment is $5,319 ($15,319–$10,000). Therefore, according to the Gerald and Nancy Investor's criteria, the modernization should be undertaken.

FIGURE 22–12 A
Douglas manor modernized: BOY 1 value of EOY 4 after-tax equity reversion, discounted at 15.00%

Disposition Price, EOY 4		$836,268
Less TC @ 7.00%		58,539
Equals Net Disposition Price		$777,730
Less Adjusted Tax Basis		
Purchase Price + Improvements	$670,000	
−Accum. S/L Tax Depreciation	126,667	543,333
Equals Long-term Capital Gain		$234,396
Minus Exclusion of 60%		140,638
Equals Taxable Portion of LTCG		$93,758
× Investor's LTCG Tax Rate		50.00 %
Equals Tax Payable on LTCG		$46,879
Disposition Price, EOY 4		$836,268
Less:		
Transaction Costs @ 7.00%	$58,539	
Loan Balance	503,056	
LTCG Taxes	46,879	608,474
Net After-Tax Equity Reversion		$227,795
Times Annual PV1 Factor: @ 15.00%		0.571753
BOY 1 Value of After-Tax Equity Reversion		$130,242

FIGURE 22–12 B
Douglas Manor modernized: Investment value of equity position and total property, if modernized

BOY1 Value of Annual CFAT to Equity	$45,889
Plus BOY1 Value of After-Tax Equity Reversion	130,242
Equals Investment Value of Equity Position	$176,131
Plus Available Mortgage Loan	520,000
Equals Total Investment Value of Douglas Manor	$696,131

FIGURE 22–13
Douglas Manor modernized: calculation of marginal revenues, and of the P.V. and IRR of the revenues

YEAR	*1*	*2*	*3*	*4*
CFAT, after modernization	$13,611	$15,420	$17,304	$247,061
CFAT, before modernization	$11,134	$12,883	$14,706	$230,379
Initial INV & Marg.Incr. ($10,000)	$2,478	$2,537	$2,598	$16,682
× PV Factor @ 15.00%	0.869565	0.756144	0.657516	0.571753
PV of Marg. Incr. in CFAT	$2,154	$1,918	$1,708	$9,538
Accum. P.V. of Modernization	$2,154	$4,073	$5,781	$15,319
A.T.I.R.R. to Marginal Equity:	$10,000	=	31.81%	

Alternatively, the internal rate of return for the marginal cash flows, based on a $10,000 initial investment, calculates to 31.81 percent. This easily exceeds the 15 percent required rate of return of the Investors, again indicating the program should be initiated.

The analysis for a major redevelopment of Douglas Manor, while more complex, would follow this same basic format. Whatever the case, the marginal revenues must justify the cost of modernization or redevelopment to be financially feasible.

SUMMARY

The reason for property development and redevelopment is land use succession. The property in the new use can absorb the cost in the old use plus improvement costs. In other words, the value created must exceed costs of development or redevelopment to be justified, according to current financial theory. Also, developers and subdividers must be ever more financially responsible because of ever-greater governmental regulation, brought about by excesses in the past.

In property development, the value created may be directly "bumped" up against total development costs, to determine if the undertaking is feasible. Property development has three distinct stages: (1) preliminary planning, (2) final planning, and (3) construction/ disposition/start-up. With modernization or redevelopment, the marginal value created must exceed the marginal costs incurred. Case examples presented in this chapter illustrate the analysis required to determine development and redevelopment feasibility.

QUESTIONS FOR REVIEW AND DISCUSSION

1. Define and explain the interrelationships among carrying costs, taxpayer, and a ripe property.
2. Distinguish between subdividing and developing property.
3. Explain briefly how the economics of land use succession leads to property development and redevelopment.
4. List five elements or considerations in site analysis and selection. Explain each as it applies to selecting a site for residential development.
5. State briefly the necessary relationship between costs and value for a property to be ripe for development.
6. Identify and discuss briefly the activities in each of the three stages of the property development process.
7. In property modernization, what is the necessary relationship between costs and value?.

8. Do zoning and other land use controls affect profits realized by a developer? If so, how? Discuss.

9. Is advance acquisition of land for development productive? Explain. Is it socially desirable?

10. Do we, as a society, need planning, zoning, subdivision regulations, and other land use controls?

11. What major areas of your community are being developed from bare land now? What type of development is it—residential, commercial, or industrial? Is such development consistent with the economic and social outlook for your community?

CASE PROBLEMS

1. Assume that NOI for Black Oaks were not expected to increase at all over the 4-year projection period, but Wendy Welloff wanted only a 12 percent after-tax rate of return. Would Black Oaks still be viable as an investment for Wendy?
2. Assume that modernizing Douglas Manor were expected to cost $35,000, with the bank still only lending $20,000. Would modernization be worthwhile from the viewpoint of the Investors, based on the IRR to their equity requirement of $15,000?

CHAPTER TWENTY-THREE
PROPERTY MANAGEMENT

Labor can do nothing without capital, capital can do nothing without labor,
and neither can do anything without the guiding genius of management;
and management, however wise its genius may be,
can do nothing without the privileges which the community affords.
W.L. MACKENZIE KING, former prime minister of Canada

IMPORTANT TOPICS OR DECISION AREAS TAKEN UP IN THIS CHAPTER

- Managing Property as an Investment
- Managing Property as a Business
- Property Assessments and Taxation
- Property Insurance
- Management Requirements by Property Type.

Considerable effort and attention are needed to make real property productive on a continuing basis. An owner must personally provide or buy (contract for) the effort and attention. This chapter provides an overview of necessary activities and decisions involved in property ownership and management; a detailed explanation of everyday routine is not intended.

The concern here is primarily with income property; therefore, attention is not given to vacant land or owner-occupied residential properties. The basic function of management, with income properties, is to lance periodic cash flow against preservation of value toward maximizing the rate of return on investment.

In Chapter 21 we noted that three of the six most important variables in income property investing are directly related to property management. These are (1) maximizing the property's gross income, (2) controlling operating expenses, and (3) maintaining leverage. They translate into balancing periodic income and obtaining capital gains from value appreciation at optimum levels.

KEY CONCEPTS INTRODUCED IN THIS CHAPTER

Assessed value
Business interruption insurance
Coinsurance
Escalation clause
Extended coverage
Levy
Minimum rated risk
Rental schedule
Specifically rated risks
Tax base

MANAGING PROPERTY AS AN INVESTMENT

Three major issues are involved in managing a property as a long-term investment:

1. *Routine administration.* Arrange for a competent manager to maintain the property's cash flow and value. The objective is to have routine details attended to by the manager while having necessary financial decisions brought to the attention of the owner at appropriate times. The results show up in the adequacy of periodic reports to the owner and the adequacy of the analysis for the financial decisions. Administrative concerns are taken up here following financial management concerns.
2. *Adapting to change.* Periodically, the property's productivity relative to changing market and environmental conditions must be analyzed. The possibility of investing additional capital to change the use, to moderize the building, or to make an addition to the property is included here. Analysis for modernization/modification is considered in Chapter 22, Development and Redevelopment. It is assumed here that the Investors did not modernize Douglas Manor so that the present analysis can be based on the familiar data introduced in Chapter 21 on investment analysis.
3. *Maintaining leverage and disinvesting.* Analysis for possible refinancing or reinvestment should also be undertaken periodically, again to assure that the owner is getting the best possible rate of return on equity, on a risk adjusted, after-

> tax rate-of-return basis. The discounted cash flow (DCF) model, introduced earlier, is highly useful for this analysis. The chance for a higher rate of return from refinancing must be weighed against the higher financial risks to be incurred. The same DCF analysis methodology also allows determination of the appropriate time for disinvestment from one property and reinvestment in another. The objective is to ascertain if a sale or exchange is in order. At such time as a higher rate of return might be earned by investing in and owning another property, a shift in investment is usually justified. The analysis must include the transaction costs involved in changing investments.

In summary then, the Investors have four basic alternatives concerning management of Douglas Manor as an investment and a financial asset. These are (1) continue without change, (2) remodel and modernize, (3) refinance, and (4) sell and reinvest. Initial analysis, along the lines shown in Chapter 22, shows what would be required for modernization to be a viable alternative. Therefore, the alternatives in this chapter are reduced to continuing as is, refinancing, and selling.

A property manager or a real estate consultant may be called upon to do much of the analysis needed for these decisions. But, because of the major, long-term implications and effects, the actual decisions should be made by the owner or owners.

Douglas Manor: EOY 4 Status

The best place for the Investors to begin is to gain knowledge of what would be likely to happen if they continued without change. Having owned Douglas Manor for four years, Gerald and Nancy Investor therefore consider it time to reevaluate their position. Douglas Manor was acquired for $640,000, with the expectation that both NOI and value would increase by 5 percent per year. See Figures 21–4 and 21–5. In fact, the increases have only been 3 percent per year. Further, because of competition and a sagging local economy, the Investors expect the 3 percent growth rate to continue. See Figures 23–1A and B. Also, The Investor's net, after-tax equity at end of year 4, is $156,215, as calculated in Figure 23–2. Again, the modernization program discussed in Chapter 22 is assumed not to have been undertaken so that this discussion can start here with the original data, and thereby keep the analysis of the alternatives on an equal footing. The Investors decide that their current after-tax net equity (EOY 4) is the appropriate base.

Cash flows for continuing "as is" for the next 4 years (years 5 to 8), are taken from Figures 23–A and B; and net after tax equity reversion at EOY 8 is taken from Figure 23–2. The NPV of the cash flows at the RRR of 15 percent is $19,914, calculated as follows:

FIGURE 23–1A
Douglas Manor: Cash flow history (years 1–4) and projections (years 5–8) and calculation of annual income tax to equity owner in 40% tax bracket

ACCOUNTING ITEM	YEAR 1	2	3	4	5	6	7	8
NOI, annual growth = 3%	$64,000	$65,920	$67,898	$69,935	$72,033	$74,194	$76,419	$78,712
− S/L tax depreciation	30,000	30,000	30,000	30,000	30,000	30,000	30,000	30,000
− Interest Paid	59,818	59,390	58,908	58,364	57,752	57,062	56,284	55,408
− Interest on loan 2					0	0	0	0
= Taxable Income	($25,818)	($23,470)	($21,010)	($18,430)	($15,719)	($12,868)	($9,865)	($6,696)
× Investor's tax rate	40.00%	40.00%	40.00%	40.00%	40.00%	40.00%	40.00%	40.00%
= Income tax payable	($10,327)	($9,388)	($8,404)	($7,372)	($6,288)	($5,147)	($3,946)	($2,678)

FIGURE23–1 B
Douglas Manor: Calculation of annual cash flows after taxes, years 1–8

ACCOUNTING ITEM	YEAR 1	2	3	4	5	6	7	8
NOI	$64,000	$65,920	$67,898	$69,935	$72,033	$74,194	$76,419	$78,712
− Annual debt service	63,193	63,193	63,193	63,193	63,193	63,193	63,193	63,193
− Annual D.S. on second debt service					0	0	0	0
= Cash flow before taxes	$807	$2,727	$4,704	$6,741	$8,839	$11,000	$13,226	$15,518
− Income tax payable	(10,327)	(9,388)	(8,404)	(7,372)	(6,288)	(5,147)	(3,946)	(2,678)
= Cash flow after taxes	$11,134	$12,115	$13,108	$14,113	$15,127	$16,147	$17,172	$18,197

FIGURE 23–2
Douglas Manor: After-tax equity at EOY

EOY		*4*	*and*	*8*
Disposition Price		$720,326		$810,733
Less Disposition Costs @ 7.00%		50,423		56,751
Equals Net Disposition Price		$669,903		$753,982
Less Adjusted Tax Basis				
BOY1 Basis	$640,000		$640,000	
+ Improvements	0		0	
− S/L Tax Depreciation	120,000	520,000	240,000	400,000
Equals Long-Term Capital Gain		$149,903		$353,982
Minus 60% Exclusion		89,942		212,389
Equals Taxable Portion of LTCG		$59,961		$141,593
Times Investor's Tax Rate on LTCG In		50.00%		50.00%
Equals Tax Payable on LTCG		$29,981		$70,796
Disposition Price, EOY		$720,326		$810,733
Less:				
Transaction Costs	$50,423		$56,751	
Loan Balance	483,707		457,440	
RRM 2nd Loan	0		0	
LTCG Taxes	29,981		70,796	
	$564,111	$564,111	$584,988	584,988
Net After-Tax Equity Reversion		$156,215		$225,745

	EOY	*CFAT*	*15% PV FACTOR*	*PV OF CFAT*	*EOY 4/BOY 5 VALUE*
	5	$ 15,127	0.869565	$ 13,154	
	6	16,147	0.756144	12,210	
	7	17,172	0.657516	11,291	
	8	18,197	0.571753	10,404	
		225,747	0.571753	129,070	
After-tax equity	8				
EOY 4/BOY 5 value of A.T. cash flows:				$176,129	$176,129
− A.T. Equity, EOY 4					−156,215
Net present value, EOY 4,					$ 19,914

These same figures provide an internal rate of return on EOY 4, current, equity of 18.94 percent. Thus, refinancing or selling and reinvesting must offer a higher NPV than $19,914 or a higher equity rate of return than 18.94 percent to be a better alternative.

Refinancing

The Investors, after some searching, determined that their best alternative for refinancing is a commitment for an interest only $80,000, RRM loan at 14 percent from the Latent Mortgage Corporation. The interest rate is to be renegotiated at the end of 5 years, with a balloon payment required at the end of 10 years. Annual interest (and debt service) would therefore come to $11,200 ($80,000 times 14 percent).

The loan would reduce their EOY 4 after-tax equity investment in Douglas Manor to $76,215 ($156,215 – $80,000). After-tax cash flows for years 5 to 8, taken from Figures 23–3 and 23–4, would be as follows: (5) ($553), (6) $467, (7) $ 1,492, and (8) $2,517. Their net after-tax equity reversion at EOY 8 would be reduced to $145,745 ($225,745 – $80,000). See Figure 23–5.

The net result of refinancing would be an IRR of 18.40 percent on their EOY 4 after-tax equity investment left in the property, $76,215. They would have $80,000 released for another venture, however. The rate of return on equity is therefore lowered slightly. An alternative investment would have to give a somewhat higher IRR or NPV on the monies released to make refinancing feasible.

Deciding to Sell and Reinvest

The last alternative open to the Investors is to sell Douglas Manor and reinvest the proceeds, which at the EOY 4, amount to $156,215 based on our earlier analysis. They have located a property, the Swift Office Building, which they can purchase for $675,000 with a downpayment of $125,000. The first year NOI is projected at $74,250. Value and NOI are expected to grow by 4 percent per year, due to differences in property type and location relative to Douglas Manor. The loan would be for $550,000 at 12 percent, compounded monthly, with amortization over 30

FIGURE 23–3
Douglas Manor refinanced: Cash flow projections (years 5–8) and calculation of annual income tax to equity owner in 40% tax bracket

	YEAR			
ACCOUNTING ITEM	*5*	*6*	*7*	*8*
NOI, annual growth = 3%	$72,033	$74,194	$76,419	$78,712
–S/L tax depreciation	30,000	30,000	30,000	30,000
–Interest on 1st	57,752	57,062	56,284	55,408
–Interest on 2nd	(11,200)	(11,200)	(11,200)	(11,200)
=Taxable income	($4,519)	($1,668)	$1,335	$4,504
× Investor's tax rate	40.00%	40.00%	40.00%	40.00%
=Income Tax payable	($1,808)	($667)	$534	$1,802

FIGURE 23–4
Douglas Manor refinanced: Calculation of annual CFAT 15%

ACCOUNTING ITEM	YEAR 5	6	7	8
NOI	$72,033	$74,194	$76,419	$78,712
−Annual Debt Service	63,193	63,193	63,193	63,193
−Annual D.S. on 2nd	11,200	11,200	11,200	11,200
=Cash Flow Before Tax	($2,361)	($200)	$2,026	$4,318
−Income Tax Payable	(1,808)	(667)	534	1,802
=Cash Flow After Tax	($553)	$467	$1,492	$2,517

years. The interest rate would be renegotiable after 5 years. The land is valued at $117,000, which means that improvements amount to $558,000, and which gives a straight-line depreciation write-off of $31,000 per year. See Figures 23–6 and 23–7 for cash flows.

Disposition at EOY 4 of owning the Swift Office Building would result in a net, after-tax equity reversion of $157,338; see Figure 23–8. The result would be a 4-year IRR of 25.70 percent, well above the 15

FIGURE 23–5
Douglas Manor refinanced

After-tax equity position at EOY		4	and EOY	8
Disposition Price		$720,326		$810,733
Less disposition costs @ 7.00%		50,423		56,751
Equals net disposition price		$669,903		$753,982
Less adjusted tax basis				
BOY 1 basis	$640,000		$640,000	
Plus: Improvements	0		0	
Less: S/L tax depreciation	120,000	520,000	240,000	400,000
Equals Long-term capital Gain		$149,903		$353,982
Less: 60% Exclusion		89,942		212,389
Equals taxable portion of LTCG		$59,961		$141,593
Times investor's tax rate on LTCG Income		50.00%		50.00%
Equals tax payable on LTCG		$29,981		$70,796
Disposition price, EOY		$720,326		$810,733
Less:				
Transaction Costs	$50,423		$56,751	
Loan Balance	$483,707		$457,440	
RRM 2nd Loan	$80,000		$80,000	
LTCG taxes	$29,981		$70,796	
	$644,111	644,111	$664,988	664,988
Net after-tax equity reversion		$76,215		$145,745

FIGURE 23–6
Swift Office Building: Cash flow projections and calculation of annual income tax to equity owner in 40% tax bracket

ACCOUNTING ITEM	*YEAR* 1	2	3	4
NOI, annual growth = 4%	$74,250	$77,220	$80,309	$85,521
−S/L tax depreciation	31,000	31,000	31,000	31,000
−Interest paid	65,893	65,639	65,354	65,033
−Interest on 2nd				
=taxable income	($22,643)	($19,419)	($16,045)	($12,512)
× Investor's tax rate	40.00%	40.00%	$40.00%	40.00%
=Income tax payable	($9,057)	($7,768)	($6,418)	($5,005)

percent RRR of the Investors. Thus, the Swift Office Building is a viable alternative for the Investors. However, in making the changeover, the Investors would have an additional $31,215 to invest; this amount is the EOY 4 after-tax equity reversion from Douglas Manor less the $125,000 down payment for the Swift Office Building. The Investors would also incur risk in the changeover in that they would be switching from a residential type property, with which they are familiar, to a business type property. In addition, considerable stress would be involved.

Making the Choice

The alternatives facing the Investors are as follows:

1. Continuing to hold Douglas Manor, as is, with an expected IRR of 18.94 percent.
2. Refinancing Douglas Manor, by borrowing an additional $80,000. This would give an IRR of 18.40 percent on the equity remaining in Douglas Manor and give them $80,000 to invest elsewhere.

FIGURE 23–7
Swift Office Building: Cash flow projections and calculation of the BOY 1 value of annual CFAT, discounted at 15%

ACCOUNTING ITEM	*YEAR* 1	2	3	4
NOI	$74,250	$77,220	$80,309	$83,521
−Annual debt service	67,888	67,888	67,888	67,888
−Annual D.S. on 2nd				
=Cash flow before taxes	$6,362	$9,332	$12,420	$15,633
−Income tax payable	(9,057)	(7,768)	(6,418)	(5,005)
=Cash flow after taxes	$15,419	$17,099	$18,839	$20,637
× PV1 factor	0.8696	0.7561	0.6575	0.5718
=P.V. of annual CFAT	$13,407	$12,930	$12,387	$11,800

FIGURE 23–8
Swift Office Building: After-tax equity position at EOY

		4
Disposition price		$789,655
Less disposition costs @ 7.00%		55,276
Equals net disposition price		$734,379
Less adjusted tax basis		
BOY1 basis	$675,000	
+Improvements	0	
−S/L tax depreciation	124,000	551,000
Equals long term capital gain		$183,379
Minus 60% exclusion		110,027
Equals taxable portion of LTCG		$73,351
Times Investor's tax rate on LTCG		50.00%
Equals tax payable on LTCG		$36,676
Disposition price, EOY		$789,655
Less:		
Transaction costs	$55,276	
Loan balance	$540,365	
LTCG taxes	$36,676	
	$632,317	632,317
Net after-tax equity reversion		$157,338

3. Selling Douglas Manor and buying the Swift Office Building. The IRR expected on the money invested in the SOB is 25.70 percent, but the Investors would have to invest an excess of about $31,000 elsewhere.

What other considerations enter in? First, Gerald and Nancy would have to find an investment for the $80,000 from the second mortgage loan that would result in an overall rate of return on the entire $156,215 higher than the 18.94 percent from Douglas Manor or the possible 25.70 percent from the Swift Office Building, other risks ignored, for refinancing to be the best choice. Risks and concerns with selling and reinvesting could be considerable. A shift in the type of property owned would involve additional risks. The Investors are already well aware of the operating requirements of Douglas Manor. Time and effort to make the change would be substantial transaction costs. Acquiring Swift Office Building would also increase the financial risk because of the larger RRM loan. Owning two properties, via the $80,000 loan, would also serve to spread the Investors' risks. These are the type of considerations facing the Investors. And each individual or group chooses a best alternative based on personal preferences, including desire to seek profit or avoid risk.

MANAGING PROPERTY AS A BUSINESS

Most owners of larger properties arrange for a property manager to handle the daily administrative routine. The property manager, if working for an owner, is an employee and acts as an agent of the owner. On the other hand, an individual managing properties for several owners is an independent contractor as well as an agent. In either case, the property manager's role is to satisfy both the owner and the tenants.

The property manager assumes all executive functions involved in the operation and physical care of the property, thereby relieving the owner of all labor and details associated with day-to-day operation of the property. The principal functions of the manager include

1. Mechandising space to secure suitable tenants at the best rents obtainable
2. Collecting rents
3. Maintaining favorable tenant relations
4. Purchasing operating supplies and equipment
5. Maintaining favorable employee relations
6. Maintaining property
7. Keeping proper accounts and rendering periodic reports
8. Looking after property assessment and taxation levels
9. Maintaining adequate insurance protection

The first seven of these functions are discussed in this section. Property taxes and insurance are so important that a separate section is devoted to each. Each function bears on the overall success of the property management effort.

Merchandising Space

The marketing of space is in essence a merchandising problem. The space-seeking tenant, as a rule, is familiar with the city, with the neighborhood in which the property is located, with prevailing rentals on a per room or per square foot basis, with availability of competitive space, and with the locational advantages and disadvantages of the subject property. To secure the prospect as a tenant, the manager or his or her representative must be able to "sell" the space by matching the service opportunities that the property has to offer with the specific needs and requirements that the prospect seeks to satisfy.

Merchandising of space, contrary to common belief, is more difficult than is outright selling. In the latter case, when a property sale is consummated the broker is through with the deal and may turn to other properties with renewed vigor and initiative. In merchandising space, the "sale" normally is for a limited time and periodically renewals must be renegotiated. The property manager is thus aware that any representations must be truthful and the services offered adequate in order that the tenant may remain sold as long as possible.

Rent schedule. The first and perhaps most important step in the marketing of space is the establishment of a *rental schedule.* In theory the price of space should be based on operating costs, fixed charges, and a fair rate of return *on* the investment and *of* the investment (amortization) over the economic life of the property. In practice, rental prices are established by space supply and demand. Although in the long run rentals must be compensatory and fully meet operating costs and investment charges (if new space is to be forthcoming), in the short run space values fluctuate widely, depending on forces affecting tenant space demand (purchasing power) in relation to the relatively inflexible space supply of apartment and commercial properties.

Rental schedules for the various units of space offered are most realistically established on a market comparison basis. This is done by rating the subject property in relation to like properties in similar neighborhoods for which accurate rental data are available. The comparison approach, though simple in application, relies on sound judgment for effective application. Comparison is generally made with a number of typical space units, and price adjustments for the subject property are based on quantitative and qualitative differences. For example, in the pricing of an apartment unit, consideration should be given to the following: area of floor space, number of bathrooms, quality of construction, decorative features, floor location, type and quality of elevator service, nature and quality of janitorial services, reputation of building and characteristics of tenants, location of building in relation to public conveniences, and quality rating of neighborhood and neighborhood trends. Assuming that a standard unit in an ideal neighborhood rents for $500 per month and the comparative rating for the subject property, after due consideration of the factors enumerated above, is 90 percent, then the estimated fair rental is judged to be $450 per month. If a detailed comparison is made for each space unit with six or more selected and comparable units, a fairly accurate and competitive rental schedule can be established and submitted for the owner's approval.[1]

Advertising and tenant selection. The next step in the marketing of space is the determination of the kind of tenants to be secured and the policy to be followed in advertising the types of units and services offered. Every effort should be made to attract qualified tenants who appear homoge-

[1]Students of management and those seeking to perfect their judgment in rental schedule preparation should study the rental formula developed by Leo J. Sheridan and William Karkow, two well-known Chicago building managers. Copies of the Sheridan-Karkow formula are available through the National Association of Building Owners and Managers, Chicago.

neous in living characteristics. Tenants react on each other and, as a whole, add or detract from the amenities of living and the congenial atmosphere that is conducive to pride of occupancy and a feeling of belonging. Some buildings may be deemed best suited for young couples with children; others may be best for older and retired people who cherish an atmosphere of quiet restfulness. The fact that an attempt is made to suit the facilities of the building to the housing needs and requirements of the tenant makes a favorable impression upon the prospect and generally contributes importantly to the development of tenant good will and to the furtherance of good public relations. If the rental schedule is properly prepared and the building space effectively advertised, one out of every five eligible prospects calling at the property should as a rule become a building tenant.[2] If the ratio of tenants to prospects is greater or smaller, the space units may be underpriced or overpriced.

Collecting Rents

The collection of rents needs not pose a problem if the credit rating of each tenant, before his or her acceptance, is carefully checked and if the collection policy is clearly explained and firmly adhered to. In most communities with a population of 10,000 and over, credit bureaus have been established, and it is possible to secure from them, at nominal cost, a credit record of the prospective tenant. Credit reports, as a rule, serve as an excellent safeguard against acceptance of tenants who have demonstrated financial instability. It is also wise policy to request references and to check with property owners from whom the applicant has rented in the immediate past. If the applicant, for instance, has not given proper "vacate" notice at a previous place of residence, or failed to pay the rent, the application should, of course, be rejected or an advance deposit of an extra month's rent be required.

A firm collection policy is basic to successful management. At the outset, tenants should be impressed with the importance of making payments on time at the start of the rental period as specified in the lease agreement. Tenants may also be informed that periodic statements are not sent and that it is their obligation to submit payment on the due date to the manager's office. In many cases, however, notices are sent. It is deemed good policy, for record purposes, to issue rental receipts even though payments are received by check. Such receipts permit uniform rental auditing and provide a ready reference for bookkeeping purposes.

A procedure for follow-up of past-due rentals should be rigidly and uniformly adhered to. A statement for past-due rents should be sent to delinquent tenants within 5 to 10 days after the rental due date. This due

[2]See James C. Downs, Jr., "Marketing and Leasing" *Principles of Real Estate Management,* 12th ed. (Chicago: Institute of Real Estate Management, 1980), Chap. 8.

notice may be followed with a final notice a week or 10 days later. If this notice is ignored or not satisfactorily acted upon, legal proceedings are then in order to obtain possesssion or to collect the unpaid rent.

Maintaining Favorable Tenant Relations

Clear communications and an open manner go far to establish and maintain cordial tenant relations. And cordial tenant relations go far in making rent collections easier, avoiding the organization of tenant unions, and obtaining tenant cooperation in general. Prompt and courteous attention to tenant requests is important in this respect, though all requests may not be met. Downs says that 90 percent of all tenant requests are reasonable.[3] If a request cannot be met, the tenant should be immediately so informed.

Purchasing Supplies and Authorizing Wages

The manager's responsibility is to supervise and authorize the prudent expenditure of money essential to the operating and maintenance of the building. Many expenditures are routine, such as the wages of employees and the bills for light, heat, power, and other recurring items. Even in meeting these expenditures, operational practices can be reviewed and economy practiced.

In meeting expenditures for repairs, the manager may refer all work to a general contractor who assumes all responsibility for carrying out the needed work, or the manager may purchase and stock required materials and hire skilled workers to attend to the repairs under his or her general supervision. The former practice is recommended when buildings under one management are small in size and number. With large buildings and extensive scope of managerial functions, the latter practice may prove more economical. Service, too, can be restored and repairs attended to more promptly where workers and technicians are subject to direct control. Where the practice of attending directly to repairs is followed, a repair voucher order should be issued for each job and an accurate record kept of labor and materials used. The owner is then billed for actual expenditures plus a nominal overhead service charge (5 to 10 percent) for job superintendence. The direct control of purchases, wages, and expenditures for repairs, provided the size and number of buildings managed warrant it, should prove more economical and more efficient in the maintenance and restoration of building service.

---

[3]Ibid., p. 355.

Maintaining Favorable Employee Relations

The success of property management depends to a great extent upon other people—that is, people upon whom the property manager must rely as employees or associates. It is therefore of utmost importance that the selection and training of personnel be given special care and consideration. Employees, although not vested with agency responsibility, indirectly represent the owner, and their conduct and serviceability affect public relations and tenant good will.

In selecting personnel, consideration should be given to the following:

1. Is the applicant technically qualified?
2. Is the person sufficiently interested in this work to make it a career?
3. Is the compensation offered at least as high as that earned for similar work in the applicant's prior position?
4. Is the applicant congenial, emotionally adjusted, and worthy of becoming a member of the firm's "family"?
5. Does the applicant display an interest in growing with the firm?

The careful selection of an employee should be followed with a well-thought-out and effective training program. The employee should be given an opportunity to meet coworkers, to sense pride in his or her work, and to acquire a feeling of belonging to an organization that "cares." Where the executive, because of stress of work, is unable to instruct the new employee, a manual should be prepared in which the overall objectives of the organization are clearly stated. The manual should also set forth the conditions of employment, hours of work, holidays, sick leave, and vacation as well as complete instructions covering duties and responsibilities of the specific job to which the employee is assigned. All employees, of course, should be informed that they are expected to give unstintingly of the time for which they are paid and that their work must prove worth their hire.

Maintaining Property

Good property management demands a thorough knowledge of building service and maintenance requirements. The building should be kept clean and attractive at all times. Inspection of the property should be made at regular intervals. It should be seen to that the janitor is on the job and carrying out janitorial duties. Halls should be kept lighted and elevators running. Heating systems and building service utilities must be kept in proper order. Constant watch should be kept for possible defects around the property. Flaws and hazards should be checked for in sidewalks, stairs, flooring, roofing, wiring, plumbing, or anywhere inattention may cause an accident. The maintenance problems and repairs referred to above apply only to buildings that are rented to a number of tenants and where the landlord controls portions of the building. In some cases, the tenant agrees to attend to all repairs, and consequently the owner is not liable for damages. The question of liability for damages is more fully discussed in the chapter on leases.

Keeping Proper Accounts and Rendering Periodic Reports

One of the prime requirements of good management is the maintenance of an adequate system of accounts by means of which an orderly presentation of monthly activities, detailed as to income and expenditures, can be submitted to the owners. Accounting, although principally intended to provide statements of assets and liabilities and interim schedules of income and expenses, is also an important aid in providing a historical record of continuing property control and occupancy as well as data useful in the determination of management policy. In selecting the appropriate accounting system, careful thought should be given to the type of forms and accounts best suited to the orderly and efficient operation of the property and to the types of records to be maintained for the reporting of required facts and figures.

Owner's statements, depending on size and number of properties managed, may be presented in summary or detailed (also known as *transcript*) form. Modern practice sanctions the detail reporting method. Under this method the owner is furnished a monthly statement which may contain property income and expense data as follows:

MONTHLY PROPERTY MANAGEMENT REPORT

Name of building ....
Location ....
Statement for the month of.. 19......
And accounts receivable as of .... 19......
Number of units rented ....
Number of units vacant..

RENTAL INFORMATION AND RECEIPTS

Property	*Name of Tenant*	*Rent per Month*	*Arrears*	*Amount Paid*	*Arrears at Close*	*Remarks*

DISBURSEMENTS AND DISTRIBUTION

Work Done or Article Bought Contractor or Vendor	*Capital or Cost*	*Payroll*	*Fuel*	*Water Gas Electricity*	*General Supplies*	*Insurance & Taxes*	*Maintenance & Repairs*	*Commissions*	*Total*

Amount Collected	$________
Less: Amount Disbursed	$________
Net Amount Deposited	$________

Where the manager is charged with the duty of maintaining social security and withholding tax records and the filing of governmental reports, auxiliary accounting records should be kept and periodically submitted for the owner's check and approval. All funds received and those held for the owner's account should be deposited in a separate trust account and under no circumstances should such monies be deposited with the manager's personal or business funds.

PROPERTY ASSESSMENT AND TAXATION

Property taxation to support local government is an unavoidable fixed cost against real estate, equal to from 1 to 8 percent of market value. New Jersey, Massachusetts, Wisconsin, and Maryland traditionally tax at high rates while Florida, Louisiana, Mississippi, and Nevada tax at comparatively low rates, according to a study by Professor Stephen E. Lile of Western Kentucky University. The best that most owners can do is get overassessments lowered to avoid overpaying taxes. The intent here is to explain property taxes as they affect ownership of realty. We do this by looking at assessment and taxation procedures, and we conclude with a discussion of challenging an assessed value.

A property can pay more or less taxes than its market value justifies because of over- or underassessment or because of being located in high or low tax rate districts. The property's value may be influenced to the amount of the capitalized value of the over- or undertaxation. That is, *tax capitalization* is the converting of all future tax payments incurred or avoided into a lump-sum present value. Assume that the assessed value of a property is higher by $8,000 than its market value justifies. In addition, annual taxes amount to 3 percent of the assessed value; thus, the property pays $240 per year too much tax. If the condition persists, and the $240 per year is capitalized into perpetuity at 10 percent, the value is influenced by $2,400. That is, if sold, the property should sell for $2,400 less than comparable properties that are taxed properly.

The Property Taxation Process

The property taxation process has three major phases, from an owner's viewpoint:

1. Property valuation and assessment
2. Budget and tax levy
3. Tax billing and collection

In the assessment phase, all real estate in a township, a city, or a county is appraised for market value. Each parcel is then assigned an assessed value, which is typically a legally required or generally agreed-upon proportion of the market value. *Assessed value* is the worth of a property for taxation purposes. Nationally, the ratio runs about one-third of market value. The ratio may run higher or lower than this. In Oregon and Florida, by state law, assessed value is 100 percent of market value. The assessed values of all properties in a tax district, when added together, constitute the *tax base* for the district.

Each fiscal year a budget summarizing the financial needs of each tax district is put together. The tax district may be a school district, a park district, a city, a village, or an entire county. The portion of the budget to be financed by property taxes is estimated and divided by the assessed value of the properties in the district to calculate the tax levy rate. The levy rate is the amount of taxes per $100 of assessed value. The *levy* is the number of dollars to be paid in taxes by a property, based on its assessed value and the tax districts in which it is located. Levying taxes on each property completes the budget and levy phase.

In the third phase, a tax roll is made up listing taxes levied against properties by section or subdivision, block, and lot. All outstanding liens for taxes (and also for special assessments for local improvements and water charges) can be readily ascertained by this method. This is preferred to listing properties by owner's name, which would necessitate a search against the names of owners for some time in the past to ascertain the existence of tax arrears. Individual property owners are also billed for taxes and assessments in the third phase. Payment of the taxes due completes the tax cycle from the viewpoint of an individual property owner. Failure to pay results in a lien against the property, which may eventually be enforced by sale of the property or some interest in it.

Valuation and assessment. The tax is apportioned to various properties in proportion to the value of each. Thus, it is necessary for the taxing body, acting through its representatives, to examine and appraise all taxable property equitably. Various methods of appraisal are used, some of which take the property at a fraction of real market value, such as one-half, two-thirds, or three-fourths. Others take the value to be the amount for which the property would sell at a forced sale, and again others use as a basis the full market value of the property. Many large cities use the last method, which is generally coming to be recognized as the only one that is fair and equitable. Full market value has been defined as "the price that one who wishes to buy, but is not compelled to buy, would pay to a seller willing but not compelled to sell." Prices paid at auction sales, particularly forced sales, do not usually measure true market value, and neither do prices paid for property by those who have a need for that particular property only.

The assessor, in valuing property, frequently separates the values of land and buildings. The land is valued on the basis of the value of a standard or typical lot, that is, a lot of the size usually marketed in the vicinity. If the assessor fairly determines the value of such a lot, the value is allocated to all similar lots. It will of course be seen that in the valuation of lots in cities and villages, each street, and in fact each block, must be considered separately. Main thoroughfares and business streets create values in excess of those on side streets and in residential districts. Corners, corner influences, plottage, and similar circumstances are taken into account in order that the assessor may make an equitable appraisement, one that is fair and just both to the taxpayer and to the community. In certain cities maps are published by the tax departments giving the front foot value of land in each block of the entire city.

Although all lots in a block may have the same value, the buildings may be different in both size and character. In the valuation of buildings, the tax assessor must consider whether they are new or old and whether they are or are not the proper improvement for the land. New buildings are usually worth their cost of production, and the assessment is computed on that basis. As the age of a building increases, allowance is made for depreciation. When the land value remains stationary and the building depreciates through age, the total valuation of land and building will tend to decrease from year to year. In many localities, land increases in value as time goes on, owing to its availability for a better building—that is, one producing a greater rental. The assessed valuation of the lot improved with an old building will increase, but the total of land and building will remain the same. In such cases the building is assessed, not at its cost less depreciation but at *the amount it adds to the value of the land.* This condition may progress so that a once valuable building adds merely a nominal amount to the value of the land.

Assessors are expected to consider the rent a building is capable of producing. It has been stated as a principle that an improved parcel of real estate is never worth more than its capitalized rental value unless the value of the land alone exceeds this capitalized sum.

After each property has been appraised by these various methods, the assessor compares and analyzes the conclusions to assign it an assessed value. Increasingly, assessed value is some proportion of market value. Therefore, the assessor's thought process in assigning an assessed value very closely parallels that discussed in the section on correlation analysis in chapter 19, Appraising For Market Value.

The assessed value assigned a property directly affects the amount of taxes to be paid on it. For example, assume a community in which the tax or levy rate runs 3 percent of the assessed value. A property assessed at $60,000 would have a tax bill of $1,800. But if the owner gets the assessed value reduced to $45,000, the tax bill drops to $1,350, a saving of $450.

Budget and tax levy. A *budget* is a statement of probable revenue and expenditure and of financial proposals for the ensuing year as presented to, or passed upon, by a legislative body. It is customary, in the preparation of a budget, for each branch or department of the government to prepare in detail an estimate of the amount it requires for the period under consideration. This estimate and those of other departments are analyzed and amended, usually decreased, by the legislative body. After consideration of all estimates, the final figures are assembled, and the total represents the amount of money the political body appropriates for its use for the period. Usually there are revenues derived from sources other than taxation, and these, estimated as closely as possible, are deducted from the total of the budget. The remaining amount represents the sum that must be raised by taxtion on property within the jurisdiction. In some states there is a tax on personal property. In others, since the enactment of income tax laws, so much personal property is exempt that the direct tax falls almost entirely upon real property.

In large cities there is usually one annual tax levy, which provides funds for all purposes for which the city raises money. In other localities there are various tax levies, which may be all or some of the following:

1. *State tax.* The expenses of the state government are met to a large extent by special taxes such as income taxes, inheritance taxes, corporation taxes, stock transfer taxes, and automobile taxes. If these taxes do not provide the state with sufficient funds, a direct tax is levied in some states by counties, based upon the value of the taxable property in each country.
2. *County tax.* Each county of the state raises money by taxation for the expenses of the county government and its courts, penal institutions, hospitals, care of the poor, roads, and bridges.
3. *Town tax.* Local town government provides for its needs by taxation. Frequently state, county, township, and town taxes are levied and collected at the same time.
4. *School tax.* The school tax is often a separate levy by school districts for the purpose of maintaining the public schools. The appropriation for which the tax is levied is usually voted by the taxpaying residents of the district.
5. *Highway tax.* The highway tax is usually made by highway commissioners for the upkeep and repair of the roads within the district.

6. *City or village tax.* Incorporated cities and villages within a county provide for their recurring expenses by a separate and independent tax levy.

To ascertain the amount of tax levied against a particular piece of property, a tax rate must be determined. To arrive at the tax rate, two factors are used: the budget or amount of money to be raised and the total valuation of taxable property within the district. The total amount to be raised by taxation divided by the total assessed valuation gives the rate, or millage. A *mill* is a monetary unit equal to one-thousandth part of the dollar. The rate, or millage, applied to the value of a particular parcel of real estate gives the amount of taxes chargeable to it. For example, assume the budget to be $9,600,000, the value of the property $80,000,000, and the amount derived from revenues other than taxes for real estate $7,200,000. The tax rate would be determined by deducting $7,200,000 from $9,600,000, which would leave $2,400,000 to be derived from property taxes. Dividing $2,400,000 by $80,000,000 gives a tax rate of 3 percent, or 30 mills per dollar, or $30 per $1,000 of assessed valuation. Calculations for a typical property tax bill are as follows:

Property of taxpayer		
Value of land		$10,000
Value of building	$35,000	
Less: Depreciation	5,000	
Depreciated building value		$30,000
Total property value		$40,000
Less: Homestead exemption	$ 5,000	
Veteran's exemption	1,000	
Total exemption		6,000
Taxable property, assessed value		$34,000

County rate =	4.4 mills
City rate =	8.6 mills
School rate =	17.0 mills
Total rate =	30.0 mills
Tax for 19___	$34,000 × 0.03 = $1,020

Billing and collection. The procedure for tax billing and collection differs among the various states. Some states bill annually on a calendar year basis; others authorize separate billing by school, municipal, county, and sanitary tax authorities. When separate tax billing is the practice, the tax burden is spread by statutory provision over budget years, which may end in spring, summer, and fall. Thus school taxes may be billed in September, sanitation taxes in April, and county taxes in July.

In some states, taxes are due when billed and become a lien against the property that takes priority over all other private liens, including mortgages, that are on public records or pending under court action.

Most states provide a grace period of 30 to 90 days, during which time taxes may be paid without penalty. Some states offer a 1 to 4 percent declining discount if taxes are paid during the first few months of billing. After the discount period, taxes are deemed due and payable, and penalties for late payment accrue in accordance with statutory law.

Challenging the Assessment Value

Each county and community generally follows a statutory tax calendar in accordance with which dates are set for the completion of the property assessment rolls, and for periods of three to six weeks, during which time the assessment rolls are open for public inspection. As a rule, notices of protest may be filed during the inspection period. Upon closing of the books, a board of review hears and considers protests made by property owners. Where relief is denied and the owner feels aggrieved, he or she may then petition the court for a judicial review.

Board of review. The value assigned to real property by a tax official is merely the opinion of that official as to its value. The owner of the property may not agree with such opinion and feel that the property has been assessed too high. The owner may challenge the assessment and is entitled to a hearing on the objections. In making a protest of this kind, the owner is advised to analyze the assessment as to land and building and see which is erroneous. Land may be assessed too high for one of two reasons: Either a mistake has been made (in which case a correction is easily obtained), or the wrong unit of value has been applied. A change in the latter requires more care, for a reduction in the unit of value will affect the assessment on neighboring property also. A reduction in the assessed valuation of one lot usually results in a reduction of the value of adjoining lots also, often of all the lots in an entire block. Evidence of value may be offered by a taxpayer by way of information as to sales, mortgages, and so forth, and his or her contention may be supported by such evidence.

Court review. The action of the tax officials is subject to review by the court. If an owner believes that the assessed value of his or her property is too high and is unable to secure a reduction upon protest to the officials, an appeal may then be made to the courts. This is a proceeding *a certiorari*; that is, it is a proceeding whereby the tax officials are required to produce their records and to certify to them to the court in order that the court may determine whether the officials have proceeded according to the principles of law by which they are bound. The court does not usually fix the assessed value, but it may criticize the administrative officers and give directions as to how they must proceed. It is, of course, also possible that the court will sustain the tax officials and find that they have proceeded according to law in fixing the assessed value, or it may direct the reduction of its assessed value.

PROPERTY INSURANCE

The primary function of insurance is to substitute certainty for uncertainty by shifting the risk of a disastrous event to an insurance company. A payment, termed an *insurance premium,* is made to the company as compensation for its acceptance of the risk. A policy contract between the individual and the company stipulates the amount of term or period of time of the insurance protection. The insurance company, of course, insures many individuals against the same risk. The overall effect is to spread the cost of the disastrous event, which normally would fall on one individual, over many individuals exposed to the same hazard.

Manager's Insurance Responsibility

The property manager's responsibility includes protecting the owner against all major insurable risks. An owner expects the management firm to relieve him or her of most details incident to the ownership of the property. As the owner's representative, the manager should be capable of determining and evaluating the risks involved and should make every effort to secure the best and most economical protection available in the insurance market.

Standard insurance coverage contracts that the manager should consider in the protection of the client's property include the following:

1. *Standard fire insurance.* This policy protects the insured against all direct losses or damages to real property by fire excepting those losses caused by perils or forces specifically excluded in the policy.
2. *Extended coverage.* The inclusion of *extended coverage* is a recommended practice. It provides for broader protection and includes risk compensation for losses due to perils of explosion, windstorm, hail, riot, civil disturbances, aircraft, vehicles, and other causes.
3. *General liability.* This policy insures the owner against liability imposed by law for damages due to injuries caused to the persons or properties of others.
4. *Workmen's compensation.* This type of employee protection against injury is mandatory in most states and varies in accordance with state law.
5. *Inland marine insurance.* This is available to cover personal property losses and, more generally, damage to property that is mobile in nature.
6. *Casualty insurance.* This protects the insured against losses due to theft, burglary, plate-glass breakage, and the failure or breakdown of elevators, steam boilers, machinery as well as other similar incidents. Under this form of insurance, policies are also issued to cover a variety of accident and health injuries.
7. *Rent insurance and consequential losses.* This type of insurance is also referred to as *business interruptions insurance.* It compensates the owner for consequential losses incident to damage or destruction of the property.

The manager's responsibility, as agent for the owner, is to keep accurate records of all insurance policies and to arrange for renewals well in advance of date of policy expiration. Care must be taken that insurance coverage is in proper relation to current property replacement costs and that dollar price changes due to increased construction costs or monetary inflation have been considered on or before the date of policy renewal. Good management, too, can assist in keeping fire insurance down to a minimum by eliminating fire hazards as much as possible. Sometimes the character of a tenant's business increases the insurance rate on the building. This fact should be recognized in setting the appropriate rent. Generally, tenants agree to pay the additional premium caused by their mode of occupancy.

A study of insurance price schedules offered by competing companies may suggest ways of securing rate reductions. As a rule, liability insurance is carried so that any claim for damages is defended by the insurance company, and loss, if any, is borne by it. Rent insurance is entirely optional with the owner. Many owners do not wish to carry it, being willing to assume the risk of a loss of rents in case of fire.

Buying Insurance

The most important consideration in obtaining insurance for the typical property owner is the selection of the agent or broker. Price, or the amount of the policy premium, and the reputation and financial capability of the insurance company are obviously important also. But the agent aids in the choice of the company and the type and adequacy of insurance coverage to be obtained. The agent helps to balance the costs against the risks to obtain the best insurance program possible within the owner's capability. The agent also services the policy on a continuing basis and is the owner's liaison with the company in the event of a claim of loss. Obviously the relationship involves considerable trust. If the trust in the relationship is lost, the owner should seriously consider changing to another agent.

Selecting the agent or broker. The very nature of the insurance business compels insurance companies to diversify their risks and to seek policyholders in far-flung areas as a safeguard against large-scale peril in a single region or community. The common-sense policy not to put all the risks in one basket necessitates insurance operations at great distances from office headquarters. Although many companies have established branch offices in the larger communities, the greater share of the insurance business is dependent on services of company agents or insurance brokers. Then too, the characteristics of the business are such that insurance must be *sold*—it is rarely bought by individual people or property owners. Generally, individuals give their insurance business to agents or brokers on the basis of professional confidence, personal acquaintance or friendship.

Legally, the agent is the representative of the insurance company and owes it his or her loyalty. An agent, too, is generally charged with the responsibility for protecting the company's interests and should confine his or her operations to the insurance offerings of the company or companies represented. For her or his services the agent is compensated by payment of a commission on new insurance and on renewals of existing policies. In fact, the agent may be called a salesperson for one or more insurance companies. The powers of such a person, as a rule, are limited to securing applications, delivering insurance policies, and collecting premiums. Acceptance of risks and settlement of losses are legally the sole responsibility of the insurance companies and not those of their agents. An important distinction is whether an agent must represent the company or whether the agent, as a broker, independent of any one insurance company, is in a position to represent the property owner. Obviously the latter is to be preferred.

An insurance broker is an independent operator and expert adviser who serves the interests of clients always. The broker generally studies the insurance needs by inspecting clients' premises and then bargains with selected insurance carriers for the best terms and lowest rate obtainable. Often the broker will suggest improvements in the physical conditions of the property, such as the installation of a sprinkler system or the elimination of a hazard that may bring about a lower class rate and thus profitable savings in insurance premiums. The broker generally, because of his or her independence, is free to place insurance business anywhere and prefers companies that he or she considers financially strong, prompt in settlement of losses, and otherwise competitive in rates and broker commission payments.

Rates. Insurance is based on the law of average. It would be difficult indeed to try to foretell, where many risks of the same nature are involved, how many would suffer loss in the period of one year and how extensive the loss would be. With 10,000 or 20,000 similar buildings, however, all with the same type risk and with proper statistics on hand, it would be easy to forecast with a great degree of accuracy the number of buildings that would suffer loss and the total extent of the damage to be expected. Knowing the total amount of the losses and the total value of the buildings, an insurance company could fairly easily calculate the rate per hundred dollars of value that should be used and, using that rate, could find the premium that should be charged each building, based on its value, to collect just sufficient funds to meet the expected loss. In actual practice, however, this rate would have to be increased to take care of the expense necessary to run an insurance company and to allow the company a fair profit from prudent underwriting.

There are a number of different types of rates, but the better known ones are minimum, or class, rates and specific rates. *Minimum rated risks* take in whole groups of buildings of similar construction and hazard and give them the same rate. For instance, brick dwellings in a certain territory would all have the same rate, frame dwellings another. Many apartments of similar construction have the same rate as well as many store and dwelling properties. These rates are the lowest that can be had unless the rate for the entire class is lowered.

Other buildings, such as mercantile and manufacturing buildings, are *specifically rated*. That means that a rate is promulgated by the use of a schedule to reflect the condition and occupancy of the building at the time it is inspected by the rating organization. Owners of properties that are specifically rated should always secure a schedule or "makeup" of their fire insurance rate. When this is received, it should be gone over thoroughly by an expert to make certain all the charges that go to make up the rate are in order. It may be that a hazardous tenant has left the building or that certain faults of management have been corrected since the rate was promulgated. If that is so, and it appears that the rate is too high, a new rate should be applied for. The expert would also make a study of existing physical conditions to determine whether fire protection devices (such as sprinklers) or building alterations (such as fireproofing) would make a sufficient rate saving to justify the high cost of installation.

Coinsurance. When rates are figured for various risks, consideration must be given to the premium those rates will produce. The premiums produced are dependent on the amount of insurance purchased. Ordinarily, the greater the amount of insurance purchased, the lower the rate that is necessary to produce sufficient reserve to meet anticipated loss. Now it is a well-known fact that in territory that enjoys fire protection, most losses are partial, and yet there is always the danger in individual cases of total loss. Knowing that most losses are partial, a person might feel that it was unnecessary to carry more than a nominal amount of insurance. On a building worth $10,000, such a person, therefore, might carry $2,000 insurance at a rate of $1 per hundred and a premium of $20. Another person, not knowing that most losses are partial, and desiring better protection, would insure for the full value, or $10,000, also at $1 per hundred, with a premium of $100. In the event of a $2,000 loss, if no *coinsurance* clause was in the policy, each would receive this amount, although the latter paid considerably more for the policy. It can be argued, of course, that the latter received a greater limit of protection; but inasmuch as most of the losses are partial, the danger of a total loss was not as great as the danger of a loss on the first few thousand at risk. Therefore, if the rate charged was the correct one for the first $2,000, it was excessive for the coverage over that amount. To equalize this distribution of the cost of insurance among policyholders and to penalize those going underinsured, the coinsurance or average clause was introduced and made a part of the policy. The clauses generally used are the 80, 90, or 100 percent average clauses. Of these, the 80 percent average clause is the one generally attached to the policy.

Many people think that an 80 percent coinsurance clause means that the insurance company will pay only 80 percent of any loss. Others feel that in the event of total loss, they would be able to collect 80 percent of the face amount of the policy. Both these ideas, of course, are wrong. The usual 80 percent coinsurance, or typical, clause reads in part, "This company shall not be liable for a greater proportion of any loss or damage to the property described herein than the sum hereby insured bears to eighty percent (80%) of the actual cash value of said property at the time such loss shall happen, nor for more than the proportion that this policy bears to the total insurance thereon."

Various factors can enter into the determination of actual cash value, but under ordinary conditions, it will be sufficient to consider actual cash value as replacement value, less depreciation. To illustrate the operation of the 80 percent average clause, consider the following example. A and B both own buildings, the actual cash value of each being $10,000. A carries $8,000 insurance, B carries $4,000 insurance. Both suffer a $2,000 loss, as shown in these calculations:

	A'S COMPANY	*B'S COMPANY*
Actual cash value of building	$10,000	$10,000
Insurance required to be carried to meet requirements of the 80% average clause (80% of $10,000)	8,000	8,000
Insurance actually carried	8,000	4,000
Actual loss	2,000	2,000

A should and did carry $8,000 insurance. His company, therefore, pays 8,000/8,000 of the $2,000 loss, or $2,000.

B should carry $8,000 insurance but only carried $4,000. His company, therefore, pays 4,000/8,000 of the $2,000 loss, or $1,000.

A carried the correct amount of insurance and therefore received the full amount of his loss without any penalty of coinsurance. B carried only one-half of the amount of insurance required by the average clause and therefore became a coinsurer with the insurance company for 50 percent of the loss.

It should be remembered that if sufficient insurance is carried to meet the requirement of the average clause, for all intents and purposes, in the event of a loss the policy can be considered as written without any coinsurance feature and will pay dollar for dollar any loss up to its face amount. The clause penalizes only when insufficient insurance is carried. It should also be noted that the average clause does not limit the amount of insurance the owner is permitted to take out. The owner can insure for full value regardless of what clause is used.

In unprotected territory—that is, territory without benefits of fire protection—the average clause is usually not required in the policy. The probable reason is that without fire protection almost any fire would in all likelihood result in a total loss, and therefore it would obviously not benefit the insurance companies to insist that large amounts of insurance be carried. In states or jurisdictions where regulations provide for "full" value insurance, the coinsurance concept is not applicable. Value for insurance purposes is ascertained by the agent. The owner may request higher coverage, but losses are limited to value as measured by cost of replacement less accrued depreciation based on age and conditions at time of loss.

Risk management and self-insurance. Ultimately, an owner is responsible for the proper management of risk. By default, an owner in effect is self-insured for risks not covered by insurance. We have discussed only a few of the many forms of insurance protection available to owners. Property owners or their managers should carefully analyze the risks they believe they are subject to and consult a broker or agent, arranging for that person to make a thorough survey of insurance needs. Then they should follow the broker's recommendations for proper coverage. If this is intelligently done, and adquate insurance is carried to meet the hazards to which an owner is subject, he or she will have purchased, at comparatively small cost, security and protection against the possibility of sudden and severe financial loss.

Loss Adjustments

When a loss occurs, the insured should immediately notify the insurance company of such loss and protect the property from further damage. He or she should then secure the estimate of several competent builders to ascertain the cost to repair the damage. One of the estimates should then be sent to the insurance company to be compared with the insurance company's estimate. If there are differences, the insured or a representative and the company adjuster discuss those differences with a view to reaching a compromise settlement. In the vast majority of cases, this settlement is reached in a friendly fashion. If by any chance the differences are so great that the insured and the insurance company cannot reconcile them, then it is necessary for each to select an appraiser. The appraisers select an umpire, but in the event they cannot agree on an umpire, then, on the request of the insured or the insurance company, one may be selected by a judge of a court of record in the state in which the property covered is located. An award arrived at by the appraisers or by the appraisers and the umpire will then determine the amount of actual cash value and loss. An insured is permitted to make temporary repairs to prevent further damage but should not proceed with the complete restoration of the damaged premises until the loss has been adjusted or at

least until the insurance company grants permission to commence the permanent repairs.

MANAGEMENT REQUIREMENTS BY PROPERTY TYPE

Each property type has some management requirements that are unique to it. Apartment buildings are the most commonly managed property types in our society, and so they serve as "the standard" in our discussion. Our look at management of alternative property types is brief, intended only to highlight differences. Much deeper study of, and experience with, alternative property types and their management requirements is needed to qualify as a professional manager. The Institute of Real Estate Management (IREM), the Building Owners and Managers Association (BOMA), the Urban Land Institute (ULI), and the International Council of Shopping Centers (ICSC) are excellent sources of more information on property management.

Residential

Much of the discussion in this chapter thus far has focused on the management of an apartment building. Lease arrangements are typically month to month or, if written, for 1 to 3 years. Physical maintenance, with periodic adjustment to changing environment or market, is needed to retain the property's tenants and therefore its value.

Many apartment buildings are being converted to condominiums or cooperatives. The physical building remains the same; yet some aspects of management take on special importance. What are these unique aspects?

Condominiums and cooperatives have almost the same operating and maintenance requirements as apartment buildings. The main difference is form of ownership and tenancy. Thus, the manager serves the tenant-owners rather than an absentee-owner. This owner-occupancy means that the interior of each unit is maintained by its owner. The manager's duties involve administration or maintenance of common areas. The security of the premises is an important area of responsibility. The managers need not be concerned with maintaining occupancy.

The administrative duties of the manager include keeping account of costs and assessing the costs to individual units. The manager also advises the owner's association, which at times means balancing opposing interests. Time-share condominiums require more intensive management than other condominium developments. Also, closer attention to payment of debt service and taxes by individual tenants is needed of a manager of a cooperative project; nonpayment by one proprietary tenant may cause a lien to be placed against the interests of all the tenants.

Commercial

Commercial space is rented in units of varying size, running from a small cubicle for a newsstand or an office to a multistory building. Except for the smallest units of space, the leases usually are complex, requiring considerable negotiation, and are for an extended number of years. Office building leases usually contain an escalation clause. An *escalation clause* increases rents to cover increasing costs of taxes, insurance, and operation. The appearance, cleanliness, and efficiency of office buildings must be carefully monitored to maintain the prestige and the rent levels. Stores and shopping centers are likely to be rented on percentage leases. Administrative reports to the owner are often involved with commercial properties because of the variety in tenants and spaces rented.

Industrial

Industrial properties, except for warehouses, tend to be special-purpose properties requiring a large capital investment. For this reason, many must be built to specification for the owner-user. That is, others are frequently not willing to incur the risk of building and leasing a special-purpose property. In turn, after the property is a going operation, the owner may enter into a sale and leaseback arrangement with an investor. Even so, the value of a special-purpose property is closely tied to the success and financial capability of the firm renting the space. Little property management is involved where a property is entirely accepted by one tenant, as the tenant is likely to be responsible for property taxes, insurance, and maintenance.

Warehouses tend to be rented on a lease for several years. And, for the most part, warehouse leases are more similar to commercial leases than to leases for other industrial property.

SUMMARY

Management of real estate as a financial asset requires (1) adapting the property to changing markets and environments, (2) maintaining leverage (which may involve sale and reinvestment), and (3) arranging for routine administration of the property. Case examples are presented to show how the discounted cash flow model may be used to make decisions in these areas.

The function of property management, in a routine sense, is to balance cash flow (keep net operating income high) against preservation of the value of the property to operate at optimum rate of return. The principal functions of a manager include (1) merchandising space, (2) collecting rents, (3) maintaining good tenant relations, (4) purchasing operating supplies and equipment, (5) maintaining employee relations, (6) keeping proper accounts and rendering periodic reports, (7) maintaining the physical property, (8) looking after the property's assessment and taxation levels, and (9) maintaining adequate insurance protection. A manager frequently needs to consult with an owner and to obtain outside assistance concerning the last two functions; each involves complex issues and is extremely important to the overall operation of the property. The three phases of the property taxation process are (1) valuation and assessment, (2) budget and tax levy, and (3) billing and collecting.

Form of ownership and tenancy is the main distinction between management and apartments as against condominiums and cooperatives. Management concerns with commercial properties derive from the greater variety in the units of space rented and form the extreme complexity of the leases negotiated. Among other things, office building leases often have escalation clauses to cover increasing costs of taxes, insurance, and operation. Retail space, on the other hand, is often rented on a percentage-of-sales lease. Being special purpose, industrial properties, as a rule, are rented on a sale and leaseback arrangement, when rented. Warehouses are more general purpose and tend to be an exception to this rule.

QUESTIONS FOR REVIEW AND DISCUSSION

1. Identify and discuss briefly the three key issues in managing a property as a long-term investment.
2. List and explain briefly five important but routine functions of a manager in operating a property as a business.
3. The property taxation process involves three distinct phases. What is the manager's (and owner's) concern about the process? What action, and when, is necessary by an owner relative to this process?
4. What is tax capitalization? How might it affect the value of a property?
5. What issues are involved in buying property insurance?
6. Explain coinsurance.
7. What criteria would be most important in hiring a property manager? Would the nature of the property make any difference?
8. How far should a property manager go in analyzing financial alternatives and recommending alternative decisions to an owner?
9. How might an owner account for time spent in seeking out and managing investment properties? Discuss.

CASE PROBLEMS

Assume that Popeye bought University Towers for $640,000 in case problems 1–4, chapter 21. He is now at the end of year 2 and considering alternatives open to him. He asks your help, as a real estate consultant, and asks you to help analyze the following alternatives:

1. What after-tax rate of return on EOY 2 after tax equity will he receive if he does nothing? Assume NOI continues to go up by $4,000 per year, and disposition price continues to go up by $40,000 per year. All other assumptions to remain as in original problem. Assume Popeye's EOY 2 after-tax equity is $160,000.
2. Popeye might modernize University Towers at a cost of $72,000. Popeye forecasts the following based on such a modernization effort:
   a. Academic A&L Association would advance $50,000 for the effort at the same terms as on the original mortgage, except the maturity date would remain unchanged.
   b. The additional outlay would be depreciated over 18 years by straight-line recovery, or $4,000 per year.
   c. NOI for the next two years would be increased $6,000 above that in case problem 1.
   d. And disposition price at the end of year four would be increased by $80,000.

   What rate of return on EOY 2 after-tax equity would Popeye receive if he modernizes and holds University Towers two more years?
3. Academic S&L Association offers to refinance the property with a $570,000 loan at 12 percent, compounded monthly, with amortization scheduled over 30 years, but with a balloon payment required at EOY 15 of the new loan. No other changes from case problem one. What is the rate of return on EOY 2 after-tax equity with this alternative?
4. Compare the likely results from the three alternatives; indicate which one you recommend, giving reasons for your choice.

CHAPTER TWENTY-FOUR
LEASES AND LEASING

The relationship of landlord and tenant is not an ideal one,
but any relation on a social order will endure if there is infused . . .
some of that spirit of human sympathy
which qualifies life for immortality.
GEORGE RUSSELL, (an open letter in the *Dublin Times* during the 1913 General Strike)

MAJOR TOPICS OR DECISION AREAS COVERED IN THIS CHAPTER

- Basic Terms and Concepts
- Kinds of Leases
- Typical Lease Covenants/Clauses
- Termination of Leases
- Tenant Unions

An owner of income property must know and understand the essence of leasing. Therefore, this chapter covers the basic terminology of, the kinds of, the typical covenants or clauses of, and the ways in which to terminate leases. Some brief attention is also given to the relative negotiating positions of the parties and to some of the broader issues involved in negotiation, mainly tenant unions.

Leasing, of course, requires no equity investment. Thus, a tenant retains or frees money for business or other purposes while also realizing greater locational flexibility. A long-term lease would negate the latter point, of course.

Locational analysis is omitted from this discussion. Location, or the relation of a site or activity to other land uses, and its general environment, is generally considered the key to value in real estate. This is true whether a property is operated by an owner or a tenant. Location, in this sense, has already been discussed in Chapter 18, on property productivity analysis.

KEY CONCEPTS INTRODUCED IN THIS CHAPTER

Actual eviction
Constructive eviction
Flat lease
Graduated lease
Gross lease
Ground lease
Index lease
Lease option
Lessee/tenant
Lessor/landlord
Net lease
Percentage lease
Reappraisal lease
Retaliatory eviction
Sandwich leasehold
Subrogation

BASIC TERMS AND CONCEPTS

As noted in Chapter 3 on ownership rights, four distinct tenancies may be held in a leasehold estate: (1) tenancy for years, (2) tenancy from period to period, or periodic tenancy, (3) tenancy at will, and (4) tenancy at sufferance. The rights of the lessee become weaker as the lessee goes from a tenancy for years to a tenancy at sufferance. The emphasis here is on tenancy for years and periodic tenancy. Tenancy, again, means the manner or conditions under which a property is held. And, in everyday language, the party that rents a property is the tenant or lessee.

The agreement under which a tenant hires a property from a landlord is a *lease.* That is, a lease is a contract under which a tenant goes into possession of a property or unit of space for a certain period of time in return for payments to the landlord. The time that the tenant may hold possession is called the *term.* The amount to be paid the landlord is known as *rent.* Rent is usually stated in dollars per month or per year.

A lease may be an oral agreement under which the property is rented for a short term, or it may be a lengthy document containing many special provisions and covenants. Most state fraud statutes require a lease for more than 1 year to be in writing. It follows that a lease for 1 year or less may be oral. Written or oral, a leasehold interest is legally personal property.

The party selling the right of occupancy and use in a lease is the *lessor* or *landlord*. The landlord or lessor is usually, but not necessarily, the owner of the property. The lessor may be a tenant of the owner who enters into an agreement to sublet the premises to subtenants. This type of agreement establishes an interest, often known as a sandwich leasehold, which is illustrated in Figure 24–1. The original tenant has become sandwiched in between the user of the premises or "top" lessee and the owner of the property or leased fee—the landlord.

Tenancies for years and a periodic tenancy are easily the most common types of rental arrangements, and therefore some additional discussion of each seems appropriate.

Tenancy for Years

A tenancy for years is usually more than 1 year and, therefore, is usually written. The term may actually be for 1 month, 6 months, 1 year, or more than 10 years. A written lease for 9 months creates a tenancy for years as well as a lease for 99 years. In both cases, the time of occupancy and use is definite.

The tenant is required to vacate the property and return possession to the landlord at the end of the lease, without any notice being required. A tenant continuing in possession beyond the end of the lease is a holdover. The landlord may dispossess or elect to hold the tenant for a further period of 1 year. The landlord may also enter into a specific agreement with the tenant that if possession continues, it is a month-to-month tenancy.

FIGURE 24–1
Sandwich leasehold

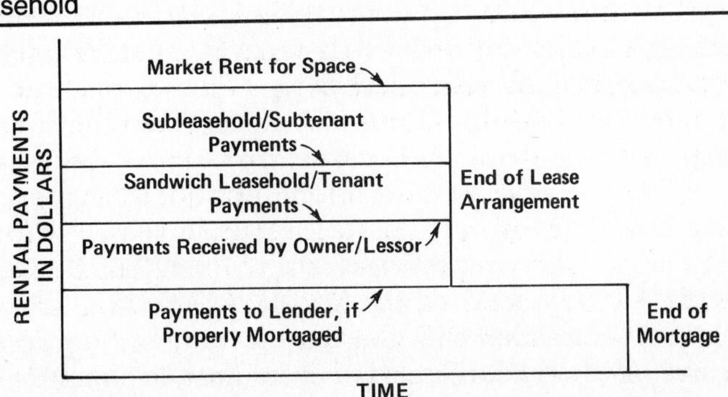

Periodic Tenancy

A tenancy of uncertain duration, for example, month to month or year to year, is termed a periodic tenancy or tenancy from year to year or period to period. The tenancy is usually from month to month in urban areas. The tenancy continues until either the landlord or tenant gives notice of termination. Usually, the rental period determines the length of notice required. That is, a week's notice is required to end a week-to-week tenancy. A month's notice is required to end a month-to-month tenancy. A notice of from 1 to 6 months is likely to be required to terminate a year-to-year tenancy. And a tenant holding over from a tenancy for years, where rental payments are accepted monthly, is likely to create a month-to-month tenancy.

KINDS OF LEASES

Broadly speaking, leases are classified as either short term or long term. This division, based upon length of time and terms of use, is rather arbitrary and has no particular legal significance. Generally, however, commercial or industrial leases extending over 10 or more years may appropriately be referred to as long-term leases. These leases, as a rule, are lengthy documents containing many special provisions and landlord-tenant convenants. At the same time, a 3-year lease for an apartment would be considered a long-term lease. And a ground lease, defined later in this section, would be considered long term only if it exceeded 21 years.

The most usual lease classification system is by rental payment method. Ground leases and sale and leaseback arrangements are also classifications of leases. Note that these classifications may overlap and, therefore, are not mutually exclusive. For example, a sale and leaseback arrangement might actually be a ground lease calling for a net rental.

Rental Payment Classifications

Flat lease. An arrangement calling for a fixed rental to be paid periodically throughout the entire life or term is a *flat lease*, but it may also be called a straight or fixed rental lease. This arrangement, which at one time enjoyed wide use and popularity, has come into gradual disuse for long-term leasing purposes because, no doubt, of inflation. Thus, when rentals are fixed in amount over a long period, a declining dollar value deprives the landlord (owner) of a competitive return in proportion to the value of the property. Consequently, the use of the flat, or straight, lease is increasingly restricted to short-term, month-to-month leases, or, at maximum, yearly leases. A flat lease calling for the lessor to pay all property carrying charges as taxes, insurance, and maintenance is a *gross lease.*

Graduated lease. A *graduated lease,* calling for periodic increases in the rental, is intended to give the tenant an opportunity to lighten operating expense during the early, formative years of a business enterprise and to give the landlord an opportunity to participate in future business growth through successively higher rental payments. This lease arrangement may result in excessive rents without growth and cause business failure or bankruptcy. This arrangement is also termed a step-up lease. Conceivably, a similar arrangement might also be used to "step down" rentals for an older property.

Percentage lease. An agreement whereby rent is a specified proportion of sales or income generated through tenant use of a property is called a *percentage lease.* A "floor" or minimum rent may be included in a percentage lease, to assure the owner of some basic income from the property.

The percentage lease based on gross sales lease has gained steadily in popularity for commercial leasing. Generally, a lease of this kind provides for a minimum rental ranging from 40 to 80 percent of amounts considered fair in relation to property value. Percentage rentals may range from as low as 2 percent of gross sales for department stores or supermarkets to as high as 75 percent for parking lot operations.

The landlord-owner's rental income is directly related to the business success of the tenant's operations. Lease clauses or covenants are generally included to ensure, insofar as possible, continuous and effective store operation. Agreement on methods of accounting for gross sales or receipts and on a periodic audit is also generally included. The landlord, in turn, is expected to promise to maintain the property in prime operating condition and to exclude competitors from other nearby owned properties.

Percentage leases are best used where changing sales figures, usually due to growth or inflation, are expected. Sometimes the percentage figures designated for rent increases; usually this occurs when the growth of sales is expected to exceed the rate of inflation because of the high rate of growth in the area. In effect, the arrangement is saying that the property has a prime location resulting in greater sales and the rent should increase more rapidly.

Index lease. Index leases, or escalation leases, have come into vogue in recent years as a result of high and continuous inflation. An *index lease* either provides for rental adjustment in direct proportion to increases in taxes, insurance, and operating costs or provides for rental increments in proportion to changes in cost-of-living or wholesale price indexes as periodically published by the U.S. Department of Commerce. Index leases are more likely to be used where property value is going up but no easy measure of its increase is available because few sales are made. Examples are warehouses, factories, or office buildings.

Net lease. A rental agreement requiring the tenant to pay all maintenance costs, insurance premiums, and property taxes is a *net lease.* Net leases generally run for 10 years or more. A net lease assures an owner of a certain rate of return from an investment while shifting the burden of meeting increasing operating costs and taxes to the tenant. Net leases are deemed suitable for large office, commercial, and industrial properties. Net leases are preferred by investment trusts and insurance companies that acquire real estate under purchase and leaseback agreements.

Reappraisal lease. The *reappraisal lease* reestablishes property value at agreed intervals, usually 3 to 5 years, so that rentals can be adjusted as a fixed percentage of the value. The reappraisal lease is rarely used today because it is expensive to maintain and has caused lengthy litigation concerning value agreements between landlords and tenants because of divergent appraisal estimates and opinions.

Ground Lease

A *ground lease* provides use and occupancy of a vacant site or unimproved land in return for rental payments. The agreement usually contains a provision that a building is to be erected by the tenant. Frequently, it contains a further provision concerning disposition of the building at the end of the term. The building, although erected at the expense of the tenant, legally becomes real estate and, therefore, unless otherwise provided, becomes the property of the landlord at the end of the lease. The lease may provide that the landlord, at the expiration of the term, will pay the tenant all or part of the cost or appraised value of the building. The term of the lease, including renewal privileges, should be long enough to allow the tenant time to amortize the entire cost of the building during the period of occupancy.

Ground rent is often a certain percentage of the value of the land. The tenant pays all taxes and other charges, the landlord's rent being net. No set rules govern ground leases. Each bargain is specifically negotiated by the parties concerned. The provisions mentioned merely suggest what may be agreed upon.

Sale and Leaseback

The transfer of title of a property for consideration (sale) with the simultaneous renting back to the seller (leaseback) on specified terms is a *sale and leaseback arrangement.* From the buyer's viewpoint, the arrangement is a purchase and leaseback. In recent years more and more businesses and corporate entities have found it profitable to sell their real estate holdings and thus free additional capital for expansion of their business operations, while leasing back the properties thus sold under custom-designed long-term agreements. Institutional investors, principally nationally known insurance companies, have found that real estate occupied on a long-term basis by reliable tenants with high credit ratings is an excellent and secure investment. Consequently, sale and leaseback transactions have increased significantly.

In arranging a sale and leaseback, the parties to the transaction exchange instruments. The seller, generally a business corporation, deeds the realty to the buyer, an insurance company, or like investor, and the buyer in turn leases the property to the seller under previously agreed-upon terms.

Such long-term leases extend from 20 to 30 years with options to renew for like periods. The lease terms usually require the tenant to pay all operating expenses, including taxes, maintenance, and insurance, thus yielding a net return or cash flow to the buyer-lessor.

The lessee-seller, in effect, obtains 100 percent financing, realizing cash far in excess of that obtainable under conventional mortgage refinancing. Further, the seller-lessee now enjoys significant income tax advantages since the entire rent becomes tax deductible as a cost of business operations. Such deductions are considerably larger than the sum of owners' deductions otherwise allowable for interest on mortgage debt, real estate taxes, and permissible deductions for depreciation on older buildings and improvements.

TYPICAL LEASE COVENANTS/CLAUSES

A lease must contain the essential elements of a valid contract to be enforceable. The rights and obligations of both the landlord and the tenant should be spelled out as much as possible. Many of these rights and obligations are standard; others must be negotiated according to the situation.

The rent to be paid is the immediate consideration in lease negotiations. The amount is negotiated against the rights and obligations of the landlord and tenant under the lease as well as against the size and quality of the space provided and the amount of services provided by the owner-landlord.

Essential Elements of a Lease

No particular wording or form of agreement is required by statute to create a valid lease. It is sufficient in law, if the intention is expressed, to transfer from one to another possession of certain real property for a determinate length of time. Substance, not form, is what counts. A contract is not a lease merely because it is designated as such.

The following items are necessary to create an enforceable lease:

1. A lessor and lessee with contractual capability
2. An agreement to let and take
3. Sufficient description of premises
4. Term

5. Consideration
6. An execution, if required by statute
7. A delivery and acceptance

Most of these provisions carry over from our ealier discussion of contracts and deeds. But a few differences need to be noted. The contract may continue to be valid even though the amount of rent and term may be omitted. Without a term, a periodic tenancy may be created rather than an intended tenancy for years. The amount of rent payable may be evidenced by actual performance of the parties even though not stated. Legally, the tenant-lessee need not sign; taking possession of the premises is evidence of acceptance and agreement. Statute requirements for execution may require witnesses, seal, acknowledgment, and recording.

Leases for 3 years or more are recordable in most states. In that possession gives actual notice of a tenant's claim in most states, recording is not always important. And some leases are not recorded because the parties wish to avoid revealing rents, terms, and other contents. See Figure 24–2 for a typical apartment lease.

Landlord Rights and Obligations

Quiet enjoyment is the covenant specifically made by a landlord. There are implied covenants of possession and sometimes fitness for use. Historically, there is no warranty in the lease of a whole or detached house of habitability or suitability. If a landlord leases an apartment in an apartment building or an office in an office building, there is an implied covenant that the portions of the building used by all tenants are fit for the use for which they are intended. Many states have recently passed landlord-tenant laws requiring that the premises be kept in good repair. Failure to maintain the property may give the tenant the right to withhold rental payments and to apply the payments toward maintainence of the premises.

The implied covenant of possession is that the tenant can hold possession against everyone, including the landlord. The lease usually allows the landlord to show the property to a prospective tenant or purchaser for a short period before expiration, with reasonable notice. Also the lease usually gives the landlord the right to enter and make necessary repairs to comply with governmental requirements. Thus, the landlord must accord possession to the tenant for the term of the lease, subject only to its conditions.

Tenant Rights and Obligations

The tenant also gets certain rights and incurs certain obligations in making a lease. The tenant gets certain automatic rights, as follows, unless otherwise agreed to in the lease: (1) right to use the premises in any legal

FIGURE 24–2
Rental Agreement

FORM No. 818
STEVENS-NESS LAW PUBLISHING CO., PORTLAND, OR. 97204
TO-BB

RENTAL AGREEMENT
(Dwelling Unit—Residence Oregon)

26-12

THIS AGREEMENT, entered into in duplicate this 10th day of September, 19 81, by and between Everready Real Estate Management Co., lessor, and Otto and Mary Mobile, lessee;

WITNESSETH: That for and in consideration of the payment of the rents and the performance of the terms of lessee's covenants herein contained, lessor does hereby demise and let unto the lessee and lessee hires from lessor for use as a residence those certain premises described as Unit 11, Douglas Manor
located at 2001 Century Drive, Urbandale, Anystate

☒ on a month to month tenancy beginning 16 September, 19 81 } (Indicate which)
☐ for a term of .... commencing ...., 19 ...., and ending ...., 19 ....

at a rental of $ 520.00 per month, payable monthly in advance on the 1st day of each and every month. Rents are payable at the following address: Everready Management Co, 41 East Third, Urbandale, Anystate 00000
It is hereby agreed that if rent is unpaid after four (4) days following due date, the lessee shall pay a late charge of $1.00 per day computed to include the first day due and continuing until both rent and late charges are fully paid. Any dishonored check shall be treated as unpaid rent and shall be subject to the same late charge plus $5.00 as a special handling fee and must be made good by cash, money order or certified check within 24 hours of notification.
It is further mutually agreed between the parties as follows:

1. Said aforementioned premises shall be occupied by no more than two adults and two children;
2. Lessee shall not violate any city ordinance or state law in or about said premises;
3. Lessee shall not sub-let the demised premises, or any part thereof, or assign this lease without the lessor's written consent;
4. If lessee fails to pay rent or other charges promptly when due, or to comply with any other term or condition hereof, lessor at lessor's option, and after proper written notice, may terminate this tenancy;
5. Lessee shall maintain the premises in a clean and sanitary condition at all times, and upon the termination of the tenancy shall surrender same to lessor in as good condition as when received, ordinary wear and tear and damage by the elements excepted; a fee is herewith paid, no part of which is refundable, for cleaning up and restoring the premises in the amount of $ 200.00.
6. There shall be working locks on all outside doors; lessor shall provide lessee with keys for same;
7. Lessee ☒, Lessor ☐ shall properly cultivate, care for and adequately water the lawn, shrubbery and grounds;
8. Lessor shall supply electric wiring, plumbing facilities capable of producing hot and cold running water and adequate heating facilities;
9. Lessee shall pay for all natural gas, electricity, and telephone service. All other services will be paid for by Lessor and Lessee as follows:

	Lessee	Lessor		Lessee	Lessor
Water	☒	☐	Garbage Service	☐	☒
Sewer	☐	☒	Cable tv	☒	☐

10. Lessee agrees to assume all liability for, and to hold lessor harmless from, all damages and all costs and fees in the defense thereof, caused by the negligence or willful act of lessee or lessee's invitees or guests, in or upon any part of the demised premises, and to be responsible for any damage or breakage to lessee's equipment, fixtures or appliances therein or thereon, not caused by lessor's misconduct or willful neglect.
11. Nothing herein shall be construed as waiving any of the rights provided by law of either party hereto;
12. In the event any suit or action is brought to collect any of said rents or to enforce any provision of this agreement or to repossess said premises, reasonable attorney's fees may be awarded by the trial court to the prevailing party in such suit or action together with costs and necessary disbursements; and on appeal, if any, similar reasonable attorney's fees, costs and disbursements may be awarded by the appellate court to the party prevailing on such appeal;
13. If the lessee, or someone in the lessee's control, irreparably endangers the health or safety of the lessor or other tenants or irreparably damages or threatens immediate irreparable damage to the dwelling unit, the lessor, after 24 hours' written notice specifying the causes, may immediately terminate the rental agreement and take possession in the manner provided in ORS 105.105 to 105.160;
14. Lessee shall not allow any undriveable vehicle to remain on the premises for more than 24 hours. No car repairs are to be made on the premises, including minor maintenance such as an oil change;
15. Property of the tenant left on the premises after surrender or abandonment of the premises, or termination of this rental agreement by any means except court order, shall be deemed abandoned. Upon 15 days notice to tenant, in writing, landlord shall have the right to store, sell or otherwise dispose of any such property as provided by law, unless within said 15-day period tenant removes the property. Failure to remove the property within 15 days will be conclusive evidence of abandonment.
16. The owner (or agent for service) is Everready Real Estate Mgt. Co.
Address 41 East Third
Urbandale, Anystate 00000 Phone 345-4330
The manager is H."Handy" Overseer
Address 41 East Third
Urbandale, Anystate Phone 345-4331
17. Any holding over by the lessee after the expiration of the term of this rental agreement or any extension thereof, shall be as a tenancy from month to month and not otherwise;
18. If this is a month-to-month tenancy only, then, except as otherwise provided by statute, this agreement may be terminated by either party giving the other at anytime not less than 30 days' notice in writing* prior to the date designated in the tenancy termination notice, whereupon the tenancy shall terminate on the date designated;
19. Lessor acknowledges receipt of the sum of $ 400.00 as a security deposit, of which the lessor may claim all or part thereof reasonably necessary to remedy lessee's defaults in the performance of this rental agreement (including nonpayment of past-due rent) and to repair damage to the premises caused by lessee, not including ordinary wear and tear. To claim all or part of said deposit, lessor shall give lessee, within thirty (30) days after termination of the tenancy, a written accounting which states specifically the basis or bases of the claim, and the portion not so claimed shall be returned to lessee within said thirty days. Lessor may recover damages in excess of said deposit to which lessor may be entitled. Lessor also acknowledges receipt of the sum of $ N.A. to insure the return of keys to said dwelling unit; said sum to be refunded upon the return of all such keys;
20. Pets are allowed ☒, not allowed ☐ (indicate which). If allowed to consist of one cat
Lessee will be held responsible for all damage caused by pets and pay an additional non-refundable fee of $ 100.00 prior to bringing a pet onto the leased premises.
21. Lessee further agrees that failure by the lessor at any time to require performance by the lessee of any provision hereof shall in no way affect lessor's right hereunder to enforce the same, nor shall any waiver by said lessor of any breach of any provision hereof be held to be a waiver of any succeeding breach of any provision, or as a waiver of the provision itself.
22. The following personal property is included and to be left upon the premises when tenancy is terminated range, refrigerator electric globes, carpeting, drapes, fire alarm.
23. Additional provisions:
Door to kitchen cabinet to be repaired

Lessee Further Agrees
1. That he has personally inspected the premises and finds them satisfactory at the time of execution of this agreement;
2. That he has read this agreement and all the stipulations contained in the lease agreement.
3. That no promises have been made to him except as contained in this agreement and lease, except the following: None

IN WITNESS WHEREOF, the parties hereto have executed this agreement in duplicate the day and year first above written and lessee, by affixing his signature hereto, acknowledges receipt of one copy of the executed documents.

/s/Handy Overseer
Lessor
for Everready Real Estate Management Co.

/s/Otto Mobile
Lessee
/s/Mary Mobile

The words lessee and lessor shall include the plural as well as the singular.

*See S-N Form Nos. 829, 971, 972, 973.

manner, (2) right to make no security deposit, (3) right to sublet, (4) right to assign, (5) right to mortgage, and (6) right of redemption.

Use of premises. Unless the lease contains a restriction, the tenant may use the premises in any legal manner. The tenant may not, however, interfere with occupants of other parts of the property. Illegal use would permit an action of dispossession by the landlord, and a lease specifically made for an illegal purpose would not be enforceable by either party. The purpose for which the premises are to be used is often stated in the lease as, for example, "private dwelling," "boardinghouse," "retail drugstore," and so on. To limit the use to a specified purpose, it is best to have the lease state that the premises shall be used for the purpose mentioned and "for no other." It has been held in court cases, where the lease simply stated that the tenant was to use the premise for a certain trade, that it could be used for other trades. The lease may contain a covenant that the premises may not be used for any purpose that is extra hazardous, objectionable, detrimental to the local neighborhood, or similarly undesirable. Note that the tenant may also vacate or give up use of the property, termed *abandonment,* before the lease expires; however the tenant continues to be liable for rental payments.

Security deposits. A landlord may properly require the tenant to furnish security performance of the terms of the lease. This security may be in the form of cash or negotiable securities, or it may be in the form of a bond executed by personal sureties or a surety company. The amount of security is usually in proportion to the rent required; thus, the required security may equal the rent for 1 month or several months, or even a year. Increasingly, the law says that tenants are entitled to receive interest on any cash security deposits.

A transfer of the property to another owner by the lessor does not, of itself, include the security deposit. The lessor's covenant to return the deposit to the lessee is personal. Of course, this liability may be otherwise stipulated in the lease.

Right to sublet. A landlord may include a clause against subletting to maintain control of property occupancy. A re-renting of space held under lease is *subletting* or *subleasing.* The re-rental may be for part or for all the premises, for part or all of the term. The right to sublet is implied unless specifically stated otherwise.

Assignment of lease. A tenant may also assign right held under a lease unless a specific covenant to the contrary is included in the lease. A landlord may rent based upon the financial worthiness of the tenant and include a clause against assignment. Even so, given a stable alternate tenant, a landlord may waive the clause and agree to a proposed assignment. A lease, once assigned, is generally considered freely assignable. In such event, the usual rule is that the original tenant-lessee can be held liable for rents under a lease even though it has be assigned and reassigned.

Mortgaging the leasehold. The tenant's rights in a lease is a leasehold, which may be mortgaged unless the lease says otherwise. In almost all states, a mortgage on a lease is a conveyance that comes under the provisions of the recording act and may, therefore, be recorded in the same manner as a mortgage on real property. In some jurisdictions a leasehold mortgage is considered a chattel mortgage. Unless otherwise agreed, the mortgage lien would not have any greater claim on the property than that held by the tenant under the lease.

Right of redemption. In some states, a tenant, dispossessed when more than 5 years of the lease are unexpired, has a right to come after the dispossession and pay up all arrears and again obtain possession of the property. That is, the lessee has a *right of redemption.* In a personally negotiated lease, the tenant usually waives this right of redemption. This enables the landlord to dispossess a tenant and to obtain another without fear of the first tenant's coming in and reclaiming possession.

Jointly Negotiated Covenants

The following points may be but are not necessarily included in a lease. If included they must usually be negotiated according to the situation.

Lease purchase option. A provision giving the tenant the right to purchase the premises at a certain price during the lease is called a *lease option* or *lease-purchase option.* Frequently, the rental for the first year applies to the purchase price if the option to purchase is exercised within the first year. A lease option is used when an owner wants to sell to a tenant, who is undecided about purchasing or who does not have an adequate down payment. A lease option has priority over any other prospective purchaser's right to purchase.

Right of renewal. A right of one or more renewals may be included in a lease. The length of each renewal and a means to determine the rent to be paid on renewal are best negotiated as part of the initial lease, to avoid uncertainty by both the tenant and the landlord. This certainty allows the tenant a more stable basis for planning operations; and it gives the owner more certainty of income and a more stable property value.

Subordination. Other liens and claims of record when the lease is made are superior to the rights of the tenant. But occupancy or recording establish the priority of the tenant's claim. A mortgage made after the lease would, therefore, be subordinate to the lease. But leases often provide that they shall be subordinate to subsequent mortgages up to a certain amount; this provision permits the landlord to increase existing mortgages up to the agreed amount. On the other hand, a vacant site may be leased on which the tenant proposes to build substantial improvements. The lessee may negotiate a clause for the investor-landlord to subordinate the fee ownership position to the proposed mortgage, up to an agreed amount.

In any event, the owner, the tenant, and a tentative lender should be aware of the significance of a subordinated position. There is a case on record in which a bank loaned $82,000 on a piece of property and ignored the rights of the people in possession. The mortgage was afterward foreclosed. It was then found that the property was occupied by tenants under a 10-year lease, with the option of further renewal of 13 years, at an annual rent of $6,000, which is entirely inadequate for a property worth $82,000.

Liability after reentry. A lease may include a provision that if a tenant is dispossessed by summary proceedings or if the tenant abandons the property, the landlord may sublease the premises as an agent of the tenant. Then, if the landlord reenters and takes possession, the landlord has the option of holding the tenant liable for the rent until the end of the term of the lease. The landlord may re-let the premises as the agent of the tenant; in such a case the landlord credits the tenant with the amount collected from the sublessee.

Improvements and repairs. Improvements become the property of the landlord when made, unless otherwise agreed. It is proper in some cases to provide that some or all improvements may be removed at, or prior to, the expiration of the lease. Trade fixtures and machinery installed by the tenant are usually considered personal property and are removable when the tenant vacates. The lease usually provides that no alterations to the building may be made without prior consent of the landlord.

The general rule is that neither party to a lease is required to make repairs, but the tenant is required to surrender the premises at the expiration of the term in as good a condition as they were at the beginning of the lease, reasonable wear and tear and damage by the elements excepted. Occasionally, the lease provides that the landlord shall make certain repairs only. There is no legal requirement that the landlord make the ordinary repairs for the upkeep of the property except that the building must be kept tenable. If a building becomes untenable, the tenant may move out on the grounds of having been constructively evicted.

Liens. The tenant may make repairs, alterations, or improvements to the premises with the consent of the landlord. Such consent may result in the tenant's neglecting to pay for work performed and the consequent filing of mechanics' liens by those who did the work. Mechanics and materialmen, under such circumstances, may enforce their liens against the landlord's property, although they may not be able to hold the landlord personally liable. At the same time, the tenant may be held personally liable.

The landlord may demand further protection from liens by requiring that the tenant deposit cash or file a bond as a guarantee that the cost of the repair or construction work will be paid. This requirement is very important in leases that require the tenant to make extensive repairs, alterations, or improvements.

Damage claims. Agreement is desirable in a lease as to which party (landlord or tenant) is liable for claims developing from ownership, occupation, or use of the property. These claims may be by persons injured on the property, or they may be by persons damaged away from the property, as when a fire spreads from the property. With liability clarified, the party bearing the risk may obtain protection through insurance.

In apartment houses or other buildings in which there are several tenants, tenants are responsbile only for injuries arising from negligence in their space, whereas the landlord is liable for injuries sustained on roof, halls, stairways, or entry.

In the absence of an agreement on damages, the general rules is that whenever a landlord would be liable to a tenant, the landlord is liable to anyone able to "stand in the tenant's shoes." This substitution of responsibility for or transference of a claim is termed *subrogation.* Thus, assume that a landlord fails to maintain a stairway properly. Claims for damages suffered by relatives, friends, employees, or business visitors of the tenant as well as by the tenant may then be filed and enforced against the landlord.

Neither the landlord nor the tenant is responsible for an accident unless it was caused by negligence on the part of either of them. Also, it must be borne in mind that neither the landlord nor the tenant is liable for an injury caused by a negligent condition unless either actually knew or should have known of the condition.

Damage/destruction of premises. Unless otherwise agreed, a lessee of land or a site must continue to pay rent even if the building thereon or other improvements are destroyed by fire, flood, wind, or other acts of God. This rule does not apply to a lease of an apartment, office, or some other portion of a building. Such an arrangement is not a lease of land.

In the event that partial destruction makes a building untenantable or unusable, the landlord must make repairs in a "reasonable" time. And if the premises are damaged and made unsuitable for occupancy before the tenant takes possession, the tenant may end the lease without liability to the landlord. A damage clause in a lease would, of course, enable the parties clearly to define their relationship and to protect themselves accordingly.

Compliance with governmental regulations. Police power allows governmental regulation of the use, occupancy, and conditions of real estate. Depending on the nature and duration of a proposed lease, a landlord and tenant may include a clause concerning responsibility for compliance with such regulations.

TERMINATION OF LEASES

Term Expiration

Written leases end on the last day of their term, without notice. Tenancies from period to period and at will continue, or are self-renewing, until notice of termination is given.

Mutual Agreement

A tenant and landlord may end a lease by a mutual arrangement of surrender and acceptance, which may be by expressed or implied agreement as well as by oral or written agreement. With a recorded lease, the parties are advised to write out, sign, and record any agreement to surrender.

Dispossess/Eviction

A breach of conditions, followed by dispossess proceedings, may terminate a lease. The conditions may be divided into two classes, those for which the landlord dispossesses the tenant by summary proceedings and those for which summary proceedings may not be brought. Summary (brief) dispossess proceedings may be used to terminate a lease for the following reasons:

1. Nonpayment of rent
2. Holding over at the end of the term
3. Unlawful use of the premises
4. Nonpayment of taxes, assignments, or other charges when, under the terms of the lease, the tenant undertook to pay them
5. When the tenant takes the benefit of an insolvent act or is adjudged a bankrupt

The right to recover possession from a tenant through the summary proceeding, known as *dispossess,* is one given by statute and is not a common law right. Upon a decision by the court that a serious breach of conditions exists, a warrant for dispossess is issued. A tenant not immediately withdrawing from the property may be forcibly removed by a local law official such as a sheriff.

For breach of other conditions of a lease, possession may be obtained only by means of a lengthy and expensive ejectment action.

An eviction may be either actual or constructive. An *actual eviction* occurs if the tenant is ousted from the premise in whole or in part by an act of the landlord or paramount title. *Constructive eviction* occurs when the physical condition of the leased premises has changed, owing to some act or failure to act of the landlord, so that the tenant is unable to occupy the premises for the purposes intended. No claim of constructive eviction will be allowed unless the tenant actually removes from the premises while the conditions exist. If the tenant removes and can prove a valid case, the lease is terminated. The tenant may also be able to recover damages for the landlord's breach of contract.

There may be some constructive eviction from a portion of the premises only. And the tenant may take advantage of the fact that a lease is a complete contract by removing from the entire premises. The tenant may also retain possession of the remainder and refuse to pay rent until restored to possession of the entire premises. A tenant's contention of constructive eviction must rest upon some act or omission of the landlord by which the tenant is deprived of the use of the property for the purpose of in the manner contemplated by the lease. The erection by the landlord of a building on adjoining property as a result of which the tenant's light was diminished would not be constructive eviction. But storage of materials on the sidewalk in front of the tenant's premise that interfere with the tenant's use of the premises may be construed as constructive eviction. Failure of the landlord to furnish steam heat or other services contemplated by the lease usually amounts to constructive eviction.

Eminent Domain

When leased property is taken for public purposes under the right of eminent domain, leases on it terminate. The tenant is given an opportunity to prove the value of the unexpired term of the lease in the proceeding under which the property is taken and may receive an award for it.

Mortgage Foreclosure

The foreclosure of a mortgage or other lien terminates a leasehold estate, provided that the lease is subsequent or subordinate to the lien being foreclosed. The lessee must be made a party in the foreclosure suit for this to occur. Also, a lease may provide for termination upon bankruptcy of the tenant or lessee.

TENANT UNIONS

Tenants and landlords need each other. Landlords have space to sell. Tenants need places to live or to do business. Both benefit when the right tenant gets the right space. The tenant gets greater satisfaction or does more business. The landlord gets higher rent and, in turn, greater property value.

At the same time, the interests of the tenants and landlords are in direct conflict in a sense comparable to that of mortgagor and mortgagee. The negotiation between them goes on continuously, in one form or another. An important development of this negotiation/competition—tenant unions—is outside the traditional landlord-tenant relationship as discussed earlier. Even so, a brief look at the nature and implications of tenant unions seems warranted.

Tenant unions came into being because of abusive practices by some landlords. In apartment house operation, particularly, the landlord is generally both more knowledgeable and stronger financially than is any individual tenant. The situation is similar to that of a large employer with many individual employees. Organizing into unions increases the bargaining power of the tenants.

Tenant unions usually seek to negotiate (1) better leases and conditions for tenants and (2) a grievance procedure for dissatisfied tenants. Tenant unions have also been instrumental in getting landlord-tenant statutes passed in many states; these statutes put tenants on a more even footing with owners.

Tenant unions have successfully called rent strikes (withholding rent payments to enforce their demands). The occasion of a rent strike might involve lack of security against criminal acts on the premises, wrongful eviction of tenants, or building code violations as when a serious hazard exists. Courts have held that if rents are paid into escrow in such strikes, retaliatory evictions are illegal. A *retaliatory eviction* is removing a tenant from a property as punishment for the tenant's asserting his or her rights. Thus landlords may not get even with tenants for joining tenant unions, for reporting violations of building codes or other local regulations, or for legally withholding rents. The movement toward tenant unions seems healthy for responsible landlords and for society as a whole as well as for tenants.

SUMMARY

A contract in which a landlord exchanges space for rent from a tenant is a lease. The main kinds of leases, based on rent payment plans, are flat, graduated, percentage, index, net, and reappraisal. The percentage lease is increasing in popularity because it provides the owner with a means of sharing in inflated property value. Ground lease and sale and leaseback arrangements are also important ways of renting property.

Typical covenants in a lease concern (1) use of the premises, (2) security deposits, (3) subletting, (4) assignment, (5) mortgaging, and (6) redemption. Covenants requiring joint negotiation by a landlord and tenant include (1) lease option, (2) rights of renewal, (3) subordination, (4) requirements for improvements and repairs, (5) damage claims by others, (6) eminent domain, and (7) property destruction.

Tenant unions negotiate leases and grievance procedures for renters more effectively than can individual tenants. Rent strikes are legal in most states if withheld rents are placed in escrow. Retaliatory eviction by landlords against tenants seeking their rights is illegal.

QUESTIONS FOR REVIEW AND DISCUSSION

1. Explain the basic nature and terminology of leasing, including a clear distinction between tenancy for years and tenancy from year to year.

2. What are the advantages and disadvantages of a written lease for years relative to a month-to-month rental from the viewpoint of the tenant.

3. List and explain these rental payment plan leases:
   a. Percentage
   b. Flat
   c. Net
   d. Graduate
   e. Index
   f. Reappraisal

4. Explain the following concepts of clauses as they relate to leasing:
   a. Use of premises
   b. Right to sublet
   c. Right to assign
   d. Right to mortgage
   e. Lease option
   f. Subordination

5. List and explain at least four ways in which a lease may be terminated.

6. A property is under lease on a long-term, step-up lease. The neighorhood deteriorates, and the property values decline. Who benefits, if anyone? Explain.

7. Compare the advantages of leasing with the advantages of buying a business property. Is there a time when either is clearly more appropriate?

8. Is there a landlord-tenant code in your state? If so, what are its main provisions? If not, where are the major laws pertaining to landlord and tenant rights found?

CASE PROBLEMS

1. Norman occupied a cabin on Henry's farm, without any provision for rent or duration. Both recognized that either could terminate the arrangement at any time. Norman died. Henry cleaned up the cabin, locked the door, and placed

Norman's belongings on the porch. William, Norman's executor, now claims the right to occupy the cabin as a continuation of the lease arrangement. Does William have this right? Explain.

2. Jean rented a luxury apartment in Tudor Towers for $1,000 per month on a 2-year lease on December 10. Shortly after, she received a job offer she could not refuse in another city. She re-rented the apartment to Edward for $1,200 per month for the remainder of the lease. Nothing is said in her original lease about whether she could assign or sublease. Now the owner of Tudor Towers objects to the re-renting and threatens to sue Jean. What are Jean's rights in this situation?
3. Carl rents a building from Eugene to establish a restaurant and tavern on a 1-year lease. Carl adds a storage room in the rear and arranges for the installation of a bar, kitchen equipment, booths, and miscellaneous other items, all of which are attached to the building. The business is unusually successful, and Carl decides to move to larger quarters at the end of the year. Upon moving, Carl starts to remove the improvements. Eugene objects and threatens to sue, saying that all improvements become property of the landlord unless otherwise agreed. And no such "other" agreement was reached. What is the result?
4. Ellen was instrumental in organizing a tenant union. As a result of the union, many tenants, including Ellen, paid their rent into an escrow account until certain improvements were made to the property. When Ellen's lease ended, the landlord refused to renew. Ellen feels that she is being punished for her actions. What rights does she have? Can she be evicted under these circumstances?

CHAPTER TWENTY-FIVE
HOMEOWNERSHIP

The fellow who owns his own home is always just coming out of the hardware store.
KIM HUBBARD, *Bartlett's Unfamiliar Quotations*

IMPORTANT TOPICS OR DECISION AREAS TAKEN UP IN THIS CHAPTER

- Determining Housing Affordability
- Federal Tax Laws and Homeownership
- Rent or Buy?
- Real Estate Settlement Procedures Act (RESPA)

It is worth noting also that in more recent years, condominiums, cooperatives, and mobile homes have become widely accepted as alternatives to detached single-family residences for homeownership. Changing life-styles as well as higher costs account for this acceptance. A part of this changing life-style is a decrease in the number of people per occupied unit, which makes housing even more expensive on a per capita basis. See Figure 25–1.

Homeownership has long been part of the Great American Dream. In 1900, 47 percent of all dwelling units were owner occupied, and in 1950, 55 percent were. Currently, about two-thirds of all residential units are owner occupied, which level may well mark the high tide of homeownership in the United States. Inflation, high interest rates, and ever-higher construction costs all act to reduce chances for the young people to realize homeownership. Hence, the percentage appears likely to decline. These forces also make it likely that the current generation will be the first that will not live in a home as large or as nice as the home in which they grew up.

Our purpose in this chapter is to take up key decisions and important knowledge relative to owning one's own home. The two basic decisions are (1) how much can I afford to pay for housing and (2) should I rent or buy? Over and above these considerations are (1) tax treatment of homeownership and (2) regulations affecting the buying and selling of personal residences, specifically the Real Estate Settlement Procedures Act.

KEY CONCEPTS INTRODUCED IN THIS CHAPTER

Adjusted sale price
Annual stabilized income, ASI
Housing expenses
"Rollover"

FIGURE 25–1
Occupied housing units—Tenure and population per occupied unit, 1900–1980 (in thousands, except percent; Hawaii and Alaska excluded prior to 1960)

		OCCUPIED UNITS					
			OWNER OCCUPIED		RENTER OCCUPIED		
YEAR	TOTAL POPULATION	TOTAL NUMBER OF UNITS	NUMBER	PERCENT	NUMBER	PERCENT	POPULATION PER UNIT
1900	76,212,168	15,964	7,455	46.7	8,509	53.3	4.8
1910	92,228,496	20,256	9,301	45.9	10,954	54.1	4.6
1920	106,021,537	24,352	11,114	45.6	13,238	54.4	4.4
1930	123,202,624	29,905	14,280	47.8	15,624	52.2	4.1
1940	132,164,569	34,855	15,196	43.6	19,659	56.4	3.8
1950	151,325,798	42,855	23,560	55.0	19,266	45.0	3.5
1960	179,323,175	53,024	32,797	61.9	20,227	38.1	3.4
1970	203,302,031	63,445	39,886	62.9	23,560	37.1	3.2
1980	226,545,805	80,390	51,795	64.4	28,595	35.6	2.8

SOURCE: U.S. Bureau of the Census, as reported in *1984 Statistical Abstract of the United States,* p. 748, Table 1339.

DETERMINING HOUSING AFFORDABILITY

An applicant's ability to pay and motivation to own are the primary considerations for a lender in making a mortgage loan. Obviously, anyone with the resources to pay cash can own whatever type of home he or she wishes. But, for most people, obtaining a loan is a necessary prerequisite to homeownership. So, over and above motivation, let us look at how a lender is likely to evaluate an applicant's ability to carry a loan, using FHLMC guidelines. We can then extend the analysis to determine how much housing can be afforded.

Annual Stabilized Income

Ability to carry a loan depends on one's recognized earning ability, which under the FHLMC guidelines is called *annual stabilized income (ASI).* Annual stabilized income begins with a person's yearly wages or salary. To wages or salary are added income from overtime, commissions, bonuses, dividends, interest, alimony, welfare, and net rents. To be consistent, payments for alimony and/or child support must be deducted in arriving at ASI. Two years' "experience" on these additions and deductions is required for the figures to be fully accepted. Let us now involve John Burgoyne in a case example.

John, we said, has an annual salary of $21,000. John and Marcia Maas, a chemist, recently became engaged. They plan to marry in about a year. Marcia earns $18,000 a year. They have little "outside" income. Together, they project, they should be earning $42,000, their annual stabilized income, at the time they want to buy a house.

Proportion for Housing

The FHLMC guidelines allow 25 percent of ASI for housing expenses. *Housing expenses* include loan interest, repayment of principal, hazard insurance premiums, and property taxes (PITI). In addition, if applicable, mortgage insurance, homeowner association dues, and ground rental payments are included. Utility charges are not included.

Alternatively, the guidelines allow up to 33 percent of ASI for housing expenses and other required periodic payments. Other payments include required outlays for utilities, housing association dues or fees, installment debt, alimony, and child support. An additional 10 percent may be added to these limits, if justified, by a large down payment, a substantial net worth, or a demonstrated ability and willingness to devote a larger portion of income for housing expense. Thus an absolute maximum of 27.5 and 36.0 percent, respectively, of income may be devoted to housing. So, what does this all mean?

The 25-percent Rule

John and Marcia inquire of the loan officer at the Urbandale Savings and Loan Association as to current lending terms. The officer tells them that RRM loans, for 80 percent of value, are now being made at 12 percent, compounded monthly, with amortization calculated on a 30-year life. The interest rate would be renegotiated every 5 years. The loan officer also informs them that property taxes and mortgage insurance typically run about 3 percent of market value in Urbandale. John and Marcia recognize that these terms may not hold next year but they do give a basis for analysis.

Under the 25 percent rule, the amount John and Marcia would have available for housing is $10,500 per year, or $875 per month. This amount must cover PITI only. Based on their conversation with the loan officer, they do not believe that they would qualify for a 10 percent bonus, to the absolute maximum, because of their short earnings record. Thus, the amount available for housing relative to purchase price would be as follows.

Amount available monthly	=	Monthly debt service for interest and principal repayment on loan	+	Amount required monthly for property taxes and hazard insurance

$875 = (80%) (purchase price) (monthly principal recovery factor—12%, 30 years) + (3%/12) Purchase price

Inserting the monthly principal recovery factor, we are in a position to solve for the purchase price of the home that is affordable by John and Marcia.

$$
\begin{aligned}
\$875 &= (0.80)\ (\text{purchase price}) \\
&\quad (0.010286) + (0.0025)\ (\text{purchase price}) \\
\$875 &= 0.008229 \text{ purchase price} \\
&\quad + 0.0025 \text{ purchase price} \\
\$875 &= 0.010729 \text{ purchase price} \\
\text{Purchase price} &= \$875/0.010289 = \$81{,}555
\end{aligned}
$$

Thus, it appears that John and Marcia can afford to pay up to $81,555 for a home. Let us see if the figures check out. The loan would be for 80 percent of $81,555, or $65,244.

Monthly debt service on loan	$671.11
Taxes and insurance at 3%/12	203.89
Total required for PITI	$875.00

Rounding to $81,500, John and Marcia suddenly realize that a cash down payment of $16,300, or 20 percent of the purchase price, would be required of them. The amount may be realized by saving, an interest-free loan from their parents (via a gift letter), "sweat equity," or some other source. At the same time, they have an initial indication of how much they can afford for housing. But they have a second way of determining the amount.

The 33 Percent Rule

Under the 33 percent rule, utilities and installment debt must be taken into account. Thus, 33 percent of ASI must cover PITI plus utility costs and installment debt. Algebraically, the relationship is as follows:

$$\text{Amount available monthly} = \text{Loan principal repayment and interest} + \text{Property taxes and home insurance} + \text{Utility costs and other installment payments}$$

Next year, John and Marcia figure that they will still be paying $212 per month on a car. Also, inquiring of the loan officer and their parents, they determine that they can expect to pay an average of $95 per month for utilities if they buy a house. The amount available is $13,860 per year or $1,155 per month, based on 33 percent of $42,000. Inserting known information into the equation gives

$$\begin{aligned}
\$1{,}155 &= (0.80)\ (\text{purchase price})\ (0.010286) + \\
&\quad (0.0025)\ (\text{purchase price}) + (\$212 + \$95) \\
\$1{,}155 &= 0.008229 \text{ purchase price} \\
&\quad + 0.0025 \text{ purchase price} + \$307 \\
\$848 &= 0.010729 \text{ purchase price} \\
\text{Purchase price} &= \$848/0.010729 = \$79{,}038
\end{aligned}$$

With a purchase price of $79,038, the loan amount would be $63,230 and the required down payment would be $15,808. Monthly debt service on the loan would be $650.40. Property taxes and hazard insurance would total to $197.60, based on the 3 percent quotation. These amounts, plus

$307 for installment payments per month, total to the $1,155 available per month.

John and Marcia are slightly surprised to find that their ability to buy is reduced because of their installment debt. After looking at available housing in the $75,000 to $80,000 range, John and Marcia decide to investigate whether they should rent or buy before making a decision. Besides everything else, they would be stretched to come up with the down payment. Thus, they would like to compare the costs of renting versus owning. Before taking up the rent or buy decision, we need a look at federal tax aspects of owning a personal residence.

FEDERAL TAX LAWS AND HOMEOWNERSHIP

The owner-occupant of a personal residence does not get all the advantages of an owner-investor in other types of real estate. For one thing, an annual depreciation allowance may not be taken on a personal residence. Also, a personal residence is not "like kind" of real estate for business or investment property in a tax-deferred exchange.

On the other hand, interest on a mortgage loan and real property taxes can both be used as direct offsets against ordinary income to reduce taxes payable. Thus, a homeowner in the 30 percent tax bracket, with property tax payments of $1,500 and interest payments of $3,000 in a given year, pays $1,350 less income tax as a result ($4,500 × 30%). Interest and tax deductions, therefore, constitute a substantial incentive to homeownership as against renting. And recognition of gain from the sale of a personal residence is postponed or "rolled over" if a replacement residence is bought or built at a cost equal to or greater than the adjusted sale price of the old residence.

Relief of "Rollover"

Congress enacted special relief provisions to minimize the tax impact on sale and repurchase of a personal residence because homeowners must occasionally relocate as a result of job transfers or of economic necessity. A U.S. Census Bureau survey indicates that one family in six moves each year, on average.[1] The moves are, therefore, not necessarily made at a time of maximum advantage or by the choice of the taxpayer.

Gain or profit on the sale of a personal residence is exempt from immediate taxation if a new residence of equal or greater value is purchased or constructed within the 48-month period beginning 24 months before and ending 24 months after the date of sale of the old residence.

---

[1] "When Did You Last Move?" *The Wall Street Journal,* December 1983, p. 25.

Date of sale is when title passes; in an installment sale, date of sale is when buyer moves into possession and is clothed with all the benefits and burdens of ownership, even though delivery of a deed is delayed to a later time.

The *adjusted sale price* equals the full price or contract price less selling expense and less "fixing-up" expense. Selling expenses are primarily brokerage fees, prepayment penalties, and legal fees. Fixing-up expenses are noncapital outlays made to assist in the sale of the residence, such as painting, minor repairs, landscaping, and so on.

Example. Bob and Betty Able bought a Denver residence for $60,000 in 1978. In November 1984, Bob's company transferred him to Chicago. The old residence was promptly sold for $94,000, with title transferred in January 1985. Selling expenses of $8,000 were incurred in the sale. Bob and Betty realized a gain of $26,000:

Sale price	$94,000
Less: Selling expenses	−8,000
Adjusted sale price	$86,000
Less: Purchase price (tax basis)	60,000
Equals long-term capital gains	$26,000

If Bob and Betty buy a home for $76,000 in Chicago, they would be taxed on $10,000 ($86,000 − $76,000), and their basis would remain at $60,000. Purchase of a new residence for $86,000 would mean no tax, and the basis would continue at $60,000. Purchase of a replacement residence for $100,000 would again mean no tax, but the basis would be increased to $74,000 ($100,000 − $26,000 unrecognized gain, or $60,000 plus $14,000 additional input).

Note that all cash proceeds from the sale need not be reinvested in the replacement residence; that is, a loan may be used to finance part of the purchase price of the new dwelling. But the new residence must be occupied within the period stipulated. And the replacement residence will not be considered a new residence if it is sold before the disposition of the old or initial residence. Finally, a condominium or a cooperative unit qualifies as a replacement residence.

Relief on Sale by Elderly

Elderly citizens, 55 and over, are entitled to a once-in-a-lifetime capital gain exclusion of $125,000 on the sale of a personal residence. The property must have been used as the principal residence for 3 of the 5 years immediately preceding the sale. This exclusion recognizes that the value in a residence may form the basic capital for retirement of senior citizens. Also, elderly citizens often need and want less living space because of smaller family size and reduced income. Thus, this option may be taken even though the move is to a smaller dwelling unit, to a retirement home, or to the home of a son or daughter.

A married couple is treated as one taxpayer under this exclusion. Both spouses are treated as satisfying the requirements, if either is 55 at the time of the sale and meets the 3- of 5-year holding provision. The "one-time exemption" means that if the exemption is used to avoid taxes on a gain of $80,000 on one sale, the taxpayer may not later claim a second exemption of up to $45,000.

Example. John and Jean, ages 56 and 57, sell their principal residence for $260,000. Their adjusted tax basis in the home is $100,000. Their fixing up and selling expenses amount to $20,000, making the adjusted sales price $240,000. Their taxable gain is $15,000, computed as follows.

Sale price	$260,000
Less: Expenses	−20,000
Equals adjusted sale price	$240,000
Less: adjusted tax basis	−100,000
Equals long-term capital gain	$140,000
Less: One-time exclusion	−125,000
Equals taxable gain	$ 15,000

John and Jean would only need to pay ordinary income taxes on $6,000, or 40 percent of the $15,000.

Conversion to Income Property

The owner of a personal residence, upon moving, may wish to convert it to an income property rather than sell it. Rental income, tax shelter, and capital appreciation might all become available as a result, while selling expenses are avoided. But the property cannot be represented as an income property, and depreciation taken, while it stands vacant and up for sale. The intent must be to convert to an income property as evidenced by the owner's affirmative actions. The property need not actually be rented; however, reaching the status of income property, rental, is prima facie proof of the conversion.

RENT OR BUY?

Unnecessarily severe sacrifices are sometimes made to achieve homeownership even though renting would be the better choice. Value may be in the eye of the beholder. But an economic comparison between renting and buying is worthwhile for anyone facing the rent or buy decision. At least the choice can then be made with full knowledge of the implications.

Also, we should note, a choice between renting or buying is generally assumed. Yet many people have no such choice. They are forced to rent for lack of down payment, of income, or of stability of income. On the other hand, ownership is sometimes forced because no rental units are available in the type of housing desired. An obvious example is that most single-family detached dwellings are owner ccupied.

Beyond the lack of choice, renting is generally regarded as a poor second choice for housing because of our great emphasis on homeownership. Therefore, before taking a detailed look at the numbers of the rent or buy decision, let us make a general comparison.

Pros and Cons of Owning

Owning is usually perceived to offer many intangibles that renting does not, such as greater status, financial security, stability, ego satisfaction, privacy, and personal freedom. Ownership is also perceived as more desirable for a family with children. Explicit financial benefits include value appreciation, taxes on which can often be deferred or avoided, and deduction of interest and property taxes as expenses on income tax returns.

The foregone return on equity invested in a home, including closing costs at purchase, is one of the most often overlooked costs of homeownership. This opportunity cost equals the rate of return that might be earned if the money were invested in stocks or bonds or some other investment media. Alternatively, the opportunity cost might be the cost of additional borrowing necessitated by the investment of the down payment in the home. Thus, if additional consumer debt is incurred at an 18 percent annual percentage rate, the opportunity cost is 18 percent.

A second opportunity cost involves the activities foregone by the owner because of the need to repair and maintain the residence. Instead of repainting the house or repairing a faucet, the owner could be watching baseball on television, traveling, water skiing, or sleeping.

Risk is a cost also. Dry rot or termites could necessitate major repairs, as could the foundation suddenly cracking or the roof developing numerous leaks. Taking out a mortgage loan adds financial risk. Some risks can be covered by insurance, as liability for injuries on the premises.

Transfer costs, financing costs, and administrative or maintenance costs must also be taken into account. Transfer costs include outlays for brokers, attorneys, title searches, surveys, recording deeds and mortgages, loan processing, and appraisals when the home is bought or sold. Transfer costs may run as high as 10 percent of value although 6 to 8 percent is more typical. Interest on borrowed money and mortgage insurance premiums are the main financing costs in owning. Administrative or maintenance costs include annual property taxes, hazard insurance premiums, and payments for repairs or replacements necessary to keep the property livable. Annual outlays for painting, yardwork, equipment maintenance, and roof repair may average 2 percent of value over a long peried. Property taxes and homeowners' insurance typically amount to 2 to 3 percent in urban areas and may often be higher.

Pros and Cons of Renting

Mobility, or ease of moving, is a major advantage of renting. Thus, adjustment to changing family size, income levels, or job locations can be easily made. In some cases, location of rental units provides greater convenience and more amenities for living. At the same time, time required to maintain the property is sharply reduced. And if the roof springs a leak, or another problem comes up, the risk and responsibility for correcting it is with the owner. Further, the money not used to buy a home may be invested in stocks, bonds, or money market certificates to enhance further the renter's income and wealth. Also, in a renter's market, as during an economic downturn, renting can be a major bargain. Finally, when a renter wants to move, it can be generally be done on short notice, with perhaps the loss of a deposit if a lease has been signed. A renter need not worry about selling a property when interest rates are extremely high or times are economically difficult.

Renters get no direct tax benefits. Indirectly, they get several benefits. Many housing expenses, not deductible by a homeowner, are deductible on residential rental properties. Obviously, an owner-investor recovers these expenses from his rental income. Thus, in a sense, maintenance, supplies, property taxes, hazard insurance, and even tax depreciation are deductible housing expenses for a renter where they are not for an owner.

The costs obviously include rent payments. Also, renter insurance premiums or the risk of loss if no insurance is carried is a cost. A renter also has the opportunity cost of not realizing value appreciation of a home; on the other hand, the risk of value depreciation is avoided. Finally, deposits for last month's rent and for security or cleaning must be made; however, if the unit is properly maintained, these are eventually recovered.

Rent Capitalization

A rent or buy decision should obviously be based on more than a simple comparison of monthly rent with monthly PITI payments on a mortgage loan. But information from mortgage lenders provides a "quick and dirty" basis for deciding whether renting is an obvious choice or more detailed analysis is in order. Some knowledge of property values is required as well. The approach works as follows.

John and Marcia, in their investigation of alternatives, have located a very nice condominium offered for rent at $800 per month. "Is it a good deal?" They consider several other comparable condominiums up for sale and, by comparison, determine that the market value of the unit they are considering is about $100,000. They already know that the mortgage loan interest rate is 12 percent, compounded monthly. Given this information, they reason as follows.

If they were to buy the unit, they would have to pay at least 12 percent per year in interest on a loan. And, since their equity position would involve more risk than that of the lender, they should expect at least a comparable rate of return on their equity. Thus, annual rental on the condominium should be at least $12,000 per year just to provide a reasonable return on the capital invested. Property taxes, insurance, and maintenace would only raise the cost of owning. Therefore, if they can rent the unit for less than $12,000 per year, or $1,000 per month, renting is clearly the better choice in the short run.

The approach may be used to determine a "break-even" market value of a unit to be rented as well. Earlier, we determined that John and Marcia could afford $875 for housing expenses. Capitalizing $875 per month, or $10,500 per year, in perpetuity, by 12 percent works out to $87,500. Thus, if a unit worth more than $87,500 can be rented for $875, renting would appear to be the better choice. As market values dropped relative to the $875 per month, owning would improve as a choice, and further analysis would be warranted.

Net After-Tax Costs

Comparison of after-tax costs and benefits provides the most accurate means of determining which alternative offers the greatest economic advantage. The analysis involves more calculation and many more assumptions than does rent capitalization. Costs and benefits discussed earlier are quantified where possible. Assumptions, calculations for a three-year projection, and results of a 10-year analysis are shown in Figures 25–2 and 25–3.

The rent or buy decision under consideration involves a dwelling offered for rent at 1 percent of its $100,000 market value. If bought, a 20 percent down payment would be required, with the balance financed by a 30-year, 12 percent, compounded monthly, loan. Closing costs are estimated to be 2 percent of the purchase price. The rental, market value, and other expenses are considered to increase by 5 percent per year. The owner's combined state and federal tax rate is 30 percent. Finally, if purchased, the owner is assumed to avoid any capital gains taxation upon disposition by buying a replacement dwelling of equal or greater value within 24 months.

Purchase and sale transaction costs are prorated over the number of years of ownership in the analysis. Thus, if the dwelling were only owned for 1 year, transaction costs of $9,000 (2 percent on purchase and 7 percent on sale) would be spread over the 1 year. If owned for 2 or 3

FIGURE 25–2
Net after tax costs of owning versus renting for one to ten years occupancy. (Based on type of analysis by authors shown in Figure 25–3)

YEAR	RENT	OWN	NET ADVANTAGE TO OWNING
1	$10,765	$16,609	−$5,844
2	11,275	12,732	− 1,458
3	11,808	11,767	41
4	12,365	11,549	816
5	12,948	11,645	1,304
6	13,558	11,911	1,645
7	14,196	12,289	1,907
8	14,862	12,747	2,115
9	15,559	13,271	2,289
10	16,288	13,851	2,437

years, the average closing costs on purchase would drop to $1,000 and $667, respectively. If sold in year 2, selling expenses of $7,350 ($105,000 times 7%) would be spread over 2 years at an average of $3,675. By a similar calculation, the average selling price for a 3-year holding period would drop to $2,573.

Other major costs of owning are interest expense, property taxes, and maintenance. Major benefits include value appreciation and tax savings on interest and tax deductions.

Monthly payments are the major cost of renting, amounting to $12,000 in year 1. A major benefit to the renter is earning on money not used for a down payment or purchase closing costs. Thus, $22,000 less

FIGURE 25–3
Net costs of owning versus renting for one to three years of occupancy

ASSUMPTIONS/INPUTS

PROPERTY AND OWNER (MARKET VALUE) COST OR PURCHASE PRICE	DOWN PAYMENT % OF M.V.	OWNER'S TAX BRACKET	ANN. CHNG. M.V., RENT EXPENSES	BUYING COSTS % OF M.V.	SELLING COSTS % OF M.V.
$100,000	20%	30%	5.00%	2.00%	7.00%

NOTE: Homeowner avoids capital gains tax by buying another unit of equal or greater value within 24 months, using "rollover."

FINANCING

LOAN TERM INT. (YEARS)	INT. RATE (NOMINAL)	LOAN TO VALUE RATIO	OPPORTUNITY COST VALUE OF CAPITAL, %
30	12.00%	80.00%	10%

RENTER DATA

FIGURE 25–3
(continued)

INITIAL MONTHLY RENTAL	REQUIRED DEPOSIT	GROSS RENT MULTIPLIER	RENTER'S CAPITAL (INVESTED)
$1,000	$1,500	100	$20,500

ANNUAL EXPENSES AS PERCENT OF MARKET VALUE

PROPERTY TAXES	HAZARD INSURANCE	MAINTENANCE	RENTER'S INSURANCE
2.00%	0.50%	2.00%	0.20%

	YEAR ONE		YEAR TWO		YEAR THREE	
BEGINNING OF YEAR M. V	$100,000		$105,000		$110,250	
MONTHLY RENTAL	$1,000		$1,050		$1,103	
GROSS RENT MULTIPLIER	100		100		100	
	RENT	OWN	RENT	OWN	RENT	OWN
COSTS						
Average buying expenses		$2,000		$1,000		$667
Interest on loan		$9,584		$9,548		$9,506
Property taxes, annual		$2,000		$2,100		$2,205
Hazard insurance at 2%		$500		$525		$551
Renter's insurance	$200		$210		$221	
Annual maintenance		$2,000		$2,100		$2,205
Equity opportunity cost		$2,000		$2,529		$3,087
Annual rent (12 × mo.)	$12,000		$12,600		$13,230	
Average selling expenses		$7,000		$3,675		$2,573
Total cost per year	$12,200	$25,084	$12,810	$21,477	$13,451	$20,793
BENEFITS						
Renter's return on money not invested in equity: at rate of 10% Minus taxes at 30%	$1,435		$1,535		$1,643	
Income tax savings:						
For interest paid		$2,875		$2,864		$2,852
For property taxes paid		$600		$630		$662
Equity build-up thru appreciation		$5,000		$5,250		$5,513
Total benefits per year	$1,435	$8,475	$1,535	$8,744	$1,643	$9,026
Net cost per year	$10,765	$16,609	$11,275	$12,732	$11,808	$11,767
Net advantage to buying		($5,844)		($1,458)		$40

$1,500 for deposits is available for investment at 10 percent in our example earning $2,050 in year 1. This $2,050 is subject to tax at 30 percent, leaving a net benefit of $1,435. The investment in year 2 is presumed to be $21,935 ($20,500 + $1,435).

Results of the analysis show that renting is nearly $6,000 less costly in year 1, $10,765 versus $16,609. In year 2, the difference has narrowed to about $1,500. And from year 3 on, owning is less costly but never by more than $2,500. See Figure 25–2 for a 10-year comparison of the net costs.

The example makes it quite clear that renting is almost certain to be less costly if occupancy is to be less than 2 years. Three years appears to be the break-even period; this is consistent with conventional wisdom. But caution is advised; a slight change in assumptions quickly changes the result. A growth rate of 3 percent would result in renting always having the lower net cost. And a 20 percent per year value increase would make ownership preferable to renting for a period as short as 2 years.

REAL ESTATE SETTLEMENT PROCEDURES ACT (RESPA)

Anyone involved in the buying or selling of a home is advised to be fully informed about the nature and implications of RESPA, the Real Estate Settlement Procedures Act. Under RESPA, the lender is at the heart of the closing process, with the following three obligations to borrowers:

1. Supply a special settlement costs information booklet, written or approved by HUD, to anyone making a written loan application. The booklet explains the basics of settlement procedures, home financing, and the functions of the various parties in the sales transaction.
2. Supply a "good faith estimate" of the costs for settlement services likely to be incurred in a closing. The intent is to indicate the approximate amount of cash likely to be needed by the buyer at closing.
3. Supply specific and actual costs of settlement to the buyer "at or before" actual settlement. Buyer may waive this requirement. At the same time, the buyer is entitled to see the settlement charges that have definitely been determined, upon request within one business day of closing.

Thus, when issuing a written loan commitment, lenders are required to give buyer-borrowers an approximation or "good faith" estimate, of local closing costs. A special HUD information booklet, *Settlement Costs and You: A HUD Guide for Homebuyers,* must also be given to the buyer along with the commitment. Actual settlement costs need not be given to the buyer-borrower until the time of settlement, and RESPA requirements may be waived by the borrower. The borrower, however, upon request one business day before settlement, must be shown any settlements costs that are known and available.

The Real Estate Settlement Procedures Act (RESPA) requires one settlement form to be used nationwide and, therefore, standardizes closing practices across the United States. See Figure 25–4. RESPA applies to sales of residential property financed with institutionally made first mortgages. Specifically, it applies only to the financing (and closing) of sales of one- and four-family homes, of individual condominium and cooperative units, and of mobile homes. RESPA was designed as consumer

FIGURE 25–4
RESPA settlement statement

ES (5-75) RESPA SETTLEMENT STATEMENT — Form Approved OMB No. 63-R1501

U.S. DEPARTMENT OF HOUSING AND URBAN DEVELOPMENT

DISCLOSURE/SETTLEMENT STATEMENT

If the Truth-in-Lending Act applies to this transaction, a Truth-in-Lending statement is attached as page 3 of this form.

B. TYPE OF LOAN:
1. ☐ FHA 2. ☐ FMHA 3. ☒ CONV. UNINS.
4. ☐ VA 5. ☐ CONV. INS.
6. FILE NUMBER 7. LOAN NUMBER
8. MORTG. INS. CASE NO.

C. NOTE: This form is furnished to you prior to settlement to give you information about your settlement costs, and again after settlement to show the actual costs you have paid. The present copy of the form is:

☐ ADVANCE DISCLOSURE OF COSTS. Some items are estimated, and are marked "(e)". Some amounts may change if the settlement is held on a date other than the date estimated below. The preparer of this form is not responsible for errors or changes in amounts furnished by others.

☒ STATEMENT OF ACTUAL COSTS. Amounts paid to and by the settlement agent are shown. Items marked "(p.o.c.)" were paid outside the closing; they are shown here for informational purposes and are not included in totals.

D. NAME OF BORROWER
Gerald & Nancy Investor
3278 Exotic Drive
Urbandale 00000

E. SELLER
Wendy Welloff
Condominium Towers, Unit 77
Urbandale, 00000

F. LENDER
Urbandale Savings & Loan Assoc.

G. PROPERTY LOCATION
Douglas Manor
2001 Century Drive
Urbandale 00000

H. SETTLEMENT AGENT
Tom Barren

PLACE OF SETTLEMENT
Hifidelity Escrow Services
221 N. Main, Urbandale 00000

I. DATES
LOAN COMMITMENT | ADVANCE DISCLOSURE | SETTLEMENT | DATE OF PRORATIONS IF DIFFERENT FROM SETTLEMENT

J. SUMMARY OF BORROWER'S TRANSACTION

100. GROSS AMOUNT DUE FROM BORROWER:	
101. Contract sales price	640,000
102. Personal property	
103. Settlement charges to borrower *(from line 1400, Section L)*	13,749.33
104.	
105.	
Adjustments for items paid by seller in advance:	
106. City/town taxes to	
107. County taxes to	
108. Assessments to	
109. Cleaning supplies to	1,800
110. Hazard insurance to	1,575
111. to	
112. to	
120. GROSS AMOUNT DUE FROM BORROWER:	657,124.33
200. AMOUNTS PAID BY OR IN BEHALF OF BORROWER:	
201. Deposit or earnest money	32,000
202. Principal amount of new loan(s)	500,000
203. Existing loan(s) taken subject to	
204.	
205.	
Credits to borrower for items unpaid by seller:	
206. City/town taxes to	
207. County taxes to	500
208. Assessments to	
209. Tenant security deposits	7,040
210. Rent prepaid 1/16 to 1/31	4,200
211. to	48
212. to	
220. TOTAL AMOUNTS PAID BY OR IN BEHALF OF BORROWER	543,788
300. CASH AT SETTLEMENT REQUIRED FROM OR PAYABLE TO BORROWER:	
301. Gross amount due from borrower *(from line 120)*	657,124.33
302. Less amounts paid by or in behalf of borrower *(from line 220)*	(543,788)
303. CASH (☒ REQUIRED FROM) OR (☐ PAYABLE TO) BORROWER:	113,336.33

K. SUMMARY OF SELLER'S TRANSACTION

400. GROSS AMOUNT DUE TO SELLER:	
401. Contract sales price	640,000
402. Personal property	
403.	
404.	
Adjustments for items paid by seller in advance:	
405. City/town taxes to	
406. County taxes to	
407. Assessments to	
408. to	
409. Cleaning supplies to	1,800
410. Hazard insurance to	1,575
411. to	
420. GROSS AMOUNT DUE TO SELLER	643,375
NOTE: The following 500 and 600 series sections are not required to be completed when this form is used for advance disclosure of settlement costs prior to settlement.	
500. REDUCTIONS IN AMOUNT DUE TO SELLER:	
501. Payoff of first mortgage loan	300,000
502. Payoff of second mortgage loan	
503. Settlement charges to seller *(from line 1400, Section L)*	29,744
504. Existing loan(s) taken subject to	
505. Accrued interest on existing loan	1,125
506.	
507.	
508. Rents collected in advance	4,200
509. Tenant security deposits held	
Credits to borrower for items unpaid by seller:	
510. City/town taxes to	
511. County taxes 1/1 to 1/15	500
512. Assessments to	48
513. Water/sewer charge	
514. to	
515. to	
520. TOTAL REDUCTIONS IN AMOUNT DUE TO SELLER:	342,657
600. CASH TO SELLER FROM SETTLEMENT:	
601. Gross amount due to seller *(from line 420)*	643,375
602. Less total reductions in amount due to seller *(from line 520)*	(342,657)
603. CASH TO SELLER FROM SETTLEMENT	300,718

HUD-1 (5-75)

protection legislation to shield homebuyers from unnecessarily high closing costs.

SUMMARY

Housing affordability is a function of ability to pay, whether from wealth or earning capacity. According to FHLMC guidelines, a borrower can afford to pay 25 percent of annual stabilized income for housing expenses, basically PITI, principal, interest, taxes, and insurance. Alternatively, a consumer should reasonably be able to devote 33 percent of income for housing expenses, utilities, and other installment debt.

Tax benefits of homeownership include deductibility of mortgage loan interest and property taxes. Also, value appreciation on a personal residence may be "rolled over" without payment of capital gains taxes if a replacement home is purchased for as much as or more than the sale price of the previous home, within 24 months of the sale.

As a rule, if the rental of a unit is less than its market value times the current mortgage loan interest rate, renting is less costly than is owning. If the rental is more than this amount, further analysis is warranted. Also, as a rule, renting is less costly than is owning if occupancy is to be less than 2 years. The main costs of owning are loan interest, maintenance, property taxes, and opportunity costs on any equity investment. The main costs of renting are the payments. A major benefit of owning is the chance for value appreciation.

QUESTIONS FOR REVIEW AND DISCUSSION

1. Explain briefly, in your own words, the relationship of annual stabilized income to the affordability of housing.
2. What is the 25 percent rule of the FHLMC? The 33 percent rule?
3. Identify and explain the tax benefits that an owner gets that a renter does not.
4. Are there any direct tax benefits that a tenant gets that an owner does not? Any indirect benefits?
5. Explain the "rollover" of a personal residence in some detail.
6. Does an owner realize any intangible benefits that a renter does not? If so, what are they?
7. What extra costs does an owner have that a tenant does not?
8. State your rights, as a buyer, under RESPA.
9. What does "home" mean? Does the wide use of "homeownership" mean that a "home" cannot be realized by one who rents a dwelling for personal use?

CASE PROBLEMS

1. Tim and Tina Turner have annual stabilized income of $50,000 and can only afford a 10 percent down payment to buy a house. Local lenders are making 90 percent loans at 12 percent, compounded monthly, with amortization over 25 years. Hazard insurance and property taxes in their community generally run about 2 percent of a house's market value. Using the FHLMC guideline, with no overage, how much housing can they reasonable afford? (About $93,500).
2. Assume that Tim and Tina have monthly installment payments of $300. Using the FHLMC 33 percent guideline, how much housing can they expect to command? (About $96,500).
3. Walter and Hazel Nutt ask you how much housing they can afford. After working with them for a while, you determine that they have an ASI of $36,000. You know that local lenders are making 90 percent, 30-year loans at 9 percent, compounded monthly. Also, property taxes and hazard insurance come to 2.4 percent per year in your experience. The Nutts tell you that they have long-term installment obligations of $240 per month.
   a. How much housing is affordable under the 25 percent rule?
   b. How much is affordable under the 33 percent rule?
   c. Check you answers by comparing the monthly payments on your answers in (a) and (b) with the amounts the Nutts can afford.
   d. How much down payment will be required of the Nutts?
4. Chech and Chung, both 55, sell their house, realizing a $75,000 long-term capital gain. They decide to take advantage of the $125,000 exemption allowed senior citizens and avoid taxes on the gain. They then buy a smaller house for $80,000, the value of which increases sharply. Six years later they sell the house for $125,000, net, after selling expenses. They take their situation to a CPA, asking that their $45,000 gain be offset by the $50,000 of the senior citizen exemption they did not use earlier. What result?
5. Local lenders are making loans at 9 percent, compounded monthly. Pritchard and Lily figure they can afford $700 per month for housing. They have located a condominium, valued at $75,000, which can be rented for $700. Based on rent capitalization, would you advise them to rent it or consider buying? What is the result if the market interest rate were 12 percent? 15 percent?
6. Rocky and Angel were recently transferred to Cambridge by Rocky's company. They expect to be here 2 years, based on previous experience. They have located a house they like and can buy for $100,000. They can rent a similar house for $1,000 per month, which is the amount they can afford for housing. Housing values in the community are expected to increase 11 percent per year for the next few years. All other information is the same as in the case problem given in the chapter. They ask you, as a housing consultant, whether they should buy or rent. Based on a 2-year net, after-tax, buy or rent comparison, what do you advise, economically speaking.
7. If John and Marcia were in the 40 percent (rather than 30 percent) tax bracket, and everything else from the problem illustrated in this chapter remained the same, would the rent or buy break-even time be shorter or longer? (*Hint*: Use calculations from the chapter, changing only those numbers affected by the different tax rate.)

CHAPTER TWENTY-SIX

REAL ESTATE TRENDS AND OUTLOOK

I never think of the future; it comes soon enough.
ALBERT EINSTEIN

Change is constant in real estate. As knowledge advances, as technology develops, and as our social and economic needs and priorities shift, the institution of real estate changes. That is, change results from these new inputs. As Emmanuel G. Mesthene, director of the Harvard Studies in Technology program, wrote, "New technology creates new opportunities for men and societies and it also generates new problems for them. It has positive and negative effects, and it usually has the two *at the same time and in virtue of each other.*"[1] Mesthene's statement certainly applies as change, from numerous sources, definitely affects how we use and value real estate.

Change means that there will be winners and losers. Winners adapt by learning the new theory, the new technology, and the new ways of making and implementing decisions. Losers will not or are not able to adapt, for whatever reasons. With a knowledge of trends and up-to-date information, one's chances of being a winner are greatly improved.

Thus, real estate decision makers and practitioners recognize their ever-greater need for information because theirs is increasingly an information-oriented business. The potential for change signaled to this chapter will, it is hoped, enable real estate analysts, decision makers, and others to be winners.

Previous chapters take up real estate as it is today. This chapter discusses bits and pieces of information that indicate what real estate will be tomorrow, as a result of changes likely to occur in the next 5 to 10

[1]Emmanuel G. Mesthene, *Technological Change: Its Impact on Man and Society* (Cambridge, Mass: Harvard University Press, 1970), p. 26.

years. New concepts and technology, and a faster pace of activity, cause a premium to be placed on having current information. This truth is becoming generally recognized. Of the ten new directions transforming our lives, noted by John Naisbett in *Megatrends,* six effectively turn on information. Naisbett's "number one" megatrend is a "megashift" from an industrial- to an information-based society.[2]

The trends identified here are based on insights and observations of the authors, both of whom have had a long association with real estate. The trends and outlook are discussed as they affect real estate as a (1) body of knowledge or field of study, (2) business activity or occupation, and (3) commodity or physical asset. The intent is to keep the discussion consistent with the three major definitions of real estate given in Chapter 1.

OUTLOOK FOR REAL ESTATE AS A FIELD OF STUDY

Several interrelated trends are having an increasingly significant impact on real estate as a field of study. Almost certainly the ever-widening use of calculators and computers in analysis for real estate decisions is the most important. Both computers and calculators make it possible to perform complex calculations quickly and accurately, and computers facilitate data storage, manipulation, and retrieval as well.[3] Computer applications in real estate are discussed at some length in the appendix to Chapter 1.

But computers are really only the vehicle that allows greater use of new theory and methodology. For example, the discounted cash flow model and statistical techniques to measure risk are now readily used today whereas they were not as of 5 years ago. In turn, it is much easier, today, to implement more sophisticated approaches to real estate such as value theory and financial management theory.

An important parallel trend is that legal concepts about real property are becoming more flexible and fluid. Syndications are increasingly converting real property into a commodity that may be bought and sold in small units. Land use controls, public and private, are causing property rights to be defined ever more precisely. And it is worth noting that decisions about real estate involve input by equity owners, lenders, tenants (users), governmental agencies, and neighbors. This trend undoubtedly reflects people's increasing awareness of the many interrelationships involved in the use of real estate.

Of course, with the availability of quick recall of data and rapid calculations, analysts and decision makers are able to take into account

---

[2]John Naisbett, *Megatrends* (New York: Warner Books, 1984), p. 1.

[3]See James Verner and Jerome Dasso, "Computer Applications in Real Estate Brokerage," *Real Estate Today,* May 1980, p. 2.

more information. But a consistent means of relating the information becomes necessary to make it meaningful. Hence, an integrated body of knowledge, largely developed around value theory becomes a logical next step. The organization and content of this book goes far toward providing an integrated framework for data collection, analysis, and decision making based on value in real estate. But much more needs to be done to develop a consistent and fully integrated theory of real estate.

If the theory and practice of real estate are brought much closer together, it is likely that the standards of performance, expected of real estate practitioners, are likely to be ever-more demanding, be the activity brokerage, property management, or investment analysis. Hence, the pressure for practitioners to update their professional knowledge and skills and to keep themselves fully informed will continue to increase.

A further indication of the importance of information is the increasing number of real estate education and research centers being established. Centers provide considerable economies to everyone as they collect, organize, and disseminate data and theory needed for improved decision analysis. They also usually provide extension courses and other services to assist practitioners and other decision makers in obtaining and understanding the information and theory as it relates to their individual needs. Centers associated with universities also project a professional image for the practitioners.[4] The number of centers is likely to continue to increase. Real estate centers are discussed at length in an article, "Research Centers: A Status Report" by Donald W. Bell and Larry E. Wofford.[5]

Outlook for Real Estate as a Business

The real estate business is moving to a new model in several ways, as a result of new technology, new theory, and new methods of organization. The change is what is known as a "paradigm shift," a concept emphasized by Thomas Kuhn in his landmark book, *The Structure of Scientific Revolutions.*[6] Kuhn argues that scientists in any field share a set of common beliefs about the state of their world, which is the dominant paradigm or model for that time. Experiments and communications are carried out under this dominant paradigm, and new knowledge is gained very slowly. A notorious example is the old belief that the world is flat and the center of the universe. The sun, stars, and moon were considered to be held in concentric circles about the earth. Copernicus and Kepler initiated a new theory—that the world is round and floats in space with other bodies—which we use today. Adoption or acceptance of the new theory constituted

---

[4]See Arthur Wright and Jerome Dasso, "Promoting Professionalism Through Real Estate Centers," *Real Estate Today*, November 1979, p. 3.

[5]Donald W. Bell and Larry E. Wofford, *Journal of Real Estate Education* (Summer 1983), p. 3.

[6]Thomas Kuhn, *The Structure of Scientific Revolutions*, 2nd ed. (Chicago: University of Chicago Press, 1970), p. 5.

a basic shift in beliefs and perceptions and a much more useful explanation of reality.

In a comparable manner, traditional beliefs and rules of thumb about real estate investing or brokerage are giving way to new concepts. Established ways of doing things—patterns—are gradually giving way to new, different, and more useful ones. In June 1984, a number of leading appraisers, users of value estimates, and academicians came together at a value colloquium in Boston to assess the implications and probable impact of this shift. The sponsoring organizations were the American Institute of Real Estate Appraisers, the Appraisal Institute of Canada, the Society of Real Estate Appraisers, and the Lincoln Institute of Land Policy. Let us look at how this shift is affecting the major areas of real estate.

Investment and Development

Old rules of thumb for valuing real estate investments are being replaced by new ones. The broker's rate of return (effectively payback period) is being replaced by after-tax, discounted cash flow analysis, with its variations of net present value or internal rate of return. An upcoming change is the incorporation of risk analysis into the model. These new concepts and techniques are increasingly being taught in colleges and universities and by professional organizations. Yet, less than a decade ago, nearly half of a number of insurance companies, real estate investment trusts, and corporations surveyed used no after-tax measures of investment desirability whatsoever.[7]

As a result of new ways of looking at legal ownership, lenders now commonly join equity investors "for a piece of the action." Likewise, real estate ownership is increasingly being syndicated, so that investors can buy and sell an interest in real property almost as easily as they can buy and sell corporate shares. At the same time, in capital markets, mortgage pools are being pioneered so that savers can invest in mortgages as easily as in bonds.

In real estate finance, RRMs and ARMs shift interest rate risk to borrowers; as of 1984, over one-half of all new real estate loans carried some means for adjusting the interest rate through time to changing market conditions. Also, interest rate hedging is becoming more widely accepted, so developers can "lock in" a feasible project that higher interest rates might suddenly convert into a "no go."

Brokerage Services

Two developments stand out as indicators of the future of brokerage operations. The first involves better selection of personnel. The second concerns the franchised brokerage.

---

[7]Robert J. Wiley, "Real Estate Investment Analysis: An Empirical Study," *The Appraisal Journal* (October 1976), pp. 5, 6.

Personnel selection. Real estate sales personnel have traditionally been hired on a random basis by brokers. Of course, some brokers were more selective and did a better job of hiring than did others. Professor B. E. Tsagris of California State University at Fullerton recently completed research concerning attributes possessed by successful sales personnel as rated by buyers.[8] Attributes that successful sale representatives invariably possess, according to the study, are professional attitude, knowledge of real estate, use of understandable terms, genuine desire to serve, willingness to keep trying, and selection of properly priced homes. According to the study, all sales representatives rate about evenly on manners, appearance, and property knowledge. And buyers apparently object strongly to excess aggressiveness in sales people.

Progressive brokers increasingly have prospective sales personnel examined by professional testing services before hiring them and putting them through a training program. The information provided by Professor Tsagris should greatly improve screening criteria for selecting people most likely to be successful in real estate sales work. The practice of test screening new personnel seems likely to continue and increase.

National brokerage services. Coldwell Banker, Century 21, Red Carpet, and similar national organizations are changing brokerage into a franchise or chain-type operation. Large brokerage organizations have the advantage of client referral from one community to another. The client benefits because of greater confidence and trust in the brokerage operation based on past experience. In the past, no easy referral system was available. These organizations have only about a 20 percent market share currently, but eventually they could dominate the market.

Independent contractor. An additional issue likely to be settled in the late 1980s is whether a salesperson is an independent contractor. Most brokerage people believe that a salesperson is an independent contractor; the IRS says not. The issue is: Are brokers responsible for withholding social security and income tax installments from commissions?

Specialized Services

Change in theory and technology is also filtering down to affect the nature of technical services rendered by real estate specialists. One likely result is that appraisers will be called on to estimate investment value, and to provide value counsel on a continuing basis, in addition to rendering estimates of market value. Effectively, the role of appraiser and counselor will be combined.

In a similar manner, property managers will be asked for information and analysis concerning the administration of real estate as a financial

---

[8]B. E. Tsagris, *The Public Image of a Real Estate Agent: An Expanded Update* (Fullerton: Real Estate Research Institute, California State University), p. 7.

asset rather than just as a business operation. They will be asked to counsel owners on when best to refinance, to remodel, and to dispose and reinvest.

And, in a third area, urban planners will be expected to take values of private owners more into account. This will represent a shift from a physical design emphasis to a value emphasis, based on social and economic considerations.

OUTLOOK FOR REAL ESTATE AS A COMMODITY

The amount of land in the United States and the world is fixed, for all practical purposes. The population of the United States is expected to climb to nearly 280 million people over the next 50 years in spite of a zero-population-growth birth rate. This means that the density of population in the 48 contiguous states will be about 90 people per square mile, compared with 60.1 in 1960 and 25.6 in 1900. In addition, the United States has changed from having a population with strong rural orientation to having a population that is nearly 75 percent urban and obviously concerned with urban problems. All this means that more and more people are crowding into a very small portion (about 3 percent) of our land area.

The crowding is reflected in the types of dwelling units occupied and the forms of ownership of dwelling units. The crowding is also reflected in an increasing concern with maintaining the quality of life and improving resource usage, both in the United States and throughout the world.

Shift in Housing Mix and Ownership

Zero population growth means smaller-sized family units. The strong movement of millions of people to the cities means a much higher density of population in urban centers. The higher density takes the form of more multifamily housing, whether apartments, cooperatives, or condominiums. A comparison of 1970 and 1977 data from the annual housing survey conducted by the Department of Housing and Urban Development and the Bureau of the Census points up the trend. (See Figure 26–1.) The trend is away from one-family and small multifamily structures. Mobile homes and larger multifamily buildings are picking up the slack. However, a large portion of the population is entering the homebuying age (30 to 44), and one-family housing construction again is increasing as a percentage of the total.

Maintaining the Quality of Life

Population growth is causing even greater pressure for ways in which to preserve and enhance the quality of life in the United States. Methods used to maintain quality of life include growth policies, legislation for

FIGURE 26–1
Types of housing units occupied year-round in the United States (percent), 1960,1970,1980

YEAR	ONE-FAMILY HOMES	MOBILE HOMES	MULTIFAMILY UNITS		TOTAL
			2–4	5 PLUS	
1960	75.0	1.3	13.0	10.7	100.0
1970	69.1	3.1	13.3	14.5	100.0
1980	67.5	4.3	12.3	15.9	100.0

SOURCE: Table 1339, page 748, *1984 Statistical Abstract of the United States.*

land use planning and environmental controls, and urban renewal programs.

Growth policies. Movement of people from one state or community to another sometimes causes severe growth problems for the receiving community or state. California and Florida were two outstanding examples of rapid-growth states in the 1950s and 1960s. Mass regional migration (from state to state) has slowed since 1970. But within states, population shifts are still occurring. For example, in 1975, the Census figures showed that populations of 37 of the nation's 58 largest cities had fallen since 1970. Heavy losers were Minneapolis, off 12.0 percent; St. Louis, off 10.3 percent; and Cleveland, off 9.6 percent.

The movement is to the suburbs for relief from crime, poor services, and high taxes. The movement to small cities in the suburbs causes traffic congestion, need for new schools and sanitation facilities, and a general lowering of quality of life for residents of the suburbs.

Petaluma, California, a suburb of San Francisco with a 1971 population of 30,500, was one city threatened with population overflow. Petaluma enacted a 5-year plan to permit no more than 500 new dwelling units per year, or to limit growth to about 2,000 new residents per year. Builders sued the city for violation of people's constitutional "right to travel" and won in district court. The case attracted national attention. A court of appeals reversed the ruling, holding that Petaluma has a right to preserve its small-town character, its open spaces, and its low density of population and to grow at an orderly and deliberate pace. The Petaluma plan serves as an indication of the strong desire of people to maintain a desired quality of life. As long as the Petaluma plan is upheld in the courts, other suburban communities are almost certain to emulate it.

Environmental quality. The desire to maintain quality of life is also evidenced in the considerable legislation introduced at the federal level to deal with land use planning, clean air and water, and energy conservation in recent years. The National Environmental Policy Act requires environmental impact statements for all major development projects. If the impact will be too detrimental to the environment, a project may be turned down.

Additional legislation proposed includes a National Land Use Planning and Resource Conservation Bill to provide financial and technical assistance to states and localities to establish standard land use planning procedures.

Also, Congress recently passed two amendments to strengthen the Clean Air Act and a separate bill to control indirect sources of air pollution by requiring preconstruction reviews of proposed facilities that attract automobiles (large multifamily projects, shopping centers, airports, and highways). Three federal programs involving pure water and waste disposal are (1) Water Quality Management Basin Plans, (2) Area Waste Treatment Management Planning, and (3) the National Pollutant Discharge Elimination System. The first is concerned with maintaining pure water, the second involves treatment of waste according to the Water Pollution Control Act Amendment, and the third is concerned with the discharge of liquid wastes into navigable waters. These three programs are likely to be expanded and coordinated in the next few years. Almost certainly, air, water, and land use controls are going to get more stringent as our population mounts and presses more strongly on our environment.

Energy conservation. Bills are introduced into every session of Congress ncerning both energy disclosure and energy conservation. An energy disclosure law would require informing prospective renters and buyers of the annual operating costs of energy systems in housing. One of the provisions of a recently passed energy conservation law is a subsidy for installation of insulation and weather stripping in housing. This type of legislation appears to be only in its beginning stages. Tax incentives seem likely to be enacted on a general basis to encourage greater use of insulation and better building design to conserve energy.

Urban renewal. The Housing and Community Development Act of 1974 provided for phasing out the federal urban renewal program. The program was initiated in 1949 to clear slums, to remove blight, and to improve the quality of the urban environment generally. According to a recent HUD study, the urban renewal program was not too successful. The program did help communities to strengthen their economies, improve their competitive positions, and expand their tax bases. Some physical blight was removed from urban areas, and a favorable climate for public and private investment was created. However, major social problems and a slow turnover of renewal lands stamped the program as generally not successful. Only projects in or near central business districts seem likely to have success in the future, according to the study.

The need for urban renewal is still with us. The means of accomplishing renewal is being shifted from direct governmental programs to governmentally assisted housing. With government assistance, all citizens should be able to afford housing of a certain minimum standard or quality. Housing codes can also be strictly enforced when governmental housing assistance is provided. The expected net result is improvement of substandard units to standard or removal of the substandard units from the housing supply. Presumably, urban renewal will, therefore, be accomplished by market forces and strict code enforcement.

Metric Conversion

The United States appears to be firmly established on a course to metric conversion. The country is out of step with the rest of the world in its system of weights and measures and needs to convert to continue to participate in world markets. Conversion will probably take at least a decade. In 1976, wines and liquors were converted to metric measure. Many machine parts for export are already designed according to metric measures. Gasoline and other domestic products seem sure to follow. And somewhere down the line, land measurements and building blueprints will be in the metric system. Tables for conversion to and from the metric systems are included in Appendix B of this book.

Time-Share Ownership of Condominiums

Recreational condominiums are generally expensive to purchase and maintain. Some developers provided management services to owners to rent the units out when they are not in use. This device was intended to generate income for the owners to cover carrying expenses as well as to give them some tax depreciation of such a unit in that it was being operated as an income property. But lack of demand for recreational units during recessions caused many owners severe cash flow problems. Some owners lost their equity in their units because of inability to meet debt-service and maintenance costs.

Developers in Hawaii and the Carolinas use a technique that gets around these problems. They sell the same condominium unit to many different owners on a time-sharing basis. For example, they build a very attractive unit for $100,000 and sell it to 24 different owners for $5,000 each or a total of $120,000. Each owner gets an exclusive right of use of the condominium for 15 days each year. That is, one owner might buy the right of use from June 16 to June 30. Under this arrangement, little financing is necessary because the people buying the units pay cash from savings or personal borrowing. Time owners must pay maintenance costs for their 15-day period only. Decorating and remodeling is done when an owner fails to use the unit during his or her time for some reason.

APPENDIX A
GENERAL REAL ESTATE INFORMATION

A-1
REAL ESTATE SALES TRANSACTION CHECKLIST

Facts to Ascertain Before Drawing a Contract of Sale

1. Date of contract.
2. Name and address of seller.
3. Is seller a citizen, of full age, and competent?
4. Name of seller's spouse and whether that person is of full age.
5. Name and residence of purchaser.
6. Description of the property.
7. The purchase price.
   a. Amount to be paid on signing contract.
   b. Amount to be paid on delivery of deed.
   c. Existing mortgage or mortgages and details thereof.
   d. Purchase money mortgage, if any, and details thereof.
8. What kind of deed is to be delivered: full convenant, quitclaim, or bargain and sale?
9. What agreement has been made with reference to any specific personal property (i.e., gas ranges, heaters, machinery, partitions, fixtures, coal, wood, window shades, screens, carpets, rugs, and hangings)?
10. Is purchaser to assume the mortgage or take the property subject to it?
11. Are any exceptions or reservations to be inserted?
12. Are any special clauses to be inserted?
13. Stipulations and agreements with reference to tenancies and rights of persons in possession, including compliance with any governmental regulatios in force.
14. Stipulations and agreements, if any, to be inserted with reference to the state of facts a survey would show (i.e., party walls, encroachments, easements, and so forth).

15. What items are to be adjusted on the closing of title?
16. Name of the broker who brought about the sale, his or her address, the amount of commission and who is to pay it, and whether or not a clause covering the foregoing facts is to be inserted in the contract.
17. Are any alterations or changes being made, or have they been made, in street lines, name, or grade?
18. Are condemnations or assessment proceedings contemplated or pending, or has an award been made?
19. Who is to draw the purchase money mortgage and who is to pay the expense thereof?
20. Are there any convenants, restrictions, and consents affecting the title?
21. What stipulation or agreement is to be made with reference to violations of sanitation laws, building code, or the like?
22. The place and date on which the title is to be closed.
23. Is time to be of the essence in the contract?
24. Are any alterations to be made in the premises between the date of the contract and the date of closing?
25. Amount of fire and hazard insurance, payment of premium, and rights and obligations of parties in case of fire or damage to premises from other causes during the contract period.

Upon the Closing of Title, the Seller Should Be Prepared with the Following

1. Seller's copy of the contract.
2. The latest receipted bills for taxes, water, and assessments.
3. Latest possible meter readings of water, gas, and electric utilities.
4. Receipts for last payment of interest on mortgages.
5. Originals and certificates of all fire, liability, and other insurance policies.
6. Estoppel certificates from the holder of any mortgage that has been reduced, showing the amount due and the date to which interest is paid.
7. Any subordination agreements that may be called for in the contract.
8. Satisfaction pieces of mechanic's liens, chattel mortgages, judgments, or mortgages that are to be paid at or before the closing.

9. List of names of tenants, amounts of rents paid and unpaid, dates when rents are due, and assignment of unpaid rents.
10. Assignment of leases.
11. Letters to tenants to pay all subsequent rent to the purchaser.
12. Affidavit of title.
13. Authority to execute deed if the seller is acting through an agent.
14. Bill of sale of personal property covered by the contract.
15. Seller's last deed.
16. Any unrecorded instruments that affect the title, including extension agreements.
17. Deed and other instruments that the seller is to deliver or prepare.

Upon the Closing of Title, the Purchaser Should Do the Following

1. Have purchaser's copy of contract.
2. Obtain abstract of title.
3. Obtain report of title.
4. Examine deed to see if it conforms to the contract.
5. Compare description.
6. See that deed is properly executed.
7. Have sufficient cash or certified checks to make payments required by contract.
8. See that all liens that must be removed are properly disposed of.
9. Obtain names and details with reference to tenants and rents.
10. Obtain assignment of unpaid rents and assignment of leases.
11. Obtain and examine estoppel certificates with reference to mortgages that have been reduced.
12. Obtain letter to tenants.
13. Obtain affidavit of title.
14. Obtain and examine authority if the seller acts through an agent.
15. Obtain bill of sale of personal property covered by the contract.
16. Examine survey.
17. See if report of title shows any convenants, restrictions, or consents affecting the title or use of the property.
18. Have bills for any unpaid tax, utilites, or assessments and have interest computed up to the date of closing.
19. Make adjustments as called for in the contract.
20. Examine purchase money mortgage and duly execute same.
21. Have damage award, if any, for public improvements assigned to the purchaser.
22. Obtain any unrecorded instruments affecting the title including extension agreements.

A-2 CODE OF ETHICS NATIONAL ASSOCIATION OF REALTORS®*

Revised and approved by the delegate body of the Association at its 67th annual convention, November 14, 1974.

PREAMBLE . . . Under all is the land. Upon its wise utilization and widely allocated ownership depend the survival and growth of free institutions and of our civilization. The REALTOR® should recognize that the interests

*Published with the consent of the National Association of REALTORS®, author and owner of all rights in the Code of Ethics of the National Association of REALTORS®, © National Association of REALTORS® 1974. All rights reserved.

of the nation and its citizens require the highest and best use of the land and the widest distribution of land ownership. They require the creation of adequate housing, the building of functioning cities, the development of productive industries and farms, and the preservation of a healthful environment.

Such interests impose obligations beyond those of ordinary commerce. They impose grave social responsibility and a patriotic duty to which the REALTOR® should dedicate himself, and for which he should be diligent in preparing himself. The REALTOR®, therefore, is zealous to maintain and improve the standards of his calling and shares with his fellow-REALTORS® a common responsibility for its integrity and honor. The term REALTOR® has come to connote competency, fairness, and high integrity resulting from adherence to a lofty ideal of moral conduct in business relations. No inducement of profit and no instruction from clients ever can justify departure from this ideal.

In the interpretation of his obligation, a REALTOR® can take no safer guide than that which has been handed down through the centuries, embodied in the Golden Rule, "Whatsoever ye would that men should do to you, do ye even so to them."

Accepting this standard as his own, every REALTOR® pledges himself to observe its spirit in all of his activities and to conduct his business in accordance with the tenets set forth below.

ARTICLE 1. The REALTOR® should keep himself informed on matters affecting real estate in his community, the state, and nation so that he may be able to contribute responsibly to public thinking on such matters.

ARTICLE 2. In justice to those who place their interests in his care, the REALTOR® should endeavor always to be informed regarding laws, proposed legislation, governmental regulations, public policies, and current market conditions in order to be in a position to advise his clients properly.

ARTICLE 3. It is the duty of the REALTOR® to protect the public against fraud, misrepresentation, and unethical practices in real estate transactions. He should endeavor to eliminate in his community any practices which could be damaging to the public or bring discredit to the real estate profession. The REALTOR® should assist the governmental agency charged with regulating the practices of brokers and salesmen in his state.

ARTICLE 4. The REALTOR® should seek no unfair advantage over other REALTORS® should and should conduct his business so as to avoid controversies with other REALTORS®.

ARTICLE 5. In the best interests of society, of his associates, and his own business, the REALTOR® should willingly share with other REALTORS® the lessons of his experience and study for the benefit of the public, and should be loyal to the Board of REALTORS® of his community and active in its work.

ARTICLE 6. To prevent dissension and misunderstanding and to assure better service to the owner, the REALTOR® should urge the exclusive listing of property unless contrary to the best interest of the owner.

ARTICLE 7. In accepting employment as an agent, the REALTOR® pledges himself to protect the interests of the client. This obligation of absolute fidelity to the client's interests is primary, but it does not relieve the REALTOR® of the obligation to treat fairly all parties to the transaction.

ARTICLE 8. The REALTOR® shall not accept compensation from more than one party, even if permitted by law, without the full knowledge of all parties to the transaction.

ARTICLE 9. The REALTOR® shall avoid exaggeration, misrepresentation, or concealment of pertinent facts. He has an affirmative obligation to discover adverse factors that a reasonably competent and diligent investigation would disclose.

ARTICLE 10. The REALTOR® shall not deny equal services to any person for reasons of race, creed, sex, or country of national origin. The REALTOR® shall not be a party to any plan or agreement to discriminate against a person or persons on the basis of race, creed, sex, or country of national origin.

ARTICLE 11. A REALTOR® is expected to provide a level of competent service in keeping with the Standards of Practice in those fields in which the REALTOR® customarily engages.

The REALTOR® shall not undertake to provide specialized professional services concerning a type of property or service that is outside his field of competence unless he engages the assistance of one who is competent on such types of property or service, or unless the facts are fully disclosed to the client. Any person engaged to provide such assistance shall be so identified to the client and his contribution to the assignment should be set forth.

The REALTOR® shall refer to the Standards of Practice of the National Association as to the degree of competence that a client has a right to expect the REALTOR® to possess, taking into consideration the complexity of the problem, the availability of expert assistance, and the opportunities for experience available to the REALTOR®.

ARTICLE 12. The REALTOR® shall not undertake to provide professional services concerning a property or its value where he has a present or contemplated interest unless such interest is specifically disclosed to all affected parties.

ARTICLE 13. The REALTOR® shall not acquire an interest in or buy for himself, any member of his family, his firm or any member thereof, or any entity in which he has a substantial ownership interest, property listed with him, without making the true position known to the listing owner.

In selling property owned by himself, or in which he has any interest, the REALTOR® shall reveal the facts of his ownership or interest to the purchaser.

ARTICLE 14. In the event of a controversy between REALTORS® associated with different firms, arising out of their relationship as REALTORS®, the REALTORS® shall submit the dispute to arbitration in accordance with the regulations of their board or boards rather than litigate the matter.

ARTICLE 15. If a REALTOR® is charged with unethical practice or is asked to present evidence in any disciplinary proceeding or investigation, he shall place all pertinent facts before the proper tribunal of the member board or affiliated institute, society, or council or which he is a member.

ARTICLE 16. When acting as agent, the REALTOR® shall not accept any commission, rebate, or profit on expenditures made for his principal-owner, without the principal's knowledge and consent.

ARTICLE 17. The REALTOR® shall not engage in activities that constitute the unauthorized practice of law and shall recommend that legal counsel be obtained when the interest of any party to the transaction requires it.

ARTICLE 18. The REALTOR® shall keep in a special account in an appropriate financial institution, separated from his own funds, monies coming into his possession in trust for other persons, such as escrows, trust funds, clients' monies, and other like items.

ARTICLE 19. The REALTOR® shall be careful at all times to present a true picture in his advertising and representations to the public. He shall neither advertise without disclosing his name nor permit any person associated with him to use individual names or telephone numbers, unless such person's connection with the REALTOR® is obvious in the advertisement.

ARTICLE 20. The REALTOR®, for the protection of all parties, shall see that financial obligations and commitments regarding real estate transactions are in writing, expressing the exact agreement of the parties. A copy of each agreement shall be furnished to each party upon his signing such agreement.

ARTICLE 21. The REALTOR® shall not engage in any practice or take any action inconsistent with the agency of another REALTOR®.

ARTICLE 22. In the sale of property which is exclusively listed with a REALTOR®, the REALTOR® shall utilize the services of other brokers upon mutually agreed upon terms when it is in the best interests of the client.

Negotiations concerning property which is listed exclusively shall be carried on with the listing broker, not with the owner, except with the consent of the listing broker.

ARTICLE 23. The REALTOR® shall not publicly disparage the business practice of a competitor nor volunteer an opinion of a competitor's transaction. If his opinion is sought and if the REALTOR® deems it appropriate to respond, such opinion shall be rendered with strict professional integrity and courtesy.

ARTICLE 24. The REALTOR® shall not directly solicit the services or affiliation of an employee or independent contractor in the organization of another REALTOR® without prior notice to said REALTOR®.

Where the word REALTOR® is used in this Code and Preamble, it shall be deemed to include REALTOR®-ASSOCIATE. Pronouns shall be considered to include REALTORS® and REALTOR®-ASSOCIATES of both genders.

The Code of Ethics was adopted in 1913. Amended at the Annual Convention in 1924, 1928, 1950, 1951, 1952, 1955, 1956, 1961, 1962, and 1974.

A-3 LAND MEASURES AND CONVERSION TABLES

Rules for Measuring Land

The following rules will be found of service in many cases that may arise in land parceling, particularly in the computation of areas:

To find the area of a four-sided tract, whose sides are perpendicular to each other (called a rectangle), multiply the length by the width. The product will be the area.

To find the area of a four-sided tract, whose opposite sides are parallel, but whose angles are not necessarily right angles (called a parallelogram), multiply the base by the perpendicular height. The product will be the area.

To find the area of a three-sided tract (called a triangle), multiply the base by half the perpendicular height. The product will be the area.

To find the area of a four-sided tract, having two of its sides parallel (called a trapezoid), multiply half the sum of the two parallel sides by the perpendicular distance between these sides. The product will be the area.

To ascertain the contents of a tract bounded by four straight lines, and in which no two lines are parallel to each other, the length of each line is known, and the two opposite angles are supplements of each other (called a trapezium), add all the four sides together and halve their sum; subtract separately each side from that sum; multiply the four remainders thus obtained continually together;

and extract the square root of the last product. The result will be the contents or area of the tract. Or divide the tract by lines into triangles and trapezoids, and ascertain and add together their several areas, the sum of which will be the area of the tract proposed.

Land bounded by an irregular line, such as a stream of water or a winding road, is measured as follows. Draw a base line as near as practicable to the actual line of the road or stream; at different places in the base line, equidistant from each other, take the distance to the line of the stream or road. Add the sum of all the intermediate lines (or breadths) to half the sum of the first breadth and the last breadth, and multiply the sum thus obtained by the common distance between the breadths. The result will be the area of the land in question.

Should the breadths be measured at unequal distances on the base line, add all the breadths together, divide their amount by the number of breadths for the mean breadth, and multiply the quotient so obtained by the length of the base line.

Measurement Tables

Table of Linear Measure

12 inches (in.)	= 1 foot	ft
3 feet	= 1 yard	yd
5½ yards or 16½ feet	= 1 rod	rd
40 rods	= 1 furlong	fur
8 furlongs, 320 rods, or 5,280 feet	= 1 statute mile	mi

Table of Area Measure

144 square inches (sq. in.)	= 1 square foot	sq ft
9 square feet	= 1 square yard	sq yd
30¼ square yards	= 1 square rod	sq rd
40 square rods	= 1 rood	R
4 rods or 43,560 square feet	= 1 acre	A
640 acres	= 1 square mile	sq mi

Table of Surveyor's Linear Measure

7.92 inches (in.)	= 1 link	l
25 links	= 1 rod	rd
4 rods or 66 feet	= 1 chain	ch
80 chains	= 1 mile	mi

Table of Surveyor's Area Measures

625 square links (sq. l.)	= 1 pole	P
16 poles	= 1 square chain	sq ch
10 square chains	= 1 acre	A
640 acres	= 1 square mile	sq mi
36 square miles (6 mi. square)	= 1 township	Tp

Note: 1 acre in square form equals 208.71 feet on each side.

Conversion to Metric Measures

U.S. UNIT	SYMBOL	MULTIPLY BY	SYMBOL	METRIC UNIT
LENGTH				
inch	in.	2.540	cm	centimeter
feet	ft	0.3048	m	meter
yard	yd	0.9144	m	meter
rod	rd	5.0292	m	meter
mile	mi	1.609	km	kilometer
AREA				
square inch	$in.^2$	6.5416	cm^2	square centimeter
square foot	ft^2	0.0929	m^2	square meter
square yard	yd^2	0.836	m^2	square meter
acre	A	0.4047	ha	hectares (10,000 m^2)
square mile	mi^2	2.590	km^2	square kilometer
VOLUME				
cubic inch	$in.^3$	16.387	cm^3	cubic centimeters
cubic foot	ft^3	0.028	m^3	cubic meters
cubic yard	yd^3	0.765	m^3	cubic meters
WEIGHT				
ounce	oz	28.350	g	gram
pound	lb	0.4536	kg	kilogram
ton, short (2,000 lb)	ton	0.9072	t	tonnes (1,000 kg)

Conversion from Metric Measures

METRIC UNIT	SYMBOL	MULTIPLY BY	SYMBOL	U.S. UNIT
LENGTH				
millimeter	mm	0.0394	in.	inch
centimeter	cm	0.3937	in.	inch
meter	m	3.2808	ft	foot
meter	m	1.0936	yd	yard
kilometer	km	0.6213	mi	mile
AREA				
square centimeter	cm^2	0.155	$in.^2$	square inch
square meter	m^2	1.196	yd^2	square yard
hectares (10,000 m^2)	ha	2.471	A	acre
square kilometer	km^2	0.386	mi^2	square mile
VOLUME				
cubic centimeters	cm^3	0.061	$in.^3$	cubic inch
cubic meters	m^3	35.714	ft^3	cubic foot
cubic meters	m^3	1.307	yd^3	cubic yard
WEIGHT				
gram	g	0.035	oz	ounce
kilogram	kg	2.2046	lb	pound
tonnes (1,000 kg)	t	1.1023	ton	short ton

A-4
FIRST AND LAST MONTHS, MORTGAGE LOAN AMORTIZATION SCHEDULE

TERM		INTEREST RATE		MONTHLY PAYMENT	INITIAL PRINCIPAL
IN YEARS	IN MONTHS	NOMINAL	MONTHLY		
25	300	12.00%	1.00%	$1.053.22	$100,000

PAYMENT NUMBER	BALANCE BEGINNING OF MONTH	LEVEL MONTHLY PAYMENT TOTAL AMOUNT	PORTION TO PRINCIPAL	PORTION TO INTEREST	BALANCE END OF MONTH
1	$100,000.00	$1,053.22	$53.22	$1,000.00	$99,946.78
2	99,946.78	1,053.22	53.76	999.47	99,893.02
3	99,893.02	1,053.22	54.29	998.93	99,838.73
4	99,838.73	1,053.22	54.84	998.39	99,783.89
5	99.783.89	1,053.22	55.39	997.84	99,728.50
6	99,728.50	1,053.22	55.94	997.29	99,672.56
7	99,672.56	1.053.22	56.50	996.73	99,616.07
8	99,616.07	1.053.22	57.06	996.16	99,559.00
9	99,559,00	1,053.22	57.63	995.59	99,501.37
10	99,501.37	1,053.22	58.21	995.01	99,443.16
11	99,443.16	1,053.22	58.79	994.43	99,384.37
12	99,384.37	1,053.22	59.38	993.84	99,324.98
13	99,324.98	1,053.22	59.97	993.25	99,265.01
296	5,111.75	1,053.22	1,002.11	51.12	4,109.64
297	4,109.64	1,053.22	1,012.13	41.10	3,097.52
298	3,097.52	1,053.22	1,022.25	30.98	2,075.27
299	2,075.27	1,053.22	1,032.47	20.75	1,042.80
300	1.042.80	1.053.22	1.042.80	10.43	(.00)

A-5
FORMS AND DOCUMENTS

These forms are typical of those used in real estate transactions. In most cases, blanks have been completed to give a clearer idea of the use of the forms. However, the completed forms are intended only as examples and not as having applicability in any particular state. We extend particular appreciation to the Stevens-Ness Law Publishing Company for their permission to use many of the forms reproduced below as well as several used in the text.

The following forms are included in this appendix:

1. Contract between real estate broker and Salesperson
2. Option to purchase
3. Binder
4. Contract for deed (land contract)
5. Acknowledgment of act or deed
6. Affidavit or voluntary written declaration sworn to before a notary public.
7. Assignment of a contract by direct endorsement on the contract
8. Satisfaction of mortgage

FIGURE A-1
Contract between Real Estate Broker and Salesperson

FORM No. 850—CONTRACT BETWEEN REAL ESTATE BROKER AND SALESMAN. STEVENS-NESS LAW PUBLISHING CO., PORTLAND, OR. 97204

TS

THIS AGREEMENT, Made and entered into this 10th day of October, 19 78, between Ivan Everready, Realtor, doing business as Everready Realty Company, hereinafter called the "broker," and Harvey Hustle, hereinafter called the "salesman";

WITNESSETH:

The broker is duly registered, licensed and actively engaged in business as a real estate broker under the laws of the state of Anystate with his principal office in said state at No. 41 East Third, City of Urbandale; said office is equipped with telephone, furnishings and facilities suitable for the said business.

The salesman is a duly registered real estate salesperson (State whether real estate salesman, associate broker, holder of a temporary permit or other appropriate description.) under the laws of said state and is duly authorized to deal with the public as a real estate salesman.

NOW, THEREFORE, in view of the premises and in consideration of the mutual promises of the parties hereinafter set forth, the parties hereto agree:

1. From the date hereof and until the termination of this agreement, the parties hereto hereby do associate themselves as broker and salesman. With respect to the clients and customers of the broker and all other persons, the salesman shall be a sub-agent only with powers limited by this agreement. It is expressly understood and agreed that the salesman is and shall be an independent contractor and not an employee, partner or joint adventurer with the broker.

2. The broker agrees to make all his listings, both current and future, available to the salesman, except those which the broker temporarily in his sole discretion may wish some other salesman to handle, and agrees to cooperate with the salesman and to assist him in his work by advice and instruction. The broker further agrees that the salesman may share with other salesmen and employees the facilities of the broker's office.

3. The salesman agrees to work diligently and use his best efforts in the name of the broker to sell, exchange, lease and rent listed properties, to purchase and take options on real estate for the broker's clients, to serve the real estate needs of the broker's clients and customers, to obtain additional listings and customers for the broker and

otherwise to promote the broker's business to the end that each of the parties hereto may derive the greatest profit possible from their association. The salesman agrees to conduct his business and regulate his habits so as to maintain his own reputation in the community and to increase the good will and reputation of the broker.

4. Both parties hereto agree to conform to and abide by all laws, rules, regulations and codes of ethics that are binding upon or applicable to real estate brokers and salesmen in their dealings with each other and with the public and other brokers and salesmen.

5. The commissions to be charged for services performed shall be at the rates generally prevalent in the community, except in those cases where in particular transactions the broker may enter into special contracts relative to items which he undertakes to handle. It is expressly understood that the broker in his discretion may arrange with other brokers to share commissions on the sale of specific properties. The parties hereto recognize that some transactions may present peculiar difficulties which require the services of surveyors, experts, specialists, accountants, attorneys, the use of the long distance telephone and telegraphic service or other expense, for the cost of which the broker is not reimbursed by the client or customer; such expenses on any transaction in which a commission is earned shall be deemed a part of the cost of that transaction and paid out of the commission thereon before any division thereof. In each transaction where services rendered by the salesman shall result in the earning by the broker of a commission, or part thereof, there shall first be deducted from the commission collected by the broker on that particular transaction the listing fee, if any is due, mentioned in the 6th paragraph of this agreement, as well as the unreimbursed expenses of that transaction hereinabove described, and the following percentage of the balance of the commission collected by the broker shall be paid to the salesman:

Except as provided in the 8th paragraph hereof, the expense of surveyors, experts, specialists, accountants, attorneys, telegrams and telephone tolls on transactions in which a commission is *not* earned shall be paid by the broker. The expense of attorney's fees and costs which are incurred in the collection of or attempts to collect a commission in which the salesman is entitled to a share shall be paid by the parties hereto in the same proportion as above provided for the division of commissions on that particular transaction. Where two or more salesmen participate in any trans-

FIGURE A-1 (cont.)

action in which a commission is earned, or claim to have done so, the salesman's said percentage or share of the commission shall accrue to the participating salesman and be divided according to agreement between them; if there is no such agreement, the share of each participating salesman shall be determined by arbitration as hereinafter provided. In those cases where the property of the broker is sold through the efforts of the salesman, the compensation of the salesman shall be agreed upon by the broker and the salesman. In those cases where property of the salesman is sold through the broker's organization, the salesman shall pay to the broker a sum equal to one-half of the regular commission on the selling price of the property so sold. In no case shall the broker be liable to the salesman for any commission, or part thereof (except in those transactions involving the broker's own property), unless the same shall have been collected by the broker. Settlements between the broker and salesman as to commissions earned and collected shall be made at the close of each transaction except as to deferred commissions or collections, on which a written accounting shall be rendered and settlement made on or before the 10th day of each month for all receipts of the previous month.

6. Where the salesman takes additional listings and if the property so listed is sold (by whomsoever sold) while this contract is in force and effect and the commission is collected by the broker, the salesman shall be entitled to a listing fee equal to the following percentages of the commission so collected:

intra office - 33-1/3%

inter office - 25%

the salesman recognizes that other salesmen in the broker's organization may become entitled to a listing fee on the sale of properties listed by them.

7. The parties further agree that on any deal when the seller or client is unable to pay the commission, or any part thereof, in cash, the broker in his sole discretion may accept notes, mortgages or securities in lieu of cash; in any such event the broker shall not be liable to the salesman for that part of the commission represented by such notes, mortgages or securities unless and until the broker shall have realized cash thereon. Upon any such collection being made, the broker's actual out-of-pocket expense in effecting such collection shall first be deducted and retained by the broker and the salesman shall be paid his said percentage of the balance of the sums (principal and interest) collected.

8. The salesman shall have no authority to bind the broker by any promise or representation, unless specifically authorized in a particular transaction. The salesman shall have no authority to hire surveyors, experts, specialists, accountants or attorneys in any transaction or to incur the expense of telegrams or long distance telephone tolls at any time without the broker's prior written approval; such expenses incurred by the salesman without such approval shall be paid by the salesman. Except as herein provided, the salesman shall not be liable to the broker for any part of the office expense or for signs, advertising, telephones or utilities and the broker shall not be liable to the salesman for any expense incurred by the salesman.

9. All advertising shall be under the direct supervision and in the name of the broker. The salesman shall not publish any advertising under his own name in any manner, either directly or indirectly. All offers to purchase, exchange, option, rent, lease or forfeit obtained by the salesman shall be submitted immediately to the broker. Closing of all transactions shall be handled by or under the direct supervision of the broker. No option shall be taken except in the name of the broker or his nominee. Suits for commissions shall be maintained only in the name of the broker. Without the broker's written consent, the salesman shall not buy for himself, either directly or indirectly, or take options to purchase any property listed with the broker or any person associated with the broker.

FIGURE A-1
(cont.)

10. The salesman shall have no power to forfeit or declare forfeited earnest money deposited by any purchaser, that power being expressly reserved to the broker. Should the broker declare any such deposit forfeited and if the salesman ultimately may be entitled to a share of the commission on the transaction, then in the absence of a settlement with and release from the depositor, the broker shall deposit the moneys so forfeited in his Clients Trust Account (if he has not already done so) and shall not be obligated to pay any share of the commission on that transaction to the salesman unless and until he has secured a written release from the depositor or has received assurances and security satisfactory to the broker that the salesman will return the salesman's share of the commission in the event it should ultimately be determined that the broker was not entitled to declare such forfeiture.

11. The broker shall have the right in his sole discretion at any time to cancel any deal signed up by the salesman, to release the parties thereto, to return deposits of earnest money and documents and generally to settle, adjust and compromise suits, actions, disputes and controversies in which the salesman is interested or to which he is a party, without the consent of the salesman and the salesman shall have no claim against the broker by reason of any such settlement, adjustment or compromise. In the event charges are made or a lawsuit is filed against the broker growing out of the conduct of the salesman in any transaction, the salesman agrees to pay the expense of defending against any such claims or law suits, to pay any judgments entered in such law suits and generally to save the broker harmless therefrom.

12. The salesman agrees to furnish his own transportation in his performance of this agreement; also, that at all times while this contract is in force and effect he will carry, maintain and keep in effect, at his own expense, public liability insurance insuring both the salesman and the broker against all liability for damage to person or property in connection with the use and operation of the salesman's car or cars in said business; the amount of said liability insurance shall be not less than $ 250,000 for injury to one person, $ 500,000 for injuries arising out of any one accident and $ 200,000 for property damage; satisfactory evidence that said insurance is in effect shall be furnished to the broker.

13. In case of a controversy between the salesman herein and another salesman in the broker's organization, which the parties to said controversy are unable to settle between themselves, the matters in dispute shall be submitted to arbitration in which the broker shall be the sole arbitrator; the decision of the broker in any such arbitration shall be final, binding and conclusive upon the salesmen involved in said controversy; the broker shall serve as arbitrator without compensation. In case a controversy should arise between the parties hereto relative to any matter arising out of this contract, which they are unable to settle between themselves, the matters in dispute shall be submitted to arbitration before a board of three arbitrators; each of the parties hereto shall select one arbitrator and the two thus chosen shall select the third arbitrator; the decision of the majority of said board of arbitration shall be final, binding and conclusive upon all parties hereto. The expense of said arbitration, including the fees of the arbitrators, shall be paid by the party or parties to such controversy as the majority of said board of arbitration may designate. In any arbitration under this paragraph each party to the controversy shall have the right to appear in person or by attorney and to summon and examine witnesses.

14. This contract and the association created hereby may be terminated by either party hereto for any reason at any time upon notice given to the other, but the right of the salesman to any commission which accrued prior to said notice shall not be divested by the termination thereof. The fact that arbitration proceedings are pending pursuant to the preceding paragraph at the time said notice is given shall not preclude either party hereto from cancelling the agreement effective forthwith. Upon such termination, (1) the salesman shall return to the broker all writings, documents and property belonging to the broker and (2) all listings of property procured by the salesman shall become the absolute property of the broker without further liability for listing commissions. After the termination of this contract, the salesman shall not use to his own advantage or to the advantage of any other person or corporation, without the broker's written consent, any information gained from the files or business of the broker.

15. If the salesman is a licensed associate broker, he agrees that while this contract is in effect he will not engage in any act in the capacity of broker.

16.

17. In construing this agreement, it is understood that the broker herein may be more than one person or a corporation and that, therefore, if the context so requires, the singular pronoun shall be taken to mean and include the plural, the masculine, the feminine and the neuter and that generally all grammatical changes shall be made, assumed and implied to make the provisions hereof apply equally to corporations and to more than one individual.

IN WITNESS WHEREOF, the parties hereto have executed these presents in duplicate on this, the day and year first above written.

....

/s/Ivan Everready
Broker

/s/Harvey Hustle
Salesman

FIGURE A-1
(cont.)

AGREEMENT

Between Real Estate Broker
and Salesman

(FORM No. 850)

....

....

....

....

Dated ...., 19.......

781 STEVENS-NESS LAW PUB. CO., PORTLAND, ORE.

FIGURE A-2
Option to Purchase

FORM No. 74—OPTION—No Commission to Agent. STEVENS-NESS LAW PUBLISHING CO., PORTLAND, OR. 97204

TT

OPTION

KNOW ALL MEN BY THESE PRESENTS, That Wendy Welloff, Unit 77, Condominium Towers, Urbandale, Anystate 00000 *hereinafter called owner, in consideration of* .... *Dollars* ($ 20,000.00) *to owner paid by* P. O. Tential, *hereinafter called the purchaser, has given and granted and does hereby give and grant unto the said purchaser, his executors, administrators and assigns, the sole, exclusive and irrevocable option to and including midnight on* 30th *day of* November, *19* 81, *to purchase the following described property in the* city of Urbandale ...., *County of* Rustic, *State of* Anystate *Zip* 00000, *to-wit:*

Douglas Manor, 2001 Century Drive
(Lots 16 and 17, Block 3, Edgewood South Subdivision)

at and for a purchase price of Seven Hundred Thousand *Dollars* ($700,000) *payable at the following times, to-wit:* $ 50,000 additional *at the time the purchaser elects to purchase said property, said sum to be paid not later than the date above fixed for the expiration of this option;* $ 30,000 *of said purchase price to be paid* by November 30th, *19* 81, *and the balance to be paid as follows, to-wit:* $600,000 at closing which is to be held on or before December 31st, 1981.

Within five (5) days after the purchaser elects to exercise this option and makes the first payment above provided, owner agrees to furnish said purchaser title insurance prepared by a reputable title insurance company insuring in the amount of said purchase price good marketable title in the owner free and clear of all incumbrances whatsoever excepting only as hereinafter stated. The purchaser shall have .... *days after the delivery of said title insurance in which to examine same, and owner is to have thirty (30) days after written notice of defects is delivered to owner to remedy same.*

Upon the payment of said purchase price, owner agrees to convey the above described property to the said purchaser by a good and sufficient deed containing covenants of general warranty, said property to be conveyed free of all incumbrances of every nature and description exccept easements of record filed as part of the subdivision

Owner further covenants and agrees to and with the said purchaser and to and with his heirs and assigns, that the undersigned are the owners of said property and have a valid right to sell and convey the same and to contract so to do.

Time is of the essence of this contract, and should the said purchaser fail for any reason whatsoever to elect to purchase said property on or before the expiration of the time above stated, then this contract shall be absolutely null and void and of no further force or effect.

DATED July 4th, *19* 81.

/s/Wendy Welloff
OWNER .... OWNER

.... OWNER .... OWNER

STATE OF ...., *County of* ....) ss. ...., *19*......

Personally appeared the within named ....

and acknowledged the foregoing instrument to be .... *voluntary act and deed.*

Before me: ....

[SEAL] *Notary Public for* .... *My Commission Expires* ....

FIGURE A-3
Binder

THIS AGREEMENT made and entered into between Wendy Welloff, as Seller, and the undersigned as Buyer. Buyer agrees to purchase Douglas Manor, 2001 Century Drive, Urbandale, Anystate at the price of \$ 640,000.00, with a deposit of \$ 16,000.00, receipt of which is hereby acknowledged, and \$ 16,000.00 when a more formal contract is agreed to by Seller and Buyer, which is to be on or about April 1st, 1982. The Buyer agrees to pay \$32,000.00 in cash at closing, and \$500,000 by assuming and agreeing to pay existing mortgage for that amount now on subject property. The balance of \$76,000 is to be paid by Buyer as follows: a five year straight term loan from seller to buyer with interest to be paid at one percent per month, secured by a second trust deed. In the event the Seller is not willing to accept the above price and terms, the deposit is to be forthwith returned. In the event the Seller accepts and the Buyer does not comply, the deposit shall be forfeited.

Closing to be in escrow, with escrow charges to be shared equally between buyer and seller. Lack of marketable title shall give buyer valid reason to void this contract.

This agreement is approved and accepted by the Seller, who agrees to pay Ivan M. Everready, Realtor, licensed real estate broker, \$28,600 ~~% of the purchase price~~ as commission.

Date: February 31st, 1982

/s/Harvey Hustle
Harvey Hustle, Sales Representative

/s/Nancy Investor
Buyer

/s/Gerald Investor
Buyer

/s/Wendy Welloff
Seller

APPENDIX B

TIME VALUE OF MONEY TABLES

These time value of money tables show annual and monthly factors at the following interest rates:

6.00%	11.00%	20.00%
7.00%	12.00%	25.00%
8.00%	13.00%	30.00%
9.00%	14.00%	40.00%
10.00%	15.00%	50.00%

SYMBOLS AND FORMULAS FOR THE FACTORS

Annual interest rate = i $m = 12$ Number of years = n

	ANNUAL FACTORS		*MONTHLY FACTORS*	
	SYMBOL	*FORMULA*	*SYMBOL*	*FORMULA*
Future value of 1 factor	FV1	$(1 + i)^n$	MFV1	$(1 + i/m)^{n \times m}$
Future value of 1 per period factor	FV1/P	$(\text{FV1} - 1)/i$	MFV1/P	$(\text{MFV1} - 1)/(i/m)$
Sinking fund factor	SFF	$i/(\text{FV1} - 1)$	MSFF	$(i/m)/(\text{MFV1} - 1)$
Present value of 1 factor	PV1	1/FV1	MPV1	1/MFV1
Present value of 1 per period factor	PV1/P	$(1 - \text{PV1})/i$	MPV1/P	$(1 - \text{MPV1})/(i/m)$
Principal recovery factor	PRF	$i/(\text{PV1/P})$	MPRF	$(i/m)/(\text{MPV1/P})$

Annual Compounding

EFFECTIVE (ANNUAL) RATE = 6.00%

YEAR	Future Value of 1 FV1	Future Value of 1 per Period FV1/P	Sinking Fund Factor SFF	Present Value of 1 PV1	Present Value of 1 per Period PV1/P	Principal Recovery Factor PRF	YEAR
1	1.060000	1.000000	1.000000	0.943396	0.943396	1.060000	1
2	1.123600	2.060000	0.485437	0.889996	1.833393	0.545437	2
3	1.191016	3.183600	0.314110	0.839619	2.673012	0.374110	3
4	1.262477	4.374616	0.228591	0.792094	3.465106	0.288591	4
5	1.338226	5.637093	0.177396	0.747258	4.212364	0.237396	5
6	1.418519	6.975319	0.143363	0.704961	4.917324	0.203363	6
7	1.503630	8.393838	0.119135	0.665057	5.582381	0.179135	7
8	1.593848	9.897468	0.101036	0.627412	6.209794	0.161036	8
9	1.689479	11.491316	0.087022	0.591898	6.801692	0.147022	9
10	1.790848	13.180795	0.075868	0.558395	7.360087	0.135868	10
11	1.898299	14.971643	0.066793	0.526788	7.886875	0.126793	11
12	2.012196	16.869941	0.059277	0.496969	8.383844	0.119277	12
13	2.132928	18.882138	0.052960	0.468839	8.852683	0.112960	13
14	2.260904	21.015066	0.047585	0.442301	9.294984	0.107585	14
15	2.396558	23.275970	0.042963	0.417265	9.712249	0.102963	15
16	2.540352	25.672528	0.038952	0.393646	10.105895	0.098952	16
17	2.692773	28.212880	0.035445	0.371364	10.477260	0.095445	17
18	2.854339	30.905653	0.032357	0.350344	10.827603	0.092357	18
19	3.025600	33.759992	0.029621	0.330513	11.158116	0.089621	19
20	3.207135	36.785591	0.027185	0.311805	11.469921	0.087185	20

Monthly Compounding

EFFECTIVE (MONTHLY) RATE = 0.500000%

MONTH	MFV1	MFV1/P	MSSF	MPV1	MPV1/P	MPRf	MONTH
1	1.005000	1.000000	1.000000	0.995025	0.995025	1.005000	1
2	1.010025	2.005000	0.498753	0.990075	1.985099	0.503753	2
3	1.015075	3.015025	0.331672	0.985149	2.970248	0.336672	3
4	1.020151	4.030100	0.248133	0.980248	3.950496	0.253133	4
5	1.025251	5.050251	0.198010	0.975371	4.925866	0.203010	5
6	1.030378	6.075502	0.164595	0.970518	5.896384	0.169595	6
7	1.035529	7.105879	0.140729	0.965690	6.862074	0.145729	7

8	1.040707	8.141409	0.122829	0.960885	7.822959	0.127829	8
9	1.045911	9.182116	0.108907	0.956105	8.779064	0.113907	9
10	1.051140	10.228026	0.097771	0.951348	9.730412	0.102771	10
11	1.056396	11.279167	0.088659	0.946615	10.677027	0.093659	11
YEAR							*YEAR*
1	1.061678	12.335562	0.081066	0.941905	11.618932	0.086066	1
2	1.127160	25.431955	0.039321	0.887186	22.562866	0.044321	2
3	1.196681	39.336105	0.025422	0.835645	32.871016	0.030422	3
4	1.270498	54.097832	0.018485	0.787098	42.580318	0.023485	4
5	1.348850	69.770031	0.014333	0.741372	51.725561	0.019333	5
6	1.432044	86.408856	0.011573	0.698302	60.339514	0.016573	6
7	1.520370	104.073927	0.009609	0.657735	68.453042	0.014609	7
8	1.614143	122.828542	0.008141	0.619524	76.095218	0.013141	8
9	1.713699	142.739900	0.007006	0.583533	83.293424	0.012006	9
10	1.819397	163.879347	0.006102	0.549633	90.073453	0.011102	10
11	1.931613	186.322629	0.005367	0.517702	96.459599	0.010367	11
12	2.050751	210.150163	0.004759	0.487626	102.474743	0.009759	12
13	2.177237	235.447328	0.004247	0.459298	108.140440	0.009247	13
14	2.311524	262.304766	0.003812	0.432615	113.476990	0.008812	14
15	2.454094	290.818712	0.003439	0.407482	118.503515	0.008439	15
16	2.605457	321.091337	0.003114	0.383810	123.238025	0.008114	16
17	2.766156	353.231110	0.002831	0.361513	127.697486	0.007831	17
18	2.936766	387.353194	0.002582	0.340511	131.897876	0.007582	18
19	3.117899	423.579854	0.002361	0.320729	135.854246	0.007361	19
20	3.310204	462.040895	0.002164	0.302096	139.580772	0.007164	20
21	3.514371	502.874129	0.001989	0.284546	143.090806	0.006989	21
22	3.731129	546.225867	0.001831	0.268015	146.396927	0.006831	22
23	3.961257	592.251446	0.001688	0.252445	149.510979	0.006688	23
24	4.205579	641.115782	0.001560	0.237779	152.444121	0.006560	24
25	4.464970	692.993962	0.001443	0.223966	155.206864	0.006443	25
26	4.740359	748.071876	0.001337	0.210954	157.809106	0.006337	26
27	5.032734	806.546875	0.001240	0.198669	160.260172	0.006240	27
28	5.343142	868.628484	0.001151	0.187156	162.568844	0.006151	28
29	5.672696	934.539150	0.001070	0.176283	164.743394	0.006070	29
30	6.022575	1004.515042	0.000996	0.166042	166.791614	0.005996	30

7.00% NOMINAL RATE

Annual Compounding

EFFECTIVE (ANNUAL) RATE = 7.00%

YEAR	Future Value of 1 FV1	Future Value of 1 per Period FV1/P	Sinking Fund Factor SFF	Present Value of 1 PV1	Present Value of 1 per Period PV1/P	Principal Recovery Factor PRF	YEAR
1	1.070000	1.000000	1.000000	0.934579	0.934579	1.070000	1
2	1.144900	2.070000	0.483092	0.873439	1.808018	0.553092	2
3	1.225043	3.214900	0.311052	0.816298	2.624316	0.381052	3
4	1.310796	4.439943	0.225228	0.762895	3.387211	0.295228	4
5	1.402552	5.750539	0.173891	0.712986	4.100197	0.243891	5
6	1.500730	7.153291	0.139796	0.666342	4.766540	0.209796	6
7	1.605781	8.654021	0.115553	0.622750	5.389289	0.185553	7
8	1.718186	10.259803	0.097468	0.582009	5.971299	0.167468	8
9	1.838459	11.977989	0.083486	0.543934	6.515232	0.153486	9
10	1.967151	13.816448	0.072378	0.508349	7.023582	0.142378	10
11	2.104852	15.783599	0.063357	0.475093	7.498674	0.133357	11
12	2.252192	17.888451	0.055902	0.444012	7.942686	0.125902	12
13	2.409845	20.140643	0.049651	0.414964	8.357651	0.119651	13
14	2.578534	22.550488	0.044345	0.378817	8.745468	0.114345	14
15	2.759032	25.129022	0.039795	0.362446	9.107914	0.109795	15
16	2.952164	27.888054	0.035858	0.338735	9.446649	0.105858	16
17	3.158815	30.840217	0.032425	0.316574	9.763223	0.102425	17
18	3.379932	33.999033	0.029413	0.295864	10.059087	0.099413	18
19	3.616528	37.378965	0.026753	0.276508	10.335595	0.096753	19
20	3.869684	40.995492	0.024393	0.258419	10.594014	0.094393	20

Monthly Compounding

EFFECTIVE (MONTHLY) RATE = 0.583333%

MONTH	MFV1	MFV1/P	MSSF	MPV1	MPV1/P	MPRF	MONTH
1	1.005833	1.000000	1.000000	0.994200	0.994200	1.005833	1
2	1.011701	2.005833	0.498546	0.988435	1.982635	0.594379	2
3	1.017602	3.017534	0.331396	0.982702	2.965337	0.337230	3
4	1.023538	4.035136	0.247823	0.977003	3.942340	0.253656	4
5	1.029509	5.058675	0.197680	0.971337	4.913677	0.203514	5
6	1.035514	6.088184	0.164253	0.965704	5.879381	0.170086	6
7	1.041555	7.123698	0.140377	0.960103	6.839484	0.146210	7

8	1.047631	8.165253	0.122470	0.954535	7.794019	0.128304	8
9	1.053742	9.212883	0.108544	0.948999	8.743018	0.114377	9
10	1.059889	10.266625	0.097403	0.943495	9.686513	0.103236	10
11	1.066071	11.326514	0.088288	0.938024	10.624537	0.094122	11
YEAR							*YEAR*
1	1.072290	12.392585	0.080693	0.932583	11.557120	0.086527	1
2	1.149806	25.681032	0.038939	0.869712	22.335099	0.044773	2
3	1.232926	39.930101	0.025044	0.811079	32.386464	0.030877	3
4	1.322054	55.209236	0.018113	0.756399	41.760201	0.023946	4
5	1.417625	71.592902	0.013968	0.705405	50.501994	0.109801	5
6	1.520106	89.160944	0.011216	0.657849	58.654444	0.017049	6
7	1.629994	107.998981	0.009259	0.613499	66.257285	0.015093	7
8	1.747826	128.198821	0.007800	0.572139	73.347569	0.013634	8
9	1.874177	149.858909	0.006673	0.533568	79.959850	0.012506	9
10	2.009661	173.084807	0.005778	0.497596	86.126354	0.011611	10
11	2.154940	197.989707	0.005051	0.464050	91.877134	0.010884	11
12	2.310721	224.694985	0.004450	0.432765	97.240216	0.010284	12
13	2.477763	253.330789	0.003947	0.403590	102.241738	0.009781	13
14	2.656881	284.036677	0.003521	0.376381	106.906074	0.009354	14
15	2.848947	316.962297	0.003155	0.351007	111.255958	0.008988	15
16	3.054897	352.268112	0.002839	0.327343	115.312587	0.008672	16
17	3.275736	390.126188	0.002563	0.305275	119.095732	0.008397	17
18	3.512539	430.721027	0.002322	0.284694	122.623831	0.008155	18
19	3.766461	474.250470	0.002109	0.265501	125.914077	0.007942	19
20	4.038739	520.926660	0.001920	0.247602	128.982506	0.007753	20
21	4.330700	570.977075	0.001751	0.230910	131.844073	0.007585	21
22	4.643766	624.645640	0.001601	0.215342	134.512723	0.007434	22
23	4.979464	682.193909	0.001466	0.200825	137.001461	0.007299	23
24	5.339430	743.902347	0.001344	0.187285	139.322418	0.007178	24
25	5.725418	810.071693	0.001234	0.174660	141.486903	0.007068	25
26	6.139309	881.024427	0.001135	0.162885	143.505467	0.006968	26
27	6.583120	957.106339	0.001045	0.151904	145.387946	0.006878	27
28	7.059015	1038.688219	0.000963	0.141663	147.143515	0.006796	28
29	7.569311	1126.167659	0.000888	0.132112	148.780729	0.006721	29
30	8.116497	1219.970996	0.000820	0.123206	150.307568	0.006653	30

8.00% NOMINAL RATE

Annual Compounding

	Future Value of 1	Future Value of 1 per Period	Sinking Fund Factor	Present Value of 1	Present Value of 1 per Period	Principal Recovery Factor	
			EFFECTIVE (ANNUAL) RATE = 8.00%				
YEAR	FV1	FV1/P	SFF	PV1	PV1/P	PRF	YEAR
1	1.080000	1.000000	1.000000	0.925926	0.925926	1.080000	1
2	1.166400	2.080000	0.480769	0.857339	1.783265	0.560769	2
3	1.259712	3.246400	0.308034	0.793832	2.577097	0.388034	3
4	1.360489	4.506112	0.221921	0.735030	3.312127	0.301921	4
5	1.469328	5.866601	0.170456	0.680583	3.992710	0.250456	5
6	1.586874	7.335929	0.136315	0.630170	4.622880	0.216315	6
7	1.713824	8.922803	0.112072	0.583490	5.206370	0.192072	7
8	1.850930	10.636628	0.094015	0.540269	5.746639	0.174015	8
9	1.999005	12.487558	0.080080	0.500249	6.246888	0.160080	9
10	2.158925	14.486562	0.069029	0.463193	6.710081	0.149029	10
11	2.331639	16.645487	0.060076	0.428883	7.138964	0.140076	11
12	2.518170	18.977126	0.052695	0.397114	7.536078	0.132695	12
13	2.719624	21.495297	0.046522	0.367698	7.903776	0.126522	13
14	2.937194	24.214920	0.041297	0.340461	8.244237	0.121297	14
15	3.172169	27.152114	0.036830	0.315242	8.559479	0.116830	15
16	3.425943	30.324283	0.032977	0.291890	8.851369	0.112977	16
17	3.700018	33.750226	0.029629	0.270269	9.121638	0.109629	17
18	3.996019	37.450244	0.026702	0.250249	9.371887	0.106702	18
19	4.315701	41.446263	0.024128	0.231712	9.603599	0.104128	19
20	4.660957	45.761964	0.021852	0.214548	9.818147	0.101852	20

Monthly Compounding

			EFFECTIVE (MONTHLY) RATE = 0.666667%				
MONTH	MFV1	MFV1/P	MSSF	MPV1	MPV1/P	MPRF	MONTH
1	1.006667	1.000000	1.000000	0.993377	0.993377	1.006667	1
2	1.013378	2.006667	0.498339	0.986799	1.980176	0.505006	2
3	1.020134	3.020044	0.331121	0.980264	2.960440	0.337788	3
4	1.026935	4.040178	0.247514	0.973772	3.934212	0.254181	4
5	1.033781	5.067113	0.197351	0.967323	4.901535	0.204018	5
6	1.040673	6.100893	0.163910	0.960917	5.862452	0.170577	6
7	1.047610	7.141566	0.140025	0.954553	6.817005	0.146692	7

8	1.054595	8.189176	0.122112	0.948232	7.765237	0.128779	8
9	1.061625	9.243771	0.108181	0.941952	8.707189	0.114848	9
10	1.068703	10.305396	0.097037	0.935714	9.642903	0.103703	10
11	1.075827	11.374099	0.087919	0.929517	10.572420	0.094586	11
YEAR							*YEAR*
1	1.083000	12.449926	0.080322	0.923361	11.495782	0.086988	1
2	1.172888	25.933190	0.038561	0.852596	22.110544	0.045227	2
3	1.270237	40.535558	0.024670	0.787255	31.911806	0.031336	3
4	1.375666	56.349915	0.017746	0.726921	40.961913	0.024413	4
5	1.489846	73.476856	0.013610	0.671210	49.318433	0.020276	5
6	1.613502	92.025325	0.010867	0.619770	57.034522	0.017533	6
7	1.747422	112.113308	0.008920	0.572272	64.159261	0.015586	7
8	1.892457	133.868583	0.007470	0.528414	70.737970	0.014137	8
9	2.049530	157.429535	0.006352	0.487917	76.812497	0.013019	9
10	2.219640	182.946035	0.005466	0.450523	82.421481	0.012133	10
11	2.403869	210.580392	0.004749	0.415996	87.600600	0.011415	11
12	2.603389	240.508387	0.004158	0.384115	92.382800	0.010825	12
13	2.819469	272.920390	0.003664	0.354677	96.798498	0.010331	13
14	3.053484	308.022574	0.003247	0.327495	100.875784	0.009913	14
15	3.306921	346.038222	0.002890	0.302396	104.640592	0.009557	15
16	3.581394	387.209149	0.002583	0.279221	108.116871	0.009249	16
17	3.878648	431.797244	0.002316	0.257822	111.326733	0.008983	17
18	4.200574	480.086128	0.002083	0.238063	114.290596	0.008750	18
19	4.549220	532.382966	0.001878	0.219818	117.027313	0.008545	19
20	4.926803	589.020416	0.001698	0.202971	119.554292	0.008364	20
21	5.335725	650.358746	0.001538	0.187416	121.887606	0.008204	21
22	5.778588	716.788127	0.001395	0.173053	124.042099	0.008062	22
23	6.258207	788.731114	0.001268	0.159790	126.031475	0.007935	23
24	6.777636	866.645333	0.001154	0.147544	127.868388	0.007821	24
25	7.340176	951.026395	0.001051	0.136237	129.564523	0.007718	25
26	7.979407	1042.411042	0.000959	0.125796	131.130668	0.007626	26
27	8.609204	1141.380571	0.000876	0.116155	132.576786	0.007543	27
28	9.323763	1248.564521	0.000801	0.107253	133.912076	0.007468	28
29	10.097631	1364.644687	0.000733	0.099033	135.145031	0.007399	29
30	10.935730	1490.359449	0.000671	0.091443	136.283494	0.007338	30

Annual Compounding

	Future Value of 1	Future Value of 1 per Period	Sinking Fund Factor	Present Value of 1	Present Value of 1 per Period	Principal Recovery Factor	
			EFFECTIVE (ANNUAL) RATE = 9.00%				
YEAR	FV1	FV1/P	SFF	PV1	PV1/P	PRF	YEAR
1	1.090000	1.000000	1.000000	0.917431	0.917431	1.090000	1
2	1.188100	2.090000	0.478469	0.841680	1.759111	0.568469	2
3	1.295029	3.278100	0.305055	0.772183	2.531295	0.395055	3
4	1.411582	4.573129	0.218669	0.708425	3.239720	0.308669	4
5	1.538624	5.984711	0.167092	0.649931	3.889651	0.257092	5
6	1.677100	7.523335	0.132920	0.596267	4.485919	0.222920	6
7	1.828039	9.200435	0.108691	0.547034	5.032953	0.198691	7
8	1.992563	11.028474	0.090674	0.501866	5.534819	0.180674	8
9	2.171893	13.021036	0.076799	0.460428	5.995247	0.166799	9
10	2.367364	15.192930	0.065820	0.422411	6.417658	0.155820	10
11	2.580426	17.560293	0.056947	0.387533	6.805191	0.146947	11
12	2.812665	20.140720	0.049651	0.355535	7.160725	0.139651	12
13	3.065805	22.953385	0.043567	0.326179	7.486904	0.133567	13
14	3.341727	26.019189	0.038433	0.299246	7.786150	0.128433	14
15	3.642482	29.360916	0.034059	0.274538	8.060688	0.124059	15
16	3.970306	33.003399	0.030300	0.251870	8.312558	0.120300	16
17	4.327633	36.973705	0.027046	0.231073	8.543631	0.117046	17
18	4.717120	41.301338	0.024212	0.211994	8.755625	0.114212	18
19	5.141661	46.018458	0.021730	0.194490	8.950115	0.111730	19
20	5.604411	51.160120	0.019546	0.178431	9.128546	0.109546	20

Monthly Compounding

			EFFECTIVE (MONTHLY) RATE = 0.750000%				
MONTH	MFV1	MFV1/P	MSSF	MPV1	MPV1/P	MPRF	MONTH
1	1.007500	1.000000	1.000000	0.992556	0.992556	1.007500	1
2	1.015056	2.007500	0.498132	0.985167	1.977723	0.505632	2
3	1.022669	3.022556	0.330846	0.977833	2.955556	0.338346	3
4	1.030339	4.045225	0.247205	0.970554	3.926110	0.254705	4
5	1.038067	5.075565	0.197022	0.963329	4.889440	0.204522	5
6	1.045852	6.113631	0.163569	0.956158	5.845598	0.171069	6
7	1.053696	7.159484	0.139675	0.949040	6.794638	0.147175	7

8	1.061599	8.213180	0.121756	0.941975	7.736613	0.129256	8
9	1.069561	9.274779	0.107819	0.934963	8.671576	0.115319	9
10	1.077583	10.344339	0.096671	0.928003	9.599580	0.104171	10
11	1.085664	11.421922	0.087551	0.921095	10.520675	0.095051	11
YEAR							YEAR
1	1.093807	12.507586	0.079951	0.914238	11.434913	0.087451	1
2	1.196414	26.188471	0.038185	0.835831	21.889146	0.045685	2
3	1.308645	41.152716	0.024300	0.764149	31.446805	0.031800	3
4	1.431405	57.520711	0.017385	0.698614	40.184782	0.024885	4
5	1.565681	75.424137	0.013258	0.638700	48.173374	0.020758	5
6	1.712553	95.007028	0.010526	0.583924	55.476849	0.018026	6
7	1.873202	116.426928	0.008589	0.533845	62.153965	0.016089	7
8	2.048921	139.856164	0.007150	0.488062	68.258439	0.014650	8
9	2.241124	165.438223	0.006043	0.446205	73.839382	0.013543	9
10	2.451357	193.514277	0.005168	0.407937	78.941693	0.012668	10
11	2.681311	224.174837	0.004461	0.372952	83.606420	0.011961	11
12	2.932837	257.711570	0.003880	0.340967	87.871092	0.011380	12
13	3.207957	294.394279	0.003397	0.311725	91.770018	0.010897	13
14	3.508886	334.518079	0.002989	0.284991	95.334564	0.010489	14
15	3.838043	378.405769	0.002643	0.260549	98.593409	0.010143	15
16	4.198078	426.410427	0.002345	0.238204	101.572769	0.009845	16
17	4.591887	478.918252	0.002088	0.217775	104.296613	0.009588	17
18	5.022638	536.351674	0.001864	0.199099	106.786856	0.009364	18
19	5.493796	599.172747	0.001669	0.182024	109.063531	0.009169	19
20	6.009152	667.886870	0.001497	0.166413	111.144954	0.008997	20
21	6.572851	743.046852	0.001346	0.152141	113.047870	0.008846	21
22	7.189430	825.257358	0.001212	0.139093	114.787589	0.008712	22
23	7.863848	915.179777	0.001093	0.127164	116.378106	0.008593	23
24	8.601532	1013.537539	0.000987	0.116258	117.832218	0.008487	24
25	9.408415	1121.121937	0.000892	0.106288	119.161622	0.008392	25
26	10.290989	1238.798495	0.000807	0.097172	120.377014	0.008307	26
27	11.256354	1367.513924	0.000731	0.088839	121.488172	0.008231	27
28	12.312278	1508.303750	0.000663	0.081220	122.504035	0.008163	28
29	13.467255	1662.300631	0.000602	0.074254	123.432776	0.008102	29
30	14.730576	1830.743483	0.000546	0.067886	124.281866	0.008046	30

Annual Compounding

EFFECTIVE (ANNUAL) RATE = 10.00%

	Future Value of 1	Future Value of 1 per Period	Sinking Fund Factor	Present Value of 1	Present Value of 1 per Period	Principal Recovery Factor	
YEAR	FV1	FV1/P	SFF	PV1	PV1/P	PRF	YEAR
1	1.100000	1.000000	1.000000	0.909091	0.909091	1.100000	1
2	1.210000	2.100000	0.476190	0.826446	1.735537	0.576190	2
3	1.331000	3.310000	0.302115	0.751315	2.486852	0.402115	3
4	1.464100	4.641000	0.215471	0.683013	3.169865	0.315471	4
5	1.610510	6.105100	0.163797	0.620921	3.790787	0.263797	5
6	1.771561	7.715610	0.129607	0.564474	4.355261	0.229607	6
7	1.948717	9.487171	0.105405	0.513158	4.868419	0.205405	7
8	2.143589	11.435888	0.087444	0.466507	5.334926	0.187444	8
9	2.357948	13.579477	0.073641	0.424098	5.759024	0.173641	9
10	2.593742	15.937425	0.062745	0.385543	6.144567	0.162745	10
11	2.853117	18.531167	0.053963	0.350494	6.495061	0.153963	11
12	3.138428	21.384284	0.046763	0.318631	6.813692	0.146763	12
13	3.452271	24.522712	0.040779	0.289664	7.103356	0.140779	13
14	3.797498	27.974983	0.035746	0.263331	7.366687	0.135746	14
15	4.177248	31.772482	0.031474	0.239392	7.606080	0.131474	15
16	4.594973	35.949730	0.027817	0.217629	7.823709	0.127817	16
17	5.054470	40.544703	0.024664	0.197845	8.021553	0.124664	17
18	5.559917	45.599173	0.021930	0.179859	8.201412	0.121930	18
19	6.115909	51.159090	0.019547	0.163508	8.364920	0.119547	19
20	6.727500	57.274999	0.017460	0.148644	8.513564	0.117460	20

Monthly Compounding

EFFECTIVE (MONTHLY) RATE = 0.833333%

MONTH	MFV1	MFV1/P	MSSF	MPV1	MPV1/P	MPRF	MONTH
1	1.008333	1.000000	1.000000	0.991736	0.991736	1.008333	1
2	1.016736	2.008333	0.497925	0.983539	1.975275	0.506259	2
3	1.025209	3.025069	0.330571	0.975411	2.950686	0.338904	3
4	1.033752	4.050278	0.246897	0.967350	3.918036	0.255230	4
5	1.042367	5.084031	0.196694	0.959355	4.877391	0.205028	5
6	1.051053	6.126398	0.163228	0.951427	5.828817	0.171561	6

7	1.059812	7.177451	0.139325	0.943563	6.772381	0.147659	7
8	1.068644	8.237263	0.121400	0.935765	7.708146	0.129733	8
9	1.077549	9.305907	0.107459	0.928032	8.636178	0.115792	9
10	1.086529	10.383456	0.096307	0.920362	9.556540	0.104640	10
11	1.095583	11.469985	0.087184	0.912756	10.469296	0.095517	11
YEAR							***YEAR***
1	1.104713	12.565568	0.079583	0.905212	11.374508	0.087916	1
2	1.220391	26.446915	0.037812	0.819410	21.670855	0.046145	2
3	1.348182	41.781821	0.023934	0.741740	30.991236	0.032267	3
4	1.489354	58.722492	0.017029	0.671432	39.428160	0.025363	4
5	1.645309	77.437072	0.012914	0.607789	47.065369	0.021247	5
6	1.817594	98.111314	0.010193	0.550178	53.978665	0.018526	6
7	2.007920	120.950418	0.008268	0.498028	60.236667	0.016601	7
8	2.218176	146.181076	0.006841	0.450821	65.901488	0.015174	8
9	2.450448	174.053713	0.005745	0.408089	71.029355	0.014079	9
10	2.707041	204.844979	0.004882	0.369407	75.671163	0.013215	10
11	2.990504	238.860493	0.004187	0.334392	79.872986	0.012520	11
12	3.303649	276.437876	0.003617	0.302696	83.676528	0.011951	12
13	3.649584	317.950102	0.003145	0.274004	87.119542	0.011478	13
14	4.031743	363.809201	0.002749	0.248032	90.236201	0.011082	14
15	4.453920	414.470346	0.002413	0.224521	93.057439	0.010746	15
16	4.920303	470.436376	0.002126	0.203240	95.611259	0.010459	16
17	5.435523	532.262780	0.001879	0.183975	97.923008	0.010212	17
18	6.004693	600.563216	0.001665	0.166536	100.015633	0.009998	18
19	6.633463	676.015601	0.001479	0.150751	101.909902	0.009813	19
20	7.328074	759.368836	0.001317	0.136462	103.624619	0.009650	20
21	8.095419	851.450244	0.001174	0.123527	105.176801	0.009508	21
22	8.943115	953.173779	0.001049	0.111818	106.581856	0.009382	22
23	9.879576	1065.549097	0.000938	0.101219	107.853730	0.009272	23
24	10.914097	1189.691580	0.000841	0.091625	109.005054	0.009174	24
25	12.056945	1326.833403	0.000754	0.082940	110.047230	0.009087	25
26	13.319465	1478.335767	0.000676	0.075078	110.990629	0.009010	26
27	14.714187	1645.702407	0.000608	0.067962	111.844605	0.008941	27
28	16.254954	1830.594523	0.000546	0.061520	112.617635	0.008880	28
29	17.957060	2034.847258	0.000491	0.055688	113.317392	0.008825	29
30	19.837399	2260.487925	0.000442	0.050410	113.950820	0.008776	30

Annual Compounding

EFFECTIVE (ANNUAL) RATE = 11.00%

YEAR	FV1 (Future Value of 1)	FV1/P (Future Value of 1 per Period)	SFF (Sinking Fund Factor)	PV1 (Present Value of 1)	PV1/P (Present Value of 1 per Period)	PRF (Principal Recovery Factor)	YEAR
1	1.110000	1.000000	1.000000	0.900901	0.900901	1.110000	1
2	1.232100	2.110000	0.473934	0.811622	1.712523	0.583934	2
3	1.367631	3.342100	0.299213	0.731191	2.443715	0.409213	3
4	1.518070	4.709731	0.212326	0.658731	3.102446	0.322326	4
5	1.685058	6.227801	0.160570	0.593451	3.695897	0.270570	5
6	1.870415	7.912860	0.126377	0.534641	4.230538	0.236377	6
7	2.076160	9.783274	0.102215	0.481658	4.712196	0.212215	7
8	2.304538	11.859434	0.084321	0.433926	5.146123	0.194321	8
9	2.558037	14.163972	0.070602	0.390925	5.537048	0.180602	9
10	2.839421	16.722009	0.059801	0.352184	5.889232	0.169801	10
11	3.151757	19.561430	0.051121	0.317283	6.206515	0.161121	11
12	3.498451	22.713187	0.044027	0.285841	6.492356	0.154027	12
13	3.883280	26.211638	0.038151	0.257514	6.749870	0.148151	13
14	4.310441	30.094918	0.033228	0.231995	6.981865	0.143228	14
15	4.784589	34.405359	0.029065	0.209004	7.190870	0.139065	15
16	5.310894	39.189948	0.025517	0.188292	7.379162	0.135517	16
17	5.895093	44.500843	0.022471	0.169633	7.548794	0.132471	17
18	6.543553	50.395936	0.019843	0.152822	7.701617	0.129843	18
19	7.263344	56.939488	0.017563	0.137678	7.839294	0.127563	19
20	8.062312	64.202832	0.015576	0.124034	7.963328	0.125576	20

Monthly Compounding

EFFECTIVE (MONTHLY) RATE = 0.916667%

MONTH	MFV1	MFV1/P	MSSF	MPV1	MPV1/P	MPRF	MONTH
1	1.009167	1.000000	1.000000	0.990917	0.990917	1.009167	1
2	1.018417	2.009167	0.497719	0.981916	1.972832	0.506885	2
3	1.027753	3.027584	0.330296	0.972997	2.945829	0.339463	3
4	1.037174	4.055337	0.246589	0.964158	3.909987	0.255755	4
5	1.046681	5.092511	0.196367	0.955401	4.865388	0.205533	5
6	1.056276	6.139192	0.162888	0.946722	5.812110	0.172055	6
7	1.065958	7.195468	0.138976	0.938123	6.750233	0.148143	7

8	1.075730	8.261427	0.121044	0.929602	7.679835	0.130211	8
9	1.085591	9.337156	0.107099	0.921158	8.600992	0.116266	9
10	1.095542	10.422747	0.095944	0.912790	9.513783	0.105111	10
11	1.105584	11.518289	0.086818	0.904499	10.418282	0.095985	11
YEAR							*YEAR*
1	1.115719	12.623873	0.079215	0.896283	11.314565	0.088382	1
2	1.244829	26.708566	0.037441	0.803323	21.455619	0.046608	2
3	1.388879	42.423123	0.023572	0.720005	30.544874	0.032739	3
4	1.549598	59.956151	0.016679	0.645329	38.691421	0.025846	4
5	1.728916	79.518080	0.012576	0.578397	45.993034	0.021742	5
6	1.928984	101.343692	0.009867	0.518408	52.537346	0.019034	6
7	2.152204	125.694940	0.007956	0.464640	58.402903	0.017122	7
8	2.401254	152.864085	0.006542	0.416449	63.660103	0.015708	8
9	2.679124	183.177212	0.005459	0.373256	68.372043	0.014626	9
10	2.989150	216.998139	0.004608	0.334543	72.595275	0.013775	10
11	3.335051	254.732784	0.003926	0.299846	76.380487	0.013092	11
12	3.720979	296.834038	0.003369	0.268747	79.773109	0.012536	12
13	4.151566	343.807200	0.002909	0.240873	82.813859	0.012075	13
14	4.631980	396.216042	0.002524	0.215890	85.539231	0.011691	14
15	5.167988	454.689575	0.002199	0.193499	87.981937	0.011366	15
16	5.766021	519.929596	0.001923	0.173430	90.171293	0.011090	16
17	6.433259	592.719117	0.001687	0.155442	92.133576	0.010854	17
18	7.177708	673.931757	0.001484	0.139320	93.892337	0.010650	18
19	8.008304	764.542228	0.001308	0.124870	95.468685	0.010475	19
20	8.935015	865.638038	0.001155	0.111919	96.881539	0.010322	20
21	9.968965	978.432537	0.001022	0.100311	98.147856	0.010189	21
22	11.122562	1104.279485	0.000906	0.089907	99.282835	0.010072	22
23	12.409652	1244.689295	0.000803	0.080582	100.300098	0.009970	23
24	13.845682	1401.347165	0.000714	0.072225	101.211853	0.009880	24
25	15.447889	1576.133301	0.000634	0.064734	102.029044	0.009801	25
26	17.235500	1771.145485	0.000565	0.058020	102.761478	0.009731	26
27	19.229972	1988.724252	0.000503	0.052002	103.417947	0.009670	27
28	21.455242	2231.480981	0.000448	0.046609	104.006328	0.009615	28
29	23.938018	2502.329236	0.000400	0.041775	104.533685	0.009566	29
30	26.708098	2804.519736	0.000357	0.037442	105.006346	0.009523	30

Annual Compounding

EFFECTIVE (ANNUAL) RATE = 12.00%

YEAR	Future Value of 1 FV1	Future Value of 1 per Period FV1/P	Sinking Fund Factor SFF	Present Value of 1 PV1	Present Value of 1 per Period PV1/P	Principal Recovery Factor PRF	YEAR
1	1.120000	1.000000	1.000000	0.892857	0.892857	1.120000	1
2	1.254400	2.120000	0.471698	0.797194	1.690051	0.591698	2
3	1.404928	3.374400	0.296349	0.711780	2.401831	0.416349	3
4	1.573519	4.779328	0.209234	0.635518	3.037349	0.329234	4
5	1.762342	6.352847	0.157410	0.567427	3.604776	0.277410	5
6	1.973823	8.115189	0.123226	0.506631	4.111407	0.243226	6
7	2.210681	10.089012	0.099118	0.452349	4.563757	0.219118	7
8	2.475963	12.299693	0.081303	0.403883	4.967640	0.201303	8
9	2.773079	14.775656	0.067679	0.360610	5.328250	0.187679	9
10	3.105848	17.548735	0.056984	0.321973	5.650223	0.176984	10
11	3.478550	20.654583	0.048415	0.287476	5.937699	0.168415	11
12	3.895976	24.133133	0.041437	0.256675	6.194374	0.161437	12
13	4.363493	28.029109	0.035677	0.229174	6.423548	0.155677	13
14	4.887112	32.392602	0.030871	0.204620	6.628168	0.150871	14
15	5.473566	37.279715	0.026824	0.182696	6.810864	0.146824	15
16	6.130394	42.753280	0.023390	0.163122	6.973986	0.143390	16
17	6.866041	48.883674	0.020457	0.145644	7.119630	0.140457	17
18	7.689966	55.749715	0.017937	0.130040	7.249670	0.137937	18
19	8.612762	63.439681	0.015763	0.116107	7.365777	0.135763	19
20	9.646293	72.052442	0.013879	0.103667	7.469444	0.133879	20

Monthly Compounding

EFFECTIVE (MONTHLY) RATE = 1.000000%

MONTH	MFV1	MFV1/P	MSSF	MPV1	MPV1/P	MPRF	MONTH
1	1.010000	1.000000	1.000000	0.990099	0.990099	1.010000	1
2	1.020100	2.010000	0.497512	0.980296	1.970395	0.507512	2
3	1.030301	3.030100	0.330022	0.970590	2.940985	0.340022	3
4	1.040604	4.060401	0.246281	0.960980	3.901966	0.256281	4
5	1.051010	5.101005	0.196040	0.951466	4.853431	0.206040	5
6	1.061520	6.152015	0.162548	0.942045	5.795476	0.172548	6
7	1.072135	7.213535	0.138628	0.932718	6.728195	0.148628	7

8	1.082857	8.285671	0.120690	0.923483	7.651678	0.130690	8
9	1.093685	9.368527	0.106740	0.914340	8.566018	0.116740	9
10	1.104622	10.462213	0.095582	0.905287	9.471305	0.105582	10
11	1.115668	11.566835	0.086454	0.896324	10.367628	0.096454	11
YEAR							*YEAR*
1	1.126825	12.682503	0.078849	0.887449	11.255077	0.088849	1
2	1.269735	26.973465	0.037073	0.787566	21.243387	0.047073	2
3	1.430769	43.076878	0.023214	0.698925	30.107505	0.033214	3
4	1.612226	61.222608	0.016334	0.620260	37.973959	0.026334	4
5	1.816697	81.669670	0.012244	0.550450	44.955038	0.022244	5
6	2.047099	104.709931	0.009550	0.488496	51.150391	0.019550	6
7	2.306723	130.672274	0.007653	0.433515	56.648453	0.017653	7
8	2.599273	159.927293	0.006253	0.384723	61.527703	0.016252	8
9	2.928926	192.892579	0.005184	0.341422	65.857790	0.015184	9
10	3.300387	230.038689	0.004347	0.302995	69.700522	0.014347	10
11	3.718959	271.895856	0.003678	0.268892	73.110752	0.013678	11
12	4.190616	319.061559	0.003134	0.238628	76.137157	0.013134	12
13	4.722091	372.209054	0.002687	0.211771	78.822939	0.012687	13
14	5.320970	432.096982	0.002314	0.187936	81.206434	0.012314	14
15	5.995802	499.580198	0.002002	0.166783	83.321664	0.012002	15
16	6.756220	575.621974	0.001737	0.148012	85.198824	0.011737	16
17	7.613078	661.307751	0.001512	0.131353	86.864707	0.011512	17
18	8.578606	757.860630	0.001320	0.116569	88.343095	0.011320	18
19	9.666588	866.658830	0.001154	0.103449	89.655089	0.011154	19
20	10.892554	989.255365	0.001011	0.091806	90.819416	0.011011	20
21	12.274002	1127.400210	0.000887	0.081473	91.852698	0.010887	21
22	13.830653	1283.065279	0.000779	0.072303	92.769683	0.010779	22
23	15.584726	1458.472574	0.000686	0.064165	93.583461	0.010686	23
24	17.561259	1656.125905	0.000604	0.056944	94.305647	0.010604	24
25	19.788466	1878.846626	0.000532	0.050534	94.946551	0.010532	25
26	22.298139	2129.813909	0.000470	0.044847	95.515321	0.010470	26
27	25.126101	2412.610125	0.000414	0.039799	96.020075	0.010414	27
28	28.312720	2731.271980	0.000366	0.035320	96.468019	0.010366	28
29	31.903481	3090.348134	0.000324	0.031345	96.865546	0.010324	29
30	35.949641	3494.964133	0.000286	0.027817	97.218331	0.010286	30

Annual Compounding

EFFECTIVE (ANNUAL) RATE = 13.00%

YEAR	FV1 Future Value of 1	FV1/P Future Value of 1 per Period	SFF Sinking Fund Factor	PV1 Present Value of 1	PV1/P Present Value of 1 per Period	PRF Principal Recovery Factor	YEAR
1	1.130000	1.000000	1.000000	0.884956	0.884956	1.130000	1
2	1.276900	2.130000	0.469484	0.783147	1.668102	0.599484	2
3	1.442897	3.406900	0.293522	0.693050	2.361153	0.423522	3
4	1.630474	4.849797	0.206194	0.613319	2.974471	0.336194	4
5	1.842435	6.480271	0.154315	0.542760	3.517231	0.284315	5
6	2.081952	8.322706	0.120153	0.480319	3.997550	0.250153	6
7	2.352605	10.404658	0.096111	0.425061	4.422610	0.226111	7
8	2.658444	12.757263	0.078387	0.376160	4.798770	0.208387	8
9	3.004042	15.415707	0.064869	0.332885	5.131655	0.194869	9
10	3.394567	18.419749	0.054290	0.294588	5.426243	0.184290	10
11	3.835861	21.814317	0.045841	0.260698	5.686941	0.175841	11
12	4.334523	25.650178	0.038986	0.230706	5.917647	0.168986	12
13	4.898011	29.984701	0.033350	0.204165	6.121812	0.163350	13
14	5.534753	34.882712	0.028667	0.180677	6.302488	0.158667	14
15	6.254270	40.417464	0.024742	0.159891	6.462379	0.154742	15
16	7.067326	46.671735	0.021426	0.141496	6.603875	0.151426	16
17	7.986078	53.739060	0.018608	0.125218	6.729093	0.148608	17
18	9.024268	61.725138	0.016201	0.110812	6.839905	0.146201	18
19	10.197423	70.749406	0.014134	0.098064	6.937969	0.144134	19
20	11.523088	80.946829	0.012354	0.086782	7.024752	0.142354	20

Monthly Compounding

EFFECTIVE (MONTHLY RATE = 1.083333%

MONTH	MFV1	MFV1/P	MSSF	MPV1	MPV1/P	MPRF	MONTH
1	1.010833	1.000000	1.000000	0.989283	0.989283	1.010833	1
2	1.021784	2.010833	0.497306	0.978680	1.967963	0.508140	2
3	1.032853	3.032617	0.329748	0.968192	2.936155	0.340581	3
4	1.044043	4.065471	0.245974	0.957815	3.893970	0.256807	4
5	1.055353	5.109513	0.195713	0.947550	4.841520	0.206547	5
6	1.066786	6.164866	0.162210	0.937395	5.778915	0.173043	6
7	1.078343	7.231652	0.138281	0.927349	6.706264	0.149114	7

8	1.090025	8.309995	0.120337	0.917410	7.623674	0.131170	8
9	1.101834	9.400020	0.106383	0.907578	8.531253	0.117216	9
10	1.113770	10.501854	0.095221	0.897851	9.429104	0.106055	10
11	1.125836	11.615624	0.086091	0.888229	10.317333	0.096924	11
YEAR							YEAR
1	1.138032	12.741460	0.078484	0.878710	11.196042	0.089317	1
2	1.295118	27.241655	0.036708	0.772130	21.034112	0.047542	2
3	1.473886	43.743348	0.022861	0.678478	29.678917	0.033694	3
4	1.677330	62.522811	0.015994	0.596185	37.275190	0.026827	4
5	1.908857	83.894449	0.011920	0.523874	43.950107	0.022753	5
6	2.172341	108.216068	0.009241	0.460333	49.815421	0.020074	6
7	2.472194	135.894861	0.007359	0.404499	54.969328	0.018192	7
8	2.813437	167.394225	0.005974	0.355437	59.498115	0.016807	8
9	3.201783	203.241525	0.004920	0.312326	63.477604	0.015754	9
10	3.643733	244.036917	0.004098	0.274444	66.974419	0.014931	10
11	4.146687	290.463399	0.003443	0.241156	70.047103	0.014276	11
12	4.719064	343.298242	0.002913	0.211906	72.747100	0.013746	12
13	5.370448	403.426010	0.002479	0.186204	75.119613	0.013312	13
14	6.111745	471.853363	0.002119	0.163619	77.204363	0.012953	14
15	6.955364	549.725914	0.001819	0.143774	79.036253	0.012652	15
16	7.915430	638.347406	0.001567	0.126336	80.645952	0.012400	16
17	9.008017	739.201542	0.001353	0.111012	82.060410	0.012186	17
18	10.251416	853.976825	0.001171	0.097548	83.303307	0.012004	18
19	11.666444	984.594826	0.001016	0.085716	84.395453	0.011849	19
20	13.276792	1133.242353	0.000882	0.075319	85.355132	0.011716	20
21	15.109421	1302.408067	0.000768	0.066184	86.198412	0.011601	21
22	17.195012	1494.924144	0.000669	0.058156	86.939409	0.011502	22
23	19.568482	1714.013694	0.000583	0.051103	87.590531	0.011417	23
24	22.269568	1963.344717	0.000509	0.044904	88.162677	0.011343	24
25	25.343491	2247.091520	0.000445	0.039458	88.665428	0.011278	25
26	28.841716	2570.004599	0.000389	0.034672	89.107200	0.011222	26
27	32.822810	2937.490172	0.000340	0.030467	89.495389	0.011174	27
28	37.353424	3355.700690	0.000298	0.026771	89.836495	0.011131	28
29	42.509410	3831.637843	0.000261	0.023524	90.136227	0.011094	29
30	48.377089	4373.269783	0.000229	0.020671	90.399605	0.011062	30

14.00% NOMINAL RATE

Annual Compounding

EFFECTIVE (ANNUAL) RATE = 14.00%

YEAR	Future Value of 1 FV1	Future Value of 1 per Period FV1/P	Sinking Fund Factor SFF	Present Value of 1 PV1	Present Value of 1 per Period PV1/P	Principal Recovery Factor PRF	YEAR
1	1.140000	1.000000	1.000000	0.877193	0.877193	1.140000	1
2	1.299600	2.140000	0.467290	0.769468	1.646661	0.607290	2
3	1.481544	3.439600	0.290731	0.674972	2.321632	0.430731	3
4	1.688960	4.921144	0.203205	0.592080	2.913712	0.343205	4
5	1.925415	6.610104	0.151284	0.519369	3.433081	0.291284	5
6	2.194973	8.535519	0.117157	0.455587	3.888668	0.257157	6
7	2.502269	10.730491	0.093192	0.399637	4.288305	0.233192	7
8	2.852586	13.232760	0.075570	0.350559	4.638864	0.215570	8
9	3.251949	16.085347	0.062168	0.307508	4.946372	0.202168	9
10	3.707221	19.337295	0.051714	0.269744	5.216116	0.191714	10
11	4.226232	23.044516	0.043394	0.236617	5.452733	0.183394	11
12	4.817905	27.270749	0.036669	0.207559	5.660292	0.176669	12
13	5.492411	32.088654	0.031164	0.182069	5.842362	0.171164	13
14	6.261349	37.581065	0.026609	0.159710	6.002072	0.166609	14
15	7.137938	43.842414	0.022809	0.140096	6.142168	0.162809	15
16	8.137249	50.980352	0.019615	0.122892	6.265060	0.159615	16
17	9.276464	59.117601	0.016915	0.107800	6.372859	0.156915	17
18	10.575169	68.394066	0.014621	0.094561	6.467420	0.154621	18
19	12.055693	78.969235	0.012663	0.082948	6.550369	0.152663	19
20	13.743490	91.024928	0.010986	0.072762	6.623131	0.150986	20

Monthly Compounding

EFFECTIVE (MONTHLY) RATE = 1.166667%

MONTH	MFV1	MFV1/P	MSSF	MPV1	MPV1/P	MPRF	MONTH
1	1.011667	1.000000	1.000000	0.988468	0.988468	1.011667	1
2	1.023469	2.011667	0.497100	0.977069	1.965537	0.508767	2
3	1.035410	3.035136	0.329475	0.965801	2.931338	0.341141	3
4	1.047490	4.070546	0.245667	0.954663	3.886001	0.257334	4
5	1.059710	5.118036	0.195387	0.943654	4.829655	0.207054	5
6	1.072074	6.177746	0.161871	0.932772	5.762427	0.173538	6
7	1.084581	7.249820	0.137934	0.922015	6.684442	0.149601	7

8	1.097235	8.334401	0.119985	0.911382	7.595824	0.131651	8
9	1.110036	9.431636	0.106026	0.900872	8.496696	0.117693	9
10	1.122986	10.541672	0.094862	0.890483	9.387178	0.106528	10
11	1.136088	11.664658	0.085729	0.880214	10.267392	0.097396	11
YEAR							*YEAR*
1	1.149342	12.800745	0.078120	0.870063	11.137455	0.089787	1
2	1.320987	27.513180	0.036346	0.757010	20.827743	0.048013	2
3	1.518266	44.422800	0.022511	0.658646	29.258904	0.034178	3
4	1.745007	63.857736	0.015660	0.573064	36.594546	0.027326	4
5	2.005610	86.195125	0.011602	0.498601	42.977016	0.023268	5
6	2.305132	111.868425	0.008939	0.433815	48.530168	0.020606	6
7	2.649385	141.375828	0.007073	0.377446	53.361760	0.018740	7
8	3.045049	175.289927	0.005705	0.328402	57.565549	0.017372	8
9	3.499803	214.268826	0.004667	0.285730	61.223111	0.016334	9
10	4.022471	259.068912	0.003860	0.248603	64.405420	0.015527	10
11	4.623195	310.559534	0.003220	0.216301	67.174230	0.014887	11
12	5.313632	369.739871	0.002705	0.188195	69.583269	0.014371	12
13	6.107180	437.758319	0.002284	0.163742	71.679284	0.013951	13
14	7.019239	515.934780	0.001938	0.142466	73.502950	0.013605	14
15	8.067507	605.786272	0.001651	0.123954	75.089654	0.013317	15
16	9.272324	709.056369	0.001410	0.107848	76.470187	0.013077	16
17	10.657072	827.749031	0.001208	0.093834	77.671337	0.012875	17
18	12.248621	964.167496	0.001037	0.081642	78.716413	0.012704	18
19	14.077855	1120.958972	0.000892	0.071034	79.625696	0.012559	19
20	16.180270	1301.166005	0.000769	0.061804	80.416829	0.012435	20
21	18.596664	1508.285522	0.000663	0.053773	81.105164	0.012330	21
22	21.373928	1746.336688	0.000573	0.046786	81.704060	0.012239	22
23	24.565954	2019.938898	0.000495	0.040707	82.225136	0.012162	23
24	28.234683	2334.401417	0.000428	0.035417	82.678506	0.012095	24
25	32.451308	2695.826407	0.000371	0.030815	83.072966	0.012038	25
26	37.297652	3111.227338	0.000321	0.026811	83.416171	0.011988	26
27	42.867759	3588.665088	0.000279	0.023328	83.714781	0.011945	27
28	49.269718	4137.404359	0.000242	0.020296	83.974591	0.011908	28
29	56.627757	4768.093467	0.000210	0.017659	84.200641	0.011876	29
30	65.084661	5492.970967	0.000182	0.015365	84.397320	0.011849	30

	Future Value of 1	Future Value of 1 per Period	Sinking Fund Factor	Present Value of 1	Present Value of 1 per Period	Principal Recovery Factor	

Annual Compounding

EFFECTIVE (ANNUAL) RATE = 15.00%

YEAR	FV1	FV1/P	SFF	PV1	PV1/P	PRF	YEAR
1	1.150000	1.000000	1.000000	0.869565	0.869565	1.150000	1
2	1.322500	2.150000	0.465116	0.756144	1.625709	0.615116	2
3	1.520875	3.472500	0.287977	0.657516	2.283225	0.437977	3
4	1.749006	4.993375	0.200265	0.571753	2.854978	0.350265	4
5	2.011357	6.742381	0.148316	0.497177	3.352155	0.298316	5
6	2.313061	8.753738	0.114237	0.432328	3.784483	0.264237	6
7	2.660020	11.066799	0.090360	0.375937	4.160420	0.240360	7
8	3.059023	13.726819	0.072850	0.326902	4.487322	0.222850	8
9	3.517876	16.785842	0.059574	0.284262	4.771584	0.209574	9
10	4.045558	20.303718	0.049252	0.247185	5.018769	0.199252	10
11	4.652391	24.349276	0.041069	0.214943	5.233712	0.191069	11
12	5.350250	29.001667	0.034481	0.186907	5.420619	0.184481	12
13	6.152788	34.351917	0.029110	0.162528	5.583147	0.179110	13
14	7.075706	40.504705	0.024688	0.141329	5.724476	0.174688	14
15	8.137062	47.580411	0.021017	0.122894	5.847370	0.171017	15
16	9.357621	55.717472	0.017948	0.106865	5.954235	0.167948	16
17	10.761264	65.075093	0.015367	0.092926	6.047161	0.165367	17
18	12.375454	75.836357	0.013186	0.080805	6.127966	0.163186	18
19	14.231772	88.211811	0.011336	0.070265	6.198231	0.161336	19
20	16.366537	102.443583	0.009761	0.061100	6.259331	0.159761	20

Monthly Compounding

EFFECTIVE (MONTHLY) RATE = 1.250000%

MONTH	MFV1	MFV1/P	MSSF	MPV1	MPV1/P	MPRF	MONTH
1	1.012500	1.000000	1.000000	0.987654	0.987654	1.012500	1
2	1.025156	2.012500	0.496894	0.975461	1.963115	0.509394	2
3	1.037971	3.037656	0.329201	0.963418	2.926534	0.341701	3
4	1.050945	4.075627	0.245361	0.951524	3.878058	0.257861	4
5	1.064082	5.126572	0.195062	0.939777	4.817835	0.207562	5
6	1.077383	6.190654	0.161534	0.928175	5.746010	0.174034	6
7	1.090850	7.268038	0.137589	0.916716	6.662726	0.150089	7

8	1.104486	8.358888	0.119633	0.905398	7.568124	0.132133	8
9	1.118292	9.463374	0.105671	0.894221	8.462345	0.118171	9
10	1.132271	10.581666	0.094503	0.883181	9.345526	0.107003	10
11	1.146424	11.713937	0.085368	0.872277	10.217803	0.097868	11
YEAR							*YEAR*
1	1.160755	12.860361	0.077758	0.861509	11.079312	0.090258	1
2	1.347351	27.788084	0.035987	0.742197	20.624235	0.048487	2
3	1.563944	45.115505	0.022165	0.639409	28.847267	0.034665	3
4	1.815355	65.228388	0.015331	0.550856	35.931481	0.027831	4
5	2.107181	88.574508	0.011290	0.474568	42.034592	0.023790	5
6	2.445920	115.673621	0.008645	0.408844	47.292474	0.021145	6
7	2.839113	147.129040	0.006797	0.352223	51.822185	0.019297	7
8	3.295513	183.641059	0.005445	0.303443	55.724570	0.017945	8
9	3.825282	226.022551	0.004424	0.261419	59.086509	0.016924	9
10	4.440213	275.217058	0.003633	0.225214	61.982847	0.016133	10
11	5.153998	332.319805	0.003009	0.194024	64.478068	0.015509	11
12	5.982526	398.602077	0.002509	0.167153	66.627722	0.015009	12
13	6.944244	475.539523	0.002103	0.144004	68.479668	0.014603	13
14	8.060563	564.845011	0.001770	0.124061	70.075134	0.014270	14
15	9.356334	668.506759	0.001496	0.106879	71.449643	0.013996	15
16	10.860408	788.832603	0.001268	0.092078	72.633794	0.013768	16
17	12.606267	928.501369	0.001077	0.079326	73.653950	0.013577	17
18	14.632781	1090.622520	0.000917	0.068340	74.532823	0.013417	18
19	16.985067	1278.805378	0.000782	0.058875	75.289980	0.013282	19
20	19.715494	1497.239481	0.000668	0.050722	75.942278	0.013168	20
21	22.884848	1750.787854	0.000571	0.043697	76.504237	0.013071	21
22	26.563691	2045.095272	0.000489	0.037645	76.988370	0.012989	22
23	30.833924	2386.713938	0.000419	0.032432	77.405455	0.012919	23
24	35.790617	2783.249347	0.000359	0.027940	77.764777	0.012859	24
25	41.544120	3243.529615	0.000308	0.024071	78.074336	0.012808	25
26	48.222525	3777.802015	0.000265	0.020737	78.341024	0.012765	26
27	55.974514	4397.961118	0.000227	0.017865	78.570778	0.012727	27
28	64.972670	5117.813598	0.000195	0.015391	78.768713	0.012695	28
29	75.417320	5953.385616	0.000168	0.013260	78.939236	0.012668	29
30	87.540995	6923.279611	0.000144	0.011423	79.086142	0.012644	30

20.00% NOMINAL RATE

Annual Compounding

EFFECTIVE (ANNUAL) RATE = 20.00%

YEAR	Future Value of 1 FV1	Future Value of 1 per Period FV1/P	Sinking Fund Factor SFF	Present Value of 1 PV1	Present Value of 1 per Period PV1/P	Principal Recovery Factor PRF	YEAR
1	1.200000	1.000000	1.000000	0.833333	0.833333	1.200000	1
2	1.440000	2.200000	0.454545	0.694444	1.527778	0.654545	2
3	1.728000	0.640000	0.274725	0.578704	2.106481	0.474725	3
4	2.073600	5.368000	0.186289	0.482253	2.588735	0.386289	4
5	2.488320	7.441600	0.134380	0.401878	2.990612	0.334380	5
6	2.985984	9.929920	0.100706	0.334898	3.325510	0.300706	6
7	3.583181	12.915904	0.077424	0.279082	3.604592	0.277424	7
8	4.299817	16.499085	0.060609	0.232568	3.837160	0.260609	8
9	5.159780	20.798902	0.048079	0.193807	4.030967	0.248079	9
10	6.191736	25.958682	0.038523	0.161506	4.192472	0.238523	10
11	7.430084	32.150419	0.031104	0.134588	4.327060	0.231104	11
12	8.916100	39.580502	0.025265	0.112157	4.439217	0.225265	12
13	10.699321	48.496603	0.020620	0.093464	4.532681	0.220620	13
14	12.839185	59.195923	0.016893	0.077887	4.610567	0.216893	14
15	15.407022	72.035108	0.013882	0.064905	4.675473	0.213882	15
16	18.488426	87.442129	0.011436	0.054088	4.729561	0.211436	16
17	22.186111	105.930555	0.009440	0.045073	4.774634	0.209440	17
18	26.623333	128.116666	0.007805	0.037561	4.812195	0.207805	18
19	31.948000	154.740000	0.006462	0.031301	4.843496	0.206462	19
20	38.337600	186.688000	0.005357	0.026084	4.869580	0.205357	20

Monthly Compounding

EFFECTIVE (MONTHLY) RATE = 1.666667%

MONTH	MFV1	MFV1/P	MSSF	MPV1	MPV1/P	MPRF	MONTH
1	1.016667	1.000000	1.000000	0.983607	0.983607	1.016667	1
2	1.033611	2.016667	0.495868	0.967482	1.951088	0.512534	2

3	1.050838	3.050278	0.327839	0.951622	2.902710	0.344506	3
4	1.068352	4.101116	0.243836	0.936021	3.838731	0.260503	4
5	1.086158	5.169468	0.193444	0.920677	4.759408	0.210110	5
6	1.104260	6.255625	0.159856	0.905583	5.664991	0.176523	6
7	1.122665	7.359886	0.135872	0.890738	6.555729	0.152538	7
8	1.141376	8.482551	0.117889	0.876136	7.431865	0.134556	8
9	1.160399	9.623926	0.103908	0.861773	8.293637	0.120574	9
10	1.179739	10.784325	0.092727	0.847645	9.141283	0.109394	10
11	1.199401	11.964064	0.083584	0.833749	9.975032	0.100250	11
YEAR							*YEAR*
1	1.219391	13.163465	0.075968	0.820081	10.795113	0.092635	1
2	1.486915	29.214877	0.034229	0.672534	19.647986	0.050896	2
3	1.813130	48.787826	0.020497	0.551532	26.908062	0.037164	3
4	2.210915	72.654905	0.013764	0.452301	32.861916	0.030430	4
5	2.695970	101.758208	0.009827	0.370924	37.744561	0.026494	5
6	3.287442	137.246517	0.007286	0.304188	41.748727	0.023953	6
7	4.008677	180.520645	0.005540	0.249459	45.032470	0.022206	7
8	4.888145	233.288730	0.004287	0.204577	47.725406	0.020953	8
9	5.960561	297.633662	0.003360	0.167769	49.933833	0.020027	9
10	7.268255	376.095300	0.002659	0.137585	51.744924	0.019326	10
11	8.862845	471.770720	0.002120	0.112831	53.230165	0.018786	11
12	10.807275	588.436476	0.001699	0.092530	54.448184	0.018366	12
13	13.178294	730.697658	0.001369	0.075882	55.447059	0.018035	13
14	16.069495	904.169675	0.001106	0.062230	56.266217	0.017773	14
15	19.594998	1115.699905	0.000896	0.051033	56.937994	0.017563	15
16	23.893966	1373.637983	0.000728	0.041852	57.488906	0.017395	16
17	29.136090	1688.165376	0.000592	0.034322	57.940698	0.017259	17
18	35.528288	2071.697274	0.000483	0.028147	58.311205	0.017149	18
19	43.322878	2539.372652	0.000394	0.023082	58.615050	0.017060	19
20	52.827531	3109.651838	0.000322	0.018930	58.864229	0.016988	20

Annual Compounding

EFFECTIVE (ANNUAL) RATE = 25.00%

YEAR	FV1 (Future Value of 1)	FV1/P (Future Value of 1 per Period)	SFF (Sinking Fund Factor)	PV1 (Present Value of 1)	PV1/P (Present Value of 1 per Period)	PRF (Principal Recovery Factor)	YEAR
1	0.250000	1.000000	1.000000	0.800000	0.800000	1.250000	1
2	1.562500	2.250000	0.444444	0.640000	1.440000	0.694444	2
3	1.953125	3.812500	0.262295	0.512000	1.952000	0.512295	3
4	2.441406	5.765625	0.173442	0.409600	2.361600	0.423442	4
5	3.051758	8.207031	0.121847	0.327680	2.689280	0.371847	5
6	3.814697	11.258789	0.088819	0.262144	2.951424	0.338819	6
7	4.768372	15.073486	0.066342	0.209715	3.161139	0.316342	7
8	5.960464	19.841858	0.050399	0.167772	3.328911	0.300399	8
9	7.450581	25.802322	0.038756	0.134218	3.463129	0.288756	9
10	9.313226	33.252903	0.030073	0.107374	3.570503	0.280073	10
11	11.641532	42.566129	0.023493	0.085899	3.656403	0.273493	11
12	14.551915	54.207661	0.018448	0.068719	3.725122	0.268448	12
13	18.189894	68.759576	0.014543	0.054976	3.780098	0.264543	13
14	22.737368	86.949470	0.011501	0.043980	3.824078	0.261501	14
15	28.421709	109.686838	0.009117	0.035184	3.859263	0.259117	15
16	35.527137	138.108547	0.007241	0.028147	3.887410	0.257241	16
17	44.408921	173.635684	0.005759	0.022518	3.909928	0.255759	17
18	55.511151	218.044605	0.004586	0.018014	3.927942	0.254586	18
19	69.388939	273.555756	0.003656	0.014412	3.942354	0.253656	19
20	86.736174	342.944695	0.002916	0.011529	3.953883	0.252916	20

Monthly Compounding

EFFECTIVE (MONTHLY) RATE = 2.083333%

MONTH	MFV1	MFV1/P	MSSF	MPV1	MPV1/P	MPRF	MONTH
1	1.020833	1.000000	1.000000	0.979592	0.979592	1.020833	1
2	1.042101	2.020833	0.494845	0.959600	1.939192	0.515679	2
3	1.063811	3.062934	0.326484	0.940016	2.879208	0.347318	3

4	1.085974	4.126745	0.242322	0.920832	3.800041	0.263155	4
5	1.108598	5.212719	0.191838	0.902040	4.702081	0.212672	5
6	1.131694	6.321317	0.158195	0.883631	5.585712	0.179028	6
7	1.155271	7.453011	0.134174	0.865598	6.451310	0.155007	7
8	1.179339	8.608283	0.116167	0.847932	7.299242	0.137001	8
9	1.203909	9.787622	0.102170	0.830628	8.129870	0.123003	9
10	1.228990	10.991531	0.090979	0.813676	8.943546	0.111812	10
11	1.254594	12.220521	0.081830	0.797070	9.740616	0.102663	11
YEAR							*YEAR*
1	1.280732	13.475115	0.074211	0.780804	10.521420	0.095044	1
2	1.640273	30.733120	0.032538	0.609654	18.736585	0.053372	2
3	2.100750	52.835991	0.018926	0.476021	25.151016	0.039760	3
4	2.690497	81.143837	0.012324	0.371679	30.159427	0.033157	4
5	3.445804	117.398588	0.008518	0.290208	34.070014	0.029351	5
6	4.413150	163.831191	0.006104	0.226596	37.123415	0.026937	6
7	5.652060	223.298892	0.004478	0.176927	39.507522	0.025312	7
8	7.238772	229.461053	0.003339	0.138145	41.369041	0.024173	8
9	9.270924	397.004337	0.002519	0.107864	42.822522	0.023352	9
10	11.873565	521.931099	0.001916	0.084221	43.957406	0.022749	10
11	15.206849	681.928746	0.001466	0.065760	44.843528	0.022300	11
12	19.475891	886.842783	0.001128	0.051346	45.535414	0.021961	12
13	24.943389	1149.282656	0.000870	0.040091	46.075642	0.021703	13
14	31.945785	1485.397684	0.000673	0.031303	46.497454	0.021507	14
15	40.913975	1915.870809	0.000522	0.024442	46.826807	0.021355	15
16	52.399819	2467.191327	0.000405	0.019084	47.083966	0.021239	16
17	67.110102	3173.284913	0.000315	0.014901	47.284757	0.021148	17
18	85.950026	4077.601254	0.000245	0.011635	47.441536	0.021079	18
19	110.078911	5235.787733	0.000191	0.009084	47.563949	0.021024	19
20	140.981536	6719.113709	0.000149	0.007093	47.659530	0.020982	20

30.00% NOMINAL RATE

Annual Compounding

EFFECTIVE (ANNUAL) RATE = 30.00%

	Future Value of 1	Future Value of 1 per Period	Sinking Fund Factor	Present Value of 1	Present Value of 1 per Period	Principal Recovery Factor	
YEAR	FV1	FV1/P	SFF	PV1	PV1/P	PRF	YEAR
1	1.300000	1.000000	1.000000	0.769231	0.769231	1.300000	1
2	1.690000	2.300000	0.434783	0.591716	1.360947	0.734783	2
3	2.197000	3.990000	0.250627	0.455166	1.816113	0.550627	3
4	2.856100	6.187000	0.161629	0.350128	2.166241	0.461629	4
5	3.712930	9.043100	0.110582	0.269329	2.435570	0.410582	5
6	4.826809	12.756030	0.078394	0.207176	2.642746	0.378394	6
7	6.274852	17.582839	0.056874	0.159366	2.802112	0.356874	7
8	8.157307	23.857691	0.041915	0.122589	2.924702	0.341915	8
9	10.604499	32.014998	0.031235	0.094300	3.019001	0.331235	9
10	13.785849	42.619497	0.023463	0.072538	3.091539	0.323463	10
11	17.921604	56.405346	0.017729	0.055799	3.147338	0.317729	11
12	23.298085	74.326950	0.013454	0.042922	3.180260	0.313454	12
13	30.287511	97.625036	0.010243	0.033017	3.223277	0.310243	13
14	39.373764	127.912546	0.007818	0.025398	3.248675	0.307818	14
15	51.185893	167.286310	0.005978	0.019537	3.268211	0.305978	15
16	66.541661	218.472203	0.004577	0.015028	3.283239	0.304577	16
17	86.504159	285.013864	0.003509	0.011560	3.294800	0.303509	17
18	112.455407	371.518023	0.002692	0.008892	3.303692	0.302692	18
19	146.192029	483.973430	0.002066	0.006840	3.310532	0.302066	19
20	190.049638	630.165459	0.001587	0.005262	3.315794	0.301587	20

Monthly Compounding

EFFECTIVE (MONTHLY) RATE = 2.500000%

MONTH	MFV1	MFV1/P	MSSF	MPV1	MPV1/P	MPRF	MONTH
1	1.025000	1.000000	1.000000	0.975610	0.975610	1.025000	1
2	1.050625	2.025000	0.493827	0.951814	1.927424	0.518827	2

3	1.076891	3.075625	0.325137	0.928599	2.856024	0.350137	3
4	1.103813	4.152516	0.240818	0.905951	3.761974	0.265818	4
5	1.131408	5.256329	0.190247	0.883854	4.645828	0.215247	5
6	1.159693	6.387737	0.156550	0.862297	5.508125	0.181550	6
7	1.188686	7.547430	0.132495	0.841265	6.349391	0.157495	7
8	1.218403	8.736116	0.114467	0.820747	7.170137	0.139467	8
9	1.248863	9.954519	0.100457	0.800728	7.970866	0.125457	9
10	1.280085	11.203382	0.089259	0.781198	8.752064	0.114259	10
11	1.312087	12.483466	0.080106	0.762145	9.514209	0.105106	11
YEAR							***YEAR***
1	1.344889	13.795553	0.072487	0.743556	10.257765	0.097487	1
2	1.808726	32.349038	0.030913	0.552875	17.884986	0.055913	2
3	2.432535	57.301413	0.017452	0.411094	23.556251	0.042452	3
4	3.271490	90.859582	0.011006	0.305671	27.773154	0.036006	4
5	4.399790	135.991590	0.007353	0.227284	30.908656	0.032353	5
6	5.917228	196.689122	0.005084	0.168998	33.240078	0.030084	6
7	7.958014	278.320556	0.003593	0.125659	34.973620	0.028593	7
8	10.702644	388.105758	0.002577	0.093435	36.262606	0.027577	8
9	14.393866	535.754649	0.001867	0.069474	37.221039	0.026867	9
10	19.358150	734.325993	0.001362	0.051658	37.933687	0.026362	10
11	26.034559	1001.382375	0.000999	0.038410	38.463581	0.025999	11
12	35.013588	1360.543518	0.000735	0.028560	38.857586	0.025735	12
13	47.089383	1843.575325	0.000542	0.021236	39.150552	0.025542	13
14	63.329985	2493.199404	0.000401	0.015790	39.368388	0.025401	14
15	85.171789	3366.871568	0.000297	0.011741	39.530361	0.025297	15
16	114.546587	4541.863497	0.000220	0.008730	39.650797	0.025220	15
17	154.052425	6122.097012	0.000163	0.006491	39.740348	0.025163	17
18	207.183385	8247.335405	0.000121	0.004827	39.806934	0.025121	18
19	278.638619	11105.544769	0.000090	0.003589	39.856445	0.025090	19
20	274.747965	14949.518599	0.000067	0.002669	39.893259	0.025067	20

40.00% NOMINAL RATE

Annual Compounding

	Future Value of 1	Future Value of 1 per Period	Sinking Fund Factor	Present Value of 1	Present Value of 1 per Period	Principal Recovery Factor	
			EFFECTIVE (ANNUAL) RATE = 40.00%				
YEAR	FV1	FV1/P	SFF	PV1	PV1/P	PRF	YEAR
1	1.400000	1.000000	1.000000	0.714286	0.714286	1.400000	1
2	1.960000	2.400000	0.416667	0.510204	1.224490	0.816667	2
3	2.744000	4.360000	0.229358	0.364431	1.588921	0.629358	3
4	3.841600	7.104000	0.140766	0.260308	1.849229	0.540766	4
5	5.378240	10.945600	0.091361	0.185934	2.035164	0.491361	5
6	7.529536	16.323840	0.061260	0.132810	2.167974	0.461260	6
7	10.541350	23.853376	0.041923	0.094865	2.262839	0.441923	7
8	14.757891	34.394726	0.029074	0.067760	2.330599	0.429074	8
9	20.661047	49.152617	0.020345	0.048400	2.378999	0.420345	9
10	28.925465	69.813664	0.014324	0.034572	2.413571	0.414324	10
11	40.495652	98.739129	0.010128	0.024694	2.438265	0.410128	11
12	56.693912	139.234781	0.007182	0.017639	2.455904	0.407182	12
13	79.371477	195.928693	0.005104	0.012599	2.468503	0.405104	13
14	111.120068	275.300171	0.003632	0.008999	2.477502	0.403632	14
15	155.568096	386.420239	0.002588	0.006428	2.483930	0.402588	15
16	217.795334	541.988334	0.001845	0.004591	2.488521	0.401845	16
17	304.913467	759.783668	0.001316	0.003280	2.491801	0.401316	17
18	426.878854	1064.697136	0.000939	0.002343	2.494144	0.400939	18
19	597.630396	1491.575990	0.000670	0.001673	2.495817	0.400670	19
20	836.682554	2089.206386	0.000479	0.001195	2.497012	0.400479	20

Monthly Compounding

			EFFECTIVE (MONTHLY) RATE = 3.333333%				
MONTH	MFV1	MFV1/P	MSSF	MPV1	MPV1/P	MPRF	MONTH
1	1.033333	1.000000	1.000000	0.967742	0.967742	1.033333	1
2	1.067778	2.033333	0.491803	0.936524	1.904266	0.525137	2

3	1.103370	3.101111	0.322465	0.906314	2.810580	0.355798	3
4	1.140149	4.204481	0.237841	0.877078	3.687658	0.271175	4
5	1.178154	5.344631	0.187104	0.848785	4.536444	0.220437	5
6	1.217426	6.522785	0.153309	0.821405	5.357849	0.186642	6
7	1.258007	7.740211	0.129195	0.794908	6.152757	0.162529	7
8	1.299941	8.998218	0.111133	0.769266	6.922023	0.144466	8
9	1.343272	10.298159	0.097105	0.744451	7.666474	0.130438	9
10	1.388048	11.641431	0.085900	0.720436	8.386910	0.119233	10
11	1.434316	13.029479	0.076749	0.697196	9.084106	0.110082	11
YEAR							*YEAR*
1	1.482126	14.463795	0.069138	0.674706	9.758813	0.102471	1
2	2.196699	35.900968	0.027854	0.455229	16.343144	0.061188	2
3	3.255786	67.673570	0.014777	0.307146	20.785634	0.048110	3
4	4.825486	114.764586	0.008713	0.207233	23.783010	0.042047	4
5	7.151981	184.559427	0.005418	0.139821	25.805358	0.038752	5
6	10.600140	288.004211	0.003472	0.094338	27.169849	0.036806	6
7	15.710749	441.322465	0.002266	0.063651	28.090479	0.035599	7
8	23.285317	668.559511	0.001496	0.042946	28.711634	0.034829	8
9	34.511785	1005.353555	0.000995	0.028976	29.130732	0.034328	9
10	51.150831	1504.524930	0.000665	0.019550	29.413499	0.033998	10
11	75.812002	2244.360048	0.000446	0.013191	29.604284	0.033779	11
12	112.362976	3340.889274	0.000299	0.008900	29.733008	0.033633	12
13	166.536143	4966.084287	0.000201	0.006005	29.819859	0.033535	13
14	246.827629	7374.828867	0.000136	0.004051	29.878458	0.033469	14
15	365.829767	10944.893015	0.000091	0.002734	29.917995	0.033425	15
16	542.205989	16236.179658	0.000062	0.001844	29.944670	0.033395	16
17	803.617859	24078.535757	0.000042	0.001244	29.962669	0.033375	17
18	1191.063316	35701.899472	0.000028	0.000840	29.974812	0.033361	18
19	1765.306491	52929.194733	0.000019	0.000566	29.983006	0.033352	19
20	2616.407513	78462.225385	0.000013	0.000382	29.988534	0.033346	20

50.00% NOMINAL RATE

Annual Compounding

EFFECTIVE (ANNUAL) RATE = 50.00%

YEAR	Future Value of 1 FV 1	Future Value of 1 per Period FV1/P	Sinking Fund Factor SFF	Present Value of 1 PV1	Present Value of 1 per Period PV1/P	Principal Recovery Factor PRF	YEAR
1	1.50000	1.00000	1.000000	0.666667	0.666667	1.500000	1
2	2.25000	2.50000	0.400000	0.444444	1.111111	0.900000	2
3	3.37500	4.75000	0.210526	0.296296	1.407407	0.710526	3
4	5.06250	8.12500	0.123077	0.197531	1.604938	0.623077	4
5	7.59375	13.18750	0.075829	0.131687	1.736626	0.575829	5
6	11.39063	20.78125	0.048120	0.087791	1.824417	0.548120	6
7	17.08594	32.17188	0.031083	0.058528	1.882945	0.531083	7
8	25.62891	49.25781	0.020301	0.039018	1.921963	0.520301	8
9	38.44336	74.88672	0.013354	0.026012	1.947975	0.513354	9
10	57.66504	113.33008	0.008824	0.017342	1.965317	0.508824	10
11	86.49756	170.99512	0.005848	0.011561	1.976878	0.505848	11
12	129.74634	257.49268	0.003884	0.007707	1.984585	0.503884	12
13	194.61951	387.23901	0.002582	0.005138	1.989724	0.502582	13
14	291.92926	581.85852	0.001719	0.003425	1.993149	0.501719	14
15	437.89389	873.78778	0.001144	0.002284	1.995433	0.501144	15
16	656.84084	1311.68167	0.000762	0.001522	1.996955	0.500762	16
17	985.26125	1968.52251	0.000508	0.001015	1.997970	0.500508	17
18	1417.89188	2953.78376	0.000339	0.000677	1.998647	0.500339	18
19	2216.83782	4431.67564	0.000226	0.000451	1.999098	0.500226	19
20	3325.25676	6648.51346	0.000150	0.000301	1.999399	0.500150	20

Monthly Compounding

EFFECTIVE (MONTHLY) RATE = 4.166667%

MONTH	MFV1	MFV1/P	MSSF	MPV 1	MPV1/P	MPRF	MONTH
1	1.04167	1.00000	1.000000	0.960000	0.960000	1.041667	1
2	1.08507	2.04167	0.489796	0.921600	1.881600	0.531463	2

3	1.13028	3.12674	0.319822	0.884736	2.766336	0.361489	3
4	1.17738	4.25702	0.234906	0.849347	3.615683	0.276573	4
5	1.22643	5.43439	0.184013	0.815373	4.431055	0.225680	5
6	1.27753	6.66083	0.150132	0.782758	5.213813	0.191798	6
7	1.33076	7.93836	0.125971	0.751447	5.965261	0.167637	7
8	1.38621	9.26912	0.107885	0.721390	6.686650	0.149552	8
9	1.44397	10.65534	0.093850	0.692534	7.379184	0.135516	9
10	1.50414	12.09931	0.082649	0.664833	8.044017	0.124316	10
11	1.56681	13.60345	0.073511	0.638239	8.682256	0.115177	11
YEAR							*YEAR*
1	1.63209	15.17026	0.065918	0.612710	9.294966	0.107585	1
2	2.66373	39.92955	0.025044	0.375413	14.990082	0.066711	2
3	4.34746	80.33904	0.012447	0.230019	18.479535	0.054114	3
4	7.09546	146.29114	0.006836	0.140935	20.617557	0.048502	4
5	11.58047	253.93117	0.003938	0.086352	21.927544	0.045605	5
6	18.90041	429.60984	0.002328	0.052909	22.730186	0.043994	6
7	30.84725	716.33395	0.001396	0.032418	23.221973	0.043063	7
8	50.34561	1184.29470	0.000844	0.019863	23.523295	0.042511	8
9	82.16878	1948.05069	0.000513	0.012170	23.707918	0.042180	9
10	134.10718	3194.57236	0.000313	0.007457	23.821039	0.041980	10
11	218.87554	5229.01306	0.000191	0.004569	23.890349	0.041858	11
12	357.22549	8549.41179	0.000117	0.002799	23.932816	0.041784	12
13	583.02563	13968.61509	0.000072	0.001715	23.958835	0.041738	13
14	951.55271	22813.26498	0.000044	0.001051	23.974778	0.041711	14
15	1553.02359	37248.56618	0.000027	0.000644	23.984546	0.041694	15
16	2534.68069	60808.33658	0.000016	0.000395	23.990531	0.041683	16
17	4136.83748	99260.09961	0.000010	0.000242	23.994198	0.041677	17
18	6751.70819	162016.99645	0.000006	0.000148	23.996445	0.041673	18
19	11019.42332	264442.15957	0.000004	0.000091	23.997822	0.041670	19
20	17984.73614	431609.66734	0.000002	0.000056	23.998666	0.041669	20

APPENDIX C
GLOSSARY

Many real estate terms use the following key words. When one of these key words appears in a term in the glossary, look up the key word first. If two or more of these key words appear in a term, the term is defined under one of them

cost, costs	**mortgage**
capital	**property**
deed	**rent**
depreciation	**tax**
equity	**tenancy**
lease	**title**
lien	**utility**
listing	**value**
market	**zoning**

Abandonment. Vacating or giving up use of, or rights in, real property. Also the vacating by a tenant of premises before a lease expires without consent of the landlord.

Absolute Fee Simple. *See* Fee.

Abstract of Title. A digest of conveyances, transfers, wills, and other legal proceedings pertinent to title of a property, such as liens, charges, or encumbrances.

Accelerated Cost Recovery System (ACRS).

Acceleration Clause. A provision in a trust deed, mortgage loan contract, or land contract giving the lender the right to declare the entire remaining balance due and payable immediately because of a violation of one of the covenants in the contract. Also known as Alienation Clause.

Acceptance. Receiving and agreeing to the terms of a deed.

Access. The approach or way to a property or the means of entrance into or out of the property.

Accessibility. Relative cost (in time and money) of getting to and from a property. A property that is easy to get to is regarded as having good accessibility (i.e., convenience of location).

Accountability. Responsibility for money or property, including the maintaining of records concerning such money or property.

Accretion. Accumulation in an owner's land area due to water action (e.g., a stream).

Accrued Expense. A charge owed and not yet paid, such as interest or property taxes.

Acknowledgment. A formal declaration by a person executing an instrument that such act is intended as a free and voluntary act made before a duly authorized officer.

Acre. A measure of area containing 43,560 square feet.

Actual Eviction. *See* Eviction.

Actual Knowledge or Notice. A claim of interest in, or ownership of, realty imputed as known to all the world because the claimant was or is in possession of the property.

Adjustable Rate Mortgage (ARM). Loan arrangement in which the interest rate may be changed periodically.

Ad Valorem. According to value; the basis of real estate taxation.

Adjusted Cost Basis. Book value in an accounting sense. Value or cost of an asset for income tax purposes. The tax basis of property after taking account of time and change involved in owning and managing of the property. Also referred to as Tax Basis.

Adjusted Sale Price. The full sale or contract price less selling expenses and less "fixing-up" expenses.

Administrative Process. A series of five steps to guide action: (1) make decision to accomplish an objective, (2) organize resources, (3) exert leadership, (4) manage operations, and (5) reevaluate periodically.

Administrator. A person appointed by a probate court to settle the estate of a deceased person.

Advance Commitment. An agreement to purchase or make a government-underwritten mortgage on a property before (in advance of) construction.

Adverse Land Use. A land use activity that is incompatible with, or has a negative effect on, nearby properties. For example, a used-car lot in a neighborhood of one-family residences.

Adverse Possession. The right of an occupant of land to acquire title against the real owner, under color of title, where possession has been actual, continuous, hostile, visible, and distinct for the statutory period.

Advertising. Promotional material and efforts intended to place the advertiser's name and business before the public.

Affidavit. A written statement or declaration sworn to before a public office holder with authority to administer an oath or affirmation.

Of Heirship. An affidavit by a person or persons claiming property through inheritance.

Of Title. An affidavit by the person or persons purporting to be the owners.

After-Tax Cash Flow to Equity. Net operating income less debt service and less tax liability on income from the investment, taken period by period.

After-Tax Equity Rate of Return. The annual yield rate earned or expected on an equity investment with taxes on income from the investment taken into account. *See* Internal Rate of Return. Also referred to as After-Tax Equity Yield Rate.

After-Tax Equity Reversion. The actual or estimated sale price of a property less transaction costs, less outstanding debt, and less disposition taxes (primarily capital gains taxes).

Agency. In real estate, a fiduciary relationship in which one party (the agent-broker) acts as the representative of the other (the principal-owner) in negotiating the sale, purchase, leasing, or exchanging of property. Also, the relationship between a broker-principal and a salesperson-agent.

Law of. The legal rights, duties, and liabilities of principal, agent, and third parties as a result of the relationships between them.

Agent. A person who represents another (a principal) by the latter's authority.

Aggravation Costs. Driver or passenger irritation and annoyance during a linkage trip caused by delay, congestion, bumping and shoving, heat, cold, and so on.

Agreement of Sale. *See* Sale Contract.

AIDA. Acronym for the intended effect of advertising: (1) attention, (2) interest, (3) desire, and (4) action (to contact owner or broker).

Air Rights. The right to inclusive and undisturbed use and control of a designated air space within the perimeter of a stated land area and within stated elevations. Such rights may be acquired for the construction of a building above the land or building of another, or for the protection of the light and air of an existing or proposed structure on an adjoining lot. The right to exclusive use, control, and quiet enjoyment of air space within stated elevations over a specific parcel of land.

Alienation. The transfer of property title to another, as by sale or gift.

ALTA Title Insurance Policy. A broad-coverage form of title insurance, suggested by the American Land Title Association, designed to protect against any defect in title not specifically excluded and whether recorded or not. Specific risks such as matters of survey, unrecorded mechanic's liens, water and mineral rights, and rights of parties in possession are automatically covered.

Alternative Minimum Tax. Payment required of taxpayer who accelerated depreciation in excess of guidelines. Insures some minimum tax is paid.

Amenities. Pleasing, nonmonetary satisfactions and benefits generated by a property, (e.g., a pleasant view).

Amortization. The systematic repayment of borrowed money.

Annual Percentage Rate (APR). The yearly cost of credit in percentage terms.

Annual Stabilized Income. Income from wages or salary, plus two-year experience of income from bonuses, commissions, and so on.

Annuity. A series of level payments to be received or paid through time.

Appraisal. An estimate or opinion of value of a property, or some interest therein, rendered by a person skilled in property analysis and valuation, usually accompanied by an appraisal report setting forth the estimate of value and any reservations or conditions attached to it. Also referred to as Valuation.

Appraisal Process. An orderly, well-conceived set of procedures for valuing real estate.

Appraiser. One who makes value estimates.

Appreciation. Increase in value or worth of a property, usually because of locational advantage or inflation; the opposite of depreciation.

Appurtenance. That which has been added to or becomes a part of property; usually passes with it when it is sold, leased, or devised, as an easement.

Architect. A person who designs and oversees construction of real estate improvements.

Assess. To place an official value on property for ad valorem tax purposes. Assessed value. *See* Value, Assessed.

Assessed Value. *See* Value, Assessed.

Assessed Value–Sales Price Ratio. Relation of assessed value of a sample of sold property to actual sales prices for the properties.

Assessment. The official value placed on a parcel of property for ad valorem tax purposes.

Assessment Roll. *See* Tax Roll.

Assessor. A government official who places assessed values on property for ad valorem tax purposes.

Assignment. A transfer of one's rights under a contract, as a transfer of lender's rights in a mortgage or of a tenant's right of occupancy on a lease.

Attachment Lien. Seizure of property by court order, usually to ensure its availability to satisfy a plaintiff or complainant in the event that a judgment against the owner is obtained in a pending suit.

Attorney-in-Fact. A person authorized to act for another under a power of attorney.

Avulsion. Transfer of property ownership by natural means, as by change in course of a stream.

Balloon Payment. The unamortized principal of a mortgage or other type of loan, which is paid off in a lump sum.

Base Activity. The economic activity producing goods or services for export outside an area or community in return for money or income.

Base Line. An imaginary east-west line through a principal meridian, north and south of which township lines are established in the government survey system.

Basis. *See* Tax Basis.

Basis, Allocation of. Assigning initial basis to land, improvements, and personal property.

Before-Tax Cash Flow to Equity. Cash available to an owner-investor, period by period, after deducting operating expenses and debt service. Also referred to as Cash Throwoff.

Before-Tax Equity Reversion. The actual or estimated sale price of a property less transaction costs and less outstanding debt, usually a mortgage loan.

Benchmark. A fixed point of known elevation used as a reference by surveyors.

Bequest. A gift of personal property through a will, a legacy.

Bigger Fool Theory. Refers to the practice by which buyers pay current prices for investments without analysis and with the expectation of reselling to a "bigger fool." The owner, when the bubble of speculation bursts, is the biggest fool.

Bill of Sale. An agreement or statement that articles of personal property have been sold or transferred to a certain person or party.

Binder. An acknowledgment of an earnest money deposit by a buyer plus a written brief agreement to enter into a longer written contract for the sale of real estate. Also referred to as an Earnest Money Receipt or an Offer to Purchase.

Blended Loan. A refinancing loan in which the interest rate on a refinancing or assumption is between old loan rate and current market rate.

Blight. The decay, withering away, or decline in the quality of a neighborhood.

Blockbusting. Inducing neighborhood residents to sell their property at depressed prices by introducing people of another race or class into the neighborhood, thereby taking advantage of fears and prejudices.

Bona Fide. In good faith, without fraud.

Book Value. *See* Adjusted Cost Basis, Tax Basis.

Boot. Cash or the market value of personal property offered or received in a tax-deferred exchange to balance equities, unlike property.

Borrower Risk. Chance of loss in mortgage lending due to perils associated with the borrower. The main items of analysis to determine the risks are (1) credit rating, (2) assests, (3) earning capacity or income, and (4) motivation.

BOY. Beginning of year, as BOY1.

Breach of Contract. Failure to perform or live up to the terms of a contract.

Broker, Real Estate. A licensed person engaged to negotiate the sale, purchase, leasing, or exchange of realty, or to arrange the financing thereof, for a fee or commission.

Broker's Bond. A bond, put up by a licensed broker or salesperson, to insure return of money, obtained fraudulently, to a client.

Buffer Strip. A parcel of land, frequently unimproved except for landscaping, to ease the transition from one land use (residential) to another (industrial) that is considered incompatible or inharmonious.

Building Code. A local or state government ordinance regulating the construction, alteration, and maintenance of structures within the jurisdiction.

Bulk Transfer. Sale of a large amount of materials, supplies, merchandise, or other inventory outside the usual course or way of doing business.

Business Interruption Insurance. Insurance to compensate a business owner for loss of income due to a fire, flood, or other peril.

Business Risk. The chance that projected levels of income will not be realized.

Buyer's Market. The supply of goods and services strongly exceeds the demand, enabling buyers to bargain for and get lower prices.

Canvassing. Contacting property owners, in person or by telephone and without a prior appointment, to obtain a listing agreement.

Capital Budgeting. Making decisions about capital and scheduling its use for long-term investments.

Capital Gains Income. The amount by which the net proceeds on resale of realty or other capital assets exceeds the adjusted cost or tax basis (book value), if held longer than one year.

Capital Market. Market in which long-term financing is arranged, as by mortgage loans, bonds, and stocks.

Capital Rationing. Allocating or budgeting financial resources to the most acceptable or desirable projects or investments.

Capitalization. The conversion or discounting of expected future income payments into a lump-sum present value.

Capitalization Rate. A ratio of income to value; a combination of discount rate and a capital recovery rate. When divided into income, as from a property, a present or capitalized value for the property results.

Carrying Cost. Expenses and outlays to be met until a property is ripe for development or redevelopment.

Cash Flow. The net result of cash receipts and disbursements taken period by period for an investment; may be on a before-tax or after-tax basis.

Cash Flow to Equity. *See* After-Tax and Before-Tax Cash Flow to Equity.

Cash Throwoff. *See* Before-Tax Cash Flow to Equity.

Caveat Emptor. "Let the buyer beware," meaning that one examines and purchases property at one's own risk.

Central Business District (CBD). The downtown or core area of an urban community where retail, financial, governmental, and service activities are concentrated.

Certificate of Occupancy. An official statement, required in many municipalities for new or rehabilitated buildings, stating that required inspections of construction, plumbing, electrical wiring, etc., have been passed and the property is fit for use.

Certification of Title. *See* Title.

Chain of Title. *See* Title.

Change, Principle of. The forces of supply and demand are constantly creating a new real estate environment, thereby leading to price and value fluctuation.

Chattel. Personal property, such as household goods or fixtures.

Client. A principal, usually a property owner, who employs a broker.

Closing. Bringing a transaction to a conclusion. Getting an interested buyer to put up earnest money and to sign an offer to purchase a property.

Closing Statement. A summary of financial adjustments between a buyer and seller, including the amount of the net difference between them, which is usually paid by cash or check at the closing.

Cloud on the Title. *See* Title, Cloud on.

Coinsurance. A clause in fire insurance policies to encourage purchase of adequate coverage. If a certain percentage of value is not insured against loss, the property owner is presumed to share the risk of loss with the insurance company.

Collateralized Mortgage Obligation (CMO). A mortgage pay-through bond, classed as short-, intermediate-, and long-term maturity.

Comingling of Funds. Illegally combining or mixing, often in the same bank account, monies held in trust for clients and personal monies.

Commission. Payment due a real estate broker or salesperson for services rendered in such capacity.

Commitment. A pledge, promise, or letter of agreement to make a loan.

Common Law. Body of law that grew up from custom and decided cases (English law) rather than from codified law (Roman law); a system of law based on precedent.

Community Property. *See* Property, Community.

Community Shopping Center. A retail trade facility, from 10 to 30 acres, that provides a limited line of shopping goods (apparel and furniture) in addition to convenience goods; often anchored by a small department store.

Comparative Economic Advantage. The activity giving the greatest gain or benefit to an area or community.

Competent Party. A person legally considered qualified or fit to enter into a binding contract.

Compound Interest. *See* Time Value of Money.

Concentric Circle Theory. An explanation of urban growth and structure in which a central city is surrounded by circles of varied economic activities.

Concession. Giving up or yielding a

right or benefit in making a contract (e.g., not requiring a security deposit in making a lease).

Condemnation. Taking private property for public use or purposes with compensation to the owner, under the right of eminent domain.

Conditional Commitment. An agreement, with certain limiting provisions, to make a loan.

Conditional Use Permit. *See* Zoning Exception.

Condominium. Fee ownership of a unit of space in developed realty plus an undivided interest in common areas owned jointly with other condominium owners in the development.

Conduit. The transfer of income from one legal entity to another when only the final recipient incurs tax liability; a form of ownership that funnels or directs profits from a property to an investor-owner without the need for payment of taxes in between. A real estate investment trust is considered a conduit; a corporation is not.

Confiscation. The taking of property by a government without compensation.

Conforming Use. A use of land that is consistent with the zoning of the property.

Consideration. Anything of value given or received in a contractual agreement. Money, services, personal or real property, and even love and affection qualify.

Construction Cycle. A regular, rhythmic rise and fall in real estate building and development activity.

Construction Loan. A short-term loan to finance construction or development of realty; upon completion of construction a permanent loan is obtained.

Constructive Eviction. *See* Eviction.

Constructive Knowledge or Notice. Notice presumed of everyone, by law, as consequence of properly making documents and other information a part of the public record.

Consumer Choice. The selection of goods and services for personal use and not for resale or use in a productive process.

Consumer Price Index. A measure of the relative costs of living, which differs from time to time or place to place.

Contingency. An event of chance, usually considered to carry negative consequences.

Contract. A legally binding agreement between competent parties calling for them to do or not to do some specific thing, for consideration.

Contract Interest Rate. The agreed rate of interest in a specific note or loan.

Contract Rent. *See* Rent, Contract.

Contract Zoning. Limiting the use by deed restriction or side agreement to a more restrictive use than allowed by a new zoning classification simultaneously granted by a public agency.

Contractor. In construction, one who contracts to build structures and other improvements to realty.

Contribution, Principle of. The value of any factor of production or component of a property depends on how much its presence adds to the overall worth of a property or its absence detracts from the overall worth.

Convenience. *See* Accessibility.

Conventional Loan. Customary or ordinary. For example, a conventional mortgage loan is made without government insurance or guarantee and conforms to accepted standards of mutual consent between a lender and a borrower.

Conveyance. The transfer of an interest in real property by deed, mortgage, or lease, but not including a will.

Cooperative Ownership. Ownership of shares in a cooperative venture entitling the owner to occupy and use specific space unit, usually an apartment; under a proprietary lease.

Corporation. An entity or organization, created by operation of law, with rights of doing business essentially the same as those of an individual. The entity has continuous existence regardless of that of its owners and limits liability of owners to the amount invested in the organization. The entity ceases to exist only if dissolved according to proper legal process.

Corporeal Right. A visible, tangible right in realty, such as occupancy.

Cost. The amount of money, or price paid or obligated, for anything.

Approach. An appraisal procedure using depreciated replacement costs of improvements and fixtures plus land value as a basis for estimating market value of the subject property. The underlying assumption is that an investor will pay no more for a property than the cost of a site, plus the cost of improvements, necessary to provide a substitute property with utility comparable to that of the subject property. Also referred to as Summation Approach.

Of Capital. The price paid for the use of money; may be an actual or imputed rate of return. For a mortgage loan, the interest rate is the cost; for equity capital, the required rate of return is set by the best alternative use of the money.

Of Replacement. The outlay or amount of money required to construct a substitute, of comparable utility, for existing buildings or improvements.

Of Replacement Less Depreciation. Cost of replacement new less decreased utility due to physical, functional, or locational causes.

Of Reproduction. The outlay or amount of money required to construct an exact duplicate of existing buildings or improvements.

Costs, Selling or Transaction. Expenses incurred in disposition of a property, such as broker's commission, escrow charges, and legal fees.

Costs of Friction. Costs of moving goods or people between linked land use activities. Included are transportation costs, time costs of travel, terminal costs, and aggravation costs.

Costs of Home Ownership. Total of all financial sacrifices to own a home, such as interest, depreciation, taxes, and maintenance.

Covenant. A promise or clause in a

contract. For example, in a warranty deed, the grantor promises that no encumbrances exist against the property being conveyed except those stated.

Credit. A bookkeeping entry in a person's favor, as in a closing statement.

Credit Financing. Making loans to others, as to help finance the purchase of a property.

Cul-de-sac. A dead-end street with a large turnaround at the closed end.

Curtesy. A husband's right or interest in his wife's real estate upon her death.

Customer. Buyer of listed property.

Cycle. *See* Construction or Real Estate Cycle.

Damages. In eminent domain, the loss in value to the remainder after a partial taking of a property.

Date of Sale. Time used to determine LTCG or rollover right; when title passes or buyer takes possession.

Dealer. One whose primary purpose and activity is to buy, develop, or hold real estate for sale to customers for profit.

Debit. On a closing statement, an entry in someone else's favor; what is owed to someone else.

Debt Financing. The borrowing of money to help pay the purchase price of a property or an investment.

Debt Service. The periodic payment on a loan for interest and principal repayment.

Decedent. A dead person.

Decision-Making Process. A series of steps for orderly decision making: (1) recognize problem situation, (2) collect pertinent information, (3) identify problem clearly, (4) pose alternatives, and (5) make decision.

Dedication. A giving of land or property to some public use and the acceptance for such use by and on behalf of the public. Example: land for a park or school.

Deed. A legal instrument that, when properly executed and delivered, transfers or conveys title, or an interest in realty, from the grantor to the grantee.

Grant. A deed in which the grantor warrants, by implication, that ownership has not already been conveyed to another, that the title is free from encumbrances except those stated, and that any title later acquired by the grantor is conveyed to the grantee.

Nonstatutory. A long form deed, written for special purposes or to cover unique situations, as when a guardian acts for a dependent or court ward.

Quitclaim. A legal instrument whereby the grantor transfers rights in a property, if any, to the grantee, without warranty of title or interest.

Release. A deed used to remove or negate a mortgage lien, a dower interest, a remainder interest, or a reverter. Also referred to as a Mortgage Re lease.

Special Warranty. A deed that only covenants that title has not been impaired, except as noted, by any acts of the grantor.

Statutory. A short form of deed in which covenants and warranties are implied as though written in full because the deed is approved or provided for in the state statutes.

Surrender. A nonstatutory deed to convey an estate for years or a life estate to a remainderman or a holder of a reversionary interest.

Trust. A legal instrument conveying title, or an interest in realty to a third party (trustee) to be held as security for a debt owed a lender-beneficiary. Also referred to as a Deed of Trust or a Trust-Deed-in-the-Nature-of-a-Mortgage.

Warranty. A deed conveying title, or an interest in realty, that covenants that the grantor has good title, free of encumbrances except as stated, which the grantee should be able to quietly enjoy and which the grantor will protect against other claimants, if necessary. Also known as General Warranty Deed.(Other types of deeds include administrator's, cession, committees, correction, executors, guardian's, referee's in foreclosure, referee's in partition, and surrender.)

Deed in Lieu of Foreclosure. An owner-borrower conveyance of equity interest to a lender when in default, to avoid foreclosure costs and procedures when equity is less than the expected costs of foreclosure.

Deed of Release. A deed from the trustee returning title to the owner-borrower-trustor to clear a trust deed; the equivalent of mortgage release or satisfaction piece. Also known as a Deed of Reconveyance.

Deed Restriction. A convenant or condition entered in the public record to limit the nature or intensity of land or realty.

Default. Failure to fulfill or live up to the terms of an agreement or contract, as a mortgage loan contract; most often the failure to make the scheduled periodic payments to service the loan.

In Prior Mortgage Clause. A provision in a second mortgage giving the mortgagee the right to pay debt service, and so on, on default of the first mortgage by the mortgagor.

Defeasance Clause. A mortgage provision returning clear title to the borrower-mortgagor after all terms of the loan, including repayment, have been met.

Defendant. The party against whom a lawsuit is filed; the party required to respond or give an answer in a legal action.

Deficiency Judgment. A judicial decree in favor of the lender for that portion of a mortgage debt that remains unsatisfied after default, foreclosure, and sale of the property pledged as security.

Delivery. An act by a grantor showing intent to make a deed effective.

Demand. A desire to own or use something, such as realty. The quantity of goods or services wanted at a given price is effective demand.

Demographic. Relating to population characteristics and study.

Demography. Study of population characteristics, trends, and patterns.

Depletion. Using up or exhausting a resource, as the taking of oil from a well.

Depreciation. Loss or decline in value of an asset; loss in market value of property because of physical deterioration, functional obsolescence, or locational obsolescence; for bookkeeping and income tax purposes, a deduction from gross income to provide for the recapture of investment in a wasting asset, or for the gradual wasting away of an asset other than land.

Accelerated. A method of calculating tax depreciation that gives a higher allowance in the early years than the straight-line method.

Curable. Describes physical deterioration or functionally obsolete items that add more to value if corrected than the cost of correction. Example: broken window.

Functional Obsolescence. The loss in value because a property cannot render a service in a given use as well as a new property designed for the use.

Functional Obsolescence, Curable. A functional deficiency that, if corrected, adds more to property value than the cost of correc tion.

Functional Obsolescence, Incurable. A functional deficiency that would cost more to correct than the correction would add to value.

Incurable. Physical deterioration or functional obsolescence items that would cost more to correct than the correction would add to value.

Locational, Economic, or Environmental Obsolescence. Diminished utility and value of a site or property because external factors and environment unfavorably affect its income or income potential. These external factors include blight, change in transportation routes, excessive taxes, or encroachment of inharmonious land uses.

Physical Deterioration. The loss in value because of physical deterioration or impairment brought about by use in service, acts of God, or actions of the elements.

Physical Deterioration, Curable. An item of physical deterioration that can be corrected at a cost less than the increase in value resulting from the correction.

Physical Deterioration, Incurable. Items of physical deterioration for which the cost to correct exceeds the increase in value resulting from the correction.

Recapture. Depreciation that has been taken by an accelerated schedule and then disallowed for income tax purposes at time of sale; this means that the owner must report the recaptured depreciation as ordinary income and pay taxes accordingly in the year of sale.

Straight Line. The annual write-off of an investment (basis) in a wasting asset by an equal amount each year over its remaining useful life.

Dereliction. Gaining land by gradual lowering of water level.

Descent. A transfer of property title according to inheritance laws because the owner died without a will.

Developer. One who prepares and improves land for use as by subdividing and adding buildings.

Development Charge. Fee imposed

on a subdivider or developer to pay the costs of new roads, utility lines, and so on, necessitated by a new subdivision or structure.

Devise. A gift of real property through a will.

Direct Income Capitalization. Determining market value by devising an overall capitalization rate from the market and applying it to the subject property in a direct or straightforward manner.

Direct Sales Comparison Approach to Value. An appraisal procedure using sale prices of properties similar to a subject property as a basis for estimating the market value of the subject property. The underlying assumption is that an investor will pay no more for a property than would have to be paid for a similar property of comparable utility. Also known as Market Approach to Value.

Direction of Least Resistance. An explanation of urban growth and structure, in which a city grows in the direction of greatest attraction or least resistance, or their resultants.

Disclosed Principal. A principal known or identified to a third party by an agent.

Discount. Reducing value of payments according to time and rate of interest or return. To reduce the value of a future payment or series of future payments, e.g., to make an adjustment for the difference in time of receipt and the rate of discounting.

Discount Rate. The percentage used in time value of money calculations to find the present value of a future payment. The percentage charge member banks must pay the Federal Reserve when borrowing.

Discounted Cash Flow Analysis. Analysis using TVM factors to solve financing problems, e.g., calculating the present value of anticipated future cash flows generated by a property by discounting them at a desired rate of return.

Discounted Rate of Return. *See* Internal Rate of Return.

Disintermediation. The process when savers withdraw money from savings or time accounts for direct investment in stocks, bonds, and other securities.

Dispersing Force. An influence for scatteration of people and activities, as for example, some people desire space and isolation.

Dispossess Proceeding. A legal action to recover possession from a tenant for default or breach of contract.

Dollar Discount. Reduction from list or face value of loan because market interest rate exceeds contract rate.

Donee. A person receiving a gift.

Donor. A person giving a gift.

Double-Entry Bookkeeping. An accounting system in which a credit entry is made for every debit entry; in turn, total debits equal total credits.

Doubling up. The occupancy of one dwelling unit by two or more families.

Dower. A wife's right in her husband's real estate; the right is "inchoate" or inactive during his lifetime. At his death, the right becomes "consummate," or effective.

Downzoning. Rezoning to less intense and less valuable use.

Dual/Divided Agency. An agency that represents two principals, which is illegal except with knowledge and consent of both.

Due on Sale Clause. *See* Acceleration/Alienation clause.

Durability. The ability of land or realty to render services or to exist for a long time.

Durability of Investment. *See* Fixity of Investment.

Duration of Loan. The life or contract period of a loan; the time over which a loan is to be repaid.

Earnest Money. A down payment of money or other consideration made as evidence of good faith in offering to purchase real estate.

Easement. A nonpossessory right or privilege to use the land of another for certain purposes such as party driveways, ingress and egress, or drainage.

Easement Appurtenant. The right of an owner of a dominant estate to use adjacent land of another, termed a servient estate, for stipulated purposes.

Easement in Gross. The right to use the land of another without the need of owning an adjacent or dominant estate. An easement granted a utility company for power or sewer lines is an example.

Easy Money. A money supply large enough to meet the economy's needs with interest rates being stable or falling.

Economic Base. The economic activity of an area or community that exports goods and/or services in return for money or income. Often the activity for which a community is famous, as beer for Milwaukee, autos for Detroit, or government for Washington,D.C.

Economic Base Analysis. The study of basic and nonbasic economic activities of an area or community to predict population, income, and demand for real estate facilities.

Economic Capacity of Land. The relative ability of a site to absorb human and capital resources in keeping with the principal of proportionality.

Economic Force. An influence for change growing out of people's efforts to use and allocate limited resources to satisfy needs and wants.

Economic Life. The number of years over which realty improvements are expected to render services of economic value (e.g., earn rents that exceed costs of operation). Also referred to as Useful Life.

Economic Rent. *See* Rent, Economic.

Economics. Science and study of the allocation and reallocation of limited resources among competing human needs to maximize human satisfactions.

Economies of Scale. Producing larger output and thereby reducing the cost per unit of output.

Effective Demand. Potential demand armed with purchasing power or the ability to pay. Demand for space that enters into and influences the market.

Effective Gross Income. Revenues actually collected in operating an income property; gross scheduled income less allowances for vacancies and credit losses (failure to collect payments even though space was rented).

Efficient Market. A market in which changes in information are quickly reflected in each property's probable selling price or value.

Emblements. Vegetation requiring annual cultivation, as for example corn, tomatoes or cabbage. They are deemed to be personal property.

Eminent Domain. The right of a government, or quasi-governmental agency, to take private property for public uses or purposes upon payment of reasonable or just compensation and without the consent of the owner.

Enabling Acts. Express authority from a state legislative body for a local governmental body to carry on a certain activity such as land use planning or zoning.

Encroachment. A building, part of a building, or other object that intrudes upon or invades a highway or sidewalk or trespasses upon property of another.

Encumbrance. Any cloud against clear, free title or property that makes it less than marketable or freely acceptable to a buyer and therefore less valuable. Outstanding mortgage loans, liens, easements, or unpaid taxes are all regarded as clouds or encumbrances on title.

Environment. The physical, legal, social, economic, and political makeup surrounding a parcel of realty that influence its value.

Environmental Impact Study (EIS). An investigation and analysis to determine the long-run effects of a proposed land use on its surroundings.

EOY. End of year, as EOY1.

Equitable Right of Redemption. A borrower's right to recover a mortgaged property, prior to foreclosure, upon payment of debt, interest, and miscellaneous costs of the lender. Also known as the equity of redemption.

Equity. The disposition value of a property less any liens or encumbrances against the property and less transaction costs; the owner's interest in a property.

Equity Buildup. The increase in the owner's interest because of mortgage loan amortization or appreciation in the total value of a property.

Equity Dividend Rate. BTCF or ATCF divided by initial equity investment.

Equity Kicker. An equity interest in a property given a mortgage lender to obtain a mortgage on said property.

Equity Rate of Return. Average annual percentage rate of earning on an equity investment expected or realized over the holding period.

Equity of Redemption. The right of a borrower to recover mortgaged property by paying the debt, even after default but before foreclosure sale. Also, the right of a tenant to reclaim occupancy, if dispossessed and more than five years remain on the lease. Also known as Equitable Right of Redemption.

Equity Yield. The total return to equity investment.

Erosion. The wearing away of land through processes of nature, as by streams and winds.

Escalation Clause. A provision in a contract, to adjust, usually increase, payments based on some index or level of costs.

Escheat. Reversion of property to the state because no heirs are available and the owner made no will disposing of the property to others.

Escrow. The depositing of money, legal instruments (deeds), or other valuables and instructions with a third party to be held until acts or conditions of a contractual agreement are performed or satisfied.

Estate. A right or interest in property. Also known as Tenancy. Also, the property of a deceased person.

Estoppel Certificate. A written statement that, when signed and given to another person, legally prevents the person signing from subsequently saying that the facts are different from those set forth.

Eviction. The removal of a tenant from possession of realty. Actual eviction results from direct actions of the landlord; constructive eviction occurs when the physical condition makes occupancy hazardous and/or makes the premises unsuitable for the purpose intended.

Excess Condemnation. The taking of more property by a public body than is physically needed for a proposed improvement under the right of eminent domain.

Excess Depreciation. Tax depreciation taken over and above straight line.

Exchange, Tax-Deferred. The trading of a productive property used in a business or held as an investment for a like kind of property for productive use in a business or held as an investment without the payment of any taxes on the economic gain or profit realized on the property transferred.

Exculpatory Clause. A provision in a mortgage that relieves the borrower of personal liability for the loan.

Executor. A person empowered by a court to carry out the terms and provisions of a will.

Expenses, Fixed Operating. Costs of operating a property that remain relatively stable during the period of concern and must be paid whether the property earns revenues or not. Property taxes and insurance are the most obvious examples.

Exposure. The environment as experienced or observed from a property and therefore a locational consideration. An aesthetic benefit, such as a good view, is termed favorable exposure. Location in a blighted neighborhood or where smoke or noxious odors prevail constitute unfavorable exposure.

Extended Coverage Insurance. Insurance against losses from other than fire; that is, from wind, rain, hail, explosion, rust, smoke, etc.

Extension. The continuation of a contract or arrangement, such as the right of renewal of a lease.

Extensive Margin. The point at which it is just barely financially feasible (profitable) to convert rural land to urban uses. The extensive margin is symbolized by land subdivision and development at the urban fringe. *See* Intensive Margin.

External Economies of Scale. Locating a production facility at a place where specialized materials and services are readily available to reduce the cost per unit.

Fair Housing Laws. Laws to ensure equality of treatment regardless of sex, race, color, religion, or national origin.

Fannie Mae. A government-sponsored, privately owned corporation that supplements private mortgage market operations by buying and selling FHA, VA, and conventional loans. Also known as FNMA or Federal National Mortgage Association.

Feasibility Analysis. The investigation to determine whether an investment or development should be undertaken. A study of the profit potential in a proposed real estate project.

Feasible. An economically reasonable, profitable, or worthwhile project, plan, or undertaking.

Federal Housing Administration (FHA) Loan. Mortgage loan insured by the FHA.

Fee, Fee Simple, Fee Simple Absolute. The most complete type of private ownership of an interest in real estate; includes all rights of possession, control, use, and disposition even by inheritance, limitations are police power, taxation, eminent domain, and escheat.

FHLMC. *See* Freddie Mac.

Fiduciary Relationship. Occupying a position of trust and confidence to handle a financial transaction for another in good faith. Examples: guardian-ward or broker-owner.

Filtering. The change in ownership and/or occupancy of housing from one income group to another. Filtering down means that lower-income groups occupy the units.

Finance Charge. Total of all costs a consumer or borrower must pay, directly or indirectly, to obtain credit.

Financial Leverage. Borrowing to finance an investment and, it is hoped, earn a higher rate of return. *See* Leverage.

Financial Management of Real Estate. Using and administering realty to maximize self-interest, which is usually taken as maximizing wealth.

Financial Markets. Creation and exchange for money of financial claims, such as bonds, bills, and mortgages.

Financial Risk. Extra uncertainty or chance of loss to an owner created by the use of debt financing (borrowing) in purchasing an investment.

Financing Statement. A legal document signifying a debt encumbrance on personal property as fixtures, prepared in accordance with the Uniform Commercial Code, for filing in the public record.

Firm Commitment. A definite offer to make a loan at stated terms and conditions.

Fixed Costs. *See* Expenses, Fixed.

Fixed-Rate Mortgage Loan (FRM). A loan at one stated interest rate over its life.

Fixing-up Expenses. Noncapital outlays made to assist in the sale of a residence, such as painting, minor repairs, or landscaping.

Fixity of Investment. An economic characteristic of realty; the long time required to recover the investment in a property.

Fixity of Location. Physical immobility of a parcel of real estate; the implication is that demand must come to the parcel for real estate to render a production service.

Fixture. An item of personal property that is annexed, attached, affixed to, or installed in real property. Examples are furnaces, plumbing fixtures, hot-water heaters, draperies, and wall-to-wall carpeting. If certain tests regarding nature of annexation, nature of use, and intent of parties are met, the item is regarded as realty. This determination is important at time of sale, of mortgaging, of lease termination, and of assessment for property tax purposes.

Flat Lease. *See* Lease, Flat.

Floor-Area Ratio (FAR) Zoning. Zoning for density by limiting the relation of building coverage to parcel area to a fixed number.

FNMA. *See* Fannie Mae.

Force. An influence for change, which involves strength or magnitude and direction.

Foreclosure. A legal process initiated by a mortgagee or other lien creditor, upon default by an owner-debtor, to force sale of the property and immediate payment of the debt.

Foundation. The supporting portion of a structure below the first-floor construction, or below grade, including the footings.

Fraud. Deceiving or misrepresenting. Using an untruth to gain an advantage in negotiations for a business transaction.

Freddie Mac. A secondary mortgage market facility affiliated with the Federal Home Loan Bank System, authorized to buy and sell conventional, FHA, and VA loans. Also known as Federal Home Loan Mortgage Corporation or FHLMC.

Freehold. An estate held in fee simple or for life.

Functional Area. A place where some specialized activity, such as retail trade, occurs in business districts and shopping centers.

Functional Efficiency. The cost and quality of services rendered by a property in a particular use relative to the cost and quality of services rendered by a new property designed for that use. A measure of how well a property is suited to its actual or intended use. *See also* Utility, Functional.

Functional Obsolescence. *See* Depreciation.

Functional Utility. In real estate, the relative ability of a property to perform in the use in which it is employed.

Fungible. Substitutable: one specimen or part may be used in place of another in satisfying an obligation or contract (e.g., money or wheat). Real property rights are often not considered fungible.

General Partner. The operating or managing partner in a limited partnership.

General Warranty Deed. *See* Deed, General Warranty.

Ginnie Mae (GNMA). A federal government corporation designed to handle special assistance functions for certain FHA and VA loans and to guarantee certain securites backed by mortgage loans. Also known as GNMA or Government National Mortgage Association.

GNMA. *See* Ginnie Mae.

Goodwill. The reputation a trade or business has built up by rendering willing, reliable service.

Graduated Lease. *See* Lease, Graduated.

Graduated Payment Mortgage Loan. A loan with debt service starting low and gradually increasing over a stated period, usually five to ten years.

Grant. Conveying an interest in property to another.

Grantee. The person or party to whom real estate is conveyed; the buyer.

Grantor. The person or party conveying an interest in realty, as in a deed signed by a seller.

Grantor-Grantee Index. Real estate filing system used in public records to keep tabs on ownership.

Gross Income. Estimated potential revenues that a property can earn before deductions for vacancies, credit losses, and expenses.

Gross Income Multiplier (GIM). The ratio between the sale price and the annual gross income of an income property.

$$\frac{\text{Sale price}}{\text{Annual gross income}} = \text{Gross income multiplier (GIM)}$$

The GIM derived in this way can be used as a means of estimating the market value of an unsold property. Gross income $\times$ GIM = indicated market value.

Gross Lease. *See* Lease, Gross.

Gross National Product (GNP). Total values of all goods and services produced in an economy at current prices.

Ground Lease. *See* Lease, Ground.

Growing Equity Mortgage (GEM). A loan arrangement with variable-sized payments tied to borrowers' ability to pay.

Guide Meridian. Imaginary north-south line parallel to principal meridian, with adjustments for earths curvature at each standard parallel.

Habendum Clause. A statement, beginning with "to have and to hold," in a deed of the interest conveyed (life estate or fee).

Hazard. The source or cause of a disastrous event, such as fire, flood, earthquake, wind, or workman's injury.

Heir. One who receives property of

a deceased person, either by will or by law of descent when an owner dies intestate (without a will).

Heterogeneity. The realty characteristic of unlikeness between one property and another in location, size and shape, topography, etc.

Highest and Best Use. The legal, possible, and probable employment of land that will give the greatest and present value to land or realty while preserving its utility. Or, roughly, that use that will give the greatest net return from land if no difference in risk is present.

Highest and Best Use, Principle of. Real estate must be appraised in its highest and best use in determining its market value.

Homestead. Real estate occupied by an owner as a home.

Homestead Exemption Right. A reservation of a homestead that precludes attachment or forced sale for nonpayment of debt, except for mortgage and tax liens. In a few states, property taxes are reduced or not applied to homesteads.

Housing Expenses. Payments for housing, as rent, debt service, hazard insurance, property taxes, and association dues.

Homogenous. Made of the same or similar kind, as a neighborhood of similar types of housing.

Hundred Percent Location. The commercial site with the greatest amount of traffic going by, hence the site likely to generate the greatest amount of sales. Presumably this is the most desirable and the most valuable site for commercial purposes.

Immobility. The characteristic of a site that it has a fixed physical location.

Improved Land. Land readied for development as by the installation of sewers, water, roads, and so on. Also, land on which buildings have been erected.

Improvements. Buildings, sewer, water and power lines, or roads to make a property marketable and/or productive.

Improvement Costs. The expenses incurred or dollar outlays to make a site productive. Outlays for buildings, driveways, and landscaping are obvious examples.

Income. *See* Gross, Net Operating, Net Spendable, Net Taxable, Ordinary.

Income Approach to Value. An appraisal procedure using capitalization of expected future income or utility (amenities) as a basis for estimating market value of the subject property. The underlying assumption is that the investor will pay no more for the subject property than would have to be paid for another property with an income stream of comparable amount, duration, and certainty.

Income Property. Realty that produces monetary income on a continuing basis.

Income Ratio. For an income property: net operating income divided by gross scheduled income.

Increasing and Diminishing Returns, Law of. An economic law relating input and output. Initially each additional unit of input is regarded as producing an increasingly larger amount of output; this is increasing returns. Eventually the amount of output per unit of input declines; this is diminishing returns. Generally, additional units of input will be added as long as the value of the marginal output exceeds the cost of the marginal input.

Independent Contractor. A person retaining control over work details while performing a service or accomplishing a result for an employer (e.g., a broker engaged to sell a property for an owner or a sales person engaged by a broker).

Indestructibility. The characteristic of land or space that it cannot be destroyed; it goes on forever.

Index Lease. A lease providing for changes in rent payments in direct proportion to changes in an independent index, such as the consumer price index.

Infrastructure. *See* Urban Infrastructure.

Injunction. A court order requiring one to pursue or to stop a certain course of action.

Installment Sale. The transfer of property to another for two or more payments, or installments.

Institution. An established principal, law, organization, custom, or belief.

Institutional Force. An influence of change generated by the acceptance by people of certain principles, laws, or beliefs.

Insurance. Shifting the risk of financial loss caused by a disastrous event (fire or death) to another party (insurance company) in return for a fee (premium).

Insurance Premium. A payment to an insurance company as compensation for its acceptance of risk.

Intensity of Use. The relative amount of human and capital resources added to a site.

Intensive Margin. The point at which it is just barely financially feasible (profitable) to use urban land more intensely (e.g., replacing old houses with a high-rise office building). *See* Extensive Margin.

Interdependence. An economic characteristic of realty; each site has a mutual interaction of uses, improvements, and value with surrounding parcels.

Interest. Rent or a charge paid for the use of money (e.g., a mortgage loan, a share or right in property).

Interest Due (in advance). Interest calculated and accruing at the beginning of each period.

Interest in Arrears. Interest accruing and calculated at the end of each period.

Interest Rate. The amount paid to borrow money, usually calculated as a percentage per month or year of the amount borrowed.

Intermediary. A go-between; one who acts between two parties, as a bank does between savers and borrowers.

Intermediation. The process that occurs when savers place monies in savings or time accounts at financial institutions, which in turn invest the funds in loans and other investments. *See also* Disintermediation.

Internal Economies of Scale. Producing a larger output, through use of specialized labor and machinery, to reduce cost per unit of output.

Internal Rate of Return (IRR). The rate of return that discounts and equates future cash flows to the initial cash investment. In more complex situations, it is the rate of discount that equates the present value of expected cash outflows (amount of investment) with expected cash inflows (return *of* and return *on* investment). It is the same return referred to as equity rate of return earned over the holding period of the investment.

Internal Revenue Code, U.S. Laws and regulations governing the filing of tax returns with the U.S. Treasury. Important sections for purposes of real estate are

453	Installment sales
1031	Tax-deferred exchanges
1231	Property used in trade or business qualifying for capital gains treatment
1245	Depreciation recapture on disposition of personal property
1250	Depreciation recapture on disposition of real property

Intestate. The legal status of a person dying without a will or last testament.

Investment. An outlay of money (or something of value) for uncertain income or profit.

Investment Value. The worth of a property to a specific investor based on available financing, desired rate of return, and other assumptions unique to the investor.

Investor. One who puts money into real estate based on careful analysis with the expectation of realizing income or profit over an extended period.

Investor's Rate of Return Method. Average annual *cash flow* from a property divided by the initial cash investment; a crude measure for ranking or accepting an investment. *See* Equity Rate of Return in contrast.

Joint Tenancy. *See* Tenancy, Joint.

Joint Venture. The development of or investment in property by two or more individuals or organizations on a partnership cooperative basis where both the risks and the benefits of ownership are shared.

Judgment. A court decree of indebtedness to another and fixing the amount.

Just Compensation. Payment to an owner for property taken in condemnation proceedings, usually the market value of the realty taken.

Labor Specialization. Labor that concentrates on a specific function or end (e.g., an electrician versus general laborer).

Land. The solid part, or crust, of the earth. Provides minerals, living and growing area, and support for buildings, and so on. Often used interchangeably with realty.

Land Contract. A written agreement for the purchase and payment of real property over an extended period of time, with title remaining in the seller until the terms of the arrangement are satisfied.

Also known as Contract for Deed or Installment Land Contract.

Land Development. Combining land and improvements to produce a completed, operational property.

Land Economics. Study of the allocation and use of land resources to meet people's needs and desires.

Land Use. The employment of land for such productive purposes as agriculture, housing, industry, or commerce. Stores, factories, houses, roads, or parks are all examples of a land use.

Land Use. *Planning.* The development of longterm schemes for the use of land together with ways and means of implementation.

Land Use Control. A means, public or private, by which to regulate and guide the use of realty.

Land Use Succession. The process of land development and redevelopment, as owners strive to maximize value of their properties.

Landlord. *See* Lessor.

Law. A body of rules and regulations established and enforced by governments.

Lease. An agreement giving possession and use of land or realty in return for a specified rental payment.

Flat, Fixed or Straight. An agreement calling for level periodic rental payments throughout its term.

Graduated or Step-up. An agreement calling for periodic rental increases during its term.

Gross. A lease calling for a single payment of rent to the landlord, who is then responsible for taxes, insurance, maintenance, and so on.

Ground. A lease giving use and occupancy of a vacant site or unimproved land.

Index or Escalated. An agreement providing for rental adjustments based on changes in a neutral index, such as the consumer price index.

Net. A lease in which all payments to the owner are equivalent to net operating income; tenant pays all property taxes, insurance, and maintenance costs.

Percentage. An agreement wherein the rental payment is based on a percentage of sales or income generated by a property.

Proprietary. A lease, with the attributes of ownership, under which a tenant-shareholder in a cooperative occupies a specific apartment or unit of space. Also known as Occupancy Agreement.

Reappraisal. An agreement with rental payments equal to a fixed percentage of market value, as determined by periodic reevaluation, usually three to five years.

Sandwich. A leasing arrangement in which a lessee rerents the property to another party putting himself or herself in the middle, or "sandwich" position.

Lease Option. A provision in a lease giving the tenant the right to purchase the property at a specific price for a specified time.

Leased Fee. The interest or position

of a landlord in a leased property, made up primarily of the rights to receive rental payments during the lease term and ultimately to repossess the property at the end of the lease term.

Leasehold/Leasehold Estate. The interest or rights or a lessee or tenant in a leased property, including rights of use and possession for a specified period of time in return for the payment of rent.

Leasehold, Sandwich. A lessee interest in real property between the user of the premises or "top" lessee and the owner of the premises or lessor.

Legacy. Personal property disposed of by a will.

Legal Description. A specific and unique identification of a parcel of real estate that is recognized and approved by law.

Lessee. A person to whom property is rented under a lease; a tenant.

Lessor. One who owns the right to use and occupy realty, which is transferred to another (a lessee) under a lease agreement; a landlord.

Leverage. Use of borrowed funds to magnify or put leverage on the rate of return on an equity investment. Economic analogy to the physical use of a lever to gain a mechanical advantage.

Levy. The amount of property tax payable on a property in a fiscal year, usually 2 to 5 percent of value, depending on the jurisdiction.

Liability. A disadvantage or drawback; a legal responsibility and obligation to another.

License. Privilege to use or enter onto premises granted by someone in legal possession of realty.

Lien. A claim, enforceable at law, to have a debt or charge satisfied out of property belonging to the debtor. Examples are mortgages, taxes, judgments, and attachments.

General. A claim that affects all property of a debtor.

Involuntary. A lien imposed against property without the owner's consent.

Judgment. A claim against property resulting from a court judgment.

Junior. A lien subsequent in priority to a lien or liens previously entered and recorded.

Mechanic's. A statutory lien in favor of those who performed work or furnished materials toward the improvement of realty.

Mortgage. A pledge of realty as security for a mortgage loan.

Specific. A claim that only applies or affects a certain property or group of properties.

Tax. A claim against property due to nonpayment of income, inheritance, or property taxes.

Vendee's. A buyer's claim against property of a seller for any money paid under a contract of sale, with subsequent default by the seller.

Vendor's. A seller's claim against a property conveyed to a buyer who subsequently failed to pay the agreed purchase price in full.

Lien Release. A legal instrument to remove or discharge a judgment, mortgage, or other lien as a claim against property.

Lien Waiver. A legal document that, if signed by a contractor, subcontractor, worker, or material supplier, signifies that payment for goods or services rendered in the construction of a property has been received and that any right to place a lien against the property for nonpayment is given up.

Life Estate. An ownership interest of use and enjoyment in real estate limited to the lifetime of a certain person.

Like-Kind Property. Property that can be traded or exchanged without any recognition of capital gains in the transaction. All real estate is like-kind property, except that owned by a dealer and that used as a personal residence.

Limited Partner. *See* Partnership, Limited.

Linkage. A relationship between two land uses that generates movement of goods or people between them.

Liquidated Damages. Penalty provided for in a contract in the event of nonperformance by one of the parties.

Liquidity. Ease of converting an asset into cash, with account taken of the ratio of cash realized relative to the value of the investment.

Lis Pen Dens. Notice of a suit pending.

Listing. An oral or written agreement between an owner and a broker employing the broker to sell or lease real estate. In most states the agreement must be in writing to be enforceable.

Certified. Employment of a broker to sell realty at an appraised (certified) value obtained from a professional appraiser.

Exclusive Agency. Employment of one broker to sell or rent realty for a commission, with the owner retaining the right to personally sell or rent the property and pay no commission.

Exclusive Right to Sell. Employment of one broker to sell or rent realty, with a commission to be paid the broker regardless of who sells or rents the property, owner included.

Multiple. The arrangement among a group of real estate brokers whereby each broker brings listings to the attention of the other members, so that if a sale results, the commission is divided between the broker bringing the listing and the broker making the sale, with a small percentage going to the multiple listing organization.

Net. Agreement whereby the owner agrees to sell or rent at a fixed or minimum price, with any excess to be considered as the broker's commission.

Open. Making opportunity to sell or rent realty available to many brokers, with compensation only to that broker who actually sells or rents the property.

Loan Commitment. *See* Commitment.

Loan Constant, Annual Mortgage. *See* Mortgage Constant.

Loan Discount. An amount off of or a reduction from the principal balance due or face amount of a loan.

Loan Premium. An amount added to or over and above the principal balance due or face amount of a loan.

Loan-to-Value Ratio (LVR). The proportion of property value financed by a mortgage loan, usually expressed as a percentage.

Location. Economically, the relationship of a property to its environment or surroundings. Important considerations are accessibility, exposure, and personal preferences. *See also* Situs. A physical or legal description of property.

Locational Analysis. Identification and study of environment, situs, linkages, accessibility, and other external factors as they relate to the use, utility, and value of a site or property.

Locational Obsolescence. *See* Depreciation.

Locational Quotient (LQ). A ratio; the percentage of local activity of an industry relative to or divided by national activity in the same industry. Any amount in the ratio in excess of one indicates base economic activity.

Lot. A distinct parcel of land.

Loyalty. Faithful performance as an agent.

Maggie Mae. A private secondary mortgage company. The legal name is Mortgage Guarantee Insurance Corporation (MGIC).

Management by Exception. Focusing attention, as an executive or manager, on substantial deviations from expected performance or results; by so doing, the manager gives attention to items or considerations of greatest concern and benefit to the operation.

Management by Objective (MBO). Making decisions and organizing resources to achieve priority-ranked objectives, such as profits or growth.

Manager. A person who operates properties for owners.

Market. The bringing together or communication between people interested in buying, selling, or exchanging a commodity or service. Real property rights constitute the commodity in the real estate market.

Market, Primary Mortgage. A market made up of lenders who supply mortgage funds directly to borrowers; examples are savings and loan associations and banks.

Market, Secondary Mortgage. A market in mortgages made up of mortgage bankers and brokers who originate loans, and lenders, such as insurance companies and mutual savings banks, who place or invest funds.

Market Analysis. A study of supply, demand, and prices to predict changes in the amount and types of real estate facilities needed in a community or area.

Market Approach to Value. *See* Direct Sales Comparison Approach to Value.

Market Area. The geographic range of competition for a particular type of real estate, taking account of physical, social, legal, and economic elements.

Market Interest Rate. Rate charged by lenders in making loans in the current market.

Market Price. The amount actually paid or payable in a buy-sell transaction.

Market Rent. *See* Rent, Economic.

Market Risk. Chance of loss due to a drop in the market value of a property.

Market Value. *See* Value, Market.

Master Plan. A comprehensive plan setting forth ways and means by which a community can adjust its physical makeup to social and economic change.

Metes and Bounds. A legal description of realty in which the boundaries are defined by directions and distances.

Middleman. A broker acting for a buyer and seller, both having full knowledge of the double agency.

Minimum-Rated Risk. A risk rating of property based on building type and other characteristics, which is the lowest rate obtainable for the property type.

Mobile Home. A year-round, fully equipped dwelling unit on wheels that may be towed from city to city without violating state highway regulations.

Modification. *See* Interdependence.

Monetary Policy. Adjustments in the nation's money supply to achieve an acceptable balance in the national goals of full employment, economic growth, and price stability.

Money Markets. The creation and exchange for money of short-term (less than one year) money instruments (e.g., notes).

Monument. A fixed object, such as a large boulder, to mark real estate boundaries.

Moral Suasion. Efforts by political leaders to tighten or ease credit without direct regulation, for instance, by persuading bankers to hold to or change certain policies.

Mortgage. A pledge of real property as security for a debt or obligation.

Amortizing. A mortgage loan contract in which the periodic debt service is expected to pay interest on the loan and to repay the principal over the life of the agreement.

Blanket. One mortgage covering two or more pieces of property pledged as security for the debt.

Construction or Building Loan. A loan to aid an owner or a builder to finance erection of a structure.

Conventional. A mortgage loan made by a financial institution without FHA insurance or a VA guarantee.

FHA. A mortgage loan in which the lender is insured against loss by the Federal Housing Administration for a fee or charge paid by the borrower.

First. A mortgage that has priority over all other mortgages as a lien on the property.

Junior. A mortgage subsequent in priority to other mortgages as a lien; this may be a third or fourth mortgage in priority.

Open-End. A mortgage contract providing for subsequent advances from a lender up to, but not exceeding, the original amount of the loan.

Package. A mortgage contract providing for accepting fixtures and building equipment as collateral.

Participation. A mortgage loan in

which two or more persons or institutions are lenders.

Purchase Money Mortgage (PMM). A mortgage given by a buyer to a seller to cover all or a portion of the purchase price of a property.

Seasoned. A mortgage loan two or three years old on which the borrower has a good record of meeting debt service and of maintaining the property.

Second. A mortgage subsequent in priority to a first mortgage as a lien.

Subject to a. Describes a case in which a buyer takes title to a property on which a mortgage loan exists but does not take over legal responsibility for the mortgage or its debt service; in case of default, the lender has no recourse against the buyer-owner for satisfaction.

Term or Straight. A nonamortizing mortgage, generally for three to five years, with interest payable quarterly or semiannually.

Trust Deed. See Trust Deed.

VA or "GI." A mortgage contract made with eligible veterans and certain others in which the lender is guaranteed against loss on loans by the Veterans' Administration.

Variable Rate. A mortgage loan interest rate that increases or decreases directly with fluctuations in an index beyond the control of the lender, such as the prime rate or bond market rate.

Wraparound. A refinancing mortgage whereby a lender assumes responsibility for debt service on an existing mortgage while making a new, larger second or junior mortgage to the property owner-borrower at a higher interest rate. In effect, the new mortgage "wraps around" the existing mortgage on the property.

Mortgage Assignment. A written transfer of ownership of a mortgage loan contract from one lender to another.

Mortgage Assumption. Agreement by the grantee (usually a buyer) of real estate to accept responsibility and become liable for payment of an existing mortgage against the property.

Mortgage Banker. A person who makes mortgage loans with the expectation of reselling them to an institutional lender while retaining the right to service them for a fee.

Mortgage Broker. A person who, for a fee, obtains mortgage money for a potential borrower or who finds a willing borrower for a potential lender.

Mortgage Consolidation Agreement. A contract whereby two or more mortgages are consolidated into a single mortgage lien.

Mortgage Constant. Total annual debt service on an amortizing mortgage loan, expressed as a proportion or percentage of the initial amount of the loan.

Mortgage Default. *See* Default.

Mortgage Extension. An agreement between the lender and the borrower to extend the life of a term loan without reduction or prepayment in the interim.

Mortgage Release. The release of part of mortgaged realty from the mortgage lien; that is, part of the mortgaged premises is no longer pledged as security for the loan.

Mortgage Satisfaction. Receipt acknowledging payment, to be recorded and thereby terminating the mortgage lien against the property. Also known as Lien Release.

Mortgage Share (Participation) Agreement. A contract setting forth the portions of a participation mortgage owned by the parties involved.

Mortgage Spreading Agreement. A contract extending a mortgage lien to properties not previously included, thereby increasing the security given a lender.

Mortgage Warehousing. An arrangement often used by mortgage bankers whereby several mortgages are initiated with funds obtained on short-term credit for later resale to a large institutional lender or investor, such as an insurance company.

Mortgagee. The lender in a mortgage loan contract, in whose favor the property is pledged as security.

Mortgagor. The borrower in a mortgage loan contract, who pledges property as security.

Mortgagor/Mortgagee Index. Public record summary showing parties giving and receiving mortgages.

Most Probable Selling Price. The amount at which a property would most likely be sold if exposed to the market for a reasonable time. Synonymous with market value.

Multiple Nuclei Theory. An explanation of urban growth and structure, in which clusters of development (functional areas) such as business districts, manufacturing districts, and residential neighborhoods combine to make up a city.

Multiple-Use Zoning. A classification allowing several compatible but different uses in the same zoning district.

Neighborhood. An area made up of a group of similar-type business enterprises, houses, or people, often surrounded by well-defined natural or manmade boundaries.

Neighborhood Shopping Center. A retail trade facility, from 5 to 15 acres in area, that primarily provides convenience goods (food, drugs, hardware) to its immediate environment or neighborhood.

Net Lease. *See* Lease, Net.

Net Operating Income (NOI). Earnings of an income property after operating and maintenance expenses are deducted but before interest and depreciation deductions are taken. Also known as Net Income Before Recapture (NIBR).

Net Present Value. The present value of future benefits from an investment less the cost of the investment.

Net Spendable Income. Money left over from a property after operating expenses and debt service have been provided for and after state and federal income taxes have been paid. Net operating income less loan payments and less federal and state income taxes.

Net Taxable Income. The income from a property actually subject to taxation; net operating income less interest on loans and less tax depreciation.

Nonassumption Clause. A clause stating that the property of an owner-borrower cannot be sold to, and the mortgage assumed by, a third party without the consent of the lender; also known as "due on sale" clause, acceleration clause.

Nonconforming Use. A land use not in agreement with the applicable zoning; may be legal or illegal.

Nonperformance. Failure to fulfill a contract or agreement; also termed breach of contract.

Nonresidential Property. Property earning *less* than 80 percent of its rental income from nontransients or "permanent" residents.

Novation. Purchaser taking over existing loan at new terms and thereby releasing original borrower of obligation. New arrangement.

Objective Value. Value of a property dependent on standards, judgments, and demands of the typical owner-user, as judged by the amount paid for similar properties in the market; synonymous with market value or value in exchange.

Obsolescence. Impairement of desirability and usefulness brought about by economic or functional changes.

Obsolete. No longer useful or desirable though physically sound.

Open Housing Law. A federal law declaring real estate a "public interest" commodity and therefore stipulating that all housing offered for sale or rent through real estate agents must be "open" to all without discrimination based on race, color, creed, or national origin.

Open Market Operations. The buying and selling of money instruments by the Fed to regulate the money supply and influence the interest rate.

Open Occupancy. Refers to residential rental property not restricted by race, creed, color, or national origin.

Operating Expenses. Out-of-pocket costs incurred to maintain a property and to keep it productive of services and income. Examples are water, electricity, supplies, redecoration outlays, taxes, insurance, and management.

Operating Income. *See* Net Operating Income.

Operating Ratio. For an income property: operating expenses divided by gross scheduled income.

Operating Statement. An accounting report of income and expenses for a property, usually based on a time period of one year. The broad format is as follows:
Gross income (GI)
Less: Vacancy and credit losses (V&CL)

Equals: Effective gross income (EGI)
Less: Operating expenses
Equals: Net operating income (NOI)

Opinion of Title. *See* Title, Certification of.

Opportunity Cost. The best alternative earning or benefit that is forgone in selecting or deciding among several alternatives.

Option. An agreement whereby an owner agrees to sell property at a stipulated price to a potential buyer within a specified length of time. The potential buyer will usually have paid a fee or price to obtain the right of purchase.

Ordinance. A law or regulation enacted by a local government unit.

Ordinary Income. Income from wages, salaries, commissions, professional fees, interest, rents, royalties, and dividends (non-capital gains income) subject to federal taxation at regular rate.

Overall Capitalization Rate. Net operating income divided by sale price, a ratio customarily designated as "R."

Partial Interest. An interest in real property that is less than a tenancy in severalty.

Partial Taking. In eminent domain, the acquisition of less than an entire property.

Partially Amortizing Mortgage Loan. A loan calling for systematic repayment of a portion of the principal, with a balloon or balance to be repaid at some future time.

Partnership. An organizational arrangement whereby two or more people join together to conduct business without forming a corporation and with profits and losses shared according to contributions of capital and expertise.

Partnership, General. *See* Partnership.

Partnership, Limited. A partnership arrangement whereby some members, termed limited or silent partners, are exempt by law from liability in excess of their contribution. Silent partners cannot participate in management under penalty of losing their limited liability status. The managing partners are termed operating or general partners.

Party Wall. A wall along the line between adjoining properties in which the respective owners share a common right of use.

Patent. A conveyance or grant of property from the U.S. government.

Payback Period. Number of years required to recover an initial capital investment.

Percentage Lease. *See* Lease, percentage.

Perfect Market. A market in which all information concerning future benefits and risks for each property is available to all participants.

Performance Bond. Insurance or security, put up by a party to a contract, to guarantee specific and proper completion of the contract.

Performance. Criteria used relative to standard land-use tests to ascertain whether a proposed land use will be acceptable in a specific zone. Tests pertain to items like noise, air pollution, and traffic generation.

Performance Zoning. Establishing zoning districts by standards relating to density, appearance, and traffic generation rather than to use.

Personal Income. Money earned by persons from all sources, with money for social security deducted.

Personalty. Any property that does not fit the definition of realty.

Physical Deterioration. *See* Depreciation.

PIIT. Acronym for payments to a lender that cover principal, interest, insurance, and taxes on a property. Sometimes PITI.

Plaintiff. The complainant or complaining party in a lawsuit.

Planned Unit Development. Development of property with overall density the same as, or slightly greater than, conventional development but in which, because of flexibility in the zoning ordinance, the improvements may be clustered, with open, common areas between.

Planner. One who coordinates community or area developement.

Planning, by City, County, Urban, State, or Regional Authorities. Devising ways and means of achieving goals and objectives considered desirable for the jurisdiction. Planning usually concerns land use, transportation, and community services and facilities.

Plat. A plan or map of a tract of land showing actual or proposed property lines, easements, setback lines, etc., entered into the public record, as for a subdivision.

Plottage. *See* Value, Plottage.

Points. Discount or premium made on the origination or the sale of mortgage loan. Each point equals 1 percent of the loan amount.

Police Power. The limitation of private rights in property by a government, without compensation to the owner, based on need to protect public health, welfare, safety, or morals.

Political Force. Influence for change generated by our efforts to organize and manage ourselves and others through government and laws.

Political Risk. Chance of loss in property ownership or value due to decisions or actions of a governmental body (e.g., a change in zoning).

Portfolio Risk. Chance of loss in owning and managing a large number of investments due to (1) administrative, (2) investment, and (3) mix or diversification perils.

Possessory Interest. A right to occupy and use realty.

POSSLQ. Census definition; persons of opposite sex sharing living quarters.

Potential Demand. Latent or unrealized desire for a good, such as real estate. Tentative quality and quantity of demand for space.

Power of Attorney. Granting authority to an agent under a formal, sealed instrument. The agent receiving this authority is called an Attorney-in-Fact.

Power of Sale. The right of a trustee

to sell property in default on a trust deed loan, without court proceedings.

Prepaid Expense. A charge paid in advance (e.g., rent or an insurance premium).

Prepayment Clause. A provision in a loan contract setting forth the conditions under which the loan can be prepaid. If the borrower can prepay any time, the contract is said to have a "prepayment privilege." If the borrower must pay for the right to prepay, such as 3 percent of the remaining or unamortized principal, the contract is said to have a "prepayment penalty."

Prescriptive Rights. *See* Adverse Possession.

Present Value. The current monetary value of future benefits or income; the discounted value of future payments.

Present Value Analysis. *See* Discounted Cash Flow Analysis.

Present Value of One (PV1). A time-value-of-money multiplier used to convert a single payment to be received in the future into a current lump-sum value.

Present Value of One per Period (PV1/P). A time-value-of-money multiplier used to convert a series of equal or level payments, to be received in the future, into a current, lump-sum value.

Price. The amount of one item or commodity traded for another, usually the amount of money.

Primary Lender. Financial institutions originating loans, thereby supplying funds directly to borrowers.

Prime Rate. The interest (or discount) rate a commercial bank charges higher-credit borowers on loans to them.

Principal. A person who employs another (an agent) as a representative. *See* Agency. Also, the capital amount of a loan or investment, which amount must be recovered over the term of the loan or investment before any interest or profit can be earned.

Principal Meridian. An imaginary north-south line in the government survey system.

Principal Recovery (PR) Factor. A time-value-of-money multiplier to convert a current, lump-sum principal value, such as a mortgage loan, into a series of equal, periodic payments, sufficient for amortization over the loan period or term.

Principal Risk. The chance that a monetary investment will be worth less than expected in terms of purchasing power when recovered.

Probate. To prove or establish the validity of a will.

Procuring Cause of Sale. A requirement for a broker to claim and collect a commission for the sale of realty from an owner-principal. A sale brought about primarily, immediately, and efficiently by the actions and efforts of a broker is considered to qualify the broker for the commission.

Productivity. In real estate, the capacity of a property to provide a flow of services and benefits in the form of shelter, fertile soil, or advantageous location.

Professional Risk Bearer. Insurance company owned and operated as a profit-making enterprise rather than as a cooperative or mutual organization operated for its members.

Profitability Index. The present value of future cash flows divided by the initial cash investment; the index must exceed 1 for the investment to be acceptable.

Promissory Note. A statement acknowledging a debt and the terms under which it is to be repaid, signed by the debtor or borrower.

Property. The right or interest of an individual in lands and chattels to the exclusion of all others. Real property rights include possession, control, enjoyment, and disposition.

Common. Land or realty owned equally by all members of a group, a community, or the public.

Community. Property, real or personal, acquired by a husband and wife, individually or jointly during their marriage, that belongs to them equally.

Personal. Ownership of or holding title to chattels or nonreal estate items such as automobiles, accounts receivable, goodwill, or clothes.

Real. Ownership of or holding title to real estate.

Property, Separate. Property that is specifically excluded from community property (e.g., property owned prior to marriage or received by gift or inheritance after marriage).

Property Brief. Written summary of pertinent information and facts about a property.

Property Discription. *See* Legal Description.

Property Risks. Chance of loss in mortgage lending due to perils of properties involved. The risk has three main sources: (1) onsite characteristics, (2) location, and (3) market.

Proportionality, Principle of. Real estate reaches its maximum productivity, or highest and best use, when factors of production are in balance with one another. Also known as principle of balance, of variable proportions, and of increasing and decreasing returns.

Proportionate Share. Allocation of taxes, maintenance, and other costs involved in a condominium or cooperative according to the relative share of value of each owner.

Proprietary Lease. A lease with the attributes of ownership.

Proration. A division or distribution of proportionate shares (e.g., the prorated adjustments of taxes, insurance, and interest in a title closing).

Public Calling. A business rendering a necessary service, such as insurance, and therefore subject to strict regulation as to formation, operation, and solicitation.

Puffing. The presentation and promotion of a property in the best light possible by a salesperson who is trying to sell the property; statements made by a salesperson about a property that tend to be exaggerated.

Purchasing-Power Risk. The chance that future dollars will be worth less than current dollars in terms of purchasing power for goods and services.

Pyramiding. A financial technique or program for controlling properties or corporations with a limited amount of equity. Also, an estate-building program whereby an investor strives to use leverage and prudent financial management to increase wealth as fast as possible.

Qualified Fee. A limitation on ownership of realty that may cause title to transfer to another person.

Quality of Use. The nature of the use and benefits to be realized from a property–an old house versus a new one.

Question of Fact. In court proceedings, the interpretation of evidence as fact or absolute reality (actual events, conditions, or actions), as by a jury in contrast to interpretation based on legal principle.

Question of Law. In court proceedings, the interpretation of evidence according to legal principles or established rules of law, as by a judge; concern with the letter of the law.

Quitclaim *See* Deed, Quitclaim.

Range. A column of townships, 6 miles wide, east or west, of a principal meridian.

Rational Being. An individual acting in a logical and reasonable manner to maximize personal advantage or self-interest.

Ready, Willing, and Able Buyer. A purchaser acceptable to a seller or capable of meeting the seller's terms.

Real Estate. An asset, commodity, or type of property, more accurately classified as "realty," that begins with land and includes all "permanent" improvements to the land. A field of study concerning the description and analysis of the physical, economic, and legal aspects of realty, or real estate as defined above. An occupation or form of business activity that involves realty or real property.

Real Estate Cycle. A rhythmic rise and fall in sales of existing real estate.

Real Estate Investment Trust (REIT). A means of holding real estate with limited liability similar to a corporation and with the ability to pass profits to owners without payment of corporate taxes: thus, the trust is said to be a 'conduit."

Real Estate Market. *See* Market.

Real Property. *See* Property, Real.

Realized Gain. A capital gain in the sale or exchange of an asset, the amount of which is received in cash or boot and is therefore subject to taxation. For contrast, *see* Recognized Gain.

Realtor®. A broker or salesperson, affiliated with the National Association of Realtors®. A word to designate an active member of a local real estate board affiliated with the National Association of Realtors®.

Realty. Land and all appurtenances and permanent improvements added thereto, such as easements and buildings.

Reappraisal Lease. *See* Lease, Reappraisal.

Recast. Keeping the same loan but modifying debt service by changing the interest rate or the amortization period.

Receiver. A person appointed by the court to take possession and control of a property involved in a legal suit, as in foreclosure.

Recognized Gain. A capital gain in the sale or exchange of an asset realized in like property; that is, not in cash or boot. Therefore not subject to taxation. *See* Realized Gain.

Reconciliation. In appraising, the process of resolving differences in indications of market value to reach a final or single estimate of value.

Reconveyance, Deed of. A deed from a trustee to a borrower to offset a trust deed; similar in function to a mortgage satisfaction.

Recording. Entering a legal instrument or document, such as a mortgage or deed, into the public record to give constructive notice to all the interests involved.

Rectangular or Government Survey. A system of land description or identification utilizing surveying lines running north and south, called meridians, and running east and west, called base lines. The system applies in thirty states.

Redemption, Equity of. *See* Equity of Redemption.

Redemption, Statutory Right of. A right to recover property for a limited time after a mortgage foreclosure sale by payment of the price plus back interest plus foreclosure costs. *See also* Equity of Redemption. Also, right to recover a leased property.

Refinance. To obtain a new, and usually larger, loan at new terms.

Regional Shopping Center. A retail trade facility, from 40 acres up, that carries a wide variety of shopping goods, with at least one large department store; the equivalent of a central business district for shopping purposes.

Regulation Z. Truth-in-lending laws concerning consumer loans, published by the Federal Reserve Boards.

Rehabilitation. The restoration of property to good condition with a change in the floor plan or style of architecture.

REIT. *See* Real Estate Investment Trust.

Reliction. Usable land becoming available to an owner owing to a gradual recession of waters. Gradual increase in land of an owner owing to the receding of water. *See also* Accretion.

Remainder. A future possessory interest in realty; what is left at the termination of a life estate.

Remainderman. The owner of a remainder interest in realty.

Remaining Economic Life. The remaining number of years over which realty improvements are expected to render services of economic value. Also known as Remaining Useful Life.

Renegotiable Rate Mortgage (RRM). A loan arrangement in which the interest rate may be adjusted to market every third or fifth year.

Rent. Consideration given for the use of space or realty, usually stated in terms of dollars per month or year.

Rent, Contract. The amount of money paid for the use of land or realty based on agreement or contract.

Rent Control. Governmental regulation of amount that may be charged as rent for dwelling units.

Rent, Economic or Market; Rental Value. The amount of money that space would bring if it were being rented currently for its highest and best use.

Rent Triangle. A schedule or graphic illustration depicting the decreasing amount of rent a land use can pay as an increasing amount of space is devoted to the use.

Rental Schedule. A listing of rents to be received for space in property.

Required Rate of Return (RRR). The rate of return necessary to compensate for time and risk of an investment.

Reserve for Replacements. An amount deducted as an expense in the annual operating statement to pay for the replacement of short-life items necessary to maintain a property's earning ability. Examples of replacement items are elevators, roofs, boilers, stoves, and washers.

Reserve Requirements. The level of monetary reserves required of financial institutions. Raising requirements tightens the money supply, and vice versa.

Residential Rental Property. For income tax purposes, property earning *more than* 80 percent of its rental income from dwelling units for nontransients.

RESPA. Real Estate Settlement Procedures Act, a federal law applying to institutionally made first-mortgage loans to finance the purchase or ownership of one-family residences.

Restrictive Condition with Reverter. A limitation on ownership that may result in the title's being returned to the grantor or to the heirs of the grantor.

Restrictive Covenant/Condition. A private limitation on the use and occupancy of realty, often included in a recorded deed or subdivision plat; it is binding on subsequent owners of the property.

Retaliatory Eviction. Removal of a tenant from a property as punishment for the tenant's asserting his or her rights; generally considered illegal.

Reverse Annuity Mortgage (RAM). Loan arrangement whereby borrower receives payments from lender and loan principal increases.

Reversion, Reversionary Right. The right to recover complete and exclusive use and/or ownership of real property, as at the end of a lease or easement.

Reverter Clause. A condition in a deed restriction calling for title to return to grantor if the restriction is violated.

Right of Eminent Domain. *See* Eminent Domain.

Right of Recission. A borrower's right to cancel or repeal a loan, as under Regulation Z.

Right of Way. A privilege or right to

cross the land of another, as with an easement for ingress-egress. Also a strip of land for a highway, railroad, or power line.

Right to Recission. Act of rescinding or canceling, as to have title reconveyed to a grantor in a buy-sell transaction.

Riparian Rights. The right of an owner of land bordering a stream or lake to continue the use and enjoyment of the waters therein.

Ripe Property. One that yields a profit to a developer after improvements have been added and all other factors of production have been satisfied.

Risk. The chance of loss on an investment or from a hazard such as fire, flood, or vandalism.

Rolling Option. An option to purchase land that remains alive as long as a certain minimum amount is purchased each year or during some stipulated time period. Often used by subdividers and developers.

Rollover Loan. Arrangement wherein a loan is renewed periodically at current market interest rates.

Rollover of Residence. Sale and repurchase of a personal residence without any payment of long-term capital gains tax.

Sale and Leaseback. The transfer of title of a property for consideration (sale) with the simultaneous renting back to the seller (leaseback) at a stipulated rent for a specified time.

Sale Contract. A written agreement concerning the transfer of ownership interests in realty, setting forth the price, the terms, and the rights and obligations of the parties, and signed by buyer and seller.

Sale Price. *See* Market Price.

Salesperson. An individual working as an agent for a broker to buy, sell, or exchange property for a fee.

Sandwich Leasehold. *See* Leasehold, Sandwich.

Satisfaction Piece. *See* Mortgage Satisfaction.

Scarcity. Inadequacy in supply of land for a given use or in a desired location.

Scenic Easement. An easement limiting use of realty in order to preserve the natural and historical attractiveness of the immediate environment or area.

Secondary Lender. A party or institution that buys existing mortgage loans or originates loans through someone else.

Secondary Mortgage Market (SMM). The buying and selling of existing mortgage loans.

Section. A square mile of land area containing 640 acres.

Secured Transaction. The pledging of personal property by a buyer to a seller or lender as collateral for a loan to buy the property.

Security Deposit. Cash, negotiable securities, or a bond placed with a landlord to assure care and maintenance by the tenant.

Seizin. Possession of realty by the owner or titleholder, who has the right to sell or convey same to another.

Self-Interest. A motivation causing each of us to strive to maximize our satisfactions.

Seller's Market. When the demand for goods and services strongly exceeds the supply, enabling sellers to bargain for and get higher prices, we have a seller's market.

Sensitivity Analysis. A study of the impact of various factors in an investment decision on the rate of return to be earned from, or the investment value of, a property.

Separate Property. *See* Property, Separate, and Property, Community.

Service Activity. The economic activity producing goods or services for consumption or use within an area or community.

Settlement. Final accounting and conclusion in a buy-sell or refinancing transaction.

Severability. A contract provision that invalidation of one clause will not affect the validity of other clauses; each clause is a distinct and independent obligation of the parties involved.

Severance Damages. The loss in market value of the remainder area after a partial taking due to the taking (severance) or the construction of the proposed improvements.

Shared Appreciation Mortgage (SAM). Arrangement whereby lender shares in any value increase in mortgaged property.

Site. A parcel of land including road improvements and public utilities that make it ready and available for use; for an improved property, the land plus road and utility improvements only.

Site Analysis. The identification and study of characteristics, such as size and shape, topography, and road improvements, that affect the value and marketability of a site.

Situs. Locational relationships external to a property that affect value. Crucial locational considerations are accessibility, exposure, and personal preference.

SMSA. *See* Standard Metropolitan Statistical Area.

Social Force. An influence for change generated by the physical and psychological needs and desires of human beings.

Soil Capability. The relative suitability of a soil for crops or for road or building support.

Special Assessment. A charge against real estate to cover the proportionate cost of an improvement, such as a street or sewer, which benefits the property.

Special-Purpose Property. A unique type of property, such as a church, cemetery, or golf course.

Special Unit Permit. The right to introduce a use not otherwise allowed in a zoning district where a definite need exists and guidelines are agreed upon.

Specific Performance. A remedy, under court order, compelling the defendant to carry out, or live up to, the terms of an agreement or contract.

Specific Rated Risk. A risk rating of a property based on the condition and occupancy at the time of inspection by a rating organization or team.

Speculator. One who buys and sells realty expecting to realize large, quick profits due to price changes.

Squatter. One who settles on land without any claim of title or right to do so.

Standard Metropolitan Statistical Area (SMSA). A central city with a minimum population of 50,000, or two contiguous cities with a combined population of 50,000 or more, and the county or counties in which they are located; may include surrounding areas if they are economically integrated with the urban centers.

Standard Parallels. Imaginary east-west lines running parallel to, and at 24-mile intervals north and south of, a base line.

Standby Commitment. An agreement to buy a loan from another lender without the other lender's being obligated to sell.

Statute of Frauds. Legislation requiring, among other things, that any contract creating or transferring an interest in land or realty be in writing. Applies to sales contracts, mortgages, creation of easements, and leases in excess of one year. The intent is to prevent perjured testimony and fraudulent proofs by not allowing oral testimony to alter or vary the terms of the written agreement.

Statute of Limitations. Legislation setting the maximum time allowed to file a legal suit after a cause of action arises. Thus, title to real property by adverse possession is gained under the statute of limitations.

Statutory Right of Redemption. *See* Redemption, Statutory Right of.

Steering. Guiding home seekers to specific properties or areas so as to create or avoid a blockbusting situation; an illegal act under fair housing laws.

Strict Foreclosure. Lender-mortgagee taking over a mortgaged property on default rather than seeking its disposition through a judicial sale.

Structural Analysis. The identification and study of characteristics, such as size, shape, layout, equipment, and physical durability, that affect a building's ability to provide services and benefits and, hence, its value.

Subdivider. One who splits land up into building sites.

Subdivision. The breaking up of a tract of land into smaller sites or plots in accordance with community regulations. Sites may be for homes, small office buildings, warehouses, and so on.

Subdivision Regulation. Local laws governing the conversion of raw land into building sites.

Subject Property. The property under study, as in a feasibility analysis or an appraisal.

Subjective Value. Value dependent on the specific judgments, standards, and demands of a user. *See* Value in Use.

Sublease/Sublet. A rerenting of space held under a lease to a third party.

Submarginal Land. Land yielding no margin of profit to an owner-operator-user.

Subordination. Clause in a lease or mortgage that stipulates that a lien, subsequent in time, is to have priority. For example, a lessee grants a right of prior claim on a property to a lender-mortgagee.

Subordination Clause. Provision in a lease or mortgage to establish priority of claim against property.

Subpoena. A legal notice requiring a

witness to appear and give testimony.

Subrogation. Substitution of one party for another, including a transfer of the rights and obligations of the first party.

Substitution, Principle of. A rational buyer will pay no more for a property than the cost of acquiring an equally desirable alternative property.

Suit for Possession. A legal action to gain or regain possession and use of a property.

Summation Approach. *See* Cost Approach.

Supply. The amount of a commodity available. The quantity of goods or services offered for sale at a given price.

Survey. The process by which a parcel of land is measured and its area ascertained. *See also* Rectangular Survey.

Syndicate. A combining of personal and financial abilities of two or more people to conduct business and to make investments; as a group they are able to accomplish ends that each alone could not undertake and complete.

Syndication. A grouping together of parties or legal entities for a business endeavor, as to develop realty.

Take-out Letter/Commitment. The statement of terms for, and agreement to make, an advance commitment for a loan, signed by the lender.

Tax Avoidance. The administration of one's affairs and the planning of transactions with income tax regulations and tax court rulings in mind to minimize the amount of taxes to be paid.

Tax Base. The total assessed value of all property in a tax district.

Tax Basis. Cost or value of a property at the time it is acquired; book value. *See* Adjusted Cost Basis.

Tax Capitalization. The discounted present value of all future taxes incurred or avoided because of over- or under-assessment.

Tax Credit. A dollar-for-dollar offset or allowance against taxes due and payable.

Tax-Deferred Exchange. The trading of a property for a *like kind* of property without taxation of economic gains.

Tax Depreciation. A deductible expense for tax purposes, to allow recovery of the cost of an asset over its useful life.

Tax Evasion. Using illegal means to escape payment of taxes, such as failure to submit a return, making false and fraudulent claims, or padding expense accounts.

Tax-Exempt Property. Property not subject to taxation because it is owned by a governmental unit or a nonprofit institution or because of statutes, such as homestead laws.

Tax Levy. A charge made against a property in the form of a tax for the operation of state or local government. Also, the total revenue to be obtained from the tax.

Tax Lien. *See* Lien, Tax.

Tax Roll. The official listing of all property in a jurisdiction, giving legal description, owner, assessed value, and the amount of taxes due and payable.

Tax Shelter. Using a bookkeeping expense of investment depreciation to protect, or avoid paying taxes on, income. It is implied or taken for granted that the investment actually maintains or increases in value during ownership.

"Taxpayer." A building of one or two stories constructed on a site to enable the property to generate enough income to pay real estate taxes until the erection of a skyscraper becomes feasible.

Tenancy. The nature of a right to hold, possess, or use property as by lease or ownership.

At Sufferance. Initially occupying or using realty by legal means and afterward remaining in possession without any justification but with implied consent of the owner.

At Will. Occupying or using realty subject to termination at the will of either the owner or tenant.

By the Entirety. Ownership of realty by husband and wife, who are regarded as one person. No disposition of any interest can take place without the consent of both. The property passes to the survivor in the event of the death of one of them.

Definite. A tenancy of certain duration.

For Years (or One Year). A tenancy for a specific period of time, usually agreed to in writing.

In Common. The ownership of realty by two or more persons, each of whom has an undivided interest, with right of inheritance upon death of the other.

In Severalty. Ownership of realty by one person.

Indefinite. A tenancy of uncertain duration.

Joint. Undivided ownership of realty by two or more persons with survivorship. That is, if one owner dies, his or her interest passes to the remaining owners and not to the heirs of the deceased.

Tenant. A person who occupies or uses real estate under a lease (lessee).

Tenant, Holdover. A tenant who remains in possession of leased property after the expiration of the lease term.

Tenement, Dominant. The benefiting property in an easement.

Tenement, Servient. The property losing rights in an easement, as by giving right of access to a dominant tenement.

Tenure. The right of use and possession of realty.

Term. The time a tenant may occupy a property under a lease. Also, the life of a mortgage loan.

Terminal Costs. Expenses and outlays required at the ends of linkage trips, such as for parking, loading docks, and loading and unloading.

Testate. Leaving a valid will at death.

Third Party. The person negotiating or contracting with the agent of a principal.

Tier. Ease-west rows of townships north or south of a baseline.

Tight Money. When money for mortgages is scarce, relatively unavailable, and lent at a high interest rate.

Time Costs of Travel. The value of the time period required to move a person or goods from one linked site to another.

Time Is of the Essence. A phrase that, if included in a contract, makes failure to perform by a specified date a material breach or violation of the agreement.

Time Value of Money (TVM). The relating of payments and value at different times by compounding or discounting at a certain interest or discount rate. The relationship depends on the rate, the frequency of compounding, and the total time period involved. Also known as Compound Interest.

Title. Ownership of property. For real estate, a lawful claim, supported by evidence of ownership.

Title, Certification of. An opinion that title is good rendered by an attorney or other qualified person who has examined the abstract of title and other records and information.

Title, Chain of. The succession of all previous holders of title (owners) back to some accepted starting point.

Title, Cloud on. An outstanding claim or encumbrance that, if valid, would affect or impair the owner's title; a mortgage or judgment.

Title, Marketable. Title to real property that is readily salable to an interested, reasonable, prudent, intelligent buyer at market value.

Title Assurance. Evidence or documentation to give confidence or certainty as to the quality of title.

Title by Accretion. Acquiring ownership to soil attaching to land as a result of natural causes, as by a river's action.

Title Closing. Final settlement in the exchange of purchase price for a deed. *See* Closing.

Title Company. A company organized to ensure title to real property.

Title Evidence. Documentary proof of ownership.

Title Examination or Search. An investigation of public records to ascertain the status of title or ownership of a specific parcel of real estate. Items of concern include liens, easements, and other encumbrances that might detract from the quality of title.

Title Insurance. Protection against financial loss due to defects in the title of real property that existed but were not known at the time of purchase of the insurance policy.

Title Report. The results of a title search. Includes the name of the owner and the legal description of a property plus the status of taxes and other liens and encumbrances affecting the property. Results of a property survey may also be included.

Torrens System. A method of land title registration in which clear title is established with a governmental authority, which subsequently issues title certificates to owners as evidence of their claims.

Tort. A wrongful or damaging act against another, for which legal action may be initiated.

Town/Township. In the rectangular survey system, an area of land 6 miles square.

Tract Index. Filing system for real property, by legal description.

Trade Area. The area from which a retail or service property draws most of its customers.

Trade Fixtures. Personal property

installed by a tenant that is removable at the end of a business lease.

Trade-off. A giving up of one alternative or advantage to gain another considered more desirable.

Trading on the Equity. *See* Leverage.

Traffic Count. The number of people or vehicles passing a given point in an hour or a day.

Transferable Development Rights (TDR). The assignment of development rights from one parcel to another parcel.

Transportation Costs. Out-of-pocket expenses for travel between linked land use activities.

Trespass. The illegal act of entering onto the land of another without permission.

Trust. A fiduciary arrangement whereby property is turned over to an individual or institution (a trustee) to be held and administered for the profit and/or advantage of another person, termed a beneficiary.

Trust Agreement. The written contract setting forth the terms of a trust arrangement.

Trust Deed. *See* Deed, Trust.

Trustee. The person or institution administering and controlling property under trust agreement.

Type of Use. Nature of land use on a site (e.g., residential—one-family, multifamily—or commercial—store, office building, or shopping center).

Undisclosed Principal. A principal, unknown to a third party, acting through an agent, who appears to be acting in self-interest.

Uniform Commercial Code. A set of laws governing the sale, financing, and security of personal property in commercial transactions.

Urban Infrastructure. The basic facilities of a community, including schools, sewer and water systems, power and communication systems (electricity and telephone services), and transportation systems (streets, freeways and subways).

Urban Land Economics. Study of the allocation and use of urban landed space to meet the needs and desires of citizens in the community.

Urban Renewal. The conservation, rehabilitation, and redevelopment of urban real estate facilities. Also, a continuing program to achieve these goals, sponsored by the federal and local governments.

Urbanizing Force. An influence toward the concentration of people, buildings, and machines (e.g., trade, education, or manufacturing).

Useful Life. *See* Economic Life; Remaining Economic Life.

Usury. Charging more than the legal rate of interest for the use of money.

Utilities. Community services rendered by public utility companies, such as providing gas, water, electricity, and telephone.

Utility. The ability of an economic good or service to satisfy human needs and desires. In real estate, the ability of a property to render services that are in demand. Also, the benefit or satisfaction that comes with owning or using realty. Utility is the basis of value.

Utility, Diminishing. Decreasing satisfaction realized with the acquisition or consumption of each succeeding unit of an economic good or service.

Utility, Functional. The ability of a property to render services in a given use based on current market tastes and standards. Depends on interior layout, sizes and types of rooms, attractiveness, and accessibility.

Utility, Marginal. The addition to total utility realized by the last unit of a good or service acquired or consumed. In general, as more units are acquired or consumed, the smaller the incremental addition to total utility.

VA (Veterans Administration). A federal government agency that aids veterans in obtaining housing, primarily by guaranteeing loans with low down payments.

Vacancy and Credit Losses (V&CL). A deduction from potential revenues of an income property because of unrented units or because of nonpayment of rent by tenants for the time they used space.

Valuation. *See* Appraisal.

Value. The worth of a thing as measured in exchange for goods, services, or money. The estimated or assigned worth of a thing because of its scarcity and desirability or usefulness. The present worth of future benefits or ownership.

Appraised. The worth of a thing (property) as estimated by a qualified appraiser. *See also* Appraisal.

Assessed. The worth or amount of dollars assigned a property for property taxation purposes usually varies with the market value of the property and may be a percentage of market value, fixed by statute.

Book. The capital amount at which a property is carried in accounting records. Usually it is original cost less deductions for depreciation plus outlays for improvements. *See* Basis, Adjusted Cost.

Capitalized. A value estimate reached through a capitalization process; the present worth of expected future benefits or income.

Market. A term synonymous with fair market value. The price at which a property will sell, assuming a knowledgeable buyer and seller both operating with reasonable knowledge and without undue pressure. The most probable selling price of a property or thing.

Plottage. Bringing two or more parcels of real estate together so that their combined value is greater than the sum of the values of the parcels when taken individually under separate owners. The increment of value created by combining two or more parcels of real estate.

Value After the Taking. Market value of the remaining lands in condemnation proceedings, assuming a partial taking and assuming the proposed improvements or changes have been completed.

Value Before the Taking. Market value of an entire property before the taking in eminent domain or condemnation proceedings.

Value in Exchange. The worth of a property in money or purchasing power (in goods and services) to the typical owner or user in the market. Synonymous with market value.

Value in Use. The worth of a property to a specific user, based on its utility to the user.

Variable Rate Mortage (VRM). Loan arrangement in which the interest rate may change based on fluctuations in a neutral index.

Vendee. The buyer or purchaser, as of real estate.

Vendor. The seller.

Veterans Administration (VA). *See* VA Mortgage Loan.

Void Contract. A contract legally invalid and unenforceable.

Voidable Contract. A contract that may be enforced or declared invalid by one of the parties, as by a minor.

Waste. Damage to property through neglect or otherwise.

Water Rights. A right to a stipulated amount of water from a stream, lake, or reservoir.

Will. A legal statement concerning the disposition of a person's property after death.

Wraparound Mortgage (WAM). A second mortgage loan arrangement in which the second lender pays the debt service on the first loan.

Yield. The rate of return or amount of return expected or earned on an investment.

Zoning. A division of a government unit into districts for regulation of. (1) nature of land use (residential, commercial, etc.), (2) intensity of land use, and (3) height, bulk, and appearance of structure.

Density. Limiting the number of families per unit of land area in a given zone rather than the number per structure.

Exclusionary. Zoning designed to keep low-income and moderately low-income groups out of a residential district by setting large minimum-lot size and floor-area requirements, and high construction-quality standards.

Spot. An area or parcel, usually small, zoned for a use that is inconsistent with the rationale of the entire zoning ordinance or plan.

Zoning Exception. Permitting a nonconforming use into a zone because of an urgent need, under conditions that protect the area and public interests. Example: a power substation in a residential neighborhood. Also known as Conditional Use Permit.

Zoning Map. A map showing the various zones of permitted land uses under a zoning ordinance.

Zoning Ordinance. Legal regulations to implement a zoning plan to control the use and character of real estate. Usually includes text and a zoning map.

Zoning Variance. A deviation from the zoning ordinance that is granted because strict enforcement would result in undue hardship on a property owner.

INDEX

C

D

E

F

G

H

I

M

N

O

P

Q

R

S

T

U

V

W

Z